1 MONTH OF
FREE
READING

at

www.ForgottenBooks.com

By purchasing this book you are eligible for one month membership to ForgottenBooks.com, giving you unlimited access to our entire collection of over 1,000,000 titles via our web site and mobile apps.

To claim your free month visit:

www.forgottenbooks.com/free1115628

ISBN 978-0-331-38362-1
PIBN 11115628

Ward 11–Precinct 1

CITY OF BOSTON

LIST OF RESIDENTS
20 YEARS OF AGE AND OVER

(NON-CITIZENS INDICATED BY ASTERISK)
(FEMALES INDICATED BY DAGGER)

AS OF

JANUARY 1, 1946

THOMAS F. SULLIVAN, *Chairman*
FREDERIC E. DOWLING, *Secretary*
WILLIAM A. MOTLEY, Jr.
ARTHUR V. COUGHLIN
EVERETT R. PROUT

Listing Board.

CITY OF BOSTON ⬥ PRINTING DEPARTMENT

1

Anita Terrace

A	Greenlaw Alice—†	5	housewife	57	1 Day
B	Kelly Ellen—†	5	at home	75	here
C	Kenney Annie—†	5	"	59	"
D	DuPrey Ethel—†	5	housewife	66	"
G	Gilligan William	6	shoeworker	59	"
H	Lynch Gerald	6	machinist	43	"
K	Hillcoat Jean—†	7	at home	69	"
L	Hillcoat William	7	plumber	32	"
M	Moore Catherine—†	7	housewife	52	"
N	Moore William	7	painter	63	
O	Gebhardt Louise—†	7	housewife	55	"
P	Papp Pauline—†	7	"	58	
R	McCarten Dudley	15	shoeworker	48	"
S	McCarten Gertrude—†	15	clerk	49	
T	McCarten Harry	15	repairman	51	"
U	Erickson Joseph	17	mechanic	51	"
V	Gasson Theodore	17	retired	68	
W	*Brown Anna—†	17	at home	73	"
X	Wineburg Otto	17	retired	70	
Y	Skinner Lester	19	laborer	40	
Z	Skinner Marion—†	19	housewife	37	"

2

A	Eldridge Mary E—†	19	"	65	
B	Eldridge William D	19	retired	70	"
C	Fiebelkorn Gerard	19	breweryworker	40	"
D	Fiebelkorn Martha M—†	19	housewife	49	"
E	Swain Albert	20	counterman	45	"
F	Swain Helen—†	20	housewife	39	"
M	Repscha John	22	woodworker	60	"
N	Repscha Lucy—†	22	waitress	35	"
P	Craig Charles	22	laborer	57	"
R	Skidmore Amy—†	22	at home	56	"
S	Skidmore Francis	22	operator	31	"
T	Skidmore John	22	shipper	27	
U	*O'Connor Bridget—†	23	housewife	47	"
V	O'Connor Cornelius	23	fireman	47	
W	O'Connor Thomas	23	clerk	20	
X	*Peterson Carl	23	mechanic	63	"
Y	Sorpewitz Andrew	23	laborer	69	
Z	Sorpewitz Elizabeth—†	23	housewife	65	"

3

Cedar Park

s	Nichols Edith—†	5	housewife	38	here
t	Nichols Jesse	5	fireman	54	"
u	Parks George	5	brazier	46	"
v	Bazner Clara—†	6	housewife	40	"
w	Bazner Jacques	6	molder	40	"
x	Pierce George N	7	constable	54	8 Hazel pk
y	Smith Frances L—†	7	sorter	47	8 "
z	MacPhee Jeanette—†	8	housewife	36	here

4

a	MacPhee Joseph	8	laborer	39	"
b	Philbrook Claude W	9	chauffeur	50	"
c	Philbrook Claude W	9	assembler	28	"
d	Philbrook Lillian B—†	9	housewife	44	"
e	Straub Joseph	10	waiter	52	
f	Straub Marie—†	10	housewife	40	"
g	Noyes Francis P	11	shipper	36	
h	Noyes Leila M—†	11	housewife	38	"
k	Shaw Elizabeth—†	12	"	25	
l	Shaw George	12	clerk	43	
m	Shaw Michael	12	"	33	
n	Starrs Bernard J	14	finisher	64	
o	Starrs Edna—†	14	operator	22	"
p	Starrs Evelyn—†	14	stenographer	20	"
r	Starrs Katherine—†	14	housewife	54	"
s	Starrs Walter	14	clerk	26	
t	Doolin Anna—†	16	housewife	53	"
u	Doolin Anna M—†	16	waitress	24	"
v	Doolin Dorothy—†	16	at home	20	"
w	Schoen Dorothy—†	16	"	33	
x	Schoen Jacob	16	laborer	74	
y	Schoen Sophie—†	16	sorter	43	"
z	Campbell John	18	engineer	47	"

5

a	Campbell Mary—†	18	housewife	40	"
b	*Buccelle Alice—†	20	"	58	"
c	Buccelle Evelyn—†	20	at home	25	"
d	Buccelle Jean—†	20	stitcher	27	"
e	*Buccelle Joan—†	20	at home	21	"
f	Buccelle John	20	laborer	26	
g	Buccelle Mario	20	U S A	24	

Cedar Park—Continued

	H	Buccelle Rosario	20	laborer	58	here
	K	Taylor John W	22	retired	83	"
	L	Taylor Katherine M—†	22	housewife	46	"
	M	Taylor William	22	watchman	50	"
	N	*MacDonald Donald	24	mechanic	34	"
	O	*MacDonald Mary—†	24	housewife	34	"
	P	Runge Edward	24	mechanic	24	"
	R	Runge George	24	presser	53	
	S	Runge Olga—†	24	housewife	49	"
	T	Runge Ruth—†	24	clerk	20	"
	U	Dolan Joseph	26	painter	28	779 Hunt'n av
	V	Dolan Ruth—†	26	housewife	25	779 "
	W	Mone Marie—†	26	"	50	here
	X	Mone Thomas	26	mason	53	"
	Y	Capone Caroline—†	28	clerk	47	"
	Z	Dowd Agatha—†	28	"	44	

6

	A	Dowd Hazel K—†	28	"	48	"
	B	Dowd Loretta—†	28	at home	43	..
	C	Dowd Lottie—†	28	"	69	
	D	Dowd William T	28	supt	41	

Cedar Street

	E	Petteway Betty—†	99	housewife	36	60 Townsend
	F	Petteway Rufus	99	U S A	24	60 "
	G	McDonald Charles	99	laborer	61	here
	H	McDonald Eunice—†	99	housekeeper	20	Framingham
	K	McDonald Rosetta—†	99	housewife	50	here
	L	McGill John	99	waiter	43	"
	M	McGill Susan—†	99	housewife	36	"
	N	James Verona—†	101	housekeeper	45	"
	O	Abbott Carolyn—†	101	factoryhand	33	"
	P	Abbott Charles	101	laborer	29	
	R	Abbott Early—†	101	housewife	52	"
	S	Abbott Joseph	101	barber	27	
	T	Abbott Leora—†	101	hairdresser	30	"
	U	Freeman Irving E	101	janitor	49	
	V	Freeman Laurena—†	101	housewife	51	"
	W	McSweeney Annie—†	103	"	59	

Cedar Street—Continued

x	McSweeney Ismay—†	103	clerk	21	here
y	McHallam Mary—†	103	housewife	44	"
z	McHallam Peter M	103	inspector	48	"

7

a	Ashe Charlotte—†	103	housewife	28	"
b	Ashe John J	103	switchman	38	"
c	Dellario Reta—†	104	clerk	38	
d	Sullivan Anna—†	104	housewife	31	"
e	Sullivan William	104	pipefitter	38	"
f	Tebeau Mary—†	104	teacher	43	"
g	Bouvie Marion—†	105	housekeeper	33	"
h	Iwanoski John	105	laborer	39	"
k	Iwanoski Loretta—†	105	housewife	33	"
l	Shine James	105	metalworker	39	"
m	Shine Nora—†	105	housewife	37	"
n	Burns Francis L	106	retired	26	
o	Burns Irene—†	106	student	23	
p	Burns Madeline B—†	106	clerk	33	
r	McGlynn Frank	106	laborer	66	
s	McGlynn Nellie—†	106	housewife	63	"
t	Cremmins Bessie—†	107	housekeeper	61	"
v	Donlon Catherine—†	107A	"	74	"
w	Manley Catherine—†	107A	"	30	
x	Nevara Francis	107A	laborer	23	
y	Curran Francis	108	U S A	28	
z	Curran Mary—†	108	clerk	25	

8

a	McDonald Mary A—†	108	housewife	72	"
b	McDonald William J	108	retired	70	
c	Pender John	108	machinist	45	"
d	Pender Ruth—†	108	housewife	35	"
e	Spinelli Clara—†	108	"	30	
f	Spinelli Patrick	108	contractor	38	"
g	Krauklis Anthony	109	laborer	63	
h	Krauklis Mildred—†	109	housewife	46	"
k	Tufankjian Catherine—†	109	housekeeper	47	"
l	Tufankjian Leon	109	shipfitter	55	"
m	Tufankjian Sadie—†	109	at home	80	"
n	Patriquin Catherine—†	109	housewife	57	"
o	Patriquin Charles S	109	mechanic	34	"
p	Patriquin Elinor—†	109	clerk	29	

Cedar Street—Continued

R	Russo James	rear 109	retired	55	here
s	Russo Margaret—†	" 109	clerk	45	"
T	Russo Mary A—†	" 109	at home	80	"
U	Russo Theresa—†	" 109	housewife	51	"
v	Brown William	110	clerk	39	
w	Small Ethel O—†	110	housekeeper	65	"
Y	Fairfield Fred	111	chauffeur	27	24 Quincy
z	Fairfield Mary—†	111	housewife	27	24 "

9

A	Brown Catherine L—†	111	"	36	here
B	Brown John	111	chauffeur	41	"
C	Heald Doris M—†	112	housewife	34	"
D	Heald John F	112	chauffeur	64	"
E	McLean Charles A	112	printer	45	
F	McLean George W	112	shipper	40	
G	McLean Veronica—†	112	housewife	70	"
H	Cameron David F	112	laborer	44	"
K	Cameron Helen R—†	112	housewife	41	"
L	Meyers John	113	chauffeur	31	139 Cedar
M	Meyers Marie—†	113	housewife	29	Vermont
O	Ski Eleanor—†	113	housekeeper	49	here
P	Crimmins Catherine—†	114	housewife	47	"
R	Crimmins John M	114	steelworker	51	"
s	Crimmins Marie R—†	114	tel operator	25	"
T	Franzow Joseph	114	retired	74	
U	Lewald Fritz	114	"	64	
v	Lewald Margaret—†	114	housewife	67	"
w	Carlson Anna—†	114	student	25	
x	Carlson Robert	114	U S A	21	
Y	Pearson Ellen I—†	114	housewife	48	"
z	Pearson John	114	laborer	60	

10

A	Pearson Richard	114	U S A	23	here
B	Taylor Goldye—†	115	clerk	34	209 W Springfield
C	Hartin Eleanor—†	115	"	21	here
D	Hartin Henry	115	U S A	26	"
E	Hartin Mary—†	115	housewife	53	"
F	Hartin William	115	bartender	53	"
G	Courtney Christina—†	115	housewife	26	"
H	Courtney Dennis	115	caretaker	32	"
K	Sickels Elinor—†	117	cook	44	125 Cedar

Cedar Street—Continued

L	Beck John W	117	student	20	here
M	Beck Joseph C	117	clerk	39	"
N	Beck Margaret A—†	117	housewife	28	"
O	Beck Sadie J—†	117	"	58	
P	Schenck Christina—†	117	saleswoman	55	"
R	Richie Margaret—†	118	housekeeper	44	16 Vinton
S	Constine Nicholas	118	baker	55	here
T	Constine Penelope—†	118	housewife	50	"
U	Goudas Gregory	118	student	23	"
V	McSherry James J	118	meatcutter	60	"
W	McSherry Margaret R—†	118	housewife	50	"
X	Arlington Dorothy—†	119	"	32	"
Y	Arlington William	119	brakeman	38	"
Z	Hansen Mary F—†	119	housewife	37	"

11

A	Hansen Richard S	119	clerk	40	
B	Hughes Frank	119	grinder	29	
C	Hughes Lillian—†	119	housewife	26	"
D	Maguire Louis	119	woodworker	63	"
E	Maguire Marie—†	119	housewife	56	"
F	Maguire Walter	119	woodworker	28	"
G	McGarry Claire—†	120	housewife	43	"
H	McGarry Matthias	120	operator	39	"
K	Crapowinski Joseph	120	laborer	59	
L	Crapowinski Pauline—†	120	housewife	48	"
M	Crapowinski Walter	120	U S A	21	
P	Kelley Agnes E—†	120	housewife	54	"
O	Dow Jeremiah G	120	U S A	32	
N	Dow Irene—†	120	housewife	26	"
R	Kelley Charles E	120	U S A	25	"
S	Kelley John H	120	cook	24	"
T	Marcella Mary—†	120	housewife	23	Brookline
U	MacFaun Ada—†	121	"	79	here
V	MacFaun Bernard	121	laborer	40	"
W	Beaudoin Marion—†	121	housewife	29	"
X	Beaudoin Rudolph	121	factoryhand	36	"
Y	O'Brien Annie M—†	121	at home	75	"
Z	Hickey George F	121	retired	72	

12

A	Hickey Marion J—†	121	housewife	59	"
B	Wilkins Charles E	121	factoryhand	28	"

Cedar Street—Continued

c	Wilkins Lillian E—†	121	clerk	29	here
d	Edwards William B	122	machinist	37	"
e	Rolfe Charles	122	chauffeur	46	"
f	Rolfe Charles O	122	U S A	25	
g	Rolfe Louise M—†	122	housewife	23	"
h	Lindsey Sadie M—†	122	housekeeper	44	"
k	Peterson Carl	122	carpenter	38	"
l	Peterson Edith—†	122	housewife	30	"
m	Spears Barbara—†	123	housekeeper	42	"
n	Galloway Julia—†	123	housewife	27	"
o	Galloway Louis	123	painter	27	"
p	Hall Mortimer	123	laborer	24	
r	Martin Naomi—†	123	entertainer	31	"
s	Wade Henry	123	porter	60	"
v	Burns Patricia—†	125	housekepper	33	32 Valentine
w	Johnston Sadie G—†	125	"	61	32 "
x	Boyd Edith—†	125	housewife	26	here
y	Boyd Raymond	125	laborer	21	"
z	Cavilla James	125	"	46	"

13

a	Hunter Gertrude—†	125	housewife	44	"
b	Hunter Robert	125	lithographer	40	"
c	Reilly Joseph	125	U S A	33	11 Newark
d	Reilly Loretta—†	125	housewife	30	11 "
g	McCoy Alma—†	127	"	30	here
h	McCoy Pedro	127	machinist	33	"
k	Dumont Alfred	127	chauffeur	36	"
l	Dumont Rose—†	127	housewife	31	"
m	Krudgel Ann—†	127	"	60	
n	Krudgel Frances—†	127	nurse	23	
o	Krudgel John	127	laborer	60	
p	Foley Michael	129	trackman	41	"
r	Foley Sarah—†	129	housewife	40	"
s	Smilewicz Joseph	129	laborer	27	
t	*Smilewicz Julia—†	129	housewife	66	"
u	Smilewicz Raymond	129	seaman	28	
v	*Smilewicz Vincent	129	clerk	57	
w	Smilewicz Walter	129	breweryworker	34	"
x	Moore Margaret—†	129	housewife	38	"
y	Moore Thomas	129	shipfitter	37	"
z	Gatt George	131	chauffeur	48	20 Linwood

Cedar Street—Continued

Page.	Letter.	FULL NAME.	Residence, Jan. 1, 1946.	Occupation.	Supposed Age.	Reported Residence, Jan. 1, 1945. Street and Number.
	A	Gatt Marie S—†	131	housewife	47	20 Linwood
	B	Gatt Roberta—†	131	supervisor	22	here
	C	Lee Mary F—†	131	housewife	38	"
	D	Lee Michael J	131	machinist	35	"
	E	Buechs Herman S	131	clerk	41	
	F	Buechs Jessie V—†	131	housewife	31	"
	G	Kirrane Margaret—†	133	"	31	
	H	Kirrane Peter	133	operator	31	"
	K	Discolo Catherine—†	133	housewife	28	"
	L	Discolo Michael	133	laborer	34	
	M	Ross Bessie—†	133	housewife	66	"
	N	Ross Chester M	133	mechanic	38	"
	O	Fay Patrick	133	laborer	43	143 Cedar
	P	Kelly Agnes—†	133	housekeeper	41	131 "
	R	Murray Bernard	133	laborer	39	Cambridge
	S	Murray Kathleen—†	133	housewife	39	131 Cedar
	T	Murray Thomas M	133	freighthandler	43	131 "
	U	Dunn Catherine—†	135	at home	60	here
	V	Dunn John	135	printer	48	"
	W	Dunn Richard R	135	teamster	24	"
	X	Dunn Rose—†	135	housewife	21	"
	Y	Ryan Enid—†	135	"	22	
	Z	Ryan Harold	135	plater	26	

15

Page.	Letter.	FULL NAME.	Residence, Jan. 1, 1946.	Occupation.	Supposed Age.	Reported Residence, Jan. 1, 1945. Street and Number.
	A	Revino Catherine—†	135	housewife	40	"
	B	Revino George	135	operator	48	"
	C	Sadoulis Margaret—†	139	housewife	20	175 Newbury
	D	Sadoulis Nicholas	139	painter	43	175 "
	E	Lynch Barbara M—†	139	clerk	20	here
	F	Lynch Josiah	139	painter	47	"
	G	*Lynch Stella—†	139	housewife	40	"
	H	Imondi Crescenzo	139	laborer	53	66 Fort av
	K	Imondi Marie—†	139	housewife	58	66 "
	L	Imondi Ruggiero	139	student	21	66 "
	M	Imondi William	139	guard	26	66 "
	N	Belfiore Dominic	140	bartender	47	here
	O	Belfiore Lillis—†	140	housewife	41	"
	P	Ryan John J, jr	140	cook	34	828 Parker
	R	Greenberg Andrew	140	retired	74	here
	S	Greenberg Elizabeth—†	140	housewife	73	"

Page.	Letter.	FULL NAME.	Residence, Jan. 1, 1946.	Occupation.	Supposed Age.	Reported Residence, Jan. 1, 1945. Street and Number.

Cedar Street—Continued

T	Goggin Anthony	140	chauffeur	46	here
U	Goggin Mary—†	140	housewife	42	"
V	Hart Agnes M—†	141	"	71	"
W	Hart Joseph A	141	laborer	31	
X	Hart Kathryn C—†	141	beautician	33	"
Y	Yerxa James	141	clerk	41	
Z	Yerxa Phyllis—†	141	housewife	27	"

16

A	Mudge Charles R	141	shoemaker	43	"
B	Mudge William F	141	surveyor	46	"
C	Mudge William F, jr	141	chauffeur	21	"
D	Gately Helen—†	143	housewife	40	"
E	Gately Margaret—†	143	secretary	20	"
F	Ellis Agnes—†	143	housewife	40	"
G	Ellis John	143	chauffeur	41	"
H	Kelly Bernard	143	U S M C	20	"
K	Kelly Lillian—†	143	housewife	46	"
L	Dunn Charles	144	painter	37	
M	Dunn Theresa—†	144	housewife	27	"
O	Little Carmen—†	145–147	"	30	
P	Little Ronald	145–147	clerk	34	
R	Fenton Herbert	145–147	bartender	38	"
S	Fenton Mary—†	145–147	housewife	37	"
T	Lee Gerald	145–147	machinist	28	131 Cedar
U	Lee John	145–147	U S A	33	131 "
V	Moriarty Frank J	146	seaman	31	here
W	Moriarty John J	146	clerk	43	"
X	Moriarty William A	146	inspector	33	"
Y	Stephens Ann—†	146	stitcher	58	"
Z	Santosuosso James A	146	inspector	46	792A Shawmut av

17

A	Santosuosso Marjorie D–†	146	housewife	36	792A "
B	Cameron John F	146	plumber	49	here
C	Doherty Mary A—†	146	housekeeper	49	"
D	Kenyon Alice—†	146	shoeworker	45	Hingham
E	Kenyon Arthur	146	cook	48	"
F	McCarthy John	146	chauffeur	40	here
G	Lieblish Bertha—†	146	operator	57	"
H	Allen Bernard	153	boatbuilder	39	"
K	Allen Palma—†	153	housewife	39	"
L	Trifiro Carmela—†	155	at home	64	"

Cedar Street—Continued

M	Trifiro Lucy—†	155	housekeeper	38	here
N	Leonard Christine—†	157	housewife	38	"
o	Leonard Peter	157	chauffeur	39	"
P	Spillane Catherine E—†	159	housewife	67	"
R	Spillane Ellen G—†	159	stenographer	65	"
T	Sorrenti Barbara—†	162	housekeeper	25	11A Jackson pl
U	Strong Josephine—†	162	waitress	51	11A "
V	Harrison Benjamin F	162	U S N	30	here
W	Sample Jenny L—†	162	housewife	51	"
X	Sample Jesse M	162	machinist	52	"
Y	Albert Alice P—†	162	housewife	40	"
Z	Albert William	162	laborer	45	

18

A	Carter Louise M—†	164	housewife	52	"
B	Carter Nicholas W	164	machinist	32	"
C	Hundert Bernice—†	164	housekeeper	26	"
D	Hundert Rudolph	164	manager	43	"
E	Buckley Florence—†	164	housewife	23	"
F	Buckley William	164	mechanic	25	"
H	McLaughlin Edward	166	laborer	54	
K	Nadelli Alice—†	166	housekeeper	21	"
L	Baker Albert	166	counterman	66	"
M	Baker Celia—†	166	at home	62	"
o	Frost Lewis	168A	storekeeper	52	"
P	Frost Ruth M—†	168A	housewife	41	"
S	Monahan Cornelius	172	laborer	67	"
T	Monahan Julia—†	172	housewife	67	"
U	Monahan Julia—†	172	SPAR	26	
V	Brown Catherine B—†	174	housekeeper	52	"
W	*McKinnon Sadie C—†	174	domestic	24	Nova Scotia
X	Remick Frank	174	salesman	27	23 Millmont
Y	Remick Irene—†	174	housewife	30	23 "
Z	Robbins Elizabeth—†	174	"	42	here

19

A	Robbins Frederick	174	laborer	48	

Centre Place

B	Apsit John J	1	machinist	71	here
C	*Apsit Minnie—†	1	housewife	64	"
D	Cromey Edward F	1	student	23	15 Highland av

11

Page.	Letter.	Full Name.	Residence, Jan. 1, 1946.	Occupation.	Supposed Age.	Reported Residence, Jan. 1, 1945. Street and Number.

Centre Place—Continued

	E	Filisen Ann—†	1	housewife	67	here
	F	Filisen John P	1	brakeman	62	"
	G	Heath Agnes—†	1	maid	66	"
	H	Bloomberg John	2	foreman	53	"
	K	Bloomberg Julia—†	2	housewife	55	"
	L	Grube Alice—†	2	"	40	..
	M	Grube August	2	brewer	53	
	N	Baneka Lola—†	2	nurse	34	
	O	Stroupe Alma B—†	3	secretary	36	"
	P	Sugar Edward J	3	painter	60	"
	R	Johnson Dorothy—†	3	housewife	31	"
	S	Johnson Ralph	3	supt	36	
	T	Herlihy Leo J	4	policeman	57	"
	V	Lamb Henry J	4	accountant	32	"
	W	Lamb Margaret—†	4	housewife	31	"
	Y	Lietner Clara—†	5	stitcher	54	"
	Z	Procopio Ann—†	5	"	38	

20

	A	Abbott Ann—†	5	saleswoman	29	"
	B	Abbott Warren	5	U S A	29	
	C	Hoye Helen—†	5	saleswoman	58	"
	D	Hoye Richard	5	welder	57	
	E	Hoefling Anton	6	retired	88	"
	F	Chapman Emily—†	6	housewife	60	1 Centre pl
	G	Timmons Mary M—†	6	at home	71	here

Centre Street

	H	Atherton James	47	retired	91	45 Centre
	K	Avon Adele—†	47	at home	62	24 Balfour
	L	Cronin John	47	retired	73	11 Revere
	M	Daley Francis D	47	chauffeur	33	103 McBride
	N	Daley Kathleen P—†	47	nurse	34	103 "
	O	Fitzpatrick Patrick	47	retired	72	407 E Fifth
	P	Garrity Austin	47	"	81	19 Maynard rd
	R	Lynch Mary—†	47	at home	73	247 Cornell
	S	Martyn Harriet—†	47	"	81	31 Edison
	T	McQuillan Nicholas	47	retired	59	495 Walnut av
	U	O'Brien Louise—†	47	at home	68	8 Elm Hill pk
	V	Oxton Rose—†	47	"	77	Braintree
	W	Oxton Walter	47	retired	78	"
	X	Pfeiffer Emma—†	47	at home	75	495 Walnut av

Centre Street—Continued

	Y	Richardson Fred	47	retired	89	56 Bakersfield
	z	Smith George	47	"	76	985 Wash'n
21						
	A	Tagney Dennis	47	"	74	34 Irwin
	B	Tinker Margaret—†	47	at home	61	Belmont
	c	Waite Oscar	47	retired	84	Winthrop
	D	Widman Elizabeth—†	47	at home	53	52 Chestnut av
	E	Wolk Charles W	47	retired	69	18 Dartmouth pl
	F	Wolk Josephine—†	47	at home	71	28 Ward
	G	Reid David	57	janitor	67	here
	H	Reid Janet M—†	57	clerk	33	"
	K	Johnson Carl R	57	retired	73	"
	N	Dolan Anna R—†	59	buyer	50	"
	o	Lindholm Mary—†	59	housewife	23	141 Centre
	P	Lindholm Robert W	59	warehouseman	24	141 "
	R*	Abolin Mary—†	61	at home	80	65 Prentiss
	s	Carrigan Paul	61	foreman	35	here
	T	Carrigan Rita—†	61	housewife	31	"
	v	MacDougall Mary—†	61	clerk	25	62 Highland
	w	MacDougall Robert	61	assembler	24	62 "
	x	Ecker Gustav G	63	machinist	39	here
	Y	Ecker Helen S—†	63	at home	71	"
	z	Pezzano Dominic	63	watchmaker	47	"
22						
	A	Pezzano Irma—†	63	housewife	45	"
	B	Armand Arnold	65	carpenter	36	"
	c	Armand Marie—†	65	housewife	30	"
	D	Denis Gladys—†	65	"	21	Connecticut
	E	Denis Lionel	65	floorman	32	582 Newbury
	F*	Robash Dora—†	67	housewife	67	here
	G	Robash Fred	67	machinist	69	"
	H	Lanigan Bridget—†	67	housewife	49	"
	K	Lanigan Robert	67	factoryhand	49	"
	L	Lanigan Robert J	67	U S A	20	"
	N	Martin Gilford	69	electrician	46	"
	o	Martin Myrtle—†	69	housewife	38	"
	P	Wik Madeline—†	69	clerk	33	
	R	Kelley Agnes M—†	71	at home	59	"
	s	Kelley Florence G—†	71	dietitian	38	"
	T	Kelley Romanzo A	71	inspector	49	"
	U	Riley Joseph	71	laborer	34	

Page.	Letter.	FULL NAME.	Residence, Jan. 1, 1946.	Occupation.	Supposed Age.	Reported Residence, Jan. 1, 1945. Street and Number.

Centre Street—Continued

v	Shamma Faris	71	proprietor	38	here
w	Shamma Mary—†	71	housewife	36	"
x	Hughes Gerard M	71	laborer	38	"
y	Hughes Marie E—†	71	at home	72	"
z	Brothers Alfred N	73	signalman	40	"

23

A	Brothers Edith M—†	73	laundress	34	"
B	Cunningham Dorothea S-†	73	social worker	31	"
c	Cunningham Thomas F	73	salesman	31	53 Beech Glen
D	Bailey Virginia—†	73	tel operator	23	here
E	Benner Ellen—†	73	housewife	57	"
F	Benner Thomas J	73	U S N	21	"
G	Murphy George A	73	engineer	66	"
H	Murphy Rosa M—†	73	housewife	65	"
K	Hiltz Marion T—†	75	pianist	46	
L	White Cecil E	75	electrician	36	"
M	White Florence G—†	75	housewife	35	"
N	Wallace Hazel—†	75	"	40	"
o	Wallace Peter J	75	toolmaker	38	"
P	Curran Anna R—†	77	housewife	44	"
R	Curran William H	77	rigger	45	"
s	Lamb John J	77	U S A	27	
T	Connors Charles J	77	laborer	50	
U	Connors Helen F—†	77	housewife	45	"
v	Woods Manuel	77	supt	41	
w	Woods Sophia—†	77	housewife	47	"
x	Barrett Ellen—†	79	"	32	
y	Barrett Thomas	79	inspector	33	"
z	Perry Clara E—†	79	housewife	57	"

24

A	Perry Roscoe F	79	chauffeur	69	"
B	Shargabian Charles	79	student	21	
c	Shargabian Isabelle—†	79	housewife	46	"
D	Shargabian James	79	U S C G	22	"
E	Mallon Anna—†	81	housewife	43	"
F	Mallon Helen—†	81	"	44	
G	Mallon Margaret—†	81	packer	73	
H	Hackett Mary—†	81	at home	74	"
K	Wheeler Alice—†	81	laundress	35	"
L	Hovhannesian Anna—†	81	housewife	35	"
M	Hovhannesian Sahag	81	laborer	48	

Centre Street—Continued

	Letter.	Full Name.	Residence, Jan. 1, 1946.	Occupation.	Supposed Age.	Reported Residence, Jan. 1, 1945. Street and Number.
	o	Peterson Annette—†	93	housewife	55	here
	p	Peterson Jacob	93	machinist	64	"
	r	Peterson Jacob A	93	electrician	25	"
	s	Peterson Alfred C	93	U S A	27	
	t	Peterson Mildred E—†	93	assembler	23	"
	u	Pettipas Catherine—†	93	"	37	54 Mozart
	v	Pitts Michael	93	waiter	35	N Hampshire
	w	Sullivan Charlotte—†	93	housewife	38	54 Mozart
	x	Sullivan James H	93	printer	44	54 "
	y	Cushman Alton D	94	clerk	21	here
	z	Ingemi Geraldine F—†	94	housewife	41	"
25						
	a	Ingemi Louis	94	foreman	45	"
	b	Lally John F	96	retired	77	
	c	Lally Julia L—†	96	at home	75	"
	d	Glennon Anna M—†	98	housewife	42	"
	e	Glennon Walter J	98	chauffeur	40	"
	f	Demetris Corrinne—†	100	housekeeper	22	"
	g	Demetris George	100	proprietor	56	"
	h	Demetris Mary—†	100	housewife	53	"
	k	O'Rourke Lucille J—†	100	factoryhand	48	"
	l	Curley Gertrude—†	107	housewife	46	"
	m	Curley Herbert	107	laborer	50	
	n	Gaffney Joseph F	107	painter	58	"
	o	Gaffney Mary A—†	107	housewife	57	"
	p	Gaffney Rita M—†	107	nurse	26	
	r	Donnelly Martin	107	bartender	53	"
	s	Kelley John J	107	U S N	48	
	t	Quinn Mary E—†	107	nurse	49	
	u	Francis Ann—†	109	instructor	30	"
	v	Francis Mary—†	109	tel operator	32	"
	w	Doyle Celia—†	109	secretary	32	"
	x	Finneran Patrick J	109	yardman	62	"
	y	McHugh Nellie A—†	109	housewife	68	"
26						
	a	McHugh Thomas H	109	guard	44	
	a¹	McHugh Thomas J	109	millhand	70	"
	b	Colby Effie—†	109	shoeworker	55	"
	c	Ela Florence—†	109	housewife	60	"
	d	Ela Marilyn L—†	109	inspector	21	"
	e	Burns James J	111	mortician	50	"
	f	Burns Mary J—†	111	housewife	54	"

15

Page.	Letter.	FULL NAME.	Residence, Jan. 1, 1946.	Occupation.	Supposed Age.	Reported Residence, Jan. 1, 1945. Street and Number.

Centre Street—Continued

	G	Daylor Daniel H	111	machinist	68	here
	H	Daylor Mary E—†	111	housewife	66	"
	K	Owens Carrie—†	111	clerk	38	"
	L	Skelly Margaret A—†	111	operator	56	"
	M	Galvin Mary L—†	117	housewife	70	"
	N	Galvin Thomas F	117	physician	72	"
	O	Gorham Rena M—†	117	domestic	40	"
	P	O'Neil Elizabeth A—†	117	teacher	73	
	R	O'Neil Katherine F—†	117	at home	77	
	S	Canavin Helen T—†	121	clerk	38	
	T	Canavin James	121	U S A	34	
	U	Canavin Mary A—†	121	housewife	71	"
	V	DeMeo Clara—†	121	"	27	
	W	DeMeo Frank	121	manager	28	"
	X	DeSimone Angelina—†	121	housewife	52	"
	Y	DeSimone Edward	121	U S N	27	"
	Z	DeSimone Martha—†	121	housewife	20	Tennessee

27

	A	DeSimone Prisco	121	carpenter	54	here
	B	DeSimone Prisco, jr	121	U S A	23	"
	C	DeSimone William	121	operator	26	"
	L	Roach Edward	123	bartender	42	"
	M	Roach Esther—†	123	housewife	32	"
	N	Wise Theresa—†	123	"	65	"
	O	Brown Jesse	125	porter	41	154 Worcester
	P	Curtis Albert	125	janitor	33	Brookline
	R	Preston Clara—†	125	housewife	25	Virginia
	S	Preston Leotis	125	laborer	28	"
	T	Pritchett Daniel E	125	cook	22	819 Col av
	U	Pritchett Mary—†	125	housewife	24	819 "
	V	Jones Emma—†	127	operator	60	here
	W	Patrick Helena—†	129	housewife	70	"
	X	Patrick Thomas W	129	physician	73	"
	Y	Greene Edith—†	131	electrician	45	"
	Z	Goldsmith Douglas L	131	janitor	34	

28

	A	Gosse Joseph	131	mechanic	54	"
	B	Gosse Mae—†	131	housewife	62	"
	D	Connelly Agnes V—†	137	"	47	
	E	Connelly Joseph F	137	foreman	48	
	F	Walsh Francis M	137	chauffeur	40	"
	G	Walsh Mary—†	137	housewife	38	"

Centre Street—Continued

H	Walsh Patrick J	137	laborer	51	here
K	Reynolds George M	137	mechanic	50	"
L	Reynolds Sarah C—†	137	housewife	47	"
M	Reynolds Theresa—†	137	saleswoman	51	"
N	Gasson George	139	carpenter	62	"
O	Gasson Lena—†	139	housewife	61	"
P	*Tiesenkoff Andrew	139	porter	60	
R	Clancy Michael	139	laborer	54	
S	Lane Mary—†	139	laundress	56	"
T	Lane Michael J	139	watchman	56	"
U	Travers George	139	musician	32	"
V	Travers Irma M—†	139	housewife	28	"
W	Wilke Helen—†	139	"	27	"
X	Wilke William A	139	inspector	29	"
Y	Galvin Cecelia—†	141	housewife	63	"
Z	Russell Margaret J—†	141	"	75	

29

A	Governor William F	141	electrician	46	"
B	Stockinger Charles J	141	rigger	27	
C	Stockinger Helen C—†	141	clerk	30	"
D	Stockinger Mary A—†	141	housewife	64	"

Columbus Avenue

W	Ross Marion—†	1263	cook	37	138 Fisher av
X	Baird John	1265	retired	81	here
Y	Baird Mary—†	1265	at home	67	"
Z	Stevenson George	1267	laborer	55	"

30

A	Hagerty Mary—†	1267	at home	81	"
B	Smith Agnes—†	1267	housewife	45	"
C	Smith Ruth—†	1267	clerk	21	
F	Walsh John	1271	foreman	40	
G	Walsh Mary A—†	1271	housewife	43	"
H	Walsh Mary M—†	1271	clerk	20	
N	Runnels Alice—†	1279	housewife	49	"
O	Holman Arthur	1279	mechanic	37	"
P	Holman Greta—†	1279	housewife	37	"
R	Holman Luther	1279	barber	60	
V	Bragel George	1299	mechanic	51	"
W	Bragel Maude—†	1299	housewife	45	"

31

L	Cyr Charles J	1362	clerk	30	

Page.	Letter.	FULL NAME.	Residence, Jan. 1, 1946.	Occupation.	Supposed Age.	Reported Residence, Jan. 1, 1945. Street and Number.

Columbus Avenue—Continued

	M	Cyr Jesse A	1362	painter	63	here
	N	Cyr Mary—†	1362	housewife	60	"
	O	Zacharchuk Leo A	1362	clerk	28	"
	P	Zacharchuk Mary—†	1362	housewife	53	"
	R	Rosenfield David	1362	salesman	57	"
	S	Rosenfield Rose—†	1362	housewife	28	"
	U	Byrne Margaret C—†	1368	"	61	
	V	Byrne William A	1368	porter	75	
	W	Parsons Margaret—†	1368	laundress	60	"
	Y	Kenney John T	1386	laborer	62	
	Z	Kenney Mary—†	1386	housewife	72	"

32

	A	Famulara Angelo	1386	janitor	63	
	C	Cardoza Joseph	1390	chauffeur	33	"
	D	Cardoza Rosimena—†	1390	housewife	27	"
	E	Earner John T	1390	chauffeur	39	"
	F	Earner Margaret—†	1390	housewife	69	"
	U	Dognazzi Edward	1400	baker	45	
	V	Dognazzi Julia—†	1400	housewife	35	"
	W	Webb Filomena—†	1400	at home	30	"
	X	Webb Walter	1400	steamfitter¹	33	"

Decatur Avenue

| | Z | Sinclair Hannah—† | 4 | housewife | 43 | here |

33

	A	Sinclair Herbert	4	chauffeur	44	"
	C	Flynn John	6	retired	66	
	D	Forlizzi Angelo	6	carpenter	39	"
	E	Forlizzi Maria—†	6	housewife	37	"

Fort Avenue

	F	Ashman Harry	17	carpenter	68	here
	G	Ashman Nathan	17	salesman	31	"
	H	*Ashman Rebecca—†	17	housewife	60	"
	K	Malis Mary—†	17	"	27	
	L	Malis Phillip	17	machinist	35	"
	M	Cusimano Morris	17	U S A	28	"
	N	DiLagami Peter	17	storekeeper	50	12 Highland
	O	DiLagami Theresa—†	17	housewife	48	12 "
	T	Judson Ida—†	23	"	50	here

Fort Avenue—Continued

U	Judson Mortimer J	23	molder	53	here
V	Washington Clara J—†	23	housewife	30	21 Highland Park av
W	Washington George W	23	machinist	31	21 "
X	Kimball Carter P	23	U S N	25	here

34

A	Simon George	27	doorman	31	"
B	Simon Mary A—†	27	housewife	40	"
C	Simon Charles J	27	U S N	20	
D	Simon William A	27	U S A	21	
E	Pirrello Evelyn F—†	27	housewife	24	"
F	Pirrello Joseph	27	U S A	24	
G	Smith Louise A—†	27	at home	62	"
H	Mahan Mary C—†	29	housewife	29	51 Fort av
K	Mahan Thomas J	29	factoryhand	32	51 "
M	Anderson Anna—†	29	cook	54	here
N	Anderson Gordon	29	laborer	25	"
O	Murphy Catherine—†	29	clerk	26	"
P	Brown Annie L—†	31	housewife	49	637 Warren
R	Brown John	31	mason	46	637 "
S	Barton Regina A—†	31	housewife	30	here
T	Barrett Thomas S	31	chauffeur	31	Brookline
U	Barrett Virginia—†	31	housewife	25	"
V	Logan Eldon	31	mechanic	21	Maine
W	Johansen Hedwig—†	35	housewife	36	147 Boylston
X	Johausen John E	35	mason	38	147 "
Y	Doiron Byron J	35	U S A	22	311 Warren
Z	Doiron Francis A	35	seaman	57	311 "

35

A	Doiron George R	35	U S N	21	311 '
B	Doiron Helen—†	35	nurse	21	311 "
C	Doiron Mary S—†	35	housewife	57	311 "
D	Michaud Elizabeth M—†	35	"	25	311 "
F	Peterson Mary A—†	37	"	53	here
G	Peterson Walter O	37	painter	57	"
H	Williamson Elizabeth—†	37	at home	64	"
K	Williamson Hans	37	cabinetmaker	65	"
L	Kahps Fritz	37	carpenter	58	"
M	*Kahps Lena—†	37	housewife	53	"
N	Koughan Anna—†	37	at home	64	"
O	Teague Evelyn—†	39	housewife	25	138 George
P	Stewart Douglas	39	laborer	39	N Hampshire

Fort Avenue—Continued

R	Stewart Martha—†	39	housewife	37	N Hampshire
S	Burke Thomas	39	machinist	61	here
T	Pettipass Mary A—†	39	laundress	54	"
V	Smith Charles R	41	machinist	60	"
W	Smith Lena—†	41	housewife	59	"
X	Smith Richard	41	laborer	21	
Y	Kenney Effie E—†	41	factoryhand	45	"
Z	Kenney Robert	41	laborer	27	

36

A	Barrett George A	41	chauffeur	35	"
B	Barrett Sarah—†	41	housewife	34	"
C	Hanf Robert	41	operator	28	"
D	Quandi Lena—†	43	at home	40	"
E	Pogeska Edna G—†	43	housewife	48	88 Lambert av
F	Monroe Elsie M—†	43	at home	45	here
G	Monroe John C	43	leatherworker	27	"
H	Gritti Angelo	43	U S A	27	"
K	*Vita Maria—†	43	at home	61	"
L	Doucet Bridget J—†	45	"	72	
M	Doucet Frank E	45	metalworker	37	"
N	Doucet John S	45	clerk	42	
O	Doucet Peter G	45	painter	36	
P	Engler Martha C—†	45	librarian	35	"
R	Engler Rudolph	45	fireman	63	
T	McGinnis Ruth H—†	45	at home	36	"
U	Mangott Gertrude V—†	47	housewife	31	"
V	Mangott John A	47	laborer	32	
W	Selmer Hermina—†	47	housewife	53	"
X	Selmer John	47	painter	59	
Y	Cloutier George E	47	cook	35	"
Z	Cloutier Irene I—†	47	housewife	35	"

37

B	Gollings Charles R	49	guard	38	
C	Gollings Eleanor M—†	49	housewife	39	"
D	Flynn Electra—†	49	"	64	
E	Flynn Francis J	49	U S A	27	
F	Moriarty Catherine—†	49	housewife	34	"
G	Moriarty Joseph	49	U S A	36	
H	Coen Mary—†	51	domestic	35	"
K	Harper Alexander A	51	laborer	40	
L	Harper Barbara E—†	51	at home	84	"

Fort Avenue—Continued

	M	Harper Viola A—†	51	bookkeeper	40	here
	N	Nolan Margaret—†	51	waitress	35	"
	O	Paquette Mary—†	51	seamstress	50	"
	P	Connor Blanche L—†	53	housewife	34	"
	R	Connor Charles	53	U S A	35	"
	S	Turner James F	53	"	26	23 Fort av
	T	Turner Mavis—†	53	housewife	23	23 "
	U	Roston Margaret F—†	53	inspector	64	here
	V	Wallace Laura R—†	53	domestic	32	"
	W	Reardon Ellen M—†	55	at home	53	59 Creighton
	X	Hallion Mary T—†	55	waitress	29	Brookline
	Y	Hallion William P	55	machinist	31	"
	Z	Reynolds Grace—†	55	waitress	25	here

38

	A	Reynolds Walter	55	U S A	29	
	B	Schlitz Catherine—†	57	leatherworker	27	"
	C	Schlitz Helen—†	57	clerk	25	
	D	Schlitz Joseph	57	shipper	61	
	E	Berbelisky Helen—†	57	housewife	56	"
	F	Berbelisky Joseph	57	machinist	61	"
	G	Tucker Annie B—†	57	housewife	75	63 Weston
	H	MacCormack Mary C—†	59	saleswoman	52	17 Highland Park av
	K	White Annie S—†	59	domestic	61	here
	L	White James H	59	electrician	27	"
	M	White Leslie D	59	rigger	55	"
	N	Postell Irene—†	61	housewife	58	"
	O	Goodrich John	61	laborer	49	
	P	Goodrich Rose—†	61	housewife	38	"
	T	Bird Mildred F—†	63	"	24	163 Highland
	U	McDonough Thomas	63	engineer	30	41 Fort av
	V	McDonough Viola—†	63	housewife	29	41 "
	W	McCall Mary E—†	65	"	23	here
	X	McCall Richard T	65	plumber	24	"
	Y	Lausier Ernest A	65	shipper	27	Pennsylvania
	Z	Lausier Grace J—†	65	housewife	22	"

39

	A	Nassiff Rose—†	65	shoeworker	31	25 Schuyler
	B	Morrill George	65	"	25	348 Ruggles
	C	Morrill Mabel—†	65	clerk	23	348 "
	G	Sullivan Delia—†	69	housekeeper	63	here
	H	Kennedy Raymond	69	welder	38	"

Fort Avenue—Continued

K	Kennedy Theresa—†	69	housewife	46	here
L	Calnan Hannah—†	69	"	69	"
M	Calnan Joseph	69	freighthandler	69	"
N	Sweeney Edward	73	laborer	45	"
O	Sweeney Eleanor—†	73	nurse	21	..
P	Sweeney Mary—†	73	housewife	42	"
R	Rogers Helen M—†	73	"	58	
S	Rogers John J	73	salesman	53	"
T	Rakauskas Helen—†	75	housewife	23	"
U	Sullivan Anna L—†	75	"	43	
V	Sullivan Percy W	75	presser	46	
W	Sullivan William D	75	U S N	21	"
X	Foye Elizabeth—†	79	housewife	28	41 Thornton
Y	Foye John	79	laborer	28	101 Dale
Z	Townsend James E	79	U S N	30	here

40

A	Townsend Marjorie—†	79	housewife	28	"
B	Wanders Francis	79	welder	25	5 Dudley
C	Hunter James	79	chauffeur	27	1 Shepherd av
D	Hunter Violet—†	79	housewife	25	Quincy
E	Mulvey Annie L—†	81	housekeeper	63	here
F	Norris Mary P—†	81	at home	66	"
G	Reynolds Edward A	81	retired	73	"
H	Cavicchi Frank	83	laborer	42	
K	Alessi Mary—†	83	housewife	29	"
L	Alessi Nicholas J	83	printer	29	
M	McDevitt Margaret—†	83	canteenworker	38	"
N	Weniger Ernest	85	metalworker	37	"
O	Weniger Gertrude—†	85	housewife	33	"
P	Lynch Eileen—†	85	clerk	21	
R	Lynch Mary—†	85	housewife	56	"
S	Gear Florence—†	85	"	35	"
T	Gear Thomas	85	clerk	35	11 Norfolk
U	Baker Helen I—†	87	stitcher	40	here
V	Connors Ellen—†	87	"	29	"
W	Cottrell Lawrence	87	laborer	55	"
X	Ericson Margaret—†	87	nurse	35	
Y	Ericson Richard	87	physician	35	"
Z	Carroll Josephine C—†	89	housekeeper	70	"

41

A	McCormick Effie—†	91	housewife	73	"

Fort Avenue—Continued

B	McCormick Joseph L	91	clerk	47	here
c	Farina James	91	U S A	20	"
D	Farina Louise—†	91	housewife	49	"
E	Farina Salvatore	91	tailor	68	"
F	Colon Mildred V—†	91	housekeeper	51	"
G	Schefchuk Alma—†	93	housewife	44	"
H	Schefchuk Frank	93	tailor	46	
K	Kopps Anna—†	93	housewife	54	"
L	Kopps George	93	breweryworker	58	"
M	Kopps Harold K	93	U S A	23	
N	Kopps Rita L—†	93	stenographer	21	"

Gardner Street

X	Olsen Harold	rear 10	painter	23	18 Letterfine ter
Y	Olsen Violet—†	" 10	housewife	21	18 "
z	Neviackas Edward	" 10	student	22	here
	42				
A	Neviackas Mary E—†	" 10	housewife	57	"
B	Scanlon Florence—†	" 10	"	45	
c	Scanlon James	" 10	U S N	44	"
D	Zahlit Arnold	12	painter	40	"
E	Zahlit Melanie—†	12	housewife	35	"
F	Feldmann Annette—†	12	at home	68	"
G	Fetler Betty—†	12	"	65	
H	Conrod Dorothy—†	16	"	39	"
K	Landers Helen—†	18	housewife	32	"
L	Landers Thomas	18	clerk	38	"
M	Mullin Doris—†	22	housewife	42	"
N	Mullin Edward T	22	storekeeper	61	"
O	Godin Blanche—†	22	operator	46	"
P	Godin Frank	22	janitor	50	"
R	Godin Ida—†	22	at home	21	"
S	Rodd Warren	22	mechanic	26	249 Roxbury
T	Whitson Alma—†	22	housewife	22	here
U	Whitson John E	22	packer	24	"
V	Hines Catherine—†	22	housewife	48	"
W	Hines Edward	22	laborer	47	
X	Hines Edward F	22	"	21	"
Y	McCarthy George	24	paperhanger	62	"
z	McCarthy Gertrude—†	24	housewife	57	130 Heath

43
Gardner Street—Continued

A	Moore James	24	U S A	37	here
B	Murphy Edith F—†	24	housewife	35	"
C	Murphy James P	24	painter	38	"
D	Bloomfield John	26	clerk	34	New York
E	Adams Armina—†	26	at home	69	here

Harrington Avenue

G	McCarthy Dorothy M—†	1	waitress	25	here
H	McCarthy Francis M	1	U S N	23	"
K	McCarthy Frank M	1	clerk	57	"
L	McCarthy Susan—†	1	housewife	60	"

Highland Street

P	Fioretti Armando	63	laborer	44	here
R	Fioretti Lena—†	63	housewife	40	"
S	Duzant Louis	63	waiter	55	"
T	Hill Edith—†	63	housewife	55	"
U	Hill John	63	mechanic	67	"
V	Meegan Bridget—†	63	at home	88	"
W	Meegan Joseph	63	painter	45	"
X	Meegan Marie—†	63	housewife	41	"
Y	Scherer Henrietta—†	65	"	41	
Z	Scherer Joseph	65	salesman	41	"

44

A	Garrity Frank	65	laborer	38	"
B	DelSette Frances—†	65	housewife	32	"
C	DelSette Thomas	65	engineer	38	"
D	Dunn Helen—†	67	housewife	30	"
E	Dunn John	67	clerk	32	
F	Hart Bridget—†	67	housewife	77	"
G	Hart James M	67	clerk	39	
H	Hart Mary E—†	67	bookkeeper	40	"
K	Hart Timothy	67	retired	73	"
L	Moore Robert	67	U S A	22	"
M	Moore Sarah—†	67	housewife	60	"
N	Bean William	69	engineer	50	"
O	Hicks Mary M—†	69	housewife	67	"
P	Hicks Thomas H	69	retired	71	

Page.	Letter.	Full Name.	Residence, Jan. 1, 1946.	Occupation.	Supposed Age.	Reported Residence, Jan. 1, 1945. Street and Number.

Highland Street—Continued

	R	Turner Clarence	69	chemist	31	New York
	s	Turner Lucille—†	69	housewife	34	"
	T	Boone Charles L	71	clerk	50	here
	U	Boone India R—†	71	housewife	48	"
	V	Branche George	71	student	20	"
	W	Branche Lillian—†	71	housewife	42	"
	X	Garrett Anna—†	71	"	50	
	Y	Ridgley Aldes	71	electrician	46	"
	Z	Ridgley Aldes	71	U S A	23	..

45

	A	Ridgley Garrett	71	student	23	
	B	Ridgley Mayme—†	71	housewife	48	"
	C	Tyson Maude G—†	71	domestic	42	"
	D	Thomas James	73	janitor	73	
	E	Thomas Jessie—†	73	housewife	70	"
	F	Colbert Samuel	73	janitor	28	99 Cedar
	G	McWilliams Lucinda—†	73	housekeeper	63	here
	H	Small Dorothy—†	75	housewife	32	"
	K	Small Fred	75	cook	39	"
	L	Taylor Mayme—†	75	housekeeper	39	"
	M	Robinson Alberta—†	75	housewife	37	"
	N	Robinson Doris—†	75	clerk	20	
	O	Robinson George	75	brakeman	40	"
	P	Sullivan Estelle—†	77	housewife	35	"
	R	Sullivan Ethelbert	77	clerk	40	"
	S	Butler Harvella—†	77	housewife	39	"
	T	Butler Sherman	77	welder	43	
	U	Fubler Mary V—†	77	housekeeper	67	"
	V	Bell Anna—†	79	housewife	33	"
	W	Bell Ernest	79	laborer	34	
	X	Wells Lucille—†	79	housewife	35	"
	Y	Wells Samuel	79	laborer	45	
	Z	Clark George	79	mechanic	34	"

46

	A	Clark Verna—†	79	housewife	32	"
	B	Kelley Harry	81	watchman	39	"
	C	Kelley Marjorie—†	81	housewife	32	"
	D	Bean Eileen—†	81	"	26	
	E	Bean Howard	81	laborer	26	
	F	Aroian Jacob	81	meatcutter	55	"
	G	Aroian John	81	U S A	27	

Page.	Letter.	FULL NAME.	Residence, Jan. 1, 1946.	Occupation.	Supposed Age.	Reported Residence, Jan. 1, 1945. Street and Number.

Highland Street—Continued

	Letter	FULL NAME	Res.	Occupation	Age	Reported Residence
	H	Aroian Mary—†	81	housewife	47	-here
	K	Aroian Mihran	81	laborer	24	"
	L	Heym Marguerite—†	81	candymaker	30	"
	N	Rautenberg George	85	shipper	31	41 Dorr
	O	Rautenberg Gertrude—†	85	housewife	25	41 "
	P	Winson Gloria—†	85	"	20	41 "
	R	Winson Raymond	85	laborer	21	41 "
	T	Gareri Anthony	101	chauffeur	32	121 Marcella
	U	Gareri Concetta—†	101	housewife	32	here
	V	Needham Marion—†	101	"	34	"
	W	Needham Mary—†	101	bookkeeper	49	"
	X	Needham Thomas	101	mechanic	47	"
	Y	Flannery Estelle—†	101	housewife	32	"
	Z	Flannery William	101	letter carrier	40	"

47

	Letter	FULL NAME	Res.	Occupation	Age	Reported Residence
	A	Hamill Francis J	103	mechanic	41	"
	B	Hamill Helen—†	103	housewife	44	"
	C	Manifase Earl	103	carpenter	48	"
	D	Manifase Mary—†	103	housewife	36	"
	E	O'Connell Joseph	103	U S A	21	
	F	O'Connell Mary—†	103	housewife	20	"
	G	Lamattini John	103	laborer	60	
	H	Lamattini Maria—†	103	housewife	62	"
	K	Lamattini Ralph	103	U S N	23	
	L	Lamattini Rocco	103	"	20	"
	M	Lamattini Louise—†	103	clerk	21	"
	N	Brooks Emerette—†	125	at home	88	"
	O	Brown Annie—†	125	"	80	
	P	Clark Anna N—†	125	"	62	
	R	Curtis Katherine—†	125	"	82	
	S	Evans Josephine—†	125	"	94	
	T	Gardner Fanny—†	125		95	..
	U	Harris Anna—†	125	"	83	
	V	Hooper Helena I—†	125	nurse	70	"
	W	Jones Mary—†	125	at home	84	193 W Springfield
	X	Langley Mary—†	125	"	77	here
	Y	Laws Emma—†	125	"	80	1 Northampton
	Z	Lee Emily—†	125		94	here

48

	Letter	FULL NAME	Res.	Occupation	Age	Reported Residence
	A	Lewis Annie—†	125		67	Everett
	B	*Mangher Josephine—†	125	"	72	here

Page.	Letter.	FULL NAME.	Residence, Jan. 1, 1946.	Occupation.	Supposed Age.	Reported Residence, Jan. 1, 1945. Street and Number.

Highland Street—Continued

c	*Mason Hannah—†	125	at home	76	here
D	Miller Lydia—†	125	"	60	Everett
E	Murphy Lottie—†	125	maid	35	here
F	Nowell Frances G—†	125	at home	72	"
G	*Peters Edith—†	125	"	63	West Indies
H	*Price Annie M—†	125	"	57	here
K	*Reid Anna—†	125	"	85	"
L	Taylor Eliza—†	125		85	Cambridge
M	Taylor Lillian—†	125		81	here
N	Walker Jennie—†	125		80	"
o	White Rosa—†	125	"	86	"
P	Wolfe Clara A—†	125	teacher	53	New York
R	Whitefield Annetta O—†	133	housewife	36	here
S	Whitefield Oliva M—†	133	"	33	"
T	Whitefield Rudolf	133	chauffeur	40	"
U	Whitefield Theodore R	133	laborer	35	
V	Haithman Irene G—†	133	housekeeper	46	"
W	Kanton Margaret—†	135	housewife	52	"
X	Azevado Emanuel	135	painter	45	"
Y	Azevado Helen A—†	135	housewife	42	"
Z	Azevado Helen A—†	135	shipper	26	

49

A	Parker Verna—†	135	clerk	36	
E	Barr Catherine—†	139	teacher	50	"
F	Crowley David F	141	checker	50	"
G	Crowley Edward G	141	U S N	21	
H	Crowley Margaret M—†	141	housewife	51	"
K	Crowley Margaret M—†	141	clerk	22	"
L	Crowley Timothy J	141	policeman	24	"
M	Urquhart Margaret—†	141	housewife	40	"
N	Urquhart Truman	141	cableworker	44	"
o	Ellison Francis	141	laborer	40	"
P	Ellison Rose—†	141	housewife	34	"
R	Cephas Charles	143	retired	70	
S	Rosa Evelyn—†	143	housewife	23	"
T	Rosa Jesse	143	porter	26	"

Highland Park Avenue

U	Rafferty Mary T—†	5	housewife	58	here
V	Rafferty Thomas J	5	clerk	61	"
W	Berweiler Bertha—†	5	housewife	73	"

Page.	Letter.	FULL NAME.	Residence, Jan. 1, 1946.	Occupation.	Supposed Age.	Reported Residence, Jan. 1, 1945. Street and Number.

Highland Park Avenue—Continued

X	Berweiler Nicholas	5	waiter	67	here
Y	Rafferty Mary F—†	5	stenographer	21	"
Z	Foye Arthur	7	chauffeur	27	10 Union av
	50				
A	Gately John J	7	carpenter	50	here
B	Gately Mary A—†	7	housewife	44	"
C	White Julia—†	7	stitcher	26	"
D	White Margaret—†	7	housewife	61	"
E	Dansereau Addie—†	8	"	66	
F	Dansereau Alfred	8	machinist	25	"
G	Goodell Henry	8	"	63	
H	Kucher Michael	8	maintenance	27	"
K	Kucher Pauline—†	8	housewife	50	"
L	Kucher Samuel	8	watchman	52	"
M	Wynohrodnyk Annie—†	8	dressmaker	28	"
N	Wynohrodnyk John	8	printer	29	
O	Slaughter Edward	9	clerk	60	
P	Slaughter Elizabeth—†	9	housewife	58	"
R	Slaughter Ernest	9	technician	32	"
S	Allen May S—†	11	domestic	68	"
T	Chappel Leonora—†	11	maid	57	
U	Davis Morris G	11	mortician	35	"
V	Davis Rosa—†	11	housewife	59	"
W	Grey Booker	13	presser	39	"
X	Benjamin Albert L	13	electrician	30	109 Sterling
Y	Benjamin Marquita—†	13	housewife	21	109 "
Z	Harris Adelaide—†	13	"	25	205 W Springfield
	51				
A	Harris William D	13	chauffeur	23	205 "
B	Kupchyk John	14	bartender	51	here
C	Kupchyk Tina—†	14	housewife	50	"
G	Homan Mary—†	16	"	34	"
H	Homan William	16	engineer	35	"
K	Bodnar Eva—†	16	housewife	65	"
L	Bodnar Peter	16	mechanic	67	"
M	Bodnar Waldemar	16	U S A	24	
N	Popowich Helen—†	16	baker	53	
O	Popowich Mary—†	16	at home	30	"
S	Durfer Frederick, jr	17	laborer	28	
T	Durfer Margaret G—†	17	housewife	29	"
U	Meyers Alice—†	18	librarian	29	"

Highland Park Avenue—Continued

v	Toorks Peter	18	carpenter	59	here
w	Toorks Wilhelmina—†	18	housewife	59	"
x	Knisbell Arthur J	19	machinist	28	845 Boylston
y	Knisbell Shirley—†	19	housewife	23	845 "
z	Malone Francis	19	U S N	26	Medford

52

A	Malone Mary—†	19	waitress	27	"
B	Richardson Lorena M—†	19	at home	78	here
c	*Rvastin Emily—†	20	stitcher	56	"
D	Rvastin Evelyn—†	20	clerk	20	"
E	Gilmore Alice—†	20	housekeeper	48	"
F	Rose Lawrence A	20	shipper	25	"
G	*Stanley John C	21	laborer	44	17 Trotter ct
H	*Stanley Lucille L—†	21	housewife	34	S Carolina
K	Gaskill Grace E—†	22	housekeeper	41	here
L	Hamilton Hugh V	22	chauffeur	46	"
M	Hunter Charles E	23	roofer	50	"
N	Hunter Ernest	23	"	52	
o	Hunter Thomas	23	foreman	61	"
P	Caulfield Anna B—†	24	cleaner	44	"
R	Lohnes George J	24	U S N	21	18 Fulda
s	Lohnes Mary E—†	24	factoryhand	21	here
T	Barrows Joseph A	25	porter	76	"
U	Simpson Reuben O	25	"	53	"
v	Simpson Winifred V—†	25	housewife	46	"
w	Caulfield James	26	clerk	39	
x	Kelly Alice J—†	26	housewife	53	"
y	Kelly Peter J	26	custodian	55	"
z	Cochis Christopher	27	storekeeper	24	"

53

A	Cochis Dennis	27	"	22	
B	Cochis Joseph	27		20	"
c	Cochis Nicholas	27	"	69	
D	Cochis Peter	27	U S A	21	
E	*Cochis Sophie—†	27	housewife	50	"
F	Gilpatrick Frank	28	janitor	65	"
G	Szemeta Anna—†	28	housewife	68	"
H	Szemeta Michael	28	painter	65	"
K	La Farge Lillian—†	29	cleaner	43	"
L	LaFarge Vivian	29	watchman	48	"
N	Gittens Alice—†	31	cleaner	49	

Page.	Letter.	FULL NAME.	Residence, Jan. 1, 1946.	Occupation.	Supposed Age.	Reported Residence, Jan. 1, 1945. Street and Number.

Highland Park Avenue—Continued

	o	Gittens Hubert	31	porter	66	here
	R	McManus Francis	32	operator	34	"
	s	McManus Margaret—†	32	housewife	33	"
	T	Riley John	32	retired	70	
	u	Riley John, jr	32	student	24	
	v	Ross Alexander	34	chauffeur	43	"
	w	Ross Elizabeth—†	34	housewife	43	"
	x	Assatly Marguerite—†	34	"	30	"
	y	Assatly William	34	laborer	31	
	z	Wadsemeek Andrew	34	retired	48	
54						
	E	Pacheco Anthony F	38	clerk	35	
	F	Pacheco Stella—†	38	housewife	28	"
	G	Zukowski Jennie—†	38	packer	23	"
	H	Zukowski Paul	38	sprayer	26	40 Blue Hill av
	K	Begee Alma—†	38	typist	21	here
	L	Begee Benjamin	38	painter	52	"
	M	Begee Mary—†	38	housewife	47	"
	N	Begee Mary R—†	38	bookkeeper	24	"
	o	Henry Mary D—†	41	housewife	35	"
	P	Henry Paul V	41	chauffeur	35	"

Highland Park Street

	s	Morrows Mary—†	40	housewife	50	here
	T	Morrows Peter	40	cleaner	44	"
	u	Zwarych George	40	machinist	52	"
	v	Zwarych Margaret—†	40	housewife	49	"
	w	Zwarych Walter	40	U S N	22	

Linwood Street

	Y	Grady Geraldine S—†	2	housewife	33	here
	z	Grady William P	2	clerk	41	"
55						
	A	Welchlin John H	2	machinist	60	Norwood
	B	Hantis Costas G	2	cook	55	here
	c	Hantis George C	2	U S A	21	"
	D	Hantis Pelagia—†	2	housewife	50	"
	E	Graham Elizabeth—†	4	clerk	40	
	F	Frohmut Caroline—†	4	housewife	57	"
	G	Frohmut George	4	toolmaker	72	"

Linwood Street—Continued

H	Grant Mary—†	4	housewife	70	here
K	Downey Elizabeth—†	6	"	63	"
L	Downey John F	6	guard	34	"
M	Lyons Arthur	6	clerk	26	"
N	Lyons Margaret—†	6	housewife	25	"
O	De Lodge Rita—†	6	"	32	"
P	Brown George	10	retired	80	"
R	Brown Simon	10	janitor	47	"
S	Buckingham Beatrice—†	10	housewife	39	"
T	Buckingham Clarence H	10	technician	38	"
U	Giunta Marquerita—†	10	bookkeeper	25	"
V	Giunta Santina—†	10	housewife	53	"
W	Giunta Santo	10	repairman	53	
X	Collins Frances—†	10	clerk	21	"
Y	Collins Louise—†	10	housewife	46	"
Z	Collins Timothy F	10	repairman	48	"

56

A	Huggins Ruth A—†	14	housewife	46	"
B	McCarthy James G	14	brakeman	51	"
C	Muise Charles A	14	welder	62	
D	Muise Gordon V	14	clerk	22	"
E	Muise Virginia A—†	14	housewife	50	"
F	Ganom Helen—†	14	shoeworker	60	"
G	Van Auken Beatrice—†	14	"	38	"
H	*Hughes Dorothy—†	16	housewife	34	"
K	Hughes James	16	chauffeur	44	"
L	Themmen Alfred T	16	printer	53	"
M	Themmen Constance—†	16	at home	23	"
N	*Themmen Frances—†	16	housewife	47	"
O	Themmen Mary—†	16	clerk	21	
P	Connors Annie E—†	16	at home	76	"
R	Connors Michael J	16	retired	72	"
S	Connors Thomas W	16	machinist	62	"
T	Leeds Katherine L—†	16	housekeeper	64	"
U	*Higgins Bridie—†	18	housewife	37	"
V	Higgins James	18	laborer	39	"
W	Goode James	18	clerk	35	"
X	Goode Marie—†	18	housewife	32	"
Y	Crowley Lillian—†	18	"	44	"
Z	Perkins Susie B—†	20	bookkeeper	62	53 Linwood

57
Linwood Street—Continued

	Letter	FULL NAME	Residence	Occupation	Age	Reported Residence
	A	Richards Louise K—†	20	at home	65	53 Linwood
	B	Manning Francis D	20	carpenter	45	here
	C	Manning Winifred E—†	20	housewife	42	"
	D	Kontanis Anna—†	20	clerk	25	"
	E	Kontanis Leon	20	shipper	26	
	F	Kontanis Nicholas L	20	laborer	60	
	G	Kontanis Stella—†	20	housewife	48	"
	H	Cronin Daniel W	24	electrician	50	51 Linwood
	K	Larkin Helen F—†	24	housewife	60	here
	L	Larkin William B	24	salesman	70	"
	M	Bradford George B	26	retired	81	"
	N	Gallagher Annie J—†	26	housewife	55	New York
	O	Gallagher Fred T	26	salesman	59	"
	P	Larkin James E	26	U S A	25	24 Linwood
	R	Larkin Madeline—†	26	housewife	22	3 Austin
	S	Lewis Fannie—†	32	"	48	here
	T	Lewis Irving	32	attorney	44	"
	U	Lewis Josiah	32	salesman	40	"
	V	Lewis Rose S—†	32	saleswoman	42	"
	W	Lewis Samuel	32	salesman	52	"
	X	Lewis Solomon	32	electrician	50	"
	Y	Curran Bessie—†	34	at home	60	"
	Z	Gormley Marie F—†	34	housewife	35	"

58

	Letter	FULL NAME	Residence	Occupation	Age	Reported Residence
	A	Gormley William J	34	mortician	37	"
	B	McKenna Elizabeth—†	40	housewife	22	Brookline
	C	McKenna Warren H	40	clergyman	27	"
	D	Currotto Gregory	44	retired	78	here
	E	Genest Joseph	44	painter	64	"
	F	Raftes Charles	44	retired	75	"
	G	*Raftes Mary—†	44	janitress	58	"
	H	Vasconcellos Theodora—†	44	housewife	28	"
	K	Vasconcellos Walter	44	U S A	29	
	L	Shea Harry F	44	policeman	58	"
	M	Shea Isabella V—†	44	housewife	43	"
	N	Dame Claudia B—†	46	at home	82	"
	O	Reilly John F	46	messenger	65	"
	P	Reilly Mary H—†	46	housewife	64	"
	R	White Margaret G—†	46	housekeeper	45	"

Linwood Street—Continued

	Letter	Full Name	Res.	Occupation	Age	Reported Residence
	s	*Comiaris George	50	baker	55	here
	t	Comiaris Pauline—†	50	clerk	24	"
	u	*Comiaris Stella—†	50	housewife	52	"
	v	Georgenes George	50	storekeeper	50	"
	w	*Georgenes Victoria—†	50	housewife	48	"
	x	Ansin Lillian—†	54	clerk	26	"
	y	Boudreault James	54	draftsman	22	157 Hemenway
	z	Boudreault Rosalie—†	54	housewife	23	157 "
59						
	A	Cousins Alma—†	54	clerk	31	here
	B	Dabol Elizabeth—†	54	housewife	60	"
	c	Dabol John	54	painter	60	"
	D	Johns John	54	accountant	43	"
	E	Downey Arthur G	56	social worker	41	"
	F	Downey Mary E—†	56	typist	50	
	G	Downey Phillip J	56	laborer	45	"
	H	Downey Walter C	56	mechanic	43	"

Merton Place

	Letter	Full Name	Res.	Occupation	Age	Reported Residence
	K	Pugsley Dora G—†	1	housewife	70	here
	L	Pugsley Frederick	1	mechanic	63	"
	N	Delehanty John F	2	clerk	35	"
	o	Delehanty Rose M—†	2	housewife	39	"
	P	Kalpowsky Emily—†	2	"	61	
	R	Kalpowsky Jacob	2	carpenter	66	"
	s	Doetch August	2	collector	43	"
	T	Doetch Norma G—†	2	housewife	37	"
	v	Potheir Ann—†	rear 2	clerk	49	
	w	Hanscom Herbert	" 2	U S N	23	
	x	Hanscom Martha—†	" 2	housewife	20	"
	y	Martin Ella—†	" 2	"	53	
	z	Martin Ora	" 2	clerk	26	
60						
	A	Reilly James	3	pipefitter	49	"
	B	Reilly Rose—†	3	clerk	40	
	c	Vilegor Anthony	3	"	29	
	D	Vilegor Mary—†	3	housewife	41	"
	E	Vilegor Vincent	3	clerk	52	
	F	Epple Mary—†	4	housewife	65	"
	G	Epple William J	4	rigger	61	"
	H	Dandrow Florence—†	4	housewife	46	"

11—1

Merton Place—Continued

K	McGee Margaret—†	4	housewife	70	here
L	Murphy Chester C	4	machinist	38	"
M	Murphy Helen E—†	4	housewife	40	"

Newark Street

N	Davidson Jeffery	6	metalworker	22	5 Bromley pk
O	Davidson Katherine—†	6	housewife	22	5 "
P	McCune James	6	pipefitter	43	here
R	McCune Rosalie—†	6	housewife	29	"
S	*Levesque Blanche—†	6	"	34	"
T	Levesque Homer	6	laborer	44	"
U	Clapp Henry A	7	machinist	40	24 Crandall
V	Clapp Ruth L—†	7	housewife	36	24 "
W	Boyajian Michael	7	laborer	50	here
X	Boyajian Rose—†	7	housewife	43	"
Y	Healy Ellen—†	7	"	72	"
Z	Healy Michael	7	laborer	60	

61

A	Hirtle Frank	8	ironworker	33	"
B	Hirtle Gertrude—†	8	housewife	32	"
C	Innocenti Charles	8	sorter	54	"
D	Innocenti Ethel T—†	8	housewife	37	133 Warren
E	Feller Helen—†	8	housekeeper	64	25 Valentine
F	Mallet Charles	8	laborer	62	25 "
H	Russell Edward	11	U S A	30	Salem
K	Russell Mary—†	11	housewife	28	"
N	Bissette Alvan	13	U S N	26	Cambridge
O	Bissette Dorothy—†	13	housewife	20	"
P	Hayward Daniel	13	attendant	35	here
R	Hayward Estelle—†	13	housewife	32	"
S	Kilroy Dorothy—†	13	operator	25	"
T	Callahan Vera—†	15	housewife	48	49 Delle av
V	Hayward Audrey—†	15	"	44	here
W	Hayward Robert	15	chauffeur	30	"
X	Gould Ethel F—†	17	housewife	42	"
Y	Gould Francis E	17	piano tuner	42	"
Z	Hagopian Arman	17	barber	50	

62

A	Hagopian Zabel—†	17	housewife	37	"
B	*Nahabedian Catherine—†	17	"	58	

34

Newark Street—Continued

c	Scott Rosemary—†	19	housewife	23	159 Readville
d	Scott William H	19	chauffeur	22	159 "
e	Pickett Frank	19	roofer	33	here
f	Pickett Helen—†	19	housewife	34	"
g	Nahabedian Dirouhi—†	19	housekeeper	43	"
h	Collins Anna E—†	21	housewife	58	"
k	Collins Mary E—†	21	assembler	23	"
l	Bairt Alva—†	21	housewife	47	56 Delle av
m	Bairt Claude	21	painter	52	56 "
n	Littlehale Milton	21	laborer	30	14 Southern av
o	Littlehale Roberta—†	21	housewife	25	14 "
p	Bourque Demerise—†	23	housekeeper	65	here
r	Shaller Bertha—†	23	at home	44	"
s	Carnation Bernadette—†	23	housewife	34	"
t	Carnation Joseph	23	U S N	30	"
u	Riley Rose E—†	23	folder	44	3 Merton pl
v	Dotolo Frank	32	driller	36	here
w	Dotolo Margaret—†	32	housewife	24	"
y	McNally Jennie—†	32	operator	39	"
z	McNally John F	32	chauffeur	40	"

63　New Heath Street

a	Cryan Mary A—†	1	housewife	55	here
b	Cryan Mary E—†	1	teacher	21	"
c	Davin Peter	1	clerk	40	"
d	Doherty Bridget M—†	1	housewife	48	"
e	Doherty John	1	clerk	48	
f	Burns Mary—†	3	housewife	57	"
g	Burns Phillip	3	machinist	58	"
h	Regan Ellen—†	3	housewife	25	"
k	Pray Irene—†	5	"	36	
l	Pray Winfred	5	painter	35	"
m	Farrell Delia T—†	5	housewife	64	"
n	Farrell James R	5	clerk	37	"
o	Farrell Joseph F	5	"	26	
p	Gray Anne—†	5	"	73	
r	Kelly William	7	retired	68	"
s	Reid Clarence	9	custodian	42	"
t	Reid Ovetta—†	9	housewife	34	"
u	Burton Embrue	9	clerk	53	

New Heath Street—Continued

v	Gibson Harold	9	U S N	29	here
w	Gibson Mildred—†	9	housewife	27	"
x	Jones Charles	11	U S A	32	"
y	Jones John	11	retired	75	64 Dudley
z	Jones Joseph S	11	seaman	38	64 "

64

A	Miller Anna T—†	11	housewife	36	here
B	Miller Thomas P	11	clerk	38	"
c	McDonald Angela—†	13	housewife	34	"
D	Uva William	13	custodian	43	"
E	Doyle Francis A	13	U S N	22	18 Lawn
F	Doyle Francis M	13	fisherman	53	18 "
G	Doyle Ida M—†	13	housewife	51	18 "
H	Doyle John P	13	policeman	25	18 "
K	Finneran Margaret—†	15	housewife	62	here
L	Finneran Margaret—†	15	clerk	21	"
M	Pray Chalmers	17	painter	41	"
N	Pray Chalmers F	17	U S A	21	

Romar Terrace

o	Noseworthy Mary—†	4	housewife	46	here
p	Noseworthy Matthias	4	fireman	54	"
R	Larson John	4	carpenter	39	"
s	*Larson Margaret—†	4	housewife	40	"
T	Larson Vera—†	4	clerk	20	
u	Antone Anthony	4	waiter	27	"
v	*Antone Nicoletta—†	4	housewife	59	"
w	Antone Paul	4	U S A	27	
x	Antone Peter	4	retired	67	
Y	Antone Sophie—†	4	clerk	31	
z	*Gurzik Mary—†	6	housewife	55	"

65

A	*Gurzik Walter	6	molder	53	
B	Ogiba Frank	6	U S N	22	
c	Sadowski Bertha—†	6	housewife	34	"
D	Sadowski Matthew	6	clerk	35	"
E	Anthony Hazen	6	chauffeur	47	68 Sherman
F	Anthony Mary T—†	6	housewife	34	53 Beech Glen
G	Lasman Albert	8	carpenter	33	2992 Wash'n

Page.	Letter.	FULL NAME.	Residence, Jan. 1, 1946.	Occupation.	Supposed Age.	Reported Residence, Jan. 1, 1945. Street and Number.

Romar Terrace—Continued

	H	Lasman Lillian—†	8	housewife	34	2992 Wash'n
	K	Duke John	8	carpenter	64	here
	L	Duke Mary—†	8	housewife	63	"
	M	Leonard Fred	8	clerk	50	"
	N	Smith Albert	8	U S A	22	
	O	Smith Alexander	8	carpenter	51	"
	P	Smith Augusta—†	8	clerk	49	

Roxbury Street

	R	Whitney Louise F—†	292	waitress	44	here
	S	Whitney Louise N—†	292	cashier	25	"
	T	Nehiley Adelaide—†	292	housewife	56	"
	U	Nehiley Joseph	292	retired	61	"
	V	Kelly Catherine—†	292	stitcher	49	1177A Tremont
	W	Kelly William J	292	chauffeur	29	1177A "
	X	LaFrenier Diana—†	294	clerk	35	here
	Y	Schilling Marion A—†	294	factoryhand	46	"
	Z	Schilling Walter J	294	U S N	20	"

66

	A	Malcolm Catherine V—†	294	clerk	49	
	B	Malcolm Veronica C—†	294	"	24	
	F	Colby Gertrude—†	298	saleswoman	55	"
	G*	Grynczel Michael	298	chef	50	
	H	Breton Adam A	298	"	67	
	K	Dunn Frances—†	298	factoryhand	59	"
	L	Summer Israel	300	tailor	43	
	M*	Zabchuk Andrew	300	cook	55	"
	P	MacLean Angus	308	carpenter	48	134 Terrace
	R	MacLean Ernest A	308	salesman	23	5 Walden
	S	MacLean Hazel—†	308	at home	21	134 Terrace
	T	MacLean Jane—†	308	cook	45	134 "

Ward 11–Precinct 2

CITY OF BOSTON

LIST OF RESIDENTS
20 YEARS OF AGE AND OVER

(NON-CITIZENS INDICATED BY ASTERISK)
(FEMALES INDICATED BY DAGGER)

AS OF

JANUARY 1, 1946

THOMAS F. SULLIVAN, *Chairman*
FREDERIC E. DOWLING, *Secretary*
WILLIAM A. MOTLEY, JR.
ARTHUR V. COUGHLIN
EVERETT R. PROUT

Listing Board.

CITY OF BOSTON ✦ PRINTING DEPARTMENT

200

Amory Street

A	Clark Gertrude—†	32	housewife	24	here
B	Clark Vendorus	32	machinist	39	"
C	Sykes Alice M—†	32	housewife	27	29 Lamartine
D	Sykes Harry L	32	retired	44	29 "
E	O'Donnell Gertrude A—†	32	housewife	44	here
F	O'Donnell James J	32	machinist	33	"
G	Mayer Loretta—†	34	housewife	53	"
H	Mayer Norman	34	shipper	25	
K	Mayer William	34	rigger	54	"
L	Hagan Priscilla—†	34	housewife	52	"
M	Hagan William F	34	chauffeur	57	"
O	Ehret Bernard	42	retired	83	
P	Gahm Christian	42	baker	38	
R	Hudlin Herman J	42	machinist	67	"
S	McEleney Beatrice A—†	44	laundress	45	"
T	McEleney Edward F	44	shipper	56	
U	Willis George	44	ironworker	42	"
V	Willis Sarah—†	44	housewife	37	"
W	Mahoney Catherine W—†	46	"	38	"
X	Mahoney Francis V	46	chauffeur	40	"
Y	Rich Louis C	48	watchman	72	"
Z	Rich Sarah E—†	48	housewife	61	"

201

A	Wagner Jason	48	machinist	63	"

Batchelder Terrace

C	Dacey Catherine—†	1	housewife	50	here
D	Dacey James	1	retired	80	"
E	Sussan Catherine—†	2	housewife	45	"
F	Sussan David	2	clerk	52	
G	Crehan Helen G—†	3	housewife	34	"
H	Crehan Matthew P	3	inspector	43	"
K	Gurney Joseph P	3	laborer	56	
L	Gurney Margaret—†	3	housewife	56	"
M	Nihan Ruth—†	3	WAC	28	
N	Rose Pauline—†	3	"	20	"
O	Gorham John P	4	carpenter	61	11 Carson
P	Joyce James J	4	entertainer	22	here
R	Joyce Julia M—†	4	housewife	47	"

Batchelder Terrace—Continued

| | s | Masterson Betty—† | 5 | housewife | 31 | here |
| | t | Masterson James | 5 | U.S N | 31 | " |

Beech Glen Street

	x	Yagjian George	21	chauffeur	34	here
	y	Yagjian Mary—†	21	at home	32	"
	w	Yagjian Richard	21	retired	67	"
	z	Yagjian Rose—†	21	housewife	56	"
202						
	a	Arzoumanian Zabar	21	proprietor	68	"
	b	DerAbrahamian Elmas—†	21	housewife	48	"
	c	DerAbrahamian Michael	21	clerk	58	"
	d	Karagozian Rubin	21	laborer	48	"
	e	Karagozian Seranough—†	21	housewife	36	"
	f	*Kevosian Mary—†	21	housekeeper	58	"
	g	Bersin Alexander	25	factoryworker	45	"
	h	Darles Helen—†	25	housekeeper	62	"
	k	Darles Waldemar	25	machinist	32	"
	l	Pehda Emily—†	25	laundress	51	"
	m	Pehda Philip	25	U S A	24	
	n	Blackten Florence—†	25	beautician	45	"
	o	Blackten Leona—†	25	teacher	22	"
	p	Parkas Basil	25	bartender	30	"
	r	Danahy Emily—†	27	housewife	48	"
	s	Danahy Timothy J	27	pipefitter	46	"
	t	Hubbard Brenda—†	27	housewife	43	5 Gloucester pl
	u	Hubbard William A	27	machinist	45	5 "
	v	Dunbar Francis J	29	plumber	38	here
	w	Dunbar Josephine G—†	29	housewife	39	"
	z	O'Leary Catherine M—†	31	"	56	"
203						
	a	O'Leary Charles T	31	attorney	28	"
	b	O'Leary Dennis J	31	letter carrier	59	"
	c	O'Leary John J	31	operator	32	"
	d	Battles Kathleen—†	31	housewife	30	"
	e	Battles William E	31	U S A	28	
	f	McGrady John	31	"	27	
	g	McGrady Josephine—†	31	housewife	25	"
	h	Majors Alta S—†	33	"	29	
	k	Majors David S	33	garageman	32	"

3

Page.	Letter.	FULL NAME.	Residence, Jan. 1, 1946.	Occupation.	Supposed Age.	Reported Residence, Jan. 1. 1945. Street and Number

Beech Glen Street—Continued

	M	Fitzgerald Helen J—†	43	operator	47	here
	N	Tjaerlis Constantine—†	43	cook	53	"
	O	O'Brien Ann M—†	43	housewife	31	"
	P	O'Brien Daniel J	43	mechanic	31	"
	R	Colleran Patrick J	45	laborer	56	
	S	Colleran Sarah—†	45	housewife	47	"
	T	Braunfield Edward J	45	chauffeur	34	"
	U	Zepurneek Edward	45	U S A	33	
	V	Zepurneek Nellie—†	45	housewife	36	"
	W	Hendershied Bertrand B	45	conductor	49	"
	X	Hendershied Irene A—†	45	housewife	46	"
	Y	Grundman John	47	laborer	67	
	z*	Otscher Lizzie—†	47	housekeeper	70	"

204

	A	Klavin Vera J—†	47	stenographer	36	"
	B	Zepurneek Frederick	47	engineer	29	"
	C	Schievink Gertrude M—†	47	housewife	49	"
	D	Schievink Johannes	47	painter	53	
	E	Coffey Annie T—†	49	stenographer	31	"
	F	Coffey Bridget F—†	49	housewife	67	"
	G	Coffey Mary A—†	49	typist	29	
	H	Cummings Bridget—†	49	housewife	50	"
	K	Cummings Lawrence J	49	mechanic	27	"
	L	Cummings Leo P	49	longshoreman	49	"
	M	Waddell Grace C—†	49	housewife	24	"
	N	Waddell John L	49	garageman	33	"
	O	Viravorian Hripsime—†	51	housewife	66	"
	P	Laughlin John J	51	salesman	40	"
	R	Laughlin Margaret H—†	51	housewife	30	"
	S	O'Leary James A	51	B F D	46	
	T	O'Leary Rita E—†	51	housewife	42	"
	U	Cunningham Elizabeth F-†	53	clerk	30	
	V	Cunningham Josephine M-†	53	housekeeper	61	"
	W	Schaefer John	53	clerk	51	"
	X	Schaefer Sarah F—†	53	housewife	51	"
	Y	Marmone Frank A	55	bookkeeper	22	"
	Z	Marmone Josephine C—†	55	saleswoman	24	"

205

	A*	Marmone Rosalle—†	55	stitcher	46	
	B*	Sarrian Mary—†	55	housewife	44	"
	C	Sarrian Peter	55	clerk	22	

Page.	Letter.	FULL NAME.	Residence, Jan. 1, 1946.	Occupation.	Supposed Age.	Reported Residence, Jan. 1, 1945. Street and Number.

Beech Glen Street—Continued

	D	Sarrian Stephen	55	proprietor	45	here
	E	Mandanici Grace—†	55	housewife	34	"
	F	Mandanici Louis	55	molder	50	"
	G	Duffy Gertrude—†	57	housewife	45	"
	H	Duffy Hugh F	57	printer	51	
	K	Becherer Charles J	57	foreman	72	"
	L	Becherer Elizabeth C—†	57	housewife	72	"
	M	Shannon Lewis	57	clerk	23	Wisconsin
	N	Kelly Jennie A—†	59	housewife	52	here
	O	Kelly Margaret F—†	59	clerk	20	"
	P	Kelly William B	59	steamfitter	52	"
	R	Reidy Mary T—†	59	nurse	45	
	S	Des Roche Florence H—†	61	housewife	41	"
	T	Des Roche John J	61	clerk	47	"
	U	Rooney Margaret M—†	61	packer	25	"
	V	Schell Beatrice I—†	61	housewife	20	"
	W	Schell Edward A	61	printer	55	
	X	Schell John L	61	"	23	
	Y	Schell Joseph F	61	electrician	23	"
	Z	Schell Mary M—†	61	housewife	56	"
		206				
	A	White Frank M	61	supt	46	
	B	Morris Elizabeth—†	63	housewife	54	"
	C	Morris John J	63	steward	64	"
	D	Collins Mary J—†	65	housewife	51	"
	E	Crowley Catherine M—†	65	"	49	
	F	Crowley David C	65	U S A	21	
	G	Crowley Joseph F	65	storekeeper	50	"

Centre Street

	H	Mitchell Jennie—†	142	housewife	62	here
	K	Mitchell John A	142	janitor	27	"
	L	Mitchell William A	142	chef	62	"
	N	Creelman Gertrude—†	149	housewife	25	"
	O	Creelman William	149	laborer	35	
	P	Flaherty Helen M—†	149	manager	29	"
	R	Flaherty Michael J	149	operator	57	"
	S	Dolan Annie—†	151	housewife	58	"
	T	Dolan Frederick J	151	clerk	23	
	U	Kilduff Mary E—†	151	"	65	

5

Page.	Letter.	Full Name.	Residence, Jan. 1, 1946.	Occupation.	Supposed Age.	Reported Residence, Jan. 1, 1945. Street and Number.

Centre Street—Continued

	v	Dimitrakis Costas M	151	waiter	55	here
	w	Dimitrakis John C	151	U S A	22	"
	x	Dimitrakis Mary—†	151	housewife	45	"
	y	Adams Catherine—†	151A	"	32	16 Mansur
	z	Adams Theodore	151A	painter	37	16 "

207

	b	Doherty Hannah J—†	153	housewife	53	here
	a	Doherty John E	153	U S A	23	"
	c	Doherty Mary J—†	153	packer	40	"
	d	Doherty Thomas F	153	retired	65	"
	e	Greene Mary G—†	153	housewife	59	"
	f	Greene Michael M	153	shipper	60	
	g	Costello James E	153A	welder	21	
	h	Costello John J	153A	"	29	
	k	Costello Margaret M—†	153A	housewife	62	"
	l	Callahan Mary—†	155	"	65	
	m	Callahan Michael	155	machinist	30	"
	n	Gallagher Catherine—†	155	clerk	26	"
	o	Gallagher Daniel J	155	U S A	28	
	p	Mulligan Alice—†	155	at home	84	"
	r	Mulligan Edward	155	chauffeur	50	"
	s	Mulligan Helen—†	155	housewife	36	"
	t	Whalen Mary A—†	155	"	52	
	u	Whalen Thomas B	155	U S A	20	
	v	Whalen William J	155	laborer	45	
	w*	Scordino Antonette—†	158	housewife	42	"
	x	Scordino Charles	158	painter	46	
	y	Scordino Francis D	158	shoeworker	20	"
	z	Puleo Mary—†	158	housewife	34	"

208

	a	Pugliese Catherine—†	158	"	25	"
	b	Pugliese Michael	158	clerk	27	
	c	Masko Samuel	158	operator	63	"
	d	Davis Alvern	160	mechanic	51	"
	e	Davis Margaret—†	160	housewife	40	"
	f	Quatrale Marion—†	160	"	25	"
	g	Quatrale Philip M	160	roofer	31	
	h	Basabe Catherine—†	160	waitress	36	
	k	Basabe James	160	U S A	3S	
	l	Bevis George	162	roofer	50	
	m	Bevis Margaret—†	162	housewife	48	"

Centre Street—Continued

	N	Murray James	162	pipefitter	39	here
	O	Normile Annie—†	162	housewife	71	"
	P	Ryan Francis	162	watchman	65	"
	R	Ryan Mary—†	162	housewife	58	"
	S	Doherty Elizabeth—†	165	cook	45	N Hampshire
	T	Guinivan Evelyn—†	165	secretary	45	here
	U	Meredith Joseph D	165	clergyman	40	"
	V	Noonan William J	165	"	34	"
	W	O'Connor Deborah—†	165	domestic	52	Milton
	X	Sullivan Mark	165	clergyman	80	here
	Z	Sullivan Catherine—†	169	housewife	23	173 Centre
209						
	A	Sullivan Edward	169	carpenter	26	173 "
	B	White Beatrice—†	169	at home	68	here
	C	Murphy Blanche—†	169A	packer	36	"
	E	Burns Frank J	171½	burner	44	"
	F	Nugent Mary J—†	171½	housewife	67	"
	G	Garrity Charles A	171½	boilermaker	58	"
	H	Garrity Mabel T—†	171½	housewife	56	"
	K	O'Brien William H	171½	clerk	23	"
	L	Galvin Roger	171½	"	30	1466 Blue Hill av
	M	Galvin Virginia—†	171½	housewife	26	1466 "
	N	McLellan Cecilia—†	173	"	43	here
	O	Dermody John	173	laborer	21	13 New Heath
	P	Dermody Mary—†	173	housewife	44	13 "
	R	Dermody William A	173	chauffeur	50	13 "
	S	Foley Dennis	173	foreman	50	here
	T	Foley Dorothy J—†	173	housewife	44	"
	U	Foley John	173	U S N	24	"
	V	Foley Robert T	173	clerk	21	
	W	Waters Alice—†	173	factoryworker	37	"
	X	Favreau Edmund	174	mechanic	31	"
	Y	Favreau Ruth—†	174	housewife	30	"
	Z	Glynn Joseph	174	clerk	22	"
210						
	A	Glynn Margaret—†	174	housewife	45	"
	B	Taylor Dorothy—†	174	clerk	22	"
	C	Taylor Mary T—†	174	housewife	50	"
	D	Casey Nora—†	175	"	45	"
	E	Casey William	175	machinist	48	"
	F	Flavin Edward	175	clerk	42	

Centre Street—Continued

G	Flavin Margaret—†	175	housewife	26	here
H	Flavin Charlotte—†	175	"	35	"
K	Flavin John	175	laborer	40	"
L	Dargenio Catherine—†	176	laundress	51	"
M	Vitale Gaetano	176	retired	78	"
N	Vitale Marion—†	176	housewife	61	"
O	Orlando Josephine—†	176	"	24	
P	Orlando Peter	176	clerk	36	
S	Curtis Catherine—†	1st r 177	housewife	26	"
T	Curtis Philip	1st " 177	engineer	32	"
U	Topping Alice—†	1st " 177	housewife	61	"
V	Topping Grace—†	1st " 177	clerk	23	
W	Newton Clifford A	1st " 177	operator	38	"
X	Newton Margaret M—†	1st " 177	housewife	31	"
Y	Travers Agnes—†	2d " 177	"	37	
Z	Rendall Antonio	2d " 177	welder	46	

211

A	Rendall Grace—†	2d " 177	housewife	39	"
B	Tobin Catherine—†	2d " 177	"	39	
C	Tobin Nichols	2d " 177	clerk	44	
D	Berrigan Bernard	178	welder	39	
E	Berrigan Patience—†	178	housewife	41	"
F	DeGregorio Florence—†	178	"	29	"
G	DeGregorio Louis J	178	chauffeur	32	"
H	Burt Delphina—†	178	housewife	26	"
K	Burt Frederick	178	engineer	27	"
L	*Tate Agnes—†	179	housewife	43	"
M	Tate Harold D	179	plumber	43	"
N	Lawrence Paul J	179	carpenter	54	"
O	Lawrence Paul J, jr	179	U S A	24	
P	Lawrence Ruth M—†	179	housewife	49	"
S	Polito Lillian M—†	180	operator	47	"
T	Polito William R	180	"	21	
U	Hartley Arthur W	180	U S A	26	
V	Hartley Mary B—†	180	manager	22	"
W	Belfiore Joseph	180	laborer	48	
X	Belfiore Josephine—†	180	housewife	41	"
Y	Smith Jean—†	181	waitress	22	"
Z	Pitts Francis	181	checker	42	"

212

A	Pitts Marie—†	181	housewife	38	"

Centre Street—Continued

B	Friscia Charles	181	U S N	25	here
c	Friscia Philomina—†	181	housewife	44	"
D	Friscia Salvatore	181	laborer	50	"
E	Dana Gertrude E—†	182	housewife	45	"
F	Corcoran Edward J	182	laborer	59	"
G	Corcoran Nora M—†	182	housewife	56	"
H	McKinnon Joseph M	182	laborer	53	"
M	Brennan Catherine—†	184	saleswoman	55	"
N	Brennan Rose—†	184	housewife	64	"
o	Mannke Howard F	184	clerk	31	Florida
P	Mannke Rita F—†	184	housewife	25	"
R	Parker Irene—†	184	"	21	here
s	Parker Robert	184	bartender	26	"
z	Lopez Manuel	197	machinist	66	"

213

A	Lopez Sarah J—†	197	housewife	69	"

Centre Street Terrace

E	Powers Helen R—†	1	housewife	46	here
F	Powers James A	1	fireman	46	"
G	Waldron John M	1	clerk	41	"
H	Waldron Josephine A—†	1	biller	42	"
K	Crothers Dorothy—†	1	clerk	25	
L	Harris Eva—†	1	"	43	"
M	*Florio Dominic	1	retired	65	
N	*Florio Judith—†	1	housewife	63	"
o	Needham Jessie—†	1	shoeworker	40	"
P	Barletto Louis	1	electrician	35	"
R	Barletto Mary—†	1	housewife	34	"
s	Lennon Annie—†	1	matron	45	
T	Lennon Florence—†	1	clerk	50	"
U	Kingston Anna—†	1	housewife	42	85 Highland
v	Ferris Freeman	1	guard	35	here
w	*Ferris Lydia—†	1	housewife	34	"
x	Rea William	1	retired	70	"
Y	Goulet Charles	1	clerk	40	
z	Goulet Monica—†	1	housewife	39	"

214

A	Doherty Leona—†	1	clerk	30	
B	Doherty Owen	1	"	38	"

Centre Street Terrace—Continued

c	Coviello Joseph	2	attorney	38	here
d	Coviello Mae—†	2	housewife	36	"
e	Hall Albert	2	fireman	30	"
f	Hall Mary—†	2	housewife	29	"
g	Hagerup Peter	2	painter	65	
h	Gaffney Josephine—†	2	housewife	29	"
k	Gaffney Stephen	2	operator	29	"
l	Kane Evelyn—†	2	housewife	28	"
m	Kane Thomas	2	clerk	30	"
n	McDonald Angus	2	painter	35	
o	McDonald Jessie—†	2	housewife	34	"
p	Florio Alphonso	2	machinist	32	"
r	Florio Florence—†	2	housewife	30	"
s	Nicosia Carmella—†	2	"	36	
t	Nicosia Guy	2	foreman	45	"
u	Leahy Catherine—†	2	clerk	30	
v	Leahy John	2	painter	40	
w	Leahy Mary—†	2	operator	40	"
x	Leahy Timothy	2	clerk	47	"
y	Leahy William	2	U S A	39	

215   Columbus Avenue

b	Coyne Delia A—†	1407	housewife	50	here
c	Coyne Philip H	1407	manager	52	"
d	Moylan John	1407	laborer	55	"
e	Moylan Robert	1407	clerk	49	
g	Simeone Guy	1410	operator	28	"
h	Simeone Mary C—†	1410	housewife	45	"
k	Simeone Salvatore	1410	storekeeper	55	"
l	Abel Arline—†	1410	housewife	28	"
m	Abel Laimon	1410	machinist	35	"
n	Freeman Fred	1410	mechanic	29	"
o	Freeman John	1410	carpenter	52	"
r	Nichols Francis	1413	chauffeur	40	"
s	Nichols Josephine M—†	1413	factoryworker	38	"
t	Dinneen James	1413	laborer	53	
u	Montgomery Josephine—†	1413	housewife	51	"
v	Montgomery Robert	1413	U S A	22	
w	Scullion Margaret—†	1414	waitress	44	"
x	Ruzzano Anthony	1414	laborer	65	

Columbus Avenue—Continued

Y	Ruzzano Josephine—†	1414	housewife	29	here
z	Barner Dorothy—†	1414	"	32	"
	216					
A	Barner Nelson	1414	pipefitter	32	"
B	Dacey Michael	1415	janitor	58	"
C	Dacey Theresa—†	1415	housewife	54	"
D	Newton Joseph	1415	laborer	37	"
E	Newton Joseph	1415	U S N	21	"
F	Newton Sadie—†	1415	housewife	38	"
G	Kelley Annie—†	1415	"	77	
H	Kelley William C	1415	painter	42	"
L	Gauthier Beatrice—†	1419	housewife	24	1413 Columbus av
M	Gauthier Philip	1419	cutter	27	1413 "
N	Kennealy William P	1419	retired	78	here
O	Kyle Gertrude—†	1419	housewife	30	"
P	Vierkant Charles	1420	retired	67	"
R	Reynolds Le Roy J	1421	laborer	23	"
S	Reynolds Le Roy W	1421	clerk	45	"
T	Reynolds Violet—†	1421	housewife	42	"
U	Flannagan James J	1421	constable	45	"
V	Marino Josephine—†	1421	domestic	22	Stoneham
W	Palermo Mabel—†	1421	housewife	26	5 Malbon pl
X	Palermo Salvatore	1421	engineer	36	5 "
Y	Canning John F	1422	U S A	21	here
z*	Canning Mary—†	1422	housewife	59	"
	217					
A	Manning Catherine F-†	1422	"	61	
B	Manning Catherine M-†	1422	domestic	21	"
C	Manning Harold W	1422	U S A	20	
D	Manning Wilfred J	1422	clerk	67	
E	Vierkant Peter	1422	laborer	63	"
F	Farrell Annie—†	1422	housewife	47	"
H	Farrell William, jr	1422	U S A	21	"
G	Farrell William N	1422	bartender	53	"
L	Little James J	1425	laborer	34	
M*	Little Mary—†	1425	housewife	68	"
N	Little Patrick	1425	retired	79	"
O	Landry Helen J—†	1425	housewife	38	"
P	Landry Joseph W	1425	laborer	43	
R	Joslyn Mae—†	1425	housewife	45	"
S	Joslyn Walter	1425	laborer	20	

Columbus Avenue—Continued

T	Amicangelo Dante	1426	shoeworker	23	here
U	Amicangelo Mary—†	1426	housewife	22	"
V	McLean Irene—†	1427	factoryworker	22	170 Heath
W	Swanson Pearl—†	1427	housewife	28	213 Eustis
X	Wirrell Adelaide—†	1427	waitress	35	here
Y	Hamilton Harold	1427	U S A	25	"
z*	Hamilton Harry	1427	laborer	51	"

218

A	Hamilton James	1427	"	20	
B*	Hamilton Jean—†	1427	housewife	50	"
F	Matarazzo Laura M—†	1431	"	36	
G*	Matarazzo Michael	1431	shipper	42	"
H	Lennihan Anna L—†	1431	housewife	47	"
K	Lennihan James J	1431	chauffeur	45	"
M	Golden Stephen J	1433	"	41	
N	Golden William A	1433	laborer	33	
O	Thomas Lewis E	1433	"	42	
P	Thomas Margaret A—†	1433	housewife	42	"
R	Barton Carrie—†	1433	"	70	
U	Ferrera James	1436	clerk	31	
V	Ferrera Mildred—†	1436	housewife	32	"
W	Scordino Anna—†	1436	beautician	23	"
X	Scordino Anthony	1436	student	22	
Y	Scordino Domenic	1436	manager	54	"
Z	Scordino Dorothy—†	1436	beautician	20	"

219

A	Scordino Rose—†	1436	housewife	51	"
B	DeGregorio Catherine-†	1436	"	34	
C	DeGregorio Louis	1436	electrician	35	"
D	DeMinico Charles	1438	shoemaker	54	"
E	DeMinico Elvira—†	1438	housewife	51	"
F	DeMinico Peter	1438	clerk	21	"
G	Marcella Anthony A	1438	student	21	
H	Marcella Frank	1438	packer	23	
K	Marcella Joseph	1438	operator	25	"
L*	Marcella Mary—†	1438	housewife	54	"
M*	Marcella Samuel	1438	janitor	56	
N	Marcella Seraphino	1438	clerk	30	

221

C	Keliher Anna—†	1475	housewife	74	"
D	Keliher James W	1475	laborer	40	

Page.	Letter.	Full Name.	Residence, Jan. 1, 1946.	Occupation.	Supposed Age.	Reported Residence, Jan. 1, 1945. Street and Number.

Columbus Avenue—Continued

N	Prizio John	1479	laborer	38	here
O	Prizio Rose—†	1479	housewife	35	"
P	*DeAngelo Anna—†	1479	"	59	"
R	*DeAngelo John	1479	baker	62	
V	Messina Esther—†	1483	housewife	50	"
W	Messina Mario J	1483	student	25	
X	Messina Thomas	1483	laborer	50	
Y	Sassi Enrico	1483	"	59	
Z	Sassi Josephine—†	1483	housewife	63	"

222

A	Bevere Guydia—†	1483	"	22	
B	Bevere John	1483	packer	24	
C	Bevere Lorenzo	1483	barber	65	
D	Bevere Louise—†	1483	housewife	58	"
K	DeGregorio Antonette-†	1487	"	67	
L	*DeGregorio Fred	1487	barber	56	
M	DeGregorio Josephine-†	1487	clerk	36	
N	DeGregorio Susie—†	1487	factoryworker	32	"
O	Denmore Edward M	1487	laborer	23	
P	Denmore John F	1487	painter	48	
R	Denmore Mary J—†	1487	housewife	49	"
S	O"Brien Edward J	1487	clerk	35	"
T	O'Brien Elizabeth—†	1487	housewife	50	"

223

U	Ryan Arthur C	1545	clerk	30	
V	Ryan Arthur J	1545	laborer	64	
W	Ryan Bernard	1545	U S A	29	"
X	Ryan Evelyn M—†	1545	housewife	29	"
Y	Ryan Raymond	1545	clerk	43	"
Z	McCarthy Louise M—†	1545	housewife	40	2495 Wash'n

224

A	VerKampen Charles	1545	laborer	39	2495 "
B	VerKampen Mary C—†'	1545	housewife	68	2495 "
C	Rago Antoinette—†	1545	"	51	here
D	Rago Jerry	1545	U S A	25	"
E	Rago John	1545	mechanic	50	"
F	Rago Nichols	1545	U S A	23	
G	Fisher James	1551	shoeworker	50	"
H	Hopwood Catherine T-†	1551	housewife	59	51 Bromley pk
K	Hopwood Charles H	1551	painter	62	51 "
L	McNeil Clarence	1551	clerk	35	124 Day

Columbus Avenue—Continued

M	*McNeil Constance—†	1551	housewife	34	124 Day
o	Bromberg Bessie—†	1575	"	45	here
p	Bromberg Joseph	1575	tailor	53	"
r	Poli Mildred E—†	1575	WAVE	23	"
s	McFarland Francis J	1575	watchman	59	"
t	Gilmartin Dorothy A—†	1575	inspector	31	"
u	Gilmartin Edward S	1575	agent	27	
v	Gilmartin James J	1575	shipper	61	
w	Gilmartin James J, jr	1575	clerk	36	
x	Gilmartin Margaret T—†	1575	housewife	59	"
y	Scully Howard C	1575	clerk	38	"
z	Scully Margaret M—†	1575	buyer	33	

225

a	Gallant Agnes T—†	1577	housewife	53	"
b	Gallant Frederick J	1577	shipper	56	"
c	Gallant James A	1577	U S N	25	
d	Ramsey Mildred S—†	1577	housewife	38	"
e	Ramsey Robert	1577	chauffeur	31	"
f	Ganey Helen C—†	1577	tel operator	51	"
g	Ganey Jennie—†	1577	matron	49	
h	Ganey Mary G—†	1577	domestic	46	"
k	Ganey Nora A—†	1577	"	48	
l	Ganey Theresa N—†	1577	clerk	41	

Echo Street

w	Derosa Antoinette—†	2	housewife	59	here
x	Derosa Joseph	2	clerk	30	"
y	Derosa Peter	2	"	22	"
z	Gelormini Jerry	2	laborer	50	

226   ## Fort Avenue

b	Kintner Mary—†	66	housewife	20	here
c	Kintner Paul	66	U S A	22	"
d	MacDonald Anna—†	66	housewife	43	"
e	MacDonald Maylo	66	millwright	54	"
f	Honour Doris A—†	66	housewife	25	Revere
g	Niles Theron S	66	repairman	37	California
h	Niles Thora H—†	66	housewife	33	"
k	Dykens Clifford F	66A	mechanic	51	here
l	Dykens Dorothy R—†	66A	housewife	41	"

Page.	Letter.	Full Name.	Residence, Jan. 1, 1946.	Occupation.	Supposed Age.	Reported Residence, Jan. 1, 1945. Street and Number.

Heath Street

o	Gismondi Alfred	6	manager	60	here
p	Gismondi Olga—†	6	housewife	48	"
s	Magliozzi Florence—†	6	"	30	"
r	Magliozzi Joseph	6	barber	30	..
u	Jackson Marie—†	8	housewife	40	"
v	Blanchard John H	8	porter	39	"
w	Carnegie Gene	8	welder	26	"

227 Highland Street

B	Harper Cora L—†	177	housewife	68	here
c	McCormack Ruth L—†	177	bookkeeper	25	"
d	Tighe Francis P	177	student	21	"
e	Tighe Margaret—†	177	housewife	47	"
f	Tighe Michael F	177	laborer	57	"
g	Gronberg Evald	177	mechanic	53	"
h	Gronberg Helen—†	177	clerk	21	"
k	Cutler Alfred	179	metalworker	51	"
l	Cutler Elizabeth R—†	179	housewife	39	"
m	Burgess David G	179	fireman	53	"
n	Burgess David S	179	clerk	24	"
o	Burgess Sarah—†	179	housewife	50	"
p	McGovern Esther H—†|	179	domestic	62	"
r	Rogers Gertrude—†	179	"	65	"
s	Healey Gene M	181	furrier	38	
t	Greatrix Crescenza—†	181	housewife	34	"
u	Greatrix Paul B	181	pipefitter	39	"
v	Burns Alice—†	181	housewife	50	"
w	Hurley Hilda M—†	187	waitress	46	"
x	Lang Frank J	187	letter carrier	34	"
y	Lang Lena—†	187	housewife	28	"
z	Dreier Elizabeth A—†	189	leatherworker	59	"

228

A	Dreier Joseph G	189	retired	62	
B	Dreier Mary F—†	189	housewife	65	"
c	Daesen Helen—†	189	"	37	
d	Lang George	189	baker	71	
e	Lang Veronica—†	189	housewife	65	"
f	Dinsmore Arthur	191	painter	56	"
g	Donnati John	191	seaman	27	"
h	Sweeney Calvin	191	student	20	"
k	Sweeney James	191	U S A	22	"

15

Highland Street—Continued ·

L	Sweeney Sarah—†	191	housewife	52	here
M	Cahill Richard	191	U S N	20	"
N	Cahill Viola—†	191	housewife	36	"
O	Cahill William J	191	painter	39	
P	Brienza Mary—†	219	housewife	59	"
R	Brienza Philip	219	U S A	30	
S	Brienza Rose—†	219	housewife	30	"
T	Brienza Ruth—†	219	"	29	
U	Mazziotti Philip	219	machinist	56	"
V	Lynch Bartholomew J	219	printer	69	
W	Lynch Catherine J—†	219	housewife	63	"
X	Lynch Gerard F	219	clerk	31	"
Y	Lynch Katherine—†	219	typist	32	..
Z	Lynch Mary G—†	219	stenographer	29	"

229

A	Lynch Rita E—†	219	"	26	"
B	Lynch Robert A	219	U S A	27	
C	Woods Ruth—†	219	housewife	26	"
D	Woods William	219	clerk	26	
E	McCluskey Lawrence J	227	mechanic	38	"
F	McCluskey Madeline—†	227	housewife	38	"
G	Allen Dorothy M—† ·	227	operator	21	"
H*	Allen Elva M—†	227	housewife	42	"
K	Allen Mobrey E	227	laborer	50	
L	Gillis Mary—†	227	housewife	31	"
M	Gillis Roy	227	mover	35	"
N	Bowles Grace—†	229	housewife	27	1431 Centre
O	Bowles William J	229	operator	26	1431 "
P	Brown Catherine M—†	229	housewife	47	here
R	Brown George M	229	pipefitter	53	"
S	Toth Gust M	229	U S N	26	"
T	Toth Margaret C—†	229	housewife	24	"
U	Warren Edda—†	229	"	35	
V	Warren Walter	229	motorman	31	"
W	Fasano Alphonse	231	shipper	32	
X	Fasano Michelina—†	231	housewife	32	"
Y	Carmen Arthur	231	chauffeur	22	"
Z	Carmen Mary—†	231	housewife	22	"

230

A	Josephs Henry	231	U S A	24	
B	Jozefowicz Helen—†	231	clerk	30	

Highland Street—Continued

c	Jozefowicz Lena—†	231	housewife	53	here
d	Amyoung Ann—†	231	operator	24	"
e	Amyoung Florence—†	231	nurse	23	"
f*	Amyoung Joseph	231	painter	47	
g	Amyoung Robert	231	accountant	25	"
h	Gallagher John J	233	storekeeper	49	"
k	Gallagher Mary E—†	233	housewife	46	"
l	Johnson Clement G	233	contractor	32	"
m	Johnson George L	233	plumber	63	"
n	Johnson George L, jr	233	salesman	34	"
o	Johnson Harold L	233	U S A	29	
p	Johnson Lydia L—†	233	housewife	53	"
r	Rogers Estelle—†	233	"	32	
s	Rogers William T	233	supervisor	34	"
t*	Ferrante Antoinette—†	235	housewife	54	"
u	Ferrante Christina—†	235	saleswoman	21	"
v	Ferrante Dominic	235	merchant	35	"
w	Ferrante Mary—†	235	housewife	34	"
x	Milani Albert	235	plater	32	
y	Milani Sabina—†	235	housewife	33	"
z	Ames Forrest	237	laborer	35	Saugus

231

a	Valinquette Albert	237	"	52	here
b	Valinquette Arthur	237	clerk	20	"
c	Valinquette Emily—†	237	housewife	50	"
d	Valinquette Pauline—†	237	buyer	21	
e	Driscoll John E	237	chauffeur	39	"
f	Driscoll John E, jr	237	clerk	24	
g	Driscoll Margaret E—†	237	housewife	46	"
h	Driscoll Mary—†	237	clerk	21	"
k	Glynn Francis A	237	laborer	29	"
l	Puzzanghera Mary—†	251	housewife	27	"
m*	Puzzanghera Samuel	251	stitcher	32	
o	Devlin Mae—†	253	housewife	40	"
p	Nee Flora—†	253	clerk	46	
r	Nee Marguerite M—†	253	operator	21	"
s	O'Rourke Charles	253	chauffeur	33	"
t	O'Rourke Irene—†	253	housewife	30	"
v	Peppard Elizabeth—†	255	"	63	
w	Peppard Helen—†	255	typist	37	

Page.	Letter.	Full Name.	Residence, Jan. 1, 1946.	Occupation.	Supposed Age.	Reported Residence, Jan. 1, 1945. Street and Number.

232
Highland Street—Continued

	Letter	Full Name	Res.	Occupation	Age	Reported Residence
	F	Gallagher John J	260	rigger	30	here
	G	Gallagher Mary E—†	260	housewife	26	"
	H	O'Toole Patrick	260	custodian	46	"
	K	Green Erwin W	261	carpenter	71	"
	L	Cashman Virginia H—†	261	housewife	36	106 Minden
	M	Cashman Willard G	261	forger	41	106 "
	N	Griffin Barbara—†	261	housewife	45	2 Wise
	O	Griffin William P	261	chef	49	2 "
	R	Egersheim Edward	263	welder	30	here
	S	Egersheim Marie—†	263	housewife	30	"
	T	McDonald John	263	laborer	48	"
	U	McDonald Mary—†	263	housewife	70	"
	V	Botulinski Mary—†	rear 263	"	70	
	W	McManamy Mary—†	269	saleswoman	38	"
	X	McManamy Robert C	269	U S A	27	"
	Y	Wall Catherine J—†	277	at home	74	1 Gouldville ter
	Z	Wall Henry E	277	retired	70	1 "

233

	Letter	Full Name	Res.	Occupation	Age	Reported Residence
	A	Collins Nellie—†	277	at home	69	here
	B	Titlebaum Jeanne—†	277	housewife	38	"
	F	Durant Veronica—†	281	"	32	174 Cedar
	G	Rowan Catherine—†	281	at home	74	here
	H	Downey Joseph	281	mechanic	51	"
	K	Hilton Asa	286	laborer	55	"
	L	McLean Clara—†	286	housewife	47	"
	M	McLean Frank	286	iceman	49	
	N	*Loyka John	286	retired	69	
	O	Blanchard Christina—†	287	housewife	27	"
	P	Blanchard James	287	laborer	32	
	R	Page Irene—†	287	at home	55	
	S	Page John D	287	U S N	24	
	T	Page Robert L	287	"	28	
	U	*Raffaele Michael	287	retired	83	
	V	Raffaele Rocco	287	U S A	40	
	W	*Raffaele Ursula—†	287	at home	62	"
	X	Reshun Olga—†	288	housewife	39	"
	Y	Eliason Frances—†	288	"	27	
	Z	Eliason George	288	laborer	33	··

234

	Letter	Full Name	Res.	Occupation	Age	Reported Residence
	A	Zeer Irene—†	288	housewife	21	1A Bickford av

Highland Street—Continued

B	Zeer Robert J	288	laborer	27	1A Bickford av
C	Hicks Dorothy—†	290	housewife	25	281 Highland
D	Hicks Wilbur	290	machinist	25	281 "
E	McGee Evelyn—†	290	waitress	34	here
F	Broughton Charles S	290	engineer	61	"
G	Broughton Henrietta—†	290	housewife	50	"
H	Newton Hannah—†	291	"	79	
K	Newton Mary—†	291	clerk	49	
L	Newton William C	291	"	41	
M	Harrington Catherine—†	292	housewife	73	"
N	Szeremeta Betty—†	292	clerk	28	
O	Szocik Helen—†	292	saleswoman	22	"
P	Szocik Joseph	292	meatcutter	49	"
R	Szocik Joseph W	292	clerk	28	"
S*	Szocik Louise—†	292	housewife	51	"
T	Szocik Mary—†	292	secretary	27	"
U	Johnson Annie—†	292	housewife	59	"
V	Johnson Erhard	292	asbestoswkr	62	"
Y	Beirot Bertha—†	294	domestic	68	"
Z	Stockman John	294	machinist	59	"

235

A	Colbert Helen—†	294	housewife	67	"
B	Drury Anna—†	294	"	68	..
C	Trainor Laura E—†	294	"	36	
D	Trainor William J	294	metalworker	38	"
F	Babula Alfred T	296	electrician	23	Connecticut
G	Babula Helen—†	296	housewife	23	"
H	Marsolini Alexander	296	U S N	23	here
K	Marsolini Fannie—†	296	housewife	46	"
L	Marsolini Louis J	296	roper	47	"
M	Marsolini Mary—†	296	operator	21	"
N	MacDonald Doris—†	296	factoryworker	45	"
O	MacDonald Marilyn—†	296	housewife	22	"
P	Marenghi Emilio	301	retired	71	
P¹	Marenghi John	301	laborer	40	
R	Marenghi Raphaela—†	301	at home	71	..
S	Kordis Alice—†	303	operator	41	"
T	Kordis John	303	laborer	21	..
U	Dawe Elizabeth M—†	303	housewife	73	"
V	Dawe James W	303	bartender	65	"
W	Lindner Anthony	303	laborer	50	

Page.	Letter.	Full Name.	Residence, Jan. 1, 1946.	Occupation.	Supposed Age.	Reported Residence, Jan. 1, 1945. Street and Number.

Highland Street—Continued

	x	Lindner Theresa—†	303	domestic	50	here
	y	*Brady Norma—†	305	factoryworker	28	Alabama
	z	Jackson Dora—†	305	housewife	22	21 Rutland sq
236						
	a	Jackson James	305	clerk	22	21 "

Marcella Street

	b	Kelly Annie—†	75	housewife	56	here
	c	Kelly Lillian—†	75	factoryworker	21	"
	d	Kelly Michael	75	oiler	60	"
	e	Kelly Thomas	75	watchman	65	"
	f	Walsh Grace—†	75	hostess	24	
	g	Cahill Anna—†	75	typist	22	
	h	*Cahill Margaret—†	75	housewife	63	"
	k	Cahill Michael F	75	plumber	28	"
	l	Cahill Peter J	75	laborer	22	
	m	Hyde Mary—†	75	typist	22	
	n	Grace Albert L	75	laborer	21	"
	o	Grace Catherine—†	75	housewife	52	"
	p	Grace William F	75	gasfitter	57	"
	r	Grace William F, jr	75	welder	22	"
	s	Day Catherine E—†	77	clerk	41	
	t	Day Patrick W	77	"	42	
	u	Morelli Mary—†	77	housewife	46	"
	v	Morelli William	77	machinist	49	"
	w	Fox Emma T—†	77	housewife	39	"
	x	Gabryelewski Jennie—†	79	examiner	50	"
	y	Gabryelewski Paul	79	stitcher	52	
	z	Arsenault Albert	79	expeditor	33	"
237						
	a	Arsenault Ethel—†	79	housewife	34	"
	b	Berran Ignatius	79	metalworker	57	"
	c	Mulvey Catherine—†	79	housekeeper	58	"
	e	*Whalen Harold J	84	laborer	44	"
	f	*Whalen Pansy E—†	84	housewife	54	"
	g	McKenzie Mary—†	84	waitress	44	"
	h	McKenzie Mary E—†	84	engraver	21	"
	k	Murphy Charles E	84	mechanic	38	"
	l	Murphy Della M—†	84	housewife	30	"
	m	Brigantino Agrippino C	86	welder	23	"

Page.	Letter.	Full Name.	Residence, Jan. 1, 1946.	Occupation.	Supposed Age.	Reported Residence, Jan. 1, 1945. Street and Number.

Marcella Street—Continued

	N	Centamore Anthony	86	laborer	61	here
	O	Centamore Croce	86	musician	31	"
	P	Centamore Joseph	86	U S N	27	"
	R	*Centamore Mary—†	86	housewife	51	"
	S	*Glennon Barbara A—†	86	"	36	∴
	T	Cordero Marion K—†	86	stitcher	29	"
	U	Cordero Salvatore	86	U S A	36	"
	V	Singarella Frank	88	printer	52	
	W	Singarella Josephine R—†	88	housewife	39	"
	X	Falcone Lucy M—†	88	"	32	
	Y	Falcone Salvatore J	88	clerk	32	
	Z	*Rock Margaret—†	88	housewife	45	"
238						
	A	Mathis Armand J	90	welder	35	
	B	Mathis Eleanor E—†	90	housewife	34	"
	C	Neilson Bella—†	90	saleswoman	35	26 Walden
	D	Neilson Harry	90	U S N	36	26 "
	E	Myers Millicent D—†	90	housewife	24	here
	F	Myers Vernon D	90	welder	25	"
	G	Perkins Abner	91	manager	26	Maine
	H	Perkins Theresa—†	91	housewife	24	"
	K	Solomon Arthur	91	manager	50	here
	L	Solomon Rose—†	91	housewife	45	"
	M	Cantillo William	91	clerk	34	"
	N	Roth Anna—†	91	housewife	35	"
	O	Roth Ralph H	91	electrician	36	"
	R	Cabozzi Alexander	rear 91	printer	45	"
	S	Cabozzi Elizabeth—†	" 91	housewife	43	"
	T	Mulvey Catherine—†	" 91	"	73	"
	U	Mulvey Joseph	" 91	painter	64	"
	W	Coady Jennie N—†	92	housewife	74	"
	X	Coady Patrick E	92	shipper	64	
	Y	Donaghue Florence M—†	92	housewife	32	"
	Z	Donaghue Harry F	92	foreman	42	"
239						
	A	Coughlin Frederick	92	U S A	36	Brookline
	B	Coughlin Nora—†	92	housewife	35	"
	C	Cornelius Frank	94	freighthandler	45	here
	D	Lindgren Robert P	94	retired	66	"
	E	Serrecchia Anthony M	94	machinist	22	"
	F	Serrecchia Irene E—†	94	housewife	20	"

Marcella Street—Continued

Page.	Letter.	Full Name.	Residence, Jan. 1, 1946.	Occupation.	Supposed Age.	Reported Residence, Jan. 1, 1945. Street and Number.
	G	Panico Dorothy—†	94	operator	31	here
	H	Szadaj Catherine—†	96	housewife	58	"
	K	Szadaj Michael	96	cleaner	59	"
	L	Szadaj Peter J	96	U S N	23	
	M	Mahoney Anna D—†	96	housewife	33	"
	N	Mahoney James C	96	roofer	30	
	O	Gauthier Mary—†	96	baker	30	
	P	Bergman Dina—†	97	housewife	20	"
	R	Bergman Harvey	97	mechanic	34	"
	S	Costanza Theresa—†	97	housewife	44	"
	T	Costanza Thomas	97	barber	63	
	U	Costanza Thomas A	97	laborer	41	"
	V	Salisbury Grace—†	97	housewife	27	17 Kingsbury
	W	Salisbury John	97	buffer	26	17 "
	X	DeLisle Frances—†	101	housewife	20	3 Myrtle pl
	Y	DeLisle Frank	101	clerk	24	3 "
	Z	Keenan Charles	101	laborer	49	2784 Wash'n
240						
	A*	Keenan Susan	101	housewife	42	2784 "
	B	Nauss Clarence	101	mechanic	40	here
	C	Nauss Mildred—†	101	housewife	41	"
	D	Dooley Stephanie—†	102	seamstress	45	"
	E	Muller Catherine—†	102	housewife	71	"
	F	Bakunas Anna—†	102	"	44	
	G	Bakunas Anthony	102	laborer	45	
	P	Olson Rose—†	106	laundress	56	"
	R	Murley Margaret—†	106	housewife	33	540 Newbury
	S	Murley Thomas J	106	painter	39	540 "
	T	Iuvarra Nicolina—†	108	housewife	63	here
	U	Iuvarra Salvatore	108	retired	66	"
	V	Petroff Catherine—†	108	housewife	58	"
	W*	Fall Delia F—†	108	"	66	"
	Y	De Board Curtis	109	mechanic	24	Kentucky
	Z	De Board Mary—†	109	housewife	28	216 Highland
241						
	A	Palingo Gertrude—†	109	"	21	30 Burrell
	B	DeVoe Laurence	109	plumber	35	here
	C	DeVoe Susan—†	109	housewife	72	"
	D	Anderson Annie S—†	110	"	78	"
	E	Mosman Verna E—†	110	domestic	41	"
	F	Sockoloff Agnes—†	110	waitress	22	1 Dudley

Page.	Letter.	Full Name.	Residence, Jan. 1, 1946.	Occupation.	Supposed Age.	Reported Residence, Jan. 1, 1945. Street and Number

Marcella Street—Continued

	G	Stanley Grace—†	110	stitcher	60	1 Dudley
	M	*DuWors Julia—†	113	housewife	36	here
	N	Hobbs Francis	113	machinist	32	30 Mercer
	o	*Hobbs Mary—†	113	housewife	39	30 "
	P	O'Toole Ruth—†	113	molder	28	here
	s	DePina John	114	chef	38	Gloucester
	T	Loughman Arthur M	114	clerk	27	here
	U	Loughman Bertha M—†	114	housewife	27	"
	V	Meichner Edith—†	114	waitress	45	Brookline
	w	Young Virgin H	114	chef	40	98 Dartmouth
	x	Libby Estelle—†	115	supervisor	51	here
	Y	Libby Kenneth M	115	machinist	51	"
	z	Libby Kenneth M, jr	115	U S A	20	"

242

	A	Turner Kathryn—†	115	clerk	30	
	B	DelGrosso Angelina—†	115	housewife	78	"
	c	DelGrosso Anthony	115	retired	76	
	D	DelGrosso Celia—†	115	supervisor	41	"
	E	DelGrosso Josephine—†	115	bookkeeper	45	"
	F	DelGrosso Laura—†	115	supervisor	28	"
	G	Giorgio Ann—†	115	housewife	34	"
	H	Giorgio Mary—†	115	stenographer	32	"
	K	Giorgio Rocco	115	salesman	36	"
	L	Giorgio Salvatore	115	U S A	32	15 Elven rd
	M	DelGrosso Louis	115	plumber	48	here
	N	DelGrosso Mary—†	115	housewife	41	"
	o	Carroll Nellie A—†	116	"	68	"
	P	Wheaton Frederick W	116	clerk	48	
	R	Wheaton Robert F	116	U S N	21	
	s	Wheaton Ruth M—†	116	housewife	43	"
	T	Finnin Rhoda—†	118	"	33	
	U	O'Brien John	118	engineer	41	"
	w	Russell Jeannette—†	121	housewife	29	"
	x	Russell Louis	121	bellhop	36	"
	Y	Falcone Jeanne—†	121	housewife	28	N Hampshire
	z	Falcone John	121	mechanic	28	"

243

	A	Buckland Lowell T	121	U S N	25	90 Marcella
	B	Buckland Ruth—†	121	housewife	22	90 "
	c	Becker Beulah—†	123	"	23	132 Marcella
	D	Becker George	123	expressman	24	132 "

Marcella Street—Continued

E	Von Kahle Bernard	123	chauffeur	26	here
F	Von Kahle Beulah—†	123	housewife	59	"
G	Von Kahle Henry	123	realtor	61	"
H	Von Kahle Paul	123	student	20	"
L	Katsiganes Charles	124	barber	33	.75 Burbank
M	Katsiganes Ruth—†	124	clerk	26	75 "
N*	McDonnell Anna—†	124	housewife	36	97 Marcella
O	McDonnell John J	124	laborer	43	97 "
P	D'Amico Angelina—†	125	packer	36	174 Bremen
R	Simboli Alex	125	driller	41	here
S	Simboli Helen—†	125	housewife	34	"
T	Palma James	125	laborer	53	"
U	Palma Rose—†	125	waitress	45	"
V	Berube Arthur	126	mechanic	23	Texas
W	Berube Ruth—†	126	housewife	21	"
X	Fall Maybelle E—†	126	at home	36	here
Y	Sherman Forest E	126	engineer	57	"
Z	Graziano Generosa—†	127	housewife	49	"

244

A	Graziano Raffaele	127	laborer	47	
B	McLellan James A	127	shipper	53	
C	McLellan Margaret—†	127	housewife	53	"
D	Luongo Lena—†	127	"	43	6 Bromley pk
E	Luongo Michael A	127	sprayer	45	6 "
H*	Campbell Lillian—†	131	housewife	38	here
K	Archambeault Florence—†	131	"	50	"
L	Archambeault Theodore	131	laborer	22	"
M	Carr Jeannette—†	131	housewife	40	"
N	Carr Richard	131	laborer	45	Somerville
O*	Cote Marie—†	131	housewife	60	here
P	Cannon Mary—†	132	clerk	73	"
R	Sullivan Jeffery H	132	chauffeur	23	Somerville
S	Sullivan Margaret—†	132	clerk	24	32 Billerica
T	Coady Catherine—†	132	domestic	28	here
U	Coady Augustine	132	laborer	29	"
W	De Fina Andrew	133	chef	34	"
X	De Fina Eda—†	133	housewife	30	"
Y	Marenghi Ambrose	133	laborer	23	
Z	Marenghi Ettore	133	shoemaker	59	"

245

A	Marenghi Gerald	133		22	

Page	Letter	Full Name	Residence, Jan. 1, 1946.	Occupation	Supposed Age.	Reported Residence, Jan. 1, 1945. Street and Number.

Marcella Street—Continued

	Letter	Full Name	Residence Jan. 1, 1946	Occupation	Age	Reported Residence
	B	Marenghi Jennie—†	133	housewife	57	here
	C	Marenghi Rita—†	133	saleswoman	29	"
	D	Turowski Helen—†	133	housewife	27	"
	E	Turowski John	133	cableman	31	"
	F	O'Donnell Charles A	134	clerk	31	
	G	O'Donnell Ethel C—†	134	typist	29	..
	H	O'Donnell Hugh	134	fireman	74	
	K	O'Donnell Isabella B—†	134	housewife	67	"
	L	DeAngelis Gertrude—†	135	"	35	"
	M	DeAngelis Joseph	135	chauffeur	34	"
	N	Tobin John J	135	dispatcher	47	"
	O	Tobin Margaret—†	135	housewife	31	"
	P	Hamrock Helen—†	135	"	54	
	R	Hamrock James	135	laborer	50	"
	S	Hamrock James S	135	U S A	23	
	T	Hamrock John P	135	"	22	"
	U	Parsons Anne M—†	136	housewife	26	Cambridge
	V	Parsons Claude J	136	chauffeur	29	"
	W*	Kirrane Mary D—†	136	waitress	30	here
	X	Kennedy Mary—†	136	cook	48	"
	Y	Cabot Beatrice—†	137	housewife	52	"
	Z	Cabot Louis	137	carpenter	59	"

246

	Letter	Full Name	Residence Jan. 1, 1946	Occupation	Age	Reported Residence
	A	Gaffey Francis C	137	retired	53	
	B	Gaffey Rosemary—†	137	stenographer	25	"
	C	Sumner Jerome	137	draftsman	22	10 New Heath
	D	Sumner Virginia A—†	137	clerk	22	here
	E	Ward Rose—†	137	"	42	"
	F	Reece Anna M—†	138	draftsman	21	"
	G	Reece Francis W	138	U S N	21	
	H	Reece Gordon W	138	steamfitter	50	"
	K	Reece Margaret S—†	138	housewife	45	"
	L	O'Brien Edith A—†	138	"	51	"
	M	O'Brien Elizabeth C—†	138	"	24	25 Regis rd
	N	O'Brien John J	138	U S N	27	here
	O	O'Brien Joseph M	138	fireman	59	"
	P	O'Brien Vincent R	138	U S N	20	"
	R	O'Brien William A	138	"	24	"
	S	Berzen Emily—†	138	housekeeper	58	"
	T	Theriault Edith—†	139	cleanser	43	611 Tremont
	U	Theriault George A	139	electrician	21	611 "

Marcella Street—Continued

v	Waldron Julia—†	139	candymaker	40	here
w	Sullivan Bridget—†	139	housekeeper	66	"
x	Blasi Alvera—†	140	housewife	65	"
y	Blasi Thomas F	140	clerk	29	
z	Blasi Anthony A	140	laborer	32	

247

A	Blasi Eva—†	140	housewife	29	"
B	Stewart Albert B	140	chauffeur	38	"
c	Stewart Rita M—†	140	housewife	29	"
D	Donelan Elizabeth B—†	141	"	63	
E	Donelan Francis X	141	student	20	"
F	Donelan George M	141	"	23	
G	Donelan James	141	surveyor	34	"
H	Donelan Mathias	141	butcher	64	"
K	Donelan Paul	141	student	26	
L	Noone Helen—†	141	teacher	39	
M	Ryan Thomas	141	meatcutter	38	"
N	Campbell Jane—†	143	housewife	57	"
o	Campbell Paul	143	U S A	23	
P	Campbell William G	143	U S M C	25	"
R	Kelty Margaret—†	143	laundryworker	64	"
s	Powers Emily—†	143	clerk	60	
U	Treiman Alida—†	145	waitress	28	"
T	Treiman Alida M—†	145	housewife	55	"
v	Simboli James	145	mechanic	55	125 Marcella
w	Treiman Anne—†	145	housewife	26	here
x	Treiman John A	145	teller	33	"
Y	Black Marie—†	147	domestic	32	Rhode Island
z	Bryant Pauline—†	147	housewife	36	19 Benton

248

A	Bryant Roosevelt H	147	U S N	45	19 "
B	Smith Daniel	147	seaman	33	here
c	Smith Ruth—†	147	housewife	29	"
D	Dinneen David	147	laborer	24	"
E	Dinneen Helen—†	147	housewife	45	"

New Heath Street

G	Murphy George	6	timekeeper	39	here
H	Murphy Helen—†	6	housewife	36	"
K	Puorro Nicola	6	retired	72	"

New Heath Street—Continued

L	Puorro Nicholas	6	laborer	29	here
M	Godsoe Rita—†	6	housewife	23	"
N	Godsoe Robert	6	laborer	27	"
O	Rodrigues Fernando	8	retired	41	2978 Wash'n
P	Rodrigues Mary—†	8	housewife	35	2978 "
R	Hanson George	8	retired	26	here
S	Hanson Priscilla—†	8	housewife	23	"
T	Lawson Harold	8	factoryworker	35	71 Green
U	Lawson Lida—†	8	housewife	29	71 "
V	Mello Francis	8	factoryworker	29	Middleboro
W	Scarlata Esther—†	10	housewife	31	here
X	Scarlata James	10	engineer	35	"
Y	Orlando Jean—†	10	housewife	36	"
Z	Orlando Michael	10	retired	37	

249

A	Prescott Arthur	10	laborer	27	
B	Raftes Doris—†	10	housewife	23	"
C	Raftes George	10	roofer	26	
D	Pelechowicz Bertha—†	10A	housewife	29	"
E	Pelechowicz Stephen	10A	welder	29	
F	*Lanza Mary—†	10A	presser	61	
G	Giannini Marie—†	10A	at home	70	"
H	Lymneos Helen—†	12	housewife	54	"
K	Lymneos Nicholas	12	retired	61	
L	Russo Alice—†	12A	housewife	34	"
M	Russo Jean	12A	tailor	35	
N	Russo Otto	12A	"	68	
O	*Russo Pasqualena—†	12A	housewife	67	"
P	Moloney Charles J	14	furrier	38	
R	Moloney Geraldine—†	14	housewife	33	"
S	Sumner Mary—†	14	cook	49	
T	*DiMarino Elizabeth—†	14	housewife	54	"
U	DiMarino Elizabeth D—†	14	stenographer	20	"
W	DiMarino Florence—†	14	"	24	"
V	DiMarino Frank W	14	U S C G	21	"
X	Liolin Edna E—†	18	housewife	55	"
Y	Liolin Thomas G	18	waiter	54	"
Z	Murphy Anne—†	18	housewife	63	53 Round Hill

250

A	Murphy Richard A	18	retired	64	53 "
B	Myers Margaret—†	18	housewife	65	here

Page	Letter	FULL NAME.	Residence, Jan. 1, 1946.	Occupation.	Supposed Age.	Reported Residence, Jan. 1, 1945. Street and Number.

New Heath Street—Continued

	c	Myers Patrick	18	clerk	37	here
	d	White Mary—†	18	stitcher	42	"
	f	DePasqua Virginia—†	20	presser	32	"
	g	Kelley James F	26	retired	70	
	h	Meally Anna Q—†	26	clerk	20	
	k	Meally John	26	laborer	60	"
	l	Meally Mary—†	26	housewife	50	"

Oakview Avenue

	o	McCallion Philip	1	watchman	66	here
	p	Schlaich Gallus C	2	clerk	67	"
	r	Schlaich Katherine A—†	2	stenographer	30	"
	s	Schlaich Theresa A—†	2	housewife	69	"
	t	Morin Mary E—†	4	domestic	48	13 Highland av
	u	Phillips Mary—†	4	clerk	43	here
	v	Silve Gerald	4	printer	39	16 Appleton
	w	Sullivan Margaret—†	4	clerk	47	here
	x	Fabio Antonetta—†	4	housewife	58	"
	y	Fabio Antonio	4	mason	57	"
	z	Fabio F Aliero	4	U S A	23	

251

	a	Fabio Faust	4		21	

Penryth Street

	b	Ciresi Joseph	1	bartender	29	here
	c	Ciresi Josephine—†	1	housewife	27	"
	d	DeLuca Anthony	1	metalworker	31	"
	e	DeLuca Marguerite—†	1	housewife	28	"
	f	Belfiore John	4	laborer	36	
	g	Belfiore Ralph	4	shoeworker	51	"
	h	Incardone Salvatore	4	"	42	
	k	Incardone Sarafina—†	4	housewife	43	"
	l	Iantosca Angelina—†	4	"	43	
	m	Iantosca Anthony	4	machinist	45	"
	n	Casey Catherine—†	5	housewife	84	"
	o	Casey Timothy J	5	retired	84	
	p	Coughlin Catherine—†	5	housewife	52	"
	r	Coughlin Eileen—†	5	clerk	21	
	s	Coughlin John	5	electrician	53	"

28

Page.	Letter.	FULL NAME.	Residence, Jan. 1, 1946.	Occupation.	Supposed Age.	Reported Residence, Jan. 1, 1945. Street and Number.

Penryth Street—Continued

	T	Whealen Edward	5	U S N	21	here
	u	Kirby Catherine—†	5	housewife	51	"
	v	Kirby John	5	clerk	46	"
	w	Donelan Richard	6	U S N	20	"
	x	Donelan Sarah A—†	6	housewife	57	"
	Y	Donelan William J	6	janitor	58	

Ritchie Street

	z	Hutton Frances M—†	10	housewife	41	32 Child
252						
	A	Sullivan Eva—†	10	"	50	here
	B	Sullivan Timothy	10	chauffeur	49	"
	c	Sullivan Timothy, jr	10	U S A	22	"
	D	Boudreau Francis	10	chauffeur	44	"
	E	Boudreau Lillian—†	10	housewife	38	"
	F	Doherty Joseph E	12	salesman	40	"
	G	Giles Edward G	12	mechanic	37	"
	H	Giles Irene—†	12	housewife	37	"
	K	Linskey Dorothy—†	12	"	33	27 Dale
	L	Linskey Martin	12	printer	36	27 "
	M	Bentley William	12	U S C G	22	31 Alton ct
	N	Roach Alice—†	12	housewife	50	1 St Alphonsus av
	o	Roach Paul	12	steamfitter	22	1 "
	P	Alexander Frederick P	15	U S A	30	here
	R	Dinault Edward	15	clerk	29	10 Dresden
	s	Dinault Grace—†	15	housewife	28	10 "
	T	Dinault Henry	15	dealer	55	here
	U	Dinault Loretta—†	15	housewife	30	"
	v	Dinault Norman	15	clerk	31	"

Thwing Street

	w	Shea Margaret—†	2	clerk	41	here
	x	Rettman Angelina—†	4	at home	76	"
	Y	Rettman Lawrence	4	custodian	40	"
	z	Rettman Martha—†	4	clerk	35	
253						
	A	Byrnes Katherine—†	5	at home	80	"
	B	Hunter Elizabeth M—†	5	operator	49	"
	c	Hunter Henry J	5	latherer	47	"

Thwing Street—Continued

D	Hunter Mary—†	5	housewife	87	here
E	Hunter Mary—†	5	saleswoman	24	"
F	Krim Anna E—†	6	at home	78	"
G	Krim Elizabeth—†	6	clerk	37	
H	Krim Joseph A	6	retired	83	
K	Krim Marie—†	6	housewife	53	"
L	Carr James V	7	electrician	48	"
M	Carr Mary L—†	7	saleswoman	52	"
N	Carr Michael X	7	laborer	44	"
O	Keane John	8	gardener	41	"
P	Keane Margaret—†	8	housewife	40	"
R	Keane Mary—†	8	clerk	26	Worcester
S	Curley Mary—†	8	housewife	45	here
T	Curley Peter	8	foreman	53	"
U	Rene Alfred A	10	laborer	24	"
V	Rene Evelyn B—†	10	housewife	22	"
W	Shaw Anne—†	10	"	41	"
X	Shaw Joseph T	10	fitter	45	
Y	Walsh Catherine—†	10	domestic	32	"
Z	Walsh Dudley	10	U S A	35	

254

A	Bates Benjamin G	12	salesman	55	"
B	Bates Benjamin G, jr	12	U S M C	27	"
C	Bates Mary M—†	12	housewife	57	"
D	Kenney Joseph	12	rigger	37	"
E	Kenney Margaret—†	12	housewife	33	"
F	Bukow John	14	retired	65	
G	Bukow Mary—†	14	housewife	62	"
H	Ellsworth Gertrude—†	14	operator	60	"
K	Peddell Alice—†	14	housewife	33	"
L	Peddell John	14	machinist	35	"
M	Crosby Fred	14	baker	60	1 Circuit sq
N	Kimbrell Mary R—†	14	housewife	24	13 Parker Hill av
O	Berrenberg Alfred	16	machinist	42	here
P	Berrenberg Rita—†	16	housewife	37	"
R	Phelan Herbert	18	machinist	28	320 Warren
S	Phelan Stella—†	18	housewife	26	320 "
T	Rettman Bertha—†	20	"	38	190 Highland
U	Rettman Henry	20	mechanic	41	190 "
V	Scanlon James J	22	U S N	21	here
W	Scanlon Palma R—†	22	housewife	43	"

Page.	Letter.	FULL NAME.	Residence, Jan. 1, 1946.	Occupation.	Supposed Age.	Reported Residence, Jan. 1, 1945. Street and Number.

Thwing Street—Continued

x	Pare Albert C	22	policeman	52	here
y	Pare Arthur	22	U S N	21	"
z	Pare Imelda—†	22	housewife	48	"

255

a	Pare Norman G	22	welder	24	
b	Pare Richard	22	U S N	22	
c	Broderick Cecelia A—†	24	housewife	53	"
d	Broderick Edith V—†	24	clerk	27	..
e	Broderick Edward P	24	repairman	23	"
f	Broderick Marie C—†	24	secretary	50	"
g	Broderick Wilhelmina—†	24	housewife	29	"
h	Broderick William F	24	plumber	28	"
k	Wood Lloyd F	24	"	29	...
l	Wood Loretta M—†	24	housewife	29	"

3

5

6

8

9

1

1

Ward 11—Precinct 3

CITY OF BOSTON

IST OF RESIDENTS
20 YEARS OF AGE AND OVER

(NON-CITIZENS INDICATED BY ASTERISK)
(FEMALES INDICATED BY DAGGER)

AS OF

JANUARY 1, 1946

THOMAS F. SULLIVAN, *Chairman*
FREDERIC E. DOWLING, *Secretary*
WILLIAM A. MOTLEY, JR.
ARTHUR V. COUGHLIN
EVERETT R. PROUT

Listing Board.

CITY OF BOSTON PRINTING DEPARTMENT

300

Bainbridge Street

A	Furkart Bessie—†	1	housewife	38	17 Bartlett
B	Furkart Robert H	1	teamster	43	17 "
C	Semonian Bagdasar	1	retired	68	here
D	Sachnovitz Ada—†	1	housewife	60	"
E	Sachnovitz Lena—†	1	presser	26	Chelsea
G	Tammaro Helen—†	3	housewife	40	126 Day
H	Tammaro John	3	polisher	30	126 "
K	Mathews Celia—†	3	housewife	39	120 Malden
L	Mathews James F	3	U S N	23	120 "
M	Stanlake Blanche—†	5	housewife	36	here
N	Gill Annie—†	5	"	59	"
O	Gill Robert F	5	laborer	31	"
P	Wallace Margaret J—†	5	housewife	66	"
S	Morgan Frank	7	seaman	22	Bridgewater
T	Johnson Louise E—†	7	housewife	21	5 Kensington
U	Manning Edna—†	7	"	27	New York
V	Manning Martin J	7	mechanic	42	"
W	Matchem James W	9	painter	49	here
X	Matchem Sarah E—†	9	housewife	42	"
Y	Pridham Edwin C	11	merchant	65	"
Z	Pridham Nina G—†	11	housewife	60	"

301

A	Pridham Ruth—†	11	at home	34	
B	MacLeod Angus	11	tailor	45	
C	MacLeod Gertrude—†	11	housewife	40	"
E	Pridham Carolyn—†	13	"	45	
F	Pridham John E	13	chauffeur	44	"
G	Pridham John W	13	U S A	22	
L	Rooney Alice H—†	17	housewife	39	"
M	Rooney Frederick M	17	retired	74	
N	Cameron Margaret M—†	19	clerk	34	
O	Raleigh Mary J—†	19	housewife	62	"
P	Raleigh Michael J	19	bartender	64	"
R	Hines Annie T—†	19	housewife	63	"
S	Hines John P	19	U S A	20	
T	Hines Joseph M	19	bookkeeper	32	"
U	Hines Michael J	19	machinist	66	"
V	Hines Theresa L—†	19	teacher	26	
W	Hurley Mary T—†	19	housewife	84	"
X	Hurley Mary V—†	19	supervisor	48	"

Bainbridge Street—Continued

	Y	Anderson Ada B—†	23	housewife	48	here
	Z	Anderson Walter K	23	porter	57	"
302						
	A	Babcock Ruth N—†	23	at home	53	"
	B	Kidd Alberta—†	23	cook	53	
	C	Miles James A	23	welder	49	
	D	Gibbs Fannie—†	23	housewife	53	"
	E	Gibbs William	23	janitor	52	
	F	Nixon Geraldine F—†	25	housewife	35	"
	G	Rose Charles W	25	laborer	44	
	H	Rose Harriett E—†	25	housewife	67	"
	K	Rose Quentin	25	U S A	27	
	L	Rose Willis W	25	machinist	71	"
	M	Hinson James	25	mechanic	42	"
	N	Booker Florence M—†	25	housewife	55	"
	O	Booker Henry F	25	U S A	25	
	P	Booker Louis H	25	machinist	57	"
	R	Booker Robert V	25	U S A	30	
	S	Hillsman Augustus C	27	presser	· 33	"
	T	Hillsman Mary L—†	27	housewife	28	"
	U	McCowan Elizabeth M—†	27	"	54	
	V	Smith Helena—†	27	presser	29	
	W	Dean Clarence C	27	waiter	33	
	X	Dean Laverne—†	27	housewife	32	"
	Y	McDonald Katherine A—†	29	"	71	
	Z	McDonald Ronald	29	clerk	41	
303						
	A	Roche David B	29	mechanic	34	"
	B	Roche Mary M—†	29	housewife	37	"
	C	Bowles Clare M—†	29	tel operator	22	"
	D	Condon Elizabeth J—†	29	housewife	41	"
	E	Condon James E	29	chauffeur	42	"
	F	Brill Patricia M—†	29	nurse	31	
	G	Martin Agnes M—†	29	housewife	62	"
	H	Martin James F	29	U S A	26	"
	K	Martin Marion F—†	29	clerk	24	"
	L	Gilman Mabel G—† ·	31	housewife	50	"
	M	Gilman Ralph J	31	chauffeur	25	"
	N	Gilman Rita M—†	31	clerk	20	
	O	Gilman Walter G	31	"	23	
	P	Brandos Adrian	31	"	46	

Page	Letter	FULL NAME.	Residence, Jan. 1, 1946.	Occupation.	Supposed Age.	Reported Residence, Jan. 1, 1945. Street and Number.

Bainbridge Street—Continued

	Letter	FULL NAME.	Residence	Occupation.	Age	Reported Residence
	R	Brandos Lillian M—†	31	housewife	51	here
	S	Hardiman Catherine F—†	31	secretary	23	"
	T	Hardiman John A	31	seaman	22	"
	U	Hardiman Leo S	31	"	25	
	V	Hardiman Thomas F	31	U S N	24	
	W	Craven Albert F	31	clerk	27	
	X	Craven Catherine A—†	31	housewife	54	"
	Y	Craven John A	31	clerk	58	
	Z	Craven John L	31	laborer	31	"
		304				
	A	McDermott Mary E—†	33	at home	66	
	B	Stapleton John W	33	U S N	24	
	C	Stapleton Mary F—†	33	housewife	22	"
	D	Gately Eleanor R—†	33	operator	25	"
	E	Gately Helen A—†	33	housewife	59	"
	F	Gately Michael J	33	clerk	55	
	G	O'Brien John T	33	custodian	49	"
	H	O'Brien John T, jr	33	U S N	22	
	K	O'Brien Margaret M—†	33	housewife	46	"
	L	Muir Dorothy B—†	35	operator	35	"
	M	Muir Ellen T—†	35	housewife	60	"
	N	Muir Francis C	35	U S A	37	
	O	Muir John S	35	accountant	40	"
	P	Muir Marion L—†	35	at home	33	
	R	Ahern Katherine E—†	35	"	68	
	S	Ryan Margaret M—†	35	nurse	46	"
	T	Keating James, jr	35	clerk	28	Watertown
	U	Keating Virginia—†	35	housewife	27	"
	V	Moccia Evelyn D—†	37	"	29	here
	W	Moccia Michael A	37	chauffeur	33	"
	X	Denisco Rosa—†	37	housewife	45	"
	Y	Denisco Vincenzo C	37	butcher	46	
	Z	Basquil Catherine M—†	37	housewife	29	"
		305				
	A	Basquil William T	37	painter	33	
	B	Sullivan Catherine J—†	39	at home	67	"
	C	Sullivan Mary L—†	39	"	70	
	D	McQuillan Albina G—†	43	housewife	27	"
	E	McQuillan William J	43	shipfitter	29	"
	F	Horgan Francis J	43	U S A	26	
	G	Horgan Jennie S—†	43	housewife	58	"

Page	Letter	Full Name.	Residence, Jan. 1, 1946.	Occupation.	Supposed Age.	Reported Residence, Jan. 1, 1945. Street and Number.

Bainbridge Street—Continued

	H	Voelker Lee	43	boilermaker	24	8 Cazenove
	K	Voelker Shirley A—†	43	housewife	21	2 "
	M	Driscoll Ella C—†	45	WAC	23	here
	N	Driscoll Esther—†	45	housewife	49	"
	O	Driscoll John F	45	carpenter	52	"
	P	Driscoll John F, jr	45	orderly	20	
	R	Driscoll William R	45	U S M C	20	"
	S	Larsen Andrew	45	checker	71	"
	T	Larsen Signe—†	45	housewife	63	"
	U	Brennan Alice—†	47	"	65	17 Kensington
	V	Glynn Thomas	47	mechanic	26	here
	W	Ryan Catherine T—†	47	housewife	53	"

Beech Glen Street

	X	Greely John J	60	agent	35	here
	Y	Greely Marguerite—†	60	housewife	31	"
	Z	Faulstick Carolyn T—†	60	tel operator	20	"

306

	A	Faulstick Charles M	60	clerk	27	
	B	Faulstick Dorothy M—†	60	operator	26	"
	C	Faulstick Marie D—†	60	housewife	50	"
	D	Faulstick Virginia—†	60	clerk	23	

Cedar Street

	E	Carrol Lorenzo	28	custodian	65	here
	F	Farben William F	28	janitor	55	"
	G	Gray Marie—†	28	housewife	35	"
	H	Gray Walter	28	laborer	44	
	K	Carrington Blanche—†	30	housewife	23	"
	L	Galloway Mildred—†	30	domestic	43	"
	M	Payton Blanche—†	30	attendant	40	"
	N	Sanford Paul	30	laborer	43	
	O	Smith Ernest	30	"	48	
	P	Green Leon G	32	retired	58	
	R	Green Mildred—†	32	housewife	51	"
	S	Smith Howard	32	laborer	54	41 Elmore
	T	Smith Mary T—†	32	housewife	49	41 "
	U	Jackson Eudora—†	32	operator	45	here
	V	Terrelonge Anita—†	34	housewife	48	"

Cedar Street—Continued

Page.	Letter.	FULL NAME.	Residence, Jan. 1, 1946.	Occupation.	Supposed Age.	Reported Residence, Jan. 1, 1945. Street and Number.
	w	Terrelonge Arnold R	34	clerk	53	here
	x	*Branker Eliza—†	34	at home	70	"
	y	Stewart Mary—†	36	housewife	63	"
	z	Clark Gladys—†	36	clerk	53	
307						
	a	Vann Edith—†	36	operator	51	"
	b	Boone James H	36	laborer	60	"
	c	Fleming Harold	36	"	36	
	d	Garrett Anderson	38	cook	37	
	e	Garrett James	38	clerk	28	
	f	Garrett Lucinda—†	38	housewife	37	"
	g	Gunderway Viola—†	38	clerk	37	
	h	Smith Alfred	38	laborer	50	
	k	Greene Hattie—†	38	beautician	34	"
	l	McCreary Anna M—†	40	factoryworker	24	Alabama
	m	McCreary Edgar	40	chauffeur	26	451 Mass av
	n	McCreary Marceline—†	40	housewife	25	451 "
	o	Oxford Emma—†	40	domestic	37	109 Northampton
	p	Williams Hermie—†	40	housewife	32	511 Mass av
	r	Williams Roosevelt	40	electrician	32	511 "
	s	Alves Laura—†	40	packer	25	451 "
	t	Gomes Minnie—†	40	housewife	26	451 "
	u	Goodridge Edena—†	42	housekeeper	25	here
	v	Goodridge James	42	inspector	65	"
	w	Robinson Fannie—†	42	machinist	22	"
	x	Robinson Leon	42	laborer	28	
	z	McNair Marion—†	44	housewife	60	"
308						
	a	Netter Phyllis—†	44	"	23	7 Harold pk
	b	Netter William	44	guard	26	353 Mass av
	c	Blithe Anna—†	46	housewife	21	here
	d	Gardella Robert	46	inspector	23	"
	e	Gardella Rose—†	46	housewife	22	"
	f	Durant John	46	U S N	21	
	g	Durant June—†	46	housewife	23	"
	h	Gibson Alexander	46½	laborer	28	
	k	Gibson Mildred—†	46½	housewife	22	"
	m	Campbell James F	54	mechanic	44	"
	n	Campbell Mary H—†	54	housewife	32	"
	o	Howard Edward	56	boilermaker	45	Somerville
	p	Howard Ruth—†	56	housewife	44	"

Cedar Street—Continued

	Full Name				
R	Knapp Theresa—†	56	housewife	44	here
S	Lamb Mary—†	56	"	30	"
T	Baldwin Adele—†	58	"	24	Vermont
U	Baldwin Emma—†	58	at home	62	here
V	Baldwin Roland	58	maintenance	27	"
W	Bushey Gertrude—†	58	housewife	31	"
X	Bushey Walter	58	manager	31	"
Y	Donahue Delia—†	60	at home	81	
Z	Fay Frances—†	60	adjuster	46	"
z¹	Emery George A	71	manager	52	"

309

	Full Name				
A	Emery Sarah—†	71	at home	85	
B	Coughlin Catherine—†	73	housewife	29	"
C	Coughlin Gerard	73	factoryworker	31	"
D	Pearson Helen—†	73	housewife	31	"
E	Pearson Robert	73	longshoreman	31	"
F	Serrecchia Diana—†	73	housewife	31	"
G	Serrecchia Pasquale	73	factoryworker	37	"
H	Howlett John	75	"	45	
K	Howlett Wanda—†	75	housewife	36	"
L	Connelly Peter	75	fireman	58	"
M	Connelly Joan—†	75	clerk	20	
N	Connelly Lena—†	75	housewife	45	"
O	Connelly William H	75	gardener	52	"
P	Nugent Florence—†	77	housewife	27	Somerville
R	Nugent Florenz	77	chauffeur	28	"
S	Esson Allen	77	checker	37	here
T	*Esson Isaac	77	"	43	"
U	Sceles Morley	77	chauffeur	37	"
V	*Sceles Muriel—†	77	housewife	33	"
W	Matthews Charles F	77	foreman	53	
X	Matthews Marion R—†	77	housewife	48	"
Y	Olsen Harold	79	painter	48	"
Z	Olsen Lottie—†	79	housewife	44	"

310

	Full Name				
A	Ranier Antonio	79	retired	78	
B	*Ranier Elizabeth—†	79	housewife	75	"
C	Ranier Joseph	79	shoeworker	43	"
D	Sciulli Mary—†	79	housewife	47	"
E	Sciulli Michael	79	cook	49	
F	Kingston Elizabeth—†	81	policewoman	42	"

Page.	Letter.	FULL NAME.	Residence, Jan. 1, 1946.	Occupation.	Supposed Age.	Reported Residence, Jan. 1, 1945. Street and Number.

Cedar Street—Continued

	G	Kingston Evelyn R—†	81	executive	53	here
	H	*Kreslin John	82	retired	61	"
	K	Lassman Anna—†	82	at home	60	"
	L	Waichel Mary—†	82	"	63	
	M	Murphy Helen—†	82	factoryworker	40	"
	N	Kalin Mary—†	82	housewife	59	"
	O	Osis Frederick	82	cutter	43	
	P	Dunn Annie—†	85	housewife	69	"
	R	Dunn James F	85	U S A	33	
	S	Fewore Frank O	85	retired	65	
	T	Fewore Mary—†	85	policewoman	33	"
	U	Hale Margaret S—†	85	at home	73	".
	V	McElroy Ann M—†	85	housewife	30	"
	W	McElroy Joseph	85	U S A	31	
	X	McGovern Mary A—†	85	at home	83	"
	Y	Shannon Margaret M—†	85	domestic	68	"
	Z	Calvin Charles	88	U S A	32	

311

	A	Calvin John	88	painter	61	
	B	Calvin Minna—†	88	housewife	60	"
	C	Sonberg John	88	painter	56	
	D	Hurley John	88	laborer	43	
	E	Hurley Margaret—†	88	housewife	44	"
	F	Hurley Mary—†	88	"	60	
	G	Doherty Daniel	88	guard .	60	"
	H	Douglas Catherine—†	89	housewife	33	631 Parker
	K	Douglas John	89	attendant	37	631 "
	L	Gaughran Anthony J	89	painter	65	here
	M	Gaughran Francis	89	U S A	27	"
	N	Gaughran Kenneth	89	clerk	32	"
	O	Gaughran Madelina—†	89	typist	25	
	P	Gaughran Nora—†	89	housewife	58	"
	R	Gaughran Theresa—†	89	saleswoman	20	"
	S	Gaughran William E	89	locksmith	21	"
	T	Mogue Amy—†	91	housewife	66	"
	U	Mogue James C	91	bartender	70	"
	V	Bartkus Anthony A	91	baker	46	
	W	Bartkus Mary—†	91	housewife	42	"
	X	Hunt Julia M—†	91	at home	72	"
	Y	Lindholm Helding	91	maintenance	45	"
	Z	Lindholm Matilda—†	91	housewife	66	"

312
Cedar Street—Continued

c	Scott Anna—†	98	housewife	42	here
d	Scott Arline—†	98	student	21	"
e	Scott Edward	98	U S N	22	"
f	Scott Eric	98	social worker	43	"
g	Copuzzo Fred	98	factoryworker	35	"
h	Copuzzo Lorreta—†	98	housewife	56	"
k	Copuzzo Paul	98	factoryworker	55	"
l	Dillon Mary—†	98	at home	66	"
m	Hermes Mary M—†	102	housewife	65	"
n	Hermes Walter J	102	student	26	
o	Milligan Dorothy—†	102	saleswoman	42	"
p	Nelson Lorna—†	102	housewife	40	"
r	Nelson Percy R	102	draftsman	45	"

Dale Street

s	Sheehan Elizabeth—†	128	housewife	86	here
t	Chappell Hattie	130	"	47	"
u	Countie Catherine—†	132	clerk	46	"
v	Countie John T	132	policeman	58	"
w	Countie Mary F—†	132	housewife	55	"

Dorr Street

x	Schrader Carl	15	engraver	49	here
y	Schrader Eloise R—†	15	clerk	20	"
z	Schrader Rose—†	15	housewife	44	"

313

a	Winterstein Frieda—†	15	at home	80	"
b	Price Louise—†	17	housewife	21	"
c	Price Richard	17	U S M C	23	"
d	Wheeler Annie L—†	17	housewife	60	"
e	Wheeler Chester L	17	janitor	62	
f	Johnson Alvhild—†	17	housewife	52	"
g	Johnson Gunnar	17	painter	45	
h	*Johnson Bertha E—†	17	housewife	52	"
k	Johnson Dorothy L—†	17	clerk	21	"
l	Johnson Norman E	17	watchman	54	"
n	McAdam Ellen—†	23	cleaner	46	"
o	McAdam Harold J	23	laborer	46	

9

Dorr Street—Continued

P	McGarroll Edward D	23	retired	39	here
R	Noseworthy Joseph F	23	pipefitter	28	"
S	Noseworthy Ruth L—†	23	housewife	25	"
U	Lyon Edward C	25	repairman	51	"
V	Roche Joseph	25	machinist	27	"
W	McInnis Neil	25	fireman	26	
Z	Daly James C	29	U S N	35	··

314

A	Daly Marie—†	29	housewife	31	"
C	Perry John	31	laborer	38	"
D	Snypes Marguerite—†	31	housewife	32	109 Sterling
E	Garland Rita—†	31	"	29	here
F	Garland Sydney	31	roofer	34	"
G	Larweneek Emily—†	33	dressmaker	55	"
H	Clark Joseph	33	retired	68	"
K	Holland Gertrude—†	33	dressmaker	50	"
L	McBride Margaret—†	35	at home	81	"
M	Desmond Mary—†	35	housewife	42	"
N	Desmond Timothy	35	laborer	48	
O	Wessling Frank	37	retired	58	
P	Wessling Marguerite—†	37	clerk	50	
R	Wessling Mary—†	37	"	53	
S	Raymond Cleo M—†	37	housewife	56	"
T	Raymond James E	37	U S N	34	
U	Raymond John R	37	"	27	
V	Raymond William C	37	fireman	60	
W	Roberts Doris R—†	37	operator	22	"
X	Baker Anna M—†	37	at home	33	··
Y	Baker John D	37	chauffeur	45	··
Z	Ritchie Caroline E—†	39	housekeeper	45	"

315

A	Champney Edward	39	retired	82	
B	Champney Mary—†	39	at home	83	··
C	Tansey William	39	U S A	26	··
D	Daly Mary—†	41	housewife	63	"
E	Nickerson Clinton	41	cutter	47	"
F	Nickerson Thelma—†	41	housewife	45	"
G	Gayton Lillian—†	41	"	43	
H	Gayton Thomas M	41	boilermaker	45	"
K	Jones Frances—†	41	housewife	22	"
L	Jones Melvin T	41	repairman	25	··

Ellis Street

M	Breen Frances—†	1	teacher	56	Canada
N	Green Helen—†	1	inspector	44	6 Greenville
O	McLellan Cecelia—†	1	housewife	42	6 "
P	McLellan John	1	carpenter	49	6 "
R	Rozanski Fred	1	operator	24	28 Sudan
S	Rozanski Pauline—†	1	housewife	22	110 Thornton
T	Sewall Stanley	1	clerk	21	Braintree
U	Williamson Carol—†	1	stenographer	27	here
V	Woodruff Ethel—†	1	housewife	51	"
W	Woodruff Thomas	1	supervisor	53	"
X	Grossman Margaret—†	9	saleswoman	27	"
Y	Grossman Robert J	9	salesman	32	"
Z	Savage Elizabeth—†	9	housewife	29	"

316

A	Savage Joseph	9	steamfitter	31	"
B	Shilladay Elizabeth—†	9	clerk	57	"
C	Shilladay Grace—†	9	housekeeper	46	"
D	Shilladay Joseph	9	retired	54	"
E	Shilladay Mabel—†	9	clerk	51	"

Elmore Street

F	Cadigan Ella—†	12	housewife	45	here
G	Cadigan James D	12	salesman	41	"
H	Cosgrove Clement B	12	"	25	"
K	Cosgrove Evelyn—†	12	housewife	21	N Carolina
L	Leahy Alice—†	12	tel operator	35	here
M	Brennan James	12	clerk	35	"
N	Brennan James J	12	painter	71	"
O	Brennan Margaret—†	12	housewife	32	"
P	Wheelock Burton	12	electrician	37	17 Dorr
R	Wheelock Lillian—†	12	housewife	24	17 "
S	Lewis James H	14	shipper	39	71 Walnut av
T	Lewis Margaret—†	14	housewife	37	71 "
U	Cossett Edna A—†	14	"	30	Malden
V	Cossett Joseph	14	chauffeur	35	"
W	Hill Constance—†	14	at home	23	Chelmsford
X	McCarthy Anna—†	14	housewife	31	here
Y	McCarthy Charles	14	U S A	30	"
Z	Looney Catherine R—†	16	bookkeeper	24	"

11

317
Elmore Street—-Continued

Letter	Full Name	Residence	Occupation	Age	Reported Residence
A	Looney Joseph P	16	salesman	33	here
B	Looney Nora T—†	16	housewife	64	"
C	Looney Paul D	16	U S A	23	"
D	Merson Laurence P	16	laborer	32	2754 Wash'n
E	Young Edward	16	shipper	34	here
F	Young Florence—†	16	housewife	34	"
G	Keohane Eleanor C—†	16	saleswoman	22	"
H	Keohane Jeremiah	16	laborer	57	
K	Keohane Mary M—†	16	housewife	60	"
L	O'Donnell Margaret M—†	16	bookkeeper	23	"
M	Lynch Lillian—†	18	waitress	43	"
N	Williams Frances—†	18	housewife	21	"
O	Irving Hilda R—†	18	waitress	22	"
P	Mitchell Edith M—†	18	housewife	32	"
R	Bass Martha—†	18	mechanic	47	10 Harold pk
S	Lopes Frances—†	18	housewife	44	here
T	Lopes Isadore J	18	U S M C	21	"
U	Lopes Manuel	18	cook	41	"
V	Lopes Manuel J	18	U S A	23	"
W	Daley Catherine K—†	20	housewife	57	"
X	Reddish Joseph F	20	U S A	32	
Y	Reddish Margaret—†	20	housewife	28	"
Z	Archilles Francis T	20	teamster	50	"

318

Letter	Full Name	Residence	Occupation	Age	Reported Residence
A	Archilles George H	20	retired	56	
B	Archilles William H	20	repairman	45	"
C	Reid Bessie M—†	20	saleswoman	59	"
D	Reid Henry F	20	student	22	
E	Kilroy Mary—†	20	bookkeeper	42	"
F	Kilroy Thomas F	20	electrician	47	"
G	Brooks Frances—†	22	housewife	60	"
H	Sanborn Franklin	22	retired	60	
K	Cunneen Helen—†	22	housewife	41	"
L	Cunneen John T	22	clerk	51	
M	McHale Edward M	22	"	58	
N	McHale Edward T	22	U S A	33	
O	McHale Mary F—†	22	housewife	52	"

Page	Letter	Full Name.	Residence, Jan. 1, 1946.	Occupation.	Supposed Age.	Reported Residence, Jan. 1, 1945. Street and Number.

Fort Avenue

	P	Philbin Anna—†	4	at home	75	here
	R	Fitzgerald Edward C	4	U S A	20	"
	S	Fitzgerald Edward T	4	foreman	55	"
	T	Fitzgerald Gladys—†	4	housewife	45	"
	U	Wilson Charles H	4	retired	66	
	V	Wilson Ernest C	4	U S N	28	"
	W	Lass Richard	4	shipper	65	"
	X	Lass Sina—†	4	housewife	46	"
	Y	Manley Mary L—†	6	"	28	
	Z	Manley Raymond D	6	oil dealer	30	"

319

	A	Roe Marion T—†	6	housewife	44	"
	B	Roe William J	6	machinist	45	"
	C	Roe William J, jr	6	U S A	22	
	D	Wilson Charles M	6	laborer	41	
	E	Wilson Marie M—†	6	housewife	34	"
	F	Arnott Emily—†	8	"	45	
	G	Arnott Howard W	8	shipper	43	
	H	Ellsworth Josephine—†	8	housewife	34	"
	K	Ellsworth Stephen	8	chauffeur	38	"
	L	Laiweneek Mildred—†	8	housewife	31	"
	M	Laiweneek Robert	8	U S A	30	
	N	Whelan Irene—†	10	housewife	26	"
	O	Whelan William	10	splicer	27	
	P	Finnell Alfreda—†	10	housewife	52	"
	R	Finnell Robert J	10	laborer	29	
	S	Kennedy Myrtle—†	10	housewife	29	"
	T	Kennedy Thomas	10	U S A	30	"

Galena Street

	U	Sullivan Frank J	2	clerk	33	here
	V	Sullivan Rachel—†	2	housewife	34	"
	W	*Kerkell Anthony	2	laborer	55	"
	X	*Kerkell Nellie—†	2	housewife	54	"
	Y	Shaknites Adele—†	2	clerk	29	
	Z	Shaknites Charles	2	laborer	59	"

320

	A	Shaknites Nellie—†	2	clerk	26	
	B	Shaknites Veronica—†	2	housewife	59	"

Galena Street—Continued

c	Porter Herbert	4	laborer	65	here
d	Squire Edith—†	4	housewife	45	"
e	Squire Elsie—†	4	clerk	21	"
f	Squire Ralph	4	machinist	20	"
g	Frenette Alice—†	4	housewife	36	"
h	Frenette Philip	4	cook	38	
k	Brooks Ada—†	4	housewife	31	"
l	Brooks William	4	electrician	44	"
m	Flagg Frank B	6	watchman	59	"
n	Flagg Mary—†	6	housewife	52	"
o	Reichert Albert G, jr	6	U S A	25	
p	Reichert Ethel—†	6	housewife	24	"
r	Grant Rose—†	6	"	40	
s	Wark Ellen L—†	6	"	49	
t	Wark Gertrude E—†	6	clerk	23	
u	Wark Robert A	6	supt	53	"
v	Wark Robert C	6	U S A	23	
w	Campbell Clarice—†	8	housewife	39	"
x	Campbell Roy	8	beltman	43	"
y	Frye Charles	8	plumber	52	"
z	Frye Kenneth A	8	seaman	22	"

321

a	Frye Maria—†	8	housewife	40	"
b	McAfee Della B—†	8	"	35	
c	McAfee George J	8	welder	38	
d	Champagne Arthur	10	machinist	52	"
e	Champagne Margaret—†	10	housewife	40	"
f	McNeil Margaret—†	10	"	45	"
g	McNeil Simon	10	carpenter	50	"
h	Ford Birchard	10	U S A	28	Ohio
k	Ford Geraldine—†	10	housewife	23	"
l	Howard Dorothy L—†	12	"	34	here
m	Howard Wallace A	12	clerk	34	"
n	Kelly Cornelius J	12	U S N	21	"
o	Kelly Margaret—†	12	housewife	52	"
p	Kelly Richard	12	clerk	52	"
r	Burnett Peter C	12	student	21	6 Romar ter.
s	Lataitis Catherine—†	12	housewife	61	6 "
t	*Mitchell Christina—†	14	"	29	here
u	Mitchell Edmund	14	shipper	36	"
v	Mullen James	14	laborer	33	"

Page	Letter	Full Name.	Residence, Jan. 1, 1946.	Occupation.	Supposed Age.	Reported Residence, Jan. 1, 1945. Street and Number.

Galena Street—Continued

w	Mullen Margaret—†	14	housewife	65	here
x	Mullen Patrick	14	watchman	66	"
y	Mullen Peter	14	laborer	37	"
z	Vosmus Barbara—†	14	housewife	32	"

322

A	Vosmus James J	14	U S C G	39	"
B	Eriksen Alfred	16	retired	70	"
C	Towers Mary—†	16	housekeeper	61	"
D	Chamberlain Jennie—†	16	housewife	67	"
E	Chamberlain Millicent—†	16	supervisor	31	"
F	Lynch Francis H	16	welder	34	"
G	Lynch Martin H	16	retired	68	
H	Lynch Mary E—†	16	housewife	56	"

Hawthorne Street

M	Mueller Joseph	12	U S A	22	here
N	Mueller Victor	12	"	22	"
O	Mueller Victor E	12	electrician	55	"
P	Duffy Anna—†	16	at home	81	"
R	Wilson Percy R	16	engraver	50	"
S	Hynes Francis T	16	clerk	29	
T	Hynes Margaret—†	16	"	33	
U	Hynes Mary—†	16	bookkeeper	31	"
V	Hynes Michael	16	laborer	60	"
X	Whittaker Eileen—†	18	clerk	40	"
Y	Whittaker Ida—†	18	buyer	33	
Z	Whittaker Mary J—†	18	at home	71	"

323

A	Whittaker Una P—†	18	secretary	45	"
B	Ruggles Hazel W—†	20	teacher	54	"
C	Hogan Lawrence J	24	U S A	23	214 Highland
D	Hogan Muriel C—†	24	housewife	39	214 "
E	Schjolden Marie—†	24	"	52	here
F	Ohlson George R	24	U S A	26	"
G	Ohlson Vivian M—†	24	housewife	25	"
H	Bickerton Isabell—†	25	stenographer	37	"
K	DeFina Anthony F	25	U S A	36	"
L	DeFina Carmela—†	25	saleswoman	28	"
M	DeFina Daniel	25	carpenter	54	"
N	DeFina Immaculate—†	25	dressmaker	24	"

Page.	Letter.	FULL NAME.	Residence, Jan. 1, 1946.	Occupation.	Supposed Age.	Reported Residence, Jan. 1, 1945. Street and Number.

Hawthorne Street—Continued

o	Rice Jane—†	26	housewife	43	here
p	Rice John F	26	fisherman	48	"
r	Alvarez Anna—†	26	housewife	41	"
s	Alvarez Marion—†	26	shoeworker	21	"
t	Alvarez Ralph W	26	chauffeur	47	"
u	Alvarez Ralph W	26	U S A	24	
v	Miller Guy	26	carpenter	63	"
w	Miller Maude I—†	26	housewife	60	"
x	Miller Roy	26	plumber	22	"
y	Morrison Francis V	26	mechanic	29	25 Horan way
z	Morrison Margaret P—†	26	housewife	24	here
	324				
a	Edwards Eddie T—†	28	laborer	25	143 Worcester
b	McRae Samuel	28	clerk	56	here
c	Priester Margaret—†	28	domestic	50	"
d	Davis Daniel W	28	laborer	41	"
e	Davis Tina—†	28	housewife	37	"
f	McLaughlin Charles H	29	salesman	59	"
g	McLaughlin Charles J	29	manager	30	"
h	McLaughlin Mary E—†	29	housewife	57	"
k	Londregan Irene A—†	29	stenographer	20	"
l	Londregan Pauline A—†	29	housewife	39	"
m	Londregan Thomas F	29	retired	43	
n	LeRiche Anna—†	30	housewife	46	"
o	LeRiche Walter	30	fireman	50	
p	Adams John J	30	manager	38	"
r	Adams Mary T—†	30	housewife	38	"
s	Misilo John	30	cook	36	
t	Misilo Mary—†	30	housewife	44	"
u	Kelly Gertrude E—† rear	31	"	35	
v	Kelly Joseph P "	31	mechanic	37	"
w	Sweney Fred J	32	guard	32	
x	Sweney Virginia A—†	32	housewife	33	"
y	York Abby—†	32	"	64	
z	York Christoff	32	brewer	66	
	325				
a	Long Agnes—†	32	clerk	50	
b	Long Alice—†	32	domestic	46	"
c	Tirrell Gertrude—†	33	clerk	38	
d	Tirrell Mary—†	33	stitcher	44	
e	Murray Charles D	33	clerk	25	

16

Hawthorne Street—Continued

	F	Murray Edwin E	33	U S A	23	here
	G	Murray James D	33	shipper	26	"
	H	Murray Mary M—†	33	housewife	45	"
	K	Antaramian George M	33	U S A	27	
	L	Antaramian Rose—†	33	housewife	50	"
	M	Antaramian Virginia—†	33	clerk	21	
	N	Connors Edward	35	steamfitter	40	"
	O	Connors Irene—†	35	housewife	38	"
	P	Murphy Catherine—†	35	"	48	
	R	Murphy John	35	engineer	49	"
	S	Murphy John J	35	shipper	21	"
	T	Avedisian Avedis	35	barber	52	"
	U	Avedisian Edna—†	35	housewife	49	"
	V	Avedisian Oscar	35	U S A	24	
	W	*Blanchard Mabel—†	36	housewife	45	"
	X	Blanchard Peter	36	painter	45	
	Y	*McDonald Irene—†	36	domestic	42	"
	Z	*Moroney Georgina—†	36	housewife	38	"

326

	A	Moroney James D	36	letter carrier	39	"
	B	McQuain George D	36	wireman	26	"
	C	McQuain Irene B—†	36	housewife	28	"
	D	Murray Catherine—†	41	"	86	"
	E	Murray Eugene	41	laborer	46	
	F	Joyce Helen—†	41	secretary	22	"
	G	Joyce Joseph	41	metalworker	26	"
	H	Joyce Patrick	41	laborer	56	"
	K	Joyce Rose E—†	41	housewife	48	"
	L	Smith Bernice M—†	51	"	43	
	M	Smith John H	51	machinist	43	"
	N	Malenfant Alice G—†	51	housewife	55	"
	O	Malenfant Joseph E	51	counterman	52	"

Highland Park

	P	Clark Helen F—†	1	teacher	37	here
	R	Clark Mary E—†	1	"	39	"
	S	Clark Sarah—†	1	housewife	74	"
	T	Geer Catherine—†	2	laundress	29	"
	U	Mulloney Arthur W	2	clerk	31	"
	V	Mulloney Paul F	2	"	21	

Highland Park—Continued

	w	Mulloney Walter V	2	clerk	20	here
	x	Mulloney William J	2	retired	72	"
	y	Mulloney William J, jr	2	U S A	28	"
	z	Concannon Catherine J—†	3	housewife	53	"
327						
	a	Concannon Francis G	3	U S N	24	
	b	Concannon Gerald	3	"	20	
	c	Concannon John F	3	auditor	26	
	d	Concannon John J	3	mechanic	55	"
	e	Concannon Mary A—†	3	clerk	22	"
	f	Zerola Aida M—†	3	"	25	159 Marion
	g	Mayer Agnes—†	3	housewife	32	here
	h	Mayer Carleton	3	B F D	32	"
	l	Wardzala Amelie—†	4½	clerk	28	"
	m	Wardzala Mary—†	4½	housewife	51	"
	n	Wardzala Walter	4½	clerk	53	
	o	Freeman Martha—†	5	at home	74	"
	p	Murphy Dennis	5	laborer	33	
	r	Murphy Julia—†	5	housewife	32	"
	s	Baier Aloyse	6	packer	43	
	t	Baier Pauline—†	6	housewife	43	"

Highland Street

	u	Kaskin Anna—†	74	housewife	62	here
	v	Kaskin Vladimir A	74	clergyman	65	"
	w	Dolan Annie—†	74	housewife	62	"
	x	Dolan Charlotte—†	74	buyer	28	
	y	Dolan John	74	letter carrier	58	"
	z	Craffey John	76	electrician	40	"
328						
	a	Craffey Lawrence	76	clerk	33	
	b	Craffey Martin	76	shipper	31	
	c	Harrington Agnes—†	76	secretary	35	"
	d	Hughes Catherine—†	76	housewife	40	"
	e	Hughes Edward	76	chauffeur	40	"
	f	Hayes Dennis	82	clerk	30	
	g	Hayes John J	82	stagehand	55	"
	h	Hayes Mary J—†	82	housewife	53	"
	k	Hoffman Charles H	82	repairman	30	"
	l	Hoffman Mary J—†	82	housewife	21	"

Highland Street—Continued

M	Kane Charles	82	porter	39	here
N	Murphy Jane V—†	82	housewife	28	"
o	Murphy Paul A	82	clerk	34	"
P	Stubbs Henry L	84	pipefitter	40	"
R	Stubbs Mildred—†	84	housewife	27	"
s	Guzelian Margaret—†	86	storekeeper	42	"
T	Guzelian Mihran	86	"	47	"
U	Lall Frances—†	86	housewife	28	14 Hubert
V	Lall Winston I	86	chauffeur	34	14 "
X	Gaynor Josiah	106	clerk	40	69 Highland
Y	Gaynor Loretta—†	106	nurse	40	69 "
Z	Reid Gaston	106	clerk	28	here

329

A	Marshman Martha—†	108	housewife	56	"
B	McPherson Ruby—†	108	"	28	
c	Michaels James A	108	policeman	49	"
D	Testa Antoinette—†	118	housewife	70	"
E	Testa Cosmo	118	retired	44	
F	Savioli Gaetano	118	laborer	54	
G	Savioli Nora—†	118	housewife	49	"
H	Crosby Anne R—†	120	at home	30	"
K	Crosby Anne D—†	120	housewife	64	"
L	Crosby Catherine M—†	120	secretary	35	"
M	Crosby Michael J	120	retired	71	"
N	Walsh John	120	clerk	60	
o	Costa John A	140	barber	36	
P	Costa Margaret—†	140	housewife	35	"
R	Fornaro John A	140	retired	39	
s	Fornaro Josephine—†	140	housewife	60	"
T	Ellis Fred	140	custodian	40	"
U	Boucher Julia A—†	140	housewife	40	"
V	Boucher Richard L	140	clerk	40	"
W	Fermino Cesar	145	"	31	63 Beech Glen
X	Fermino Mary—†	145	housewife	34	63 "
Y	Fermino Jose J, jr	145	laborer	34	63 "
Z	Fermino Olive—†	145	housewife	27	63 "

330

B	Green Henry J	151	steamfitter	79	here
c	Green Mary C—†	151	housewife	66	"
D	Feran Marguerite E—†	151	secretary	22	"
E	Feran Mary E—†	151	housewife	55	"

Highland Street—Continued

F	Feran William C	151	shipper	60	here
G	Crehan Elizabeth—†	151	operator	27	"
H	Crehan Matthew	151	retired	31	"
K	Crehan Nora—†	151	clerk	25	
L	*Albert Louise—†	153	housewife	44	"
M	Hogan Mary—†	153	waitress	48	..
N	Aronson Esther—†	153	student	21	"
O	*Aronson Harold	153	carpenter	57	"
P	*Aronson Lina—†	153	housewife	59	"
R	Aronson Ruth—†	153	clerk	20	
S	*Aronson Vincent	153	metalworker	23	"
V	Hurley Dorothy M—†	158	housewife	43	"
W	Hurley John C	158	storekeeper	40	"
X	Martineau Amy—†	158	housewife	45	"
Y	Martineau Ubaldric	158	metalworker	45	"
Z	Tincoe Mary—†	158	housewife	28	"

331

A	Tincoe Willard	158	clerk	28	
B	Blaxland Bessie—†	160	housewife	40	"
C	Blaxland John, jr	160	clerk	40	
D	Boehmer Antoinette—†	162	"	21	
F	Boehmer M Hedwig—†	162	housewife	61	"
E	Boehmer Mary L—†	162	"	29	
G	Boehmer William	162	clerk	61	
H	Boehmer William J	162	teacher	32	..
K	Lenberger Mary N—†	162	housewife	30	"
L	Lenberger Sidney, jr	162	U S A	34	
M	McGillicuddy John J	162	"	28	
N	McGillicuddy Roberta P-†	162	housewife	28	"
O	Callahan Francis W	163	policeman	32	"
P	Callahan Helen L—†	163	housewife	30	"
R	Allen Amy E—†	163	"	48	
S	Allen Harold B	163	salesman	49	"
T	Boyle Elizabeth C--†	165	secretary	23	165 Highland
U	Boyle Helen F—†	165	housewife	54	165 "
V	Boyle Joseph M	165	salesman	55	165 "
W	Boyle Rita L—†	165	nurse	26	165 "
X	O'Neill Marie H—†	165	housewife	28	165 "
Y	O'Neill Martin J	165	salesman	30	165 "
Z	Iverson Louise—†	174	housewife	24	Dedham

332
Highland Street—Continued

A	Reiss Anna—†	174	housewife	55	here
B	Zentgraf Isabelle—†	174	"	65	"

Kensington Street

C	Petrie Anna—†	1	housewife	39	17 Wakullah
D	Petrie William	1	roofer	43	17 "
E	Peterson Mary—†	1	housewife	31	9 Shafter
F	Peterson William C	1	retired	50	9 "
G	Carney Mary—†	1	housewife	36	3 Kingsbury
H	Kent Mary G—†	3	"	45	here
K	Kent Thomas H	3	chauffeur	46	"
L	Williams Catherine—†	3	housewife	54	"
M	Williams Francis G	3	machinist	27	"
N	Williams Frank	3	metalworker	57	"
O	Williams George E	3	clerk	24	"
P	Williams Joseph	3	U S N	21	"
R	Williams Robert C	3	"	20	"
S	Heelan Mary R—†	3	stenographer	28	87 High
T	Merritt Fred	5	janitor	70	here
U	Merritt Margaret—†	5	housewife	63	"
V	Robinson Edward	5	laborer	43	"
W	Getherall Annie—†	5	housewife	57	17 Albion pl
X	Getherall James	5	shipper	22	17 "
Y	Getherall Rita F—†	5	packer	21	17 "
Z	Getherall Robert	5	mover	25	17 "

333

A	Getherall Thomas H	5	U S A	26	17 "
B	Getherall William J	5	shipper	29	17 "
C	Burke Edna C—†	5	secretary	35	2756 Wash'n
D	Burke Elizabeth—†	5	housewife	65	2756 "
E	Burke James F	5	policeman	27	2756 "
F	Burke Virginia—†	5	secretary	21	2756 "
G	Calway Helen E—†	5	housewife	28	2756 "
H	Dubin Benjamin	7	waiter	45	here
K	Dubin Dorothy—†	7	housewife	43	"
L	McGonagle Frances E—†	7	"	50	"
M	McGonagle Francis J	7	clerk	53	
N	McGonagle Frank X	7	U S M C	24	"

21

Kensington Street—Continued

o	McGonagle Mildred—†	7	clerk	22	here
p	McGonagle William L	7	"	30	"
r	Shwartz Benjamin	7	salesman	47	"
s	Shwartz Bessie—†	7	housewife	46	"
t	Shwartz Charles	7	clerk	26	
u	Shwartz Estelle—†	7	stenographer	21	"
v	Tobin John	9	painter	40	"
w	*Tobin Mary—†	9	housewife	35	"
x	Casavant Clarence G	9	laborer	48	
y	Casavant Grace S—†	9	housewife	48	"
z	Campbell Cora—†	9	"	57	

334

A	Campbell Paul	9	U S A	22	
B	Hartnet Alice D—†	11	housewife	47	"
C	Hartnet Alice T—†	11	clerk	20	
D	Hartnet James E	11	foreman	46	
E	Hartnet James E	11	U S N	24	
F	Hartnet Rita M—†	11	clerk	21	
G	Gately Doris M—†	11	"	21	
H	Gately Jane L—†	11	laundress	25	"
K	Gately Joseph P	11	U S A	24	"
L	Gately Mary E—†	11	housewife	52	"
M	Gately Patrick J	11	laborer	52	
N	Abelson Max	11	storekeeper	55	"
o	*Abelson Sarah—†	11	housewife	55	"
P	Effelberg Dora—†	11	clerk	34	
R	Frasier Roderick	13	laborer	48	
S	Murphy Daniel J	13	bartender	50	"
T	Murphy Julia—†	13	housewife	41	"
U	Morse Lillian M—†	13	mechanic	33	"
V	Walker Charles E	13	U S N	26	
W	Walker Meada A—†	13	housewife	55	"
X	Walker Richard L	13	manager	24	"
Y	Walker William L	13	chauffeur	56	"
Z	Walker William L, jr	13	mechanic	28	"

335

D	Woodbarn George W	17	woodworker	45	"
E	Woodbarn Mary E—†	17	housewife	35	"
F	Coyle Patrick J	17	retired	73	
G	Glynn Eugene P	17	laborer	35	
H	Glynn Mary E—†	17	housewife	30	"

Kingsbury Street

K	Stella Arthur	4	machinist	39	here
L	Stella Mary—†	4	housewife	37	"
M	McPhee Mary L—†	4	"	43	"
N	McPhee Peter A	4	clerk	44	
O	Davis Emma—†	4	housewife	44	"
P	Davis Michael G	4	U S N	20	
R	Lihzis Anna—†	4	at home	77	"
S	DiNardo Lillian—†	6	clerk	25	"
T	Jarvis Arthur	6	U S A	34	"
U	Jarvis Margaret—†	6	housewife	55	"
V	Wincus Eleanor—†	6	at home	30	"
W	Forsyth Mary—†	6	housewife	28	97 Bragdon
X	Forsyth William	6	clerk	28	97 "
Y	Glynn Owen	6	laborer	59	here
Z	Glynn Theresa—†	6	housewife	43	"

336

A	Glynn Thomas	6	U S A	22	"
B	Ridlon Oscar G	8	chauffeur	40	6 Kensington
C	Ridlon Stella N—†	8	housewife	34	6 "
D	Hines Helen—†	8	at home	42	here
E	Waters Helen—†	8	clerk	21	"
F	Waters Marion—†	8	housewife	45	"
G	Waters Patrick	8	laborer	52	"
H	Corr Francis O	10	U S A	26	"
K	Corr Margaret Z—†	10	housewife	62	"
L	Corr Peter E	10	carpenter	72	"
M	Parker Emily—†	10	housewife	67	"
N	Parker William H	10	laborer	25	"
O*	Powers Nora A—†	10	garmentworker	52	139 Marcella
P	Cunningham Edna M—†	12	housewife	22	17 Batchelder
R	Cunningham Gerald J	12	chauffeur	24	17 "
S	Cunningham Edith—†	12	housewife	44	102 Howard av
T	Cunningham Francis A	12	clerk	21	102 "
U	McKean Wendell E	12	"	52	4 Circuit sq
V	Ritchie Lena A—†	14	housewife	30	here
W	Ritchie William	14	mechanic	35	"
X	Carpluk Alfred E	14	student	21	"
Y	Carpluk John	14	carpenter	50	"
Z*	Carpluk Mary—†	14	housewife	44	"

337

A	Zaiatz John F	14	U S N	26	

Kingsbury Street—Continued

B	Garland Mary L—†	14	housewife	24	here
C	Garland Philip W	14	rigger	27	"
D	Leon Anna J—†	14	housewife	57	"
E	Leon Georgene E—†	14	saleswoman	21	"
G	Ciano Michael	16	laborer	56	
H	Ciano Rose—†	16	housewife	38	"
K	Loll Marguerite L—†	16	stenographer	22	"
L	McInnis Gerald L	16	U S N	20	"
M	McInnis Isabelle—†	16	housewife	47	"
N	Pike Agnes M—†	16	"	47	
O	Davis Bessie—†	17	"	32	
P	Davis Myer	17	merchant	35	"
R	Manna Anthony W	17	leatherworker	44	"
S	Manna Victoria—†	17	housewife	37	"
T	O'Neil Anna M—†	17	"	32	New Jersey
U	O'Neil William F	17	machinist	34	"
V	Goodrich Genevieve H—†	18	"	29	here
W	Goodrich Milton F	18	engineer	30	"
X	Davis Barbara M—†	18	housewife	22	"
Y	Davis Joseph F	18	shipper	30	
Z	Wagner Charles E	18	chauffeur	21	"

338

A	Wagner St Clair S	18	U S A	23	
B*	Wagner Wilfred	18	machinist	59	"
C	Crowell Charles F	21	retired	72	
D	Peters John D	21	steamfitter	52	"
E	Peters Mary A—†	21	housewife	76	"
F	O'Brien Bernard A	21	mechanic	50	"
G	O'Brien Ermina J—†	21	tel operator	44	"
H	Alston Eugene J	21	U S N	26	
K	Alston Mary S—†	21	housewife	20	"
L	Bucevich Charles	21	shoeworker	63	"
M	Bucevich Katherine P—†	21	housewife	54	"
N	Hardway Anna E—†	21	"	29	
O	Hardway Doyle R	21	U S N	24	
P	Cunningham Harriet A—†	25	housewife	27	"
R	Cunningham James L	25	U S A	31	
S	Gerus Adela A—†	25	machinist	53	"
T	Gerus Edward I	25	"	25	
U	Wegeler Adele E—†	25	housewife	54	"
V	Wegeler George H	25	millwright	53	"

Kingsbury Street—Continued

w	Wegeler George H, jr	25	clerk	21	here
x	Wegeler Geraldine M—†	25	bookkeeper	26	"
y	Wegeler Virginia I—†	25	machinist	24	"
z	Devlin Mary A—†	29	housewife	72	"

339

A	Devlin Richard B	29	retired	73	
B	Dillon Mary—†	29	housewife	64	"
c	Dillon Mary E—†	29	tel operator	26	"
D	Dillon William H	29	janitor	76	
E	Dillon William H, jr	29	salesman	35	"
F	Leonard Catherine—†	29	housewife	62	"
G	Leonard Edward T	29	checker	23	"
H	Leonard James E	29	shipper	33	"
K	Leonard Joseph A	29	printer	28	"
L	Leonard Katherine M—†	29	tel operator	21	"
M	Leonard Mary H—†	29	cashier	31	
N	Pulver Albert W	33	U S A	21	"
o	Pulver Frank J	33	chauffeur	50	"
P	Pulver Margaret E—†	33	housewife	44	"
R	Sullivan James J	33	bricklayer	59	"
s	Sullivan Mary E—†	33	housewife	51	"
T	Sullivan Mary E—†	33	student	23	"
U	Sullivan Rita J—†	33	WAVE	21	
v	Arruda Phyllis C—†	33	presser	59	"
w	Bush Gertrude E—†	33	housewife	48	"
x	Bush Thomas J	33	carpenter	37	"
Y	Foreman John H	33	U S A	27	"
z	Foreman Joseph E	33	rigger	25	47 W Walnut pk

340 **Lambert Avenue**

A	Ahlgren Charles J	63	shipper	40	here
B	Flannery Mary A—†	63	at home	74	"
c	*Baker Edward	63	retired	75	"
D	Teahan Arleen—†	63	housewife	41	"
E	Teahan Richard	63	chauffeur	40	"
F	Salmon Mary A—†	63	housewife	55	"
G	Salmon Michael	63	laborer	57	
H	Bobin Mary V—†	65	cook	68	
K	Wasielewsky Josephine A—†	65	waitress	39	"
L	Wasielewsky Mathew J	65	mechanic	52	"

Lambert Avenue—Continued

M	King Albert E	65	painter	47	here
N	King Helena—†	65	housewife	47	"
O	King Josephine—†	65	secretary	25	"
P	Townsend Charles A	65	U S N	23	..
R	Townsend Frank G	65	leatherworker	59	"
S	Townsend Grace—†	65	bookkeeper	20	"
T	Townsend Jenny—†	65	housewife	57	"
U	Anderson Frances E—†	67	clerk	20	
V	Anderson Frank	67	machinist	67	"
w*	Anderson Jane B—†	67	at home	59	..
x*	DeHaro Dorothea—†	67	housewife	36	"
Y	DeHaro Francis E	67	U S N	32	
Z	Reckard Barbara R—†	67	at home	28	"

341

A	Reckard Richard E	67	U S C G	32	"
B	Root Ida B—†	67	housewife	69	"
C	Root Marcia E—†	67	WAVE	32	..

Oakland Street

D	Morris David H	4	brazier	38	here
E	Morris Edith—†	4	housewife	34	"
F	DiMarino Leopold	4	laborer	41	"
G*	DiMarino Tranquilla—†	4	housewife	55	"
H	Sheed Esther—†	6	"	29	N Carolina
K	Sheed Frank	6	machinist	38	"
L	Berzon Harry	6	baker	29	here
M	Berzon Sadie—†	6	housewife	27	"
N	Riordan Irene K—†	8	"	36	"
O	Riordan Michael J	8	letter carrier	41	"
P	Forte Anna—†	10	clerk	22	
R	Forte Charles	10	barber	50	
S	Forte Dorina—†	10	housewife	45	"
T	Crognolia Angelo	10	student	24	15 Oakland
U	Crognolia Nina—†	10	housewife	24	here
V	Doyle Annie C—†	12	"	63	"
w	Kenney James W	12	packer	23	"
x	Kenney Shirley I—†	12	operator	20	"
Y	Joyce Martin	12	U S N	20	
Z	Joyce Mary—†	12	housewife	48	"

342
Oakland Street—Continued

A	Joyce Patrick	12	laborer	52	here
B	Gaul Frances L—†	14	manager	31	"
c	*Gaul Mary A—†	14	at home	53	"
D	*Taylor Amos	14	laborer	63	
E	McPherson John	16	chauffeur	43	"
F	McPherson Sadie—†	16	housewife	45	"
G	Mulkay Mary—† †	18	"	39	"
H	Mulkay Patrick	18	laborer	39	
K	*Blackstead Margaret—†	18	housewife	39	"
L	*Blackstead Raymond	18	painter	39	"
M	Cote Margaret—†	20	housewife	32	Ohio
N	Callahan Alice—†	20	"	46	here
o	Simpson James A	20	chauffeur	56	"
P	Abbis Anna—†	22	housewife	45	"
R	Abbis Anthony	22	U S N	21	"
s	Abbis Dominic	22	U S A	22	.

Thornton Street

T	Clapp Catherine A—†	75	at home	49	here
U	Clapp Elmer A	75	steamfitter	48	"
V	Clapp Rita C—†	75	teacher	22	"
W	Dolan Catherine—†	75	housewife	68	"
X	Dolan Michael A	75	starter	68	
Y	Jones Gertrude—†	81	housewife	37	"
Z	Jones John	81	B F D	41	

343

'A	Thomas Catherine—†	81	at home	53	Maryland
B	Thomas Eugene	81	laborer	44	"
c	Nurse St Clair	81	clergyman	41	Cambridge
D	Eckman Elsie M—†	rear 83	supervisor	46	here
E	Eckman Julia—†	" 83	housewife	86	"
F	Filipowicz Anna—†	85	stitcher	46	"
G	Filipowicz Jennie—†	85	technician	23	"
H	Filipowicz Peter	85	carpenter	57	"
K	Maloney George	85	U S M C	24	"
L	Maloney Mary—†	85	housewife	22	"
M	*McLellan Annie—†	85	matron	55	
N	McLellan Joseph	85	shipper	26	"
o	Patti Catherine—†	91	housewife	32	126 Bremen

Thornton Street—Continued

P	Patti Joseph	91	barber	34	126 Bremen
S	Cook Florence—†	96	nurse	25	here
T	Cook Lelia—†	96	housewife	54	"
U	Cook William F	96	porter	27	"
V	Kearney Marion—†	96	at home	31	26 Cedar
W	Kearney Peter	96	roofer	35	26 "
Y	French Anna J—†	102	clerk	22	here
Z	French Chester W	102	musician	48	"

344

A	French Mary—†	102	housewife	46	"
B	DeGraan Anita—†	108	cook	35	
C	DeGraan George	108	chauffeur	40	"
D	Johnson Arthur	108	clerk	44	
E	Johnson Elsa—†	108	housewife	41	"
F	Sullivan Charles W	108	inspector	34	"
G	Sullivan Edith—†	108	housewife	28	"
H	Bonanno Frances—†	110	"	26	
K	Bonanno John	110	electrician	29	"
L	Carrazza Nicholas	110	laborer	54	
M	Connor Anna—†	110	WAVE	26	
N	Connor Elizabeth—†	110	housewife	56	"
O	Irving Charles	112	painter	45	
P	Irving Ida—†	112	housewife	41	"
R	O'Connor Cornelius	112	machinist	43	101 Highland
S	O'Connor Margaret—†	112	housewife	40	101 "
T	Boucher Lorenzo	112	stevedore	42	here
U	Boucher Vera—†	112	housewife	32	"
V	Carrazza Frank	114	U S N	20	"
W	Pender Mary—†	114	clerk	21	"
X	Pender Thomas	114	laborer	24	
Y	Pender William	114	"	51	
Z	Brunetto Florence—†	116	bookkeeper	22	"

345

A	Brunetto Harriet—†	116	electrician	41	"
B	Brunetto Joseph	116	boilermaker	50	"
C	Grogan Elizabeth—†	116	at home	26	"
D	Grogan William	116	U S A	26	
E	Leazott Helen M—†	116	housewife	46	"
F	Leazott Ralph	116	roofer	50	
G	Leazott Victor	116	mechanic	22	"
H	*Kanes Katina—†	120	textile worker	49	"

Thornton Street—Continued

Page.	Letter.	Full Name.	Residence, Jan. 1, 1946.	Occupation.	Supposed Age.	Reported Residence, Jan. 1, 1945. Street and Number
	K	Kocourek Harold	120	U S N	28	here
	L	Kocourek Mildred—†	120	beautician	25	"
	M	Kolivas Nicholas	120	chauffeur	28	"
	N	Kolivas Olga—†	120	beautician	23	"
	O	Connelly Edmund A	120	laborer	47	17 Julian
	P	Connelly Mary B—†	120	housewife	47	17 "
	R	Sullivan Catherine M—†	120	"	39	12 Walnut pk
	S	Sullivan Francis G	120	chauffeur	43	12 "
	T	Carson Charles R	126	retired	72	here
	U	Carson Jamila—†	126	at home	53	"
	V	Carson Marjorie—†	126	operator	29	"
	W	Lippi Angelo	126	manager	59	"
	X	Lippi Elizabeth T—†	126	housewife	65	"
	Y	Campbell Margaret—†	132	at home	72	"
	Z	Gavell Alma—†	132	housewife	41	"

346

Page.	Letter.	Full Name.	Residence, Jan. 1, 1946.	Occupation.	Supposed Age.	Reported Residence, Jan. 1, 1945. Street and Number
	A	Gavell Bertram	132	engineer	38	"
	C	Nestor Edwin	140	repairman	71	"
	D	Nestor Ellen T—†	140	auditor	24	
	E	Stillman Charles J	142	student	20	
	F	Stillman Flora—†	142	housewife	57	"
	G	Stillman George	142	U S M C	21	"
	H	Stillman Joan—†	142	cashier	24	"
	K	Bishop Edward	152	chauffeur	27	4 Hubert
	L	Bishop Gertrude—†	152	housewife	27	4 "
	M	Carrington Bernice—†	152	"	28	here
	N	Carrington James	152	instructor	32	"
	O	Gomes Anna—†	152	laundress	34	"
	P	Collins Melvin	152	laborer	20	
	R	Curtis James	152	retired	38	
	S	Curtis Marion—†	152	housewife	38	"
	T	Carey Eugenia—†	154	at home	37	"
	U	Carey William H	154	retired	49	
	V	Eikerenkoetter Helen—†	154	housewife	36	"
	W	Eikerenkoetter Jethro	154	porter	36	
	X	Tucker Walton	154	machinist	24	"
	Y	Bibbins James	156	presser	45	563 Mass av
	Z	Jones Daniel	156	grinder	54	here

347

Page.	Letter.	Full Name.	Residence, Jan. 1, 1946.	Occupation.	Supposed Age.	Reported Residence, Jan. 1, 1945. Street and Number
	A	Jones Irene—†	156	domestic	47	"
	B	Townes Carrie—†	156	"	65	

Thornton Street—Continued

c	Dorsey Henry	156	garageman	33	here
d	Dorsey Myrtle—†	156	domestic	34	"

Valentine Street

f	Pridham Arthur W	4	cleaner	34	here
g	Pridham Violet—†	4	housewife	33	"
h	Schneider Harry	6	fireman	42	"
k	Schneider Sara—†	6	housewife	41	"
l	MacFarlane Donald J	6	carpenter	41	"
m	MacFarlane Mary M—†	6	housewife	44	"
n	Lynch Catherine—†	6	"	35	
o	Lynch James	6	chauffeur	35	"
p	Blaney Ruth—†	8	housewife	25	"
r	Marcun Anthony	8	plumber	49	"
s	Marcun William	8	U S A	22	
t	Rock Michael	8	janitor	64	
u	O'Leary Eva—†	8	housewife	26	"
v	O'Leary Francis A	8	plumber	29	"
w	Boutin Homer	8	mechanic	35	"
x	Boutin Margaret—†	8	dressmaker	33	"

348 · Washington Street

a	Cummings John	2717	policeman	29	here
b	Cummings Mary—†	2717	housewife	25	"
c	Murphy Agnes—†	2717	seamstress	41	"
d	Murphy Dorothy—†	2717	clerk	20	
e	Murphy William	2717	repairman	43	"
h	*Ross Dora—†	2727	housewife	40	"
k	*Ross John	2727	mechanic	45	"
l	*Capuzzo Jennie—†	2727	housewife	69	"
m	Capuzzo William	2727	laborer	31	"
n	*Capuzzo Evelyn—†	2727	housewife	39	"
o	*Capuzzo Peter	2727	laborer	48	"
p	Turcotte Elizabeth—†	2727	housewife	53	Weymouth
r	Fasulo John J	2729	laborer	63	here
s	Fasulo Mary—†	2729	seamstress	35	"
t	Smith Donald A	2729	U S N	20	"
u	Smith John	2729	roofer	53	
v	Smith Margaret—†	2729	housewife	45	"

Washington Street—Continued

w	Oliver Doris—†	2732	housewife	24	here
x	Oliver James T	2732	welder	27	"
y	*Oliver Mary—†	2732	housewife	55	"

349

A	Tarquini Arthur	2737	baker	36	..
B	Tarquini Dorothy—†	2737	housewife	27	"
C	Tarquini James V	2737	baker	27	"
D	Tarquini Josephine—†	2737	housewife	22	Fall River
E	Tarquini Pasquale	2737	baker	65	here
F	Tarquini Regelo	2737	buffer	24	"
G	*Alleyne Daisy—†	2741	housewife	43	"
H	Benford Mabel—†	2741	domestic	40	"
K	Bruce Gloria—†	2741	housewife	20	"
L	Miller Evelyn—†	2741	clerk	20	
M	Jones Alice—†	2747	housewife	40	"
N	Jones James	2747	clerk	40	
O	Turnage Alexander	2747	porter	60	
P	Turnage Margaret—†	2747	housewife	60	"
R	King Catherine—†	2751	"	49	
S	King Russell T	2751	molder	53	
T	O'Rourke Edward M	2751	painter	45	
U	O'Rourke Francis—†	2751	laborer	37	
w	Chancholo Alice—†	2754	housewife	57	"
x	Chancholo Anthony J	2754	painter	47	"
y	Chancholo Edward	2754	janitor	59	
z	Chancholo Frank	2754	electrician	22	"

350

A	Chancholo Thomas J	2754	mechanic	35	"
B	Chancholo William	2754	weaver	27	
C	McDermott George J	2754	roofer	50	
D	McDermott Loretta R—†	2754	housewife	45	"
E	Keith George	2756	realtor	55	107 Fellows
F	Keith Pauline M—†	2756	housewife	46	107 "
G	Devin Mary—†	2756	"	22	here
H	Devin Richard	2756	clerk	30	"
K	Cotter John	2756	mechanic	48	"
L	Mazzeo John L	2756	chauffeur	53	"
M	Mazzeo Marie—†	2756	housewife	49	"
N	Mazzeo William	2756	clerk	24	..
O	Forsyth Charles	2756	lather	55	
P	Forsyth Charles E	2756	laborer	21	

Washington Street—Continued

R	Forsyth Florence E—†	2756	housewife	45	here
s	Forsyth Frank	2756	laborer	23	"
T	Zeigler Lillian M—†	2756	housewife	64	"
u	Riley Melissa—†	2757	student	24	
v	Riley Rudolph	2757	operator	24	"
w	Peay Cecelia—†	2757	secretary	21	"
x	Peay Ophelia—†	2757	stenographer	27	"
y	Peay Rose—†	2757	housewife	57	"

351

A	Daniels George F	2761	technician	24	"
B	Daniels Grace F—†	2761	inspector	33	"
c	Daniels Mary F—†	2761	housewife	53	"
D	Thompson Lorraine E—†	2761	"	23	
E	Ferguson Gerald	2761	brakeman	36	"
F	Ferguson Lorraine—†	2761	housewife	31	"
M	Morris Alonzo	2767	painter	39	
N	Morris Virginia—†	2767	housewife	35	"
P	McDonough Bertha—†	2773	"	28	New York
R	McDonough Donald	2773	clerk	30	"
s	Murphy Francis	2773	"	35	"
T	Murphy Margaret—†	2773	housewife	32	"
u	Prause August	2773	cook	59	"
v	*Gianelis Argiro—†	2773	housewife	56	here
w	Gianelis Irene—†	2773	stitcher	28	"
x	Gianelis Nicholas	2773	laborer	31	"
y	Kefalis James	2773	"	22	
z	*Kefalis Permathia—†	2773	housewife	57	"

352

c	Doyle Charles	2775	guard	53	
D	Doyle Grace—†	2775	housewife	53	"
F	Beigel Frances—†	2777	bookkeeper	44	"
G	Beigel Samuel	2777	retired	70	"
H	Spellman Isaac	2777	storekeeper	72	"
K	Dee Joseph W	2777	retired	60	"
L	Dillion Francis K	2777	artist	28	
M	Dillion John H	2777	electrician	33	"
N	Dillion Joseph W	2777	mechanic	22	"
o	Dillion Sarah—†	2777	housewife	58	"
P	Wethington Bertha—†	2777	"	24	
R	Wethington Nelson	2777	U S N	26	"
T	Flanders Gloria—†	2781	waitress	21	2779 Wash'n

Page.	Letter.	Full Name.	Residence, Jan. 1, 1946.	Occupation.	Supposed Age.	Reported Residence, Jan. 1, 1945. Street and Number.

Washington Street—Continued

u	Flanders John	2781	painter	59	2779 Wash'n
v	Flanders John F	2781	laborer	20	2779 "
x	Mahoney Jeremiah	2787	operator	61	here
y	Mahoney Julia—†	2787	housewife	55	"
z	Mahoney Timothy	2787	U S A	29	"

353

A	McGrath Margaret—†	2787	typist	24	
B	McGrath Thomas	2787	U S A	26	
c	Moschos George	2787	cook	47	
D	Moschos Velma—†	2787	housewife	44	"
E	Coggins Frederick	2789	cabinetmaker	55	"
F	Werth Ann—†	2789	housewife	30	"
G	O'Loughlin Alice—†	2789	"	53	
H	O'Loughlin John	2789	manager	51	"
K	O'Loughlin John T	2789	U S A	24	"
L	O'Loughlin Michael	2789	manager	53	"
M	O'Loughlin William	2789	pipefitter	30	"
N	Hobson Viola—†	2789	dressmaker	54	20 Dean
o	McCleary Gerald	2789	U S N	23	here

5

6

8

9

1

1.

Ward 11–Precinct 4

CITY OF BOSTON

5

LIST OF RESIDENTS
20 YEARS OF AGE AND OVER

(NON-CITIZENS INDICATED BY ASTERISK)
(FEMALES INDICATED BY DAGGER)

AS OF

JANUARY 1, 1946

THOMAS F. SULLIVAN, *Chairman*
FREDERIC E. DOWLING, *Secretary*
WILLIAM A. MOTLEY, JR.
ARTHUR V. COUGHLIN
EVERETT R. PROUT

Listing Board.

CITY OF BOSTON ⬥ PRINTING DEPARTMENT

400

Ellis Street

	A	Ross Gertrude—†	2	housewife	37	here
	B	Ross Gordon	2	clerk	40	"
	C	Ross Gordon	2	U S N	21	"
	D	Ross Stanley	2	"	22	
	E	Bower Bernard A	2	welder	52	
	F	Bower Marcella T—†	2	housewife	47	"
	G	Sprague Charles	2	painter	53	
	H	Sprague Margaret—†	2	housewife	53	"
	K	McNamara Annie V—†	4	housekeeper	74	"
	L	Kamp Alphonsus F	4	manager	45	"
	M	Kamp Margaret—†	4	housewife	45	"
	N	Cullinane Edward G	4	B F D	50	
	O	Cullinane Julia M—†	4	housewife	53	"
	P	Cullinane William J	4	U S A	23	
	R	Campbell Mary—†	6	housewife	25	"
	S	Hanlon Anna—†	6	"	42	
	T	Hanlon Marie—†	6	WAVE	22	
	U	Hanlon Walter	6	stevedore	41	"
	V	Hannon Delia A—†	6	housewife	65	"
	W	Hannon John	6	laborer	23	
	X	Hannon Josephine M—†	6	clerk	24	
	Y	Alger Catherine—†	10	matron	40	
	Z	Berlo Catherine M—†	10	teacher	55	

401

	A	Bernhardt Catherine—†	10	"	61	
	B	Cann Margaret M—†	10	"	36	"
	C	Gemperli Agnes M—†	10	"	44	
	D	Hogan Anna M—†	10	"	34	
	E	Jerolymack Catherine—†	10	"	73	
	F	Lindermier Walburga—†	10	"	45	
	G	Mahoney Margaret T—†	10	"	31	
	H	Murphy Helen G—†	10	"	58	
	K	Quinn Bridget—†	10		67	
	L	Schoenwald Catherine M-†	10	"	54	
	M	Sullivan Rita M—†	10		30	
	N	Weisser Gertrude—†	10		36	

Elmore Street

	O	McCarthy Frederick	4	clerk	33	here
	P	McCarthy Justin	4	retired	70	"

Elmore Street—Continued

R	McCarthy Justin, jr	4	clerk	37	here
T	Cotter Mary E—†	6	housewife	66	"
U	Hankard Robert	6	laborer	45	"
W	Nichols Edith M—†	8	housewife	33	"
X	Nichols William J	8	supervisor	33	"
Y	Bopp Elizabeth G—†	8	housewife	58	"
Z	Bopp Emil J	8	foreman	58	"

402

A	Bopp Geraldine E—†	8	bookkeeper	35	"
B	Bopp Jeanette G—†	8	at home	37	"
C	Bopp Joseph E	8	U S A	31	
D	Collins Frederick B	10	mechanic	56	"
E	Collins John F	10	U S A	26	
F	Collins Leo F	10	clerk	23	
G	Collins Margaret M—†	10	housewife	52	"
H	Mellyn Mary—†	10	"	54	
K	Mellyn Thomas	10	B F D	50	

Fulda Street

L	Kimmel Frank A	12	painter	60	here
M	Kimmel Rose—†	12	housewife	60	"
N	Poninske Julia A—†	12	saleswoman	54	"
O	*Blakstad Erling	16	painter	41	
P	*Blakstad Nancy E—†	16	housewife	42	"
R	O'Neil John J	16	fireman	29	'
S	O'Neil Marie—†	16	housewife	28	"
T	Fitzgerald Mary—†	16	"	50	'
U	Fitzgerald Michael	16	clerk	28	
V	Hebdon Frederick	16	U S N	32	
W	Hebdon Mary—†	16	housewife	31	"
X	Krim George F	17	clerk	51	
Y	Krim Mary C—†	17	housewife	45	"
Z	Kimmel Eleanor L—†	17	"	23	415 S Hunt'n av

403

A	Kimmel Francis A	17	painter	24	415 "
B	Swendeman Ignatius	17	repairman	60	here
C	Carey Anna M—†	18	housewife	41	"
D	Carey John J	18	chauffeur	45	"
E	Lohmes George	18	laborer	58	
F	Lohmes Theresa—†	18	housewife	52	"
H	Canisius Anna J—†	19	"	38	

Fulda Street—Continued

K	Canisius Joseph	19	baker	38	here
L	Seegraber Andrew F	19	machinist	63	"
M	Seegraber Emma K—†	19	housewife	53	"
N	Seegraber Marie A—†	19	clerk	23	
O	Seegraber Theresa—†	19	tel operator	32	"
P	Kohler Gertrude—†	19	housewife	53	"
R	Kohler Joseph P	19	janitor	53	
S	Catarius George F	20	welder	34	
T	Catarius Margaret H—†	20	housewife	24	"
U	Flanigan Mabel A—†	20	"	42	"
V	Flanigan William	20	brushmaker	46	"
W	Becker Joseph P	20	shoecutter	57	"
X	Becker Nellie E—†	20	housewife	57	"
Y	Kuhner Carl L	23	fireman	47	2 Ellis
Z	Lee Mary A—†	23	cutter	45	2 "

404

A	McAlenden Paul F	23	salesman	24	here
B	McAlenden Rose M—†	23	housewife	27	"
C	Kuhner Helen—†	23	"	41	"
D	Kuhner John	23	brewer	40	
F	Wehner Charles E	25	U S A	23	
G	Wehner Charles F	25	accountant	50	"
H	Wehner Marie G—†	25	nurse	21	
K	Wehner Robert J	25	U S A	22	
L	DiAngelo Edna M—†	25	housewife	31	"
M	DiAngelo Patrick J	25	salesman	34	"
N	Wehner Ann M—†	25	secretary	44	"
O	Wehner Mary—†	25	housewife	44	"
P	Whyte Delia—†	26	"	41	
R	Kast Alice—†	26	"	45	
S	Kast John	26	machinist	21	"
T	Lavers George	26	foreman	35	"
U	Lavers Mary—†	26	housewife	35	"
V	Sullivan James	33	laborer	40	43 Fulda
W	Sullivan Margaret—†	33	housewife	35	43 "
X	Neary Francis M	33	laborer	25	here
Y	Neary Jeanette E—†	33	housewife	24	"
Z	Ryan Francis J	33	repairman	37	"

405

A	Ryan Helena—†	33	housewife	37	"
B	McGarry Bernard D	35	expressman	21	"

Fulda Street—Continued

c	McGarry Frances T—†	35	housewife	21	here
d	Kingston Donald F	35	chauffeur	25	"
e	Kingston Gertrude M—†	35	housewife	28	"
f	Corkery Margaret M—†	35	"	30	
g	Corkery William J	35	machinist	35	"
l	McDougall Elizabeth—†	41	housewife	67	"
n	Gavin Barbara—†	43	housekeeper	68	"
o	Ryan Joseph	43	retired	65	
p	Kriegesman J Hattie—†	43	housewife	73	"
r	Gillespie Jean P—†	43	"	27	New York
s	Gillespie Willis S	43	clerk	32	"
w	Hawley Charles E	47	laborer	44	here
x	Hawley Sophie—†	47	housewife	39	"

406

b	Grinnell Catherine E—†	49	"	28	
c	Grinnell Otto A	49	laborer	30	
d	McGuire Virginia M—†	49	housewife	24	"
e	McGuire William B	49	chauffeur	27	"
g	DeBest Katherine V—†	74	housewife	32	"
h	DeBest Richard F	74	laborer	45	
k	Winston Charles E	74	retired	76	
l	Winston Esther M—†	74	housewife	66	"
m	Winston Frederick R	74	shoeworker	37	"
n	Winston Helen M—†	74	waitress	25	
o	Selfridge Marion—†	76	operator	43	"
p	Dugan Margaret—†	76	housewife	36	"
r	Dugan Vincent A	76	chauffeur	37	"
s	Tucker Rota L—†	78	housewife	21	"
t	Tucker Russell W	78	U S A	26	
u	Bernard Grace—†	78	housewife	78	"
v	Dalton Herbert	78	clerk	33	
w	Dalton Mary—†	78	housewife	28	"
x	Cogill Frances M—†	80	"	21	229 Highland
y	Cogill James W	80	machinist	25	229 "
z	Baier Francis A	80	repairman	36	here

407

a	Baier Helen M—†	80	operator	32	"
b	Mason Elizabeth L—†	80	housewife	45	"
c	Mason Frank C	80	chauffeur	38	"
d	White Mary—†	80	housewife	48	"
e	White Patrick	80	U S N	50	"

Fulda Street—Continued

F	Leonard Dorothea F—†	82	housewife	22	here
G	Leonard Francis R	82	machinist	23	"
H	Willis Caroline F—†	82	housewife	40	"
K	Willis Henry	82	millwright	46	"
L	Doucette Mary—†	82	waitress	34	
N	McGarry Bernard	83	chauffeur	48	"
O	McGarry Mary—†	83	housewife	45	"
P	Kingston Anna—†	83	"	54	
R	Kingston Harold	83	U S A	21	
S	Curley Lillian T—†	85	housewife	32	"
T	Curley Walker T	85	painter	37	
U	Haggerty Priscilla A—†	85	housewife	25	"
V	Grosberg Eric	85	retired	60	
W	Grosberg Jenny—†	85	housewife	55	"
X	Tedeski Jean—†	85	"	30	
Y	Tedeski Thomas	85	laborer	35	

408   Galena Street

A	Carney Kathlene—†	1	housewife	35	71 Regent
B	Johnson Helen J—†	3	clerk	24	here
C	Johnson Mary A—†	3	housewife	47	"
D	Nemet Anna J—†	3	"	35	2969 Wash'n
E	Martin Harold	5	U S A	20	9 Vale
F	Patriquin George W	5	clerk	32	9 "
G	Patriquin Helen L—†	5	housewife	30	9 "
H	Southers Myrtle—†	5	"	21	9 "
K	Brooks Josephine—†	5	"	35	here
L	*Coffran Florence—†	7	housekeeper	65	"
M	Lake Mae—†	7	housewife	48	"
N	Lake Scholley	7	policeman	53	"
O	Cherry Margaret E—†	13	housewife	39	"
O¹	Cherry Michael F	13	electrician	42	"
P	Cherry Michael J	13	salesman	21	"
R	Chetwynd Catherine—†	13	housewife	69	"
S	Chetwynd Mitchell	13	janitor	75	"
T	Kinlin Edward J	15	checker	62	
U	Kinlin Stella—†	15	housewife	46	"
V	Hurley Anna—†	17	"	41	
W	Hurley John	17	U S A	20	
X	Healey Catherine—†	17	housekeeper	40	"

Galena Street—Continued

Y	Healey John	17	retired	81	here

409

A	Cunningham Jane—†	19	housewife	40	"
B	Cunningham Patrick	19	chauffeur	43	"
C	White George	19	manager	45	"
D	DeGregorio Christina M—†	19	housewife	29	Texas
E	DeGregorio Fred T	19	U S A	28	"
F	Draper Annie M—†	19	housewife	59	here
G	Draper Frank W	19	machinist	25	"
H	Draper Richard E	19	U S A	20	"
K	Howard Mary—†	19	clerk	26	
L	Howard Maude—†	19	housewife	60	"
M	Baldasare Nicholas	21	ice dealer	30	"
N	Baldasare Rita—†	21	housewife	28	"
O	Holland Eliza—†	21	"	70	22 Dana
P	Quinn James H	21	salesman	54	22 "
R	Quinn Winifred—†	21	housewife	33	22 "
S	Megel Elizabeth—†	21	clerk	24	here
T	Megel John	21	"	25	"
U	Megel Peter	21	baker	62	"
V	Crosby Nina M—†	23	housewife	63	"
W	Crosby Samuel L	23	electrician	66	"
X	Kelley Henry W	23	laborer	51	
Y	Kelley Lillian C—†	23	nurse	45	

410

A	Kane Henry	23	retired	55	
B	Kane Mary—†	23	operator	26	"
C	Kane Rose—†	23	housewife	50	"
D	Finn Anna—†	25	"	32	
E	Finn George	25	chauffeur	32	"
F	Hall Arathusa J—†	25	housewife	65	"
G	Miller Harriet E—†	25	attendant	57	"
H	Sexton Della—†	25	housewife	56	"
K	Sexton John	25	clerk	60	
L	Sexton John, jr	25	"	23	

Highland Street

O	Engram Olive—†	188	housewife	45	here
P	Engram Ralph	188	carpenter	47	"
R	Horne Bertha—†	188	housewife	25	777 E Fifth

Page.	Letter.	FULL NAME.	Residence, Jan. 1, 1946.	Occupation.	Supposed Age.	Reported Residence, Jan. 1, 1945. Street and Number.

Highland Street—Continued

s	Horne Leo	188	cook	26	777 E Fifth
T	Donovan Catherine—†	188	housewife	62	here
U	Donovan Joseph	188	carpenter	21	"
V	Donovan Michael	188	retired	66	"
W	Higgins Mary L—†	188	housewife	51	"
X	Murphy Nora—†	190	"	36	22 Marcella
Y	Murphy Timothy	190	operator	45	22 "
Z	Hennessey Joseph	190	bartender	34	here

411

A	Hennessey Julia—†	190	clerk	32	
B	Crowley Albert	190	laborer	49	
C	Crowley Caroline—†	190	packer	49	
D	Bernard Anna—†	192	housewife	60	"
E	Bernard Carl	192	supt	33	"
F	Bernard Thelma—†	192	secretary	30	510 Mass av
G	Howard Ann—†	192	housewife	30	here
H	Howard George H	192	U S N	40	"
K	Sullivan Rose A—†	192	clerk	22	"
L	Sullivan Theresa C—†	192	housewife	59	"
M	Becker Dorothy K—†	192	librarian	26	"
N	Becker Emma C—†	192	housewife	60	"
O	Becker Godfrey J	192	shoeworker	58	"
P	Schmidt Mary E—†	194	at home	57	"
R	Vallmar Amelia H—†	194	housewife	61	"
S	Vallmar Charles W	194	glassworker	61	"
T	Wall Josephine L—†	194	housewife	37	84 W Newton
U	Wall William F	194	shipper	39	84 "
V	Doherty Margaret—†	196	housewife	40	here
W	Doherty Patrick	196	rigger	45	"
X	Winters Dorothy—†	196	housewife	37	"
Y	Winters George	196	stonecutter	39	"
Z	Hession Delia—†	196	housewife	68	"

412

A	Hession Henry J	196	policeman	28	"
B	Hession Thomas A	196	shipper	33	
C	Hession William J	196	printer	33	"
D	Crehan Grace E—†	198	housewife	30	"
E	Crehan John J	198	machinist	33	"
F	McLeod Charles	198	laborer	35	
G	Yanulis Adam	198	chauffeur	30	"
H	Yanulis Eleanar—†	198	draftsman	22	"

Page.	Letter.	FULL NAME.	Residence, Jan. 1, 1946.	Occupation.	Supposed Age.	Reported Residence, Jan. 1, 1945. Street and Number.

Highland Street—Continued

K	Yanulis George	198	machinist	29	here
L	Yanulis Richard	198	seaman	32	"
M	Yanulis Victoria—†	198	housewife	52	"
N	Mueller John A	198	watchman	52	"
O	Mueller Mary A—†	198	housewife	51	"
P	Halpin Arthur J	200	machinist	64	"
R	Halpin Elizabeth—†	200	housewife	73	"
S	McGaffigan Charles	200	laborer	30	
T	McGaffigan Florence—†	200	housewife	30	"
U	Jorgensen Dorothy—†	200	"	34	
V	Jorgensen Hanson	200	laborer	38	
W	Stevens Audrey—†	202	bookkeeper	22	"
X	Stevens David J	202	engineer	63	"
Y	Stevens Ethel—†	202	bookkeeper	46	"
Z	*Allfrey Charles	202	painter	46	Malden

413

A	Allfrey Irene D—†	202	housewife	21	"
B	Carr Helen—†	202	laundress	64	here
C	Wooding Roy	202	bricklayer	44	"
D	Wooding Sadie—†	202	housewife	62	"
E	Fennel Doris—†	204	"	31	
F	Fennel Henry	204	laborer	37	
G	Saltmarsh Charles	204	chauffeur	46	"
H	Saltmarsh Charles	204	U S A	22	
K	Saltmarsh Esther—†	204	housewife	47	"
L	Saltmarsh William	204	iceman	21	
M	Greenal Joseph P	204	expressman	45	"
N	Greenal Josephine—†	204	housewife	51	"
O	Giacobbi Andrew	206	U S N	25	
P	Giacobbi Angelina—†	206	operator	20	"
R	Giacobbi Anthony	206	U S A	21	
S	Giacobbi Dominic	206	laborer	53	
T	Giacobbi Phyllis—†	206	housewife	50	"
V	*Cutrone Grace—†	206	"	41	
W	*Cutrone Paul	206	barber	50	
X	Ricci Catherine—†	206	housewife	22	"
Y	Ricci Dewey	206	U S A	22	
Z	Conrad Elsie B—†	208	clerk	23	"

414

A	Conrad Margaret F—†	208	housewife	62	"
B	Conrad Samuel	208	laborer	69	

9

Page.	Letter.	FULL NAME.	Residence, Jan. 1, 1946.	Occupation.	Supposed Age.	Reported Residence, Jan. 1, 1945. Street and Number.

Highland Street—Continued

	C	Kadlick Mary—†	208	housewife	52	here
	D	Kadlick Rita—†	208	clerk	25	"
	E	Kadlick Stephen J	208	inspector	50	"
	F	Kadlick Stephen J, jr	208	U S A	23	
	G	Emery Mary—†	208	housewife	24	"
	H	Emery Thomas	208	laborer	29	
	L	O'Keefe Viola—†	210	housewife	35	"
	M	Murphy Anna—†	210	"	40	
	N	Murphy John	210	laborer	43	
	O	McCafferty Catherine—†	210	housewife	51	"
	P	McCafferty John J	210	custodian	51	"
	R	McCafferty Mary C—†	210	housewife	21	"
	S	McCafferty Thomas H	210	U S A	22	
	T	Mulhearn Mary—†	210	at home	80	"
	U	Coughlin Joseph	212	laborer	35	"
	V	Coughlin Winifred—†	212	housewife	29	"
	W	Mitchel Charles	212	retired	60	
	X	Mitchel Margaret—†	212	housewife	61	"
	Y	Pinn Carl	212	U S A	40	
		415				
	A	Pinn Lucy—†	212	housewife	43	"
	B	Kelly Sarah—†	212	clerk	46	
	D	Marshall Frank	214	laborer	45	"
	E	Keefe Evelyn—†	214	counter girl	31	183 Centre
	F	Keefe Richard	214	laborer	32	183 "
	G	Carpentier Myrtle—†	216	housewife	44	here
	H	Carpentier Paul	216	laborer	40	"
	K	Pepi Alfred	216	"	37	"
	L	Pepi Lillian—†	216	housewife	25	"
	M	Pepi Sebastiana—†	216	at home	78	"
	N	Squizzero Joseph P	216	cutter	26	69 River
	O	Squizzero Rosemary—†	216	housewife	24	69 "
	P	Tagliaferro Pauline—†	218	laundress	30	here
	R	Tagliaferro Salvatore	218	toolmaker	35	"
	T	Fitzgerald Catherine—†	218	housewife	38	"
	U	Fitzgerald Thomas	218	packer	32	
	V	Duncan Frank J	226	U S A	32	
	W	Duncan Virginia A—†	226	clerk	46	
	X	Estella Evelyn L—†	226	housewife	43	"
	Y	Estella Robert A	226	painter	48	
	Z	Theall Catherine—†	226	housewife	45	"

416
Highland Street—Continued

A	Bray Ethel—†	226	housewife	46	here
B	Bray John	226	laborer	39	"
C	Clark Jay	226	mechanic	22	Pennsylvania
D	Warren Louise—†	228	housewife	58	here
E	*McKay Catherine—†	228	"	40	"
F	*McKay Fred E	228	machinist	41	"
G	Quinn Anna—†	228	bookkeeper	23	"
H	Quinn Margaret—†	228	clerk	20	"
K	Quinn Mary J—†	228	housewife	48	"
L	Quinn Michael	228	laborer	54	

Kingsbury Street

M	Thoma Mary L—†	3	housewife	22	9 Cedar pk
N	Thoma Robert L	3	chauffeur	23	here
O	Floran Anna—†	3	housewife	50	"
P	Floran Joseph	3	oiler	40	"
R	*Janusoni John	3	baker	57	
S	Casey James M	3	chauffeur	39	"
T	Casey Mary E—†	3	clerk	51	
U	Chancholo Helen—†	5	housewife	30	"
V	Chancholo James M	5	U S A	32	
W	Allen Lillian L—†	5	at home	70	"
X	O'Driscoll Frederick T	5	mechanic	24	"
Y	O'Driscoll Gertrude V—†	5	cleaner	47	
Z	O'Driscoll William F	5	mechanic	26	"

417

A	Jarvis Leo A	7	distiller	24	"
B	Jarvis Margaret—†	7	housewife	28	14 Harvard av
C	Sekula Basil	7	painter	38	here
D	Sekula Julia—†	7	housewife	34	"
E	Moynihan Joseph E	7	supervisor	52	"
F	Moynihan Mary B—†	7	housewife	51	"
G	Foley Anna D—†	9	"	43	
H	Tracy Gladys R—†	9	machinist	47	"
K	Lawhorn Joel A	9	packer	44	44 Whitney
L	Lawhorn Lillian V—†	9	housewife	25	44 "
M	Lear John E	11	chauffeur	33	here
N	Lear Rose P —†	11	housewife	31	"
O	Rosenmayer Helen—†	11	housekeeper	63	"

Kingsbury Street—Continued

P	Durfee Anna L—†	11	housewife	26	here
R	Durfee George A, jr	11	dyer	25	"
S	Fisher Beatrice L—†	11	housewife	48	"
T	Fisher Earl F	11	U S N	20	
U	Fisher William A	11	machinist	48	"
V	Fisher William A, jr	11	"	24	

Marcella Street

X	Chandler Corinne—†	3	housewife	21	here
Y	Chandler Sylvanus	3	U S N	25	"
Z	Leverone Helen A—†	3	housewife	43	"
	418				
A	Leverone John J	3	painter	49	
B	Leverone John J, jr	3	U S N	23	
C	Leverone John R	3	retired	76	"
D	Bucalis Charles	4	cook	25	37 Dorset
E	Bucalis Helen—†	4	housewife	25	23 Gray
F	McKinnon Annie E—†	4	stitcher	64	here
G	McKinnon Mary A—†	4	at home	72	"
K	Krauklis Alson E	5	collector	37	"
L	Krauklis Mary A—†	5	packer	35	
M	Krauklis Bertha T—†	5	housewife	64	"
N	Krauklis John D	5	shipfitter	64	"
O	Krauklis Leone L—†	5	housekeeper	30	"
P	Carrigan Ann—†	6	housewife	23	"
R	Carrigan William	6	baker	48	"
S	Sweeney Eugene M	6	laborer	26	48 Codman pk
T	Sweeney Katherine M—†	6	nurse	58	13 Elmore
W	Bane Patrick, jr	8	fitter	20	here
X	Marenghi Bertha—†	8	hairdresser	45	"
Y	White Elizabeth—†	8	at home	79	"
	419				
A	Walsh Frances—†	10	housewife	38	"
B	Walsh John W	10	clerk	41	
C	Holmes Dorothy—†	11	housewife	34	"
D	Holmes Joseph D	11	carpenter	35	"
E	Owens John A	12	retired	80	"
F	Owens Leo G	12	engineer	31	Quincy
G	Owens Tena—†	12	housewife	24	"
H	Blackman Charles J	13	shoemaker	61	here

Marcella Street—Continued

K	Blackman Mary A—†	13	housewife	62	here
L	Kenney Edith—†	13	clerk	42	"
M	McGinnis John A	13	retired	79	"
N	*Bethune Mabel P—†	14	housekeeper	43	"
O	Bigelow Francis O	14	supt	78	..
P	Codding Thelma—†	15	waitress	39	''
R	Codding Valentine	15	carpenter	42	"
S	Kidling Gerald	15	U S N	21	Pennsylvania
T	Minkevicz Adolphus	16	machinist	37	here
U	Minkevicz Lydia—†	16	housekeeper	32	"
V	Atkins David	16	machinist	63	"
W	Atkins Frances—†	16	teacher	32	
X	Atkins Mary—†	16	housewife	63	"
Y	Centamore Anthony M	17	baker	24	Florida
Z	Centamore Elizabeth A—†	17	housewife	25	"

420

A	Centamore Jennie—†	17	"	27	here
B	Centamore Ross	17	musician	29	"
C	Farrenkopf Anna B—†	18	housewife	58	"
D	Farrenkopf John C	18	manager	58	''
E	Calhoun Mary E—†	20	housewife	59	"
F	Calhoun Walter E	20	collector	61	''
G	Varley John E	20	shipper	57	
H	Moloney Charles P	21	retired	71	
K	Moloney Paul V	21	U S N	33	
L	Reichert Helen M—†	21	housewife	40	"
M	Reichert Joseph D	21	furrier	42	"
N	Matthews Alice M—†	22	housewife	32	18 Marcella
O	Matthews Thomas F	22	U S N	34	18 "
P	Mons Marie—†	22	waitress	54	here
R	Thomas Margaret A—†	22	housewife	56	"
S	Thomas Warren J	22	U S A	22	"
T	D'Eon Anna—†	23	housewife	47	"
U	D'Eon Grace E—†	23	clerk	21	
V	D'Eon Maxim J	23	fishcutter	47	''
W	Gilmore Leo	23	warehouse	50	"
X	Gilmore Marie—†	23	secretary	47	"
Y	Rasch Florence H—†	24	housewife	46	"
Z	Rasch Frederick V	24	guard	53	

421

A	Davis Abigail—†	25	housewife	56	"

Marcella Street—Continued

B	Davis Joseph P	25	papercutter	62	here
C	Huston Anna A—†	25	housewife	59	"
D	Huston Charles V	25	retired	67	"
E	Hoehle Marie L—†	27	at home	62	··
F	Yetter Emilie H—†	27	housewife	70	"
G	Yetter Otto	27	retired	69	
H	Copatch Felicie L—†	28	housewife	54	"
K	Copatch Gordon M	28	U S N	20	
L	Copatch John M	28	mechanic	57	"
M	Frizzell Jennie I—†	29	housewife	34	"
N	Frizzell John C	29	shipper	26	"
O	Frizzell Ernest	29	chauffeur	32	67 Marcella
P	Frizzell Madeline E—†	29	glassblower	24	here
R	Frizzell Rose Y—†	29	housewife	51	67 Marcella
U	Campbell Kathleen E—†	31	"	23	here
V	Campbell Thomas H	31	machinist	25	"
W	Danforth Ethel M—†	31	saleswoman	22	"
X	Danforth Sarah M—†	31	housewife	49	"
Y	Sharkey John W	31	metalworker	65	"
Z	Stratford Arthur J	31	meatcutter	32	"
	422				
A	Stratford Helen—†	31	housewife	27	8 Elmore
C	Kelly Frank D	32	fireman	54	here
D	Kelly Gladys L—†	32	housewife	40	"
E	Will Emily F—†	34	"	55	"
F	Will Frances J—†	34	secretary	21	"
G	Will Leo F	34	machinist	57	"
H	Will Leo J	34	U S A	24	
K	Mueller Henry W	34	clerk	48	
L	Mueller Louise M—†	34	housewife	55	"
M	Brophy Helen L—†	rear 34	"	32	
N	Brophy Walter	" 34	electrician	33	"
O	Tallier Joseph E	35	U S A	21	
P	Tallier Lewis	35	painter	65	
R	Tallier Nora E—†	35	housewife	61	"
S	Rollins Alfred	35	painter	60	
T	Rollins Edith—†	35	housewife	60	"
U	Caddle Emily—†	35	"	62	
V	Caddle John	35	polisher	61	"
W	Flynn Frank	36	clerk	58	
X	Flynn Mary F—†	36	housewife	64	"

14

Marcella Street—Continued

	Letter	Full Name	Res.	Occupation	Age	Reported Residence
	z	Harvey Gertrude—†	37	housewife	27	here
423						
	A	Harvey Samuel	37	chauffeur	25	"
	B	Wallin Edna—†	37	packer	37	
	D	Hendsbee Fielding	39	dehydrator	42	"
	E	Hendsbee Gilbert	39	seaman	21	
	F	*Hendsbee Mary—†	39	housewife	38	"
	G	Diaz Benjamin	42	welder	31	1865 Col av
	H	Diaz Lucia—†	42	housewife	26	1865 "
	K	Saiza Paul	42	barber	57	53 Chambers
	L	Saiza Ralph	42	operator	28	53 "
	M	Saiza Victoria—†	42	housewife	59	53 "
	N	Morrison Helen—†	43	"	38	61 Horadan way
	O	Morrison Phillip	43	laborer	43	61 "
	P	Ware Minnie A—†	43	housekeeper	68	here
	R	Casey Edward J	43	student	25	"
	S	Casey Joseph P	43	clerk	62	"
	T	Casey Julia A—†	43	housewife	56	"
	U	Friel Walter H	43	steamfitter	40	"
	V	Fairbanks Bridie—†	47	housewife	35	"
	W	Fairbanks Frank	47	electrician	40	"
	X	Rivers Henry G	51	factoryworker	23	"
	Y	Rivers Theresa M—†	51	matron	58	
	z	Rivers Virginia M—†	51	stitcher	34	
424						
	A	Denault Abigail—†	51	housekeeper	53	15 Ritchie
	B	Diaz Katherine M—†	51	housewife	53	here
	C	Diaz Walter W	51	chauffeur	34	"
	D	Ackerson George	51	operator	26	"
	E	Devon Helen—†	51	housewife	51	"
	F	Devon Thomas	51	machinist	22	"
	G	*Riendeau Florence—†	53	housewife	37	"
	H	Riendeau Frank	53	sorter	38	
	K	Serrechia Armando	53	decorator	20	"
	L	*Serrechia Maria—†	53	housewife	58	"
	M	Serrechia Salvatore	53	laborer	58	
	N	Hennessey Elizabeth—†	53	housewife	26	"
	O	Hennessey Thomas	53	mechanic	31	"
	P	Persons Harold	55	porter	38	
	R	Persons Lucille—†	55	housewife	42	"
	S	*Walter Clifford	55	laborer	44	703 Shawmut av

15

Marcella Street—Continued

T	Walter Florence—†	55	machinist	20	703 Shawmut av
U	Walter Norris	55	U S N	23	703 "
V	*Walter Thomasina—†	55	housewife	42	703 "
W	Flowers Ina—†	57	secretary	31	here
X	Nicholas Elisha	57	painter	70	"
Y	Nicholas Hilda—†	57	housewife	55	"
Z	Nicholas Huntley	57	student	20	

425

A	Nicholas Joyce—†	57	clerk	23	
B	Mahoney James	rear 57	welder	28	
C	Mahoney Ruby—†	" 57	housewife	28	"
D	Smolenski Alphonso	59	machinist	30	"
E	Smolenski Laura—†	59	housewife	30	"
F	DePaoli Anthony	59	painter	52	
G	DePaoli Celestina—†	59	housewife	49	"
H	DePaoli Loretta—†	59	"	23	Missouri
K	Driscoll Alta—†	61	"	37	here
L	Driscoll Joseph	61	chauffeur	44	"
M	Carey Elizabeth D—†	65	waitress	40	"
N	*Carey Michael D	65	chauffeur	45	"
O	Levesque Claire—†	65	housewife	39	"
P	Levesque Joseph E	65	chauffeur	42	"
R	White Helen M—†	65	housewife	39	"
S	White John F	65	laborer	41	"
T	*Shtika Dimitri	67	storekeeper	49	315 Hunt'n av
U	*Shtika George	67	"	23	315 "
V	*Shtika Pieno—†	67	housewife	45	315 "
W	Curran Catherine—†	67	"	83	here
X	Curran John F	67	laborer	40	"
Y	Curran Patrick	67	printer	53	"

426   Merriam Place

A	Mulhern Barbara—†	1	housewife	41	here
B	Mulhern John	1	U S N	24	"
C	Mulhern Martin	1	clerk	45	"
D	Mulhern Patrick	1	"	45	

Thornton Place

E	Kilcoyne Anna—†	1	housekeeper	50	here
F	Kilcoyne Anna T—†	1	housewife	60	"

16

Thornton Place—Continued

G	Kilcoyne John J	1	U S A	30	here
H	Kilcoyne Patrick J	1	laborer	60	"
K	Ollen Mary—†	1	housewife	28	"
L	Ollen Walter	1	clerk	24	
M	Dahoney Rose B—†	3	housewife	39	"
N	Hohmann Anna E—†	3	clerk	40	
O	Hohmann Carl E	3	retired	77	
P	Hohmann Edmund	3	chauffeur	35	"
R	Hohmann Loretta C—†	3	bookkeeper	38	"
S	Hohmann Mary A—†	3	clerk	41	"
T	McNally Mary—†	4	housewife	32	"
U	McNally Robert L	4	florist	32	
V	Levitsky Arthur	4	clerk	22	
W	Levitsky Fannie—†	4	housewife	59	"
X	Levitsky Joseph	4	plumber	59	"
Y	Efford Alice—†	5	WAC	22	"
Z	Efford Charlotte—†	5	housewife	66	2775 Wash'n

427

A	Efford Thomas	5	student	23	here
B	Pedersen Frederick L	5	operator	50	"
C	Pedersen Marie M—†	5	at home	82	"
. D	Kilcoyne John	7	clerk	59	

Thornton Street

E	McPhee Henry B	133	machinist	44	here
F	McPhee Sadie—†	.133	housewife	46	"
G	Glynn Josephine—†	133	"	47	"
H	Glynn Marie—†	133	stenographer	21	"
K	Glynn Thomas P	133	machinist	54	"
L	Locke Dorothy—†	133	clerk	20	
M	Locke John	133	U S A	33	
N	Locke Joseph	133	U S N	27	"
O	Locke Julia—†	133	housewife	58	"
P	Locke William	133	machinist	55	"
R	Pope Edythe—†	135	housewife	58	"
S	Pope Harold V	135	machinist	55	"
T	Parks Lillian—†	135	housewife	38	"
U	Parks Robert	135	machinist	35	"
V	Townsend Frank G, jr	137	auditor	31	
W	Townsend Paula—†	137	housewife	34	"

Thornton Street—Continued

x	Schuerkamp Clara—†	137	examiner	63	here
y	Wright Anna J—†	137	housewife	50	"
z	Wright George H	137	expressman	60	"

428

A	Finnegan James J	137	metalworker	65	"
B	Finnegan James M	137	U S A	33	"
C	Finnegan Margaret—†	137	housewife	69	"
D	Nehiley James W	139	metalworker	37	"
E	Siegel August	139	laborer	40	
F	Siegel Augusta—†	139	housewife	43	"
G	Dillon Edna—†	139	"	29	
H	Dillon William	139	pipefitter	30	"
K	Burke Joseph	143	chauffeur	38	"
L	Burke Margaret—†	143	housewife	35	"
M	Bross Rosina—†	143	"	74	
N	Bross William J	143	laborer	53	
O	Foote Mary—†	143	housewife	50	"
P	Foote Michael	143	machinist	51	"
S	O'Brien Amelia M—†	151	housewife	32	"
T	Howard Sylvia M—†	151	machinist	36	162 Humboldt av
U	Gordon Hans	151	clerk	34	162 "
V	Gordon Lucille—†	151	housewife	32	162 "
W	Walker Ariel—†	153	"	29	Medford
X	Salisbury Elizabeth—†	153	operator	50	here
Y	Francis Fred	153	painter	47	Florida
Z	Francis Pinkey—†	153	housewife	30	"

429

A	Perry Martha—†	155	housekeeper	65	548 Wash'n
B	Ryan Winifred—†	155	housewife	39	here
C	Harris Arthur	155	chauffeur	20	7 Auburn
E*	Lopey Antonio	163	laborer	44	Onset
F	Lopey Nora—†	163	housewife	23	"
G	Carter Consuela—†	163	"	31	here
H	Carter James	163	U S A	25	"
L	Keating Daniel	178	welder	30	"
M	Keating Edna—†	178	factoryworker	28	"
N	Keating Ellen—†	178	"	25	
O	Keating Constance—†	178	housewife	28	"
P	Keating Timothy D	178	U S A	31	
R	Dooley John E	180	machinist	38	"
S	Dooley Mary—†	180	housewife	35	"

Thornton Street—Continued

T	Keaveney Edward	180	welder	25	here
U	Keaveney James	180	U S A	24	"
V	Keaveney John	180	U S N	24	"
W	Keaveney Mary—†	180	housewife	54	"
X	Keaveney Michael J	180	shoeworker	59	"
Y	Keaveney Rita—†	180	clerk	29	"
Z	Keaveney Robert	180	U S N	20	"

430

A	Kraby Donald J	182	"	22	"
B	Kraby Dorothy M—†	182	saleswoman	25	1025 Bennington
C	Kraby Edna L—†	182	housewife	20	16 Vale
D	Kraby Edward T	182	U S N	20	here
E	Kraby Elizabeth—†	182	housewife	50	"
F	Kraby Joseph W	182	salesman	29	"
G	Kraby Thurston O	182	policeman	57	"
H	Rogers Clayton	184	mechanic	34	"
K	Rogers Ruth—†	184	housewife	33	"
L	Rogers Silas	184	laborer	65	"
M	Barrett Catherine—†	184	housewife	72	"
N	Barrett Mary E—†	184	machinist	42	"
O	Gibney Edna—†	185	buyer	51	
P	Gibney Fred J	185	shipper	30	"
R	Lysaght James	188	gardener	53	"
S	Lysaght Nellie—†	188	housewife	55	"
T	Evangelist Anthony	188	baker	36	"
U	Evangelist Helen—†	188	housewife	28	"
V	Pierce Ida C—†	192	"	29	"
W	Pierce Joseph	192	chauffeur	30	"
X	Carew Charles R	192	student	24	"
Y	Carew Charles T	192	bookkeeper	47	"
Z	Carew Gertrude V—†	192	housewife	45	"

431

A	Carew Joseph	192	U S N	23	"
B	Sargent Rose—†	192	housekeeper	36	"
C	*Matthews Aphrodite—†	194	housewife	29	"
D	*Matthews Athena—†	194	housekeeper	62	"
E	Matthews Christo	194	retired	73	
F	Matthews Nicholas	194	storekeeper	40	"
G	Schnabel Harold J	194	at home	27	"
H	Schnabel Mary M—†	194	housewife	61	"
K	Schnabel Oscar A	194	shoeworker	59	"

Page.	Letter.	Full Name.	Residence, Jan. 1, 1946.	Occupation.	Supposed Age.	Reported Residence, Jan. 1, 1945. Street and Number.

Vale Street

	L	McLaughlin Gladys—†	9	housewife	28	51 Vale
	M	McLaughlin John	9	goldplater	31	here
	N	Martin Anna—†	9	housewife	27	5 Galena
	O	Martin Charles	9	engineer	60	here
	P	Martin Harry	9	chauffeur	25	5 Galena
	R	Winston Blanche—†	9	waitress	31	here
	S	Goessl Florence M—†	12	housewife	65	"
	T	Goessl John A	12	roofer	62	"
	U	Lawrence Helen E—†	12	housewife	22	"
	V	Lawrence John W	12	U S N	23	
	W	Finneran Annie—†	16	housekeeper	55	"
	X	Finneran Rita—†	16	"	27	"
	Y	Ryan Ethyl—†	16	"	22	California
	Z	Ryan George	16	U S N	24	"

432

	A	Carey Mary—†	18	housewife	30	here
	B	Carey Peter	18	diesetter	35	"
	C	Kelley Francis	18	U S N	25	"
	D	Kelley Mary—†	18	housewife	23	"
	F	McLellan Joseph	20	chauffeur	41	"
	G	McLellan Mary—†	20	housewife	41	"
	H	McKay George	20	agent	62	
	O*	Nicholson James	24	retired	77	
	P	Nicholson Marion—†	24	housekeeper	35	"
	R*	Nicholson Mary—†	24	housewife	70	"
	S	Prime John	24	houseman	28	Vermont
	T	Prime Margaret—†	24	housewife	27	"
	X	Catarius Frank	34	operator	62	here
	Y	Catarius Mary—†	34	housewife	56	"
	Z	Catarius Paul	34	U S N	21	"

433

	A	Conley Helen—†	34	housewife	24	"
	B	Conley Joseph	34	mechanic	25	"
	C	Dabrowski Ann M—†	38	housewife	34	"
	D	Dabrowski Walter J	38	bricklayer	36	"
	E	Plunkett Edward C	40	operator	39	"
	F	Plunkett John J	40	technician	40	"
	G	Plunkett Julia—†	40	housewife	37	"
	H	Merrill Walter M	42	entertainer	40	9 Winchester
	K	MacDonnell Angus J	44	carpenter	61	here
	L	MacDonnell Jeanette—†	44	housewife	52	"

M	MacDonnell Marjorie—†	44	bookkeeper	22	here
N	Maloney Alice—†	46	housewife	38	"
O	Maloney Phillip C	46	steamfitter	42	"
P	Ross James C	48	maintenance	46	"
R	Ross Mildred I—†	48	housewife	42	"
S	Walter James	48	photographer	22	"
T	Ross Margaret H—†	50	clerk	41	"
U	Ross Rachael—†	50	housewife	39	"
V	Ross Walter	50	retired	85	"
W	Ross Walter	50	carpenter	49	"
X	Foshey Charlotte—†	51	assembler	45	"
Y	Foshey George	51	photographer	46	"
Z	Foshey George W, jr	51	U S N	22	"

434

A	Foshey Marion—†	51	housewife	44	"
B	Sweeney Florence—†	51	"	34	"
C	Sweeney John	51	machinist	44	"
D	Lutton Ernest	51	guard	46	51 Marcella
E	Lutton Louise—†	51	housewife	50	51 "
F	O'Keefe Joseph J	53	agent	37	here
G	O'Keefe Mary C—†	53	housewife	36	"
H	Kennedy John	57	steamfitter	60	"
K	Wilfert Edwin J	61	lineman	35	"
L	Wilfert Martha S—†	61	housekeeper	73	"
M	Bagley Anna T—†	63	housewife	39	"
N	Bagley Joseph F	63	expressman	40	"
O	Raciti Frances—†	63	housewife	35	"
P	*Brady Bridget—†	63	"	43	
R	*Brady John F	63	laborer	42	"

Valentine Street

S	*Lynch Annie—†	3	domestic	60	here
T	Lynch Henry	3	laborer	28	"
U	Lynch Marion—†	3	housewife	28	"
V	Barter Joseph	5	laborer	47	"
W	Davis Claire—†	5	housewife	22	"
X	Davis Harry	5	U S N	27	
Y	McCarthy Alice—†	5	dishwasher	45	"
Z	McCarthy John	5	U S M C	23	"

435
Valentine Street—Continued

I	A	Calevro Della—†	5	housewife	48	here
	B	Calevro John	5	butcher	50	"
	C	Corriea Bella—†	5	dressmaker	42	"
	D	Corriea Millie—†	5	cashier	21	
	E	Pierce Anna M—†	7	clerk	20	
	F	Pierce Arthur E	7	chauffeur	56	"
	G	Pierce Margaret—†	7	housewife	54	"
	H	Burns Margaret—†	7	"	28	
	K	Emmett Agnes—†	7	"	25	
	L	Leach Charles	9	pipefitter	34	"
	M	Leach William	9	retired	76	"
	N	Long Jessie—†	9	housewife	37	"
	O	Long William	9	mechanic	39	"
	P	LeCours Alphonse	9	musician	50	"
	R	LeCours Winifred—†	9	housewife	46	"
	S	Burns Anna—†	11	boxmaker	52	"
	T	Burns Dorothy—†	11	tel operator	38	"
	U	Burns Frances—†	11	secretary	42	"
	V	Gunn Anne—†	11	housewife	72	"
	W	*Dube Celina—†	13	"	47	
	X	Dube Emil	13	operator	20	"
	Y	*Dube Philip	13	"	48	

436

	A	Dorgan Elizabeth—†	15	housewife	27	"
	B	Gibson Edythe—†	15	dancer	28	"
	H	Hagen Alvah F	20	laborer	51	28 Valentine
	K	Hagen Mary—†	20	housewife	54	28 "
	L	Grasse Lillian M—†	20	"	33	here
	M	Grasse Maynard S	20	operator	42	"
	N	Bedard Mabel—†	20	factoryworker	52	"
	S	Munroe Charles G	22	mechanic	60	3510 Wash'n
	T	Munroe Ora E—†	22	housewife	76	3510 "
	U	Luks Anna—†	22	"	68	here
	V	Luks Leopold	22	shoeworker	70	"
	W	Keating Ellen—†	22	housewife	70	"
	X	Keating Michael J	22	rigger	70	
	Y	McCarthy Mary—†	23	clerk	65	
	Z	Reynolds Ethel L—†	23	housewife	53	"

437

	B	Flynn Arthur	24	clerk	41	4½ Sumner pl
	C	Flynn Mary—†	24	housewife	39	4½ "

Valentine Street—Continued

D	Barry Anne—†	24	housewife	59	here
E	Barry James	24	laborer	64	"
F	Barry James, jr	24	U S A	22	"
H	McEachem Angus	25	retired	81	
K	Gorman Mary—†	25	housewife	26	Maine
L	Gorman Wallace	25	clerk	34	"
M	Bunnell Agnes M—†	25	housewife	58	here
N	Bunnell Francis X	25	clerk	22	"
O	Bunnell Frederick	25	painter	59	"
P	Bunnell Frederick J	25	U S A	24	"
R	Curwen Charles T	26	rigger	64	"
S	Starrett Sarah—†	26	clerk	52	"
U	Scott Charlotte—†	27	housewife	53	"
V	Pritchard Catherine—†	27	"	68	"
W	Buckley Cornelius F	27	watchman	63	"
X	Buckley Helen F—†	27	housewife	64	"
Z	McDonald Catherine—†	28	"	39	

438

A	McDonald Joseph	28	laborer	38	
B	Curley Catherine—†	28	at home	71	"
C	Cavanaugh Bertha—†	29	factoryworker	21	6 Flagg
D	Cavanaugh John	29	janitor	63	6 "
E	Cavanaugh Mary—†	29	housewife	53	6 "
F	Dinan Mary—†	29	at home	77	here
G	Mansfield Catherine—†	29	housewife	70	"
H	Mansfield Joseph	29	clerk	33	"
K	Mansfield Rita—†	29	operator	25	"
L	Vandenberg John A	29	retired	77	"
M	Mahoney Charlotte—†	30	housewife	26	Pennsylvania
N	Mahoney Walker	30	U S A	32	"
O	Dixon Dorothy—†	30	housewife	22	111 Bower
R	Alabiso Carmelia—†	31	factoryworker	25	here
S	Alabiso Catherine—†	31	"	43	"
T	Alabiso Charles	31	laborer	23	"
U	McDermott John J	31	operator	33	"
V	McDermott Mary	31	housewife	29	"
W	McNamara Bertha—†	31	"	54	"
X	McNamara John	31	factoryworker	52	"
Y	McNamara Thomas F	31	clerk	26	
Z	Wood David	32	U S A	38	"

439

A	Wood Maria—†	32	factoryworker	34	"

Washington Street

M	Sheehan Daniel E	2774	carpenter	66	here
N	Sheehan Helen M—†	2774	housewife	46	"
O	Nadeau Elmer J	2774	billposter	38	"
P	*Nadeau Mary A—†	2774	housewife	33	"
R	McDonald Evelyn V	2776	machinist	40	"
S	McDonald Murdoch J	2776	carpenter	46	"
T	Bangui Helena G—†	2776	clerk	29	Louisiana
U	Bangui Mariano A	2776	U S N	49	"
X	Monteiro Dorothy M—†	2782	housewife	35	18 Trotter ct
Y	*Douglas Dorcas M—†	2782	"	53	206 W Springfie
Z	Douglas Mabel B	2782	waitress	25	206 "

440

A	Douglas Reginald S	2782	orderly	27	here
C	Furr Irma E—†	2784	packer	33	2455 Wash'n
D	Williams Roy R	2784	laborer	29	109 Ruggles
G	Forchiea Thomas F	2788A	U S A	24	here
H	Forchiea Veronica L—†	2788A	housewife	20	151 Thornto
K	Fallon John F	2788A	carpenter	59	here
L	*Ferri Arleen C—†	2788A	housewife	30	204 Highland
M	Ferri Louis	2788A	laborer	36	204 "
N	McCambly John H	2788A	carpenter	73	here
O	Currie Eva M—†	2788A	housewife	40	"
P	Currie John B	2788A	sorter	38	"
R	Sears Carrol C	2788A	steamfitter	40	"
S	Sears Theresa J—†	2788A	housewife	42	"
U	Lee Young	2792	laundryworker	40	1944 Wash'n
V	Cylinski Joseph W	2792	laborer	30	Needham
W	D'Amore Claire M—†	2792	housewife	29	here
X	Donovan Ella V—†	2792	cleaner	64	235 Bolton
Y	Grove Franklin A	2792	chauffeur	37	here
Z	Grove Irene R—†	2792	housewife	30	"

441

B	Hahir Ellen E—†	2794	"	45	
C	Hahir Priscilla F—†	2794	electrician	22	"
F	Cichon Helen M—†	2796	housewife	24	"
G	Lorden Catherine V—†	2796	factoryworker	23	"
H	Lorden Francis J	2796	rigger	21	
K	Lorden Helena T—†	2796	housewife	47	"
L	Lorden John J	2796	clerk	46	
M	McLean Louis H	2796	U S N	22	
N	McLean Minnie A—†	2796	housewife	53	"

Washington Street—Continued

o	McLean Nancy D—†	2796	saleswoman	20	here
p	McLean Wellington P	2796	U S N	23	"
r	O'Connell Daniel E	2796	chauffeur	46	"
s	O'Connell Mary G—†	2796	machinist	20	"
t	O'Connell Mary T—†	2796	housewife	41	"
v	Daniels Callie M—†	2800½	teacher	27	
w	Daniels Titus	2800½	salesman	34	"
x	Jones Annie L—†	2800½	housewife	21	"
y	Jones Roberta—†	2800½	"	46	
z	Thompson Joseph E	2800½	clerk	33	

442

a	Thompson Mary—†	2800½	housewife	22	"
b	Gamer Ada B—†	2800½	florist	35	..
c	Gamer Elizabeth—†	2800½	housewife	68	"
d	Gamer John J	2800½	florist	48	"
f	Kristo Elizabeth T—†	2806	operator	25	80 Fulda
g	Masse Ellen E—†	2806	supervisor	52	here
h	Boyd Barbara—†	2806	housewife	45	"
k	Boyd James	2806	steamfitter	49	"
l	Johnson Carrie V—†	2806	dressmaker	28	Pennsylvania
m	Johnson Isaiah	2806	salesman	47	"
p	Sauve Leo A	2808	laborer	42	here
r	Bergland Corrine A—†	2808	clerk	24	"
s	Bergland Ruth V—†	2808	housekeeper	47	"
t	Browne Perley A	2808	U S A	21	"
u	Browne Phyllis E—†	2808	housewife	22	"
v	Douglass James M	2808	laborer	26	"
w	Crosby Augusta—†	2808	housekeeper	28	Illinois
x	Griggs Wilbur O	2808	laborer	43	here
y	Fitzgerald John	2809	"	30	"
z	Fitzgerald Mary L—†	2809	housewife	25	"

443

a	Smith Donald	2809	operator	30	"
d	Mitchell George H	2812	clerk	43	
e	Mitchell Valeda A—†	2812	housewife	38	"
f	Daley Jennie I—†	2812	"	29	..
g	Daley Robertson M	2812	laborer	34	
h	Wong Florence—†	2815	housewife	42	"
k	Wong George F	2815	laborer	44	
m	Dekas Anna B—†	2817	housewife	48	"
n	Dekas James A	2817	gardener	52	"

Washington Street—Continued

P	Kelley Gladys M—†	2821½	saleswoman	48	here
R	Chartsand Lillian I—†	2821½	"	48	"
W	McMahon Michael J	2831A	storekeeper	73	"
X	McMahon Nora—†	2831A	housewife	78	"
Y	Pettigrew Alice—†	2831A	"	59	
Z	Pettigrew Archibald	2831A	clerk	60	

444

B	Paul Matilda—†	2837	housewife	64	"
C	Stravinos Emma—†	2837	"	43	
D	Stravinos Stephen	2837	"	45	
E	Bennett Charles A	2837	retired	68	"
F	Bennett Charles C	2837	clerk	32	
G	Bennett Mary C—†	2837	housewife	74	"
H	Bennett Mildred—†	2837	"	29	
K	Doherty Annie M—†	2839	"	34	
L	Doherty Bernard	2839	laborer	41	
N	Delaney Joseph M	2843	"	55	
O	Delaney Mary L—†	2843	housewife	62	"
R	Campbell Duncan B	2843	watchman	69	"
S	Campbell Duncan S	2843	shoeworker	22	"
P	Campbell Etta—†	2843	housewife	54	"
T	Duval Claire L—†	2843	"	24	
W	O'Dwyer Elizabeth C—†	2855	"	72	
X	O'Dwyer Myles	2855	retired	75	"
Y	Kapinos Martha—†	2855	housewife	25	215 Amory
Z	Kapinos Michael J	2855	physician	31	215 "

445

A	Long Edna—†	2855	teacher	56	here
B	McCall Frances M—†	2855	housewife	40	"
C	McCall Thomas F	2855	operator	44	"
D	Bloomfield Mary E—†	2855	housewife	55	"
E	Kelley Katherine—†	2855	"	66	632 Dudley
F	Todesco Mildred C—†	2855	"	32	here
G	Duncan Elsa—†	2857	stenographer	32	"
H	Duncan William	2857	clerk	35	"
K	Grinnell Robert E	2859	salesman	27	"
L	Grinnell Ruth F—†	2859	housewife	25	"
M	Jefferson Peter	2859	mechanic	47	"
N	Foley Cornelius	2859	clerk	44	"
O	Duncan Selina—†	2859	"	57	"
P*	Abraham Ellen M—†	2893	teacher	63	Peabody

Washington Street—Continued

	Letter.	Full Name	Residence	Occupation	Age	Reported Residence
	R	Brogan Anna—†	2893	housekeeper	35	here
	S	Brogan Cecelia M—†	2893	teacher	48	"
	T	Buckley Margaret—†	2893	stitcher	84	"
	U	Callahan Catherine—†	2893	teacher	50	
	V	Callahan Grace A—†	2893	"	34	
	W	Carroll Claire—†	2893	"	47	
	X	Cawley Alice G—†	2893	"	35	
	Y	Cullinane Anna—†	2893	matron	69	
	Z	Daley Mary A—†	2893	teacher	24	"

446

	A	Donavan Mary E—†	2893	domestic	70	"
	B	Dooley Bridget—†	2893	"	77	"
	C	Dowling Anna E—†	2893	teacher	34	
	D	Dwight Sarah C—†	2893	"	60	
	E	Fallon Clara M—†	2893	"	58	"
	F	Farrell Agnes P—†	2893	"	37	"
	G	Flaherty Elizabeth A—†	2893	"	27	
	H	Fleming Mary—†	2893		71	
	K	Fleming Mary—†	2893	"	29	
	L	Gallagher Helen D—†	2893	"	32	
	M	Gannon Mary C—†	2893	"	27	
	N	Gorham Ann A—†	2893	"	36	
	O	Gutowski Helen—†	2893	cook	26	
	P	Hall Mary M—†	2893	teacher	39	"
	R	Hummel Lillian C—†	2893	"	51	"
	S	Kelcher Theresa M—†	2893	"	26	
	T	Kennedy Mary—†	2893	domestic	69	"
	U	Kingston Mary E—†	2893	teacher	42	"
	V	Lamb Marie L—†	2893	domestic	52	"
	W	Langlois Mary V—†	2893	teacher	37	Peabody
	X	LaValley Marion—†	2893	domestic	24	here
	Y	Lynch Florence C—†	2893	teacher	42	"
	Z	Lyons Helen—†	2893	"	47	"

447

	A	Mahan Anna R—†	2893	"	50	
	B	Mahoney Margaret L—†	2893	"	47	"
	C	Malone Margaret L—†	2893	"	27	"
	D	McBride Evelyn E—†	2893	"	71	
	E	McCann Theresa L—†	2893	"	43	
	F	McCarthy Mary C—†	2893	"	39	"
	G	McClaskey Regina—†	2893	"	66	"

Washington Street—Continued

Page.	Letter.	FULL NAME.	Residence, Jan. 1, 1946.	Occupation.	Supposed Age.	Reported Residence, Jan. 1, 1945. Street and Number.
	H	McDonough Catherine P—†	2893	teacher	23	here
	K	*McDonough Bridget—†	2893	housekeeper	63	"
	L	McGillivray Mary—†	2893	teacher	47	"
	M	McQuade Helen E—†	2893	"	38	
	N	Melchionda Anna—†	2893	"	36	
	O	Meuse Marie L—†	2893	"	38	
	P	Mullen Mary A—†	2893	"	38	
	R	Mulvaney Kate T—†	2893	domestic	44	"
	S	Murphy Margaret B—†	2893	teacher	37	
	T	Naze Mary M—†.	2893	"	30	
	U	O'Connor Alice—†	2893	housekeeper	76	"
	V	*O'Connor Catherine—†	2893	domestic	57	"
	W	Otis Aloyse M—† '	2893	teacher	38	Andover
	X	Palinkas Juha M—†	2893	housekeeper	45	here
	Y	Piela Jane C—†	2893	teacher	30	"
	Z	Quill Dorothy—†	2893	"	28	"
448						
	A	Quinn Grace V—†	2893	"	55	
	B	Quinn Nora—†	2893	"	30	
	C	Reilly Mary R—†	2893		36	
	D	Shaw Agnes I—†	2893	"	47	
	E	Smith Ellen—†	2893	domestic	73	"
	F	Stark Lucille—†	2893	teacher	21	Waltham
	G	Steinmeyer Mary A—†	2893	"	25	here
	H	Sullivan Mary G—†	2893	"	33	"
	K	Tobin Gertrude M—†.	2893	"	58	"
	L	Walsh Mary E—†	2893	"	38	
	M	Ward Sarah—†	2893		82	
	N	Watson Margaret M—†	2893	"	42	
	O	Wessling Mary O—†	2893	"	69	

5

6

8

9

12
13

Ward 11—Precinct 5

CITY OF BOSTON

LIST OF RESIDENTS
20 YEARS OF AGE AND OVER

(NON-CITIZENS INDICATED BY ASTERISK)
(FEMALES INDICATED BY DAGGER)

AS OF

JANUARY 1, 1946

THOMAS F. SULLIVAN, *Chairman*
FREDERIC E. DOWLING, *Secretary*
WILLIAM A. MOTLEY, JR.
ARTHUR V. COUGHLIN
EVERETT R. PROUT

Listing Board.

CITY OF BOSTON PRINTING DEPARTMENT

500
Brinton Street

A	Leach Theresa R—†	9	housewife	31	here
B	Leach William F	9	machinist	36	"
C	Cormier Helen—†	9	housewife	23	"
D	Cormier Joseph L	9	welder	31	
E	Belban Edmund	9	watchman	75	"
F	Belban Laura R—†	9	housewife	62	"
G	Rentel Leonard	9	U S N	30	"
H	Rentel Pauline—†	9	housewife	25	"
K	Thompson Grace—†	9	operator	45	"
L	Marino Antonio	9	machinist	31	"
M	Marino Margaret—†	9	housewife	26	"
N	Wantman Bernard	10	salesman	30	29 McLellan
O	Wantman Mollie—†	10	housewife	30	29 "
P	Dietchman Anna—†	10A	"	68	here
R	Dietchman Samuel	10A	drawtender	44	"
S	O'Leary Jeremiah F	11	laborer	67	"
T	O'Leary Mary V—†	11	milliner	69	
U	O'Leary Nellie G—†	11	housewife	64	"
V	Shumilla Adam	11	clerk	60	
W	Shumilla Anna—†	11	chemist	54	
X	Shumilla Mabel—†	11	housewife	33	"
Y	Woods Edgar F	11	chauffeur	27	"
Z	Woods Irene M—†	11	housewife	23	"

501

A	Shumilla Edward S	11	chauffeur	35	"
B	Venetskas Beatrice—†	11	stitcher	43	
C	Venetskas Boleslaw	11	barber	53	
D	King Earl V	11	maintenance	54	"
E	King Mary H—†	11	housewife	54	"
F	Daly Dorothy—†	14	"	25	
G	Daly Thomas F	14	switchman	26	"
H	Harris Mabel—†	14	housewife	50	"
K	Harris William B	14	clerk	57	
L	Winder Frances—†	14A	housewife	61	"

Cardington Street

M	DeFrancesco Andrew R	1	chauffeur	34	here
N	DeFrancesco Mary—†	1	housewife	35	"

Cardington Street—Continued

o	Falso Fred	1	cablemaker	37	here
p	Falso Nicoletta—†	1	housewife	40	"
r	MacKay Emma—†	2	at home	83	"
s	MacKay Mary—†	2	saleswoman	56	"
t	MacKay William	2	clerk	26	
u	Flaherty Charles C	2	policeman	47	"
v	Flaherty Minnie—†	2	housewife	43	"
w	Toland Frances—†	3	"	36	
x	Toland Patrick	3	engineer	44	"
y	Crosby Clare—†	3½	housewife	30	"
z	Crosby Walter T	3½	mechanic	33	"

502

a	McCarthy Charles W	4	machinist	34	"
b	McCarthy Margaret—†	4	housewife	31	"
c	Foley Anna—†	4	bookkeeper	31	"
d	Foley Catherine—†	4	"	33	"
e	Foley Joseph	4	clerk	38	
f	Foley Mary—†	4	bookkeeper	35	"
g	Amirault Amanda—†	5	housewife	36	"
h	Amirault Samuel	5	fisherman	42	"
k	Burkhardt Anna K—†	5	housewife	71	"
l	Burkhardt Carl I	5	clerk	42	
m	O'Connell Ellen M—†	6	housewife	57	"
n	O'Connell Thomas I	6	laborer	53	
o	Sullivan Edward	6	U S A	22	
p	Sullivan Mary A—†	6	inspector	52	"
r	Farmer George T	6	printer	48	
s	Farmer Helen L—†	6	housewife	52	"
t	Varley Walter	6	laborer	49	
u	Wiehe Albert L	7	clerk	38	
v	Wiehe Emma—†	7	housekeeper	61	"
w	Hurney Francis I	7	U S A	22	"
x	Hurney Michael F	7	retired	69	
y	Hurney Winifred T—†	7	housewife	53	"
z	McFarland James F	9	U S A	51	

503

a	McFarland James F	9	laborer	22	
b	McFarland Pauline G—†	9	housewife	47	"
c	McFarland Robert W	9	student	21	
d	Golden George	9	chauffeur	48	"
e	Golden Harriet—†	9	clerk	38	"

Cobden Street

F	Wolff Albert G	1	attorney	61	here
G	Wolff Nellie B—†	1	housewife	52	"
H	Baker Arline—†	1	"	53	"
K	Baker Julia—†	1	"	75	
L	Baker Virgil	1	laborer	42	
M	Frazier Lawrence	1	porter	52	
N	Frazier Rachel—†	1	housewife	32	"
O	Alexis Mabel—†	3	"	52	
P	Alexis Milton	3	student	25	
R	Alexis Spiro	3	beautician	54	"
S	Turcotte Catherine—†	3	housewife	55	"
T	Turcotte Charles D	3	retired	54	
U	Turcotte Charles J	3	U S N	21	
V	Turcotte Marie—†	3	teacher	25	
W	DeFrancesco Angeline—†	5	housewife	35	"
X	DeFrancesco Attore	5	chauffeur	37	"
Y	Krokmen Robert	5	U S A	29	
Z	Runzio Ernest	5	chauffeur	30	"
	504				
A	Klett Anna—†	15	housewife	53	"
B	Klett Gertrude—†	15	bookkeeper	26	"
C	Klett Henry	15	custodian	63	"
D	Coughlin Dennis I	15	machinist	58	"
E	Coughlin Helen E—†	15	instructor	50	"
F	Ruck Francis M	15	laster	58	
G	Ruck Honora T—†	15	housewife	57	"
H	Imbrogna Arsenio I	17	U S M C	20	"
K	Imbrogna James	17	barber	55	
L	Imbrogna Stella—†	17	housewife	46	"
M	Friese Gustav	19	operator	51	"
N	Friese Heinz	19	student	26	
O	Friese Martha—†	19	housewife	50	"
P	Rosche Albert	19	laborer	53	
R	Sobasco Edward	21	clerk	29	
S	Zelan Hilda—†	21	housewife	46	"
T	Zelan Ludwig	21	repairman	64	"
U	Comeau Ethel F—†	25	housewife	39	"
V	Comeau John W	25	electrician	39	"
W	Nolan Ellen F—†	25	housewife	65	"
X	Nolan Valentine B	25	fireman	65	
Y	Nolan William R	25	clerk	40	

Cobden Street—Continued

		Name	Res.	Occupation	Age	Reported
	z	Swanson Arnold T	27	machinist	37	here
505						
	A	Swanson Esther—†	27	housewife	37	"
	B	David Agnes—†	27	"	26	
	C	David Aram A	27	U S A	28	
	D	Libby Alice—†	27	waitress	60	
	E	MacDonald Allan	29	laborer	45	
	F	MacDonald Mary A—†	29	housewife	41	"
	G	MacDonald Mary A—†	29	stenographer	21	"
	H	Regan Charles I	29	clerk	39	"
	K	Regan Margaret M—†	29	housewife	38	"
	L	Regan William F	29	porter	38	
	M	Reiser George	33	chauffeur	38	"
	N	Reiser Mary—†	33	housewife	34	"
	O	Bray James F	33	chef	36	
	P	Bray Mary J—†	33	housewife	33	"
	R	Bocanfuso Alfred	33	laborer	25	
	S	Bocanfuso Antonio	33	cook	62	
	T	Bocanfuso Joseph	33	laborer	27	
	U	Bocanfuso Pasquale	33	glazier	31	
	V	Bocanfuso Theresa—†	33	housewife	59	"
	W	Enos Leonard	33	manager	25	"
	X	Berggren Erik	35	janitor	38	
	Y	Berggren Helen—†	35	housewife	32	"
	Z	Daley Lorraine—†	35	at home	21	"
506						
	A	Clish Fred	35	janitor	60	
	B	Clish Mary—†	35	housewife	59	"
	C	Fillips Anna—†	35	"	41	
	D	Fillips Stephen	35	counterman	47	"
	E	McDonald Virginia—†	37	housekeeper	27	"
	F	Glassett Dennis	37	shipper	70	18 Byron
	G	O'Donnell Mary—†	37	housewife	39	18 "
	H	O'Donnell William F	37	chauffeur	40	18 "
	K	Thompson Alice T—†	37	housewife	28	57 Horan way
	L	Thompson Vincent	37	shipfitter	29	57 "
	M	Gannon William A	39	machinist	36	here
	N	Long Alfred	39	carpenter	58	"
	O	Long Catherine F—†	39	housewife	63	"
	P	Foley Catherine—†	39	"	64	
	R	Foley Timothy	39	laborer	67	

Cobden Street—Continued

	s	Shea Michael	39	porter	55	here
	t	Moran Thomas J	39	laborer	49	"
	u	Moran Thomas J	39	"	20	"

Codman Park

	v	Doyle Annie—†	5	housewife	49	here
	w	Doyle Louis T	5	painter	49	"
	x	O'Keefe Margaret—†	5	clerk	28	"
	y	O'Keefe Richard	5	"	32	
	z	Ratelle Catherine—†	5	housewife	39	"
507						
	a	Golden Mabel—†	5	clerk	35	
	b	Golden Patrick	5	"	40	
	c*	Carignan Fabiola—†	5	housewife	43	"
	d	Carignan Lucien	5	laborer	41	
	e	Gray Ella T—†	5	housewife	42	"
	f	Gray Ernest	5	laborer	41	
	g	Gass Francis L	6	engineer	50	"
	h	Gass Mary A—†	6	housewife	53	"
	k*	Dalton Catherine A—†	6	"	37	
	l	Dalton Oswald F	6	paymaster	38	"
	m	Stewart Lena—†	6	housewife	68	"
	n	Stewart Maurice J	6	laborer	24	
	o	Stewart Robert R	6	"	21	
	p	Stewart Vivian A—†	6	clerk	27	
	r	Gibbons John F	6	operator	50	"
	s	Gibbons Joseph F	6	U S C G	24	"
	t	Gibbons Mary E—†	6	housewife	52	"
	u	Houghton Florence M—†	6	buyer	55	
	v	Houghton Jean M—†	6	nurse	21	
	w	Houghton Virginia—†	6	student	20	
	x	DiMarino Helen B—†	6	housewife	36	"
	y	DiMarino John	6	laborer	34	
	z	Fales Lester T	9	retired	73	
508						
	a	Fales Mabel E—†	9	housewife	**74**	"
	b	Fales Russell L	9	clerk	48	"
	c	Rawinski Ada—†	9	housewife	56	Connecticut
	d	Rawinski Julius	9	retired	62	"
	e	Key Ora—†	9	housewife	48	here

Codman Park—Continued

F	Key Percy W	9	shoeworker	48	here
G	O'Laughlin Eli	9	engineer	52	"
H	McAuliffe Elizabeth—†	9	housewife	38	"
K	McAuliffe Jeremiah	9	clerk	46	
L	Brawley John H	9	U S A	28	
N	Ghomas Catherine—†	9	housewife	50	"
M	Ghomas John H	9	letter carrier	52	"
O	Guinessy Joseph F	9	laborer	36	
P	Guinessy Mary G—†	9	housewife	35	"
R	D'Entremont Beatrice A—†	10	"	40	
S	D'Entremont Robert	10	laborer	41	
T	D'Eon Isaie L	10	operator	40	"
U	D'Eon Redina A—†	10	housewife	37	"
V	Wile Arthur	10	laborer	48	
W	Wile Jean—†	10	housewife	45	"
X	Boyle Beatrice—†	10	"	36	
Y	Boyle Hugh	10	laborer	38	
Z	Andrews Lillian L—†	10	housewife	71	"

509

A	Mulcahy Alice J—†	10	"	60	
B	Mulcahy Michael B	10	laborer	61	"
C	Conaghan John	15	fireman	40	Somerville
D	Conaghan Rose—†	15	housewife	35	"
E	Price Michael	15	clerk	39	here
F	Price Sevilla—†	15	housewife	29	"
G	Nielsen Hans C	15	laborer	61	"
H	Nielsen Petra—†	15	housewife	59	"
K	Yankowski Caroline—†	15	"	38	
L	Yankowski Felix	15	chauffeur	36	"
M	Freeman Anna M—†	15	housewife	55	"
N	Freeman George M	15	chauffeur	57	"
O	Freeman Leona G—†	15	clerk	21	
P	Wojciechowski Anna—†	15	housewife	41	"
R	Wojciechowski John	15	U S N	24	
S	Lombardelli Anita—†	30	secretary	26	"
T	Lombardelli Peter	30	laborer	59	"
U	Guerriero Eileen—†	30	housewife	31	769 Dor av
V	Guerriero William	30	entertainer	29	769 "
W	Vecchia Eleanor L—†	30	housewife	27	7 Frawley
X	Vecchia John P	30	laborer	34	7 "
Y	Vecchia Randolph W	30	"	33	7 "

510
Codman Park—Continued

B	Conley Eugeñe J	32	plumber	37	112 Amory
C	Conley Pauline H—†	32	housewife	38	112 "
D	Mellon Agnes—†	34	"	46	here
E	Mellon Alexander A	34	machinist	47	"
F	Mellon James F	34	laborer	21	"
G	Pierce Albert G	34	"	24	
H	Coyle Mary—†	35	housewife	52	"
K	Coyle Robert	35	mechanic	51	"
L	Nehiley Dorothy—†	35	housewife	33	"
L¹	Nehiley Wilfred	35	plater	39	
M	Brown John	36	retired	62	"
N	Doherty Anthony	36	laborer	60	"
O	Pearson Iver	36	machinist	50	"
P	Pearson Margaret—†	36	housewife	50	"
S	Neary Irene—†	37	"	50	
T	Neary Leo M	37	clerk	50	
U	Moritz Albert J	38	mechanic	34	"
V	Moritz Helen M—†	38	housewife	29	"
W	Maier Christian	38	painter	73	
X	Davis Mattie—†	39	housewife	34	"
Y	Bonito Margaret—†	39	housekeeper	66	"
Z	Morrison Dorothy—†	39	housewife	40	"

511

A	Morrison Louis	39	porter	41	"
B	Madden Margaret—†	40	housewife	36	"
C	Madden Thomas	40	laborer	40	"
D	McGough Ruth H—†	40	housewife	30	"
E	McGough William H	40	cutter	39	
F	Cotter Brendan R	41	U S M C	20	"
G	Cotter Francis W	41	U S A	21	
H	Cotter Helen L—†	41	housewife	51	"
K	Cotter Patricia—†	41	clerk	25	
L	Shaughnessy Edna—†	42	housewife	35	"
M	Shaughnessy John J	42	laborer	38	
N	Sullivan James M	42	"	38	
O	Sullivan Nancy—†	42	housewife	29	"
P	Banks Charles S	43	welder	39	Quincy
R	Banks Katherine P—†	43	housewife	34	"
S	Finer Harry	43	retired	60	here
T	Simon Morris	43	laborer	31	"

8

Codman Park—Continued

u	Simon Rose—†	43	housewife	32	here
v	Marshall Edna L—†	44	"	31	"
w	Bowman Albert	44	laborer	45	"
x	Bowman Dorothy—†	44	housewife	42	"
y	Mendall Louis R	45	U S N	42	
z	Mendall Ruth—†	45	housewife	39	"

512

b	Jackson Aina—†	46	"	30	
c	Jackson John J	46	laborer	31	
d	Buckman William H	46	plumber	30	"
e	Buckman Winifred M—†	46	housewife	31	"
f	Riley Margaret—†	47	"	70	
h	Sweeney Daniel J	48	molder	32	
k	Sweeney Marjorie R—†	48	housewife	32	"
l	Good Albina—†	48	laborer	51	
m	Cullinane Jeremiah	48	"	55	
n	Cullinane Mary J—†	48	housewife	45	"
o	McCarthy Catherine E—†	49	"	69	
p	McCarthy Charles	49	laborer	60	
r	McCarthy Rita M—†	49	clerk	24	
s	McCarthy Theresa F—†	49	"	21	"
t	Greenfield Frank	51	proprietor	53	"
u	Greenfield Ida—†	51	housewife	40	"
v	Greenfield Lillian—†	51	"	45	
w	Smith Catherine D—†	51	"	20	"
x	Smith Harry	51	welder	25	
y	Mulvey Elizabeth—†	52	housewife	54	"
z	Mulvey Elizabeth E—†	52	"	75	

513

a	De'Eon Jean—†	53	clerk	20	..
b	De'Eon Theresa M—†	53	housewife	39	"
c	D'Entremont Lucien	53A	clerk	45	
d	Arnold Benjamin J	53A	retired	65	
e	Smith Laura—†	53A	housewife	47	"
f	*Waters John	54	retired	74	
g	DeValle Lidia—†	55	housewife	41	"
h	DeValle Rufino	55	seaman	51	
l	DePina Amancio	57	cook	44	
m	*DePina Caroline—†	57	housewife	31	"
n	McMillan Margaret E—†	57	"	28	
o	McMillan Walter L	57	retired	61	..

Codman Park—Continued

P	Colby Charles E	57	clerk	46	here
R	Colby Edward C, jr	57	brakeman	27	"
S	Colby Gloria C—†	57	housewife	21	N Hampshire
T	Colby Maude C—†	57	"	42	here
U	Lunde Richard	58	painter	65	"
V	Jenkins Alfred	59	clerk	28	"
W	Jenkins Martin	59	retired	69	
X	Thibault Felix	59	diesetter	69	"
Y	Thibault Leona—†	59	housewife	60	"
Z	Thibault Mary L—†	59	clerk	28	

514

A	Griffin Mary—†	59	housewife	46	"
B	Griffin Rita—†	59	clerk	21	
D	McGrane Joseph	61	chef	55	
E	*Murphy Mary—†	61	housewife	68	"
F	*Murphy William	61	cook	72	
G	*O'Connor Esther—†	61	housewife	56	"
H	O'Connor Thomas	61	boilermaker	69	"
K	Kimtis Hilda—†	61	housewife	30	"
L	Kimtis Joseph	61	carpenter	34	"
M	Wilfert Andrew	62	laborer	32	"
O	*Finn Beatrice—†	64	housewife	36	2 Folsom av
P	Finn Patrick J	64	chauffeur	37	2 "
R	Franzi Margaret—†	65	housewife	49	here
S	Corrigan Margaret J—†	65	"	34	"
T	Corrigan Philip H	65	pipefitter	38	"
U	Fazio Grace—†	65	housewife	70	"
V	Cooper Annette V—†	66	"	29	"
W	Cooper Edward C	66	laborer	34	"
X	Jennings Margaret C—†	66	housewife	34	"
Y	Jennings Martin	66	conductor	36	"
Z	Cottreau Genevieve M—†	67	housewife	34	"

515

A	Cottreau Mark E	67	cook	35	"
B	Bylander Anna—†	67	housewife	45	"
C	Benjaminson Marion—†	67	"	35	
D	Benjaminson Oscar	67	painter	43	"
E	Johnson Constance—†	68	housewife	25	"
F	Johnson Lawrence	68	U S A	27	
G	Cordice Conrad	68	engineer	55	"
H	Cordice Florence—†	68	inspector	48	"

Codman Park—Continued

K	Cordice Richard	68	draftsman	21	here	
L	Moore John	69	warehouse	31	Weymouth	
M	Moore Muriel C—†	69	housewife	36	"	
N	DeCosta Eva—†	69	"	71	here	
O	Mooney Gladys—†	69	clerk	32	"	
P	Armington Clara J—†	69	housewife	43	"	
R	Armington George C	69	chauffeur	50	"	
S	Armington George F	69	printer	25		
T	Armington Katherine—†	69	housewife	21	"	
U	Armington Richard W	69	U S A	23		
V	Walsh Hugh	70	laborer	42	"	
W	Walsh Minnie—†	70	housewife	40	"	
X	Rabita Ella—†	70	"	49	"	
Y	Rabita Liborio	70	laborer	56	"	
Z	Johnson Anna M—†	71	housewife	58	"	

516

A	Johnson Fritz J	71	carpenter	69	"	
B	Johnson Harry M	71	welder	24		
C	DeBury Cora E—†	71	housewife	54	"	
D	DeBury Cyril C	71	salesman	58	"	
F	McDonough Barbara—†	72	housewife	51	"	
G	McDonough Michael	72	carpenter	55	"	
H	McDonough Patrick F	72	U S A	21		
K	Carter Marjorie—†	73	housewife	39	"	
L	Carter Reginald	73	clerk	42	"	
M	Lafond Gertrude—†	73	housewife	24	40 Ottawa	
N	Lafond Wilfred	73	U S A	32	here	
O	Tulley Albert	73	mechanic	38	15 Alhambra rd	
P	Tulley Laura E—†	73	housewife	37	15 "	
R	Hughes Bernard T	74	retired	72	here	
S	Hughes James J	74	student	28	"	
T	Hughes Mary D—†	74	housewife	65	"	
U	Hughes Peter F	74	laborer	23		
V	Hughes Thomas M	74	student	28		
W	Sears Matilda J—†	76	housewife	59	"	
X	Sears Otto A	76	U S A	27		
Y	Williams Mary M—†	76	clerk	22		
Z	Williams Raymond J	76	U S A	23		

517

A	Spillane Anna F—†	78	clerk	25	"	
B	Spillane Patrick J	78	student	29		

11

Codman Park—Continued

c	Spillane Keven F	78	student	22	here
d	Spillane Thomas F	78	U S N	23	"
e	Hanlon John	80	laborer	60	"
f	Tornberg Emily L—†	80	housewife	50	"
g	Tornberg Henry E	80	clerk	53	"
h	Dew Hartford C	82	U S N	24	Virginia
k	Dew Ramona M—†	82	housewife	23	"
l	*Webb Hazel—†	82	"	28	here
m	*Webb Norman R	82	laborer	28	"
n	Mendall Lewis R, jr	84	seaman	20	"
o	Mendall Mildred W—†	84	housewife	21	"
p	*Webb Hilda E—†	84	"	46	
r	Webb Owen L	84	carpenter	47	"
s	Webb Stewart F	84	U S M C	23	"
t	*Campbell Christina R—†	85	housewife	25	"
u	Campbell Francis, jr	85	machinist	33	"
v	Walsh James M	85	student	21	
w	Walsh Martin F	85	foreman	49	"
x	Walsh Mary—†	85	housewife	49	"
y	Walsh Mary F—†	85	bookkeeper	22	"

Codman Place

z	DiBella Cecilia—†	1	clerk	25	Cambridge
	518				
a	DiBella Charles	1	salesman	55	"
b	DiBella Isabella—†	1	housewife	56	"
c	Hill Kathleen—†	2	"	29	here
d	Hill Thomas	2	pipefitter	26	"
f	*Downey James	3	clerk	58	"
g	*Lyle Ellen—†	3	domestic	53	"
h	Mason Freeman	5	manager	69	"
k	Mason Sarah—†	5	housewife	67	"

Corliss Street

l	Cahill John T	2	salesman	27	here
m	Cahill Mary V—†	2	housewife	27	"
n	Carroll Evelyn M—†	2	clerk	20	"
o	Carroll Helen—†	2	hostess	26	
p	Carroll Josephine—†	2	housewife	59	"

Page.	Letter.	FULL NAME.	Residence, Jan. 1, 1946.	Occupation.	Supposed Age.	Reported Residence, Jan. 1, 1945. Street and Number.

Corliss Street—Continued

R	Carroll Paul	2	U S N	23	here
S	Carroll William F	2	clerk	28	"
T	Diggins Dennis T	2	"	27	"
U	Diggins Josephine M—†	2	housewife	30	"
V	Hassett Arthur T	2	retired	72	
W	Hassett Walter T	2	laborer	70	
X	Boyd Ann—†	3	housewife	44	"
Y	Boyd Hugh	3	telegrapher	44	"
Z	Chigas Helen—†	3	clerk	22	

519

A	Chigas Jack	3	stitcher	55	
B	Chigas Mary—†	3	"	49	
C	Elliott John	3	mechanic	29	"
D	Elliott Theresa—†	3	housewife	29	"
E	Hamilton Janet—†	4	"	32	85 Bernard
F	Taft Helen—†	4	"	20	85 "
G	Taft Kenneth	4	clerk	27	85 "
H	Murphy Agnes—†	4	housewife	42	here
K	Murphy William	4	machinist	42	"
L	Berretti Ella—†	4	housewife	44	"
M	Berretti Max	4	clerk	46	
N	Jackson Lillian—†	5	housewife	57	"
O	Jackson Owen	5	U S N	25	
P	Kamelis Anthony	5	machinist	57	"
R	Kamelis Edward	5	clerk	44	
S	Kamelis Emily—†	5	housewife	44	"
T	Gamble George	5	mechanic	24	"
U	Gamble Janet—†	5	housewife	22	"
V	Greeley Catherine—†	6	"	51	"
W	Greeley John	6	clerk	23	
X	Greeley Peter	6	U S N	20	"
Y	Greeley Sarah—†	6	clerk	22	"
Z	Greeley Thomas	6	mechanic	54	"

520

A	Sullivan Anna M—†	6	housewife	26	"
B	Sullivan Gerard	6	clerk	26	
C	Haley Eva—†	7	housewife	46	"
D	Haley David	7	painter	52	
E	Giangrande Pasquale	7	shipper	54	
F	Giangrande Sadie—†	7	housewife	29	"
G	Rabita Vincent	7	clerk	21	

13

Corliss Street—Continued

H	Turner Harold	7	retired	70	here
K	Turner Mary—†	7	housewife	70	"
L	Schiffer Bertha—†	9	"	31	"
M	Schiffer Sigwald	9	salesman	30	"
N	LeBlanc Edgar	9	mechanic	34	"
O	LeBlanc Estelle—†	9	housewife	32	"
P	Noumi Anthony	9	welder	28	74 Codman pk
R	Noumi Gertrude—†	9	housewife	28	74 "
S	Smith Effie—†	11	"	48	2888 Wash'n
T	Smith William	11	cook	51	2888 "
U	Kickham Hilda—†	11	housewife	34	here
V	Kickham Ralph	11	mechanic	40	"
W	Jameson Joy—†	11	clerk	25	"
X	Jameson Katherine—†	11	housewife	47	"

Dennison Street

Y	Cipriano Bessie—†	4	secretary	40	here
Z	Mirkin Mitchell	4	agent	46	"
	521				
A	Mirkin Vera B—†	4	housewife	36	"
B	Alpert Harry J	4	tester	41	"
C	Alpert Riva B—†	4	bookkeeper	38	"
D	Rubenstein Lisa—†	4	housewife	62	"
E	Rubenstein Louis	4	leatherworker	60	"
F	Feinzig Anna—†	5	housewife	25	"
G	Feinzig Leonard	5	accountant	28	"
H	Rabinowich Ella A—†	5	housewife	47	"
K	Rabinowich Isaac	5	accountant	49	"
L	*Casipit Felix S	6	engineer	44	398 Mass av
M	Casipit Mary J—†	6	housewife	28	398 "
N	Lichtman Anna—†	6	"	45	here
O	Lichtman Doris B—†	6	WAVE	21	"
P	Lichtman Israel	6	presser	47	"
R	Rubinowich Caroline—†	6	housewife	25	37 Robeson
S	Rubinowich William	6	lithographer	28	5 Dennison
T	Graglia Angelo C	7	mechanic	25	here
U	Graglia Eleanor—†	7	operator	29	"
V	Graglia Felix	7	laborer	66	"
W	Graglia Mary—†	7	clerk	26	"
X	Graglia Melinia—†	7	housewife	62	"

Dennison Street—Continued

	Y	Zimmerman Blanche—†	7	housewife	22	here
	z	Zimmerman Jerome	7	baker	24	"
522						
	A	Markham George F	8	advertising	34	3 Spruce
	B	Murdock Mildred—†	8	housewife	30	here
	C	Murdock William F	8	assembler	37	"
	D	McKinney Aubrey	8	electrician	33	"
	E	McKinney Eva—†	8	housewife	55	"
	F	McKinney Eva D—†	8	teacher	24	"
	G	McKinney George	8	clerk	26	"
	H	McKinney Jean—†	8	nurse	33	"
	K	Harrison George T	9	U S A	27	7 Auburn
	L	Lamm Lillian S—†	9	clerk	23	here
	M	Smith Hyman M	9	merchant	52	"
	N	Smith Mary R—†	9	housewife	52	"
	O	DaLomba Helen B—†	9	"	25	7 Auburn
	P*	DaLomba Joseph N	9	cook	45	7 "
	R	Harrison Olive C—†	9	housewife	53	7 "
	S	Ehrlich Josephine—†	9	seamstress	58	here
	T	Sheer Minnie H—†	10	housewife	48	5 Normandy
	U	Sheer Rubin	10	clerk	57	5 "
	V	Gruber Ethel—†	10	housewife	30	here
	W	Lefkowith Freida—†	10	"	32	"
	X	Lefkowith Max	10	agent	34	"
	Y	Sooper Ida—†	10	housewife	29	"
	z	Sooper Simon	10	salesman	31	"
523						
	A	Spillane Edna N—†	27	housewife	26	"
	B	Spillane John F	27	carpenter	27	"
	C	Smith Beatrice H—†	28	clerk	36	"
	D	Smith Charles H	28	shipper	42	
	E	Van Dernoot Anna—†	28	housewife	52	"
	F	Van Dernoot Morris L	28	merchant	49	"
	G	Van Dernoot Paul H	28	U S N	24	
	H	Markowitz Aura	28	technician	32	"
	K	Markowitz Sarah—†	28	housewife	33	"
	L	Croke Anna M—†	29	"	30	
	M	Croke Patrick F	29	engineer	46	"
	N	Hankard Edward J	29	salesman	33	126 Fellows
	O	Hankard Helen M—†	29	housewife	32	126 "
	P	Gerstein Lillian M—†	32	"	32	here

Page.	Letter.	FULL NAME.	Residence, Jan. 1, 1946.	Occupation.	Supposed Age.	Reported Residence, Jan. 1, 1945. Street and Number.

Dennison Street—Continued

R	Gerstein Manuel	32	merchant	33	here
S	Solov Benjamin	32	welder	61	"
T	Solov Harry	32	technician	30	"
U	Solov Pauline—†	32	housewife	57	"
V	Frank Abraham	32	U S A	23	
W	*Frank Lena—†	32	housewife	49	"
X	*Frank Louis	32	merchant	54	"
Y	Bergman Frances—†	32	housewife	37	"
Z	Bergman Jacob L	32	salesman	45	"
	524				
A	D'Entremont Ethel N—†	32	housewife	36	"
B	D'Entremont Theodore G	32	fisherman	41	"
C	Brown Celia—†	32	housewife	51	"
D	Brown Celia G—†	32	stenographer	22	18 Abbot
E	Brown Herbert S	32	U S A	22	here
F	Brown James A	32	merchant	51	"
G	Halpern Clara—†	32	housewife	58	"
H	Halpern Louis	32	salesman	60	"
K	Thompson Elizabeth A—†	35	cashier	62	"
L	Thompson Margaret A—†	35	domestic	61	"
M	Thompson Mary—†	35	housewife	76	"
N	Thompson Anna—†	35	"	58	
O	Thompson Arthur W	35	grocer	65	"
P	Wagner Emma R—†	36	housewife	75	"
R	Wagner Isiah E	36	retired	79	
S	Asmous Eugenia A—†	38	housewife	46	"
T	Asmous Vladimir C	38	librarian	54	"
U	*Toulinoff Elizabeth N—†	38	housewife	77	"

Dunford Street

V	David Julia A—†	1	housewife	65	here
W	David Oscar A	1	retired	71	"
X	David Satineg—†	1	clerk	37	"
Y	Carey Andrew	2	painter	70	
Z	Carey Andrew I	2	"	40	
	525				
A	Carey Anna B—†	2	clerk	34	
B	Cary James	2	"	29	
C	Carey Mary—†	2	housewife	72	"
D	Carey Mary—†	2	bookkeeper	41	"

Dunford Street—Continued

E	Priest Esmeralda—†	3	housewife	78	here
F	Priest Ruth A—†	3	bookkeeper	38	"
G	Kearns Lillian—†	3	"	26	"
H	Russell Andrew	3	mechanic	54	"
K	Russell Catherine—†	3	housewife	53	"
L	Harnett Francis T	4	auditor	50	
M	Harnett James F	4	U S N	23	
N	Harnett Mary E—†	4	housewife	50	"
O	Connolly Ellen—†	4	housekeeper	61	"
P	McLeod Dorothy E—†	4	housewife	25	"
R	McLeod Roderick D	4	clerk	33	
S	Egan Raymon W—†	6	housewife	34	"
T	Egan William M	6	proprietor	65	"
U	McBurney Madeline—†	6	clerk	34	
V	Fisher Henry	6	engineer	55	"
W	Fisher Margaret—†	6	housewife	47	"
X	Hagan Mary H—†	6	"	21	
Y	Hagan Oliver C	6	engineer	21	"

Elmore Park

Z	Powers Elsie—†	1	housewife	40	here
	526				
A	Powers John	1	chauffeur	40	"
B	Sweeney Dorothy—†	1	housewife	32	"
C	Sweeney John P	1	U S A	35	"
D	Jordan John J	1	laborer	38	"
E	Jordan Mary E—†	1	housewife	36	"
F	Cadlick Andrew	2	cutter	42	"
G	Cadlick Margaret—†	2	housewife	41	"
H	Maxwell Annie K—†	2	"	62	
K	Maxwell Thomas L	2	retired	62	
L	Maxwell Wallace R	2	technician	29	"
M	Fichtner Leatrice E—†	2	saleswoman	22	"
N	Fichtner Louis N	2	shipper	52	
O	Fichtner Loüis N, jr	2	laborer	22	
P	Fichtner Sarah M—†	2	stitcher	42	"
R	Giambo Josephine—†	3	housekeeper	39	"
S	McCormack Robert J	3	laborer	29	"
T	McCormack Ruth G—†	3	housewife	26	"

Page.	Letter.	FULL NAME.	Residence, Jan. 1, 1946.	Occupation.	Supposed Age.	Reported Residence, Jan. 1, 1945. Street and Number.

Elmore Park—Continued

U	Basta Joseph	3	presser	27	Cambridge
V	Basta Marion—†	3	housewife	24	"

Elmore Street

W	Clement Donald G	3	salesman	31	here
X	Clement Helen M—†	3	housewife	27	"
Y	Smith Agnes—†	3	"	25	"
Z	Smith Forrest F	3	engineer	28	"
	527				
A	Sosna Catherine—†	3	operator	21	"
B	Sosna Joseph	3	plumber	33	"
C	Sosna Mary M—†	3	clerk	33	
D	Sosna Pauline—†	3	housewife	57	"
E	Foley Margaret M—†	5	"	35	"
F	Foley Patrick	5	laborer	40	"
G	Bopp James F	5	salesman	22	8 Elmore
H	Bihl Alfred	5	chauffeur	59	here
K	Bihl Wilhelmina—†	5	housewife	64	"
L	Pinkul Adela N—†	9	"	31	"
M	Pinkul Gustav A	9	engineer	38	"
N	Ryan Ellen A—†	9	housewife	57	"
O	Ryan John	9	U S N	20	
P	Ryan Ruth—†	9	U S A	29	
R	*Janczanski Anna—†	9	housewife	50	"
S	Janczanski Bernard	9	U S A	24	
T	Janczanski Joseph	9	"	28	
U	*Janczanski Roman	9	laborer	52	
V	Janczanski Stella—†	9	saleswoman	20	"
W	Apsit Albert J	11	printer	28	"
X	Apsit Mathilda J—†	11	housewife	27	"
Y	Lekas Eva—†	11	"	59	
Z	Lekas Jacob	11	laborer	64	
	528				
A	Sieberg Frederick H	11	engineer	34	"
B	Sieberg Palmira E—†	11	housewife	30	"
C	Bozadjian Abraham	11	U S A	22	
D	Bozadjian Krikor	11	molder	54	
E	Bozadjian Sarkis	11	U S A	26	
F	Bozadjian Setrag	11	laborer	56	
G	Cunningham Anna—†	11	housewife	24	"

18

Elmore Street—Continued

H	Cunningham Richard	11	U S A	24	here
K	Maher Edward	13	laborer	40	40 Danube
L	McKeever Alice—†	13	housewife	68	13 Palmer
M	McKeever Arthur	13	chauffeur	38	13 "
N	Jordan Leo	13	U S A	26	here
O	Jordan Margaret—†	13	housewife	56	"
P	Thom Frances—†	13	"	25	"
R	Thom Horace	13	U S N	34	"
S	John Johanna—†	15	housewife	43	"
T	John Peter	15	molder	45	
U	Cushing Esther—†	15	housewife	56	"
V	Cushing Walter	15	retired	63	
W	Flynn William	15	chauffeur	53	"
X	MacLean Annie—†	15	housewife	40	"
Y	MacLean Elizabeth—†	15	"	79	
Z	Guisti Betty—†	17	housekeeper	30	"

529

A	Carey Bridget—†	17	housewife	75	"
B	Carey Patrick	17	retired	75	
C	Carey Terrance	17	painter	40	
E	Madden George	21	chauffeur	36	"
F	Madden Kathleen—†	21	housewife	27	"
G	Curris Charles D	21	shipper	38	55 Park Drive
H	Curris Helene J—†	21	housewife	28	55 "
K	Gates John H	21	laborer	62	here
L	Rumrill Lawrence G	21	"	38	"
M	Rumrill Phyllis G—†	21	housewife	30	"
N	Anctil Clarence	23	laborer	37	
O	Anctil Lillian—†	23	housewife	39	"
P	Foley Amanda L—†	23	"	51	
R	Foley Thomas M	23	laborer	58	
S	Kerr John A	23	"	32	
T	Kerr Mary A—†	23	housewife	58	"
U	Kerr William J	23	chauffeur	31	"
V	Campbell Mary A—†	29	housewife	47	"
W	Campbell William E	29	laborer	42	
X	*Senier Richard	29	retired	76	"
Y	Bean Arthur H	29	janitor	59	
Z	Bean Chester E	29	"	61	

530

A	Bean Lillian—†	29	clerk	26	

Elmore Street—Continued

B	Bean Nellie F—†	29	housewife	61	here
C	Dench Grace V—†	29	clerk	42	"
D	Russo Alice C—†	29	housewife	53	"
E	Russo Frank F	29	chauffeur	56	"
F	Gilman Mary K—†	31	housewife	64	"
G	Gilman Thomas S	31	operator	63	"
H	Amoling Louise E—†	31	housekeeper	59	"
K	Stabers John	31	U S N	35	"
L	Stabers Wallia B—†	31	housewife	26	"
M	McElroy Joseph H	31	retired	73	
N	Whittaker Dorothea A—†	31	clerk	20	
O	Whittaker Margaret T—†	31	housewife	48	"
P	Bentley Arthur D	33	U S N	24	
R	Bentley Helen—†	33	housewife	48	"
S	Bentley Irene—†	33	operator	22	"
T	Bentley John F	33	U S N	21	
U	Wagner Charles R	33	chauffeur	33	"
V	Wagner Frederick W	33	laborer	69	
W	Wagner James F	33	"	37	
X	Wagner Mary E—†	33	housewife	65	"
Y	Piotrowicz Alexander	33	baker	35	
Z	Piotrowicz Helena—†	33	housewife	33	"

531

A	McCarthy Katherine—†	35	clerk	26	
B	McCarthy Margaret—†	35	saleswoman	25	"
C	McCarthy Mary A—†	35	housewife	63	"
D	McCarthy Michael J	35	retired	65	
E	Corrigan Helen V—†	35	operator	44	"
F	Corrigan Margaret—†	35	housewife	65	"
G	McCusker Eleanor A—†	35	bookkeeper	21	"
H	McCusker John	35	salesman	52	"
K	McCusker Margaret C—†	35	housewife	47	"
L	McCusker Mary M—†	35	bookkeeper	22	"
M	Wylie Beatrice—†	39	housewife	37	115 Dale
N	Wylie Ernest	39	salesman	42	115 "
O	Moore Edwin A	41	"	57	here
P	Moore Edwin A, jr	41	U S A	27	"
R	Moore Mabelle F—†	41	housewife	57	"
S	Moore William W	41	U S A	22	"
T	St Lawrence John	41	laborer	38	Chelsea
U	Washington Bessie M—†	41	housewife	44	here

Elmore Street—Continued

v	Washington Henry F	41	mechanic	23	here
w	Bradley Anna—†	43	housekeeper	42	"
x	Brothers Stanley	43	laborer	41	Cambridge
y	Skeeter Huron	43	porter	51	here
z	Carney Anne—†	45	social worker	58	51 Elmore

532

a	Searle Lilly—†	45	bookkeeper	42	here
b	Sedlin Charles	45	carpenter	56	"
c	Sedlin Elizabeth—†	45	housewife	46	"
d	Payne John	47	retired	70	15 Wellington
e	Thomas Ethel—†	47	housewife	51	15 "
f	Thomas Manza	47	porter	53	15 "
g	West Dorothy—†	47	secretary	29	New York
h	Gillis Alexander	47	U S A	21	here
k	Gillis Daniel	47	carpenter	47	"
l	Gillis Margaret—†	47	housewife	48	"
m	Riley Gastrel	49	plumber	60	"
n	Riley Ruth E—†	49	housewife	51	"
o	Calvin Arthur	49	clerk	39	7 Wellington
p	Calvin Doris—†	49	housewife	36	7 "
r	Guilford Margaret—†	49	"	24	here
s	Guilford Richard	49	laborer	25	"
t	Prentice Ernest	51	buffer	35	Malden
u	Prentice Grace—†	51	housewife	30	109 Harrishof
v	Prentice Leonard	51	clerk	32	109 "
w	Prentice Mattie—†	51	housewife	63	Malden
x	Prentice Thelma—†	51	"	31	"
y	MacInnes Gladys—†	51	"	32	here
z	MacInnes William H	51	clerk	40	"

533   Fenner Street

a	LaBrecque Fred A	1	porter	48	745 Tremont
b	LaBrecque Marion B—†	1	housewife	37	745 "
c	Logan Claire—†	1		24	here
d	Logan Frank	1	chauffeur	27	"
e	Buzzell Thelma—†	7	jeweler	21	"
f	Gary Odessa—†	7	presser	39	
g	Gary Richard	7	laborer	20	"
h	Petroski Irene—†	7	at home	21	"
k	Petroski Paul P	7	laborer	42	"

Fenner Street—Continued

L	Petroski Peter	7	cleaner	44	here
M	Ploof Margaret—†	7	assembler	29	"
N	Haight Marie—†	7	at home	23	"
O	Lanouette Charles F	7	U S N	23	
P	Lanouette Louisa—†	7	housewife	22	"
R	Strand Angeline—†	16	"	29	
S	Strand Floyd	16	chauffeur	28	"
T	Chamberlain Elizabeth H–†	16	housewife	32	"
U	Chamberlain William H	16	electrician	36	"
V	Cleary Helen—†	18	domestic	52	"
W	Robinson Mary—†.	18	housekeeper	33	"

Haley Street

X	Golden Louis	1	metalworker	48	here
Y	Golden Sadie R—†	1	housewife	45	"
Z	Imbrogna Lillian—†	5	"	37	"

534

A	Imbrogna Pasquale	5	barber	42	
B	Harris Fannie W—†	6	housewife	45	"
C	Harris Henry D	6	janitor	47	
D	Harris Henry J	6	laborer	25	
E	Harris Sally—†	6	teacher	22	"
F	Mason Luoneal	6	clerk	37	
G	Mason Mildred—†	6	housewife	37	"
H	Quarles Lorenzo	6	waiter	35	
K	Quarles Margaret—†	6	housewife	35	"
L	Coleman Estelle R—†	7	"	24	
M	Coleman Leona J—†	7	student	21	"
N	Coleman Luella B—†	7	housewife	49	"
O	Coleman Ralph M	7	actor	47	
P	Coleman Riche J	7	social worker	27	"
R	Williams Mae A—†	7	housewife	22	"
S	Cummings Esther B—†	7	draftsman	35	"
T	Spencer James L	7	physician	42	New York
U	Spencer Rita E—†	7	housewife	41	"
V	Stoney Pauline E	7	retired	82	"
W	Naiman Isadore S	8	pharmacist	32	here
X	Naiman Miriam—†	8	housewife	29	"
Y	Naiman Bertha—†	8	"	56	"
Z	Naiman Melvin S	8	U S A	24	

535
Haley Street—Continued

A	Naiman Raphael	8	merchant	60	here
B	Naiman Robert	8	U S N	25	Springfield
C	Naiman Rose—†	8	nurse	24	"
D	Lindsey Archibald L	9	decorator	50	here
E	Lindsey Ruth D—†	9	housewife	43	"
F	Anderson Christine—†	9	"	70·	"
G	Anderson Evelyn I—†	9	secretary	30	. "
H	Burgess Gertrude H—†	9	bookkeeper	28	"

Harrishof Street

K	Hoole Charles W	167	mechanic	59	here
L	McKinney John D	167	agent	30	"
M	McKinney Marguerite V–†	167	housewife	26	"

Rochdale Street

N	Robery Daniel	2	welder	59	50 Savin
O	Robery Daniel	2	"	37	50 "
P	Walker Olivia K—†	2	housekeeper	61	50 "
R	Murphy Christine M—†	2	housewife	37	here
S	Murphy Peter R	2	chauffeur	40	"
V	Davis Louis	2	retired	58	"
T	Harris Allan A	2	expeditor	59	"
U	Harris Helen F—†	2	housewife	55	"
W	Melville Earle	4	musician	30	"
X	Morrissey Mary—†	4	nurse	48	
Y	Donofrio Anthony	4	plasterer	25	"
Z	Donofrio Mary—†	4	housewife	23	"

536

A	Mann George F	4	U S A	30	
B	Mann Mary A—†	4	housewife	27	"
C	Tatum James	5	proprietor	36	"
D	Tatum Thelma—†	5	housewife	35	"
E	Busby Golburn	5	machinist	55	"
F	Busby Ottilie—†	5	housewife	42	"
G	Harrison Anita—†	5	"	40	
H	Harrison John M	5	printer	36	"
K	West Anna—†	6	housewife	24	Maine
L	West Paul	6	clergyman	36	"

Rochdale Street—Continued

M	MacLean Hilda—†	6	housekeeper	55	here
N	Norris Joseph	6	retired	91	"
O	Hodkvist Anna C—†	6	at home	76	"
P	Rasmussen Anna D—†	6	housekeeper	42	"
R	Rogers Aubrey	8	welder	26	··
S	Rogers Elsie—†	8	housewife	23	"
T	Cutter George J	8	metalworker	56	"
U	Cutter Sadie B—†	8	hostess	61	
V	Malloy Agnes—†	8	housewife	30	"
W	Malloy William	8	boilermaker	33	"
X	Reid Dora—†	9	housewife	38	"
Y	Reid Harry	9	welder	39	
Z	Chace Robert	11	chauffeur	23	"

537

A	Chace Ruth—†	11	housewife	22	"
B	King Charles	15	chauffeur	46	··
C	Prout Arthur B	15	janitor	65	":
D	Prout Viola B—†	15	housewife	51	"
E	Lewis Floyd	17	chauffeur	31	182 Northampt
F	Lewis Margaret—†	17	housewife	34	182 "

Townsend Street

G	Burroughs Edith N—†	8	housewife	52	here
H	Burroughs George A	8	caretaker	56	"
K	Burns Maude—†	8	at home	66	"
L	McNair James L	8	machinist	43	"
M	McNair Margaret G—†	8	housewife	32	"
N	McKenna James	8	mason	56	
O	McKenna James E	8	clerk	27	
P	McKenna Margaret C—†	8	at home	29	··
R	McKenna William E	8	U S A	22	
S	Riley Fergus A	8	starter	53	
T	Riley Florence L—†	8	stenographer	22	"
U	Riley John B	8	operator	31	"
V	Riley Mary D—†	8	timekeeper	25	"
W	Riley Mary R—†	8	housewife	53	"
X	Hayes Rose B—†	8	"	33	
Y	Hayes Vincent	8	engineer	41	"
Z	Hannon Ellen—†	11	housewife	40	"

538
Townsend Street—Continued

A	Hannon Leonard	11	attendant	43	here
B	Audrey Annie—†	14	shoeworker	61	"
C	Audrey Charles	14	iceman	57	"
D	Cowley Johanna—†	14	housewife	35	"
E	Cowley Patrick C	14	fisherman	41	"
F	Dunphy Flora E—†	14	housewife	40	"
G	Dunphy Raymond E	14	mechanic	42	"
H	French George A	14	salesman	67	Malden
K	French Josephine R—†	14	at home	67	here
L	Parker Selma E—†	14	housewife	43	"
M	Parker Weston W	14	rigger	45	"
N	Fougere Albert J	14	mechanic	36	"
O	Whitley Dorothy F—†	14	seamstress	61	"
P	Keane John L	14	retired	46	
R	Booth Alice—†	15	at home	68	"
S	Booth Anna S—†	15	operator	49	"
T	Marsh John H	15	janitor	71	
U	Gross Dora—†	19	stitcher	50	
V	Gross Matthew	19.	shipper	50	
W	Kelly Catherine M—†	19	clerk	20	
X	Kelly Christina T—†	19	tel operator	30	"
Y	Kelly James F	19	machinist	35	"
Z	Kelly Joseph P	19	U S A	33	

539

A	Kelly Mary A—†	19	housewife	66	"
B	Kelly Paul A	19	printer	25	"
C	Kelly Phillip J	19	machinist	23	"
D	Kelly Rose M—†	19	clerk	36	"
E	Kelly Veronica C—†	19	chemist	28	"
F	Brigham Gladys E—†	23	housewife	40	"
G	Brigham James E	23	accountant	35	"
H	Michaels Dorothy V—†	23	presser	20	"
K	Moccia Angelo G	23	electrician	56	"
L	Moccia Ella C—†	23	housewife	56	"
M	Moccia Emma—†	23	presser	24	"
N	Moccia Marie M—†	23	"	24	
O	Jordan George L	27	draftsman	48	"
P	Jordan Irene A—†	27	housewife	45	"
R	Dacey Theresa A—†	27	director	67	"
S	McCann Cecelia M—†	27	at home	75	"

Townsend Street—Continued

T	Barrows Adassa—†	28	housewife	41	here
U	Barrows Conrad	28	supt	41	"
V	Gray Arthur	30	machinist	30	"
W	Gray Eunice A—†	30	at home	27	"
X	Smith Dagmar L—†	30	housewife	46	"
Y	Smith James L	30	machinist	47	"
Z	Smith Mildred B—†	30	at home	21	"

540

A	Sweeney Gertrude M—†	31	housewife	40	"
B	Sweeney Lawrence T	31	electrician	39	"
C	Gour Kathleen—†	31	housewife	35	"
D	Gour William	31	inspector	35	"
E	Millett Mildred M—†	31	tracer	35	
F	Linehan Gertrude—†	35	operator	40	"
G	Linehan Katherine E—†	35	housewife	37	"
H	Linehan William J	35	U S N	37	"
K	Rogers Hortense J—†	35	housewife	27	"
L	Thebado Charles H	35	grinder	68	
M	Thebado Charles O	35	machinist	34	"
N	Thebado Ernest A	35	chauffeur	33	"
O	Thebado Mary—†	35	housewife	33	"
P	Brown Christina A—†	44	at home	76	"
R	Brown Wanda F—†	44	housewife	37	"
S	Brown William H	44	machinist	40	"
T	Young Irene R—†	44	operator	21	"
U	Young Isabella—†	44	housewife	40	"
V	Young James	44	laborer	41	"
W	Abramovitz David	45	tailor	78	42 Intervale
X	Abrams Rebecca—†	45	at home	73	Chelsea
Y	*Baker Rebecca—†	45	"	72	here
Z	Barres Eli	45	presser	79	"

541

A	*Belston Joseph	45	laborer	70	
B	Berger Minnie—†	45	at home	65	"
C	Berlin Flora—†	45	"	68	33 Wenonah
D	Berman Simon	45	merchant	74	Lynn
E	*Berson Eva—†	45	at home	77	Quincy
F	*Brown Hilda—†	45	"	75	11 Mt Hood rd
G	*Brown Sarah—†	45	"	69	71 Phillips
H	Butkovitz Philip	45	furrier	55	Malden
K	Chaskelson Mamie—†	45	at home	68	Chelsea

Townsend Street—Continued

L	Cohen Abram	45	tailor	81	45 Dover
M	*Devore Gertrude—†	45	domestic	54	here
N	Dores Andre	45	machinist	39	"
O	*Epstein Fannie—†	45	at home	75	154 Chambers
P	Ernst Lilly—†	45	"	64	here
¹R	*Fine Minnie—†	45	"	63	9 Balsam
S	*Finkel Sarah—†	45	"	69	here
T	Frank Annie—†	45	housewife	59	Revere
U	Frank Phoebe—†	45	at home	75	Cambridge
V	*Freedman Rebecca—†	45	"	· 67	here
W	Friedenberg Sarah—†	45	"	69	Brookline
X	Gabriel Morris	45	salesman	63	15 Richfield
Y	*Gabriel Rachael—†	45	at home	72	here
Z	Gale Simon	45	mechanic	77	46A Cheney

542

A	*Geltman Minnie—†	45	at home	62	here
C	*Gitstein Aaron	45	retired	50	"
D	*Glassman Nathan	45	baker	73	"
E	Glazer Rebecca—†	45	at home	66	"
F	Glick Anna—†	45	domestic	46	"
G	Golden Simon	45	caterer	77	"
H	*Guralnick Sarah—†	45	housewife	57	"
K	Harrison Hyman	45	contractor	89	"
L	*Hill Annie—†	45	housewife	66	"
M	Hoffman Sarah—†	45	nurse	56	
N	Hollander Jessie—†	45	housewife	44	"
O	*Hullman Abraham	45	rabbi	81	
P	*Indeck Bessie R—†	45	housewife	68	"
R	*Isenberg William	45	laborer	68	
S	*Kittner Jacob	45	retired	80	
T	Koplovitz Lena—†	45	at home	74	"
U	Lander Sadie—†	45	domestic	48	899 Morton
V	Learner Dora—†	45	clerk	42	here
W	Levine Harry	45	machinist	48	"
X	Levine Samuel	45	carpenter	65	"
Y	Levy Abraham	45	tailor	67	"
Z	*Licht Jacob	45	cutter	54	127 Howland

543

A	*Masse Jacob	45	salesman	65	1619 Com av
B	*Mazzin Morris	45	expressman	71	here
C	Raitman Samuel	45	shoeworker	66	"

Page.	Letter.	FULL NAME.	Residence, Jan. 1, 1946.	Occupation.	Supposed Age.	Reported Residence, Jan. 1, 1945. Street and Number.

Townsend Street—Continued

D	Resnick Max	45	tailor	61	here
E	*Rosenthal Hyman	45	"	73	"
F	Rubenstein Harry	45	salesman	67	"
G	Rudman Nimon	45	junk dealer	82	Everett
H	Rutherford Celia—†	45	domestic	34	125 Ruthven
K	Sarver Rose—†	45	at home	55	here
L	Schacher Eva—†	45	"	75	"
M	Schwartz Pearl—†	45	"	71	Chelsea
N	*Schwartz Rose—†	45	"	75	31 Leston
O	*Sherman Jennie—†	45	domestic	60	here
P	*Sidel Solomon	45	tailor	69	"
R	*Singer Sarah—†	45	at home	73	Revere
S	Slanger David	45	merchant	64	here
T	Slobodkin Frances—†	45	domestic	43	"
U	Solomon Joseph	45	druggist	60	Brookline
V	Spin Isaac	45	capmaker	82	374 Harrison av
W	Stroyman Maurice	45	retired	67	here
X	Tappan Henry	45	baker	52	"
Y	*Tatelman Carl	45	coppersmith	68	"
Z	*Tobin Etta—†	45	domestic	64	Chelsea

544

A	Trilling Etta—†	45	clerk	56	here
B	*Walter Morris	45	janitor	76	"
C	*Weinstein Eva—†	45	operator	40	534 Blue Hill av
D	Ritchie George S	46	machinist	34	here
E	*Ritchie Jean A—†	46	housewife	30	"
F	Varnerin Emma M—†	47	physician	40	"
G	Varnerin Frank S	47	manager	38	"
H	Varnerin Helen F—†	47	housewife	33	"
K	Varnerin Henry P	47	manager	46	"
L	Varnerin Ida E—†	47	clerk	41	
M	Varnerin William J	47	mechanic	34	"
N	Swerling Arthur	50	clerk	28	
O	Swerling Ethel—†	50	housewife	26	"
P	Hartman Evelyn—†	50	"	30	
R	Hartman George	50	salesman	31	"
S	Himmel Dora—†	50	housewife	55	"
T	Himmel Harold D	50	U S C G	24	"
U	Himmel Israel	50	fitter	55	
V	Kennedy Francis J	50	U S N	26	

Townsend Street—Continued

Page.	Letter.	FULL NAME.	Residence, Jan. 1, 1946.	Occupation.	Supposed Age.	Reported Residence, Jan. 1, 1945. Street and Number.
	w	Kennedy Lena M—†	50	housewife	23	here
	x	Kasin Ruth A—†	52	beautician	32	"
	y	Kasin Sydney A	52	mechanic	33	"
	z	Weiner David	52	bartender	33	"
545						
	a	Weiner Gertrude—†	52	nurse	29	
	b	Weiner Marcia M—†	52	housewife	34	"
	c	Feldman Isaac	52	stitcher	57	
	d	Feldman Rose—†	52	stenographer	29	"
	e	Feldman Sydney	52	photographer	27	"
	f	Baker David	52	tailor	47	"
	g	Etique Georgette—†	54	clerk	45	
	h	Grebe William	54	mechanic	45	"
	k	Walter Elizabeth—†	54	housewife	44	"
	l	Walter Henry A	54	engineer	52	"
	m	*Epstein Rose—†	58	housewife	72	"
	n	Epstein Samuel N	58	retired	73	
	o	Horowitz Celia—†	58	housewife	51	"
	p	Horowitz Louis J	58	cleaner	51	
	r	Horowitz Myer G	58	student	21	
	s	Penn Esther—†	58	housewife	45	"
	t	Penn Phillip R	58	clerk	48	
	u	Anderson Ada M—†	60	housewife	48	"
	v	Hooks Alexander C	60	chef	53	
	w	Lamb Dorothy—†	60	domestic	33	"
	x	Medley Earl	60	porter	50	
	y	Richardson Thomas R	60	machinist	49	"
	z	Tillery Elizabeth—†	60	domestic	52	"
546						
	a	Williams Estelle—†	60	"	37	
	b	Randolph Austin L	67	U S A	23	
	c	Randolph Effie M—†	67	stitcher	48	
	d	Randolph Marion B—†	67	welder	26	"
	e	Randolph Ralph C	67	chipper	51	"
	f	Lane James T	67	patternmaker	27	"
	g	Lane John T	67	attorney	45	"
	h	Lane Ruth M—†	67	housewife	42	"
	k	Lane Ruth M—†	67	student	21	
	l	Pugatch Gertrude--†	71	housewife	33	"
	m	Pugatch Henry J	71	laundryman	35	"

Townsend Street—Continued

N	Goldberg Aaron	71	roofer	49	here
o	Goldberg Fannie—†	71	housewife	47	"
P	Goldberg Harriet—†	71	operator	26	"

Walnut Avenue

R	Hosten Mabel R.—†	221	housewife	58	here
s	Hosten Steadford R	221	seaman	68	"
T	Phillibert Cuthbert E	221	physician	40	"
U	Phillibert Marjorie P—†	221	housewife	33	"
V	Freeman George W	221A	court officer	56	"
W	Freeman Josephine T—†	221A	housewife	58	"
X	Williams Conover	221A	laborer	49	
Y	Williams Louise—†	221A	housewife	57	"
z	Council Elsie—†	223	domestic	49	"

547

A	Ruffin Rosalia—†	223	"	50	"
B	Moore Corinne D—†	223A	housewife	29	Alabama
c	Moore Walter E	223A	clerk	28	"
D	Avery Blanche E—†	223A	beautician	36	here
E	Avery George	223A	butcher	37	"
F	Hughes Rosalie—†	225	stitcher	43	"
G	Roberts Erskine C	225A	retired	71	"
H	Roberts Lillian M—†	225A	clerk	37	
K	Roberts Ruth H—†	225A	housewife	53	"
L	Whiting Ella—†	225A	domestic	63	"
M	Corey Michael J	227	merchant	25	"
N	*Corey Sadie—†	227	housewife	51	"
o	Corey Sideed J	227	painter	63	
P	Grossman Ida—†	227A	housewife	67	"
R	Grossman Jacob	227A	retired	69	
s	Gordon Etta—†	227A	housewife	49	"
T	Gordon Samuel	227A	carpenter	53	"
U	Brown Rosanna—†	237	at home	72	"
V	Cox James	237	retired	76	
W	Crowley Mary A—†	237	nurse	32	"
X	Cummings Duncan	237	retired	70	756 Tremont
Y	Cunningham Elizabeth-†	237	at home	77	here
z	Doherty John	237	retired	78	"

548

A	Field Margaret—†	237	at home	80	93 Sedgwick

Page.	Letter.	FULL NAME.	Residence, Jan. 1, 1946.	Occupation.	Supposed Age.	Reported Residence, Jan. 1, 1945. Street and Number.

Walnut Avenue—Continued

	B	Finneran Thomas	237	retired	86	here
	C	Gallagher Edward	237	"	70	"
	D	Griffin Hyland	237	laborer	60	"
	E	Hallaren Mary T—†	237	nurse	22	241 Walnut av
	F	Heanue William	237	retired	80	here
	G	Henderson Ellen—†	237	attendant	64	30 Newbern
	H	Hinds Helen—†	237	nurse	25	here
	K	Hogan John	237	retired	68	"
	L	Hurley Michael	237	"	82	"
	M	Keane Daniel	237	"	82	
	N	Logan Margaret—†	237	nurse	59	
	O	MacKillip Kenneth	237	retired	76	
	P	McManus James	237	"	81	"
	R	McQuaid Margaret—†	237	at home	67	131 Pembroke
	S	Quigley David	237	retired	78	here
	T	Ross Thomas	237	"	74	"
	U	*Sarno Louis	237	"	82	"
	V	Semenza Sabato	237		75	
	W	Spring Harry	237	"	75	"
	X	Webster Elizabeth—†	237	at home	79	"
	Y	*Aikens Elizabeth—†	241	"	70	11 Elm Hill pk
	Z	Bournazos Gregory	241	retired	65	18 Bulfinch

549

	A	Brett John	241		89	here
	B	Callahan Timothy	241	"	83	"
	C	Collyer Edwin	241		79	"
	D	Crane Thomas	241	"	74	"
	E	Davis Bertha—†	241	at home	79	"
	F	DeShon Leona—†	241	"	59	9 Caulfield
	G	Domigan Frederick	241	retired	69	here
	H	Flynn Elizabeth—†	241	at home	81	"
	K	Hallaran Jeremiah A	241	architect	56	"
	L	Hallaran Rose M—†	241	proprietor	62	"
	M	Hanlon Mary—†	241	at home	82	"
	N	Hannon Annie—†	241	"	83	
	O	Henry Myrtle—†	241	domestic	68	"
	P	Leonard Elizabeth—†	241	at home	84	"
	R	Madden Mary—†	241	"	69	"
	S	Masionis Julius	241	retired	76	17 O
	T	McCleave Mary—†	241	at home	79	6 Atherstone
	U	McSweeney Dennis	241	retired	77	here

Page.	Letter.	Full Name.	Residence, Jan. 1, 1946.	Occupation.	Supposed Age.	Reported Residence, Jan. 1, 1945. Street and Number.

Walnut Avenue—Continued

v	Miskelly Prudence—†	241	retired	80	here
w	Murphy Ellen—†	241	at home	78	"
x	O'Brien Michael	241	retired	72	85 Warren av
y	Parker Mary—†	241	at home	83	here
z	Posner Marian—†	241	"	73	"

550

A	Quigley Anna—†	241		76	"
B	Rosenberg Matilda—†	241	"	59	"
C	Shine Daniel J	241	retired	89	
D	Thayer Mary—†	241	at home	63	"
E	Ward George	241	retired	69	"
F	Warren Alfred	241	"	84	118 Hemenway
G	Lamont Joseph J	247	janitor	41	here
H	Lamont Margaret R—†	247	housewife	36	"
K	Richman Bedelle—†	247	"	22	Florida
L	Richman Charles K	247	jeweler	28	here
M	*Richman Helen—†	247	housewife	47	"
N	*Richman Leo	247	retired	50	"
O	Linsky Beatrice—†	247	housewife	40	"
P	Linsky Chester	247	U S A	21	
R	Linsky Leonard	247	"	24	
S	Linsky Louis	247	salesman	50	"
T	Scherer Albert	247	"	40	
U	Scherer Lillian—†	247	bookkeeper	38	"
V	Rabinovitz Max	247	agent	55	"
W	Rabinovitz Thelma A—†	247	housewife	46	"
X	Cohen Israel	247	merchant	50	"
Y	Cohen Lillian—†	247	housewife	45	"
Z	Sacks Celia—†	247	"	52	

551

A	Sacks Jacob	247	merchant	49	"
B	Shapiro Dora—†	247	housewife	51	11 Waldren rd
C	Shapiro Morris	247	tailor	58	11 "
D	Lang Harman	247	shoeworker	37	here
E	Lang Nellie—†	247	housewife	30	"
F	Sandler Ben	247	merchant	45	"
G	Sandler Sarah—†	247	housewife	36	"
H	*Zisken Esther—†	247	"	70	
K	Zisken Hyman	247	retired	70	
L	Fox Celia C—†	247	housewife	28	"
M	Fox Sidney H	247	pharmacist	31	"

Walnut Avenue—Continued

N	Kushner Anna—†	247	housewife	42	here
o	Kushner Joseph	247	manufacturer	45	"
P	Cohen Jennie—†	247	housewife	50	"
. R	Sawyer Fanny—†	255	"	66	
s	Sawyer James	255	agent	68	
T	Milgram Aaron	255	electrician	26	"
u	Milgram Ida E—†	255	housewife	26	"
v	Wald Jennie—†	255	"	62	
w	Wald Louis	255	tailor	67	"
x	Goren Frances—†	255	housewife	26	Salem
y	Goren Sydney	255	salesman	29	
z	Bell Henry J	273	U S A	28	169 Townsend

552

A	Bell Viola—†	273	stitcher	27	169 "
B	Jones Benjamin	273	U S A	27	169 '
c	Jones Elizabeth—†	273	stitcher	22	169 "
D	Warren Mary—†	273	housewife	28	here
E	Warren Paul	273	laborer	30	"
F	Young Gertrude—†	273	welder	49	"
G	Jigarjian Annie—†	275	clerk	20	250 Walnut av
H	Santucci Anthony G	275	U S M C	27	Lynn
K	Santucci Nevart R—†	275	housewife	24	"
L	Fritz Herman H·	275	electrician	32	here
M	Fritz Vivian H—†	275	housewife	29	" "
N	Godfrey Elsie G—†	275	"	28	91 Harrishof
o	Godfrey William F	275	painter	25	91 "
P	Berenberg Bella—†	275A	WAVE	28	here
R	Berenberg Joseph	275A	merchant	63	"
s	Berenberg Leah—†	275A	housewife	60	"
T	Ehrlich Gertrude W—†	275A	stitcher	27	24 Homestead
u	Ehrlich Hans	275A	cutter	28	24 "
v	Berry Bertha L—†	277	housewife	42	139 Harrishof
w	Berry Ernest O	277	clerk	54	139 "
x	Murphy Marie—†	277	shipfitter	36	139 "
Y	Price Arthur J	277	porter	53	139 "
z	Robinson Nellie B—†	277	social worker	30	139 "

553

A	Keay Katherine T—†	277A	operator	21	here
B	Shea Helen M—†	277A	"	41	"
c	Shea Mary A—†	277A	guard	22	"
D	Sheridan Helen F—†	277A	housewife	20	"

Walnut Avenue—Continued

E	Sheridan Joseph P	277A	student	22	here
F	Andelman Evelyn M—†	279	housewife	30	"
G	Andelman Manuel	279	merchant	33	"
H	Green Edward M	279	electrician	29	"
K	Green Shirley R—†	279	housewife	26	"
L	Metcalf Charles	279	merchant	65	"
M	Metcalf Jennie—†	279	stitcher	60	
P	Cuzzens Lorena M—†	283	secretary	43	"
N	Shaw Anna P—†	283	housewife	54	"
O	Shaw Clarence F	283	embalmer	54	"
R	Yates Everett C	283	teacher	50	
S	Yates Thelma M—†	283	housewife	40	"
T	Wharton Harriet B—†	285	teacher	45	
V	Tynes Alfred C	287	realtor	45	
W	Tynes Dorothy E—†	287	housewife	44	"
X	Tynes Dorothy E—†	287	teacher	22	"
Y	Tynes Timothy G	287	clerk	49	
Z	Tynes Virginia F—†	287	housewife	45	"

554

A	Douglas Bessie A—†	289	"	43	
B	Douglas Steven A	289	clerk	48	
C	Hathaway Julia A—†	289	at home	61	
D	Nelson Lulu E—†	289	domestic	45	"
E	Averett Katherine—†	291	at home	67	
F	Holt George E	291	waiter	54	
G	Holt Mary F—†	291	housewife	37	"
H	Lauretano Vera E—†	291	teacher	21	
K	McAdoo Gladys A—†	291	clerk	42	
L	McAdoo Martha G—†	291	student	20	

Washington Street

M	Carter Morris	2818	laborer	32	here
N	Carter Phyllis—†	2818	housewife	20	Illinois
O	Methot Armand G	2818	U S A	22	here
P	Methot Elsie M—†	2818	housewife	29	"
R	Methot Joseph	2818	machinist	57	"
S	Methot Lavina—†	2818	housewife	55	"
T	Methot Omar D	2818	jeweler	32	
Y	*Parone Mary—†	2820A	housewife	76	"
Z	Parone Pasquale	2820A	agent	34	

34

555
Washington Street—Continued

B	Crisp Edward T	2822	U S N	21	here
C	Egan Catherine—†	2822	at home	42	"
D	McRae Joseph P	2822	clerk	42	"
E	McRae Margaret M—†	2822	operator	43	"
F	Owens Paul T	2822	U S N	36	
G	Owens Susan E—†	2822	clerk	41	
H	Kelley Florence N—†	2822	waitress	53	"
L	Williams Phichol C	2826	laborer	24	59 Rockland
M	Johnson Farrington D	2826	seaman	31	here
N	Johnson Margaret—†	2826	domestic	37	43 Elmore
O	Johnson Margaret L—†	2826	housewife	63	Cambridge
P	Shavers Inez E—†	2826	"	28	"
R	Shavers Robert F	2826	U S N	29	here
S	Mahar Helen—†	2828	saleswoman	55	"
T	Stanley Arthur	2828	mechanic	63	"
U	Vaughan Mary L—†	2828	at home	48	"
V	Thomas Flora S—†	2828	housewife	32	65 Bower
W	Thomas Percy L	2828	U S N	39	here
X	Washington Dorothea L—†	2828	housewife	20	32 Humboldt **av**

556

A	Cotton Barbara N—†	2842	"	35	here
B	Cotton Laura M—†	2842	"	64	"
C	Cotton Robert T	2842	manager	37	"
D	Billings Eleanor Y—†	2842	secretary	48	"
E	Billings Walter F	2842	proprietor	45	"
F	Rehm William J	2870	clerk	49	9 Kenney
G	Douglas Ellen F—†	2888	housewife	29	14 Edgeworth
H	*Douglas John W	2888	mechanic	25	35 Hunt'n av
K	Curtis Agnes C—†	2888	seamstress	38	985 Col av
L	Curtis Albert L	2888	seaman	20	985 "
M	Mack Gladys M—†	2888	housewife	25	S Carolina
N	Mack Leggett	2888	machinist	25	Wash'n D C
O	Ware Beatrice—†	2890	housewife	49	45 Waumbeck
P	Ware Daniel	2890	chauffeur	49	45 "
R	Daum Arthur J	2890	laborer	38	2894 Wash'n
S	Duncanson Frederick W	2890	"	51	2894 "
T	Duncanson Lulu—†	2890	housewife	40	2894 "
U	Duncanson William T	2890	U S A	21	here
V	Natorp Herman E	2890	machinist	51	"
	Natorp Sisley M—†	2890	packer	53	"

Page.	Letter.	FULL NAME.	Residence, Jan. 1, 1946.	Occupation.	Supposed Age.	Reported Residence, Jan. 1, 1945. Street and Number.

Washington Street—Continued

	x	Moroney Agnes—†	2892	laundress	45	here
	y	Moroney Mary V—†	2892	secretary	21	"
	z	*Twohig Bridie A—†	2892	at home	54	"
557						
	a	Twohig James J	2892	U S A	23	"
	b	Twohig John A	2892	laborer	29	
	c	Donovan Alice—†	2892	housewife	45	"
	d	Donovan Alice—†	2892	operator	28	"
	e	Donovan Francis H	2892	chauffeur	32	"
	f	Donovan Vincent S	2892	laborer	33	"
	g	Estabrooks Elizabeth T—†	2894	housewife	29	Springfield
	h	Estabrooks Norman H	2894	baker	35	"
	k	McKenzie Alexander F	2894	operator	43	here
	l	*McKenzie Cecelia H—†	2894	housewife	37	"
	m	Ouellette Alice R—†	2894	"	38	"
	n	Ouellette Joseph B	2894	painter	41	
	p	*Jamieson Mary A—†	2898	at home	59	
	r	*Jamieson Sydney J	2898	laborer	59	
	s	Little Mary E—†	2898	housewife	27	"
	t	Little William D	2898	U S N	33	
	u	Memos James J	2898	waiter	47	"
	v	Memos Mary M—†	2898	housewife	45	"
	x	Methot Florence H—†	2928	"	30	
	y	Methot William L	2928	chauffeur	29	"
	z	Rockwell Annie J—†	2928	housewife	77	"
558						
	a	Rockwell William H	2928	retired	75	
	b	Bowlen Robert E	2928	electrician	40	"
	c	Geelin Margaret M—†	2928	domestic	54	71 Bickford
	d	Falter Ellen T—†	2930	housewife	40	Needham
	e	Falter John P	2930	chauffeur	41	"
	f	Falter Norma M—†	2930	saleswoman	20	"
	g	Yatt Alfred	2930	laborer	45	Rhode Island
	h	Yatt Florence M—†	2930	housewife	44	"
	k	Keegan John F	2930	welder	37	12 Flagg
	l	Keegan Letitia—†	2930	housewife	32	12 "
	m	Christensen Jean E—†	2932	operator	28	6 Marcella
	n	Witham George W	2932	U S A	38	here
	o	Witham Mary M—†	2932	cook	68	3 Dimock
	p	Frank Florinda A—†	2932	housewife	21	870 Hyde Park
	r	Kelly Elissa—†	2932	saleswoman	40	here

Washington Street—Continued

T	Murphy Francis J	2944	mechanic	35	2983 Wash'n
U	Murphy Mary A—†	2944	at home	57	2983 "
V	O'Hare William	2944	plumber	50	2983 "
W	Finn Ethel J—†	2944	housewife	42	here
X	Finn George F	2944	bartender	50	"
Y	Finn George F, jr	2944	salesman	20	"

559

A	Botolinsky George	2946	motorman	32	"
B	Botolinsky Margaret J–†	2946	housewife	34	"
C	Glorioso Eleanor—†	2946	domestic	38	"
D	DeRosa Clarinda S—†	2946	at home	38	"
E	Greenlaw Mildred W—†	2948	housewife	28	"
F	Greenlaw Percy H	2948	laborer	36	
G	Reis Benvinda—†	2948	operator	37	"
H	Reis Caesar	2948	steward	51	"
K	Harwood Albert W	2948	fireman	65	"
L	Harwood Esther F—†	2948	stitcher	52	"
O	Tebeau Joseph R	2956	machinist	44	"
P	Tebeau Mary B—†	2956	housewife	45	"
S	MacDonald Charles B	2958	fireman	59	
T	Gay Mary A—†	2958	housewife	33	"
U	Freiwald Fritz R	2960	bookkeeper	35	"
V	Freiwald Miram A—†	2960	housewife	27	"
W	Conrad Ada—†	2960	cook	58	"
X	McAllister Helen E—†	2960	housewife	32	2 Copeland pl

560

E	Knapp Ivory E	2966	retired	74	here
F	West Christine M—†	2966	housewife	25	"
G	West Willard C	2966	plumber	33	"
H	Reilly Catherine—†	2966	housewife	35	"
K	Reilly Joseph	2966	chauffeur	33	"
L	Caddis Mildred M—†	2974	housewife	27	New Jersey
M	Caddis Richard B	2974	U S N	27	"
N	Conrad Florence L—†	2974A	housewife	44	here
O	Conrad Frederick T	2974A	mechanic	47	"
P	Gentsch Herbert W	2974A	seaman	20	"
R	Gentsch Marjorie A—†	2974A	housewife	20	"
S	Norton Mary—†	2976	at home	55	2890 Wash'n
T	Engeran Margaret T—†	2976A	housewife	31	here
U	Engerau Peter S	2976A	mechanic	36	"
V	Kavavas Nicholas P	2976A	waiter	60	"

Page.	Letter.	Full Name.	Residence, Jan. 1, 1946.	Occupation.	Supposed Age.	Reported Residence, Jan. 1, 1945. Street and Number.

Washington Street—Continued

w	Gately George T	2978	printer	31	2828 Wash'n
x	Gately James E	2978	cleaner	39	4 Corliss
y	Reinhardt Geraldine L—†	2978	at home	61	4 "
z	Reinhardt Julius T	2978	retired	65	4 "

561

A	Gately Ada E—†	2978	housewife	32	here
B	Gately Herbert F	2978	shipper	42	"
c	McGowan Delia A—†	2978	housewife	64	"
D	McGowan Esther T—†	2978	operator	24	"
E	McGowan Helen J—†	2978	bookkeeper	28	"
F	McGowan Owen	2978	laborer	73	"
H	Humphries Edward R	2980A	baker	31	
K	Humphries Virginia K—†	2980A	housewife	31	"
L	Thomas Eunice A—†	2980A	presser	28	Wash'n D C
M	Wayne Dorothy M—†	2980A	housewife	33	here
N	Wayne Norman	2980A	welder	38	"
o	DeGloria Albert R	2982	repairman	34	"
P	DeGloria Frances L—†	2982	housewife	31	"
R	Smith Dorothy J—†	2982	"	30	6 Symphony rd
w	*Jelalian Cayane—†	2986	"	41	here
x	Jelalian Hopet	2986	proprietor	49	"
y	Jelalian Seta—†	2986	saleswoman	21	"
z	*Evlian Elmas—†	2986	stitcher	60	

562

A	Evlian Krikor	2986	attendant	75	"

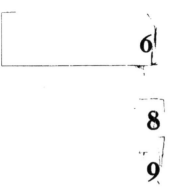

6

8

9

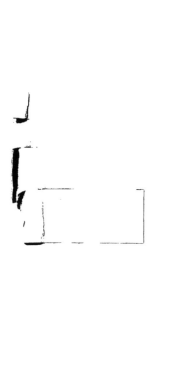

Ward 11–Precinct 6

CITY OF BOSTON

LIST OF RESIDENTS
20 YEARS OF AGE AND OVER

(NON-CITIZENS INDICATED BY ASTERISK)
(FEMALES INDICATED BY DAGGER)

AS OF

JANUARY 1, 1946

THOMAS F. SULLIVAN, *Chairman*
FREDERIC E. DOWLING, *Secretary*
WILLIAM A. MOTLEY, JR.
ARTHUR V. COUGHLIN
EVERETT R. PROUT

Listing Board.

CITY OF BOSTON ⬦ PRINTING DEPARTMENT

600

Amory Avenue

A	Larosa Andrew	2	laborer	41	here
B	Larosa Mary—†	2	housewife	30	"
c	*Mullen Doris—†	2	"	37	Oxford
D	Mullen Harry M	2	manager	36	"
E	Manning John T	2	attendant	23	54 Mattapan
F	Manning Patrick J	2	laborer	49	54 "
G	Manning Patrick J, jr	2	metalworker	24	54 "
H	Evju Walter	4	U S A	22	here
K	*Hansen Aagot—†	4	laundress	57	"
L	Hansen George	4	electrician	28	"
M	Hansen Regina—†	4	housewife	26	"
N	Fisher Christopher	4	chauffeur	47	"
O	Fisher Gertrude—†	4	housewife	36	"
P	Lohnes Gertrude—†	4	"	36	
R	Lohnes Harry	4	machinist	47	"
S	Moylan Edward F	20	baler	46	
T	Moylan Mildred E—†	20	housewife	39	"
U	Sullivan Lillian T—†	20	"	35	
V	Fallon Rita—†	20	"	28	
W	Fallon Stephen	20	U S A	32	
X	Keady James T	20	laborer	23	"
Y	Langner Anna—†	24	housewife	42	56 Day
Z	Langner Richard	24	steward	37	56 "

601 Amory Street

E	Magnant Edward L	81	shipper	37	here
F	Magnant Eva M—†	81	matron	34	"
G	Wilson Blanche—†	81	"	50	"
H	Wilson Jessie—†	81	"	45	
K	Flaherty John J	81	foreman	37	"
L	Flaherty Mary J—†	81	housewife	39	"
M	Boehner Elsie M—†	83	"	54	
N	Boehner Fred J	83	entertainer	57	"
O	Boehner Fred J, jr	83	student	24	
P	Boehner Russell H	83	"	21	
R	O'Connell Judith—†	83	housewife	58	"
S	O'Connell Thomas	83	roofer	49	
V	Curley Anna G—†	91	housewife	34	"
W	Curley James M	91	operator	38	"

Amory Street—Continued

	x	Silver John W	91	machinist	43	here
	y	Silver Loretta T—†	91	housewife	41	"
	z	Cook John W	93	operator	36	"
602						
	a	Cook Mary A—†	93	housewife	36	"
	b	Lingoes Vera—†	93	waitress	41	"
	c	Hirtle Arthur L	95	attendant	52	"
	d	Hirtle Margaret E—†	95	housewife	54	"
	e	Hirtle Robert A	95	U S A	24	
	f	McCarthy Alfred	95	laborer	24	
	g	McCarthy Margaret L—†	95	forewoman	21	"
	h	Kelley John J	112	chef	44	
	k	Kelley Mary E—†	112	housewife	36	"
	l	Moriarty John J	112	U S A	25	
	m	Moriarty Nellie—†	112	housewife	46	"
	n	Sullivan Bridget C—†	112	"	61	
	o	Wickman John	112	laborer	64	"
	p*	Wickman Julia—†	112	housewife	59	"
	r	Geary Della M—†	112	"	45	
	s	Geary Joseph H	112	U S N	26	"
	t	Carey Audrey—†	112	housewife	23	41 Dorr
	u	Carey James	112	chauffeur	25	41 "
	v	Malone Florence L—†	114	housewife	23	here
	w	Malone John J	114	manager	36	"
	x	Tripp Zaidie—†	114	factoryworker	36	48 Magnolia
	y	Forman Edward	114	laborer	34	here
	z	Forman Mary—†	114	housewife	30	"
603						
	a	McCann Thomas J	114	supervisor	48	"
	b	Bonito Arthur	114	operator	26	"
	c	Bonito Rose—†	114	housewife	26	"
	d	Daley Kathleen—†	114	"	21	33 Goldsmith
	g	Block David	153	clerk	49	here
	h	Block Dorothy—†	153	housewife	37	"
	k	Burkart Emily M—†	153	"	48	"
	l	Burkart Joseph R	153	manager	49	"
	m	Hopfgarten Marie E—†	153	housekeeper	71	"
	n	Tibbetts Gladys—†	155	housewife	50	"
	o	Tibbetts Henry G	155	clerk	51	
	p	Anderson Dorothy—†	155	typist	22	
	r	Anderson Dorothy E—†	155	housewife	38	"

Amory Street—Continued

s	Anderson Gustave	155	brewer	49	here
T	Mitchell Catherine F—†	155	packer	58	"
U	Bock Edith G—†	171	housewife	53	"
V	Bock Henry W	171	clergyman	60	"
w	Smith Elsie—†	171	secretary	31	"
x	Lemieux Charles	173	machinist	27	"
Y	Lemieux Elizabeth—†	173	housewife	25	"
z	Richards Margaret—†	173	operator	22	"

604

A	*Richards Margaret A—†	173	housewife	60	"
B	Richards William N	173	machinist	24	"
C	Keenan Robert	173	laborer	50	14 Dixwell
D	Koeble Alfred	173	retired	86	here
E	McEleney Josephine—†	173	housekeeper	56	"
F	McLaughlin Edward	173	laborer	54	"
G	McLaughlin Elizabeth—†	173	typist	26	
H	*Nicol Ernestine—†	175	housekeeper	59	"
K	MacDonald Alice M—†	175	housewife	61	"
L	MacDonald Hugh	175	carpenter	70	"
M	Glennon Edward L	181	splicer	42	
N	Glennon Ruth E—†	181	housewife	41	"
O	Glennon Timothy F	181	machinist	50	"
P	Southwick Eugene	181	retired	62	"
R	Southwick Eugene, jr	181	butcher	28	"
S	Southwick Laura—†	181	housewife	53	"
T	Southwick Marie—†	181	"	28	
U	Boyden Clifton	183	guard	58	
V	Boyden Harold	183	laborer	30	
w	Boyden Kenneth	183	cutter	21	
x	Boyden Stella—†	183	housewife	56	"
Y	Daniels Elsie—†	183	operator	24	"
z	Daniels Francis	183	polisher	23	"

605

A	Shea Dorothy—†	183	housewife	26	"
B	Shea John	183	painter	27	
C	Trull Elizabeth—†	183A	housewife	30	"
D	Trull Harry E	183A	mechanic	35	"
F	Guariglia Marion—†	187	housewife	22	"
G	Guariglia Vincent	187	U S A	26	
H	Toro Jennie—†	187	housewife	45	"
K	Toro Joseph	187	custodian	52	"

Amory Terrace

Letter.	FULL NAME.	Residence, Jan. 1, 1946.	Occupation.	Supposed Age.	Reported Residence, Jan. 1, 1945.
N	Roukey Arthur	1	painter	41	here
O	Roukey Corinne—†	1	housewife	41	"
P	Reno Elmer E	1	clerk	48	"
R	Reno Sarah M—†	1	housewife	58	"
S	Tucker Dorothy F—†	1	waitress	35	"
T	Tucker Robert T	1	laborer	31	"
U	Eno Angela E—†	1	housewife	47	24A Whitney
V	Eno Henry J	1	machinist	58	24A "
W	French Ellen—†	1	housewife	21	24A "
X	Leonard Mary T—†	3	housekeeper	80	here
Y	Sweetland Nancy—†	3	housewife	86	"
Z	Lesch Caroline A—†	3	"	50	"

606

Letter.	FULL NAME.	Residence, Jan. 1, 1946.	Occupation.	Supposed Age.	Reported Residence, Jan. 1, 1945.
A	Lesch Hans	3	bartender	51	"
B	Sakowich Anna—†	3	clerk	31	"
C	*Sakowich Constance—†	3	housewife	55	"
D	Sakowich Ellen—†	3	clerk	25	
E	Sakowich John J	3	U S A	32	"
F	*Sakowich Joseph	3	metalworker	59	"
G	Sakowich Mary—†	3	stenographer	28	"
H	Laflin John	10	machinist	23	Rhode Island
K	Laflin Ruth M—†	10	housewife	26	"
L	Kuroputkin Martha—†	10	housekeeper	61	here

Atherton Place

Letter.	FULL NAME.	Residence, Jan. 1, 1946.	Occupation.	Supposed Age.	Reported Residence, Jan. 1, 1945.
M	*Holmes Agnes C—†	1	housewife	58	here
N	Holmes Alexandriana—†	1	clerk	29	"
O	Holmes Edward F	1	machinist	59	"
P	Costa Ella—†	2	housewife	65	"
R	Costa Helen—†	2	operator	30	"
S	Hogan Thomas D	3	fireman	34	"
T	Hogan Winifred C—†	3	housewife	30	"
U	Appoldi Salvatore	4	florist	38	
V	Lauro Anna—†	4	clerk	30	
W	Lauro Carmella—†	4	teacher	32	"
X	Lauro Frances—†	4	clerk	30	"
Y	Lauro John	4	barber	63	
Z	Lauro Mary—†	4	housewife	62	"

607

Letter.	FULL NAME.	Residence, Jan. 1, 1946.	Occupation.	Supposed Age.	Reported Residence, Jan. 1, 1945.
A	Lauro Salvatore R	4	U S A	23	

Atherton Place—Continued

	Letter.	FULL NAME.	Residence, Jan. 1, 1946.	Occupation.	Supposed Age.	Reported Residence, Jan. 1, 1945. Street and Number.
	B	Hasenfuss Agnes—†	5	housekeeper	66	here
	C	Hasenfuss Clara E—†	5	"	62	"
	D	Hasenfuss Mary R—†	5	"	59	"
	E	Vincent Cornelius	6	retired	76	
	F	Vincent Cornelius, jr	6	U S A	25	
	G	Vincent Mathilda R—†	6	housewife	59	"
	H	Vincent Muriel R—†	6	student	20	
	K	Williams Damin	6	U S A	29	
	L	Williams Ruth G—†	6	housewife	27	"

Atherton Street

	Letter.	FULL NAME.	Residence, Jan. 1, 1946.	Occupation.	Supposed Age.	Reported Residence, Jan. 1, 1945. Street and Number.
	M	Keough John J	2	operator	37	here
	N	Keough Ruth E—†	2	housewife	34	"
	O	Boggiar Dolores—†	2	operator	27	"
	P	Boggiar Jennie—†	2	at home	69	"
	R	Ford Catherine—†	2	housewife	63	"
	S	Ford Herbert E	2	electrician	38	"
	T	Ford Mary A—†	2	typist	33	
	U	Fest Hedwig—†	2	housewife	45	"
	V	Fest Oscar F	2	baker	61	
	W	Duffy Celia M—†	3	matron	40	
	X	Kenney Edward T	3	clerk	37	
	Y	Kenney John F	3	inspector	42	"
	Z	Kenney Mary A—†	3	housewife	65	"

608

	Letter.	FULL NAME.	Residence, Jan. 1, 1946.	Occupation.	Supposed Age.	Reported Residence, Jan. 1, 1945. Street and Number.
	A	Kenney Paul W	3	mechanic	35	"
	B	Poulos Bessie—†	4	housewife	29	"
	C	Poulos Evelyn—†	4	at home	68	
	D	Poulos George P	4	manager	33	"
	E	Atsales Arthur	4	counterman	53	"
	F	Atsales Evelyn—†	4	operator	21	"
	G	Atsales Helen—†	4	bookkeeper	22	"
	H	Atsales Pauline—†	4	housewife	40	"
	K	Barca Allie—†	5	"	31	3 Bishop
	L	Barca Rosario	5	U S A	32	3 "
	M	Martin George	5	student	26	Gloucester
	N	McGrath John J	5	mechanic	33	8 Northam pk
	O	McGrath Leila E—†	5	housewife	31	8 "
	P	Genes Lefkoula—†	6	"	39	here
	R	Genes Nicholas	6	merchant	51	"

Atherton Street—Continued

s	Whitney Letitia E—†	7	housewife	46	here
T	Whitney Thomas R	7	finisher	52	"
U	Whitney Violet—†	7	cashier	20	"
V	Shea Francis E, jr	7	clerk	23	
W	Shea Lawrence A	7	"	22	
X	Shea Mary R—†	7	packer	25	"
Y	Shea Sarah—†	7	housewife	50	"
Z	Davey Elizabeth—†	8	"	44	

609

A	Davey John J	8	operator	49	"
B	Kirchgassner Barbara—†	8	at home	68	
C	Willgoose Harold	8	retired	74	"
D	Brown Chester A	9	carpenter	50	"
E	Doneghy Eleanor O—†	9	housewife	23	"
F	Doneghy James F	9	U S A	30	
G	Hamilton John J	9	retired	79	"
H	Morin Grace—†	9	housewife	49	"
K	Morin Lawrence	9	U S N	21	
L	Morin Oliver	9	painter	51	"
M	Norris Charles F, jr	10	chauffeur	51	"
N	Norris Sadie C—†	10	housewife	72	"
O	Morrow Florence M—†	10	at home	58	"
R	Gisetto Lena—†	11	housewife	34	3 Sheridan pl
S	Gisetto William	11	operator	34	3 "
T	*Mennella Angelina—†	11	housewife	62	3 "
U	Cadorette Antonio J	12	plumber	55	here
V	Cadorette Ruth L—†	12	typist	22	"
W	Cadorette Theresa A—†	12	clerk	20	"
X	Cadorette Theresa M—†	12	housewife	50	"
Y	Freiwald Chester F	13	mechanic	33	"
Z	Freiwald Marie C—†	13	housewife	33	"

610

A	Lasdow Daniel	13	longshoreman	49	"
B	Lasdow Olga—†	13	housewife	43	"
C	Almon Doris—†	14	operator	33	"
D	Konetzny Mary R—†	14	secretary	25	"
E	Konetzny Walter J	14	student	26	Newton
F	O'Donnell Julia E—†	14	teacher	23	here
G	O'Donnell Margaret R—†	14	housewife	56	"
H	O'Donnell Thomas F	14	operator	58	"
K	O'Donnell Thomas J	14	student	20	

Atherton Street—Continued

L	Rhodes Meda C—†	15	operator	38	here
M	Wisnioski Sarah—†	15	"	37	"
N	Wisnioski William W	15	"	50	"
O	Hannaford Anna S—†	16	housewife	71	"
P	Hannaford J Frank	16	retired	63	
R	Lipshultz Nellie A—†	16	at home	79	
S	Brown Delia A—†	17	housewife	55	"
T	Brown John	17	inspector	58	"
U	Lagrew Clyde	17	engineer	40	"
V	Whiteman William	17	manager	64	"
W	McBirney Flora M—†	18	housewife	39	"
X	McBirney Joseph	18	manager	40	"
Y	McBirney Ellen M—†	18	housewife	68	"
Z	McBirney Peter J	18	retired	46	

611

A	Connor Bernard	19	bartender	60	"
B	Connor Bernard U	19	"	29	
C	Connor Edmund G	19	student	25	"
D	Connor Rebecca M—†	19	housewife	55	"
E	Ganley Mary—†	19	housekeeper	50	"
F	Cass William	20	realtor	62	"
G	Abel Mary E—†	20	housewife	65	"
H	Abel William S	20	retired	66	
K	Jensen Hedwig D—†	21	housewife	40	"
L	Jensen Thomas D	21	rigger	48	
M	Kardinal Emil	21	seaman	25	"
N	Lindholm Ivar	21	"	48	
O	*Trabish Mary—†	25	housewife	51	"
P	Trabish William	25	salesman	52	"
R	O'Leary Daniel H	37	teacher	39	
S	O'Leary Marguerite—†	37	housewife	29	"
T	Colburn Ellen M—†	39	"	70	
U	Colburn Eugene J	39	salesman	39	"
V	Osterberg George	41	engineer	39	Michigan
W	Osterberg Mary—†	41	housewife	35	"
X	Biewend Adolf	41	attorney	46	here
Y	Biewend Ruth—†	41	housewife	42	"
Z	De Entremont Leah—†	45	laundress	44	"

612

A	Derau Richard	45	draftsman	31	Dedham
B	Fox Josephine A—†	45	housewife	56	here

Page.	Letter.	FULL NAME.	Residence, Jan. 1, 1946.	Occupation.	Supposed Age.	Reported Residence, Jan. 1, 1945. Street and Number.

Atherton Street—Continued

	c	Fox William W	45	printer	68	here
	d	McLaughlin Susan—†	45	laundress	49	"
	e	Weldon Eugene	45	electrician	37	"
	f	Kennison Harry	49	merchant	45	"
	g	Livingston Charlotte—†	49	nurse	30	
	h	Tracy Francis X	49	U S A	23	
	k	Tracy Mary C—†	49	housewife	59	"
	l	Tracy Mary J—†	49	teacher	28	"
	m	Tracy Philip A	49	U S A	31	
	n	Kelley Bridget J—†	51	housewife	32	"
	o	Kelley Thomas M	51	shipper	39	
	p	Marenghi Americo	55	foreman	50	"
	r	Marenghi Henrietta—†	55	housewife	41	"
	s	Mongillo Emma—†	55	operator	33	"
	t	Mongillo Frank	55	"	39	
	u	Coughlan Helen F—†	59	bookkeeper	43	"
	v	Hartnett Floretta M—†	59	tel operator	38	"
	w	Kelley Margaret J—†	59	"	42	"
	x	Kelley Robert E	59	clerk	46	
	y	Hart George B	61	pedler	65	"
	z	Hart Myrtis C—†	61	housewife	50	"

613

	a	Clem Edward	75	steamfitter	31	"
	b	Clem Gertrude—†	75	housewife	32	"
	c	Galvin James J	75	fireman	44	
	d	Galvin Mary—†	75	housewife	45	"
	e	Richmond Lawrence F	75	maintenance	24	"
	f	Richmond Marie—†	75	housewife	23	"
	g	Sullivan John J	75	janitor	62	
	k	Egan Evelyn M—†	79	stenographer	22	"
	l	Egan John B	79	U S A	23	"
	m	Egan Mary J—†	79	housewife	53	"
	n	Galvin George M	79	salesman	31.	"
	o	Galvin Gladys—†	79	housewife	30	"
	p	Galvin Mary—†	79	"	65	"
	r	Healey James M	79	diemaker	27	"
	s	Healey Mary—†	79	housewife	27	"
	t	Bishop Elsie H—†	83	housekeeper	60	"
	u	Keeble Dorothy W—†	83	housewife	51	"
	v	Keeble Herbert W	83	student	21	
	w	Tracy Emma F—†	83	housewife	83	"

9

Page.	Letter.	FULL NAME.	Residence, Jan. 1, 1946.	Occupation.	Supposed Age.	Reported Residence, Jan. 1, 1945. Street and Number.

Atherton Street—Continued

	x	Harris Donald	83	diesetter	25	94 Forbes
	y	Harris Lorraine—†	83	housewife	22	94 "
	z	Bearisto Ernest B	87	salesman	46	here
		614				
	A	Bearisto Johanna W—†	87	housewife	46	"
	B	Bearisto Ruth D—†	87	clerk	20	
	C	Bearisto William E	87	student	21	"
	D	Ogilvie John	87	machinist	50	Connecticut
	E	Ogilvie John G	87	chauffeur	23	"
	F	Ogilvie Rose—†	87	housewife	50	"
	G	Mamigonian Margaret M–†	87	stenographer	21	here
	H	Mamigonian Terrante M–†	87	waitress	36	"

Bancroft Street

	K	Sullivan Dorothy—†	1	housewife	37	here
	L	Sullivan John J	1	U S A	37	"
	M	*McNulty John J	1	plasterer	54	"
	N	*McNulty Mary J—†	1	housewife	58	"
	O	McNulty Patricia—†	1	clerk	21	
	P	Gallagher Arthur	1	laborer	62	
	R	Ward Alpheus J	1	steamfitter	51	"
	S	King Charles H	3	investigator	39	"
	T	King Charlotte F—†	3	operator	39	"
	U	King John F	3	retired	64	560 Centre
	V	Richards Annie E—†	3	housekeeper	65	here
	W	Burns Margaret—†	3	housewife	54	"
	X	Frattone Beatrice—†	3	"	28	"
	Y	Frattone Joseph	3	U S N	25	
	Z	Norton Elizabeth—†	3	housewife	45	"
		615				
	A	Norton John W	3	manager	43	"
	B	Norton Josephine—†	3	housewife	39	"
	C	McFadden Delbert	5	chauffeur	42	"
	D	McFadden Mildred—†	5	housewife	35	"
	E	Linnehan Frederick	5	butcher	32	"
	F	Linnehan Marie—†	5	housewife	31	"
	G	Murphy Mary I—†	5	housekeeper	71	"
	H	Mulcahy Agnes—†	7	housewife	68	"
	K	Mulcahy John	7	retired	72	
	L	Nilson Arthur	7	salesman	49	"

Bancroft Street—Continued

M	Nilson Arthur, jr	7	chef	26	here
N	Nilson Edward	7	clerk	22	"
O	Nilson Frederick	7	U S N	20	"
P	Nilson Ruby—†	7	housewife	49	" .
R	Finley Katherine E—†	7	"	68	
S	Finley Mary F—†	7	tel operator	65	"
T	Ward Mary—†	9	housewife	37	"
U	Ward Thomas G	9	brakeman	34	"
V	Clark Esther—†	9	housewife	22	California
W	Clark Jennie—†	9	"	47	13 Bartlett
X	Clark William	9	chauffeur	26	13 "
Y	Dietrich Caroline—†	9	housewife	48	here
Z	Dietrich Robert O	9	chauffeur	48	"

616

A	Steele Hugh F	11	inspector	66	"
B	Steele Mary—†	11	housewife	62	"
C	Ward Mary A—†	11	"	53	
D	Ward Thomas B	11	laborer	56	
E	Brown Mary—†	11	housekeeper	61	"
F	Dern Joseph	11	chauffeur	36	"
G	Dern Marion—†	11	housewife	38	"
H	Kontrouba Gertrude—†	15	"	44	
K	Kontrouba Michael	15	carpenter	48	"
L	Radiches Marie—†	15	clerk	23	
M	Lemieux Ruth—†	15	housewife	29	"
N	Lemieux Wilbrod	15	carpenter	28	"
O	Costa Anna—†	18	housewife	31	"
P	Costa John	18	carpenter	35	"
R	*Costa Venera—†	18	housewife	71	"
S	Wakefield Anna E—†	20	operator	30	"
T	Wakefield Dorothy L—†	20	"	32	
U	Wakefield Mary T—†	20	housewife	28	"
V	Wakefield Matilda E—†	20	operator	26	"
W	Wakefield Rita J—†	20	"	21	
X	Wakefield Walter A	20	shipper	54	

Beethoven Street

Z	Catenacci Anthony	6	mechanic	59	here

617

A	Catenacci Susan—†	6	housewife	54	"

Beethoven Street—Continued

B	Guadalupe Esther—†	6	packer	23	here	
C	Cushing Edna B—†	8	housewife	36	"	
D	Cushing Sherman J	8	merchant	41	"	
E	Fallon Bernard J	8	laborer	37	"	
F	Gibbons Peter E	8	fitter	47	47 School	
G	Mills Arthur	8	chef	50	here	
H	McGovern Anna P—†	8½	secretary	28	"	
K	McGovern Helen S—†	8½	collector	43	"	
L	McGovern Mary W—†	8½	housewife	74	"	
M	Buckley Timothy D	9	plumber	53	2401 Wash'n	
N	Cook Eva J—†	9	housewife	55	2401 "	
O	Cook William G	9	foreman	65	2401 "	
P	Collins Arthur J	10	chauffeur	55	here	
R	Collins Arthur V	10	U S A	30	"	
S	Collins Bertha J—†	10	housewife	54	"	
T	Doyle Bridget T—†	10	at home	67		
U	Doyle Dominick	10	foreman	39	"	
V	Doyle Mary K—†	10	housewife	38	"	
W	Zaimes Elena K—†	11	"	45		
X	Zaimes Stilios	11	mechanic	57	"	
Y	*Lucyk Annie—†	12	waitress	62		
Z	Lucyk Michael	12	retired	73		

618

A	Trabish Sophie H—†	12	housewife	31	"	
B	Trabish William	12	electrician	33	"	
C	Mulloy Mildred V—†	14	housewife	28	"	
D	Mulloy William M	14	machinist	37	"	
E	Martin Florence R—†	14	housewife	48	52 Atherton	
F	Martin Harold E	14	carpenter	50	52 "	
G	Botolinski Catherine—†	15	housewife	62	here	
H	Botolinski Joseph	15	chauffeur	35	"	
K	Botolinski Michael	15	packer	37	"	
M	Cummings Hannah M—†	16	clerk	21		
N	Cummings John J	16	repairman	70	"	
O	Cummings Susan A—†	16	housewife	64	"	
P	Ulrich Dorothy G—†	16	"	25		
R	Ulrich John F	16	machinist	29	"	
S	Emery Harris P	17	operator	57	"	
T	MacDonald Felicia—†	17	housewife	61	"	
U	Ronan Frederick J	18	investigator	48	43 Hampstead rd
V	Ronan James W	18	operator	62	43 "	

Page.	Letter.	FULL NAME.	Residence, Jan. 1, 1946.	Occupation.	Supposed Age.	Reported Residence, Jan. 1, 1945. Street and Number.

Beethoven Street—Continued

	w	Ronan Mildred C—†	18	clerk	46	43 Hampstead rd
	x	Smith Stuart W	18	"	57	16 John A Andrew
	y	Bagley Cecile A—†	19	housewife	40	here
	z	Bagley George E	19	laborer	45	"

619

	a	Bagley Norman E	19	U S N	20	
	b	Bagley Theresa—†	19	nurse	21	
	c	Bourgoin Marie—†	19	beautician	31	"
	d	Bongartz John	20	laborer	59	"
	e	Hertel Frederick	20	retired	80	176 School
	f	Kloser Gertrude E—†	20	housewife	61	here
	g	Kloser Oswald J	20	machinist	59	"
	h	Lunderville Phoebe—†	20	at home	93	"
	k	Short Thomas	20	laborer	45	"
	l	Van Tassel Charles J	21	salesman	73	"
	m	Teare Bertha—†	21	housewife	50	"
	n	Teare William	21	foreman	51	
	o	Thompson Bertha—†	21	housewife	59	"
	p	Thompson Edward	21	salesman	61	..
	r	MacDonald Alexander L	22	U S A	30	
	s	MacDonald John E	22	manager	32	"
	t	MacDonald Mary—†	22	at home	70	
	u	*Easter Dorothy L—†	24	housewife	42	"
	v	*Easter George R	24	foreman	40	..
	w	Collins Adelard	25	engineer	60	"
	x	Driscoll Arthur	25	laborer	56	
	y	Galvin Patrick	25	engineer	55	"
	z	Gibbs Matthias	25	retired	81	

620

	a	Gibbs Matthias E	25	manager	46	Medford
	b	Joyce Thomas	25	chauffeur	36	here
	c	Whitman Dorothy—†	25	manager	36	Medford
	d	Whitman Lillian B—†	25	housewife	56	"
	e	Gamble Charlotte—†	26	"	26	49 Elmore
	f	Gamble Harry A	26	presser	32	49 "
	g	Melton William	26	clerk	32	49 "

Boylston Street

| | l | *Lavoie Oliver | 128 | laborer | 59 | here |
| | m | Lavoie Rose—† | 128 | housewife | 57 | " |

Boylston Street—Continued

N	White Charles H	128	chauffeur	35	here
O	White Germaine M—†	128	housewife	31	"

Bragdon Street

P	DeBenedeto Orlando	9	chauffeur	42	here
R	DeBenedeto Rose—†	9	housewife	28	"
S	Manning Helen—†	9	"	24	2975 Wash'n
T	Manning Joseph	9	electrician	28	2975 "
U	Downs Anna M—†	15	housewife	35	here
V	Downs John J	15	shipfitter	30	"
W	Normandin Carmella—†	15	housewife	27	52 Haverford
X	Davis Frederick	25	chemist	50	here
Y	Ganley Thomas F	25	painter	49	"
Z	Reed Gertrude—†	25	housewife	48	"

621

A	Brown Kenneth	56	supt	38	
B	Brown Rita—†	56	housewife	31	"
C	Cowie Helen C—†	56	"	43	"
D	Cowie William	56	baker	45	
E	Stern Dorothy A—†	56	housewife	42	"
F	Stern Morris	56	bookbinder	47	"
G	Hogan Catherine E—†	56	housewife	25	"
H	Hogan Thomas E	56	chauffeur	43	"
K	Lowder Mark F	56	laborer	23	
L	Lowder Mark T	56	retired	64	
M	Fulton Jessie—†	56	housewife	30	"
N	Fulton Robert	56	clerk	40	
O	Corcoran James L	56	U S A	28	
P	Corcoran Justine H—†	56	WAC	25	
R	Pierce Andrew J	56	pipefitter	48	"
S	Pierce Helen G—†	56	housewife	52	"
T	Pierce Robert H	56	U S A	20	
U	Woodson Irene—†	60	housewife	24	"
V	Woodson Newton	60	chauffeur	42	"
W	Murphy Edward	60	artist	32	"
X	Murphy Mary—†	60	secretary	30	"
Y	Murphy Winifred—†	60	housewife	55	"
Z	Kearns Florence E—†	60	"	42	

622

A	Kearns Harold J	60	electrician	43	"

Page.	Letter.	Full Name.	Residence, Jan. 1, 1946.	Occupation.	Supposed Age.	Reported Residence, Jan. 1, 1945. Street and Number.

Bragdon Street—Continued

	Letter.	Full Name.	Residence	Occupation	Age	Reported Residence
	B	McAuliffe Chester A	60	packer	40	here
	C	McAuliffe Margaret—†	60	housewife	38	"
	D	Kleuber Elizabeth—†	60	"	69	"
	E	DeBassio Hermina F—†	60	"	39	
	F	Brunelle Alfred	70	laborer	27	
	G	Brunelle Lillian—†	70	housewife	29	"
	H	Glennon James	70	chauffeur	33	"
	K	Glennon Rita—†	70	housewife	24	"
	L	Cunniffe Herbert F	70	chauffeur	37	"
	M	Cunniffe Mary—†	70	housewife	35	"
	N	Paige Grace—†	72	"	26	
	O	Paige Jerome	72	operator	32	"
	P	Kimball Francis G	72	U S N	20	"
	R	Kimball Howard U	72	stevedore	31	40 W Walnut pk
	S	Kimball Margaret T—†	72	housewife	61	40 "
	T	Kimball Thomas E	72	operator	61	40 "
	U	Soule Harold	72	U S M C	28	here
	V	Soule Ruth—†	72	housewife	27	"
	W	Lemon Veronica—†	74	"	37	114 Amory
	X	Cavelius Gertrude—†	74	"	27	here
	Y	Cavelius Paul	74	machinist	30	"
	Z	Gronberg Edwin	74	"	29	"

623

	Letter.	Full Name.	Residence	Occupation	Age	Reported Residence
	A	Gronberg Sylvia—†	74	housewife	29	"
	B	Lemeiux Peter	76	mechanic	53	"
	C	Lemeiux Robert	76	"	23	"
	D	Lemeiux Rose—†	76	housewife	50	"
	E	Neary Grace—†	76	"	27	1871 Col av
	F	Neary Joseph F	76	machinist	31	1871 "
	G	DiPaolo Lena—†	76	housewife	34	here
	H	DiPaolo William	76	shipper	35	"
	K	Leger Madeline—†	78	housewife	20	26 Egleston
	L	Leger Roland	78	chauffeur	24	26 "
	M	Grueter George E	78	"	25	39 W Walnut pk
	N	Grueter Mary H—†	78	housewife	24	39 "
	O	Parrelli Daniel	78	machinist	24	Quincy
	P	Parrelli Ruth—†	78	clerk	23	"
	R	Wilson Loretta—†	78	housewife	30	here
	S	Williams Elmer R	80	machinist	32	"
	T	Williams Florence M—†	80	housewife	27	"
	U	Knighten Francis L	80	U S A	23	

Bragdon Street—Continued

v	Knighten Lloyd	80	carpenter	54	here
w	Knighten Sarah—†	80	housewife	49	"
x	Barden Anthony	80	U S A	21	25 Rockland
y	Barden Margaret—†	80	housewife	40	25 "
z	Sullivan Claudia—†	82	"	29	here

624

a	Sullivan Edward B	82	laborer	36	
b	Belton Theodore D	82	chauffeur	52	"
c	Lydon Antoinette—†	82	housewife	27	"
d	Lydon Ralph L	82	U S A	21	
e	Lydon William	82	chauffeur	26	"
f	Beissner Frederick L	82	inspector	53	"
g	Beissner Stella—†	82	housewife	58	"
h	Cadigan Catherine E—†	91	clerk	39	
k	Powers Irene G—†	91	"	46	
l	Schwarz Louise M—†	91	housewife	57	"
m	Schwarz William F	91	salesman	26	"
n	Houde Albert	91	machinist	24	"
o	Houde Margaret—†	91	housewife	56	"
p	Houde Mary—†	91	"	25	510 E Sixth
r	Dunn Gertrude—†	92	"	35	282 Amory
s	Dunn William C	92	fireman	29	282 "
t	Greggs Claud O	92	B F D	54	here
u	Greggs Nettie—†	92	housewife	53	"
v	Johnson Thomas	92	salesman	54	"
w	Johnson Thomas, jr	92	U S A	23	
x	McRae Dorothy F—†	93	housewife	31	"
y	McRae George A	93	supt	35	
z	Krikorian Mary—†	93	housewife	35	"

625

a	Krikorian Walter	93	printer	35	
b	Andrews Margaret—†	93	housewife	56	"
c	Andrews William	93	shipfitter	47	"
d	McGuire Catherine E—†	94	housewife	50	213 Boylston
e	McGuire Peter J	94	custodian	52	213 "
f	Pearson Eleanor—†	94	housewife	30	here
g	Wernig George	94	chauffeur	36	"
h	Wernig Mary—†	94	housewife	36	"
k	Campana Frances—†	94	"	23	310 Centre
l	Campana Joseph J	94	machinist	23	Brookline
m	Powers Henry J	94	baker	36	here

16

Bragdon Street—Continued

N	Powers Ruth E—†	94	housewife	32	here
P	Stinson Charlotte—†	95	"	38	"
R	Smith Helen M—†	95	"	36	"
T	Miller Minerva—†	97	"	41	
U	Rockel Albert	97	U S N	22	
V	Rice Ethel M—†	97	housewife	53	"
W	Rice Ethel M—†	97	tel operator	27	"
X	Rice Lawrence H	97	engineer	52	"
Y	Rice Lawrence J	97	U S N	21	

Columbus Avenue

Z	Allison Edith—†	1841	nurse	21	14 Dimock
	626				
A	Anton Clotilda—†	1841		34	Brookline
B	Beaumont Mary—†	1841	"	20	14 Dimock
C	Carson Erna—†	1841	"	24	here
D	Clayton Lillian—†	1841	"	21	14 Dimock
E	Cooley Phyllis—†	1841		20	14 "
F	Coyle Ruth—†	1841		20	14 "
G	Damon Alfreda—†	1841		20	14 "
H	Delaney Marion—†	1841	"	20	14 "
K	Devine Mona—†	1841		20	14 "
L	Douglas Dorothy—†	1841	"	30	here
M	Francis Marion—†	1841	"	20	14 Dimock
N	Franklin Jean—†	1841		20	14 "
O	Gillis Virginia—†	1841	"	20	14 "
P	Griffin Margaret C—†	1841	"	33	here
R	Hamilton Elizabeth—†	1841	"	20	14 Dimock
S	Hoffman Jeanette—†	1841	"	20	14 "
T	Hourihan Alice—†	1841		20	14 "
U	Jodoin Marianne—†	1841	"	22	14 "
V	Lyons Mary—†	1841	"	20	14 "
W	Matherson Priscilla—†	1841	"	24	here
X	May Mary—†	1841		20	14 Dimock
Y	Metzger Helen—†	1841		20	14 "
Z	Parker Virginia—†	1841	"	20	14 "
	627				
A	Poole Betty—†	1841	"	21	14 "
B	Ross Agnes—†	1841		23	New York
C	Savage Effie—†	1841		22	14 Dimock

Columbus Avenue—Continued

D	Scheinfeldt Jeanne—†	1841	nurse	21	14 Dimock
E	Young Elizabeth—†	1841	"	24	14 "
F	Ziebrinski Irene—†	1841	"	21	14 "
G	McCloskey Catherine—†	1845–47	housewife	48	here
H	McCloskey James V	1845–47	chauffeur	58	"
K	McMahon Florence—†	1845 47	housewife	55	"
L	Currier Hilda—†	1845–47	"	24	
M	Currier John	1845–47	U S A	26	
N	Mulkern William	1845–47	clerk	58	
O	Kelly Catherine—†	1845–47	housewife	68	"
P	Kelly Elizabeth—†	1845–47	bookkeeper	70	"
R	Sprague Catherine–†	1845–47	housewife	56	"
S	Jackley Anna—†	1845–47	"	72	
T	Jackley Theodore	1845–47	retired	80	
U	Mullen Frederick	1845 47	manager	60	"
V	Mullen Theresa—†	1845–47	housewife	55	"
W	Golay Leon	1845–47	U S N	30	
X	Golay Marion—†	1845–47	housewife	24	"
Y	Dinsmore Mary—†	1845–47	cook	45	1859 Col av
Z	Dale Irene—†	1845–47	housewife	31	here

628

A	Dale John	1845–47	plumber	34	"
B	Gaffney Alice—†	1845–47	clerk	23	
C	Gaffney Anna—†	1845–47	housewife	50	"
D	Lucas George H	1849–51	machinist	68	"
E	Lucas James	1849–51	clerk	26	
F	Johnson Charles	1849–51	machinist	26	"
G	Johnson Florence—†	1849–51	housewife	26	"
H	Guiva Ernest	1849–51	chauffeur	45	"
K	Guiva Mary C—†	1849–51	housewife	38	"
L	Burgess Clarence	1849–51	salesman	52	"
M	Gregorie Alexander	1849–51	retired	70	"
N	Gregorie Blanche—†	1849–51	cashier	51	
O	Scott Ida M—†	1849–51	operator	49	"
P	Holland Arthur J	1849–51	"	50	
R	Holland Helen T—†	1849–51	housewife	49	"
S	Simpson Florence—†	1849–51	clerk	43	
T	Palmeter Muriel—†	1849–51	nurse	38	
U	Palmeter Vera—	1849–51	"	40	
V	Roche John	1849–51	operator	48	"
W	Roche Vera—†	1849–51	housewife	38	"

Columbus Avenue—Continued

x	Schermerhoran Caroline—†	1853	housewife	58	here
y	Schermerhoran Donald	1853	U S M C	23	"
z	Schermerhoran Ford	1853	attendant	65	"
	629				
a	McGuire Doris—†	1853	checker	41	"
b	McGuire Marie—†	1853	secretary	24	"
c	Devanney Margaret—†	1853	housewife	40	"
d	Riley Eva M—†	1853	secretary	44	"
e	Riley John E	1853	student	22	"
f	Shea Charlotte M—†	1853	collector	53	"
g	Bennett Marie E—†	1855	housewife	42	"
h	Larivee Armand	1855	laborer	46	"
k	Larivee Valentine—†	1855	housewife	45	"
l	Sohijian Ethel A—†	1855	beautician	23	"
m	Sohijian Isabel—†	1855	housewife	44	"
n	Sohijian Louis M	1855	painter	25	
o	Sohijian Richard	1855	laborer	56	
p	Thomas Agnes D—†	1855	beautician	27	"
r	Thomas Roscoe P	1855	waiter	28	
s	Doyle Jane—†	1857	housewife	54	"
t	Keefe George	1857	shipper	26	"
u	Keefe Helen—†	1857	operator	25	"
v	Twigg Pauline—†	1857	clerk	31	
w	Bartasch Edith—†	1857	housewife	26	"
x	Bartasch Raymond C	1857	U·S A	25	"
y	O'Reilly James P	1857	merchant	59	"
z	O'Reilly John M	1857	chauffeur	57	"
	630				
a	O'Reilly John W	1857	"	34	
b	O'Reilly Mabel E—†	1857	housewife	51	"
c	O'Reilly Mary L—†	1857	clerk	31	
d	*Logavich Samuel	1859	laborer	54	
e	*Logavich Victoria—†	1859	housewife	53	"
f	Mayeski Anna M—†	1859	"	41	
g	Mayeski William W	1859	inspector	40	"
h	Murphy Bartholomew	1859	retired	56	"
k	Murphy Charles J	1859	chauffeur	40	"
l	Murphy Mary—†	1859	housewife	44	"
m	Donahue Annie—†	1861–63	"	68	
n	Donahue David F	1861–63	engineer	63	"
o	Bernstein Bertha—†	1861–63	housewife	74	"

Columbus Avenue—Continued

	P	Coletti Marie—†	1861–63	nurse	30	here
	R	Bowers Mary—†	1861–63	operator	33	"
	S	Plovnick Gladys—†	1861–63	housewife	31	"
	T	Plovnick Isadore	1861–63	machinist	30	"
	U	King Margaret—†	1861–63	housewife	45	"
	V	King Thomas	1861–63	retired	52	
	W	Valliere Catherine F—†	1861–63	housewife	58	"
	X	Anderson Helen T—†	1861–63	"	27	Virginia
	Y	Anderson Ralph G	1861–63	U S A	28	"
	Z	Ashe Ida F—†	1861–63	nurse	37	here

631

	A	O'Neil Madeline—†	1861–63	"	54	
	B	Birkwald Pauline—†	1861–63	forewoman	62	"
	C	Phillips Caroline—†	1861–63	cashier	61	"
	D	Brown Donald	1861–63	U S N	28	Malden
	E	Brown Margaret—†	1861–63	operator	22	"
	F	Grossman Anna C—†	1861–63	housewife	52	here
	G	Grossman William J	1861–63	steamfitter	53	"
	H	Melanson Josephine—†	1861–63	waitress	49	"
	K	O'Hara Mary—†	1861–63	housewife	60	"
	L	Sadoski Frank J	1865	operator	56	"
	M	Sadoski James G	1865	U S M C	22	"
	N	Maloney Helen T—†	1865	housewife	49	"
	O	Maloney James	1865	clerk	52	
	P	Costello Catherine A—†	1865	W A V E	23	"
	R	Costello James E	1865	U S A	28	
	S	Costello Mary A—†	1865	housewife	46	"
	T	Costello Michael F	1865	shipper	50	
	U	McLaughlin Rita M—†	1865	typist	26	
	V	Gallagher Catherine—†	1865	housewife	65	"
	W	Gallagher Helen—†	1865	bookkeeper	27	"
	X	Parent Grace—†	1865	nurse	40	"
	Y	Cameron Grace—†	1865	operator	52	"
	Z	Highet Andrew	1865	meter reader	56	"

632

	A	Highet Edith G—†	1865	housewife	35	"
	B	Loomis Constantine	1865	laborer	62	
	C	Loomis Sarah—†	1865	teacher	22	
	D	*Loomis Stella—†	1865	housewife	59	"
	E	Harrington Helen A—†	1865	"	38	California
	F	Harrington John L	1865	driller	38	here

Columbus Avenue—Continued

	Letter	FULL NAME	Residence Jan. 1, 1946	Occupation	Supposed Age	Reported Residence, Jan. 1, 1945. Street and Number
	G	Murray Donald J	1865	U S A	33	here
	H	Murray Helen L—†	1865	housewife	59	"
	K	Murray Raymond A	1865	clerk	29	"
	L	Shepard Gladys M—†	1865	"	35	87 School
	M	Kelley James	1865	operator	51	here
	N	Gillogley Esther—†	1865	clerk	21	"
	O	Gillogley Marie—†	1865	"	23	"
	P	Gillogley Rose—†	1865	housewife	50	"
	R	Montville Dorothy—†	1865	waitress	21	Vermont
	S	Montville Elizabeth—†	1865	housewife	40	"
	W	McLaughlin John	1871	clerk	28	1865 Col av
	X	McLaughlin Rita—†	1871	"	26	1865 "
	Y	McCoy Jessica—†	1871	housewife	50	94 Bragdon
	Z	McCoy Raymond	1871	U S A	25	94 "
633						
	A	McCoy Raymond J	1871	machinist	49	94 "
	B	Hill Barbara A—†	1871	waitress	22	22 W Walnut pk
	C	Hill Joseph A	1871	porter	62	22 "
	D	Hill Kathleen—†	1871	housewife	54	22 "
	E	Reveliotis Alexander	1871	U S A	30	22 "
	F	Reveliotis Elizabeth—†	1871	waitress	27	22 "
	G	Fay Florence—†	1873	housewife	43	here
	H	Fay Henry	1873	operator	58	"
	K	Fay Paul L	1873	clerk	20	"
	L	Horgan Mary—†	1873	housewife	60	"
	M	Horgan Maurice	1873	laborer	60	"
	N	McNamara Catherine—†	1873	housewife	65	1538 Tremont
	O	McNamara Joseph	1873	electrician	27	1538 "
	P	McNamara Kathleen—†	1873	clerk	25	1538 "
	R	McNamara Mary—†	1873	typist	23	1538 "
	S	McNamara Timothy	1873	clerk	66	1538 "
	W	Freeman Mary E—†	1899	domestic	40	here
	X	Johnson Benjamin F	1899	janitor	61	"
	Y	Johnson Edith S—†	1899	housewife	58	"
	Z	Johnson Henry S	1899	U S A	32	"
634						
	A	Coles Arthur	1899	bartender	52	"
	B	Coles Mabel—†	1899	housewife	48	"
	C	Coles Charles	1901	retired	79	
	D	Coles Sarah—†	1901	housewife	72	"
	E	Pierre Manuel	1901	mechanic	38	"

Columbus Avenue—Continued

F	Pierre Secornal—†	1901	housewife	29	here
G	Gray Helen—†	1901	domestic	47	"
H	Hall Florence—†	1901	housewife	53	"
K	Hill Minnie—†	1901	domestic	49	"
L	Logan Gladys—†	1901	housewife	43	"
M	Lambert James A	1903	musician	54	"
N	Lambert John T	1903	U S N	24	"
O	Lambert Margaret M—†	1903	secretary	22	"
P	Lambert Mary A—†	1903	housewife	54	"
R	Papastavros George P	1903	laborer	55	"
S	Papastavros Helen—†	1903	operator	45	"
T	Barrio Mary J—†	1903	housewife	48	"
U	McElhinney Rose A—†	1903	matron	51	
V	Lambert George H	1905	musician	52	"
W	Lambert Virginia I—†	1905	clerk	29	
X	Driscoll Claire A—†	1905	teacher	21	
Y	Driscoll Loretta M—†	1905	housewife	59	"
Z	Driscoll Paul S	1905	clerk	20	

635

A	Cusick Edward A	1905	"	30	
B	Powers Albert J	1905	painter	50	
C	Powers Anna F—†	1905	housewife	49	"
D	Bennett John	1907	florist	39	
E	Bennett Saville—†	1907	housewife	35	"
G	Baker Caroline—†	1907	operator	50	"
H	Twing Esther J—†	1909	waitress	35	
K	Egan Mary—†	1909	clerk	48	"
L	McLaughlin Jessie—†	1909	at home	66	New York
O	Glynn Winifred—†	1922	clerk	47	here
P	*Stanislawzyk Anna—†	1922	housewife	49	"
R	Stanislawzyk Jennie—†	1922	clerk	24	"
S	Stanislawzyk Joseph	1922	"	21	
T	*Stanislawzyk Stanley	1922	operator	50	"
U	Graham Agnes—†	1922	housewife	53	"
V	Graham Clarence	1922	laborer	54	
W	Jack Mary—†	1922	housewife	26	"
Z	King Mary—†	1937	at home	83	

636

A	Williams Emily—†	1937	housewife	58	"
B	Williams Mathias	1937	painter	58	
C	Williams Mathias	1937	laborer	25	

22

Columbus Avenue—Continued

D	Miller Jean—†	1937	clerk	24	here	
E	Miller Mary—†	1937	"	45	"	
H	Chin Sam	1951	manager	41	"	
K	MacDonald Earl L	1953	photographer	43	"	
L	MacDonald Mildred—†	1953	housewife	42	"	
M	Macauley Margaret—†	1953	"	23		
N	Macauley Robert	1953	chauffeur	29	"	
O	Egan Beatrice—†	1953	housewife	27	"	
P	Egan Thomas F	1953	chauffeur	27	"	
R	Boivin Madeline—†	1955	housewife	20	41 Houghton	
S	Boivin Roger	1955	laborer	24	41 "	
T	Fryer Mary—†	1955	waitress	39	here	
U	Henry David	1955	student	21	"	
V	Henry Helen—†	1955	beautician	48	"	
W	Harzbecker Frank C	1955	chauffeur	53	"	
X	Harzbecker Grace J—†	1955	clerk	38		
Y	*Gallagher Elizabeth—†	1957	housewife	48	"	
Z	Gallagher James P	1957	retired	64	"	

637

A	Zinck Delphine—†	1957	housewife	30	"	
B	Zinck William S	1957	fishcutter	33	"	
C	Harzbecker Robert G	1957	mechanic	50	"	
D	Harzbecker Robert G, jr	1957	U S N	22		
G	Black Herbert K	1963	clerk	28		
H	Swazdowich Daisy—†	1963	housewife	49	"	
K	Swazdowich Michael	1963	bartender	54	"	
L	Pasek Eleanor—†	1963	housewife	60	"	
M	Pasek Frank	1963	assembler	65	"	

Copley Street

N	Cokinos Spiros J	16	salesman	56	here	
O	Eck Beatrice E—†	16	housekeeper	49	"	
P	Fallon Elizabeth C—†	16	at home	86	"	
R	Sulfaro Tomaso	16	retired	61	"	
S	Barca Mary—†	17	housewife	36	"	
T	Barca Peter M	17	cutter	35	"	
U	Haasis Frederick W	18	U S A	21		
V	Haasis Helen—†	18	housewife	51	"	
W	Haasis Helen M—†	18	operator	23	"	
X	Haasis William N	18	carpenter	48	"	

23

Page.	Letter.	FULL NAME.	Residence, Jan. 1, 1946.	Occupation.	Supposed Age.	Reported Residence, Jan. 1, 1945. Street and Number.

Copley Street—Continued

	Y	Mileski Michael	18	U S A	32	here
	z	Mileski Theo—†	18	housewife	31	"
638						
	A	Fisher Frances—†	19	wrapper	23	"
	B	Fisher Lillian—†	19	waitress	23	"
	c	Fisher Mary—†	19	cashier	25	
	D	Fisher Mary D—†	19	housewife	43	"
	E	Devine Anastasia A—†	20	"	61	
	F	Devine Simon P	20	dentist	37	
	G	Devine Walter J	20	printer	40	
	H	Devine Walter S	20	retired	63	
	K	Devine Hugh S	22	shipper	50	
	L	Devine Katherine M—†	22	secretary	47	"

Dimock Street

	M	McMahon Elizabeth G—†	1	housewife	40	here
	N	McMahon James P	1	bartender	44	"
	o	Cunningham Mary—†	1	housewife	31	"
	P	Cunningham Richard	1	pipefitter	29	"
	s	Curley Elsie I—†	2	housewife	30	"
	T	Curley John J	2	porter	34	
	U	Maxwell John L	3	foreman	61	"
	v	Silva Catherine M—†	4	housewife	49	"
	w	Silva Constance B—†	4	clerk	28	
	x	Silva Gabriela C—†	4	"	25	
	Y	Silva Helen E—†	4	"	31	
	z	Silva Julius	4	chef	60	
639						
	A	Braid Effie—†	8	nurse	46	
	B	Murphy Esther—†	8	"	34	
	c	Shaw Marjorie—†	8	"	34	
	D	Eastman Helen A—†	N E Hosp	housekeeper	52	"
	E	Grauer Ruth—†	"	technician	28	"
	F	Mann Arlene M—†	"	nurse	24	
	G	Mulville Josephine A—†	"	supt	64	
	H	Stephens Ada—†	"	technician	30	"
	K	Blakeman Priscilla—†	14	nurse	23	"
	L	Brady Florence—†	14	"	23	New Bedford
	M	Burtt Eudora—†	14	"	22	here
	N	Cleland Gertrude—†	14	"	33	"

24

Dimock Street—Continued

o	Dunbrach Elsie—†	14	nurse	42	here
p	Everett Edith—†	14	"	23	166 Boylston
R	Kingston Elizabeth—†	14	"	27	here
s	Lacey Phyllis—†	14	"	21	"
T	Maki Helen M—†	14		32	"
u	Markham Elsie—†	14		26	
v	Martin Jean F—†	14		60	
w	McDermott Barbara—†	14	"	22	
x	O'Grady Frances—†	14		25	"
Y	O'Toole Anne M—†	14	"	21	Randolph
z	Perkins Miriam L—†	14	"	35	here

640

A	Shennet Anne—†	14	"	27	"
B	Smith Esther—†	14		47	"
c	Stirling Charlotte—†	14	"	27	Maryland
D	Wilkie Kathleen L—†	14	"	42	here
E	Wyse Elizabeth—†	14	"	33	"
F	Day Alice—†	84	housewife	39	"
G	Day Ernest	84	mechanic	45	"
H	Sykes Esther—†	84	housewife	24	"
K	McGillicuddy James F	84	chauffeur	57	"
L	McGillicuddy Mary E—†	84	housewife	47	"
M	Solohonides Kermon	84	operator	55	"
N	Larecy Eulalia—†	86	"	50	
o	Larecy Matilda—†	86	at home	80	"
P	Thorson George	86	painter	45	
R	Thorson George, jr	86	laborer	22	
s	Thorson Viola—†	86	housewife	40	"
T	Reissfelder Emma G—†	86	"	41	"
u	Reissfelder George	86	foreman	43	"

Ernst Street

v	Seale Helena—†	1	housewife	28	here
w	Seale William	1	calker	30	"
x	Benson Constance—†	1	housekeeper	73	"
Y	Owen Grace—†	1	housewife	29	"
z	Owen Robert	1	rigger	32	

641

A	Bartels Edith L—†	1	housewife	39	"
B	Bartels William K	1	U S N	27	"

Ernst Street—Continued

c	Graham Blanche—†	2	housewife	48	here
d	Daley Francis T	2	U S A	37	Cambridge
e	Gallagher James T	2	operator	38	here
f	Gallagher Margaret G—†	2	housewife	35	"
g	Graham William	2	painter	49	"
h	Kelley Louis F	2	engineer	45	"
k	Kelley Mary W—†	2	housewife	35	"
l	Johnston Alfred J	4	fireman	64	
m	Kelley James F	4	maintenance	38	"
n	Kelley Ruth M—†	4	housewife	34	"
o	Hartzbecker Marie—†	4	"	40	"
p	Hartzbecker Walter	4	machinist	45	"
r	Armstrong John E	4	chauffeur	33	"
s	Armstrong Wanda—†	4	housewife	27	"
t	Gallagher Daniel F	6	chauffeur	39	"
u	Gallagher Mary T—†	6	housewife	42	"
v	Rhodes Fotika—†	6	"	51	
w	Rhodes George T	6	pedler	61	
x	Senecal Edward	6	boilermaker	58	"
y	Senecal Eva—†	6	housewife	55	"
z	Senecal Reginald	6	U S A	36	"

642

a	Blue Helen G—†	8	housewife	58	"
b	Blue John D	8	mechanic	55	"
c	Daley Mary—†	8	housekeeper	62	"
d	Coleman Francis	8	brewer	43	"
e	Coleman Helena—†	8	housewife	37	"
f	Davis Catherine—†	8	"	61	
g	Davis Francis	8	mechanic	35	"
h	Davis William R	8	seaman	32	
k	DeEntremont David	10	chauffeur	36	"
l	DeEntremont Regina—†	10	housewife	36	"
m	Drown Donald	10	operator	24	Nebraska
n	Sjoquist Axel	10	metalworker	54	here
o	Sjoquist Karen V—†	10	clerk	20	"
p	Sjoquist Reynold	10	shipper	24	"
r	Sjoquist Tekla—†	10	housewife	57	"
s	Withers Aaron D	10	pedler	26	Malden
t	Withers Edith M—†	10	housewife	22	"
u	Greenhow Joseph	12	watchman	45	here
v	*Greenhow Mary—†	12	housewife	43	"

Ernst Street—Continued

w	Hodgson Eric	12	operator	28	2997 Wash'n
x	Duosrzko Stanley	12	machinist	51	here
y	Niedzwicki Felix	12	painter	51	"
z	Niedzwicki Malvina—†	12	housewife	50	"

643

a	Fallon Daniel E	12	porter	56	
b	Fallon Helen—†	12	housewife	53	"
c	Cantellis Constantina—†.	14–16	"	46	
d	Cantellis James	14–16	salesman	55	"
e	Cantellis John	14–16	shipper	23	
f	Stella James	14–16	musician	39	"
g	Stella Leona—†	14–16	housewife	36	"
h	DeFilippo Anthony G	15–17	manager	44	"
k	DeFilippo Elizabeth—†	15–17	housewife	39	"
l	Bartlett Eva A—†	15–17	"	52	
m	Bartlett Everett N	15–17	foreman	58	"

Mahn's Terrace

n	Horgan Catherine—†	1	housewife	34	here
o	Horgan John	1	attendant	38	"
p	Campbell Mildred—†	1	housewife	33	"
r	Morrill Hollis	1	mechanic	38	"
s	Carleson Charlotte—†	1	housewife	40	"
t	Carleson Robert	1	machinist	44	"
u	Partridge Dorothy—†	2	housewife	35	"
v	Partridge Horace E	2	chauffeur	39	"
w	Groves Mary—†	2	housewife	25	Worcester
x	Groves Victor	2	chauffeur	25	"
y	Sadoski Elvira L—†	2	housewife	27	here
z	Sadoski Joseph	2	operator	27	"

644   Marbury Terrace

a	Langone Carmella—†	2	at home	64	Woburn
b	Lovallo Grace—†	2	housewife	31	"
c	Lovallo Leonard	2	engineer	34	30 Peterboro
d	Moylan Anna J—†	2	housewife	63	here
e	Moylan James	2	operator	69	"
f	Moylan James, jr	2	U S A	25	"
g	Lasinsky Ernest	2	retired	73	"

Page.	Letter.	FULL NAME.	Residence, Jan. 1, 1946.	Occupation.	Supposed Age.	Reported Residence, Jan. 1, 1945. Street and Number.

Marbury Terrace—Continued

H	Lasinsky Frederick	2	electrician	36	here
K	Fowles Lillian—†	4	housewife	40	"
L	Fowles Priscilla—†	4	"	56	"
M	Fowles Wilbur	4	clerk	61	
N	Poeld Lillian—†	4	teacher	41	
O	Poeld Oscar	4	draftsman	51	"
P	Wenstein Bella—†	4	at home	68	"
R	Blood Arthur J	4	machinist	28	"
S	Blood Louise—†	4	housewife	24	"
T	Deininger Anna—†	8	"	66	
U	Deininger Frederick E	8	guard	41	
V	Deininger Otto C	8	watchman	68	"
W	Deininger Ruth C—†	8	clerk	28	
X	Kelley Alma D—†	8	"	39	
Y	Callahan Alice M—†	8	housewife	55	"
Z	Callahan Joseph E	8	salesman	29	"
	645				
A	Callahan Joseph P	8	carpenter	55	"
B	DeCoste Albert W	8	foreman	29	"
C	DeCoste Virginia—†	8	housewife	26	"
D	Crowley Claire M—†	8	operator	24	"
E	Crowley Daniel	8	laborer	49	
F	Crowley Nora T—†	8	housewife	48	"
G	Cahill Allida—†	10	"	39	229 Highland
H	Cahill Frederick W	10	machinist	31	229 "
K	Graham Hannah M—†	10	housekeeper	71	here
L	Waterman Albert	10	shipper	30	"
M	Waterman Anne—†	10	housewife	29	"
N	Kilduff Celia—†	18	"	40	
O	Kilduff John	18	carpenter	47	"
P	McKay Mary—†	18	housewife	32	"
R	McKay William	18	carpenter	37	"
S	Murphy John	18	clerk	35	Cambridge
T	Mercer Mary—†	18	housewife	51	here
U	Mercer Sidney	18	carpenter	55	"
V	*Miller Barbara—†	20	housewife	33	"
W	Miller Walter	20	printer	38	"
X	McKay Mary E—†	20	at home	60	2 Marbury ter
Y	Morrison Helen—†	20	housewife	34	here
Z	Morrison Woodbury W	20	clerk	34	"

Page.	Letter.	FULL NAME.	Residence, Jan. 1, 1946.	Occupation.	Supposed Age.	Reported Residence, Jan. 1, 1945. Street and Number.

646
Marbury Terrace—Continued

A	Sashe Jacob	20	machinist	66	here
B	Sashe Lizette—†	20	housewife	69	"

Miles Street

C	Mangan Etta—†	1	assembler	34	here
D	Mangan James	1	U S A	32	"
E	Frizzell Anna—†	1	housewife	53	"
F	Frizzell Lillian—†	1	clerk	21	"
G	Frizzell Mary—†	1	"	29	
H	Lee Isabelle—†	1	housewife	36	"
K	Lee Joseph	1	U S N	35	"
L	Maloney James	2	salesman	31	16 Westminster av
M	Maloney Mary—†	2	housewife	28	16 "
N	Gartland Estelle—†	2	"	55	here
O	Gartland George	2	clerk	57	"
P	Tierney Arthur	2	electrician	30	"
R	Fest Carl H	2	jeweler	24	
S	Fest Christine—†	2	housewife	22	"
T	*MacIver Catherine A—†	2	"	41	
U	MacIver John M	2	carpenter	47	"
V	Pizza Lillian—†	14–16	housewife	32	"
W	Pizza Ralph	14–16	pipefitter	39	"
X	Kearney Michael J	14–16	fireman	40	
Y	Kearney Rose A—†	14–16	housewife	44	"

647 Notre Dame Street

C	Butler Bertha—†	10	housewife	38	here
D	Butler Viola—†	10	"	35	"
E	Walker Walter	10	U S N	20	"
F	Miller Louella—†	10	housewife	32	"
G	Jordan Arthur	10	U S N	33	
H	Jordan Theresa—†	10	housewife	33	"
K	Miner Ella—†	12	"	51	
L	Gregg Helen—†	12	"	38	
M	Gregg Wellington	12	porter	44	
N	Snowden Jane G—†	12	housekeeper	38	"
O	Janey Clara M—†	20	housewife	52	"

29

Notre Dame Street—Continued

P	Janey Daniel B	20	laborer	55	here
T	Sheehy Velma—†	26	clerk	37	105 Munroe
U	Fanning Caroline—†	28	housewife	27	here
V	Fanning Andrew	28	letter carrier	33	"
X	Pearson Bertha—†	29	housewife	35	"
Y	Pearson George	29	letter carrier	35	"
Z	Stuckey Alexander	29	machinist	40	"

648

A	Stuckey Marjorie—†	29	housewife	40	"
B	White Caroline—†	31	"	59	
C	White John A	31	clerk	60	
D	White John A, jr	31	U S A	28	"
E	White Ralph A	31	"	24	
F	White Virginia L—†	31	stitcher	22	
G	McKnight Chester	35	laborer	48	
H	Thomas Edward	35	retired	76	
K	Thomas Lillian—†	35	housewife	67	"
L	Williams Isaac	37	laborer	32	
M	McFall Ethel—†	43	housewife	52	"
N	McFall Oscar	43	pharmacist	60	"
O	Muncey Henry	45	retired	76	..
P	Thornton Josephine—†	45	housekeeper	64	"
R	Thornton Martha—†	45	"	69	"
S	Toomey Helen—†	47	housewife	50	"
T	Toomey William	47	clerk	24	
U	Toy Arthur	47	U S N	20	
V	Toy Caroline—†	47	housewife	56	"
W	Toy Edwin	47	clerk	23	..
X	Toy George	47	chef	63	

School Street

Z	Coulton Gordon S	101	chemist	33	here

649

A	Coulton Josephine L—†	101	housewife	70	"
B	Coulton Lillian J—†	101	clerk	30	
C	Downey George	101	machinist	50	"
D	Ryder Margaret—†	101	housewife	44	"
E	Ryder Owen A	101	meter reader	44	"
F	Baxendale George T	103	metalworker	38	"

School Street—Continued

G	Baxendale Lillian—†	103	housewife	38	here
H	Preston Pearl—†	103	stenographer	22	"
K	Terwilliger Elizabeth—†	103	housewife	44	"
L	Terwilliger Frances—†	103	stenographer	25	"
M	Terwilliger Thomas	103	U S C G	50	"
N	Fitzgerald Catherine M-†	105	housewife	56	"
O	Fitzgerald John F	105	fireman	60	
P	Fitzgerald John M	105	U S N	20	
R	Fitzgerald Mary M—†	105	clerk	24	
S	Fitzgerald Monica—†	105	at home	21	"
T	O'Brien John	105	painter	46	
U	Harzbecker Frank	105	retired	80	
V	Hughes Elizabeth T—†	105	floorwoman	44	"
W	Roache Marie A—†	105	housewife	42	"
X	Roache Nicholas F	105	painter	46	
Y	Domahowski Edith—†	105	housewife	21	"
Z	Eldridge Loretta—†	105	cook	43	

650

A	Natale Evelyn—†	105	housewife	20	"
B	Fox James	107	electrician	42	"
C	Mahoney Mary E—†	107	nurse	29	
D	*Martell Rose M—†	107	housekeeper	60	"
E	Seward Charles	107	retired	81	"
F	Esson Catherine—†	107	housewife	54	"
G	Esson Elizabeth—†	107	tel operator	21	"
H	Esson Thomas	107	attendant	61	"
K	Hufnagle Charles	107	laborer	48	13 Weld av
L	McGee Alexander D	107	retired	76	here
M	McGee Eleanor J—†	107	housewife	64	"
N	Stegemann Herman	107	clerk	64	"
O	Daly Edith V—†	111	housewife	35	"
P	Daly James R	111	guard	47	"
R	Fiore Alphonso	111	baker	28	
S	Fiore Amelia—†	111	teller	31	
T	Fiore Edith—†	111	secretary	29	"
U	Fiore Gerardo	111	clerk	26	"
V	Fiore Helen—†	111	"	33	
W	Fiore Lucy—†	111	housewife	53	"
X	Fiore Salvatore	111	barber	62	
Y	Silton Edward	115	manager	36	"
Z	Silton Margaret M—†	115	housewife	33	"

651
School Street—Continued

A	Donnelly Alice—†	115	housewife	36	here
B	Donnelly Harold	115	mechanic	39	"
C	McCormack George A	117	U S A	27	"
D	McCormack Gertrude E–†	117	housewife	53	"
E	McCormack John R	117	foreman	53	"
F	Kuehnel Emily—†	117	housewife	69	"
G	Kuehnel Minnie—†	117	clerk	43	"
H	Joyce Catherine—†	119	inspector	43	105 School
K	Reams Anna B—†	119	housewife	40	here
L	Reams William H	119	foreman	44	"
M	Bauman Matilda—†	119	housewife	70	"
N	Gimel Frieda—†	119	at home	70	"
O	Kardinal Emil W	121	baker	69	21 Atherton
P	Kardinal Hedwig—†	121	housewife	65	21 "
R*	Sandelind Alexander	121	painter	66	here
S	Sandelind May—†	121	housewife	55	"
T	Conroy Anna G—†	125	broker	55	"
U	Conroy Jennie L—†	125	at home	73	"
X	McLaughlin John F	125	teacher	26	"
Y	McLaughlin John G	125	custodian	64	"
V	McLaughlin Mary H—†	125	housewife	67	"
W	McLaughlin Mary K—†	125	teacher	34	
Y¹	Gately Margaret—†	127	at home	71	"
Z	Farrington Alice C—†	127	teacher	45	

652

A	Farrington Wendell M	127	laborer	51	
C	Colburn Mary K—†	131	housewife	36	"
D	Roche Lawrence B	131	metalworker	39	"
E	Roche Mary F—†	131	housewife	73	"
F	Roche Nicholas J	131	retired	76	
G	Roche Raymond	131	laborer	41	
H	French Joseph H	135	physician	54	"
K	French Katherine—†	135	supervisor	56	"
L	Maxwell Clement	135	teacher	50	
M	McEntee Ellen J—†	135	housekeeper	58	"
N	McFarland Robert J	135	U S N	25	"
O	Brickley Edith C—†	137	housekeeper	47	"
P	Morris Florence M—†	137	assembler	29	"

Washington Street

T	Pryor Hattie—†	2937	housewife	40	here
U	Pryor Moses	2937	janitor	47	Louisiana
W	Cox Amanzo	2941	"	35	22 Hollander
X	Cox Julia—†	2941	housewife	20	22 "
Y	Gibson Marie—†	2941	housekeeper	79	here
Z	Jones Alice—†	2947A	housewife	24	"
	653					
A	Jones William	2947A	laborer	49	"
B	Bush Cynthia M—†	2947A	housekeeper	25	"
C	Bush Mary E—†	2947A	"	51	"
D	Muse Harriet—†	2947A	housewife	27	2941 Wash'n
F	Jackson Elizabeth—†	2949	"	31	here
G	Jackson James	2949	laborer	30	"
H	Driscoll Kathleen—†	2949	supervisor	22	"
L	*Gallagher Catherine—†	2963	housekeeper	65	"
M	Johnson Portia—†	2963	housewife	22	67 Sharon
N	Johnson William	2963	laborer	28	67 "
O	Barnett Edna—†	2963	housewife	38	32 Hammond
P	Barnett Norwell	2963	chef	50	32 "
R	Hamilton Bessie—†	2965	housekeeper	58	here
S	Shea Mildred—†	2965	housewife	32	"
T	Turner George	2965	chauffeur	25	"
U	Turner Shirley—†	2965	housewife	22	"
W	*DeFrancisco Mary—†	2969	housekeeper	67	73 Bromley
X	Hansen Henry	2969	mechanic	36	here
Y	*Hansen Margaret—†	2969	housewife	42	"
Z	DiPaola Alfred	2969	packer	37	"
	654					
A	DiPaola Marie—†	2969	housewife	30	"
B	*Blanchard Oscar	2971	laborer	60	26 Notre Dame
C	Hart Mary—†	2971	housewife	44	here
D	Hart Patrick	2971	fireman	43	"
E	*Zogas Charles	2871	chef	59	"
F	Zogas Pauline—†	2971	housewife	43	"
G	DiCarlo Rose—†	2971	operator	27	"
H	Kelley Alan	2973	chauffeur	35	"
K	Kelley Frances—†	2973	housewife	32	"
L	Baxter Edward	2973	chauffeur	51	"
M	Baxter Florence—†	2973	housewife	49	"
N	*Visconti Mary—†	2973	"	67	"

Page.	Letter.	FULL NAME.	Residence, Jan. 1, 1946.	Occupation.	Supposed Age.	Reported Residence, Jan. 1, 1945. Street and Number.

Washington Street—Continued

	o	Henry Evelyn M—†	2973	housewife	40	here
	p	Henry Francis E	2973	porter	50	"
	r	McKay Mary—†	2975	housekeeper	72	2989 Wash'n
	s	Doucette Alexandra—†	2975	housewife	41	here
	t	Doucette Willis	2975	painter	37	"
	u	McCarthy Ruth—†	2975	housewife	32	"
	v	McCarthy William F	2975	chauffeur	32	"
	w	Esaian Elias K	2981	shoemaker	54	"
	x	Johnson Rose—†	2983	laundress	34	108 W Springfield
	y	Boghosian Agnes—†	2983	housewife	46	here
	z	Boghosian Krikor	2983	machinist	20	"

655

	a	Boghosian Toros	2983	carpenter	65	"
	b	Munroe Beatrice—†	2985	housewife	33	2 Ditmus ct
	c	Munroe Edward	2985	porter	35	1 "
	d	*Albuzetian Nartonke—†	2985	housewife	47	here
	e	Albuzetian Sarkis	2985	operator	52	"
	f	*Nigohosian Virginia—†	2985	housewife	32	"
	g	Nigohosian Zabel—†	2985	finisher	31	
	k	Carr Francis J	2989	trainman	22	"
	l	Carr Margaret A—†	2989	housewife	62	"
	m	Frawley Charles	2989	retired	79	
	o	Brooks Michael J	2991	painter	63	"
	p	Grogan Edward F	2991	chauffeur	31	4 Dighton
	r	Grogan Rita E—†	2991	housewife	29	4 "
	s	Doyle Bridget—†	2991	"	58	10 Beethoven
	t	Doyle John J	2991	U S M C	30	10 "
	u	Hagen John F	2991	metalworker	48	4 Jess
	v	Hagen John F, jr	2991	U S A	24	4 "
	w	Hagen Rose B—†	2991	housewife	48	4 "
	x	Rivers Lucy—†	2993	cook	32	Maine
	y	Standish Ada—†	2993	"	47	here
	z	Chute Leonora J—†	2993	housewife	52	9 Cornwall

656

	a	LaVasseur Julia—†	2993	"	50	Cambridge
	b	LaVasseur Louis	2993	chauffeur	50	"
	c	Chamberlain Mary—†	2995	housekeeper	40	here
	d	Pauley Charles J	2995	mechanic	21	Florida
	e	Pauley Shirley—†	2995	housewife	21	"
	f	Tatem Catherine M—†	2995	"	24	Malden
	g	Tatem Vernon A	2995	U S N	26	"

Washington Street—Continued

H	Gincola Theresa—†	2995	housewife	28	2971 Wash'n
K	McCormack Helen J—†	2997	housekeeper	48	8 Gloucester
L	Morris Havlin J	2997	boilermaker	63	here
M	Morris Isabelle—†	2997	housewife	56	"
N	Monkewicz Frank	2997	chef	34	Canton
O	Monkewicz Hester—†	2997	housewife	31	here
P	Mosher Mabel—†	2997	saleswoman	65	"
R	Darby Edna M—†	2999	housewife	24	4 Thornton pl
S	Darby Paul	2999	machinist	29	4 "
T	Hubbard Ernest	2999	salesman	29	Texas
U	Hubbard Jane—†	2999	housewife	22	"
V	Stanyiani Angela—†	2999	"	23	30 Codman pk
W	Stanyiani Walter	2999	printer	23	30 "
X	Stoddard Rose—†	2999	housewife	23	here
Y	Walsh Edward F	3001	U S A	24	"
Z	Walsh Emily E—†	3001	housewife	51	"

657

A	Walsh William J	3001	U S A	28	"
B	Drummond Jennie—†	3001	housekeeper	62	"
D	Bruton Mattie—†	3003	"	66	"
E	McCraw Howard	3003	machinist	51	"
F	Williams Ellen—†	3003	housekeeper	73	"
G	Charles Ethel—†	3003	"	60	"
M	Williams Nora—†	3069	housewife	62	"
N	Williams Robert H	3069	laborer	61	
O	Chaney Mary E—†	3069	housewife	58	"
P	Ippolito Salvatore H	3069	clerk	36	"
R	Lennon Thomas J	3069	U S N	25	1865 Col av
S	Lydon Madeline—†	3069	housewife	26	1865 "
T	McCarty Margaret M—†	3069	"	46	1865 "
U	McCarty Robert H	3069	letter carrier	47	1865 "
V	Davey Delia—†	3069	operator	56	here

658

M	Miller Adam J	3103	baker	50	"
N	Miller Emma F—†	3103	housewife	52	"
R	Harmon Blanche E—†	3109	knitter	39	
S	Harmon Frank L	3109	mechanic	42	"
T	Flynn Kathleen—†	3109	operator	29	"
U	Flynn Nina—†	3109	housewife	50	"
V	Hutchins Edith—†	3111	"	63	
W	Hutchins Eugene S	3111	U S A	22	

Washington Street—Continued

x	Hutchins Joseph	3111	chef	54	here
y	Tumulty Catherine M–†	3111	housewife	48	6 W Cottage

659

b	Carey Phyllis—†	3117	packer	21	here
c	Reynolds Albert J	3117	laborer	47	"
d	Reynolds Julia—†	3117	operator	45	"
e	Colley Alice—†	3117	housewife	35	"
f	Colley Frank	3117	chauffeur	37	"
g	Arvan Anna T—†	3117	stitcher	49	
h	Arvan Henry D	3117	U S M C	27	"
k	Banks Charlotte M—†	3117	housewife	58	"
l	Banks Enock	3117	machinist	50	"
m	Lowder Alice M—†	3117	clerk	39	
n	Lowder James F	3117	chauffeur	38	"
o	Johnson Dorinda G—†	3117	housewife	77	Woburn
p	Johnson William H	3117	retired	77	"
t	George Celia—†	3123	housewife	33	here
u	George Edward	3123	chauffeur	38	"
v	Grant Dorothy C—†	3123	collector	58	14 Dixwell
w	Reynolds Gertrude—†	3123	packer	54	here
x	Reynolds Louise—†	3123	housewife	77	"
y	Reynolds Thomas F	3123	ropemaker	75	"
z	Hanes Joseph E	3123	agent	49	

660

a	Haines Margaret V—†	3123	housewife	67	"
b	Dekesian Anna—†	3123	clerk	30	
c	Dekesian Kerop	3123	"	50	
d	Cunniff Catherine—†	3123	housewife	33	"
e	Cunniff Patrick	3123	shipper	35	

West Walnut Park

f	Kennedy Clara—†	20	housewife	38	2946 Wash'n
g	Kennedy Joseph	20	shipper	38	2946 "
h	Cahill Catherine B—†	20	housewife	68	here
k	Cahill James F	20	retired	75	"
l	Cahill Lillian E—†	20	operator	28	"
m	Fallon Hildred M—†	20	housewife	40	"
n	Fallon William A	20	foreman	44	"
o	Edmiston Eleanor C—†	22	housewife	53	"
p	Edmiston Olive—†	22	WAC	24	

West Walnut Park—Continued

Page.	Letter.	FULL NAME.	Residence, Jan. 1, 1946.	Occupation.	Supposed Age.	Reported Residence, Jan. 1, 1945. Street and Number.
	R	Edmiston William	22	foreman	52	here
	S	Edmiston Anna—†	22	housewife	57	"
	T	Edmiston James	22	carpenter	58	"
	U	Edmiston James M	22	U S A	22	"
	V	Landrigan Mary—†	22	operator	32	52 School
	W	Murphy Michael	22	welder	30	52 "
	X	Murphy Sabina A—†	22	housewife	69	52 "
	Y	Barker Vernon F	24	operator	27	here
	Z	Barker Walter	24	U S A	30	"
661						
	A	Connell Harris D	24	salesman	58	"
	B	Connell Marion—†	24	housewife	57	"
	C	Lindsay John	24	shipfitter	49	"
	D	Lindsay Mary—†	24	housewife	45	"
	E	Lindsay Robert	24	clerk	20	"
	F	Stewart Robert	24	retired	76	
	G	Lloyd Freda—†	28	housewife	32	"
	H	Lloyd William	28	attendant	38	"
	K	Paige James R	28	clerk	21	170 Amory
	L	Paige Margaret—†	28	laundress	56	170 "
	M	Bois Josephine—†	30	housewife	25	167 School
	N	Bois Marcel J	30	machinist	23	167 "
	O	Parevoliotes Christine—†	32	housewife	38	20 W Walnut pk
	P	Parevoliotes Manoles	32	chauffeur	36	20 "
	R	Allen Ann—†	33	bookkeeper	20	here
	S	Allen Paul D	33	U S C G	20	N Carolina
	T	Foster Charles	33	chauffeur	59	here
	U	Slade Lydia W—†	33	housewife	43	"
	V	Slade William R	33	brakeman	49	"
	W	Sullivan James	33	painter	65	
	X	Gatturna William	34	salesman	50	"
	Y	O'Brien Edward G	34	engineer	60	"
	Z	Wesely Ernest	34	carpenter	70	"
662						
	A	Wesely Mary—†	34	housewife	41	"
	B	Byron Martha—†	35	housekeeper	58	31 Glendower rd
	C	Carpenter Charles F	35	shipper	27	31 "
	D	Carpenter Martha—†	35	housewife	37	31 "
	E	Holbrook David	37	U S C G	50	here
	F	Holbrook Louise—†	37	housewife	48	"
	G	Perino Catherine—†	37	operator	44	"

West Walnut Park—Continued

H	Perino Mary—†	37	housewife	41	here
K	Eichner Agnes—†	38	"	38	"
L	Eichner John	38	metalworker	43	"
M	Moreau Flora—†	38	housewife	22	"
N	Moreau Joseph	38	metalworker	24	"
O	Forbes Edward D	39	operator	25	"
P	Forbes Mary B—†	39	housewife	23	"
R	Broderick Josephine—†	39	operator	42	"
S	Moran Edward J	39	printer	32	3 Atherton pl
T	Moran Phyllis—†	39	housewife	29	3 "
U	Bell Gertrude—†	40	"	38	here
V	Bell Mary J—†	40	"	70	"
W	Bell William V	40	clerk	45	"
X	Shields Mary—†	40	housewife	71	"
Y	Shields Vincent	41	chauffeur	45	"
Z	Annis Fred G	41	pedler	26	

663

A	Annis Joseph R	41	mechanic	21	100 Regent
B	Annis Lillian I—†	41	housewife	23	here
C	Cunniffe Catherine A—†	41	housekeeper	62	"
D	Clark Joseph M	43	shipper	25	245 Roxbury
E	Clark Mary N—†	43	housewife	23	245 "
F	Stuteville Olive—†	43	"	34	here
G	Stuteville Overton	43	manager	41	"
H	Sacco Elizabeth—†	44	housewife	42	"
K	Sacco Joseph J	44	refinisher	41	"
L	Paige Charles W	46–48	brakeman	30	20 Elton
M	Paige Mary C—†	46–48	housewife	28	20 "
N	Waters Abbie D—†	46–48	"	39	here
O	Waters Nicholas J	46–48	policeman	46	"
P	Kearns Edward F	47–49	manager	43	"
R	Kearns Margaret H—†	47–49	housewife	41	"
S	O'Brien Annie M—†	47–49	housekeeper	72	"
T	Henneberry Elizabeth J—†	47–49	housewife	43	"
U	Henneberry James J	47–49	mechanic	53	"
V	Henneberry Mary P—†	47–49	stenographer	23	"
W	Walsh Lillian M—†	50–52	housewife	38	"
X	Walsh William	50–52	custodian	38	"
Y	Fournarakis Lillian—†	50–52	secretary	20	84 W Walnut pk
Z	Fournarakis Nicholas	50–52	waiter	54	84 "

Page.	Letter.	FULL NAME.	Residence, Jan. 1, 1946.	Occupation.	Supposed Age.	Reported Residence, Jan. 1, 1945. Street and Number.

664
West Walnut Park—Continued

A	*Fournarakis Olympia–†	50–52	housewife	39	84 W Walnut pk
B	Hardiman George	51	chauffeur	37	here
C	Hardiman Mary—†	51	housewife	36	"
D	Gounis Angelo	51	manager	47	"
E	*Gounis Dimitra—†	51	housewife	48	"
F	Mirageos George	51	U S A	22	"
G	Mirageos Mendo	51	"	22	
H	Parsons Louise E—†	54–56	housewife	42	"
K	Parsons Walter M	54–56	letter carrier	48	"
L	Bellows Albert M	54–56	electrician	43	"
M	Bellows Albert M	54–56	U S N	20	
N	Bellows Ebba I—†	54–56	housewife	42	"
O	McCullough Jennie—†	54–56	housekeeper	72	"
P	Nelson Hilda C—†	54–56	"	72	"
R	*Carota Catherine—†	55	housewife	58	"
S	Carota John	55	laborer	68	
T	Caruso Grace—†	55	packer	38	"
U	Ladas Panagota—†	55.	housewife	62	46 W Walnut pk
V	Ladas Peter	55	clerk	36	46 "
W	Ladas William	55	operator	64	46 "
X	Oberlander Mary T—†	58–60	housewife	40	here
Y	Oberlander Warren	58–60	retired	46	"
Z	Rohanna Florence—†	58–60	stitcher	47	"

665

A	Cutler Isabelle—†	58–60	housewife	56	"
B	Cutler Lawrence	58–60	carpenter	30	"
C	Cutler Mildred—†	58–60˙	secretary	32	"
D	Cutler Samuel	58–60	carpenter	58	"
E	Ghiza Charles	59	cleaner	54	63 Compton
F	Ghiza Evelyn—†	59	housewife	43	63 "
G	Ghiza Florence—†	59	shipper	21	63 "
H	Falcone Domenic	59	milliner	47	here
K	Falcone Minnie—†	59	housewife	37	"
L	Shedrick Hannah E—†	62–64	"	57	"
M	Shedrick Ivan B	62–64	machinist	60	"
N	Cavallaro Carmella—†	62–64	housewife	30	"
O	Cavallaro Raymond	62–64	painter	32	
P	Donabedian Ashod	66–68	carpenter	43	"
R	Donabelian Florence—†	66–68	housewife	42	"

West Walnut Park—Continued

s	*Margosian Elmeas—†	66–68	housekeeper	74	here
T	Burns John F	66–68	roofer	59	"
U	Burns Mary A—†	66–68	housewife	53	"
V	Burns Mary A—†	66–68	supt	23	..
W	Sheridan John J	66–68	painter	47	
X	Anagnos Anna—†	70–72	housewife	33	"
Y	*Anagnos Bessie—†	70–72	"	82	
Z	Anagnos William	70–72	merchant	41	"

666

A	Mayman Margaret—†	70–72	housekeeper	29	"
B	*Barnett Alfreda—†	70–72	housewife	70	"
C	Barnett Alice—†	70–72	stenographer	37	"
D	Barnett Mary—†	70–72	typist	42	"
E	Williams Andrew	71–73	metalworker	27	"
F	Williams Phyllis—†	71–73	housewife	24	"
G	Zombick Irma—†	71–73	housekeeper	51	"
H	Lolos Aphrodite—†	71–73	housewife	35	"
K	Lolos Charles	71–73	baker	47	
L	Woleyko Louise—†	74–76	housewife	26	"
M	Woleyko Victor	74–76	foreman	30	"
N	Jung Anna M—†	74–76	WAVE	23	
O	Jung Carl	74–76	chauffeur	65	"
P	Jung Gertrude C—†	74–76	stenographer	32	"
R	Jung Sophie C—†	74–76	housewife	59	"
S	Triantos Arthur	75–77	machinist	26	"
T	Triantos Athena—†	75–77	stenographer	22	"
U	*Triantos Bessie—†	75–77	housewife	51	"
V	Triantos George	75–77	U S A	25	
W	Triantos Harry	75–77	mechanic	27	"
X	Triantos Nicholas	75–77	rigger	56	
Y	Papadinis Mary—†	75–77	housewife	45	"
Z	Papadinis Rosment	75–77	U S A	21	

667

A	MacLeod Alexander D	78–80	chauffeur	58	"
B	MacLeod Margaret A—†	78–80	housewife	51	"
C	Sullivan Catherine F—†	78–80	stenographer	33	"
D	Sullivan Florence	78–80	retired	66	"
E	Ponn Alice—†	79–81	housewife	32	"
F	Ponn Julius	79–81	steamfitter	38	"
G	Deligianis Stamatis	79–81	chef	50	
H	*Deligianis Timothea—†	79–81	housewife	35	"

West Walnut Park—Continued

K	Sylvester Anna—†	82–84	housewife	34	20 Wise
L	Sylvester Joseph	82–84	operator	34	20 "
M	DiNicola Dominic	82–84	retired	65	here
N	DiNicola John	82–84	clerk	25	"
O	DiNicola Louis	82–84	U S A	21	"
P	DiNicola Mary—†	82–84	housewife	52	"
R	Silverio Concetta—†	82–84	"	23	"
S	Silverio John	82–84	operator	27	Beverly
T	Nichols Charles L	83–85	machinist	25	55 Brookley rd
U	Nichols Emma R—†	83–85	housewife	26	55 "
V	Christopoulos Arthur	83–85	carpenter	21	here
W	Christopoulos Charles	83–85	chef	45	"
X	Field Sarah E—†	86–88	housekeeper	58	"
Y	Nelson Edith—†	86–88	housewife	22	"
Z	Richardson Agnes—†	86–88	"	54	

668

A	Costa Frank	86–88	operator	50	"
B	Costa Grace—†	86–88	"	23	
C	Costa Ida A—†	86–88	housewife	45	"
D	Hourihan Edward J	87–89	electrician	41	"
E	Hourihan Mary E—†	87–89	housewife	35	"
F*	Kostavan Catherine—†	87–89	housekeeper	76	"
G	Pappas Eva—†	87–89	housewife	36	"
H	Pappas George	87–89	chef	45	
K	Paraskos Catherine—†	90–92	housewife	35	"
L	Sarruda Angelo	90–92	retired	62	
M	Sarruda Bertha—†	90–92	housewife	26	"
N	Sarruda Charles	90–92	U S N	27	
O	Sarruda George	90–92	"	20	
P	Sarruda John	90–92	operator	23	"
R	Sarruda Mary—†	90–92	stenographer	22	"
S*	Sarruda Sophie—†	90–92	housewife	57	"
U	Stockman Carl A	94–96	U S A	27	
V	Stockman Edward E	94–96	U S C G	22	"
T	Tumshais Carl A	94–96	carpenter	56	"
W	Tumshais Mollie—†	94–96	housewife	42	"
X*	Adasis Andramarki—†	94–96	housekeeper	46	"
Y	Barkus Constantinos J	94–96	manager	54	"
Z	Barkus Helen—†	94–96	bookkeeper	26	"

669

A	Barkus Mary C—†	94–96	housewife	48	"

West Walnut Park—Continued

B	Menechios Catherine—†	95–97	housewife	47	here
C	Menechios Frances—†	95–97	clerk	24	"
D	Menechios Kaliope—†	95–97	"	21	"
E	Menechios Thomas K	95–97	merchant	53	"
F	Zervas Christie	95–97	U S A	21	
G	Zervas Effie—†	95–97	housewife	46	"
H	Zervas Mary—†	95–97	clerk	24	"
K	Zervas William	95–97	chef	56	
L	McKinnon Helen—†	99–101	housewife	52	"
M	McKinnon Philip	99–101	mechanic	52	"
N	Kearney John J	99–101	carpenter	43	"
O	O'Donnell Bernard A	99–101	U S A	25	
P	O'Donnell John J	99–101	supervisor	50	"
R	O'Donnell John J	99–101	U S N	21	
S	O'Donnell Rose G—†	99–101	housewife	50	"
T	Howard Eugene A	103–105	machinist	60	"
U	Howard Nancy—†	103–105	stitcher	60	
V	Sturgis Leonidhas	103–105	waiter	46	
W	Sturgis Margaret—†	103–105	housewife	38	"
X	Sawyer Carrie—†	109	housekeeper	80	86 Pembroke
Y	*Toland Carmella—†	109	housewife	46	86 "
Z	Toland Philip J	109	butcher	49	86 "

670

A	Toronto Joseph	109	laborer	30	here
B	Toronto Yvette—†	109	housewife	28	"
C	Gordon James	109	agent	65	"
D	Lemack Edward	109	machinist	28	"
E	Lemack Hannah—†	109	housewife	47	"
F	Lemack Samuel	109	clerk	22	
G	Opochinsky Pauline—†	109	housewife	85	"
H	Sandri Philip	109	chauffeur	25	45 Holworthy
K	Sandri Reno	109	"	27	45 "
L	Dolan James F	109	"	27	here
M	Dolan Josephine B—†	109	housewife	28	"
N	Kemmett Helen—†	109	"	30	Falmouth
O	Pursley Josephine—†	109	tester	37	here
P	Kanter Josephine M—†	109	housewife	38	"
R	Kanter Paul L	109	laborer	40	"
S	Welland Ruth—†	109	housewife	41	"
T	Welland Werner	109	accountant	46	"
U	Armstrong Grace F—†	109	housekeeper	80	"

West Walnut Park—Continued

v	Webber Frances G—†	109	librarian	39	here	
w	Webber Helen—†	109	housewife	68	"	
x	Jago Edna—†	109	waitress	33	"	
y	Jago Frank	109	chauffeur	29	"	
z	Jago Gertrude J—†	109	housewife	71	"	

671

A	Burnham Anna R—†	109	operator	62	"	
B	Krasnoff Etta—†	109	housewife	29	"	
c	Krasnoff Samuel	109	clerk	33		
D	*Epstein Frances—†	109	housekeeper	65	"	
E	Gerson Edward	109	clerk	38	"	
F	Gerson Gertrude—†	109	housewife	32	"	

8

9

1

1

Ward 11–Precinct 7

CITY OF BOSTON

LIST OF RESIDENTS
20 YEARS OF AGE AND OVER

(NON-CITIZENS INDICATED BY ASTERISK)
(FEMALES INDICATED BY DAGGER)

AS OF

JANUARY 1, 1946

THOMAS F. SULLIVAN, *Chairman*
FREDERIC E. DOWLING, *Secretary*
WILLIAM A. MOTLEY, JR.
ARTHUR V. COUGHLIN
EVERETT R. PROUT

Listing Board.

CITY OF BOSTON PRINTING DEPARTMENT

700

Ashworth Park

A	Alexander Orca—†	6	housekeeper	38	here
B	Rockwell Anna—†	8	housewife	38	"
C	Rockwell William	8	proprietor	39	"
D	McDonald Lloyd P	10	electrician	22	"
E	McDonald Maurice G	10	"	20	
F	McDonald Michael	10	salesman	25	"
G	McDonald Russell A	10	shipwright	53	"
H	McDonald Walburga—†	10	housewife	48	"

Cleaves Street

K	Ruddy Anna—†	5	clerk	51	here
L	Lagerborg Ruth—†	5	typist	47	"
M	Proctor Laura—†	5	housewife	64	"
N	Rawitz Jacob	5	salesman	54	"
O	Rawitz Leonard	5	student	23	"
P	Rawitz Rebecca—†	5	housewife	46	"
R	Levin Theodore	6	manager	31	"
S	Levin Tina—†	6	housewife	28	"
T	Solomon Morton M	6	manufacturer	36	"
U	Solomon Violet—†	6	housewife	37	"
V	Facktoroff Augusta—†	6	"	46	
W	Facktoroff Henry	6	salesman	49	"
X	Cohen Emma—†	7	housewife	40	"
Y	Cohen Maurice	7	salesman	40	"
Z	Dorsick Jack	7	chauffeur	35	"

701

A	Dorsick Martha—†	7	housewife	36	"
B	Chyet Ethel—†	7	"	32	
C	Chyet Irving S	7	salesman	37	"
D	Solomon Charlotte C—†	8	housewife	34	"
E	Solomon Leo	8	manager	34	"
F	Helman Dora—†	8	housewife	39	"
G	Helman Philip	8	accountant	39	"
H	Levison Bessie—†	8	housewife	84	"
K	Levison Manuel	8	salesman	41	"
L	Kaplan Bernard	9	roofer	47	
M	Kaplan Gertrude—†	9	saleswoman	45	"
N	Kaplan Leonard	9	buyer	21	"
O	Albert Bessie—†	9	stitcher	58	

Page.	Letter.	FULL NAME.	Residence, Jan. 1, 1946.	Occupation.	Supposed Age.	Reported Residence, Jan. 1, 1945. Street and Number.

Cleaves Street—Continued

	P	Albert Samuel	9	stitcher	63	here
	R	Swiechowicz Theodore	9	shoeworker	36	"
	S	Swiechowicz Wanda—†	9	housewife	33	"
	T	Balkan Ida—†	10	"	71	
	U	Krovitsky Evelyn—†	10	clerk	37	
	V	Krovitsky Harry	10	mechanic	42	"
	W	Golner Ann N—†	10	manager	37	Chelsea
	X	Golner Nathan	10	clerk	43	here
	Y	Russell John	10	student	20	"
	Z	Goldman Bertha—†	10	housewife	36	"

702

	A	Ross Bradford	11	manager	41	"
	B	Ross Evelyn—†	11	housewife	36	"
	C	Malamut Irving	11	salesman	34	"
	D	Malamut Molly—†	11	housewife	30	"
	E	Flood Dorothy—†	11	librarian	32	"
	F	Flood Florence—†	11	housewife	51	"
	G	Higgins Fred B	12	janitor	31	New Jersey
	H	Higgins Ruth—†	12	housewife	27	"
	K	Goldberg Gertrude—†	12	clerk	32	here
	L	Goldberg Hendla—†	12	at home	69	"
	M	Goldberg Joel	12	manager	44	"
	N	Kennedy Martha—†	12	housewife	24	"
	O	Kennedy Robert	12	foreman	32	"
	P	Nadler Edwin B	14	agent	47	
	R	Nadler Gertrude—†	14	housewife	41	"
	S	Fritz Anna—†	14	"	26	"
	T	Fritz Nathan	14	operator	34	"
	U	Colpas Mary—†	14	housewife	30	12 Dixwell
	V	Colpas Philip A	14	salesman	37	12 "
	W	Fritz Bernard	15	"	38	here
	X	Fritz Jean—†	15	housewife	39	"
	Y	Chyet Ella—†	15	"	32	"
	Z	Chyet Hyman B	15	cutter	34	"

703

	A	Davis Emma L—†	15	housewife	45	"
	B	Davis Samuel	15	druggist	50	
	C	Savransky Idelle—†	16	housewife	37	"
	D	Savransky Louis	16	clerk	42	
	E	Brickman Jacob	16	barber	65	
	F	Brickman Mildred—†	16	housewife	60	"

3

Cleaves Street—Continued

G	Joseph Frances—†	16	housewife	43	here
H	Joseph Louis	16	foreman	54	"
K	Sallop Max	17	"	26	Revere
L	Sallop Rebecca—†	17	housewife	27	"
M	Harris Barney	17	carpenter	57	here
N	Harris Irene—†	17	stenographer	20	"
O	Harris Mary—†	17	housewife	48	"
P	Saltzman Annette—†	17	chemist	24	
R	Saltzman Theodore	17	agronomist	28	"
S	Lavin Katherine—†	17	housewife	52	"
T	Lavin Virginia—†	17	clerk	21	

Cobden Street

U	Archer Carrie E—†	4	housewife	52	here
V	Archer James A	4	clerk	56	"
W	Nordahl Carl E	8	"	37	"
X	Nordahl Ruth L—†	8	housewife	37	"
Y	Strom Ellis C	8	gardener	72	"
Z	Strom Esther E—†	8	housewife	71	"

704

A	Garrity Dennis	16	retired	90	
B	Garrity John	16	bartender	50	"
C	Garrity Margaret—†	16	matron	43	
D	Molloy Henry	18	plumber	69	"
E	Molloy Thomas	18	metalworker	61	"
F	LaTorre John	20	merchant	55	55 W Walnut
G	Mosgofian Catherine—†	20	housewife	26	here
H	Mosgofian Katchik	20	painter	40	"
K	Ross Genevieve L—†	20	housewife	42	59 W Walnut
L	Allard Albert	22	laborer	22	here
M	Kelleher Dorothea M—†	22	WAVE	23	"
N	Kelleher Frances C—†	22	housewife	53	"
O	Kelleher Patrick J	22	operator	60	"
P	McCraith James F	22	retired	87	
R	Ruff Arthur G	24	chauffeur	47	"
S	Ruff George W	24	U S A	22	
T	Ruff Martha E—†	24	housewife	47	"
U	Murphy Edward D	26	supt	51	
V	Murphy Helen A—†	26	housewife	48	"
W	Murphy Maureen—†	26	dietitian	21	"

Cobden Street—Continued

x	Rooney Eugenia—†	28	housewife	44	here
y	Rooney Walter J	28	accountant	51	"

705

A	McIntyre Hugh C	30	supervisor	49	"
B	McIntyre Janet R—†	30	at home	80	"
D	Coleman George H	32	student	22	
E	Coleman Mary E—†	32	housewife	46	"
F	Coleman Ralph J	32	coremaker	47	"
G	Coleman Ralph J, jr	32	clerk	27	
H	Pollard Mary J—†	32	typist	23	
K	Brennell Emma—†	32	at home	81	
L	Brennell Kenneth	32	chauffeur	47	"
M	Cavarnos Constantine	32	student	26	
N	Cavarnos Irene—†	32	at home	61	
O	Cavarnos John	32	student	29	
P	Cavarnos Peter	32	merchant	65	"
R	Varney Frances—†	34	housewife	25	"
S	Varney Milton	34	U S A	27	
T	O'Leary Eva—†	34	housewife	58	"
U	O'Leary Thomas	34	laborer	48	
V	MacKinnon Colin F	34	"	49	
W	MacKinnon Martha—†	34	housewife	40	"
X	Watson Esther—†	36	"	54	
Y	Watson Peter J	36	laborer	59	
Z	Watson Richard F	36	printer	21	

706

A	Kelly Anna—†	36	operator	33	"
B	Kelly John E	36	retired	63	
C	Kelly John F	36	"	37	
D	Kelly Margaret—†	36	housewife	60	"
E	Kelly Marguerite—†	36	operator	25	"
F	Santoro Agnes R—†	36	housewife	37	"
G	Santoro Charles J	36	chauffeur	37	"
H	Hillen John J	38	laborer	56	
K	Hillen John J, jr	38	U S A	21	"
L	Hillen Maria—†	38	housewife	44	"
M	Keller Edward	38	U S N	25	
N	Agretelis Metaxia—†	38	typist	31	
O	Hatzimanolis Pelagia—†	38	housewife	65	"
P	Hatzimanolis Theogue	38	student	30	"
R	*Campbell Donald	38	chauffeur	51	21 Oakdale

Cobden Street—Continued

s	Campbell Florence—†	38	housewife	33	21 Oakdale
T	*Richard Florence—†	40	"	70	here
U	Richard Frank	40	laborer	70	"
V	Koutsaftis Frances—†	40	housewife	30	"
W	Koutsaftis James	40	machinist	31	"
X	Ferrara Louise—†	40	housewife	37	"
Y	Ferrara Rocco	40	cobbler	37	
Z	Jackson Frances M—†	44	housewife	44	"

707

A	Jackson Herbert L	44	baker	49	
B	Jackson Herbert L, jr	44	musician	22	"
c	Blanchette Adolphe	44	painter	48	
D	Blanchette Prudence—†	44	housewife	42	"
E	Colin Wilfred	44	painter	59	
F	Hurder Arthur	44	mechanic	27	"
G	Hurder Cecelia—†	44	operator	36	"
H	Hurder John	44	carpenter	64	"
K	Hurder Julia—†	44	housewife	65	"
L	Hurder Mary—†	44	operator	37	"
M	Walsh George A	46	custodian	32	"
N	Walsh James J	46	"	63	
o	Walsh Pauline—†	46	housewife	26	"
P	Spero Margaret—†	46	"	50	
R	Leet Kathleen—†	48	saleswoman	22	"
s	Leet Robert H	48	chauffeur	57	34 Cobden
T	Leet Robert H	48	laborer	21	here
U	Leet Sarah—†	48	housewife	55	34 Cobden

708 Columbus Avenue

E	Wallace Louis	1990	merchant	66	here
F	Wallace Minnie—†	1990	housewife	67	"
G	Pimental Alice—†	1990	"	40	"
H	Pimental John L	1990	policeman	49	"
K	DeCosta Celia R—†	1990	housewife	30	"
L	DeCosta Herman	1990	operator	42	"
M	Sullivan Mary H—†	1991	housewife	61	4 Page's ct
N	Christopher L Urban	1991	dentist	67	here
o	Aramian Mary R—†	1991	housewife	40	"
P	Aramian Sarkis	1991	tailor	50	"
R	Yiannacopoulos Anna V—†	1991	bookkeeper	26	"

Page.	Letter.	FULL NAME.	Residence, Jan. 1, 1946.	Occupation.	Supposed Age.	Reported Residence, Jan. 1, 1945. Street and Number.

Columbus Avenue—Continued

	s	Yiannacopoulos Dorothy—†	1991	housewife	44	here
	t	Yiannacopoulos Helen–†	1991	clerk	26	"
	u	Yiannacopoulos Peter A	1991	bartender	59	"
	v	Tingus Constantine	1991	clerk	28	
	w	Tingus Diamond—†	1991	housewife	57	"
	x	Tingus Olga—†	1991	"	24	Newburyport
	y	Tingus Stephen	1991	merchant	66	here
	z	Grattin Grace—†	1991	waitress	45	"

709

	a	Harkins Joseph	1991	chef	55	"
	b	Shaw Jeremiah	1991	laborer	65	"
	c	Flanders Alton L	1996	physician	82	"
	d	Mohla Maria I—†	1996	housekeeper	60	"
	e	Murray Dorothy L—†	1996	saleswoman	32	"
	l	McMaster Bruce	2012	U S A	21	"
	m	McMaster Ida M—†	2012	housewife	60	"
	n	McMaster Stanley E	2012	shipper	64	"
	o	McMaster Thelma—†	2012	artist	25	
	p	Walsh Verna M—†	2012	housewife	28	"
	r	Connor Thomas T	2026	court officer	41	"
	t	Mulhern Anna E—†	2029	at home	65	"
	u	Mulhern Louise M—†	2029	teacher	45	"
	v	Cunningham Harriet—†	2029	floorwoman	37	"
	w	Cunningham James	2029	salesman	48	"
	x	Byron Russell E	2029	clerk	23	29 School
	y	Lorden Esther—†	2029	operator	21	N Hampshire
	z	Robinson Donald E	2029	laborer	47	here

710

	a	Robinson Gladys A—†	2029	nurse	42	"
	b	Robinson Sydney G	2029	retired	79	Maine
	c	Burke Catherine M—†	2031	cook	54	here
	d	Burke Christine M—†	2031	entertainer	22	Texas
	e	Gillis John J	2031	carpenter	52	here
	f	Starobin Morris M	2031	painter	52	"
	g	Starobin Sarah I—†	2031	housewife	44	"
	h	Catherwood Catherine A—†	2031	"	39	
	k	Catherwood Donald P	2031	student	21	
	l	Catherwood William J	2031	guard	49	
	m	Kurth Elizabeth D—†	2032	at home	40	"
	n	Kurth Katherine D—†	2032	housewife	72	"
	o	Kurth William I	2032	attorney	75	"

Page.	Letter.	FULL NAME.	Residence, Jan. 1, 1946.	Occupation.	Supposed Age.	Reported Residence, Jan. 1, 1945. Street and Number.

Columbus Avenue—Continued

P	Porter Effie—†	2033	clerk	63	here
R	Porter Victor •	2033	watchman	73	"
S	Flaherty Dora—†	2033	housewife	49	"
T	Flaherty William	2033	engineer	53	"
U	Nelson Clara—†	2033	housewife	61	"
V	Nelson Gertrude—†	2033	"	33	
W	Nelson Peter W	2033	engineer	64	"
X	Nelson Robert E	2033	machinist	29	"
Y	Hughes Julia J—†	2035	housewife	62	"
Z	Hughes Peter J	2035	salesman	57	"

711

A	Clooney Arthur J	2035	clerk	22	
B	Clooney Catherine—†	2035	housewife	49	"
C	Clooney James	2035	manager	57	"
D	Clooney James L	2035	operator	27	"
E	Jones Theodosia M—†.	2035	housewife	66	"
F	Alexander Fannie V—†	2037	at home	73	
G	Clark Gertrude P—†	2037	collector	55	"
H	Clark Walter J	2037	supervisor	29	9 Wren
K	Baker Harry J	2037	laborer	36	10 Elgin
L	Gannon Katherine—†	2037	tel operator	57	here
M	McLaughlin Marion—†	2037	operator	47	"
N	Spencer William R	2037	engineer	38	Rhode Island
O	Bell Antoinette—†	2037	housewife	39	here
P	Bell Frank W	2037	collector	51	"
R	Gettis Arthur J :	2041	millwright	41	"
S	Gettis Lillian S—†	2041	housewife	43	"
T	Nugent Arthur J	2041	checker	42	
U	Nugent Arthur J, jr	2041	U S N	21	
V	Nugent Florence M—†	2041	housewife	41	"
W	Nugent Thomas W	2041	U S N	23	
X	Aikens Jennie M—†	2041	housewife	67	"
Y	Hood Mae—†	2041	bookkeeper	46	"
Z	Magee Mary—†	2043	clerk	63	"

712

A	Bourgeois Concetta—†	2043	housewife	25	"
B	Bourgeois Emile	2043	metalworker	32	"
C	Bourgeois Joseph	2043	mechanic	23	Watertown
D	Kelly James F	2043	student	26	70A South
E	Kelly Rita L—†	2043	stenographer	25	5 Mission
F	Dahl Elizabeth—†	2044	housekeeper	79	here

8

Page.	Letter.	FULL NAME.	Residence, Jan. 1, 1946.	Occupation.	Supposed Age.	Reported Residence, Jan. 1, 1945. Street and Number.

Columbus Avenue—Continued

	G	Dahl Rosina—†	2044	housekeeper	78	here
	H	Serago Doris—†	2045	housewife	22	Pennsylvania
	K	Serago Frank J	2045	seaman	23	"
	L	Ryan Mary W—†	2045	at home	65	here
	M	Ryan Natalie C—†	2045	secretary	35	"
	N	Hayes James J	2045	U S A	27	"
	O	Hayes Nora S—†	2045	housewife	52	"
	P	Hayes Robert L	2045	laborer	25	
	R	Carey Mary—†	2047	at home	80	"
	S	McDonald James P	2047	chauffeur	46	109 W Walnut pk
	T	McDonald Rose—†	2047	housewife	33	109 "
	U	McDonnell James J	2047	retired	73	109 "
	V	Bennett Henry	2047	oiler	43	here
	W	Bennett Sarah E—†	2047	housewife	40	"
	X	Schiraga Harry	2047	custodian	38	"
	Y	Roundoerg John	2049.	draftsman	72	"
	Z	Barnes Rita M—†	2049	inspector	25	"
		713				
	A	Barnes Samuel A	2049	U S A	26	"
	B	Merlin Edward J	2049	"	28	
	C	Merlin Mary F—†	2049	housewife	57	"
	E	McGeoch Margaret—†	2049	operator	41	160 Boylston
	F	McGeoch Robert	2049	carpenter	42	160 "
	D	McGougen Jean—†	2049	housewife	63	160 "
	G	Adams Fred A	2055	retired	91	here
	H	Allen Minnie M—†	2055	supt	60	"
	K	Ashton Helen—†	2055	at home	68	"
	L	Bacon Cora—†	2055	"	77	
	M	Baker Hattie A—†	2055	"	66	
	N	Barker Daniel	2055	porter	65	
	O	Bateman Carrie T—†	2055	at home	81	"
	P	Bemis Elizabeth—†	2055	"	72	
	R	Bemis Ernest	2055	retired	74	
	S	Brackett George R	2055	"	85	
	T	Brennion Florence—†	2055	domestic	26	"
	U	Briggs Benjamin	2055	retired	72	
	V	Brown Edith—†	2055	waitress	62	"
	W	Bullard Carrie—†	2055	at home	83	"
	X	Bullard George A	2055	retired	79	
	Y	Burgstahler Elsie—†	2055	at home	76	"
	Z	Butterfield William A	2055	retired	83	

Page.	Letter.	FULL NAME.	Residence, Jan. 1, 1946.	Occupation.	Supposed Age.	Reported Residence, Jan. 1, 1945. Street and Number.

714
Columbus Avenue—Continued

	Letter.	FULL NAME.	Residence	Occupation	Age	Reported Residence
	A	Carson Adella—†	2055	at home	79	here
	B	Chadwick Catherine A–†	2055	"	80	Marblehead
	C	Chambers Johanna—†	2055	"	79	here
	D	Chambers John T	2055	retired	77	"
	E	Cheever Nellie R—†	2055	at home	80	"
	F	Colby Sarah R—†	2055	"	68	"
	G	Crosby Addie L—†	2055	"	90	Harwich
	H	Crosby Herbert M	2055	retired	78	"
	K	D'Annikov Alexander	2055	"	82	here
	L	D'Annikov Sophie—†	2055	at home	75	"
	M	Dickson Rose—†	2055	"	76	"
	N	Dizer Hattie H—†	2055	"	84	
	O	Dizer Wendell T	2055	retired	88	
	P	Drake Ella—†	2055	at home	85	"
	R	Evans Elizabeth A—†	2055	"	67	
	S	Evans Frederick S	2055	retired	79	"
	T	Farrar Etta E—†	2055	at home	83	"
	U	Fernald Nellie A—†	2055	"	82	
	V	Gardner Nellie—†	2055	"	76	
	W	Gardner Walter	2055	retired	84	
	X	Greenwood Frank	2055	"	85	"
	Y	Hager Clifford	2055	"	83	"
	Z	Hager Ella—†	2055	at home	83	"

715

	Letter.	FULL NAME.	Residence	Occupation	Age	Reported Residence
	A	Henderson Grace—†	2055	"	73	
	B	Henderson Henry	2055	retired	76	
	C	Hewitt Alice—†	2055	at home	85	"
	D	Hewitt Chauncy	2055	retired	81	"
	E	Hill Joanna—†	2055	at home	79	"
	F	Hill Walter F	2055	retired	90	
	G	Hinckley Edward	2055	"	87	
	H	Hoadley Ruth—†	2055	nurse	53	
	K	Hodgson Benjamin	2055	retired	81	
	L	Holmes Caroline—†	2055	at home	74	"
	M	Hubbard Edith—†	2055	"	75	
	N	Hyde Ida A—†	2055	"	81	
	O	Hyde William	2055	retired	83	
	P	Jaycock William	2055	"	91	
	R	Jones Louise—†	2055	at home	74	"
	S	King Mary W—†	2055	"	66	

Columbus Avenue—Continued

	T	King William	2055	retired	80	here
	U	Knowles Annie C—†	2055	at home	78	"
	V	Knowles Ernest H	2055	retired	80	"
	W	MacAdam Daniel J	2055	"	76	19 Idaho
	X	MacAdam Martha M—†	2055	at home	75	19 "
	Y	MacAskill Anna—†	2055	domestic	32	here
	Z	MacAskill Katherine—†	2055	cook	35	"

716

	A	MacAskill Roderick	2055	retired	83	
	B	MacDonald Katherine—†	2055	cook	61	
	C	MacLean Margaret—†	2055	at home	86	"
	D	Macomber George W	2055	retired	85	
	E	Mayo Charles W	2055	"	85	"
	F	McInnis Neil	2055	"	82	
	G	McLeod Agnes—†	2055	domestic	60	"
	H	McQueen Katherine—†	2055	nurse	69	
	K	Morse William H	2055	retired	76	
	L	Moulton Frederick C	2055	"	86	
	M	Murphy Elizabeth—†	2055	tel operator	57	"
	N	Nolan Edith M—†	2055	at home	68	"
	O	Owens Annie—†	2055	"	79	
	P	Pierce Ada C—†	2055	"	82	
	R	Pierce Warren C	2055	retired	79	"
	S	Poindexter Eskar	2055	engineer	49	Missouri
	T	Poindexter Viola—†	2055	domestic	46	"
	U	Ringer Archibald	2055	retired	66	here
	V	Ringer Ella M—†	2055	at home	66	"
	W	Schiertz Ferdinand A	2055	retired	75	"
	X	Schiertz Hedwig—†	2055	housewife	74	"
	Y	Severence George E	2055	retired	86	
	Z	Severence Mariette—†	2055	at home	78	"

717

	A	Shorey Blanche M—†	2055	"	76	"
	B	Shorey Leonard H	2055	retired	66	
	C	Sidebottom John	2055	"	86	
	D	Smith Albert O	2055	"	83	
	E	Smith Ella E—†	2055	at home	79	"
	F	Speakman Amanda V—†	2055	"	88	
	G	Speakman Frederick	2055	retired	90	"
	H	Stafford David	2055	"	85	
	K	Stearns Alice W—†	2055	at home	74	"

11

Page.	Letter.	Full Name.	Residence, Jan. 1, 1946.	Occupation.	Supposed Age.	Reported Residence, Jan. 1, 1945. Street and Number.

Columbus Avenue—Continued

	L	Stone Atwell	2055	retired	79	here
	M	Stone Luella—†	2055	at home	88	"
	N	Thoms Annie—†	2055	"	87	"
	O	Tuell Francis	2055	retired	84	..
	P	Walsh Albert	2055	"	73	..
	R	Walsh Alice H—†	2055	at home	67	..
	S	Weston Anne—†	2055	"	85	
	T	Wilder Elizabeth M—†	2055	"	80	
	U	Wilder George M	2055	retired	80	
	V	Wilmot George E	2055	"	82	
	W	Wilmot Theresa—†	2055	at home	75	"
	X	Wolfe Mabel—†	2055	nurse	59	
	Y	Wraight Percival	2055	retired	81	

Dixwell Street

	Z	Tingus Andrew G	4	clerk	26	here

718

	A	Tingus George	4	merchant	70	"
	B	Tingus Helen—†	4	housewife	56	"
	C	Tingus Theodore	4	U S A	20	
	D	Kevorkian Arthur	4	molder	22	
	E	Kevorkian John	4	barber	51	
	F	Kevorkian Mary—†	4	housewife	44	"
	G	MacDonald Helen—†	6	"	45	
	H	MacDonald Robert W	6	meatcutter	22	"
	K	MacDonald Stewart	6	manager	49	"
	L	Peppin Arthur J	6	merchant	63	"
	M	Higgins Elizabeth—†	6	housewife	57	"
	N	Higgins Fred L	6	constructor	64	"
	O	Bravaco Mary—†	6	housewife	30	"
	P	Bravaco Ralph	6	chauffeur	33	"
	R	MacKay Alice—†	7	housewife	68	"
	S*	MacKay Jessie G—†	7	nurse	57	
	T	Bakalor Gertrude—†	7	housewife	62	"
	U	Bakalor William	7	retired	63	
	V	Kanserstein Celia—†	7	housewife	35	"
	W	Kanserstein Samuel	7	druggist	38	"
	X	Gazzam Goldie—†	9	housewife	54	"
	Y	Gazzam Robert A	9	pharmacist	70	"
	Z	Lane Lynne A—†	9	housewife	38	"

719
Dixwell Street—Continued

A	Lane Moses H	9	buyer	30	here
B	Weiner Evelyn—†	9	housewife	38	"
C	Weiner Moses L	9	laborer	34	"
D	Lindsay Mary A—†	9	housewife	49	"
E	Lindsay Thomas A	9	mechanic	51	"
F	Leavitt Frances—†	11	saleswoman	42	"
G	Leavitt Walter	11	mechanic	45	"
H	Rubinstein John	11	U S A	37	
K	Rubinstein Lillian—†	11	housewife	32	Ohio
L	Bander Edward	11	U S N	22	here
M	Goldstein Harry	11	messenger	41	"
N	Goldstein Ida—†	11	housewife	50	"
O	Yahnis Helen—†	11	machinist	47	"
P	Yahnis James	11	florist	53	
R	Kaplan Dorothy—†	12	housewife	25	"
S	Kaplan Morris	12	chauffeur	28	41 Kingsley
T	Dickey George P	12	mechanic	33	560 E Fifth
U	Dickey Phyllis—†	12	housewife	30	560 "
V	Hall Vera—†	12	secretary	32	New Mexico
W	Brown Blanche L—†	12	"	26	here
X	Brown Murdena—†	12	WAC	28	"
Y	Brown William C	12	printer	24	"
Z	Brown William F	12	inspector	62	"

720

A	Sokol Albert H	13	counterman	33	"
B	Sokol Anne—†	13	housewife	29	"
C	Portman Abraham	13	tailor	55	
D	Portman Edith—†	13	waitress	47	"
E	Portman William	13	student	20	
F	Zwirm Louis	13	barber	34	
G	Zwirm Renee—†	13	housewife	34	"
H	Rochford Albina—†	14	"	48	77 Chambers
K	Rochford Leonard	14	jaintor	48	77 "
L	Casci Ameigo	14	U S A	38	here
M	Casci Blanche—†	14	manager	39	"
N	Cunniff James P	14	retired	68	3234A Wash'n
O	Cunniff Phillip F	14	inspector	56	3234A "
P	Cunniff Robert E	14	retired	66	3234A "
R	Heffron Isadore	17	chauffeur	35	here
S	Heffron Mary—†	17	housewife	29	"

13

Dixwell Street—Continued

	T	*Fabiano Bella—†	17	housewife	40	here
	U	*Fabiano James	17	jeweler	42	"
	V	Belasco Bertha—†	17	checker	25	"
	W	Belasco Phillip	17	U S A	40	"
	X	Newmark Alberta—†	17	WAVE	24	
	Y	Newmark Beulah—†	17	housewife	46	"
	Z	Newmark Helen—†	17	machinist	22	"

721

	A	Newmark Lawrence	17	student	21	
	B	Newmark Samuel	17	operator	49	"
	C	Bautze Anna—†	18	housewife	52	"
	D	*Bautze Gustave A	18	glassblower	58	"
	E	Antopoulos Arthur	18	salesman	57	"
	F	Souretis Christine—†	18	housewife	28	"
	G	*Souretis James	18	teacher	38	"
	H	Reynolds Bernard	18	plumber	45	"
	K	Reynolds Julia—†	18	housewife	43	"
	L	Reynolds Robert	18	U S N	23	
	M	Emanuel John A	19	painter	36	"
	N	Emanuel Louise—†	19	housewife	30	"
	O	MacIsaac Dorothy—†	19	"	38	
	P	MacIsaac Roland E	19	guard	38	
	R	Lombardini Constante	19	porter	53	
	S	Lombardini Therese—†	19	housewife	45	"
	T	Chadbourne Horace	20	pressman	42	"
	U	Chadbourne Violet—†	20	housewife	36	"
	V	Geracoulis Eva—†	20	"	29	
	W	Geracoulis George	20	merchant	31	"
	X	Brennan Raymond P	20	manager	42	45 School
	Y	Hurd Harry C	20	waiter	60	here
	Z	Hurd Robert E	20	operator	63	"

722

	A	Pengeroth Andrew	21	welder	59	
	B	Pengeroth Irving	21	painter	31	
	C	Pengeroth Maxine—†	21	secretary	27	"
	D	Pengeroth Patrick	21	machinist	21	"
	E	Pengeroth Rose—†	21	housewife	58	"
	F	*McElman Edna M—†	21	clerk	49	
	G	McElman Edna P—†	21	WAVE	26	
	H	McElman Thomas A	21	operator	55	"
	K	McElman Thomas A, jr	21	clerk	28	

14

Dixwell Street—Continued

L	Coulouris Bertha—†	21	housewife	52	here	
M	Coulouris Emanuel	21	waiter	47	"	
N	Coulouris George	21	clerk	59	"	
O	Chatelain Ernest	23	electrician	61	"	
P	Chatelain Harriet—†	23	housewife	60	"	
R	Chatelain Lorraine—†	23	stenographer	26	"	
S	Chatelain Robert E	23	salesman	27	"	
T	Coulouris Helen—†	23	housewife	31	"	
U	Coulouris Peter	23	chauffeur	40	"	
V	Rose Anna M—†	23	housewife	57	"	
W	Rose Harold A	23	diesinker	56	"	

School Street

X	Lennon Catherine G—†	27	at home	62	here	
Y	Lennon Elizabeth F—†	27	clerk	64	"	
Z	Lennon Margaret A—†	27	at home	66	"	
	723					
A	Snyder Helen T—†	27	"	60	"	
B	Koelsch Emma M—†	29	housewife	66	5 Bismarck	
C	Butler Charles V	29	painter	56	here	
D	Butler Eliza—†	29	housewife	59	"	
E	Just Anna—†	31	at home	70	29 School	
F	Morgan Mary—†	31	housewife	57	here	
G	Morgan William A	31	retired	34	300 Newbury	
H	Starke Anna—†	31	clerk	25	here	
K	Mullen Helen L—†	33	secretary	38	"	
L	Mullen Mary F—†	33	at home	73	"	
M	Walsh Catherine R—†	33	housewife	67	"	
N	Walsh Richard P	33	plumber	80	"	
O	MacDonald Agnes—†	35	nurse	33	33 Wolcott	
P	Lynch Lorne	35	roofer	22	37 W Selden	
S	MacKenzie Mary E—†	35	nurse	46	here	
T	Priola Barbara—†	35	stitcher	26	"	
U	Priola Catherine—†	35	"	25	"	
V	Priola Guy	35	laborer	24		
W	Priola Helen—†	35	housewife	49	"	
X	Priola Vincent	35	U S A	20	"	
Y	Dewar Mary—†	35	housewife	26	3 Valentine	
Z	Maxim Arthur S	37	retired	75	here	

724
School Street—Continued

A	Maxim Margaret J—†	37	housewife	72	here
B	Cull Freeman M	37	painter	45	"
C	Rafuse Evalena—†	37	at home	79	"
D	Rafuse Nina E—†	37	corsetiere	45	"
E	Rafuse Rose I—†	37	stitcher	49	"
F	Mason Anna—†	37	housewife	46	"
G	Mason George	37	laborer.	47	"
H	Cripps Dorothy—†	41	clerk	30	Brookline
K	McGowan Charles F	41	technician	46	2 Glines av
L	McGowan Honora B—†	41	housewife	39	2 "
M	Ginkus John J	41	shipper	40	here
N	Ginkus Mary—†	41	stitcher	46	"
O	Machakos Bessie—†	43	stenographer	23	"
P	*Machakos Eleanora—†	43	housewife	50	"
R	Machakos Rita—†	43	stenographer	21	"
S	Machakos Trifon	43	barber	55	"
T	*Comelchook Joseph	43	laborer	35	
U	*Kala Anna—†	43	housewife	29	"
V	*Kala Oscar	43	seaman	38	
W	Gilfeather Charles T	43	shipper	36	
X	Gilfeather Marion C—†	43	housewife	39	"
Y	Blodgett Inez M—†	45	at home	67	35 School
Z	Fletcher Ella—†	45	"	60	35 "

725

A	*Silberberg Edward	45	seaman	30	here
B	*Silberberg Marguerite—†	45	clerk	32	"
C	Boulter Edward	45	janitor	53	"
D	Boulter Laura—†	45	housewife	53	"
E	Hanlon Evelyn R—†	47	"	31	
F	Hanlon John J	47	roofer	34	"
G	*Milne Jean—†	47	housewife	43	"
H	Milne William	47	meatcutter	49	"
K	Bentley Edward F	47	seaman	22	7 Asylum
L	Ellis George	47	roofer	22	45 Oswego
M	Ellis Irene—†	47	clerk	23	117 E Newton
O	Flynn Mary C—†	69	housewife	54	here
P	Flynn William J	69	guard	57	"
R	Manley Harold	69	clerk	24	1585 Wash'n
S	Manley Lillian—†	69	"	22	18 Dixwell
T	Bourke Joseph T	71	"	66	here

School Street—Continued

U	Bourke Martha A—†	71	operator	63	here
V	Kelleher Hannah—†	71	housewife	62	"
W	Kelleher Timothy J	71	foreman	62	"
X	Pettigrew Archibald K	71A	laborer	37	
Y	Pettigrew Evelyn S—†	71A	housewife	33	"
Z	*Vlachos Minnie—†	73	"	42	

726

A	Vlachos Theodore	73	waiter	50	
B	Vlachos Theodore, jr	73	clerk	20	
C	*Rydings Elizabeth—†	73A	housewife	54	"
D	Rydings Florence G—†	73A	at home	23	
E	Rydings James A	73A	painter	52	"
F	Rydings John J	73A	clerk	27	Randolph
G	Rydings Joseph A	73A	"	24	"
H	Boue Jean	73A	mechanic	61	here
K	*Boue Louise—†	73A	housewife	60	"
L	Beyea Elizabeth L—†	81	student	20	"
M	Blodgett Lena E—†	81	technician	53	"
N	Rider Lillian D—†	81	secretary	65	"
O	Stringe Dorothy M—†	83	housewife	26	"
P	Stringe Edward W	83	U S A	26	
R	Scher Gertrude B—†	83	operator	47	"
S	Calvin Agnes T—†	85	clerk	34	"
T	Calvin Charles J	85	U S A	32	New York
U	Dolan Alice B—†	85	matron	60	here
V	Haskins Ernest C	85	clerk	30	New York
W	Haskins Frances M—†	85	housewife	31	here
X	Dolan Sara F—†	87	at home	63	"
Y	Wildberger Charles	87	retired	70	"
Z	Wildberger Emma—†	87	at home	44	

727

A	Wildberger Ethel—†	87	typist	46	
B	Wildberger May—†	87	clerk	49	"
C	Coleman Mary J—†	87	housewife	35	607 Shawmut av
D	McHoul Jacqueline M—†	87	"	26	here
E	McHoul James N	87	U S M C	27	"
F	Chernack Benjamin R	87	proprietor	33	"
G	Chernack Marguerite A—†	87	clerk	29	
H	Nathan Andrew	87	operator	59	"
K	Nathan Elizabeth A—†	87	clerk	59	
L	Nathan Louise A—†	87	shipper	25	

School Street—Continued

M	Nathan Mark A	87	clerk	31	here
N	Bella John J	87	inspector	49	"
O	Bella Josephine—†	87	at home	70	"
P	Bella Josephine M—†	87	operator	24	"
R	Bella Ruth—†	87	housewife	29	"
S	Clark Charles	87	retired	71	
T	Shea Ellen V—†	87	at home	63	
U	Gardner Emma—†	87	housewife	56	"
V	Gardner Marion E—†	87	assembler	29	1841 Dor av
W	Gardner Robert F	87	"	66	here
X	Lane John	87	operator	43	9 Bancroft
Y	Prindeville William F	87	retired	70	116 School

School Street Place

Z	Kohl Otto	2	retired	68	here
	728				
A	Kohl William C	2	carpenter	54	"
B	Bigelow Harold B	4	engineer	60	"
C	Dean Andrew	4	painter	33	
D	Dean Phyllis L—†	4	housewife	28	"
E	Parker Etta J—†	4	"	56	
F	Parker Harriet B—†	4	"	86	"
G	Byrnes Evelyn F—†	4	nurse	30	
H	Kinsman William	4	chauffeur	55	"
K	Kutz Mary A—†	4	housewife	59	"
L	Olsen Maud C—†	4	domestic	61	"
M	Murray Alice L—†	7	housewife	37	"
N	Murray Walter J	7	lineman	37	
O	Anderson Othelia T—†	7	at home	66	
P	Donahue Catherine L—†	8	housewife	51	"
R	Donahue William L	8	printer	53	
S	Donahue William L, jr	8	U S A	22	
T	Gulino Angelo	9	operator	48	"
U	Gulino Mary C—†	9	housewife	36	"
V	Gaffey Bridget A—†	11	"	80	
W	Gaffey Helen M—†	11	accountant	35	"
X	Gaffey Henry P	11	laborer	37	
Y	Stabin Fred	27	carpenter	55	"
Z	Stabin Martha A—†	27	housewife	48	"

18

729
School Street Place—Continued

A	Flynn Rachel D—†	27	housewife	29	5 Morrow rd
B	Flynn Thomas F	27	mechanic	31	5 "
c*Deschenes Mary A—†	27A	housewife	40	Salem
D	Deschenes William J	27A	machinist	46	"
E	Goyea George A	27A	"	46	New Jersey
F	Goyea Sarah M—†	27A	housewife	38	"

Waldren Road

G	Weinfeld Charles W	7	engineer	29	here
H	Weinfeld Frederick D	7	U S A	22	"
K	Weinfeld Matilda—†	7	housewife	53	"
L	Weinfeld Morris	7	salesman	55	"
M	Butler Ann—†	7	housewife	51	"
N	Butler Samuel	7	salesman	52	"
O	Ganak Julian	7	clerk	26	"
P	Ganak Shirley—†	7	housewife	26	"
R	Tannenbaun Jacob	7	designer	62	"
S	Tannenbaun Tillie—†	7	housewife	61	"
T	Grodsky David	7	U S A	32	
U	Grodsky Jennie—†	7	clerk	33	"
V	Grodsky Lillian—†	7	secretary	28	"
W	Grodsky Rose—†	7	teacher	35	"
x*Bender Ida—†	7	housewife	60	"
y*Bender Joseph	7	retired	65	"
Z	Brecker Ann—†	7	housewife	39	"

730

A	Brecker Robert	7	laborer	39	"
B	Aptaker Alexander	7	tailor	63	74 Ruthven
C	Aptaker Edward	7	student	23	74 "
D	Aptaker Mary—†	7	housewife	54	74 "
E	Trager Abraham	7	presser	58	80 McLellan
F	Becker Mary—†	11	bookkeeper	35	11 Brookledge
g*Biller Clara—†	11	housewife	52	here
H	Ebb Harry	11	salesman	62	"
K	Ebb Lawrence	11	student	27	"
L	Ebb Rachel S—†	11	housewife	58	"
M	Kaufman Beatrice—†	11	"	30	
N	Kaufman Samuel	11	pipecoverer	35	"
o*Zunder Esther—†	11	housewife	54	"

19

Waldren Road—Continued

P	Zunder Morris	11	U S A	33	here
R	Mintz Beatrice—†	11	housewife	39	"
S	Mintz Morton	11	salesman	41	"
T	Figur Benjamin	11	cutter	52	225 Norfolk
U	Figur Reba—†	11	housewife	45	225 "
V	Simon Meyer	15	tailor	48	50 Wardman rd
W	*Simon Sylvia—†	15	housewife	41	50 "
X	*Prager Ida—†	15	"	36	here
Y	Prager Jacob	15	clerk	38	"
Z	Bronstein Samuel	15	U S A	28	"

731

A	Bronstein Sarah—†	15	housewife	28	"
B	Codish Adolph	15	tailor	66	
C	Codish Esther—†	15	bookkeeper	30	"
D	*Codish Ida—†	15	housewife	61	"
E	Cohen David	15	salesman	49	"
F	Schechtman Harold	15	U S A	38	
G	Schechtman Harriet—†	15	housewife	23	"
H	Fishman Phillip	15	mechanic	37	"
K	Fishman Winifred—†	15	housewife	37	"
L	Arkin Julia—†	15	"	75	
M	Arkin Sonia—†	15	bookkeeper	40	"
N	Winner Isadore	15	furrier	46	"
O	Salvin James	15	salesman	54	"
P	Salvin Louis	15	photographer	24	"
R	Salvin Minnie—†	15	housewife	52	"

Walnut Avenue

S	Rosenberg Anna—†	297	housewife	58	here
T	Rosenberg Phillip	297	salesman	65	"
U	Brown Leonard	297A	broker	40	"
V	Brown Samuel	297A	cleanser	72	"
W	Israelson Evelyn—†	297A	housewife	41	"
X	Israelson Jack	297A	clerk	42	
Y	Robbins Ida R—†	297A	housewife	44	"
Z	Robbins Israel	297A	printer	48	

732

A	Rotefsky Ida—†	297A	housekeeper	71	"
B	Stamler Morris	297A	shipfitter	39	"
C	Stamler Sarah F—†	297A	housewife	39	"

Walnut Avenue—Continued

D	*Campbell Mary—†	315	cook	44	Brookline
E	Hersey Ada H—†	315	at home	87	here
F	McCorry Sarah J—†	315	domestic	61	Newton
G	Pearse Alice W—†	317	housekeeper	64	here
H	Richardson Elizabeth M—†	331	at home	75	"
K	Richardson Laura E—†	331	"	77	"
L	Shute Mary C—†	331	"	74	..
N	Reines Eva—†	361	housekeeper	63	"
O	Krasnow Abraham	361	furrier	34	"
P	Krasnow Annette—†	361	housewife	34	"
R	Beeman Abraham S	361	broker	38	
S	Beeman Annette—†	361	housewife	34	"
T	Rose Esther—†	361	"	65	
U	Rose Max	361	bookbinder	70	"
V	Baker Henry R	361	U S A	26	
W	Baker Marion—†	361	housewife	24	"
X	Blumsack David	361	shipper	20	
Y	Blumsack Fannie—†	361	housewife	57	"
Z	Hurwitz Daniel	361	engineer	40	"

733

A	Hurwitz Hilda—†	361	housewife	41	"
B	Gudowsky Arthur	361	clothier	65	"
C	Gudowsky Fannie—†	361	housewife	62	"
D	Pike Frances Y—†	361	"	31	
E	Pike George M	361	U S A	35	
F	Rommell Beatrice—†	361	housewife	33	"
G	Rommell Julius	361	salesman	37	"
H	Spack Allan	361	attorney	28	"
K	Bluestein Lena—†	361	housewife	29	"
L	Bluestein Louis	361	shipper	31	"
M	Miseph Anna—†	361	housewife	44	"
N	Miseph Joseph	361	presser	47	
O	Miseph Lillian E—†	361	clerk	26	
P	Miseph Samuel	361	U S M C	25	"
R	Eavzan Ann—†	361	housewife	28	"
S	Eavzan George	361	salesman	30	"
T	Shapiro Betty—†	361	housewife	28	"
U	Shapiro Carl	361	clerk	30	
V	Herman Isaac	363	salesman	56	"
W	Herman Sophie—†	363	housewife	50	"
X	Michelson Sarah—†	363	at home	80	"

Walnut Avenue—Continued

Y	Ufland Jeannette—†	363	housewife	32	here
Z	Ufland Phillip	363	electrician	39	"
	734				
A	Stern Eleanor I—†	363	housewife	36	"
B	Stern Samuel H	363	foreman	50	"
C	Spector Estelle I—†	363	housewife	24	Maine
D	Spector Max	363	salesman	31	"
E	Lissack Maurice	363	buyer	35	here
F	Lissack Thelma—†	363	housewife	33	"
G	*Yaffe Max	363	tailor	62	"
H	*Yaffe Sophie—†	363	housewife	60	"
K	Sherman Hyman	363	manager	61	"
L	Sherman Joseph	363	salesman	33	"
M	Rubin Bernard	363	U S A	25	
N	Rubin Charles	363	salesman	52	"
O	Rubin Lillian—†	363	housewife	48	"
P	Sawyer Arthur	363	counterman	61	"
R	Sawyer Esther—†	363	housewife	61	"
S	Shapiro Rose—†	363	"	33	
T	Shapiro Simon	363	salesman	35	"
U	Oven Joseph	363	U S A	35	"
V	Oven Ruth—†	363	housewife	30	"
W	Sidman Abraham	363	tailor	58	
X	Sidman Lillian—†	363	housewife	58	"
Y	Glasberg Jean—†	363	"	26	
Z	Glasberg Lester	363	machinist	28	"
	735				
A	Broderick Ann V—†	367	teacher	29	"
B	Broderick Anna G—†	367	housewife	67	"
C	Broderick Paul D	367	contractor	26	"
D	Finnegan Charles A	377	clergyman	70	"
E	Reynolds Mary—†	377	housekeeper	40	"
F	Sullivan Daniel F	377	clergyman	30	"

736   Walnut Park

A	Hagimamole Emanuel	8	retired	60	Florida
B	Hagimamole Mary—†	8	at home	57	"
C	Tsavaris Emanuel	8	engineer	20	"
D	Tsavaris John	8	U S N	43	
E	Tsavaris Sylvia—†	8	housewife	37	"

Page.	Letter.	FULL NAME.	Residence, Jan. 1, 1946.	Occupation.	Supposed Age.	Reported Residence, Jan. 1, 1945. Street and Number.

Walnut Park—Continued

	F	Young Alexander	8	engineer	46	10 Westminster av
	G	Young Christina—†	8	housewife	46	10 "
	H	Mahan Helen—†	10	stitcher	21	243 Lamartine
	K	Stack Dorothy—†	10	saleswoman	42	243 "
	L	Voutselas Angelina—†	12	at home	85	here
	M	Voutselas Gerald	12	salesman	45	"
	N	Voutselas Katherine—†	12	housewife	35	"
	O	Swift Elizabeth N—†	12	"	52	
	P	Swift John H	12	salesman	71	"
	R	Swift Pauline E—†	12	analyst	33	
	S	Karimbakas Anastasia—†	14	housewife	38	"
	T	Karimbakas Charles	14	merchant	48	"
	U	Houpis James	15	clerk	38	"
	v*	Houpis Peter	15	retired	80	"
	W	Houpis Samuel	15	clerk	34	
	X	Koumarianos Helen—†	15	housewife	32	"
	Y*	Koumarianos James	15	cook	44	
	Z	Finneran John V	15½	student	21	"
		737				
	A	Finneran Thomas F	15½	salesman	29	California
	B	Glennon Katherine M—†	15½	housewife	30	here
	C	Glennon William G	15½	U S A	28	"
	D	Visvis Christie	15½	U S N	20	"
	E*	Visvis Mary A—†	15½	housewife	43	"
	F	Visvis Sophie—†	15½	clerk	21	
	G	Johnson Ernest	17	musician	50	"
	H	Johnson Ethel M—†	17	housewife	48	"
	K	Williamson Ernestine L—†	17	"	25	
	L	Williamson Rufus T	17	clerk	35	
	M	Booker Manuel	19	waiter	37	
	N	Marchioni Albino J	20	shoemaker	57	"
	O	Marchioni Rose—†	20	stitcher	46	"
	P	Shaw Mary—†	20	bookkeeper	46	"
	R	Shaw William	20	salesman	56	"
	S	Hanbury Adeline—†	24	assembler	29	"
	T	Hanbury Catherine—†	24	housewife	56	"
	U	Hanbury Thomas	24	printer	31	
	V	Foye Jodie H	24	supt	50	"
	W	Foye Rose M—†	24	housewife	47	"
	X	Brown Bertha—†	24	stitcher	41	"
	Y	Singer Goldie—†	24	typist	25	"

Page.	Letter.	FULL NAME.	Residence, Jan. 1, 1946.	Occupation.	Supposed Age.	Reported Residence, Jan. 1, 1945. Street and Number.

Walnut Park—Continued

	z	Clayman Benjamin	24	pharmacist	37	here
		738				
	A	Clayman Ida—†	24	housewife	36	"
	B	Landa Mary—†	24	"	52	
	C	Landa Maurice	24	merchant	60	"
	D	Rovner Hannah—†	24	housewife	40	"
	E	Rovner William	24	realtor	43	
	F	Brown Dora—†	24	housewife	31	"
	G	Brown Eugene	24	manager	32	"
	H	Davis Ida—†	24	at home	74	"
	K	Silkman Sophia—†	24	housewife	69	"
	L	Strumph Bettina—†	24	"	36	
	M	Strumph Leonard	24	florist	40	
	N	Ross Ethel—†	24	cashier	52	
	O	Ross Nathan	24	merchant	57	"
	P	Darcy Katherine—†	24	operator	44	"
	R	Mosher Mary—†	24	stenographer	42	"
	S	Goldberg Albert	24	manager	35	"
	T	Goldberg Rose—†	24	housewife	32	"
	U	Eagerman Charles	24	accountant	27	"
	V	Eagerman Gladys—†	24	housewife	26	"
	W	Cherner Beatrice—†	24	"	30	"
	X	Cherner Michael	24	cleanser	31	"
	Y	Dahl Edward	25	instructor	68	"
	z	Dahl George J	25	salesman	70	"
		739				
	A	Dahl Lorenz	25	clerk	72	
	B	Metten Harriet D—†	25	housewife	58	"
	C	Metten William H	25	engineer	34	"
	D	Kasoff Jennie—†	30	housewife	36	"
	E	Kasoff Theodore	30	agent	43	
	F	Green Bernard	30	electrician	47	"
	G	Green Dora—†	30	stitcher	44	
	H	Goldberg Bertha—†	30	housewife	50	"
	K	Goldberg Harry	30	operator	51	"
	L	Rutman Anna—†	30	stitcher	41	
	M	Rutman Louis	30	"	41	"
	N	Manascalco Dominic	30	operator	37	"
	O	Manascalco Josephine—†	30	housewife	33	"
	P	Freeman Hilda—†	30	"	45	
	R	Freeman Ralph	30	merchant	49	"

Page.	Letter.	Full Name.	Residence, Jan. 1, 1946.	Occupation.	Supposed Age.	Reported Residence, Jan. 1, 1945. Street and Number.

Walnut Park—Continued

s	Cohen Julia—†	30	housewife	30	here
t	Cohen Louis S	30	manager	31	"
u	Bernstein Rose—†	30	housewife	50	"
v	Bernstein Solomon	30	merchant	50	"
w	Kirsten Arnold	30	U S A	23	
x	Kirsten Mark S	30	manufacturer	65	"
y	Kirsten Sadie—†	30	clerk	50	
z	Deitch Ida—†	30	housewife	35	"

740

a	Deitch Louis	30	merchant	34	"
b	Cohen Hannah—†	30	housewife	65	"
c	Cohen Hyman	30	clerk	67	
d	Cohen Victor	30	merchant	36	"
e	Gray Abraham	30	salesman	61	"
f	Gray Fannie—†	30	housewife	55	"
g	Gray Milton B	30	U S N	28	"
h	Glutman Goldie—†	30	housewife	52	"
k	Glutman Joseph	30	egg candler	54	"
l	Moshcovitz Ethel H—†	30	housewife	33	"
m	Moshcovitz Samuel J	30	accountant	38	"
n	Eskot Emma—†	30	housewife	29	"
o	Eskot Reuben	30	painter	33	
p	Cohen Frank	30	stitcher	53	
r	Cohen Lena—†	30	housewife	50	"
s	Chofnas Ida E—†	30	"	56	
t	Chofnas Irving	30	physician	29	"
u	Chofnas Jacob W	30	manager	56	"
v	Cummings Maurice	30	merchant	29	"
w	Cummings Norma—†	30	housewife	29	"
x	Ruddman Mary—†	30	housekeeper	53	"
y	Siegel Rae—†	30	housewife	22	"
z	Siegel Solomon	30	carpenter	26	"

741

a	Hyman Jacob	30	salesman	37	"
b	Hyman Sylvia—†	30	housewife	32	"
c	Segel Bernard	30	paperhanger	57	"
d	Segel Mollie—†	30	housewife	50	"
e	Balkan Arnold	30	decorator	32	"
f	Balkan Hilda—†	30	housewife	32	"
g	Malk Mary—†	30	bookkeeper	36	40 Forest
h	Malk Mildred—†	30	stenographer	40	40 "

Page.	Letter.	Full Name.	Residence, Jan. 1, 1946.	Occupation.	Supposed Age.	Reported Residence, Jan. 1, 1945. Street and Number.

Walnut Park—Continued

K	Wilson Esther—†	30	housewife	29	40 Forest
L	Wilson George	30	agent	33	4 Fort av
M	Freedman Rose—†	37	housewife	33	here
N	Freedman Samuel	37	jeweler	44	"
O	Snider Alice—†	37	housewife	30	"
P	Snider Harry	37	retired	74	"
R	Snider Samuel	37	salesman	44	"
S	Snider Sarah—†	37	bookkeeper	35	"
T	Wekstein Abraham	38	attorney	26	"
U	Wekstein Helen—†	38	housewife	54	"
V	Wekstein Louis	38	teacher	28	
W	Cohen Hyman	38	reporter	52	"
X	Cohen Samuel	38	realtor	82	
Y	Korins Elliot L	38	salesman	33	"
Z	Korins Gwendolyn—†	38	housewife	30	"
	742				
A	Pollen David	38	clerk	37	"
B	Pollen Mary—†	38	secretary	34	"
C	Goodman Meyer	38	student	29	"
D	Goodman Ruth—†	38	bookkeeper	26	"
E	Pruzan Zelda—†	38	housekeeper	57	"
F	Nesson Ada—†	38	housewife	37	"
G	Nesson Harold	38	decorator	40	"
H	Miller Charles	38	salesman	36	"
K	Miller Dorothy—†	38	housewife	32	"
L	Schindler Joseph	38	instructor	28	"
M	Schindler Lillian—†	38	housewife	26	"
N	Ratihn Lillian—†	38	"	23	
O	Ratihn Samuel	38	clerk	24	
P	Miller Joseph	38	metalworker	52	"
R	Miller Rena—†	38	housewife	38	"
S	Gilbert Frank J	38	accountant	39	"
T	Gilbert Naomi—†	38	housewife	30	"
U	Goldman Albert B	38	attorney	40	"
V	Goldman Tessie—†	38	clerk	30	"
W	Gould George	38	musician	29	"
X	Gould Marion—†	38	housewife	28	"
Y	Goldberg Leah—†	39	saleswoman	38	"
Z	Housman Gertrude—†	39	"	40	
	743				
'A	Ladoulis Etta—†	39	housewife	45	"

Walnut Park—Continued

B	Ladoulis Theodore	39	merchant	48	here
c	*Ladoulis William	39	retired	83	"
D	Krock Mitchell S	41	student	22	"
E	Krock Nathan R	41	printer	56	
F	Krock Rebecca R—†	41	housewife	53	"
G	Krock Ruth—†	41	teacher	27	
H	*Rosen Bessie—†	41	housewife	56	"
K	Rosen Samuel	41	clerk	56	
L	Rosen Sydney	41	U S A	27	
M	Miller Harry	42	salesman	40	"
N	Miller Tillie—†	42	housewife	40	"
O	Cardoza Henry	42	clerk	24	Fall River
P	Cardoza Lena—†	42	stitcher	22	here
R	Lachapelle Mary—†	42	at home	80	"
S	Lachapelle William	42	retired	77	"
T	Menard Edgar	42	janitor	47	
U	Menard Florida—†	42	housewife	43	"
V	Menard Lorraine—†	42	stitcher	20	"
W	Love Marie H—†	46	housewife	50	3 Glenvale ter
X	Love Thomas W	46	tailor	53	3 "
Y	Love William M	46	U S A	28	3 "
Z	Roberts Chester	46	"	21	231 Amory

744

A	Roberts Irma—†	46	housewife	44	231 "
B	Hite Arnold	50	merchant	34	here
C	Hite Sylvia—†	50	housewife	30	"
D	Gale Harry	50	foreman	57	"
E	Gale Melvin	50	U S N	23	
F	Gale Ruth—†	50	inspector	30	"
G	Gale Sarah—†	50	saleswoman	51	"
H	Lipschitz Abraham	50	U S A	26	
K	Lipschitz Pearl—†	50	housewife	26	"
L	Levitt Ruth R—†	50	"	44	38 Walnut pk
M	Levitt William J	50	clerk	47	38 "
N	Praise Anna—†	50	stenographer	35	38 "
O	Barsky Freida—†	50	housewife	57	here
P	Barsky Louis	50	U S A	21	"
R	Barsky Samuel	50	realtor	64	"
S	Lerman Frank	50	foreman	50	"
T	Lerman Rose—†	50	housewife	50	"
U	Rottenberg Alice—†	50	"	50	

Walnut Park—Continued

v	Rottenberg Charlotte—†	50	secretary	30	here
w	Rottenberg Hyman	50	barber	51	"
x	Hersh Jessie C—†	51	clerk	26	"
y	Schneiderman Jacob	51	"	46	
z	Schneiderman Rose—†	51	housewife	38	"

745

A	Scudney Gertrude—†	57	clerk	43	
B	Scudney Hannah—†	57	housekeeper	38	"
E	Revis Mildred—†	60	housewife	27	"
F	Revis Solomon	60	U S A	27	
G	Rottenberg Eva—†	60	at home	57	..
H	Rottenberg Norma J—†	60	bookkeeper	23	"
K	Rottenberg Victor	60	machinist	66	- "
L	Gries Sophie—†	60	at home	61	.,
M	Harkins Clara C—†	60	"	66	
N	Card Rose—†	60	housewife	44	"
O	Card William	60	woodworker	44	"
P	Stern Levi	60	salesman	67	"
R	Stern Rose—†	60	housewife	63	"
S	Wolff Harry	60	clerk	39	
T	Wolff Henny—†	60	at home	37	..
U	Schwartz Bella—†	60	housewife	71	"
V	Schwartz Ida—†	60	bookkeeper	43	"
W	Brittain Annette S—†	60	stenographer	21	"
X	Brittain Dora—†	60	housewife	63	"
Y	Brittain Leon	60	printer	58	
Z	Brittain Miriam H—†	60	bookkeeper	28	,,

746

A	Brittain Saul M	60	metalworker	21	"
B	Fink Charles F	61	clothier	52	
C	Fink Martin B	61	decorator	24	,,
D	Fink Norman	61	U S A	22	
E	Fink Rhea—†	61	housewife	49	"
F	Finkelstein David	61	presser	77	
G	Johnson Calvin L	61	clerk	21	
H	Johnson Clarence L	61	mechanic	47	"
K	Johnson Louise A—†	61	housewife	45	"
L	Shaw Martha—†	61	housekeeper	50	"
M	Wright Ruby—†	61	seamstress	27	"
N	Hogan Irene—†	61	housewife	28	"
O	Hogan John B	61	salesman	30	,,

Page.	Letter.	Full Name.	Residence, Jan. 1, 1946.	Occupation.	Supposed Age.	Reported Residence, Jan. 1, 1945. Street and Number.

Walnut Park—Continued

P	*Lourie Bessie—†	61	housewife	56	here
R	Lourie Jacob	61	machinist	61	"
S	Lourie Miriam—†	61	clerk	21	"
U	Foilb Helen R—†	67	housewife	53	"
V	Foilb Morris L	67	merchant	55	"
W	Foilb Robert L	67	clerk	29	..
X	Goss Louis	67	manager	53	"
Y	Goss Sarah—†	67	housewife	50	"
Z	Labourene Elliot J	67	salesman	32	"

747

A	Labourene Marcia—†	67	housewife	26	"
B	Rodman Barbara J—†	67	"	20	"
C	Rodman George	67	U S A	21	
E	Oberman Nathan	71	clerk	40	
F	Oberman Shirley—†	71	housewife	35	"
G	Rosenbaum Rose—†	71	inspector	33	Revere
H	Greenstein Gertrude—†	71	housewife	39	here
K	Greenstein Louis	71	clerk	41	"
L	Knoff Phillip	71	salesman	47	"
M	Speigel Gladys—†	71	housewife	26	"
N	Speigel Samuel	71	waiter	49	..
O	Cohen Anne R—†	72	housewife	35	"
P	Cohen George	72	salesman	37	"
R	Brock Rose—†	72	housewife	37	"
S	Brock Samuel	72	buyer	41	"
T	Levine Florence R—†	72	saleswoman	29	38 Deckard
U	Levine Yetta—†	72	housewife	64	38 "
V	Price Annette—†	72	"	23	here
W	Price Harold D	72	salesman	25	"
X	Rosenberg Israel	72	"	44	"
Y	Rosenberg Lillian—†	72	housewife	42	"
Z	Brown Calvin	72	salesman	31	"

748

A	Brown Evelyn—†	72	housewife	27	"
B	Grodensky David	72	roofer	43	
C	Grodensky Lena—†	72	housewife	42	"
D	Brock Esther—†	72	tel operator	45	"
E	Brock Maxwell	72	salesman	50	"
F	Brock William	72	tailor	75	
G	Glick Helen—†	72	housewife	31	"
H	Glick Max S	72	welder	33	

Walnut Park—Continued

K	Brown Lena—†	72	housewife	43	here
L	Brown Samuel	72	butcher	45	"
M	Golden Lillian—†	73	housewife	36	"
N	Golden Louis	73	chauffeur	38	"
O	Spivack Ralph	73	manager	48	"
P	Spivack Rose—†	73	housewife	41	"
R	Bendersky Freda—†	73	teacher	23	
S	Bendersky Reuben	73	photographer	54	"
T	Bendersky Sarah—†	73	housewife	53	"
U	Possick Leo	76	plumber	27	"
V	Possick Selma—†	76	housewife	25	"
W	Black Harry	76	meatcutter	61	"
X	Black Rebecca—†	76	housewife	56	"
Y	Tristman Jeanette—†	76	"	27	
Z	Tristmas Seymour	76	auditor	28	

749

A	Gorenstein Bella—†	76	housewife	36	"
B	Gorenstein Harry	76	musician	32	"
C	Reed Jack	76	operator	51	"
D	Reed Rachael—†	76	housewife	44	"
E	Bromfield Ethel—†	76	"	39	
F	Bromfield Samuel	76	salesman	41	"
G	Herson Gladys—†	76	housewife	28	"
H	Herson Harold	76	salesman	31	"
K	Esner Herbert	76	shipper	39	
L	Esner Ida—†	76	housewife	39	"
M	Cantor Bessie—†	76	"	47	
N	Cantor Joseph	76	salesman	53	"
O	Ladin Blanche—†	77	housewife	41	"
P	Ladin Charles	77	salesman	45	"
R	Stone Herbert L	77	U S A	20	
S	Stone Lena—†	77	housewife	46	"
T	Stone William	77	merchant	51	"
U	Hill Emma—†	77	clerk	48	"
V	Gantman Edna—†	77	nurse	20	"
W	Gantman Louis	77	salesman	56	"
X	Gantman Milton	77	U S M C	23	"
Y	Gantman Norma—†	77	housewife	51	"
Z	Gantman Sydney D	77	U S A	25	

750

A	Gollis Hannah—†	77	at home	67	"

Page.	Letter.	Full Name.	Residence, Jan. 1, 1946.	Occupation.	Supposed Age.	Reported Residence, Jan. 1, 1945. Street and Number.

Walnut Park—Continued

	B	Michelman John H	77	salesman	76	here
	c	Michelman Katherine E—†	77	housewife	70	"
	D	Michelman Theresa—†	77	clerk	44	"
	E	Mitchell Sarah—†	77	housewife	64	"
	F	Woods Bertha B—†	77	"	32	
	G	Woods Walter L	77	U S A	34	
	H	Meltzer Edward	77	embalmer	48	"
	K	Meltzer Ida—†	77	housewife	47	"
	L	Meltzer Ruth E—†	77	bookkeeper	21	"
	M	Glick Abraham A	77	salesman	53	"
	N	Glick Dorothy R—†	77	housewife	47	"
	o	Glick Estelle—†	77	clerk	21	
	P	Glick Monroe S	77	salesman	24	"
	R	Smokler Barney	77	"	42	
	s	Smokler Sophie—†	77	housewife	42	"
	T	Kleinbart Betty—†	77	"	31	"
	U	Kleinbart Leonard	77	salesman	36	"
	V	Schneider Barnet	77	clerk	51	
	W	Schneider James B	77	engineer	24	"
	X	Schneider Phillip J	77	U S N	21	
	Y	Schneider William M	77	machinist	22	"
	z	Schneider Winifred M—†	77	housewife	47	"

751

	A	Neckes Edith H—†	77	secretary	32	"
	B	Neckes Eva—†	77	bookkeeper	30	"
	c	Neckes Sarah—†	77	housewife	66	"
	D	Lazarus Betty—†	79	"	47	
	E	Lazarus Edward	79	U S A	21	
	F	Lazarus John	79	machinist	49	"
	G	Weinshell Betty—†	79	nurse	50	
	H	Rosen Jacob	79	accountant	51	",
	K	Rosen Rebecca—†	79	housewife	48	"
	L	Kahn Jeanette R—†	79	housekeeper	53	"
	M	Ratkowsky Charles F	79	salesman	61	"
	N	Drucker Arlene D—†	79	bookkeeper	20	"
	o	Drucker Betty—†	79	housewife	44	"
	P	Drucker Marvin	79	U S A	24	
	R	Drucker Murray	79	salesman	48	"
	s	Harrison Lottie S—†	79	housewife	44	"
	T	Harrison Louis P	79	meteorologist	44	"
	U	Simes Ethel—†	79	bookkeeper	42	"

Page.	Letter.	Full Name.	Residence, Jan. 1, 1946.	Occupation.	Supposed Age.	Reported Residence, Jan. 1, 1945. Street and Number.

Walnut Park—Continued

	v	Simes Florence—†	79	stenographer	38	here
	w	Chase Morton	79	butcher	26	"
	x	Chase Natalie—†	79	housewife	24	"
	y	Shore Anne—†	79	bookkeeper	30	"
	z	Shore Bessie—†	79	housewife	60	"
752						
	a	Shore Hyman	79	U S A	29	"
	b	Weinstein Dora—†	79	housewife	53	"
	c	Weinstein Ethel G—†	79	teacher	24	
	d	Weinstein Herbert	79	U S N	27	
	e	Weinstein Ruth S—†	79	housewife	24	"
	f	Berry Evelyn—†	79	"	24	
	g	Berry Nelson H	79	merchant	25	"
	h	Klein Bessie—†	79	housewife	59	"
	k	Klein David	79	chauffeur	23	"
	l	Swerdlove Ethel—†	79	housewife	25	"
	m	Swerdlove Morris	79	salesman	26	"
	n	Tucker Esther—†	79	housewife	27	"
	o	Tucker Nathaniel	79	U S N	26	
	p	Wheeler Freida—†	79	housewife	25	"
	r	Wheeler Joseph	79	pharmacist	27	"
	s	Alpert Ann—†	79	housewife	34	"
	t	Alpert Joseph	79	engineer	38	"
	u	Segal Morris J	79	salesman	60	"
	v	Brutman Barbara E—†	80	WAVE	24	
	w	Brutman Charles	80	metalworker	59	"
	x	Brutman Earl M	80	"	21	
	y	Brutman Jennie—†	80	housewife	57	"
	z	Viner Nathan	80	retired	87	
753						
	a	Role Morris	81	engineer	51	"
	b	Role Rae—†	81	housewife	50	"
	c	Kaplan Ephraim	81	salesman	69	"
	d	Kaplan Fannie—†	81	housewife	69	"
	e	Horwitz Morris	81	pedler	64	
	f	Horwitz Myron	81	merchant	33	"
	g	Horwitz Selma—†	81	housewife	28	"
	h	Baker Nathaniel	81	manager	44	"
	k	Baker Tessa—†	81	housewife	44	"
	l	Caplan Rae—†	81	"	44	
	m	Caplan Richard	81	manager	42	"

Walnut Park—Continued

N	Caplan Sidney	81	U S A	20	here
O	Osobow Rose—†	81	housewife	37	"
P	Osobow Samuel	81	salesman	41	"
R	Rosen Mollie—†	81	housewife	33	"
S	Rosen William J	81	clerk	38	
T	Weinrebe Paul	81	salesman	29	"
U	Weinrebe Rose—†	81	housewife	27	"
V	Bouchard Augustine	81	mechanic	29	"
W	Bouchard Eleanor—†	81	housewife	24	"
X	Epstein Boris	81	retired	69	"
Y	Epstein Celia—†	81	housewife	62	"
Z	Kahn Doris—†	81	manager	36	2 Holborn ter

754

A	Finkelstein Frances—†	81	housewife	42	here
B	Finkelstein Max	81	accountant	38	"

Wardman Road

C	Goldstein Bertha—†	3	housewife	28	here
D	Goldstein George	3	pharmacist	30	"
E	Sanderson Benjamin	3	chauffeur	37	"
F	Sanderson Eva D—†	3	housewife	34	"
G	Williams Benson	3	U S N	20	
H	Williams Lewis	3	salesman	53	"
K	Williams Mae—†	3	housewife	46	"
L	Jacobs Bedonna B—†	3	WAC	24	
M	Jacobs Florence S—†	3	"	26	
N	Jacobs Irving	3	salesman	57	"
O	Jacobs May—†	3	housewife	54	"
P	Rubin Bernard	3	shipper	63	"
R	Rubin Evelyn—†	3	bookkeeper	26	"
S	Rubin Irene F—†	3	"	24	"
T	Rubin Norman S	3	student	21	
U	Rubin Rose C—†	3	housewife	61	"
V	Brown Esther—†	3	clerk	49	
W	Brown Irving	3	machinist	47	"
X	Brown Rose—†	3	housewife	76	"
Y	Kalus Celia—†	7	"	20	178 Harold
Z	Kalus Samuel	7	assessor	25	178 "

755

A	Hyman Benjamin	7	accountant	30	here

Wardman Road—Continued

B	Hyman Etta—†	7	housewife	63	here
C	Hyman Julius	7	metalworker	61	"
D	Haffer Herbert R	7	presser	40	"
E	Haffer Zelma—†	7	housewife	36	"
F	Daley Ruth E—†	7	bookkeeper	25	"
G	Glynn John F	7	accountant	57	"
H	Glynn Nettie—†	7	housewife	45	"
K	Rosenthal Mildred—†	7	"	27	..
L	Rosenthal Ralph	7	U S A	30	
M	Bornstein Rose—†	7	saleswoman	49	"
N	Goldman Joseph	7	salesman	39	"
O	Goldman Ruby—†	7	housewife	29	"
P	Fearer Benjamin	7	merchant	50	"
R	Sharfman Freida—†	8	housewife	45	"
S	Sharfman Maurice	8	printer	49	"
T	Block Ada—†	8	housewife	42	"
U	Block Herman L	8	physician	34	..
V	Block Max H	8	realtor	45	
W	Volinn Ruth—†	8	chemist	27	
X	*Volinsky Ada—†	8	housewife	50	"
Y	Volinsky Jacob	8	baker	54	
Z	Baker Dora—†	9	housewife	50	"

756

A	Baker Jacob	9	presser	59	
B	Gootman Alter	9	agent	58	
C	Gootman Miriam—†	9	housewife	32	"
D	Gootman Solomon J	9	chemist	35	
E	Iserovitz David I	9	U S A	27	
F	Barsky Celia—†	9	housewife	45	"
G	Barsky Erwin	9	U S A	20	
H	Barsky Louis	9	merchant	45	"
K	Hoffman Abraham	9	salesman	54	..
L	Hoffman Edward	9	student	22	
M	Hoffman Rose—†	9	housewife	45	"
N	Hoffman Samuel	9	U S N	20	..
O	Levine Dorothy—†	9	housewife	39	"
P	Levine George	9	stitcher	42	..
R	Langson Frances—†	9	bookkeeper	23	"
S	*Langson Jennie—†	9	housewife	54	"
T	Langson Philip	9	salesman	30	"
U	Pearlstein Abraham	10	broker	47	"

Wardman Road—Continued

v	Pearlstein Esther H—†	10	housewife	42	here
w	Fisher Gertrude—†	10	"	46	"
x	Fisher Walter	10	foreman	50	"
y	Allen Saul	10	chauffeur	51	"
z	Berger Irving S	10	clerk	32	

757

a	Berger Muriel—†	10	housewife	23	"
b	Prolman Beatrice—†	10	"	25	
c	Prolman Harry	10	U S A	26	
d	Bearson Betty—†	11	housewife	35	"
e	Bearson Harry	11	salesman	34	"
f	*Freedman Celia—†	11	housewife	57	"
g	Freedman Joseph	11	tailor	60	
h	Bennett Katherine—†	11	operator	54	"
k	Bennett Martin	11	attorney	29	"
l	Bennett Phyllis—†	11	clerk	23	"
m	Laskey Evelyn—†	11	housewife	27	"
n	Laskey Sigmund	11	foreman	30	"
o	Olken Charlotte—†	11	housewife	27	Nebraska
p	Olken Harry A	11	clerk	28	here
r	Rogoff Joseph S	11	U S A	30	"
s	Rogoff Rita—†	11	housewife	25	"
t	Zides Rebecca—†	11	"	59	
u	Lerner Abraham	11	florist	55	
v	Lerner Hattie—†	11	housewife	52	"
w	Lerner Natalie—†	11	at home	20	"
x	Antick Bernice—†	11	bookkeeper	20	"
y	Antick Ida—†	11	housewife	49	"
z	Antick Sidney H	11	accountant	49	"

758

a	Feinberg Robert	12	tailor	37	
b	Feinberg Sarah—†	12	housewife	32	"
c	Feinberg Alice—†	12	"	32	
d	Feinberg Jacob	12	operator	37	"
e	Gardner Maurice H	12	retired	79	"
f	Edelstein Elizabeth—†	12	dressmaker	55	Rhode Island
g	Goodman Ida—†	12 ·	housewife	54	here
h	Goodman Reuben	12	merchant	55	"
k	Simon Elizabeth—†	15	typist	22	"
l	Simon Etta—†	15	housewife	49	"
m	Simon Irving	15	laborer	50	

Wardman Road—Continued

	N	Gunders Henry	15	U S A	21	here
	O	Gunders Herta—†	15	housewife	46	"
	P	Gunders Paul L	15	accountant	50	"
	R	Baker Joseph	15	printer	50	
	S	Weiner Israel	15	cutter	53	
	T	Weiner Rena—†	15	housewife	46	"
	U	Clayman Sadie—†	15	clerk	40	
	V	Silverman Bessie—†	15	housewife	68	"
	W	Shepett Hyman	15	decorator	25	"
	X	Shepett Lena—†	15	housewife	48	"
	Y	Shepett Sidney	15	electrician	21	"
	Z	Neidle Frank H	15	welder	50	

759

	A	Neidle Helen—†	15	clerk	20	
	B	Neidle Rose—†	15	housewife	48	"
	C	Kopel Bessie—†	16	"	70	
	D	Lieberman Dinah—†	16	"	72	
	E	Lampert Abraham	16	clerk	30	..
	F	Lampert Anne—†	16	saleswoman	32	..
	G	Wheeler Ida--†	16	housewife	56	"
	H	Wheeler Maurice D	16	salesman	64	"
	K	Cohen Lorraine—†	16	housewife	25	"
	L	Cohen Wolfe	16	salesman	27	"
	M	Slepian Ida—†	17	housewife	69	"
	N	Slepian Louis	17	retired	71	
	O	Wolff Elsa—†	17	housewife	35	"
	P	Wolff Paul	17	chemist	49	
	R	*Lemack Bessie—†	17	housewife	36	"
	S	Lemack David	17	cutter	40	
	T	Miller Abraham	17	salesman	45	"
	U	Miller Hannah—†	17	housewife	45	"
	V	Davis Florence—†	17	"	29	N Carolina
	W	Davis Maurice D	17	U S A	31	"
	X	Riter Ida—†	17	housewife	54	here
	Y	Riter Shirley—†	17	saleswoman	36	"
	Z	Riter Solomon	17	mechanic	62	"

760

	A	Press Celia—†	17	at home	54	
	B	Sobel Abraham	17	machinist	30	"
	C	Sobel Anne— †	17	housewife	27	"
	D	Glass Ann—†	18	"	54	

Wardman Road—Continued

E	Glass Harry	18	merchant	62	here
F	Burger Jean—†	18	bookkeeper	35	"
G	Burger Maurice	18	merchant	44	"
H	Levine Ida—†	18	housewife	66	"
K	Beckman Charlotte—†	18	"	36	
L	Beckman Joseph	18	merchant	42	"
M	Block Nancy—†	19	housewife	53	"
N	Block Samuel	19	guard	53	"
O	Leventhal Julius	19	jeweler	58	"
P	Leventhal Leon	19	attorney	32	"
R	Leventhal Sarah—†	19	housewife	58	"
S	Gold Samuel	19	meatcutter	44	"
T	*Gold Tillie—†	19	housewife	42	"
U	Glick Bessie—†	19	"	53	
V	Glick Irving	19	student	23	"
W	Glick Philip	19	foreman	60	"
X	Adwin David	19	operator	45	"
Y	Adwin Ida—†	19	housewife	38	"
Z	Goldstein Maurice	19	caterer	39	

761

A	Goldstein Minnie—†	19	housewife	36	"
B	Simons Lillian—†	20	clerk	30	
C	Simons Sarah—†	20	housewife	69	"
D	Gilman Julius	20	cutter	46	"
E	Gilman Nettie—†	20	housewife	45	"
F	Gilman Selma—†	20	secretary	22	"
G	Abrams Ruth J—†	20	saleswoman	38	"
H	Glazer Harry	20	merchant	47	"
K	Glazer Minnie—†	20	housewife	47	"
L	Lewis John H	20	welder	42	

Washington Street

M	Hughes John	2990	operator	35	here
N	Hughes Olive—†	2990	housewife	40	"
O	Burnie Avis—†	2990	"	60	"
P	Burnie Douglas	2990	chef	55	
R	Burnie Douglas, jr	2990	U S A	20	"
S	Feeney Anna—†	2990	housewife	43	2888 Wash'n
T	Feeney Daniel	2990	fireman	54	2888 "

Page.	Letter.	Full Name.	Residence, Jan. 1, 1946.	Occupation.	Supposed Age.	Reported Residence, Jan. 1, 1945. Street and Number.

Washington Street—Continued

	u	McMahon John A	2992	laborer	34	2890 Wash'n
	v	Thomas Sarah—†	2992	at home	67	here
	w	*Hayes Rita—†	2992	housewife	34	"
	x	Hayes Robert F	2992	laborer	44	"
	y	Bailis Alice—†	2992	housewife	51	5 Glines av
	z	Bailis Anthony J	2992	finisher	54	5 "

762

	a	Herman Helen—†	2992	housewife	31	5 "
	b	Herman Herbert	2992	clerk	25	Virginia
	c	Lynch Dorothy —†	2994	housewife	23	12 Hollander
	d	Lynch Joseph F	2994	waiter	24	12 "
	e	Hunt Douglas	2994	clerk	21	here
	f	Hunt Mildred—†	2994	housewife	41	"
	g	Daley Charles J	2994	laborer	38	123 Green
	h	Daley Elizabeth A—†	2994	housewife	43	123 "
	k	McGee Ruth V—†	2994	saleswoman	22	123 "
	l	Factoroff Catherine—†	2996	housewife	46	here
	m	Factoroff Cecil	2996	chauffeur	46	"
	n	Gatturna Elizabeth—†	2996	operator	40	"
	o	Greene Catherine E—†	2996	housewife	45	"
	p	Greene John, jr	2996	chauffeur	21	"
	r	Greene John R	2996	machinist	53	"
	s	Greene Mary A—†	2996	assembler	24	"
	t	Bulger Charles	2998	baker	55	
	u	Bulger Mary—†	2998	housewife	45	"
	v	Burnham George	2998	operator	23	"
	w	Burnham Minnia—†	2998	housewife	20	"
	x	Murch Anita—†	2998	operator	21	"
	y	Murch Mary—†	2998	packer	43	
	z	Montgomery Cecil	2998	janitor	42	

763

	a	*Montgomery Mary—†	2998	housewife	29	"
	b	*Buccelli Annie—†	3000	at home	70	"
	c	Buccelli Camillo	3000	laborer	56	
	d	*Nelson Margaret—†	3000	at home	85	"
	e	Russell Frances I—†	3000	housewife	39	"
	f	Russell Patrick J	3000	seaman	20	
	h	Williams Florence—†	3028	clerk	35	
	k	Williams Martha—†	3028	at home	75	"
	l	Fisher Myrtle—†	3042	housekeeper	50	"
	m	McCullough Richard	3042	retired	83	
	n	Nash Clifford	3042	mechanic	45	"

Page.	Letter.	Full Name.	Residence, Jan. 1, 1946.	Occupation.	Supposed Age.	Reported Residence, Jan. 1, 1945. Street and Number.

	w	Kilroy John T	3088	laborer	57	here
	x	Kilroy Lena—†	3088	housewife	74	"
	y	Daly Eileen—†	3088	"	24	"
	z	Ferreira Vincent	3088	painter	46	
764						
	a	Ferreira Vincent J	3088	buffer	21	
	c	Davis Alice M—†	3090	housewife	47	"
	d	Davis Dewey C	3090	laborer	48	
	e	Grueter Anna M—†	3090	inspector	27	"
	f	Grueter Anne V—†	3090	housewife	64	"
	g	Grueter Edward J	3090	machinist	29	"
	t	MacDonald Mildred—†	3110	housewife	51	"
	u	MacDonald Norman A	3110	U S A	21	
	v	Acres Chester S	3110	"	25	
	w	Acres Veronica—†	3110	housewife	23	"
	x	Owens Elizabeth V—†	3110	"	50	
	y	Owens James L	3110	steamfitter	52	"
765						
	b	Gaskill Frank	3118	janitor	46	
	c	Gaskill Hilda—†	3118	housewife	43	"
	d	Young Catherine J—†	3118	typist	21	
	e	Young Fred	3118	fireman	68	
	f	Young Fred, jr	3118	chauffeur	25	"
	g	Young Mary—†	3118	housewife	56	"
	h	Boyd Helen W—†	3118	clerk	21	
	k	O'Connell Daniel F	3118	retired	59	''
	l	O'Connell Davina S—†	3118	housewife	48	"
	m	O'Connell Rita F—†	3118	clerk	22	"
	n	Smith Mildred—†	3118	"	20	35 School
	o	Thompson Paul A	3118	laborer	25	here
	p	Green Isabelle—†	3118	executive	73	79 Warren
	r	Wilson Myra—†	3118	housekeeper	64	here
	s	Melanson Dorothy—†	3118	operator	28	"
	t	Wright Beatrice—†	3118	housewife	46	"
	u	Wright Mervin E	3118	inspector	49	"
	v	Duda Joseph	3118	clerk	57	
	w	Helms Charlotte—†	3118	housewife	31	"
	x	Helms Walter M	3118	meatcutter	38	"
	y	Hurley Daniel	3118	operator	48	"
	z	Wesa Beatrice—†	3118	housewife	24	Rhode Island
766						
	a	Wesa Emil	3118	U S A	41	''

Weld Avenue

D	Adler Althea—†	1	housewife	32	here
E	Adler John F	1	pipefitter	35	"
F	Fantasia Helen H—†	2	housewife	27	"
G	Hastings Charles M	2	advertiser	57	"
H	Hastings Lillian S—†	2	housewife	58	"
K	Hastings Walter C	2	laborer	28	
L	Mullen Florence A—†	2	laundress	23	"
M	Patten John D	3	janitor	55	
N	VanDyck Charles D	3	machinist	63	"
O	VanDyck Margaret P—†	3	housewife	53	"
P	McClutchy Clara E—†	4	"	37	
R	McClutchy Herbert S	4	salesman	54	"
S	Brady Isabel—†	4	housewife	61	"
T	Brady William	4	painter	65	"
U	Rodiches Alexander A	4A	foreman	25	
V	Rodiches Daniel A	4A	U S N	20	"
W	*Rodiches Nazira—†	4A	housewife	52	"
X	Lynch Bernard	4A	metalworker	59	"
Y	Lynch Rose A—†	4A	housewife	45	"
Z	Smith Elizabeth—†	4A	at home	75	

767

A	Ayer Frederick N	4A	technician	35	"
B	Ayer James W	4A	retired	70	
C	Regan Timothy F	4A	supervisor	64	"
D	Lane Alice A—†	5	inspector	53	"
E	O'Handley Daniel	5	chauffeur	52	"
F	O'Handley John J	5	U S A	22	
G	O'Handley Joseph P	5	policeman	50	"
H	O'Handley Joseph P, jr	5	U S A	24	
K	O'Handley Mary E—†	5	housewife	48	"
L	Rafter Elizabeth A—†	6	at home	78	
M	DiOrio Angelo	6	janitor	58	
N	DiOrio Elvira—†	6	secretary	20	"
O	DiOrio Mary—†	6	housewife	56	"
P	McIntyre Peter	7	retired	75	
R	McIntyre Rose—†	7	cashier	59	
S	Embree Fredonia E—†	7	housewife	70	"
T	Walker Dorothea E—†	7	designer	47	"
U	Crossman Violet—†	8	at home	52	
V	McClarity George R	8	fireman	40	
W	McClarity Hazel D—†	8	housewife	35	"

Weld Avenue—Continued

x	Cecil Adrian L	9	laborer	21	Ohio
y	Horrigan Annie T—†	9	housewife	46	here
z	Horrigan John J	9	manager	50	"

768

A	Quigley Francis W	10	fireman	33	
B	Quigley Mary F—†	10	housewife	55	"
c	Quigley William F	10	fireman	65	
D	Bickford Agnes M—†	11	housewife	40	"
E	Bickford Lorraine M—†	11	operator	24	"
F	Doyle Martin E	11	printer	48	
G	Gallagher Mary K—†	11	manager	48	"
H	Twoomey Mary—†	11	merchant	29	"
K	McGuinness Joseph W	13	technician	28	"
L	McGuinness Theresa C—†	13	at home	45	
M	Maloley Alice L—†	14	saleswoman	28	"
N	Maloley Lillian E—†	14	clerk	26	
o	*Maloley Mary—†	14	at home	48	
P	Maloley Nora M—†	14	cashier	33	
R	Maloley Thomas G	14	U S N	24	
T	Stanley George A	16	plumber	44	"
U	Stanley Isabelle M—†	16	at home	42	"
S	Stanley Odley H	16	plumber	26	"
V	Stanley Susan F—†	16	at home	65	
W	Caddle Barbara L—†	17	housewife	24	"
X	Caddle Howitson W	17	printer	24	"
Y	Stringe Beulah M—†	17	housewife	51	"
Z	Stringe Edward I	17	steamfitter	51	"

769

A	Lydon Helena M—†	18	housewife	46	"
B	Lydon Thomas F	18	retired	51	
c	DeStefano Dominic J	22	clerk	36	
D	DeStefano Mary J—†	22	secretary	31	"
E	DeStefano Carmela—†	22	at home	61	"
F	DeStefano Victor F	22	musician	27	"

Westminster Avenue

G	Carlos Mary E—†	4	housewife	50	here
H	DeVault William	4	clerk	30	"
K	Henderson Raymond	4	U S N	20	9 Laurel
L	Halloran Ellen—†	6	housewife	64	here

11—7

41

Westminster Avenue—Continued

M	Johnson Margaret—†	6	housewife	68	here
N	Erasme Albana—†	6	"	49	"
O	Erasme Jenny—†	6	clerk	23	"
P	Orbit Anton	6	"	53	175 Boylston
R	Orbit Elizabeth L—†	6	housewife	52	175 "
S	Lotto Gertrude—†	8	"	52	here
T	Lotto Samuel H	8	clerk	24	"
U	Fliegelman George	8	plumber	49	"
V	Fliegelman Sadie—†	8	housewife	37	"
W	Joyce Etta—†	8	"	58	"
X	Davis Anna M—†	10	"	20	Virginia
Y	Davis James R	10	mechanic	26	Amherst
Z	Hunter Frank L	10	clerk	45	89 Munroe

770

A	Johnson Alexander D	10	mechanic	45	89 "
B	Johnson Amy E—†	10	housewife	36	89 "
C	Ginn Susan—†	12	"	70	here
D	Hoye Mary L—†	12	"	82	"
E	Bradley George	16	clerk	39	Quincy
F	Davis Elizabeth—†	16	nurse	32	here
G	D'Entremont Justinian	16	carpenter	45	"
H	D'Entremont Linden—†	16	clerk	41	"
K	Lowe Catherine—†	16	"	53	"
L	Wynott Charles	16	operator	53	10 Westminster av
M	Wynott Myrtle—†	16	housewife	50	10 "
N	Henderson Hulda A—†	18	"	74	here
O	Henderson Laurence H	18	clerk	45	"
P	Henderson Myrtle C—†	18	housewife	39	"
R	Valoni Dorothy—†	19	"	40	
S	Seifert Edward E	19	clerk	34	
T	Seifert Ruth—†	19	housewife	27	"
U	Belgrave Donald E	19	nurse	31	
V	Winter Constance—†	19	housewife	64	"
W	Dow Charles	19	clerk	49	
X	Dow Mary—†	19	housewife	39	"
Y	Prodan Marie—†	19	"	39	
Z	Prodan Theodore	19	cleaner	36	

771

A	Sullivan Elizabeth—†	19	housewife	28	"
B	Sullivan John J	19	clerk	35	
C	Freiwald Mary N—†	19	housewife	32	"

Page.	Letter.	FULL NAME.	Residence, Jan. 1, 1946.	Occupation.	Supposed Age.	Reported Residence, Jan. 1, 1945. Street and Number.

Westminster Avenue—Continued

	D	Freiwald Robert E	19	painter	32	here
	E	Bell Mary—†	22	housewife	60	78 Holworthy
	F	Bell Thomas	22	retired	68	78 "
	G	Pasco Bertha E—†	22	housewife	67	here
	H	Pasco Louis	22	guard	67	"
	K	Pasco Louis E, jr	22	clerk	35	"
	L	Pasco Ruth G—†	22	"	34	"
	M	Field Charles H	24	manager	45	N Hampshire
	N	Field Mary—†	24	housewife	54	"
	O	Miller George	24	carpenter	54	here
	P	Miller Nettie—†	24	housewife	34	"
	R	Sadowsky Florence—†	24A	"	25	"
	S	Sadowsky Leo	24A	clerk	29	
	T	Crafin Benjamin	24A	"	57	
	U	Crafin Lillian—†	24A	housewife	25	"
	V	Crafin S Isadore	24A	jeweler	29	
	W	Dolan Agnes—†	65	housewife	49	"
	X	Dolan Edna—†	65	clerk	21	"
	Y	Kessler Barnet	65	retired	60	
	Z	Kessler Rose—†	65	housewife	50	"

772

	A	Balisok Julian	65	clerk	49	
	B	Balisok Rebecca—†	65	housewife	45	"
	C	Lucas Anna P—†	65	"	42	
	D	Lucas Hugo F	65	salesman	44	"
	E	Singer Irving	65	clerk	35	
	F	Singer Judith—†	65	housewife	27	"
	G	Jackson Betty—†	65	"	52	
	H	Jackson Myer	65	salesman	62	"
	K	Kahan David	65	"	59	
	L	Kahan Sarah—†	65	housewife	57	"
	M	Weiner Anna—†	65	"	42	
	N	Weiner Louis	65	salesman	45	"
	O	Plotkin Bernard	65	accountant	23	"
	P	Plotkin Rebecca—†	65	housewife	24	"
	R	Bernstein Barney	65	clerk	48	
	S	Bernstein Rose—†	65	housewife	48	"
	T	Madoff Isadore H	65	jeweler	60	"
	U	Rubin Louis	65	printer	38	
	V	Rubin Shirley—†	65	housewife	28	"
	W	LeMann Rose—†	65	clerk	30	

Page.	Letter.	FULL NAME.	Residence, Jan. 1, 1946.	Occupation.	Supposed Age.	Reported Residence, Jan. 1, 1945. Street and Number.

Westminster Avenue—Continued

x	Archibald James	65	clerk	50	here
y	Pass Lillian—†	71	"	36	"
z	Pass Ray	71	inspector	36	"

773

A	Johanson Harris L	71	repairman	50	"
B	Johanson Harris L, jr	71	U S A	22	
c	Alban Gertrude—†	71	housewife	38	"
D	Alban Oscar	71	shipper	50	
E	Cohen Arnold C	71	U S A	21	
F	Cohen Julius	71	tailor	65	
G	Cohen Mildred F—†	71	bookkeeper	33	"
H	Cohen Rose—†	71	housewife	60	"
K	Resnick Rae—†	71	"	43	
L	Resnick Rita—†	71	saleswoman	21	"
M	Resnick Rubin	71	merchant	45	"
N	Anopolsky Rose—†	71	at home	62	"
o	Stone Anna C—†	71	housewife	50	"
P	Zimering Mark A	71	printer	58	
R	St Germain Albert	71	seaman	36	
s	St Germain Marie—†	71	housewife	36	"
T	Levinson Gertrude—†	77	"	50	
u	Levinson Julius S	77	merchant	58	"
v	Levinson Melvin	77	U S A	25	
w	Steinberg Arthur	77	clerk	29	
x	Steinberg Selma—†	77	housewife	27	"
y	Levin Annie—†	77	"	80	
z	Prager Israel	77	clerk	48	

774

A	Prager Minnie—†	77	housewife	55	"

Westminster Terrace

B	Snyder Mary—†	3	clerk	45	here
c	Warshawsky Anna—†	3	housewife	78	"
D	Gateman Ida—†	3	"	40	"
E	Gateman Jacob	3	clerk	42	
F	Silverman Ella—†	3	"	38	
G	Silverman Harold	3	student	26	
H	Silverman Lillian—†	3	clerk	32	
K	Silverman Minnie—†	3	housewife	62	"
L	Silverman Zelda—†	3	clerk	35	

Westminster Terrace—Continued

M	*Katz Sarah—†	5	housewife	65	here
N	Kaufman Lillian—†	5	clerk	37	"
O	Kaufman Saul	5	"	41	"
P	Baker Bernard	5	U S A	24	
R	Baker Celia—†	5	housewife	55	"
S	Baker Marshall	5	clerk	55	"
T	Baker Walter	5	"	30	..
U	Rubinowitz Esther—†	5	housewife	57	"
V	Rubinowitz Myer	5	clerk	67	
W	Stern Jennie—†	7	housewife	49	"
X	Stern Melvin	7	U S N	25	
Y	Stern Sylvia—†	7	bookkeeper	22	"
Z	Bowers Charles	7	accountant	40	"

775

A	Bowers Miriam—†	7	housewife	38	"
B	Cohen Clara—†	7	"	23	"
C	Cohen Harold	7	meatcutter	25	"
E	*Kerber Etta—†	9	housewife	62	"
F	Levine Harry	9	agent	51	..
G	Levine Rae—†	9	housewife	39	"
H	Marcus Benjamin	9	printer	36	
K	Marcus Leah—†	9	housewife	33	"

8
9

1.
1

Ward 11–Precinct 8

CITY OF BOSTON

LIST OF RESIDENTS
20 YEARS OF AGE AND OVER

(NON-CITIZENS INDICATED BY ASTERISK)
(FEMALES INDICATED BY DAGGER)

AS OF

JANUARY 1, 1946

THOMAS F. SULLIVAN, *Chairman*
FREDERIC E. DOWLING, *Secretary*
WILLIAM A. MOTLEY, JR.
ARTHUR V. COUGHLIN
EVERETT R. PROUT

Listing Board.

CITY OF BOSTON ⬥ PRINTING DEPARTMENT

800

Boylston Street

A	McIsaac Eunice—†	209	factoryworker	21	here
B	McIsaac Hector E	209	longshoreman	58	"
C	McIsaac Margaret—†	209	housewife	55	"
D	McIsaac Mary M—†	209	factoryworker	20	"
E	Quinn Antoinette H—†	209	housewife	32	"
F	Quinn William A	209	policeman	35	"
G	Curran Mary B—†	209	housewife	54	"
H	Curran Thomas F	209	waiter	53	
K	Curran Thomas F, jr	209	U S N	22	
L	Amerault Florence—†	211	housewife	20	"
M	Amerault Lloyd	211	foreman	34	"
N	Corbett Catherine—†	211	housekeeper	74	"
O	Gilson Ellen B—†	211	housewife	65	"
P	Gilson Naomi C—†	211	teacher	36	"
R	Gilson Richard A	211	bookkeeper	66	"
S	Holden James	213	chauffeur	40	3224 Wash'n
T	Holden Margaret—†	213	housewife	39	here
U	Meade William J	213	baker	48	"
V	Meade William J, jr	213	U S N	20	"
W	Smith Elizabeth—†	213	housekeeper	62	"
X	Sheehan Frank F	213	chauffeur	27	316 Belgrade av
Y	Sheehan Isabel—†	213	housewife	26	316 "
Z	Gately Thomas F	215	guard	64	here

801

A	Gately Winifred M—†	215	at home	85	"
B	Gately Winifred W—†	215	clerk	32	
C	Thorne Helen—†	215	housewife	29	"
D	Arnott Margaret J—†	215	"	23	115 Paul Gore
E	Arnott Willard J	215	U S N	24	115 "
F	Yarnella Alice M—†	217	at home	77	here
G	Emerson Donald	217	laborer	43	"
H	Emerson Gertrude—†	217	housewife	35	"
K	Philbin Sarah—†	217	housekeeper	50	"
M	Smith Herbert	219	laborer	50	"
N	Smith Marion N—†	219	housewife	45	"
O	MacDonald Allan	219	lineman	42	Winthrop
P	MacDonald Catherine—†	219	housewife	43	here

	Letter.	Full Name.	Residence, Jan. 1, 1946.	Occupation.	Supposed Age.	Reported Residence, Jan. 1, 1945. Street and Number.

Byron Court

	R	Cannata Anna M—†	7	housewife	58	here
	S	Cannata Jeannette M—†	7	bookkeeper	39	"
	T	Cannata Joseph R	7	barber	69	"
	U	Caruso Domenic	9	"	49	
	V	Caruso Mary—†	9	housewife	41	"
	W	MacNeil Lena—†	9	capmaker	44	"
	X*	MacNeil William	9	shipper	65	"
	Z	Moylan Lillian—†	10	housewife	42	Braintree

802

	A	Moylan Matthew	10	U S N	21	"
	B	Moylan Matthew J	10	chauffeur	48	"
	C	Busa Alfred S	11	baker	38	here
	D	Busa Natalie M—†	11	housewife	24	"
	E	Busa Charles F	11	baker	26	"
	F	Busa Elizabeth—†	11	clerk	21	
	G	Busa John	11	shoemaker	43	"
	H	Busa Joseph	11	"	69	
	K	Busa Pasqua—†	11	housewife	65	"
	L	Cannata Charles J	14	U S N	35	
	M	Cannata Mary L—†	14	housewife	39	"
	N	McArthur Gabriel C—†	14	"	34	Alabama
	O	McArthur Wilbur W	14	laborer	39	"
	P	Crowley John	15	operator	57	here
	R	Crowley Michael	15	student	20	"
	S	Crowley Nora M—†	15	housewife	53	"
	T	Buckley Anna—†	16	technician	45	"
	U	Flora Frank R	16	welder	24	
	V	Flora Gloria—†	16	housewife	24	"
	W	Mills Catherine—†	16	stenographer	26	"
	X	Stoia Mary—†	16	waitress	25	"
	Y	Sproul Christine—†	18	housewife	27	Somerville
	Z	Sproul William J	18	foreman	27	"

803

	A	Spada George J	19	musician	23	10 Perch
	B*	Balliro Isabella—†	19	housewife	38	here
	C	Balliro Salvatore	19	woodworker	44	"
	D	McCann Josephine E—†	19	inspector	22	"
	E	McCann Nicholas	19	U S A	22	

Byron Court—Continued

	F	Berti Dorothy E—†	20	housewife	30	here
	G	Berti Victor A	20	salesman	34	"
	H	Penning Bridget—†	20	housewife	80	"
	K	Penning Ruth B—†	20	"	43	
	L	Penning William F	20	laborer	45	
	M	Giannetti Antonio	22	U S A	27	"
	N	Giannetti Jeanette—†	22	housewife	29	"
	O	Manfredi Joseph	22	retired	66	
	P	Manfredi Louis	22	U S A	24	
	R	Manfredi Frank	22	laborer	63	
	S	Manfredi Philomena—†	22	housewife	85	"
	T	Manfredi Theresa—†	22	"	56	
	U	Donovan Henry L	23	U S M C	26	"
	V	Donovan Lucille E—†	23	housewife	26	"
	W	DeMarinis John	23	mattressmaker	49	31 Snow Hill
	X	Colton Florence D—†	23	housewife	35	here
	Y	Colton Leo	23	printer	45	"
	Z	DeSimone Jennie—†	23	stitcher	51	"

804

	A	DeSimone Matteo	23	retired	75	
	B	Lamberti Celia—†	23	packer	28	
	c*	DiCarlo Antonio	23	laborer	68	

Chilcott Place

	D	Gallagher Grace M—†	3	housewife	25	33 Dalrymple
	E	Gallagher Hugh T	3	salesman	29	33 "
	F	Handren Martha—†	3	housewife	47	33 "
	G	Handren Patrick J	3	laborer	49	33 "
	H	Gibbons John J	3	manager	58	here
	K	Gibbons Mary T—†	3	housewife	51	"
	L	Varney Harold L	3	U S A	26	"
	M	Varney Ruth—†	3	at home	25	
	N	Brennan Gertrude L—†	3	clerk	47	
	O	Glennon John J	3	U S A	25	
	P	Glennon Madeline S—†	3	housewife	47	"
	R	Glennon Marion L—†	3	clerk	22	
	S	Glennon William E	3	operator	51	"
	T	Glennon William E, jr	3	U S A	28	
	U	Magee Ellen E—†	5	housewife	62	"
	V	Magee Joseph F	5	printer	64	

Chilcott Place—Continued

w	McKinnon Joseph A	5	craftsman	39	here
x	McKinnon Margaret—†	5	housewife	34	"
y	Wronski Elizabeth—†	5	"	53	"
z	Wronski Michael	5	blacksmith	56	"

805

A	Yachinsky Blanche—†	5	at home	22	
B	Yachinsky Julia—†	5	operator	25	"
c	Yachinsky Stephen	5	U S N	27	
D	Cameron Gertrude S—†	6	housewife	34	"
E	Cameron John	6	plasterer	39	"
F	Saunders Hugh	6	engineer	62	"
G	Saunders Hugh N	6	accountant	27	8 Primrose
H	Saunders Mary—†	6	housewife	52	here
K	Aspacher Ruth—†	6	bookkeeper	24	"
L	Aspacher William	6	metalworker	25	"
M	Emrick Elizabeth C—†	7	clerk	21	
N	Emrick Emma F—†	7	"	51	"
o	Donovan William J	7	"	24	Cambridge
P	Murray Joseph L	7	secretary	52	here
R	Murray Mary A—†	7	buyer	68	"
s	Murray Thomas F	7	plumber	56	"
T	Booth Simpson	7	retired	80	
U	Prescott Arthur T	7	policeman	50	
v	Prescott Gladys B—†	7	housewife	50	"
w	Kelly Beatrice—†	9	bookkeeper	21	"
x	Kelly John J	9	U S C G	22	41 Iffley rd
y	Tedeschi Albino	9	cook	53	here
z	Tedeschi Louis	9	U S N	24	"

806

A	Tedeschi Providenza—†	9	housewife	46	"
B	Carmichael Anne—†	9	clerk	31	
c	Forsyth Annie—†	9	housewife	69	"
D	Forsyth William	9	retired	75	"
E	Lavers Lillie—†	9	at home	78	
F	Margeson Eltha—†	9	housewife	55	"
G	Margeson Welner	9	chauffeur	60	"
H	Zager John	10	clerk	42	
K	Zager Ruth—†	10	housewife	38	"
L	Faubert Martha C—†	10	"	37	
M	Faubert Raymond L	10	engineer	31	"
N	Crapo John A	11	electrician	56	"

Chilcott Place—Continued

o	MacDonald Tryphena—†	11	housewife	72	here
P	Mahoney Tryphena—†	11	clerk	48	"
R	Mahony Josephine M—†	11	housewife	55	"
S	Mahony Margaret L—†	11	bookkeeper	25	"
T	Mahony Robert W	11	clerk	32	"
U	Dross Anna—†	11	housewife	34	"
V	Dross Bernard A	11	mechanic	43	"
W	Larson Hans P	12	laborer	53	
X	Lieber Ernest	12	"	54	"
Y	Lieber Wanda—†	12	housewife	51	"
Z	Carter Barbara E—†	15	waitress	24	"

807

A	Carter Harry D	15	druggist	66	"
B	Carter Lloyd	15	mover	32	
C	Carter Mabel E—†	15	housewife	59	"
D	Olson Dorothy S—†	15	secretary	25	"
E	Stewart Horace G	15	mechanic	48	"
F	Stewart Lillian A—†	15	housewife	47	"
G	Stewart Parker E	15	finisher	47	
H	Mills Anne F—†	15	housewife	47	"
K	Mills Thomas	15	machinist	48	"
L	Mills Thomas F	15	U S N	22	
M	Smith Howard A	16	mason	34	"
N	Smith Madge—†	16	housewife	34	Florida
O	Smith Warren E	16	retired	72	here
P	Roemer Alice E—†	16	housewife	44	"
R	Roemer William J	16	builder	49	"
S	Johnstone James	16	laborer	44	
T	Johnstone Josephine—†	16	housewife	36	"
U	Dolan John E	17	chauffeur	30	"
V	Dolan Marjorie A—†	17	housewife	28	"
W	Cohen Esther—†	17	"	40	"
X	Cohen Rubin	17	proprietor	46	"
Y	Buckley Katherine G—†	17	clerk	50	190 Perham
Z	Glynn Margaret V—†	17	"	48	190 "

808

A	Kenney Daniel J	19	tel worker	58	here
B	Kenney Lillian M—†	19	housewife	37	"
C	Doody D Ernest	19	supt	58	"
D	Wolfrum Eleanor M—†	19	housewife	31	"

Page.	Letter.	Full Name.	Residence, Jan. 1, 1946.	Occupation.	Supposed Age.	Reported Residence, Jan. 1, 1945. Street and Number.

Chilcott Place—Continued

	E	Wolfrum Walter F	19	engineer	33	here
	F	Noonan Nora M—†	19	at home	66	11 Atherton
	G	Smith Margaret V—†	19	housewife	33	11 "
	H	Smith Thomas M	19	brakeman	34	11 "
	K	Layton George	20	machinist	64	here
	L	Layton Nellie—†	20	housewife	63	"
	M	McDevitt Henry T	20	laborer	39	"
	N	McDevitt Mary M—†	20	housewife	36	"
	O	Fox Margaret M—†	21	at home	74	"
	P	O'Hare Mary L—†	21	"	55	
	R	Kelly Alice T—†	21	manager	61	"
	S	Kelly Eileen A—†	21	clerk	26	
	T	Kelly Ferdinand F	21	U S N	32	
	U	White Albert R	23	bartender	46	"
	V	White Gerald W	23	U S N	21	
	W	White Harriet E—†	23	housewife	39	"
	X	White James H	23	U S A	21	
	Y	Rausa Sabastina—†	24	housewife	40	"
	Z	Scarpaci Frank	24	butcher	28	"

809

	A	Scarpaci Rose—†	24	housewife	23	"
	B	Tringalia Antoinette—†	24	dressmaker	35	"
	C	Tringalia Dominic	24	machinist	28	"
	D	Tringalia Gaetano	24	fisherman	65	"
	E	Tringalia Marie—†	24	housewife	60	"
	F	Tringalia Mary—†	24	dressmaker	25	"
	G	Tringalia Salvatore	24	laborer	31	
	H	Haddigan Josephine R—†	25	housewife	30	"
	K	Haddigan Raymond L	25	salesman	42	"
	L	Baker J Murray	25	teacher	70	"
	M	Campbell Charles A	25	carpenter	74	"
	N	Campbell Margaret L—†	25	housewife	62	"
	O	Davis Grace R—†	26	"	38	
	P	Davis Lewis K	26	machinist	38	"
	R	Kouroyen Irene—†	26	at home	45	"
	S	Kouroyen Ralph	26	clerk	36	
	T	Quinn Ellen J—†	26	housewife	74	"
	U	Cuttillo Marie—†	26	"	46	
	V	Cuttillo Sabino	26	shoemaker	45	"
	W	Redden Walter L	26	laborer	52	

Chilcott Place—Continued

x	Zager Aurelia—†	27	at home	70	here
y	Zager Harold A	27	teacher	48	"
z	Zager Louis A	27	retired	74	"

810   Ellsworth Street

A	Dunn Herbert G	5	chauffeur	34	here
B	Dunn Marjorie B—†	5	housewife	32	"
C	Hennessey Olive F—†	5	"	54	"
D	Elias Assad J	7	cleaner	56	"
E	Elias Joseph P	7	technician	20	"
F	Elias Martha M—†	7	housewife	41	"
G	Hardiman Isabelle M—†	9	"	40	
H	Hardiman Joseph C	9	checker	44	"
K	Foran John J	14	steelworker	57	"
L	Foran John T	14	clerk	20	"
M	Foran Mary—†	14	housewife	56	"
N	Foran Mary N—†	14	operator	24	"
O	McLain Martha—†	18	housewife	71	"
P	Scott Charles E	18	porter	63	
R	McLain Alonzo	18	mechanic	46	"
S	McLain Gertrude—†	18	housewife	41	"
T	Brauner Elizabeth—†	22	"	29	
U	Brauner Frederick	22	fireman	31	"
V	Kenny Catherine A—†	22	housewife	41	"
W	Kenny Charles M	22	U S A	30	
X	Kenny John J	22	pipefitter	43	"
Y	Kenny Robert F	22	U S A	35	
Z	Kenny Thomas J	22	retired	74	

811

A	*Shaughnessy Kathleen—†	26	housewife	37	"
B	Shaughnessy Michael	26	plumber	50	"
C	Peterson Freda—†	26	housewife	58	"
D	Peterson Ralph	26	U S A	30	

Erie Place

E	*Pavarunas Alezas	4	machinist	55	here
F	*Pavarunas Minnie—†	4	housewife	50	"
G	MacLellan Frank W	4	mechanic	37	"
H	MacLellan Mildred—†	4	housewife	39	"

Page.	Letter.	Full Name	Residence, Jan. 1, 1946.	Occupation.	Supposed Age.	Reported Residence, Jan. 1, 1945. Street and Number.

Erie Place—Continued

	k	Wilson Elsie M—†	9	housewife	31	39 Sheridan
	l	Wilson Ralph W	9	auditor	48	39 "
	m	Wilson Robert E	9	seaman	20	39 "
	n	*Wilson Ann—†	10	housewife	50	here
	o	Wilson Horace S	10	electrician	38	"
	p	Wilson Rebecca—†	10	at home	70	"
	r	DeFronzo Anthony	15	laborer	42	
	s	DeFronzo Giuseppe	15	clerk	39	"
	t	DeFronzo Susie—†	15·	housewife	44	"
	u	DeIorio Joseph	15	ironworker	47	"
	v	*DeIorio Philomena—†	15	housewife	40	"

Forest Hills Street

	w	Mulcahy Mary—†	10	housewife	27	here
	x	Mulcahy Stephen	10	engineer	28	"
	y	McCarthy Frederick L	10	laborer	53	"
	z	McCarthy Leah G—†	10	housewife	46	"
812						
	a	Welby Martin, jr	10	mechanic	20	"
	b	Welby Martin J	10	packer	54	
	c	Welby Mary—†	10	clerk	23	
	d	Shields Alice—†	12	operator	42	"
	e	Twomey Eva—†	12	housewife	46	"
	f	Molloy Kathleen—†	12	"	39	
	g	Reynolds Nora—†	12	"	47	
	h	Reynolds Patrick	12	engineer	61	"
	k	Harvey Hugh	14	electrician	42	"
	l	Higgins Jane—†	14	housewife	45	"
	m	Higgins Phillip	14	reporter	43	"
	n	Haddigan Phoebe—†	14	housewife	68	"
	o	Mills John F	14	cutter	41	
	p	Mills Mary M—†	14	housewife	41	"
	r	Quinn Catherine—†	19	"	40	5 Torrey
	s	Quinn Francis X	19	machinist	40	5 "
	t	McLaughlin James J	20	laborer	28	here
	u	McLaughlin Mary A—†	20	housewife	69	"
	v	McLaughlin Mary E—†	20	operator	31	"
	w	McLaughlin William	20	retired	79	
	x	McLaughlin William J	20	clerk	22	
	y	Mahoney Dennis	20	policeman	50	"

9

Page.	Letter.	FULL NAME.	Residence, Jan. 1, 1946.	Occupation.	Supposed Age.	Reported Residence, Jan. 1, 1945. Street and Number.

Forest Hills Street—Continued

	z	Mahoney Ella—†	20	housewife	45	here
813						
	a	Sloan Catherine—†	20	operator	50	"
	b	Leehan Ellen—†	20	housewife	55	"
	c	Leehan Mary L—†	20	U S M C	23	"
	d	Leehan Rose P—†	20	clerk	20	
	e	Leehan William E	20	mechanic	54	"
	g	Kelly Mary—†	21	bookkeeper	42	"
	k	Tripp Dorothy E—†	22	clerk	20	"
	l	Tripp Edith E—†	22	housewife	51	"
	m	Tripp Edward R	22	tinsmith	55	"
	m¹	Tripp Edward R, jr	22	operator	24	"
	n	Brigandi Mary—†	22	housewife	31	"
	o	Brigandi Victor	22	shipwright	39	"
	p	Ford Catherine—†	22	housewife	45	"
	r	Ford Joseph	22	packer	47	
	s	Banks Edward	23	salesman	53	"
	t	Gamble William	23	janitor	61	
	u	Therrien Ruby—†	23	housewife	55	"
	v	Boyd James	23	retired	80	
	w	Boyd Mary—†	23	housewife	65	"
	x	Dolan Edward	23	chauffeur	53	Connecticut
	y	Morrow Thomas	23	clerk	70	here
	z	Cronin John	24	salesman	25	Texas
814						
	a	Cronin Patricia—†	24	housewife	22	"
	b	Clark Frank M	24	electrician	44	here
	c	Clark Margaret—†	24	housewife	42	"
	d	Klau Louise—†	24	cook	64	"
	e	Ramm Peter	24	carpenter	70	"
	f	Farrell Mary—†	25	housewife	36	"
	g	Farrell Neal J	25	pressman	38	"
	h	Leonard Ann—†	25	nurse	36	
	k	Leonard Catherine—†	25	clerk	42	
	l	Crowley Alice B—†	25	checker	27	"
	m	Crowley Catherine A—†	25	housewife	58	"
	n	Crowley Louise A—†	25	bookkeeper	22	"
	o	Crowley Mary C—†	25	operator	33	"
	p	Crowley William D	25	janitor	62	
	r	Crowley William J	25	U S A	25	"
	s	Malley Edward W	26	manager	53	76 Causeway
	t	Malley Mary K—†	26	housewife	41	here

Forest Hills Street—Continued

	U	Bensen Arne	26	waterproofer	49	here
	V	Bensen Margot—†	26	housewife	45	"
	W	Sorensen Arthur	26	mechanic	23	"
	X	Kenney Elizabeth T—†	26	housewife	69	"

Glines Avenue

	Y	Haile Dorothea—†	1	housewife	31	14 Dixwell
	Z	Haile Lacett	1	mechanic	44	14 "
		815				
	A	Ward John	rear 2	clerk	53	198 Fisher av
	B	Ward Viola—†	" 2	housewife	46	198 "
	C	McDonough Walter	" 2	retired	67	here
	D	Wirrell Mary T—†	" 2	housewife	60	"
	E	Wirrell Robert J	" 2	glazier	66	"
	F	*Petrie Patrick	3	painter	36	1 Fenner
	G	Petrie Rita—†	3	housewife	30	1 "
	H	Mullen Marcus C	3	inspector	44	47 Dalrymple
	K	Mullen Margaret A—†	3	housewife	41	47 "
	L	Burke Mary—†	4	supervisor	38	here
	M	Dunn Agnes—†	4	housewife	32	"
	N	Dunn John F	4	clerk	36	"
	O	Dunn John	4	machinist	69	"
	P	Dunn Mary—†	4	housewife	64	"
	R	Hardiman Martin	5	clerk	31	..
	S	Hardiman Mary—†	5	housewife	28	"
	T	Mahoney Catherine J—†	5	"	40	New York
	U	Mahoney Henry A	5	operator	39	"
	V	Meyer Herbert E	6	clerk	50	here
	W	Meyer Mary K—†	6	housewife	46	"
	X	Schmidt Emil	6	ironworker	44	"
	Y	Schmidt Hildegarde—†	6	housewife	34	"
	Z	Martin Edward	7	doorman	27	"
		816				
	A	Martin Eleanor—†	7	housewife	23	"
	B	*Maslanka Mary—†	7	"	48	
	C	Maslanka William	7	carpenter	59	"

Haverford Street

	D	Johnson Kathryne—†	35	housekeeper	27	here
	E	McKee Elizabeth E—†	35	clerk	31	"

11

Page.	Letter.	Full Name.	Residence, Jan. 1, 1946.	Occupation.	Supposed Age.	Reported Residence, Jan. 1, 1945. Street and Number.

Haverford Street—Continued

	F	Rowen Estelle M—†	35	housekeeper	63	here
	G	Hamilton Albert	37	janitor	59	"
	H	Hamilton Pauline—†	37	housewife	42	"
	K	Miller Eben	37	longshoreman	44	"
	L	Murphy Edward J	41	U S N	21	
	M	Murphy John J	41	laborer	52	"
	N	Murphy John J, jr	41	chauffeur	24	"
	O	Murphy Margaret L—†	41	WAC	26	
	P	Murphy Mary M—†	41	housewife	51	"
	R	Downey Catherine V—†	43	housekeeper	53	"
	S	Downey Mary A—†	43	clerk	24	"
	T	Downey Nora T—†	43	"	20	
	U	Wheeler Charles	45	laborer	52	
	V	Wheeler Mary—†	45	housewife	23	"
	W	Campanella Frank	47	barber	62	
	X	Campanella John A	47	U S A	29	"
	Y	Campanella Mary A—†	47	housewife	62	"

817   Iffley Road

	B	Angers Albertine R—†	18	housewife	47	here
	C	Angers Emeric J	18	metalworker	50	"
	D	Angers Emeric O, jr	18	U S N	23	"
	E	Eastman Frederick W	18	jeweler	21	California
	F	Mulhern George J	18	clerk	50	52 Walnut pk
	G	Mulhern Mary A—†	18	secretary	45	52 "
	H	Matthew Frederick H	18	constable	67	here
	K	Sweeney Blanche L—†	18	housewife	47	"
	L	Sweeney Edward J	18	manager	49	"
	M	Jacomin Isidore	19	retired	78	
	N	Jacomin Stephen F	19	machinist	49	"
	O	O'Connor Charles A	19	electrician	61	"
	P*	Mathony Amelia—†	19	manager	66	"
	R	Bassett Earle S	19	chef	57	
	S	Bassett Lillian J—†	19	housewife	57	"
	T	Barrett John F	22	teacher	37	
	U	Hesselschwerdt John J	22	clerk	25	
	V	Hesselschwerdt Margaret—†	22	housewife	24	"
	W	O'Brien John	22	machinist	65	"
	X	O'Brien John D	22	student	21	
	Y	O'Brien Margaret—†	22	housewife	64	"

Iffley Road—Continued

		FULL NAME.	Residence, Jan. 1, 1946.	Occupation.	Supposed Age.	Reported Residence, Jan. 1, 1945.
	z	Edmands Minnie E—†	22	at home	65	here
818						
	A	Swansburg Frank L	22	machinist	62	"
	B	Swansburg Louise S—†	22	housewife	62	"
	c	Warecki Julius	22	baker	53	
	D	Warecki Olga—†	22	housewife	47	"
	E	Gerlacher Edward B	23	foreman	71	"
	F	Gerlacher Flora—†	23	housewife	60	"
	G	Moore Thomas F	23	operator	65	"
	H	Saunders Mabel C—†	23	nurse	35	New York
	K	Tipping Ethel—†	23	housewife	55	here
	L	Tipping Stanley	23	U S N	23	"
	M	Baker James J	26	U S A	29	"
	N	Baker Mabel L—†	26	housewife	27	"
	o	Bruce Ada B—†	26	"	68	
	P	Bruce Fred E	26	retired	67	
	T	Craven Katherine M—†	26	housewife	59	"
	U	Craven Patrick J	26	foreman	61	"
	R	Farrell Madeline J—†	26	housewife	26	"
	S	Farrell Patrick J	26	salesman	26	"
	V	Coffey Daniel J	27	fireman	65	"
	w	Coffey Dorothea L—†	27	operator	26	"
	X	Coffey Joseph L	27	seaman	29	"
	Y	Coffey Rose E—†	27	housewife	60	"
	z	MacLeod Eleanor—†	27	operator	28	"
819						
	A	MacLeod James	27	electrician	28	"
	B	Garrity Margaret—†	27	housewife	43	"
	c	Garrity Patrick J	27	policeman	50	"
	D	Sundberg John V	27	storekeeper	56	"
	E	Sundberg Mary—†	27	clerk	56	"
	F	Morse Augusta E—†	30	housewife	63	"
	G	Morse Charles F	30	retired	64	"
	H	Morse Edward C	30	factoryworker	24	"
	K	Hassett Anna—†	31	housewife	58	"
	L	Hassett Eleanor A—†	31	clerk	20	"
	M	Hassett George H	31	fireman	61	
	N	Hassett Marie A—†	31	bookkeeper	21	"
	o	Fitzpatrick Alice M—†	31	at home	34	"
	P	Fitzpatrick William H	31	retired	74	
	R	Fitzpatrick William J	31	timekeeper	32	"

13

Page	Letter	FULL NAME.	Residence, Jan. 1, 1946.	Occupation.	Supposed Age.	Reported Residence, Jan. 1, 1945. Street and Number.

Iffley Road—Continued

	Letter	FULL NAME	Res.	Occupation	Age	Reported Residence
	s	Fahey Ellen—†	31	housewife	57	here
	t	Fahey James C	31	U S N	22	"
	u	Fahey Joseph M	31	packer	24	"
	v	Fahey Martin J	31	rigger	61	
	w	Kelly Barbara—†	31	packer	25	"
	x	Kelly Francis J	31	U S A	28	41 Iffley rd
	y	Smith Alfred E	32	engineer	41	53 Wentworth
	z	Smith Anne R—†	32	housewife	29	35 Iffley rd
		820				
	A	Fleming Katherine—†	32	"	72	here
	B	Fleming Patrick J	32	retired	73	"
	C	Savini Jennie—†	32	housewife	57	"
	D	Savini Salvatore	32	manager	57	"
	E	Young Alexander	35	chauffeur	47	"
	F	Young Mary F—†	35	clerk	30	
	G	McLaughlin Joseph J	35	"	27	
	H	McLaughlin Katherine—†	35	housewife	56	"
	K	McLaughlin Theresa D—†	35	clerk	30	
	L	Nolan Katherine—†	35	"	38	
	M	Nolan Teresa—†	35	at home	65	"
	N	Fay Daniel J	36	guard	59	
	O	Fay Mary F—†	36	housewife	55	"
	P	Thyne Josephine A—†	36	"	44	
	R	Thyne Josephine A—†	36	student	20	
	S	Thyne Martin A	36	gateman	46	"
	T	Green Catherine E—†	36	clerk	32	
	U	Green Francis J	36	chauffeur	33	"
	V	Green Margaret J—†	36	housewife	63	"
	W	Green Mary M—†	36	clerk	31	
	X	Green Michael J	36	guard	65	
	Y	Bamberry Eben H	39	chauffeur	33	"
	Z	Bamberry Margaret H—†	39	housewife	31	"
		821				
	A	Landry Alma R—†	39	attorney	33	"
	B	Landry Francis X	39	retired	83	"
	C	Landry Francis X	39	chef	31	
	D	Landry Jane M—†	39	clerk	32	
	E	*Landry Margaret R—†	39	housewife	80	"
	F	Brogna Alexander S	39	reporter	29	California
	G	Brogna Lila J—†	39	housewife	23	"
	H	Jackson Carl J	39	machinist	48	here

Iffley Road—Continued

K	Jackson Selma M—†	39	housewife	40	here	
L	Jackson Thelma A—†	39	clerk	22	"	
M	Hemeon Florence J	40	housewife	40	"	
N	Hemeon Roy M	40	factoryworker	41	"	
O	Tuohey John	40	ironworker	70	"	
P	Tuohey Katherine C—†	40	stenographer	32	"	
R	Tuohey Margaret M—†	40	factoryworker	35	"	
S	Tuohey Mary A—†	40	housewife	70	"	
T	Tuohey Mary C—†	40	stenographer	30	"	
U	Hurley Mary L—†	40	housewife	55	"	
V	Turley Rose G—†	40	bookkeeper	59	"	
W	Kelly Marion E—†	41	housewife	47	"	
X	Kelly Thomas F	41	steamfitter	48	"	
Y	Clark Allen T	41	engineer	27	"	
Z	Clark James C	41	"	25		

822

A	Clark Louis C	41	"	61		
B	Clark Rose E—†	41	housewife	54	"	
C	Clark Rose E—†	41	operator	22	"	
D	Dinkelberg Margaretha A—†	41	housewife	71	"	
E	Dinkelberg Marguerite M—†	41	clerk	34		
F	*Barnes Alice A—†	43	housewife	58	"	
G	Barnes George R	43	student	22		
H	Barnes Melvin L	43	U S A	20		
K	Barnes Samuel H	43	supervisor	58	"	
L	Kenney Lillian F—†	43	housewife	35	"	
M	MacDonald Alexander	43	contractor	62	"	
N	MacDonald Charlotte M—†	43	housewife	57	"	
O	MacDonald Katherine D—†	43	nurse	36		
P	MacDonald Leonard W	43	painter	34	"	
R	MacDonald Ronald A	43	clerk	24		
S	Chakarian Mabel—†	43	housewife	35	"	
T	Chakarian Warren	43	manager	40	"	
U	Clifford Jeremiah J	44	bartender	46	"	
V	Clifford Mary A—†	44	housewife	40	"	
W	McCarthy Catherine A—†	44	checker	42	"	
X	Yanus Ann G—†	44	housewife	39	"	
Y	Yanus Bronislaw	44	foreman	35	"	
Z	Tipping Clara—†	44	housewife	53	"	

823

A	Tipping Leonard	44	machinist	55	"	

Iffley Road—Continued

B	Tipping Leonard, jr	44	U S A	26	here
C	Alasevicius Joseph S	45	welder	57	"
D	Alasevicius Veronica—†	45	operator	36	"
E	Colliontzis Peter	45	bartender	62	"
F	Colliontzis Veronica A—†	45	dressmaker	35	"
G	Buckland Cleveland B	45	welder	42	
H	Hayes Carlton	45	technician	30	"
K	Hayes Mae—†	45	housewife	45	"
L	Kolka Alvina—†	47	"	51	"
M	Kolka George H	47	sign maker	27	"
N	Kolka Harry W	47	electrician	21	"
O	*Kolka John	47	sign maker	61	..
P	Kolka John F	47	U S A	26	..
R	Kolka Lawrence R	47	laborer	23	"
S	Kolka Ruth C—†	47	clerk	20	
T	Scally Elizabeth N—†	47	housewife	33	"
V	Scally Joseph W	47	social worker	34	"
U	Scally Josephine A—†	47	saleswoman	58	"
W	Quinn James F	47	retired	75	"
X	Quinn Margaret A—†	47	secretary	35	"
Y	Quinn Margaret E—†	47	housewife	73	"
Z	Ricker Anna V—†	48	"	55	

824

A	Ricker Elizabeth A—†	48	teacher	25	
B	Ricker George V	48	agent	55	
C	Wood Calvin S	48	machinist	39	"
D	Wood Georgiana B—†	48	housewife	34	"
E	Baker Barbara L—†	48	secretary	25	"
F	Baker Ernest F	48	tester	26	"
G	Baker Mary C—†	48	housewife	55	"
H	Hester John J	50	clerk	50	
K	Hester Mary M—†	50	housewife	40	"
L	Doherty Catherine E—†	50	"	72	
M	Doherty Kathleen L—†	50	teacher	37	
N	Doherty Timothy C	50	U S A	36	
O	Sullivan Alma G—†	50	saleswoman	20	"
P	Sullivan Eli	50	engineer	47	"
R	Sullivan Elsie M—†	50	housewife	40	"
S	Egersheim George F	55	mason	32	
T	Egersheim Leonora—†	55	bookkeeper	29	"
U	Pezzulo Anne—†	55	stenographer	31	"

16

Iffley Road—Continued

v	Pezzulo Julia—†	55	teacher	27	here
w	*Pezzulo Maria—†	55	at home	67	"
x	O'Neil Charles C	55	steward	60	"
y	O'Neil Frances M—†	55	adjuster	29	"
z	O'Neil Mary A—†	55	housewife	55	"

825

A	Matthews Mary—†	55	"	50	
B	Matthews Michael	55	mattressmkr	53	"
c	Zevitas George A	60	checker	68	"
D	Zevitas Louis G	60	U S A	31	
E	Zevitas Mary G—†	60	housewife	56	"
F	Zevitas Minerva G—†	60	operator	22	"
G	Zevitas Paskalia G—†	60	clerk	29	
H	Pappas John	60	counterman	44	"
K	Pappas Nafsica—†	60	housewife	33	"
L	George Charles A	60	U S A	34	
M	George Mary A—†	60	housewife	30	"
N	Kouloplos Charles	60	U S A	32	
O	Feinberg David	64	capmaker	65	"
P	Feinberg Rebecca—†	64	housewife	65	"
R	Grosberg Evelyn—†	64	"	33	159 Kelton
S	Grosberg Jacob	64	manager	36	159 "
T	Jacobson Lee—†	64	housewife	37	here
U	Jacobson Max	64	realtor	50	"
V	Tobey Mitchell	64	manager	48	"
W	Tobey Rose—†	64	clerk	45	"
X	*Kasloff Benjamin	64	manager	54	"
Y	*Kasloff Sylvia E—†	64	housewife	46	"
Z	Levenson Arthur	64	tailor	55	"

826

A	Levenson Esther—†	64	housewife	48	"
B	Lipsky Selma—†	64	bookkeeper	24	"
c	Badavas Angela—†	68	housewife	28	"
D	Badavas Charles	68	engineer	24	"
E	Badavas Percival	68	salesman	29	"
F	Jacobs Jacob	68	"	49	
G	Jacobs Lena C—†	68	housewife	48	" .
H	Rubot Charles	68	tailor	53	
K	Rubot Ethel L—†	68	housewife	51	"
L	Rubot Howard E	68	U S N	24	
M	*Cohen Irving D	68	plumber	52	"

Page.	Letter.	FULL NAME.	Residence, Jan. 1, 1946.	Occupation.	Supposed Age.	Reported Residence, Jan. 1, 1945. Street and Number.

Iffley Road—Continued

	N	Cohen Leonard A	68	U S A	27	here
	o	Cohen Nell I—†	68	housewife	26	Arizona
	P*	Cohen Sadie E—†	68	"	41	here
	R	Feingold Bessie—†	68	"	49	"
	s	Feingold Doris—†	68	saleswoman	21	"
	T	Feingold George	68	tailor	52	
	U	Curwin Ann—†	68	housewife	37	"
	v	Curwin Louis J	68	manager	43	"
	w	Gorodetzky Rose—†	72	housewife	38	"
	x	Gorodetzky Saul	72	musician	42	"
	Y	Litsky Ethel—†	72	housewife	30	"
	Y¹	Litsky Howard	72	student	29	
	z	Litsky Jack	72	salesman	34	"

827

	B	Svetkey David	72	printer	39	
	c	Svetkey Shirley—†	72	housewife	37	"
	D	Scholnick Julia—†	72	"	33	"
	E	Scholnick Theodore	72	agent	37	"
	F	Hargrove Beatrice—†	72	stenographer	26	"
	G	Karp Dorothy—†	72	bookkeeper	28	"
	H	Karp Jacob	72	junk dealer	58	"
	K*	Karp Rose—†	72	housewife	55	"
	L	Castaline Harry	72	butcher	36	
	M	Castaline Veda—†	72	housewife	36	"

Montebello Road

	N	DeBassio Joseph	28	clerk	28	15 Marmion
	o	DeBassio Ruth—†	28	housewife	26	15 "
	P	Spellman Dorothy—†	28	"	28	here
	R	Spellman John	28	operator	27	"
	s	Callahan Ann T—†	28	housewife	67	"
	T	Callahan Dennis J	28	retired	69	
	U	Harkins Gertrude M—†	28	housewife	24	"
	v	Harkins John H	28	accountant	30	"
	w	Devine Rose E—†	28	operator	29	"
	x	Devine Rose H—†	28	housekeeper	62	"
	Y	Devine Margaret H—†	28	clerk	24	"
	z	Devine William J	28	student	25	

828

	A	McDermott Bridget—†	30	housekeeper	52	"

Page.	Letter.	Full Name.	Residence, Jan. 1, 1946.	Occupation.	Supposed Age.	Reported Residence, Jan. 1, 1945. Street and Number.

Montebello Road—Continued

	B	Murray Joseph	30	chauffeur	34	43 McGreevey way
	C	Murray Mary—†	30	housewife	35	43 "
	D	Patterson Douglas	30	student	20	Maine
	E	Flynn John	30	laborer	63	here
	F	Flynn Josephine—†	30	housewife	63	"
	G	Diggins Catherine—†	30	clerk	24	231 Lamartine
	H	Diggins John J	30	policeman	23	231 "
	K	Diggins Margaret—†	30	housewife	47	231 "
	L	Diggins Michael	30	laborer	58	231 "
	M	Antry James	47	fitter	52	here
	N	Kelley Josephine—†	47	hostess	45	"
	O	Degregorio Anne—†	47	housewife	56	"
	P	Degregorio Rocco	47	barber	57	
	R	Marciano Domonic	47	driller	33	
	S	Marciano Tomasina—†	47	housewife	31	"
	T	Taxier Elias A	47	manager	47	"
	U	Taxier Theresa—†	47	housewife	46	"
	V	Smith Lydia—†	51	"	22	"
	W	Smith Warren	51	U S A	24	"
	X	Welch Catherine F—†	51	housekeeper	75	58 Southbourne rd
	Y	Welch John L	51	salesman	42	58 "
	Z	Welch Marguerite—†	51	secretary	21	58 "

829

	A	Hindle Margaret—†	51	housewife	35	35 Cheshire
	B	Hindle Thomas J	51	engineer	39	35 "
	C	Kohl Bertram	51	agent	42	here
	D	Kohl Sarah L—†	51	housewife	36	"
	E	O'Sullivan Andrew	51	policeman	33	"
	F	O'Sullivan Elizabeth—†	51	housewife	36	"
	G	Welch James	51	mechanic	52	"
	H	Weleh Jeannette—†	51	housewife	48	"
	K	Schmidt Clara M—†	52	"	73	"
	L	Schmidt Otto H	52	retired	73	"
	M	Glavin Harold F	52	laborer	41	"
	N	Glavin Victoria P—†	52	housewife	37	"
	O	Colter Miriam—†	52	supervisor	56	"
	P	Soderberg Albert W	52	coppersmith	38	"
	R	Soderberg Alice E—†	52	housewife	37	"
	S	Kalinowski Anna G—†	52	"	26	
	T	Kalinowski Stanley J	52	supervisor	25	"
	U	Hart Angela—†	52	housewife	25	"

19

Montebello Road—Continued

v	Hart James J	52	operator	29	here
w	Cairnes D Joseph	55	bottler	66	"
x	*Cards Edith R—†	55	housewife	24	Nova Scotia
y	*Cards Norman W	55	Canad'n Army	26	"
z	Storey Raymond L	55	chauffeur	47	here

830

A	Storey Theresa—†	55	housewife	38	"
B	*Armakaucis Elizabeth—†	55	housekeeper	52	"
C	Armakaucis Peter	55	electrician	60	"
D	Kerle Paul	55	clerk	29	
E	Walker Alice—†	55	housewife	28	"
F	Walker John	55	meatcutter	31	"
G	Turley Albert A	61	salesman	54	"
H	Turley Rose—†	61	housewife	47	"
K	Marquard John R	61	manager	39	"
L	Marquard Sylvia—†	61	housewife	39	"
M	Marshall Daniel F	61	janitor	37	
N	Marshall Mary—†	61	housewife	31	"
O	Gannum Edna M—†	62	stitcher	44	162 Metropolitan av
P	Gannum Nicholas	62	executive	27	162 "
R	Malouf Afife N—†	62	stitcher	22	here
S	Malouf Allia S—†	62	at home	61	"
T	Malouf Faris S	62	attorney	52	"
U	Malouf Hanny F—†	62	housewife	61	"
V	Malouf Rasheedy M—†	62	stitcher	29	"
W	Scoff Theodora B—†	62	librarian	46	162 Metropolitan av
X	Griffin Anna B—†	69	housewife	33	here
Y	Griffin Thomas H	69	salesman	38	"
Z	Finneran Mary—†	69	secretary	33	"

831

A	Finneran Thomas	69	draftsman	33	"
B	Leonard Bridget B—†	69	housekeeper	61	"
C	Luby Elizabeth N—†	69	housewife	50	"
D	Luby Thomas F	69	teacher	47	"
E	Cloherty Martin	70	clerk	44	"
F	Cloherty Nora—†	70	housewife	45	"
G	Galvin Agnes M—†	70	"	51	
H	Galvin John T	70	agent	30	
K	Galvin Mary A—†	70	supervisor	25	"
L	Galvin Thomas J	70	fireman	52	"
M	Lynch Catherine—†	70	housekeeper	55	27 Denton

Montebello Road—Continued

N	Lynch Helen—†	70	clerk	23	27 Denton
O	Lynch Michael J	70	student	21	27 "
P	Coffey Bridget—†	73	housewife	55	here
R	Coffey Matthew J	73	watchman	60	"
S	Sullivan Margaret M—†	73	housekeeper	63	"
T	Sullivan Timothy F	73	inspector	63	"
U	Manuel Mary M—†	73	housewife	39	"
V	Manuel Wallace E	73	operator	52	"
W	Laffey Ellen—†	74	housewife	48	"
X	Laffey Patrick	74	steamfitter	65	"
Y	Tarvizian Anna—†	74	at home	59	"
Z	Tarvizian Bertev	74	U S A	34	"

832

A	Tarvizian Charles	74	salesman	38	"
B	Tarvizian Vahan	74	printer	36	
C	Leonard Helen—†	74	housewife	60	"
D	Leonard James J	74	retired	65	
E	Leonard Marjorie—†	74	secretary	23	"
F	Northway George F	77	accountant	32	"
G	Northway Mary A—†	77	housewife	72	"
H	Northway William J	77	retired	83	
K	Peasley Margaret—†	77	at home	50	"
L	Mathony Ida C—†	77	secretary	50	"
M	Mathony Mary E—†	77	housekeeper	70	"
N	Grady Mary—†	78	housewife	38	"
O	Grady Walter	78	clerk	40	"
P	Rowan Sara—†	78	"	48	
R	Bowen Laura—†	78	housewife	37	"
S	Bowen Thomas	78	gas worker	40	"
T	Burke John F	78	laborer	41	"
U	Power Joseph A	78	retired	67	
V	Power Mary—†	78	clerk	38	
W	Conlon Patrick	78	fireman	47	
X	Conlon Theresa—†	78	housewife	49	"
Y	Tighe Patrick	81	policeman	46	"
Z	Tighe Sadie J—†	81	housewife	45	"

833

A	Smallcombe John H	81	accountant	29	83 Wellsmere rd
B	Smallcombe Paula—†	81	housewife	23	83 "
C	Cardock James	81	salesman	45	here
D	Cardock Nora—†	81	housewife	38	"

Montebello Road—Continued

E	Thornton Margaret—†	82	housewife	46	here
F	Thornton Michael	82	janitor	48	"
G	MacDonald Helen—†	82	operator	26	".
H	MacIsaac Archie D	82	lineman	39	
K	MacIsaac Sadie—†	82	housewife	24	"
L	Hillcoat Grace—†	82	"	27	
M	Hillcoat Robert	82	shipfitter	29	"
N	Margot Ida—†	85	housewife	36	"
O	Rodney Anne—†	85	saleswoman	34	"
P	Rich Elizabeth—†	85	housewife	33	"
R	Rich James	85	accountant	33	"
S	Leonard Leona E—†	86	housewife	35	"
T	Leonard William J	86	U S A	37	"
U	Stoddard Dorothy—†	86	adjuster	25	Vermont
V	McCoy Floyd	86	manager	33	here
W	McCoy Gertrude—†	86	housewife	26	"
X	Wolfe Celia—†	86	"	54	"
Y	Wolfe Esther H—†	86	stenographer	28	"
Z	Wolfe Max	86	shipper	58	"

834

A	Wolfe Sylvia—†	86	stenographer	22	"
B	Rasmussen Clara—†	89	teacher	39	"
C	Rasmussen Eleanor—†	89	secretary	29	"
D	Rasmussen Nicoline—†	89	housewife	66	"
E	Rasmussen Rasmus C	89	agent	65	"
F	Petti Dominic	89	salesman	56	"
G	Petti Josephine—†	89	housekeeper	48	"
H	Rogers Margaret—†	89	secretary	42	"
K	Walsh Dorothy—†	89	"	24	"
L	Walsh Dorothy V—†	89	housewife	52	"
M	Walsh William	89	policeman	52	"
O	Spack Abraham A	90	teacher	36	
P	Spack Phyllis—†	90	housewife	31	"
R	Meehan Margaret T—†	90	"	64	
S	Meehan Richard	90	retired	64	
T	Stearns Frances—†	93	housewife	33	"
U	Stearns Jacob	93	merchant	33	"
V	Conviser Benjamin	93	contractor	38	"
W	Conviser Sophie—†	93	housewife	38	"
X	Feldman Esther—†	93	at home	60	
Y	Feldman Joseph	93	tailor	62	"

Page.	Letter.	FULL NAME.	Residence, Jan. 1, 1946.	Occupation.	Supposed Age.	Reported Residence, Jan. 1, 1945. Street and Number.

Montebello Road—Continued

z	Reubens Anna S—†	93	housewife	55	here

835

A	Reubens Emil M	93	merchant	57	"
B	Sullivan Agnes C—†	94	housewife	46	"
C	Sullivan Barbara J—†	94	clerk	22	
D	Sullivan John J	94	"	50	
E	Sullivan John J	94	U S N	22	
F	Haven John	94	merchant	45	"
G	Keegan Elizabeth—†	94	housewife	31	Belmont
H	O'Connor Eileen—†	94	"	40	here
K	O'Connor Timothy	94	laborer	45	"
L	Connolly Martin	94	watertender	58	"
M	Kelleher Mary—†	94	housewife	28	"
N	Kelleher Patrick J	94	manager	36	"
O	Carty Hermena W—†	97	housewife	38	"
P	Carty William L	97	timekeeper	40	"
R	Morgan Frances T—†	97	clerk	36	"
S	Morgan Stephen J	97	checker	53	"
T	Murray Mildred M—†	97	secretary	38	"
U	Murray Vincent M	97	U S N	21	"
V	McClaren Donald E	97	U S A	23	"
W	McClaren James E	97	retired	70	
X	McClaren Josephine L—†	97	housewife	60	"
Y	Blake Bridget—†	97	at home	74	"
Z	Finley Catherine—†	97	stenographer	70	"

836

A	Diettrich Bernard F	97	machinist	54	"
B	Diettrich Margaret—†	97	housewife	54	"
C	Perry Mary—†	97	operator	56	"
D	Perry Robert	97	machinist	57	"
E	Kearns Agnes R—†	98	housewife	53	"
F	Kearns James	98	technician	20	"
G	Kearns James E	98	collector	50	"
H	Pow A Florence	98	teacher	53	"
K	Pow Catherine F—†	98	housewife	78	"
L	Nelson Alexander G	98	foreman	55	"
M	Nelson Charlotte R—†	98	housewife	52	"
N	Nelson James A	98	student	27	"
O	Nelson Jean R—†	98	SPAR	24	"
P	Nelson Robson	98	U S N	23	"
R	Wallace Dorothea M—†	100	operator	30	"

Page.	Letter.	Full Name.	Residence, Jan. 1, 1946.	Occupation.	Supposed Age.	Reported Residence, Jan. 1, 1945. Street and Number.

Montebello Road—Continued

	s	Wallace Joseph F	100	retired	60	here
	T	Wallace Mary F—†	100	housewife	54	"
	U	Kussmaul Marguerite—†	100	housekeeper	77	"
	V	Collatos Angelino	100	foreman	21	"
	W	Collatos Charles	100	publisher	28	"
	X	Collatos George	100	"	24	
	Y	Collatos Peter	100	U S A	23	
	Z	*Collatos Vasilike—†	100	housekeeper	44	"
837						
	A	Connaughton James R	101	agent	40	
	B	Connaughton Theresa—†	101	housewife	41	"
	C	Gavin Grace—†	101	"	32	
	D	Gavin Martin W	101	U S A	33	
	E	Cohen Esther—†	104	housewife	38	"
	F	Cohen Jacob	104	manufacturer	42	"
	G	Barry Louis	104	merchant	66	"
	H	Barry Rose—†	104	housewife	57	"
	K	Barry Samuel	104	U S A	30	
	L	Goldstein Benjamin	104	merchant	45	"
	M	Goldstein Clara R—†	104	housewife	45	"
	N	Wells Charles D	105	retired	82	
	O	Nitkin Claire—†	106	housewife	33	"
	P	Nitkin Samuel	106	cutter	34	
	R	Eldridge Loretta—†	106	WAC	22	
	S	Meshon Frances—†	106	at home	65	
	T	Phillips Anna—†	106	housewife	31	"
	U	Phillips George	106	salesman	40	"
	V	Smith Henry H	106	cutter	49	
	W	Smith Irene E—†	106	artist	22	
	X	Smith Leonard	106	mechanic	26	"
	Y	Smith Ruth—†	106	housewife	25	New York
	Z	Smith Sadie J—†	106	"	47	here
838						
	A	Domey Dagny—†	109	stitcher	39	
	B	Emblom Arthur	109	cabinetmaker	45	"
	C	Emblom Margaret—†	109	housewife	45	"
	D	Kearney Anna L—†	109	"	39	
	E	Kearney Clarence B	109	collector	42	"
	H	Dupont Marjorie—†	109	mechanic	20	"
	K	Dupont Robert H	109	U S A	23	
	L	Dupont Ruth—†	109	welder	21	

Montebello Road—Continued

F	Gowans Loretta—†	109	housekeeper	44	here	
G	Goyette Peter	109	barber	77	Worcester	

Olmstead Street

M	Moller Alva—†	8	housewife	50	here	
N	Moller Maurice	8	contractor	55	"	
O	Ornstedt Signe—†	8	housewife	55	"	
P	Samuelson Laura—†	8	artist	29	Maryland	
R	Erlandson Karen L—†	8	housewife	27	here	
S	Erlandson Ralph	8	craftsman	25	"	
T	Teichmann Emil	10	butcher	62	"	
U	Teichmann Selina M—†	10	housewife	62	"	
V	Owen Alice—†	10	clerk	45	8 Laurel	
W	Owen Ann—†	10	stenographer	21	8 "	
X	Owen Ernest	10	technician	50	8 "	
Y	Johnston Eleanor—†	10	housewife	48	here	
Z	Johnston Eleanor—†	10	stenographer	21	"	

839

A	Johnston John	10	inspector	52	"	
B	Johnston Thomas	10	student	23		
C	Cate Lottie—†	11	housewife	65	"	
D	Cate Walter	11	molder	70		
E	Gabrielson Gustaf A	11	assembler	69	"	
F	Gabrielson Sophie C—†	11	housewife	69	"	
G	Eckstrom Eric	11	engineer	36	"	
H	Eckstrom Ruth L—†	11	nurse	32		
K	Pearson Emil	12	mechanic	70	"	
L	Pearson Ethel—†	12	stenographer	24	"	
M	Pearson Marion—†	12	"	22	::	
N	Pearson Selma—†	12	housewife	62	"	
O	McGovern John L	12	oiler	46		
P	O'Donnell Catherine—†	12	housewife	44	"	
R	O'Donnell Edwin J	12	laborer	23	"	
S	Eckholm Valborg—†	12	housewife	59	"	
U	Cunningham Lila—†	15	"	70		
V	Doyle Francis	15	manager	55	"	
W	Doyle Mary—†	15	at home	63	"	
X	Sullivan Anna M—†	16	clerk	21	"	
Y	Sullivan Catherine J—†	16	housewife	60	"	
Z	Sullivan Helen C—†	16	clerk	24		

Page.	Letter.	FULL NAME.	Residence, Jan. 1, 1946.	Occupation.	Supposed Age.	Reported Residence, Jan. 1, 1945. Street and Number.

840
Olmstead Street—Continued

A	Sullivan Julia M—†	16	at home	36	here
B	Sullivan Michael J	16	U S A	29	"
C	Sullivan Patrick J	16	retired	65	"
D	Sullivan Thomas F—†	16	clerk	32	
E	Ulrich Anna L—†	18	housewife	68	"
F	Ulrich James L	18	student	27	
G	Ulrich Martha A—†	18	bookkeeper	33	"
H	Ulrich Mary E—†	18	secretary	37	"
K	DerHohannesian Agavnie-†	19	housewife	63	"
L	DerHohannesian Ann—†	19	clerk	27	
M	DerHohannesian Harry	19	"	37	
N	DerHohannesian Levon	19	social worker	39	"
O	Read Edwin S	19	electrician	43	"
P	Murray Agnes—†	20	housewife	59	"
R	Murray Margaret—†	20	saleswoman	65	"
S	Moriarty Catherine M—†	23	clerk	35	
T	Moriarty Hannah M—†	23	housewife	69	"
U	Moriarty John E	23	clerk	32	
V	Moriarty Margaret K—†	23	stenographer	38	"
W	Moriarty Timothy J	23	warehouse	31	"
X	Callanan Joan E—†	24	housewife	48	"
Y	Callanan Kathleen F—†	24	tel operator	21	"
Z	Callanan Lawrence J	24	chauffeur	47	"

841

A	Callanan Mary E—†	24	clerk	24	"
B	Santos Joan E—†	24	housewife	23	Wash'n D C
C	Cairnes Arthur	28	butler	59	here
D	Cairnes Bertha M—†	28	housewife	60	"
E	Cairnes Edward F	28	clerk	24	"
F	Cairnes Gertrude L—†	28	saleswoman	24	"
G	Cairnes Robert L	28	machinist	33	"
H	Cairnes Walter T	28	U S A	39	Needham
K	Flynn Edward J	34	manager	46	here
L	Flynn Marguerite L—†	34	housewife	46	"
M	Flynn Natalie J—†	34	secretary	24	"
N	Foley Mary F—†	38	housewife	75	"
O	Lyons Florence R—†	38	"	44	
P	Lyons John J	38	engineer	45	"
R	Lyons Joselyn M—†	38	secretary	21	"
S	McGoff Gloria M—†	38	housewife	22	"
T	Sullivan James F	38	mechanic	48	"

Page.	Letter.	Full Name.	Residence, Jan. 1, 1946.	Occupation.	Supposed Age.	Reported Residence, Jan. 1, 1945. Street and Number.

Park Lane

u	Deveney Martin F	4	salesman	54	here
v	Deveney Minnie R—†	4	housewife	50	"
w	Hamilton Gertrude—†	6	"	31	"
x	Hamilton Julia M—†	6	at home	70	"
y	Hamilton Thomas E	6	restaurateur	45	"
z	Bellamy Arthur	7	engineer	63	"

842

a	Bellamy Gladys H—†	7	housewife	53	"
b	Ormsby Daisy J—†	8	"	73	
c	Cooke Margaret—†	9	housekeeper	40	"
d	Crosby Alice B—†	9	housewife	91	"
e	West Alice—†	9	at home	64	"
f	Finklestein Sara—†	10	housewife	63	"
g	Rosenthal Helen E—†	10	dietitian	35	"
h	Rosenthal Joseph	10	physician	42	"
k	Nitz Anna L—†	12	housewife	72	"
l	Nitz William H	12	retired	72	
m	Schuerer Anna C—†	12	clerk	49	"
n	Bonifaci Robert	14	U S A	23	Washington
o	Iverson Dorothy—†	14	housewife	31	Melrose
p	Iverson Theodore L	14	mechanic	32	"
r	Novotny Albert	14	U S A	21	Illinois
s	Sherman Daisy E—†	14	teacher	55	here
t	Williams Ralph	14	U S A	21	California
u	Zavon Mitchel	14	"	22	New York
v	Donovan Edward M	15	shipper	49	here
w	Donovan Katherine R—†	15	housewife	44	"
x	Howe Joseph B	18	gardener	67	"
y	Keane Helga M—†	18	housewife	50	"
z	Seabury Ruth I—†	19	secretary	53	"

843

a	*Vakar Gertrude—†	19	housewife	41	"
b	*Vakar Nicholas P	19	teacher	51	
c	Davidmeyer Frank H	28	watchman	70	"
d	Davidmeyer M Gladys—†	28	clerk	33	
e	Davidmeyer Mary A—†	28	housewife	58	"
f	Hartin Catherine—†	28	at home	66	"

Peter Parley Road

g	McLaughlin Catherine I—†	2	housewife	45	here
h	McLaughlin Charles J	2	mechanic	23	"

Peter Parley Road—Continued

K	McLaughlin Charles P	2	clerk	47	here
L	Turner Arthur E	2	"	38	"
M	Turner Frank S	2	retired	72	"
N	Turner Nellie T—†	2	housewife	72	"
O	Campanella Blanche—†	4	"	37	
P	Campanella Joseph J	4	accountant	39	"
R	*Minihan Catherine—†	6	at home	80	"
S	Sheehan Annie J—†	6	housewife	60	"
T	Sheehan John J	6	guard	60	
U	Sheehan John M	6	student	20	
V	McCarthy Dorothy O—†	22	at home	38	"
W	McCarthy Thomas N	22	U S A	36	
X	McCready Leo P	22	"	24	
Y	McCready Leo T	22	physician	65	"
Z	McCready Margaret J—†	22	housewife	61	"

844

A	Sheridan Edmond C	22	foreman	29	"
B	Sheridan Marguerite M—†	22	at home	43	"
C	Sweeney Anne—†	30	clerk	43	
D	Sweeney Peter	30	"	58	
E	Parlon Grace E—†	32	teacher	40	
F	Parlon Mary A—†	32	housewife	40	"
G	Parlon Thomas A	32	cotton grader	59	"
H	Parlon William J	32	chauffeur	48	"
K	Hays Elizabeth—†	34	at home	84	"
L	Herron Isabelle—†	34	housewife	47	"
M	Herron Ruth A—†	34	clerk	21	
N	Coleman George S	42	engineer	61	"
O	Coleman Jacqueline—†	42	clerk	20	
P	Coleman Mary A—†	42	housewife	55	"
R	Coleman Paul S	42	student	25	
S	Coleman Winifred B—†	42	clerk	31	
T	Talbot Mary C—†	42	teacher	28	
U	Dyott Alfred R	44	machinist	41	"
V	Dyott Mary—†	44	housewife	37	"
W	Hennigan George F	48	retired	77	Taunton
X	Hennigan Mary A—†	48	housewife	75	here
Y	McLaughlin Eileen B—†	48	secretary	38	New York
Z	McLaughlin Joseph D	48	salesman	73	here

845

A	McLaughlin William T	48	retired	76	

28

Peter Parley Road—Continued

B	March Hazel G—†	56	housewife	51	here
C	March John A	56	teacher	65	"
D	Kelly Ellen E—†	64	at home	65	"
E	McCarthy Mary E—†	64	teacher	56	
F	Sullivan Mary V—†	70	" .	56	
G	Welch Grace S—†	70	housewife	49	"
H	Welch John F	70	executive	50	"

School Street

M	Stone Ann	4	housewife	44	here
N	Stone Myer	4	manufacturer	43	"
K	Otto Paul E	4	mechanic	32	"
L	Otto Rita—†	4	housewife	34	"
O	Irving Dorothy F—†	6	"	41	
P	Irving John P	6	chauffeur	41	"
R	Reardon Mary—†	6	at home	69	"
S	Shine Jeremiah	6	manager	66	"
T	Shine Margaret—†	6	housekeeper	70	"
V	*MacEachern John A	8	cutter	38	"
W	*MacEachern Sarah—†	8	housewife	39	"
X	Grimm Frederick	8	guard	60	
Y	Grimm Laurence	8	U S N	21	"
Z	Grimm Marie—†	8	housewife	50	"

846

B	Frazer Catherine—†	10	waitress	53	"
D	White Forrest	12	chauffeur	34	"
E	White Georgia—†	12	housewife	34	"
F	Pasquale Bernard	18	carpenter	26	"
G	Pasquale Josephine—†	18	housewife	25	"
H	Scipione Anna—†	18	"	63	
K	Scipione Nicola	18	retired	72	
L	Melino Nicola	18	laborer	56	"
M	Melino Palmina—†	18	housewife	54	"
N	Gurry John F	22	operator	29	"
O	Gurry Lillian—†	22	housewife	25	"
P	Donnelly Andrew R	22	U S A	28	
R	Donnelly Ellen V—†	22	housewife	60	"
S	Donnelly Francis	22	electrician	60	"
T	Magnifico Joseph	22	jeweler	35	
U	Magnifico Marie—†	22	housewife	25	"

29

School Street—Continued

v	Hollinger Otto	22	painter	48	here
w	Hollinger Willa—†	22	housewife	48	"
x	Fardie Evelyn U—†	22	"	22	24 Brookside av
y	Fardie William C	22	clerk	25	Medford
z	Norton Helen—†	22	housewife	26	here

847

a	Norton William J	22	roofer	27	
b	Kelley James F	26	clerk	22	
c	Kelley Jennie—†	26	housewife	50	"
d	Kelley Marguerite—†	26	clerk	20	
e	Kelley Mertin	26	policeman	50	"
f	Fitzgerald Rebecca—†	26	housewife	39	"
g	Fitzgerald Walter E	26	repairman	43	"
h	Foster Elizabeth—†	26	housewife	31	"
k	Foster George	26	chauffeur	31	"
l	Blackadar Charles	26	machinist	27	"
m	Blackadar Frances—†	26	housewife	26	"
n	White Arthur	26	U S A	21	
o	White Freda—†	26	housewife	46	"
p	Conkey Herbert F	26	clerk	58	
r	Conkey Lillian—†	26	housewife	57	"
s	Havey John	36	shipfitter	47	"
t	Havey Josephine—†	36	housewife	33	"
u	McGrath Ellen—†	36	clerk	31	
v	McGrath Herbert	36	electrician	38	"
w	McGrath May—†	36	housewife	44	"
x	McGrath Viola P—†	36	manager	41	"
y	Bradley Hugh	38	steelworker	30	51 Monument
z	Bradley Rita—†	38	housewife	29	51 "

848

a	Hulden Fred	38	electrician	65	51 "
b	Hatch Katherine—†	42	at home	64	New York
c	Regan Muriel E—†	42	supervisor	45	here
d	Weaver Sadie—†	42	housekeeper	61	"
e	Hamilton Francis J	46	seaman	22	"
f	Hamilton Rose—†	46	housewife	45	"
g	Bonner Alice I—†	46	"	39	3 Glines av
h	Bonner John	46	laborer	50	3 "
k	Bonner Mary A—†	46	clerk	20	3 "
l	Kayikjian Sarkis	48	carpenter	59	here
m	Kayikjian Vartouhy—†	48	housewife	48	"

School Street—Continued

N	Woods Lucy E—†	48	housewife	65	here
O	Woods William P	48	inspector	55	"
R	Murphy Anne—†	50	housewife	53	"
S	Murphy Michael	50	fireman.	50	
T	Shields Robert S	50	supt	53	
U	Sweeney Ellen—†	50	housewife	52	"
V	Sweeney John	50	policeman	22	"
W	Slattery Delia M—†	50	housewife	53	"
X	Slattery John J	50	guard	57	
Y	Bowen Cornelius	52	bottler	61	
Z	Bowen Mary E—†	52	housewife	57	"

849

A	Khachadourian David	52	brazier	45	20 Cobden
B	Wagner Jason	52	policeman	32	here
C	Wagner Lucille—†	52	housewife	26	"
D	Waters Elmer F	54	shipper	26	"
E	Waters Emery J	54	painter	35	
F	Waters Mary E—†	54	housewife	59	"
G	Waters Myrtle M—†	54	spinner	30	
H	McGowen Herbert R	54	chauffeur	24	"
K	McGowen Isabelle—†	54	housewife	55	"
L	McGowen Lloyd R	54	janitor	49	..
M	McGowen William H	54	U S N	22	
N	Buckley Timothy	54	mechanic	43	"
O	Redmond Arthur P	56	electrician	58	"
P	Redmond Mary E—†	56	housewife	52	"
R	*Maniatis Catherine—†	56	clerk	55	
S	Hachadoorian Balsam	56	retired	67	
T	Hachadoorian Helen Y—†	56	housewife	66	"
V	Foote Elizabeth R—†	60	"	40	
W	Foote James H	60	plater	42	
X	Villari Joseph	60	barber	29	
Y	Villari Ruth—†	60	housewife	29	"
Z	McCool Catherine M—†	60	"	42	..

850

A	McCool Floyd	60	painter	43	
B	Watkins Theresa—†	60	at home	53	"
C	Butterfield Albert	64	salesman	49	5 Johnson pk
D	Butterfield Francis	64	student	23	5 "
E	Butterfield Howard	64	paperworker	26	5 "
F	Butterfield Louise—†	64	housewife	46	5 "

School Street—Continued

G	DeCoste Bernard B	64	retired	21	here	
H	DeCoste Elizabeth—†	64	housewife	58	"	
L	Ranney Edwin	66	electrician	36	"	
M	Ranney Ethel M—†	66	housewife	33	"	
N	Ranney George	66	electrician	38	"	
O	Rice George	68	"	38		
P	Rice Jean—†	68	housewife	31	"	
R	Backman Ellen J—†	70	"	51		
S	Backman Gustav A	70	molder	62		
T	Backman Helen E—†	70	clerk	27		
U	MacKinnon George M	70	steamfitter	28	"	
V	MacKinnon Malvina M—†	70	housewife	24	"	
W	Kohler William F	74	manager	43	62 Seaverns av	
X	Messina Ella—†	74	housewife	25	22 School	
Y	Messina Frank R	74	musician	25	22 "	

851   Walnut Avenue

B	*Stone Dora—†	427	housewife	71	here	
C	Stone Samuel	427	manager	75	"	
D	*Donelan Margaret—†	429	housewife	53	"	
E	Donelan Michael	429	plasterer	53	"	
F	Donelan Michael R	429	U S N	23	"	
G	Forester David	rear 429	tree surgeon	28	431 Walnut av	
H	Forester Helen—†	" 429	housewife	25	431 "	
K	Ambler Herbert R, jr	431	laborer	28	20 Byron ct	
L	Ambler Margaret E—†	431	housewife	23	20 "	
M	Cohen Martin	431	salesman	68	here	
N	Cohen Rose—†	431	housewife	52	"	
O	Cooper Bessie—†	431	"	48	"	
P	Cooper Ernest S	431	technician	21	"	
R	Guba Edward L	433	clerk	57	46 Fisher av	
S	Guba Mary—†	433	housewife	71	46 "	
T	*Shapiro Bessie—†	433	at home	75	here	
U	Shapiro Nathan	433	retired	75	"	
V	*Rossi Margaret—†	433	housewife	32	23 Byron ct	
W	*Rossi Pasquale	433	waiter	42	23 "	
X	Ludwig Deborah—†	435	buyer	32	here	
Y	Ludwig Melvin S	435	"	34	"	
Z	Abrams Bessie—†	435	housewife	71	"	

852
Walnut Avenue—Continued

A	Abrams Isadore	435	dressmaker	38	here
B	Abrams Thomas	435	manager	72	"
C	Harris Aaron	435	tailor	76	"
D*| Harris Bertha—†	435	housewife	74	"
E	Rich Bertha—†	435	"	66	"
F	Rich Saul A	435	salesman	67	"
G	Weener Joseph	435	dentist	53	
H	Weener Minnie M—†	435	housewife	51	"
K	Weener Sumner S	435	U S A	23	
L	Gordon Emma—†	435	housewife	35	"
M	Gordon Irving	435	salesman	36	"
N	Bronkhorst Julia—†	435	saleswoman	50	"
O	Bronkhorst Nathan	435	repairman	52	"
P	Fried Rose—†	435	at home	62	"
R	Goldberg Frances—†	435	housewife	32	"
S	Goldberg Samuel	435	pipefitter	42	"
T*| Goldman Beatrice R—†	435	housewife	31	"
U	Goldman Philip	435	broker	30	
V	Supraner Mary—†	435	housewife	60	"
W	Starr Florence—†	435	"	30	
X	Starr Milton	435	book jobber	33	"
Y	Vigor Mildred—†	435	housewife	29	"
Z	Vigor Moses H	435	manager	36	"

853

A	Slade Celia—†	435	housewife	32	
B	Slade Samuel	435	manager	38	"
C	Singer Dora—†	439	housewife	40	"
D	Singer Paul	439	salesman	42	"
E	Shaffer Annie F—†	439	housewife	29	"
F	Shaffer Michael	439	merchant	29	"
G	Forsdahl Bertha—†	441	housewife	55	"
H	Forsdahl Carl	441	shipper	55	"
K	Haney Dennis	445	U S A	29	125 Boylston
L	Haney Gertrude—†	445	housewife	31	125 "
M	Cosgrove Joseph P	445	printer	45	here
N	Cosgrove Rose M—†	445	housewife	37	"
O	Shire Sadie M—†	445	at home	72	"
P	Karklin Emily—†	447	housewife	59	"
R	Karklin Jacob	447	polisher	73	"
S	Sessler Aagot—†	447	housewife	63	"

11—8
33

Walnut Avenue—Continued

T	Sessler Jacob	447	retired	68	here	
U	Catron Rudolph	449	janitor	38	"	
V	Newsome Archie	449	"	55	"	
W	Raymond Morris	449	manager	39	"	
X	*Raymond Rita—†	449	housewife	35	"	
Y	Alexander Esther—†	449	secretary	40	"	
Z	Alexander Fannie—†	449	at home	62	"	
	854					
A	Alexander Henrietta—†	449	secretary	30	"	
B	Alexander Marie—†	449	at home	22	"	
C	Leeder Anna—†	449	stenographer	43	"	
D	Leeder Celia—†	449	housewife	68	"	
E	Leeder Louis	449	accountant	41	"	
F	Leeder Simon	449	manufacturer	71	"	
G	Waldorf Abraham	449	painter	64	"	
H	Waldorf Eleanor—†	449	bookkeeper	39	"	
K	Waldorf Esther—†	449	housewife	64	"	
L	Waldorf Harry L	449	U S A	38	"	
M	Reitman David	449	retired	80	"	
N	Sadow Bella—†	449	at home	47	"	
O	Sadow Joseph	449	chauffeur	47	"	
P	Feldman Dorothy—†	449	housewife	34	"	
R	Feldman Ellis	449	photographer	34	"	
S	Lowenstein Benjamin	451	salesman	39	"	
T	Lowenstein Ruth—†	451	housewife	35	"	
U	Risman Frances—†	451	at home	71	"	
V	Kanter Mae—†	451	housewife	49	"	
W	Kanter Nathan	451	manager	50	"	
X	Kanter Selma—†	451	secretary	25	"	
Y	Krafsur Jeanette T—†	451	stenographer	42	"	
Z	Krafsur Lewis	451	investigator	49	"	
	855					
A	Vernick Elizabeth—†	451	housewife	38	"	
B	Vernick Victor H	451	manager	40	"	
C	Brooker Anna—†	451	bookkeeper	28	"	
D	Brooker Etta—†	451	housewife	58	"	
E	Brooker Ida—†	451	stenographer	25	"	
F	Brooker Rose—†	451	bookkeeper	27	"	
G	Holtze Abraham	451	salesman	48	"	
H	Levitan Harold	451	U S A	21	"	
K	Levitan Nettie—†	451	factorywkr	45	"	

Walnut Avenue—Continued

L	Gaull Edith H—†	451	housewife	36	here
M	Gaull Maurice	451	furrier	38	"
N	*Berman Ethel—†	461	at home	72	"
O	Weiner Lena B—†	461	housewife	38	"
P	Weiner Samuel J	461	attorney	43	"
R	Russell Leo	461	U S N	35	"
S	Russell Margaret—†	461	housewife	32	"
T	Sokol Harry	461	jobber	30	36 Maple
U	Sokol Laura—†	461	housewife	23	36 "
V	Goffin Gerald	461	furrier	27	here
W	Goffin Rose—†	461	housewife	27	"
X	Karp Anita B—†	461	saleswoman	21	"
Y	Karp John	461	manager	55	"
Z	Karp Mary—†	461	housewife	55	"
	856				
A	Gross Jeanne—†	461	"	24	"
B	Gross Sumner A	461	accountant	26	"
C	Lynn Isabella—†	489	housekeeper	60	"
D	Scannell David	489	physician	68	"
E	Scannell David, jr	489	attorney	31	"
F	Scannell Elizabeth—†	489	housewife	65	"
G	Sencabaugh Margaret—†	489	attendant	67	"
H	Gross Constance—†	493	housewife	45	"
K	Gross Max	493	realtor	43	"
L	Bradley Gerald W	495	U S M C	25	"
M	Bradley Kathleen L—†	495	nurse	32	"
N	Bradley Marjorie—†	495	at home	27	"
O	Bradley Mary F—†	495	"	57	"
P	Bradley Warren F	495	U S A	29	"
R	Bruno Catherine—†	495	at home	75	48 Revere
S	Bukata Zigmond	495	retired	69	54 Montgomery
T	Candee Leverett	495	"	84	here
U	Dole Helen C—†	495	at home	78	21 Fairfield
V	Fay Mary—†	495	"	75	here
W	Golden Mary—†	495	"	74	"
X	Henry Thomas	495	retired	78	69 Thomas pk
Y	Johnson Jennie E—†	495	at home	65	here
Z	McGilvary Thomas	495	retired	55	10 Summer
	857				
A	Nourse Carrie—†	495	at home	75	4 Alpine
B	O'Brien Francis	495	retired	71	69 Thomas pk

Page.	Letter.	Full Name.	Residence, Jan. 1, 1946.	Occupation.	Supposed Age.	Reported Residence, Jan. 1, 1945. Street and Number.

Walnut Avenue—Continued

	c	O'Meara David	495	retired	83	94 Rollins
	d	Pearson Walter G	495	"	80	here
	e	Pfeiffer Emma—†	495	at home	77	247 Beech
	f	Pignotti Luigi	495	retired	59	162 Lexington
	g	Risser Marion—†	495	at home	85	here
	h	Trott John W	495	retired	71	"

Washington Street

	k	McDonough Mark	3140	U S A	35	here
	l	McDonough Mary—†	3140	housewife	70	"
	m	McLaughlin Annabelle F—†	3140½	"	39	"
	n	McLaughlin Timothy	3140½	chauffeur	51	"
	r	Hartman Eileen—†	3142B	housewife	28	"
	s	Hartman Ora	3142B	machinist	33	"
	t	McLaren Agnes—†	3142B	"	37	
	u	McLaren Lillian—†	3142B	factorywkr	31	"
	v	*McLaren Sarah—†	3142B	cleaner	61	"
	w	McLaren Thomas	3142B	retired	30	
	x	*McLaren Thomas	3142B	"	63	
	y	Morris Amelia C—†	3144A	maid	55	
		858				
	a	Livingston Annie—†	3144A	housewife	53	"
	b	Livingston Louis	3144A	salesman	58	"
	c	Webster Catherine—†	3144A	factorywkr	45	"
	d	Deveney Charlotte—†	3144A	machinist	54	"
	e	Johnstone James	3144A	laborer	63	185 Boylston
	f	Crawford Astrid E—†	3144A	housewife	33	here
	g	Crawford Robert G	3144A	switchtender	36	"
	h	Hollis Charles D	3144A	retired	72	"
	k	Richards Ebba—†	3144A	housewife	26	"
	l	Richards Nicholas	3144A	bottler	29	
	n	Mackey Isabelle—†	3144C	housewife	70	"
	o	Mackey Kenneth M	3144C	retired	76	"
	p	Ripley Charles	3146	cook	50	886 Hunt'n av
	r	Ripley Charles, jr	3146	U S N	23	886 "
	s	Ripley Della—†	3146	housewife	48	886 "
	t	Ripley Frank	3146	bellboy	22	886 "
	v	Fleming Margaret E—†	3146	housewife	50	here
	w	Scriven Helen J—†	3146	at home	25	"

Page.	Letter.	Full Name.	Residence, Jan. 1, 1946.	Occupation.	Supposed Age.	Reported Residence, Jan. 1, 1945. Street and Number.

Washington Street—Continued

x	Corey George	3148	retired	81	8 Tupelo
y	Corey Margaret—†	3148	housewife	80	8 "
z	Carson Elizabeth K—†	3148	"	47	here

859

a	Carson John R	3148	retired	20	..
b	McNealy Albert	3148	laborer	41	"
c	McNealy Arthur A	3148	laundrywkr	48	"
d	Dolbeare Cyril	3148	"	38	
e	Dolbeare Ella—†	3148	housewife	37	"
g	*Ferguson Mary—†	3150	at home	59	"
h	*MacAuley Annie—†	3150	nurse	37	
k	*MacAuley John	3150	laborer	39	"
l	Horne Patricia—†	3150	housewife	21	4 Linwood
m	Horne Theodore	3150	machinist	21	36 Greenough av
v	Pratt George H	3163	laborer	23	here
w	Pratt Mary M—†	3163	housewife	25	"
x	O'Leary Gerald	3163	coppersmith	39	"
y	O'Leary Mary—†	3163	housewife	39	"

860

a	Licciardi Elizabeth R—†	3165	"	26	"
b	Licciardi Peter J	3165	warehouse	46	"
c	Collum Catherine—†	3165	waitress	42	"
d	O'Toole John B	3165	laborer	37	
w	McGonagle Annie—†	3189	housewife	45	"
x	McGonagle Hugh	3189	laborer	45	
y	*Kelly Helen—†	3189	housewife	35	"
z	Kelly Philip	3189	janitor	37	"

861

l	Donahue Joseph	3224	mechanic	33	"
m	Donahue Ruth—†	3224	housewife	32	"
n	Holden Catherine C—†	3224	"	69	
o	Holden William J	3224	laborer	39	
p	Briscoe John	3226	chauffeur	46	"
r	Briscoe Margaret—†	3226	housewife	48	"
s	Briscoe Mary—†	3226	machinist	25	"
t	Callahan Joseph D	3226	shipper	28	
u	McDermott Helen—†	3226	at home	24	"
v	McDermott Walter	3226	U S A	28	
w	Kilroy John	3226	laborer	40	
x	Kilroy Veronica—†	3226	housewife	37	"

Washington Street—Continued

Y	Tetreault Catherine—†	3226A	housewife	42	here
Z	Tetreault Raymond	3226A	chauffeur	35	"

862

A	Sanger Calvin	3228	retired	75	
B	Sanger Joseph	3228	chauffeur	46	"
C	Sanger Nora—†	3228	housewife	75	"
D	Urquhart David	3228A	porter	25	"
E	Urquhart Gertrude—†	3228A	housewife	58	"
F	Patch Jessie—†	3228A	at home	27	"
G	Goode Annie I—†	3230	housewife	34	"
H	McElroy Mary G—†	3230	"	31	15 Jess
K	Blair Josephine—†	3230	inspector	43	here
L	McBride Francis	3230A	chauffeur	34	"
M	McBride Marie R	3230A	housewife	36	"
¹M	Dudley Ida—†	3232	"	31	"
N	Koenig Edwin P	3232A	instructor	42	3234 Wash'n
O	Koenig Lila—†	3232A	housewife	52	3234 "
P	Wetterhan David	3232A	roofer	33	here
R	Wetterhan Jeanette—†	3232A	housewife	28	"
S	Molloy Margaret F—†	3234	"	43	"
T	Molloy Timothy	3234	packer	47	"
U*	McGinn Effie—†	3234	domestic	34	"
V	McGinn James	3234	retired	30	
W	McGrath Rita—†	3234	housewife	26	"
X	Austin William	3234A	machinist	45	"
Y	Tetreault Willa—†	3234A	bookkeeper	36	17 Hamilton
Z	Gaura Alfred	3236	operator	27	3238 Wash'n

863

A	Gaura Alice—†	3236	housewife	27	3238 "
B	Kent Agnes—†	3236	"	46	here
C	Kent James	3236	fireman	43	"
D	Sawyer Emma—†	3236	housewife	49	"
E	Stevens Doris—†	3238	"	27	"
F	Stevens Frances K—†	3238	clerk	29	"
G	Weymouth Florence—†	3238	"	22	
H	Weymouth Ruth—†	3238	housewife	25	"
K	Finn Ronald O	3238	U S A	29	"
L	Finn Teresa G—†	3238	housewife	58	"
M	Finn Theodore	3238	steamfitter	26	"
N	Betz Doris—†	3240	housewife	22	212 Boylston
O	Betz Hayes	3240	U S A	28	212 "

Washington Street—Continued

P	Craig Catherine M—†	3240	housewife	44	here
R	Craig Edward D	3240	retired	21	"
S	Craig Edward H	3240	machinist	44	"
T	*Rodgers Ronald G	3240	retired	24	Canada
U	Bock Jeanne—†	3240	housewife	48	here
V	Bock Robert C	3240	U S N	50	"

9

Ward 11—Precinct 9

CITY OF BOSTON

LIST OF RESIDENTS
20 YEARS OF AGE AND OVER

(NON-CITIZENS INDICATED BY ASTERISK)
(FEMALES INDICATED BY DAGGER)

AS OF

JANUARY 1, 1946

THOMAS F. SULLIVAN, *Chairman*
FREDERIC E. DOWLING, *Secretary*
WILLIAM A. MOTLEY, JR.
ARTHUR V. COUGHLIN
EVERETT R. PROUT

Listing Board.

CITY OF BOSTON PRINTING DEPARTMENT

900
Adams Circle

A	Lohrer Elizabeth L—†	3	housewife	55	here
B	Lohrer Leo	3	engineer	56	"
C	Lohrer Martin R	3	teacher	28	"
D	Lohrer Ruth L—†	3	secretary	24	"
E	Bastable Mary—†	5	housewife	30	"
F	Bastable William	5	electrician	32	"
G	Costello John J	5	expressman	34	11 Egleston
H	Costello Lena M—†	5	housewife	56	11 "
K	Titus Doris—†	7	"	28	here
L	Titus James L	7	clerk	33	"
M	Ingram Alice—†	7	inspector	39	"
N	Ingram Frank	7	chauffeur	43	"

Amory Street

O	Frasse Americo	170	floorman	28	66 Bromley
P	Frasse Theresa—†	170	housewife	24	66 "
R	LaRusso Alexander	170	laborer	29	66 "
S	LaRusso Angelo	170	U S A	21	66 "
T	LaRusso Ferdinand	170	"	27	66 "
U	LaRusso Josephine—†	170	housewife	58	66 "
V	LaRusso Luigi	170	laborer	57	66 "
W	Collin Albert	186	painter	54	here
X	Collin Evelyn—†	186	housewife	54	"
Y	Collin Leo	186	chauffeur	27	"
Z	Meier Alice—†	186	housewife	54	"

901

A	*Meier Robert	186	baker	52	
B	McEleney Anne—†	186	teacher	23	
C	McEleney Neil	186	laborer	63	"
D	Paschal Archie	188	"	52	372 Amory
E	Paschal Robert	188	U S M C	24	372 "
F	Griffin Daniel	190	laborer	50	here
G	Griffin Elizabeth—†	190	housewife	48	"
H	Cummings Mary—†	190	"	64	"
K	Cummings Veronica—†	190	operator	37	"
L	Cummings William	190	U S A	33	
M	Bates Albert	192	clerk	55	
N	Bates Bella—†	192	housewife	53	"

2

Amory Street—Continued

o	Bates George	192	U S A	21	here
p	Bates Sophie—†	192	operator	23	"
r	Butler Thomas	192	laborer	60	"
s	*Kileen Delia—†	192	housewife	60	"
t	Kileen Francis	192	U S A	24	
u	Kileen Marie—†	192	operator	26	"
v	Kileen Patrick	192	laborer	59	
w	Meyers Anna—†	194	nurse	31	
x	Meyers Helen—†	194	"	28	
y	Meyers Nellie—†	194	housewife	66	"
z	Rivard Emile	196	engineer	48	"

902

a	Rivard Hermine—†	196	housewife	50	"
b	Blood Bertha—†	196	"	52	
c	Blood James E	196	fireman	56	
d	McCoy Edwin	198	operator	31	"
e	McCoy Helen—†	198	clerk	25	
f	McCoy Loretta—†	198	operator	28	"
g	McCoy Margaret—†	198	domestic	32	"
h	McCoy Mary—†	198	housewife	62	"
k	McCoy Mary—†	198	operator	33	"
l	McCoy Walter	198	U S A	27	
m	Connolly Mary—†	200	teacher	51	
n	Fitzpatrick Edmund	200	student	33	
o	Fitzpatrick Mary—†	200	operator	28	"
p	Gallagher James	200	carpenter	65	"
r	Gallagher Margaret—†	200	housewife	57	"
s	Doherty Eileen—†	200	clerk	32	
t	Doherty Margaret—†	200	housewife	63	"
u	Sullivan Anna—†	210	"	40	
v	Sullivan John	210	salesman	40	"
w	Cowen Lillian—†	210	operator	38	"
x	Anderson Gertrude—†	210	clerk	37	
y	Anderson James	210	laborer	40	
z	Hamilton Aubrey	210	welder	58	

903

a	Hamilton Christine—†	210	housewife	49	"
b	Lamond Freda—†	210	"	42	
c	Lamond George	210	shipper	45	
d	Drozd Helen—†	210	saleswoman	50	"
e	Zalis Lena—†	210	secretary	35	"

3

Amory Street—Continued

	G	Clark Bertha—†	213	housewife	62	here
	H	Clark Walter	213	chauffeur	68	"
	K	Horn Caroline —†	213	housewife	31	"
	L	Baden Geraldine—†	213	"	22	288 Dudley
	M	Baden Ivan	213	U S N	30	288 "
	N	McCone Mary—†	215	housewife	69	here
	O	Hachey Catherine—†	215	"	30	"
	P	McLean Isabel—†	215	"	43	"
	R	McLean Jennie—†	215	housekeeper	65	"
	S	Schwollman William	215	laborer	72	"
	U	Doherty Andrew	217	engineer	48	"
	V	Doherty William	217	"	21	
	W	Harvey Catherine—†	217	housewife	57	"
	X	Harvey Peter	217	laborer	60	
	Y	Manley Isabel—†	217	housewife	40	"
	Z	Brinkert Alice—†	219	"	42	

904

	A	Brinkert Frederick	219	packer	44	
	B	Casserino Frank	219	U S N	35	
	C	Casserino Mary—†	219	housewife	35	"
	D	Kincannon Grace—†	219	clerk	25	
	E	Kincannon Mary—†	219	"	48	
	F	Jacomb Edward	221	chef	39	"
	G	Jacomb Irene—†	221	housewife	33	125 Boylston
	H	Bell Alfred	221	chef	22	here
	K	Bell Anna—†	221	housewife	44	"
	L	Cirino Henry	221	laborer	41	2 Glendale ter
	M	Walter Emily—†	221	housewife	47	here
	N	Walter Louis	221	foundryman	24	"
	O	Walter Warren	221	"	27	"
	P	Sullivan Ethel—†	222	housewife	50	"
	R	Sullivan Sidney	222	bottler	56	
	S	Murray Francis	223	shipper	31	
	T	Murray Joseph	223	U S N	27	
	U	Murray Rose—†	223	housewife	53	"
	V	Murray Thomas	223	bartender	56	"
	W	Harzbecker Edwin	225	packer	37	
	X	Harzbecker Martha—†	225	housewife	77	"
	Y	Harzbecker William	225	laborer	38	"
	Z	Jenner John	226	painter	45	Watertown

905
Amory Street—Continued

A	Jenner Violet—†	226	housewife	40	Watertown
C	Semonsen Margaret—†	226	"	41	25 Worcester sq
D	*Semonsen Ole	226	carpenter	53	25 "
E	DeCoste Augustus	227	steelworker	59	here
F	DeCoste Elizabeth—†	227	housewife	49	"
G	DeCoste Warren	227	steelworker	23	"
H	Saunders Augusta—†	229	at home	55	..
K	Estabrook Donald	230	chauffeur	21	"
L	Estabrook Lena—†	230	housewife	42	"
M	Estabrook Leon	230	chauffeur	43	"
N	Wiegold Arthur	230	laborer	36	
O	Wiegold Clara—†	230	housewife	70	"
P	Madden Andrew	230	laborer	20	
R	Madden Paul	230	U S N	28	
S	Madden Thomas C	230	brewer	31	
T	Madden Thomas J	230	"	51	
U	Madden Viola—†	230	housewife	50	"
V	Rhone Vivian—†	231	"	23	557 Col av
W	Rhone Warren	231	clerk	23	557 "
X	Powell Joshua	233	chemist	22	here
Y	Powell Mattie—†	233	housewife	23	"
Z	Wells Bronie—†	234	"	29	Stoughton

906

A	Wells Richard	234	U S N	26	"
B	Nelson Albertina—†	234	housewife	61	here
C	Powers Marie—†	234	"	46	"
D	Powers Michael	234	pipefitter	50	"
E	Perrotta Biagio	235	laborer	48	
F	Perrotta Secondina—†	235	housewife	40	"
G	Gallant Charles	236	laborer	26	Milford
H	Gallant Helen—†	236	housewife	25	"
K	Auclair Amos	236	brewer	52	here
L	*Buckley Regina—†	236	housewife	36	34 Burnett
M	Breen David	237	retired	73	here
N	Breen Selina—†	237	housewife	60	"
O	Manning John	239	rigger	43	"
P	Manning Margaret—†	239	housewife	39	"
R	O'Rourke Joseph M	241	clerk	21	
S	O'Rourke Susan—†	241	housewife	47	"
T	*Wieland Oscar	247	laborer	65	

Arcadia Street

w	Festel Arthur	1	U S A	32	here
x	Festel Gertrude H—†	1	secretary	32	"
y	Sawyer Harold I	1	clerk	40	"
z	Sawyer Ida—†	1	"	40	

907

A	Conway Eugene	2	metalworker	36	"
B	Conway Mary I—†	2	housewife	29	"
c	Lueth Clara—†	2	"	45	
D	Lueth Henry	2	watchman	47	"
E	Langer Herman	3	retired	95	69 Spring Park av
F	Simpson Ella A—†	3	nurse	66	here
G	Simpson George E	3	"	66	"
H	Raulston Amos C	4	blacksmith	64	"
K	Raulston Bertha M—†	4	housewife	60	"
L	Turner Eleanor M—†	4	"	28	"
M	Turner Frank H	4	clerk	30	Missouri
N	Senf Emma—†	4	housewife	63	here
o	Coghlin Josephine M—†	5	housekeeper	60	"
P	Danner Irene—†	5	machinist	42	17 Beethoven
R	Lonigan William H	5	fireman	59	here
s	Smith Catherine—†	5	clerk	42	11 Egleston
T	Cushing Dorothy—†	6	teacher	36	here
u	Lyons Francis C	6	U S N	38	"
v	Lyons Helen C—†	6	at home	32	"
w	Day Dorothy H—†	7	teller	23	
x	Day Margaret C—†	7	housewife	52	"
y	Day Walter E	7	laborer	58	
z	MacDonald Lillian D—†	7	housewife	32	"

908

A	MacDonald Robert	7	clerk	34	

Atherton Street

B	Quinn Alexander	28	retired	67	here
c	Quinn Josephine—†	28	housewife	65	"
D	Plasko Chester	28	chauffeur	28	"
E	Plasko Theresa—†	28	machinist	28	"
F	Juenger Ernest G	30	clerk	57	
G	Koehler Emma L—†	30	cook	63	"
H	Payne Berna—†	30	housewife	23	Pennsylvania
K	Payne R Howard	30	clergyman	23	"

Atherton Street—Continued

L	Feeley Gertrude—†	36	teacher	50	here
M	Feeley Mary—†	36	social worker	25	"
N	Fettig Emma—†	36	housewife	51	"
O	Fettig Henry	36	draftsman	20	"
P	Fettig Joseph	36	waiter	52	
R	Forbes Elizabeth—†	38	nurse	56	
S	Haymer Joseph A	38	retired	59	
T	Haymer Marie—†	38	housewife	56	"
U	Mullen Ada F—†	42	"	58	
V	Mullen James E	42	druggist	63	"
W	Fotch Gisela—†	46	housewife	84	" .
X	Schmitz Henry J	46	foreman	64	"
Y	Schmitz Henry T	46	shipper	25	
Z	Schmitz Olga—†	46	housewife	64	"
Z¹	Haffenreffer Christine M—†	48	at home	82	"

909

A	Sessler Annie—†	48	housekeeper	64	"
B	Stevens Martha C—†	48	dressmaker	52	Missouri
C	Crockett David W	50	draftsman	22	here
D	Crockett George R	50	manager	64	"
E	Crockett Jennie E—†	50	housewife	64	"
F	Colvin William J	52	shipper	46	Attleboro
G	Ferris James	52	dentist	24	69 Emerald
H	Sullivan Grace—†	52	housewife	41	here
K	Sullivan John J	52	shipwright	41	"

Bismarck Street

L	DeMotte Elmer	5	laborer	35	3 Hoffman
M	DeMotte Mary—†	5	housewife	32	3 "
N	Clark Ethel I—†	5	"	54	173 Boylston
O*	Clark Thomas O	5	electrician	52	173 "
P	Toenjes Constance—†	5	housewife	24	173 "
R	Toenjes John W	5	seaman	24	173 "
S	Mills Barbara—†	5	housewife	24	here
T	Mills Harvey S	5	mechanic	25	"
U	Wallace Patrick	5	laborer	56	"
V	Wallace Robert P	5	"	21	"
Y	Evans James D	13	brewer	36	
Z	Evans Lillian M—†	13	housewife	41	"

910
Bismarck Street—Continued

A	Connell Margaret M—†	13	domestic	41	here
B	Connell Thomas F	13	chauffeur	53	"
C	Cappel Carl	13	brewer	52	"
D	Cappel Laura R—†	13	housewife	45	"

Boylston Place

E	Dunne Celia A—†	1	housewife	33	here
F	Dunne William F	1	laborer	31	"
G	Speierman Alma—†	1	housewife	69	"
H	Speierman Arthur	1	buffer	38	
K	Speierman Elizabeth—†	1	housewife	29	"
L	Taylor Dorothy—†	1	"	39	
M	Taylor Sidney	1	laborer	45	"
N	Tennihan Anna—†	3	housekeeper	67	"
O	Tennihan Joseph H	3	laborer	76	"
P	Mahoney Eva B—†	3	at home	70	
R	McCarthy Mary—†	3	"	74	
S	Sharpe Clara L—†	4	housewife	58	"
T	Sharpe Percy	4	shoeworker	58	"
U	Woodside Alfred A, jr	4	agent	37	
V	Woodside Helen C—†	4	housewife	30	"
W	McManus Caroline A—†	4	packer	27	
X	McManus Thomas J	4	clerk	28	
Y	Morrison Evelyn—†	4	"	36	
Z	Thornton Mary—†	8	housewife	28	"

911

A	Thornton Michael	8	operator	41	"
B	McLellan Gordon	8	carpenter	62	"
C	McLellan Magdalene—†	8	housewife	63	"
D	Frey Dorothy—†	rear 8	bookkeeper	33	"
E	Frey Marie—†	" 8	housewife	60	"

Boylston Street

F	Marshman Mildred M—†	123	housewife	67	here
G	*Marshman William	123	painter	69	"
H	Doyle Michael J	123	retired	71	"
K	Reardon Leonard F	123	chauffeur	41	"
L	Reardon Mary E—†	123	housewife	37	"

Boylston Street—Continued

M	Reardon William J	123	U S N	20	here
N	Moore Anna M—†	123	stitcher	21	"
O	Moore Joseph A	123	meatcutter	62	"
P	Moore Joseph F	123	mortician	31	"
R	Moore Mary A—†	123	housewife	55	"
S	Desmaries Moses	125	chauffeur	32	Cambridge
T	Desmaries Virginia—†	125	housewife	26	"
U	Dustin Edward	125	electrician	60	here
V	Dustin Mary—†	125	housewife	44	"
W	Gadman Arlene V—†	125	"	29	212 Chestnut av
X	Gadman Harold E	125	chauffeur	26	212 "
Y	McCarthy Jeremiah	129	clerk	38	7 Rand pl
Z	McCarthy Marion E—†	129	housewife	20	7 "

912

A	Gowans James H	129	electrician	40	here
B	McKellar Robert E	129	fireman	26	1849 Hyde Park av
C	Osier Gerald	129	contractor	31	here
D	Osier Leola—†	129	housewife	30	"
E	Johnson Kathleen T—†	129	"	31	114 Marcella
F	Johnson Kenneth M	129	shipfitter	28	114 "
G	McCarthy Marguerite—†	129	waitress	41	here
H	McCarthy William	129	bartender	42	"
K	Kennedy Claire E—†	129	housewife	21	"
L	Kennedy Larson W, jr	129	laborer	23	
M	Baker Irving E	129	chauffeur	36	"
N	Brainerd Cornelia E—†	129	housewife	41	"
O	Moore Marion L—†	131	at home	31	"
P	MacDonald Carmella T—†	131	waitress	29	Texas
R	MacDonald Vincent S	131	chauffeur	24	"
S	Anderson Mary J—†	131	waitress	30	36 Greenleaf
T	Connors Charles	131	seaman	34	32 Westland av
U	Connors Marguerite—†	131	housewife	26	32 "
V	Center Mary—†	131	machinist	50	here
W	DeFranco Mary C—†	131	operator	37	55 Greenbrier
Z	Limmer Francis	135	shoemaker	22	here

913

A	Limmer Mary—†	135	housewife	47	"
B	Limmer Peter	135	shoemaker	50	"
C	Limmer Peter	135	"	25	
F	Long Charles W	145	printer	41	
G	Long Veronica R—†	145	housewife	41	"

Boylston Street—Continued

H	Schofield Anna—†	145	housewife	43	here	
K	Schofield Joseph	145	builder	45	"	
L	Ryder Donald D	146	letter carrier	27	31 Armstrong	
M	Ryder Roberta—†	146	housewife	24	31 "	
N	Berry Catherine F—†	146	"	36	here	
O	Berry James C	146	painter	37	"	
P	Lindblad Aile—†	146	housewife	34	"	
R	Lindblad Otto	146	electrician	42	"	
S	Downes James E	146	salesman	25	"	
T	Downes Laura P—†	146	housewife	21	"	
U	Chitro Eileen—†	146	clerk	23	44 Buswell	
V	Chitro John	146	welder	28	44 "	
W	Godfrey John	146	baker	25	196 Amory	
X	Quirk Bridget—†	146	housewife	55	here	
Y	Quirk John	146	retired	54	"	
Z	Ishkanian Hagop	147	shoemaker	46	Rhode Island	

914

A	Ishkanian Queenie—†	147	housewife	36	"	
C	*Sweeney Patrick J	150	brewer	41	here	
D	*Sweeney Sarah—†	150	housewife	40	"	
E	*Kilduff Mary—†	150	at home	69	44 Haverford	
F	*Apolon Adolf	150	painter	47	here	
G	*Apolon Jennie—†	150	housewife	74	"	
H	Danca Gertrude—†	151	"	27	"	
K	Danca Salvatore	151	burner	31		
L	*Connors Catherine—†	152	at home	78	"	
M	McDonald George	152	laborer	45		
N	McDonald Margaret—†	152	housewife	42	"	
O	Richardson Harry W	152	engineer	30	6 Brookford	
P	Richardson Mary—†	152	housewife	25	6 "	
R	Giunta Antoinette—†	153	"	57	here	
S	Giunta Julius C	153	laborer	63	"	
T	Martin Guy	153	retired	66	"	
U	Ihlefeldt Doris L—†	153	typist	22		
V	Ihlefeldt Edmund G	153	laborer	50		
W	Ihlefeldt Harold G	153	clerk	25		
X	Ihlefeldt Madeline L—†	153	housewife	49	"	
Y	Oxford Alma—†	153	"	44		
Z	Gerstel Freida L—†	154	"	63		

915

A	Gerstel Walter H	154	janitor	34		

Boylston Street—Continued

B	Gerstel William C	154	janitor	63	here
C	Sears Catherine W—†	154	housewife	32	"
D	Sears Daniel E	154	toolmaker	52	"
E	Hargraves George H	154	printer	54	
F	Hargraves Lauretta H—†	154	housewife	51	"
G	Kelly Margaret—†	156	"	30	
H	Kelly William J	156	shipper	32	"
K	King George	156	busboy	30	"
L	King Pauline—†	156	housewife	30	"
M	Sites Catherine E—†	156	"	57	"
N	Sites George A	156	clerk	65	"
O	Sites William J	156	foreman	37	24 Maple
P	Roth Charles	157	draftsman	75	here
R	McCarthy Edwin	158	U S A	36	"
S	McCarthy Elizabeth—†	158	saleswoman	25	"
T	Dowd Christina—†	158	domestic	58	"
U	Dowd Frank	158	chauffeur	58	"
V	Kupzok Gertrude—†	158	housewife	46	"
W	Kupzok William	158	brewer	47	
X	Barrett Agnes J—†	159	saleswoman	45	"
Z	Barrett Mary E—†	159	clerk	49	
Y	Barrett Richard	159	shipper	42	

916

A	Steele Jean—†	160	housewife	39	"
B	Steele John	160	machinist	39	"
C	Craven Anna M—†	160	housewife	44	"
D	Craven William F	160	starter	49	"
E	Hall John	160	mechanic	26	"
F	Rist Barbara—†	160	clerk	20	
G	Rist Bernard J	160	machinist	44	"
H	Rist Frances—†	160	housewife	42	"
K	Mahoney Agnes—†	162	operator	28	"
L	Raeke Barbara C—†	162	housewife	29	"
M	Raeke Robert R	162	lather	27	
N	McGrath Florence M—†	162	housewife	28	"
O	McGrath William J	162	paint mixer	31	"
P	Randall Reginald D	162	packer	33	
R	Evans Dorothy—†	162	housewife	25	"
S	Evans Hugh	162	molder	30	
T	Dunlap Ann L—†	163	typist	23	"
U	Stumpf Marie F—†	163	stenographer	26	"

Boylston Street—Continued

v	Stumpf Mary J—†	163	domestic	50	here
w	Stumpf Robert J	163	chauffeur	21	"
x	Stumpf Bridget J—†	163	housewife	52	"
y	Stumpf John J	163	janitor	55	
z	Smyth Michael J	163	"	40	
	917				
a	Conway Anne—†	165	housewife	35	"
b	Conway John	165	burner	35	
c	Stacey Walter R	165	painter	45	
d	O'Toole Joseph	166	builder	47	
e	O'Toole Mary—†	166	housewife	42	"
f	Brower Anna V—†	166	operator	50	"
g	O'Hara Alice—†	166	factoryworker	55	"
h	Everett Edith V—†	166	nurse	23	
k	Everett Edward M	166	electrician	55	"
l	Everett Mary A—†	166	housewife	53	"
m	Rae Frederick N	166	factoryworker	71	"
n	O'Brien Edward J	167	machinist	46	"
o	O'Brien Edward J, jr	167	laborer	25	
p	O'Brien Ethel E—†	167	clerk	23	
r	O'Brien Mary J—†	167	housewife	45	"
s	O'Brien Mary J—†	167	candymaker	21	"
t	Lehan Arthur R	167	laborer	20	
u	Lehan John F	167	"	21	
v	Lehan Mary J—†	167	housewife	40	"
w	Richburg Albert	167	laborer	56	37 Moreland
x	Munck Gretchen—†	169	factoryworker	48	here
y	Cohen Hyman	169	salesman	45	"
z	Long Rhoda—†	169	checker	45	"
	918				
a	*Rogers Jean—†	169	manager	23	"
b	Noseworthy Anne G—†	169	housewife	42	"
c	Noseworthy James	169	engineer	43	"
d	LeBlanc Clair W	172	operator	28	"
e	LeBlanc Rita M—†	172	housewife	23	"
f	Flynn Arthur	172	lawyer	34	88 Gardner
g	Flynn Rita P—†	172	housewife	27	178 Boylston
h	Carey Helen—†	172	clerk	35	here
k	Carey Mildred—†	172	factoryworker	36	"
l	Lamond John	173	operator	29	N Hampshire
m	Lamond Mary E—†	173	housewife	27	"

Page.	Letter.	Full Name.	Residence, Jan. 1, 1946.	Occupation.	Supposed Age.	Reported Residence, Jan. 1, 1945. Street and Number.

Boylston Street—Continued

	N	Burke Marion E—†	173	housewife	20	here
	O	Burke Walter M	173	machinist	24	"
	P	Jefferson Emma J—†	173	housewife	41	"
	S	Nicholas Anthony	rear 173A	cook	48	
	T	Nicholas Catherine—†	" 173A	housewife	37	"
	U	Gerstel Anna M—†	" 173A	"	27	
	V	Gerstel Charles H, jr	" 173A	buffer	28	
	W	Weiland Henry	174	brewer	55	
	X	Patch Henry	174	operator	32	"
	Y	Patch Rose—†	174	housewife	58	"
	Z	O'Neil Mary A—†	175	housekeeper	54	"
919						
	A	Willworth Charles J	175	U S M C	27	"
	B	Willworth Mary G—†	175	bookkeeper	27	"
	C	Wolfe Glanda—†	175	housewife	28	Colorado
	D	Wolfe Herbert	175	mechanic	31	"
	E	Gerstel Dorothy A—†	175	packer	27	here
	F	Gerstel Gladys L—†	175	housewife	49	"
	G	Gerstel Mildred E—†	175	at home	21	"
	H	Gerstel Richard E	175	operator	24	"
	K	Sweeney Delia A—†	176	housewife	46	"
	L	Sweeney James	176	brewer	47	
	M	Maguire Bridget—†	178	housewife	74	"
	N	Maguire Thomas	178	retired	82	
	O	Welch Frances D—†	178	housewife	35	"
	P	Welch John E	178	inspector	35	"
	R	Sullivan Hilda—†	178	housewife	38	"
	S	Sullivan Richard J	178	janitor	42	
	T	Dooley John J	180	brewer	45	
	U	Homer Charles C	180	janitor	73	
	V	Springer Rudolph	180	egg candler	57	"
	W	Mulrey Catherine J—†	180	housewife	54	"
	X	Tedeschi Mary K—†	180	typist	22	
	Y	Dudley George	180	brewer	36	
	Z	West Henry F	180	realtor	67	"
920						
	A	West Magdalena—†	180	housewife	63	"
	B	Gormley Marie—†	182	clerk	38	
	C	Weed Francis	182	teletyper	36	"
	D	Weed Mildred—†	182	tel operator	42	"
	E	Goode Cecelia—†	182	housewife	56	"

13

Boylston Street—Continued

F	Goode Dorothy L—†	182	typist	27	here
G	Goode Thomas E	182	printer	57	"
H	Goode Thomas N	182	guard	26	"
K	McGrath Madge—†	182	housewife	46	"
L	McGrath Maurice	182	operator	47	"
M	Sertory Hubert	183	retired	79	
N	Wortmann Maria—†	183	buffer	37	
O	Wortmann Mary—†	183	at home	65	
P	Fickeis Caroline—†	183	clerk	52	
R	Fickeis Eva—†	183	at home	44	
S	Pilkington Hannah C—†	183	operator	40	"
T	Russell Chester W	183	laborer	28	78 Mozart
U	*MacDonald John	184	tree surgeon	57	140 W Newton
V	*MacKenzie Catherine—†	184	housekeeper	55	167 Roxbury
W	MacKenzie Evelyn—†	184	clerk	21	167 "
X	Henning Lillie—†	184	housewife	81	here
Y	Baxter Sarah—†	184	"	45	"
Z	Baxter William	184	woodworker	53	"

921

A	Dempsey Agnes—†	185	housewife	42	"
B	Dempsey George	185	machinist	49	"
C	Bisset Jennie—†	185	housewife	32	"
D	Bisset John	185	salesman	32	"
E	Corchemny Fred	185	carpenter	64	"
F	*Corchemny Julia—†	185	at home	64	
G	Carter John D	185	U S A	21	
H	Carter John J	185	foreman	49	
K	Carter Joseph F	185	clerk	25	
L	Carter Margaret M—†	185	housewife	43	"
M	Harkins George A	185	electrician	23	"
N	Harkins Helen M—†	185	inspector	23	"
O	Rankin Helen—†	186	housewife	26	"
P	Rankin Margaret—†	186	"	61	
R	Rankin Thomas	186	agent	31	
S	Blair Allan	186	machinist	64	"
T	Blair Isabella—†	186	housewife	65	"
U	Blair Thomas W	186	storekeeper	44	"
V	Larson Ada—†	186	housewife	53	"
W	Larson Russell	186	U S N	20	
X	Smith Edith—†	186	housewife	24	"
Y	Smith George	186	molder	29	

14

Page.	Letter.	FULL NAME.	Residence, Jan. 1, 1946.	Occupation.	Supposed Age.	Reported Residence, Jan. 1, 1945. Street and Number.

Boylston Street—Continued

	z	Reppucci Ethel—†	187	housewife	41	here
922						
	A	Reppucci Michael A	187	electrician	47	"
	B	Lyons James E	187	auditor	37	"
	c	Lyons Margaret L—†	187	housewife	35	"
	D	Hall Margaret—†	187	stitcher	46	
	E	Neumann Mary—†	187	at home	80	"
	F	Yanarella Louise—†	188	housewife	38	"
	G	Yanarella Warren M	188	attendant	38	"
	H	DiCarlo Anna L—†	188	housewife	66	"
	K	DiCarlo John	188	laborer	46	
	L	Moriarty Clarence W	188	mechanic	38	"
	M	Moriarty Theresa—†	188	housewife	39	"
	N	DiCarlo Bridget—†	188	"	35	..
	o	DiCarlo Emilio	188	laborer	31	"
	P	DiCarlo Samuel	188	contractor	36	"
	R	Doherty Bernard	189	laborer	42	
	S	Doherty Winifred—†	189	housewife	40	"
	T	Rehm Anna L—†	189	stitcher	28	
	U	Rehm George F	189	boxmaker	60	."
	V	Rehm Luella—†	189	housewife	52	"
	W	Rehm Mary J—†	189	stitcher	26	
	X	Rehm William T	189	U S A	20	
	Y	Burton Joseph	189	laborer	60	"
	z	Burton Louise—†	189	housewife	61	"
923						
	A	Desrochers Bernard	189	millhand ·	30	"
	B	Desrochers Evelyn—†	189	housewife	26	"
	c	Tennihan Mary L—†	191	"	48	
	D	Tennihan Ralph E	191	rubberworker	50	"
	E	Tennihan Ralph E	191	U S N	22	
	F	Rogers Frank W	191	shipper	57	
	G	Rogers Robert	191	U S N	21	"
	H	Burney Anna C—†	191	housewife	30	"
	K	Burney George E	191	chauffeur	33	"
	L	Oppelaar Jennie G—†	191	at home	53	"
	M	Krug Florence—†	192	housewife	41	"
	N	Krug Henry	192	inspector	45	"
	o	Krug Marion—†	192	clerk	21	
	P	O'Leary Bridget J—†	192	housewife	70	"
	R	O'Leary James J	192	retired	74	"

15

Page.	Letter.	FULL NAME.	Residence, Jan. 1, 1946.	Occupation.	Supposed Age.	Reported Residence, Jan. 1, 1945. Street and Number.

Boylston Street—Continued

	s	O'Leary James J	192	U S A	34	here
	t	O'Leary Marguerite A—†	192	clerk	32	"
	u	O'Leary Timothy J	192	U S A	38	"
	v	Splaine Anna—†	192	housewife	42	"
	w	Splaine John C	192	houseman	44	"
	x	Lynch Mary—†	193	housewife	33	"
	y	Lynch Matthew	193	engineer	40	"
	z	Dempsey Mabel—†	193	waitress	42	"

924

	a	Dempsey Nellie—†	193	matron	45	
	b	Poulos Catherine—†	193	housewife	38	"
	c	Poulos James P	193	manager	49	"
	d	Lowder Marie J—†	194	housewife	39	"
	e	Lowder Thomas J	194	plumber	43	"
	f	Walther George W	194	retired	65	
	g	Landry Elizabeth M—†	194	housewife	79	"
	h	Landry Thomas S	194	welder	35	
	k	Carlson Jennie C—†	194	clerk	62	
	l	Gudjons Julius	195	retired	69	"
	m	Schumann Barbara M—†	195	secretary	27	"
	n	Schumann Beatrice M—†	195	housewife	55	"
	o	Schumann Philip L	195	retired	57	"
	p	Doherty James M	196	laborer	60	
	r	*Doherty Margaret M—†	196	housewife	52	"
	s	Dwyer Patrick J	196	laborer	58	
	t	Lucey William	196	"	56	
	u	Herron Anna—†	196	housewife	72	"
	v	Herron Arthur N	196	retired	72	
	w	Matthei Eva—†	198	housewife	71	"
	x	Holt Stanley F	198	mechanic	23	"
	y	Jamison Florence—†	198	housewife	32	"
	z	Jamison George	198	painter	37	

925

	a	Stephansky Helen M—†	200	secretary	26	"
	b	Stephansky Lillian E—†	200	printer	37	"
	c	Stephansky Marie M—†	200	stenographer	32	"
	e	May Evelyn C—†	201	housewife	30	"
	f	May William	201	ironworker	46	"
	g	Perry Alma—†	201	saleswoman	21	"
	h	Perry Catherine—†	201	housewife	45	"
	k	Perry Edward J	201	U S M C	23	"

Page.	Letter.	FULL NAME.	Residence, Jan. 1, 1946.	Occupation.	Supposed Age.	Reported Residence, Jan. 1, 1945. Street and Number.

Boylston Street—Continued

	L	Perry John	201	steelworker	55	here
	M	Perry Robert J	201	U S A	21	"
	N	Clay Madeline—†	203	housewife	25	"
	O	Clay Reginald G	203	U S A	26	
	P	Hannan Anna L—†	203	housewife	53	"
	R	Hannan Ellen F—†	203	secretary	21	"
	S	Hannan Frank A	203	janitor	61	..
	T	Hannan John A	203	electrician	31	"
	U	Perry Mary—†	203	housewife	47	"
	V	Perry Peter	203	operator	51	"
	W	Walsh Delia—†	203	housekeeper	40	"
	X	Walsh Nora—†	203	saleswoman	21	"
	Y	Richburg Elizabeth—†	205	housekeeper	52	"
	Z	Riese Elizabeth—†	205	housewife	27	"

926

	A	Riese Paul	205	U S A	29	Ohio
	B	Koelsch Catherine—†	205A	housewife	38	here
	C	Koelsch Edgar	205A	laborer	47	"
	D	Koelsch Frank	205A	carpenter	77	"
	E	Koelsch Frank	205A	mechanic	38	"
	G	Anderson Carl D	212	salesman	29	"
	H	Anderson Louise M—†	212	housewife	24	"
	K	Morin Alice H—†	212	clerk	21	
	L	Morin Grace—†	212	housewife	48	"
	M	Morin Walter C	212	painter	52	"
	N	Morin Walter C, jr	212	printer	27	
	O	Crawford Albert B	212	retired	65	"
	P	Crawford Valerie J—†	212	housewife	50	"

927 Brookside Avenue

	A	Walraven Cornelius	2	carpenter	47	here
	B	Walraven Tena—†	2	housewife	84	"
	C	Bausch Frank G	2	laborer	21	"
	D	Bausch George C	2	brewer	64	
	E	Bausch Helen M—†	2	housewife	42	"
	F	Haggerty Frances M—†	2	"	31	
	G	Haggerty William J	2	carpenter	31	"
	H	Sheehan Clifford C	5	shipper	26	15 King
	K	Sheehan Ellen E—†	5	housewife	21	15 "
	L	Salisbury Charles D	5	laborer	48	here

Page.	Letter.	FULL NAME.	Residence, Jan. 1, 1946.	Occupation.	Supposed Age.	Reported Residence, Jan. 1, 1945. Street and Number.

Brookside Avenue—Continued

M	*Salisbury Margaret—†	5	housewife	47	here
N	Smith Ernest P	5	U S A	26	"
O	Smith Margaret—†	5	housewife	62	"
P	Smith Robert E	5	laborer	29	
R	*Smith Thomas	5	retired	74	
S	Sloane Arthur T	7	U S A	24	
T	Sloane Margaret M—†	7	housewife	60	"
U	Sloane Thomas V	7	U S N	20	"
V	Carpenter Albert	7	brewer	36	20 Germania
W	Carpenter Helen—†	7	housewife	29	20 "
X	MacEachern Irene—†	7	stenographer	21	here
Y	MacEachern Margaret—†	7	housewife	45	"
Z	MacEachern Roderick	7	carpenter	47	"

928

A	Kunan Katharine—†	8	housewife	60	"
B	Kunan Richard	8	U S A	37	"
C	Piper Charles	8	retired	80	3 St John
D	Dugal Anna—†	8	housewife	65	here
E	Dugal Victor G	8	accountant	35	"
F	Faretra Josephine—†	8	housewife	25	"
G	Faretra Michael	8	printer	26	
K	Moulton George W	9	coppersmith	57	"
L	Moulton Helen F—†	9	housewife	56	"
M	Wood Vivian I—†	9	domestic	64	"
N	Greenough Clifford	9	foreman	53	"
O	Farrell Edith D—†	10	housewife	37	"
P	Farrell Lawrence M	10	chauffeur	40	"
R	Boyle Dorothy L—†	10	housewife	25	"
S	Boyle James A	10	chipper	27	"
T	O'Hear Charles	10	chauffeur	43	"
U	O'Hear Margaret—†	10	housewife	45	"
V	*Duncan Rebecca—†	11	operator	43	"
W	Kelley Clara—†	11	housewife	44	"
X	Kelley Thomas	11	electrician	44	"
Y	MacPherson Hugh	11	painter	60	
Z	MacPherson Martha F—†	11	housewife	63	"

929

A	Imbescheid Otto	22	salesman	54	"
B	Mills Henry B	22	chauffeur	33	"
C	Mills Lillian C—†	22	housewife	31	"
D	Foster Catharine—†	22	benchworker	38	"

Brookside Avenue—Continued

E	Foster Edward L	22	shipper	39	here
F	Rodd Anna R—†	22	housekeeper	59	"
G	Murphy Catharine J—†	22	housewife	37	"
H	Murphy Eugene	22	waiter	45	"
K	Jager Edward G	24	electrician	37	"
L	Jager Ethel I—†	24	housewife	36	"
M	Albach Anna M—†	24	"	47	
N	Albach Harry	24	mechanic	49	"
O	DeMinico Angelo	24	chauffeur	46	"
P	DeMinico Julia—†	24	housewife	43	"
R	Reusch Katharine—†	28	"	82	
S	Reusch Louis	28	retired	70	"
T	Caley John	28	clerk	23	30 Archdale rd
U*	Caley Mary C—†	28	secretary	20	here
V	Nash Dorothy A—†	28	housewife	22	Texas
W	Nash John J	28	retired	67	here
X	Nash Lawrence R	28	machinist	23	"
Y	Nash Nora G—†	28	dressmaker	56	"
Z	Goode Mary E—†	28	housewife	56	"

930

A	Goode William F	28	U S A	28	
B	Burwell Alfred	32	laborer	67	
C	Burwell Mary E—†	32	housewife	69	"
D	Haley Anne L—†	32	nurse	32	
E	Haley Francis E	32	machinist	34	"
F	Haley Minetta J—†	32	housewife	69	"
G	Marich Edna M—†	32	"	24	30 Iffley rd
H	Marich Rodie D	32	clerk	28	30 "
K	Pearl Edward J	32	agent	34	here
L	Pearl Marion E—†	32	housewife	35	"
M	Laffey Ellen A—†	34	"	34	"
N	Laffey James J	34	buffer	34	
O	Roemer Carl O	34	fireman	55	
P	Roemer Elizabeth M—†	34	photographer	21	"
R	Roemer Freda C—†	34	housewife	50	"
S	Roemer Helen E—†	34	saleswoman	22	"
T	Wortmann Elizabeth—†	34	housewife	40	"
U	Wortmann Fritz	34	machinist	40	"
V	Cullen Bertha—†	36	housewife	54	"
W	Cullen James P	36	steelworker	58	"
X	Cullen Marie A—†	36	operator	24	"

Page.	Letter.	FULL NAME.	Residence, Jan. 1, 1946.	Occupation.	Supposed Age.	Reported Residence, Jan. 1, 1945. Street and Number.

Brookside Avenue—Continued

Y	Turnbull Rose M—†	36	housewife	21	here
Z	Turnbull William R	36	policeman	31	"

931

A	Cosgrove Martin	38	laborer	75	
B	Cosgrove Mary A—†	38	housewife	73	"
C	Costello John J	46	clergyman	50	"
D	DeCourcey Daniel C	46	"	43	
E	Kelly James F	46	"	73	
F	McCarthy Mary H—†	46	housekeeper	71	"
G	Mulligan Edward	46	clergyman	30	Scituate
H	Scannell Annie—†	46	domestic	66	here

Copley Street

K	DeBenedetto Anna—†	1	housekeeper	46	here
L	DeBenedetto Ottavio	1	clerk	21	"
M	Blotner Bessie—†	2	saleswoman	47	"
N	Gerofski Jennie—†	2	housekeeper	58	"
O	Weis Juhus A	5	clerk	76	"
P	Weis Louise B—†	5	housewife	75	"
R	Beal Frederick W	6	retired	67	"
S	Beal Vera M—†	6	housewife	67	"
T	Cox Charles B	7	U S A	39	
U	Cox Frederick J	7	retired	71	
V	Cox Louise M—†	7	housewife	68	"
W	Hantz Beatrice G—†	8	teacher	42	"
X	Hantz Helen M—†	8	housekeeper	56	"
Y	Hantz John J, jr	8	agent	45	"
Z	Hantz Louis A	8	repairman	54	"

932

A	Davison Catherine M—†	9	housekeeper	54	"
B	Scipione Alfred D	9	metalworker	37	"
C	Scipione Grace V—†	9	housewife	33	"
D	O'Hearn Katharine E—†	11	housekeeper	86	"
E	O'Hearn Katharine E—†	11	pharmacist	49	"
F	O'Hearn Mary M—†	11	teacher	51	
G	O'Hearn William W	11	U S A	43	
H	Saliba Elizabeth K—†	12	housewife	30	"
K	Saliba Ned J	12	optometrist	33	"
L	Cottle Clara V—†	15	at home	68	"
M	Cottle George T	15	manager	65	"

Copley Street—Continued

N	Cottle Louise M—†	15	at home	71	here
o	Cottle Phoebe C—†	15	housekeeper	65	"

Dalrymple Street

P	Hession Charlotte M—†	4	housewife	73	here
R	Hession Henry M	4	retired	72	"
S	Schmuck Erwin	4	clerk	64	"
T	Schmuck Erwin, jr	4	student	23	
U	Schmuck Johanna B—†	4	housewife	59	"
V	Fitzgerald James P	4	operator	30	"
W	Fitzgerald Margaret—†	4	housewife	32	"
X	McGinnis Annie—†	4	at home	71	
Y	McGinnis Robert A	4	manager	30	"
Z	Franz Edward J	5	shipper	46	"

933

A	Franz Sabina E—†	5	housewife	60	"
B	Antonowitz Nellie—†	5	"	50	
C	Antonowitz Walter	5	gardener	51	"
D	Keaveney Joseph R	6	U S N	28	
E	Keaveney Josephine—†	6	nurse	24	"
F	Egersheim Adriana J—†	6	housewife	49	"
G	Egersheim Carl G	6	artist	54	
H	Murphy Francis G	6	shipper	31	"
K	VanGemert Warren	6	U S N	20	
L	Arnold Ethel V—†	6	nurse	57	
M	Arnold Marjorie—†	6	student	27	
N	Kasper Herman P	7	clerk	53	
o	Blye Mary—†	7	stitcher	65	"
P	Gartland Sabina—†	7	saleswoman	49	"
R	Kasper Margaret E—†	7	housewife	56	"
S	Wolfrum Alice C—†	10	"	41	
T	Wolfrum Carl A	10	engineer	40	"
U	Condon Christine—†	10	housewife	58	"
V	Lehman Louis	10	factoryworker	41	"
W	Lehman Margaret—†	10	housewife	39	"
X	Hasink George	11	laborer	53	100 Rossmore rd
Y	Hasink Magdalena—†	11	cook	51	100 "
Z	Lako Catherine—†	11	hairdresser	31	100 "

934

A	Lako William	11	U S A	36	100 '

Dalrymple Street—Continued

B	Starr Bernard	11	supervisor	41	here
C	Starr Wilma—†	11	housewife	37	"
D	McPartlan Alice—†	11	"	25	"
E	McPartlan Patrick	11	laborer	36	"
F	Finnegan George E	12	boilermaker	48	"
G	Finnegan George E, jr	12	U S M C	23	"
H	Finnegan Hannah—†	12	housewife	47	"
K	Sawdy James	12	U S M C	25	687 Walk Hill
L	Sawdy Rita—†	12	nurse	25	here
M	Herlihy Michael	12	laborer	40	"
N	Herlihy Norah—†	12	housewife	33	"
O	Dorney Caroline J—†	12	secretary	27	"
P	Dorney Caroline W—†	12	waitress	44	"
R	Neumann Dorothy E—†	14	secretary	23	"
S	Neumann Edith M—†	14	housewife	49	"
T	Neumann Harry L	14	mechanic	54	"
U	Haussler Irwin J	14	machinist	48	Quincy
V	Haussler Margaret M—†	14	housewife	52	"
W	Caskie Elise—†	14	"	82	here
X	Caskie John	14	retired	83	"
Y	Moriarty Daniel F	15	bricklayer	42	"
Z	Moriarty Mary R—†	15	housewife	40	"

935

A	Mulhern Frederick F	15	U S N	21	
B	Mulhern Harold J	15	clerk	38	"
C	Foley Mabel—†	15	housewife	51	"
D	Foley Peter A	15	chauffeur	58	"
E	MacDonald Irene—†	15	housewife	41	"
F	MacDonald Peter J	15	shipper	42	
G	Allgaier John	16	laborer	54	
K	Allgaier Marie E—†	16	manager	22	"
H	Allgaier Mary—†	16	housewife	51	"
L	Wolfrum Adam	16	loomfixer	68	"
M	Wolfrum Sophie—†	16	housewife	71	"
N	Strick Margaret—†	16	"	42	
O	Strick Rudolph P	16	machinist	47	"
P	Starr Anna—†	17	supervisor	44	"
R	Starr James H	17	operator	45	"
S	Perkins Edward R	17	printer	50	
T	Perkins Margaret M—†	17	housewife	38	"
U	Tingus Constantine G	17	burner	34	

Page.	Letter.	FULL NAME.	Residence, Jan. 1, 1946.	Occupation.	Supposed Age.	Reported Residence, Jan. 1, 1945. Street and Number.

Dalrymple Street—Continued

v	Tingus Mimi T—†	17	housewife	33	here
w	West Joseph E	18	custodian	53	"
x	West Olga A—†	18	housewife	50	"
y	West Warren W	18	student	21	"
z	Anderson Arthur O	18	chauffeur	45	"

936

a	Anderson Dorothy C—†	18	housewife	36	"
b	Rooney John H	18	pressman	53	"
c	Rooney Lillian T—†	18	housewife	40	"
d	Brennan Alice—†	20	stenographer	29	"
e	Brennan Mary—†	20	housewife	74	"
f	Brennan Walter J	20	clerk	37	
g	Shea Margaret—†	20	packer	42	
h	Mills Daniel A	20	accountant	28	"
k	Mills Francis J	20	clerk	58	
l	Mills Katherine V—†	20	housewife	65	"
m	Rau Joseph F	20	retired	78	
n	Rau Louise W—†	20	factoryworker	46	"
o	Rau Wilhelmina—†	20	housewife	70	"
p	Carty Agnes—†	22	bookkeeper	20	"
r	Carty Eleanor—†	22	secretary	20	"
s	Carty John	22	repairman	56	"
t	Carty John J	22	clerk	28	
u	Carty Mary E—†	22	housewife	50	"
v	Carty Rita—†	22	secretary	23	"
w	Carty Thomas	22	repairman	26	"
x	Griffin Gertrude—†	22	hairdresser	38	"
y	Connolly Delia—†	22	housewife	54	"
z	Connolly James	22	U S A	30	"

937

a	Connolly John	22	boilermaker	60	"
b	Connolly Joseph	22	U S N	23	"
c	Connolly Margaret—†	22	operator	25	"
d	MacLeod Dolly—†	23	waitress	41	"
e	Martin Edgar W	23	steelworker	34	"
f	Martin Margaret I—†	23	housewife	34	"
g	Barbour George	23	laborer	61	
h	Barbour George T	23	"	25	
k	Barbour Joseph J	23	accountant	25	"
l	Barbour Margaret—†	23	housewife	58	"
m	McHugh Charles J	23	manager	38	"

Dalrymple Street—Continued

N	McHugh Frances L—†	23	housewife	33	here	
O	Sheridan Louise L—†	24	housekeeper	34	5A Adams Circle	
P	Schumann Ada M—†	24	housewife	70	here	
R	Schumann Frederick	24	clerk	70	"	
S	Stone Lydia M—†	24	domestic	74	"	
T	Enders Marie—†	24	at home	75	"	
U	O'Rourke Lena—†	24	saleswoman	40	"	
V	Englemann Lillian—†	25	housewife	35	"	
W	Englemann Robert T	25	electrician	35	"	
X	Cronin Alice—†	25	housewife	35	"	
Y	Cronin Philip	25	clerk	38		
Z	Harrington Mary P—†	25	housewife	35	"	

938

A	Harrington William A	25	mechanic	36	"	
B	Campbell Hannah E—†	26	secretary	38	"	
C	Campbell Mary J—†	26	at home	67	"	
D	Campbell Ralph J	26	executive	25	"	
E	Dwyer James E	26	agent	38		
F	Dwyer Mary C—†	26	housewife	40	"	
G	Quigley Catherine—†	26	"	69		
H	Quigley Francis A	26	mechanic	46	"	
K	Vail Mary J—†	26	housewife	48	"	
L	Vail Maurice F	26	dispatcher	55	"	
M	Clarke Anne—†	26	housewife	64	"	
N	Clarke Francis	26	salesman	29	"	
O	Clarke James	26	U S A	30		
P	Clarke Joseph	26	clerk	33		
R	Clarke Owen	26	watchman	64	"	
S	Clarke Owen L	26	clerk	31		
T	Matthews Arthur R	28	manager	42	"	
U	Matthews Margaret L—†	28	housewife	36	"	
V	Coffey Edward	28	foreman	44	"	
W	Coffey Margaret—†	28	housewife	30	"	
X	Benkart Frank	28	machinist	59	"	
Y	Benkart Isabel—†	28	housewife	57	"	
Z	Keenan Margaret—†	29	"	37		

939

A	Keenan Michael	29	manager	38	"	
B	McDonald Ann M—†	29	housewife	33	"	
C	McDonald Peter S	29	chauffeur	39	"	
D	McViney Howard	29	policeman	41	"	

Dalrymple Street—Continued

E	McViney Mary—†	29	housewife	37	here
F	Mangone Joseph	30	inspector	56	"
G	McCarthy Virginia—†	30	housewife	28	"
H	McCarthy William	30	painter	32	
K	Tower Harold W	30	shipper	50	"
L	Tower Ruth—†	30	housewife	48	"
M	Olson Gustave	30	mechanic	74	"
N	Olson Hilda A—†	30	housewife	63	"
O	Olson June M—†	30	stenographer	27	"
P	Browne Arthur W	31	clerk	26	"
R	Browne Emma L—†	31	housewife	25	46 School
S	*Drabentowicz Ignac	31	shipper	52	46 "
T	*Drabentowicz Louise—†	31	housewife	54	46 "
U	Saville Josephine—†	33	"	33	25 Tower
V	Saville Sydney	33	expeditor	35	25 "
W	Knowland Arthur K	35	clerk	41	here
X	Knowland Susanna M—†	35	housewife	38	"
Y	Marshall Ephraim	35	carpenter	69	"
Z	Mangan Margaret—†	36	at home	71	"

940

A	Mangan William K	36	machinist	67	"
B	Scipione Guerino F	36	policeman	30	"
C	Scipione Mary A—†	36	housewife	26	"
D	Johnson Carl I	36	foreman	38	"
E	Johnson Margaret M—†	36	housewife	38	"
F	Bolingbroke Emily—†	36	"	31	
G	Bolingbroke Richard	36	mechanic	31	"
H	Generazzo Francis	36	shoeworker	39	"
K	Generazzo Gertrude—†	36	housewife	35	"
L	Logan Beatrice—†	36	"	39	
M	Logan John	36	laborer	42	
N	Harroun Elaine—†	37	operator	20	"
O	Harroun Harriet—†	37	housewife	38	"
P	Harroun William	37	inspector	41	"
R	Gurley Margaret E—†	39	housewife	37	"
S	Gurley Patrick J	39	fireman	41	
T	Callela Angelo	39	shipper	39	
U	Callela Elmer	39	upholsterer	36	"
V	Callela Mary—†	39	at home	55	..
W	Smith George A	39	roofer	36	
X	Smith Philomena M—†	39	factoryworker	35	"

Page.	Letter.	FULL NAME.	Residence, Jan. 1, 1946.	Occupation.	Supposed Age.	Reported Residence, Jan. 1, 1945. Street and Number.

Dalrymple Street—Continued

	Y	Murray Andrew J	40	guard	40	here
	z	*Murray Catherine—†	40	housewife	39	"
941						
	A	Murray Thomas J	40	salesman	39	"
	B	Kudrick Eugene	40	welder	32	
	C	Kudrick Sonia—†	40	housewife	30	"
	D	Ostopchuk Katherine—†	40	cook	55	'
	E	Ferguson Charles	40	foreman	40	"
	F	*Ferguson Mary—†	40	housewife	40	"
	G	Pomeranz Bernice—†	43	secretary	20	"
	H	Pomeranz Daniel	43	storekeeper	54	"
	K	*Pomeranz Tillie—†	43	housewife	55	"
	L	Harris Ernest L	43	salesman	49	"
	M	Harris Margaret—†	43	housewife	30	"
	N	Callela Louis	43	roofer	33	
	O	Callela Margaret—†	43	housewife	28	"
	P	Belben Laura H—†	47	"	65	
	R	Belben Rodman G	47	laborer	64	"
	S	Wallace John	47	machinist	36	"
	T	*Wallace Nora—†	47	housewife	36	"
	U	Reardon Bridget—†	47	"	38	
	V	Reardon John J	47	fireman	38	

Egleston Street

	W	Alexander Gertrude—†	10	housewife	21	6 Ashworth pk
	X	Levreault Catherine A—†	10	"	45	here
	Y	Levreault William A	10	technician	43	"
	Z	Brown Harold B	10	laborer	24	"
942						
	A	Brown Rita—†	10	housewife	22	"
	B	Rasmussen Agnes J—†	10	"	48	
	C	Corey Daniel F	11	operator	38	"
	D	Corey Mary J—†	11	housewife	33	"
	E	Shire Edward	11	chauffeur	41	10 Egleston
	F	Shire Ruth—†	11	housewife	37	10 "
	G	Duffy Mary—†	14	"	30	here
	H	Duffy William	14	chauffeur	32	"
	K	Gilson Christina—†	14	housewife	53	"
	L	Gilson Horace M	14	machinist	51	"
	M	Kirstein Frederick E	14	painter	61	

26

Egleston Street—Continued

N	Kirstein Martha C—†	14	housewife	57	here
O	McElhill Frank	15	shopkeeper	52	"
P	McElhill Gertrude—†	15	housewife	45	"
R	McElhill Margaret—†	15	clerk	22	
S	Walsh Beatrice M—†	16	housewife	74	"
T	Walsh Edward	16	messenger	75	"
U	Walsh Patrick E	16	laborer	44	"
V	Cella Emma E—†	16	operator	22	"
W	Cella Gino J	16	machinist	54	"
X	Cella Helen D—†	16	housewife	20	169 Boylston
Y	Cella Henry J	16	driller	24	here
Z	Cella Mary L—†	16	housewife	48	"
z¹	Marsalini Henry A	16	hatter	44	"

943

B	Flaherty Patrick	18	laborer	44	
C	Flaherty Mary—†	18	housewife	34	"
D	Gavin Alice—†	18	clerk	25	
E	Gavin Anne J—†	18	"	27	
F	Gavin Catherine—†	18	"	29	
G	Gavin Edward	18	U S A	24	"
H	O'Neil Margaret—†	18	clerk	45	50 Boylston
K	Bannon Joseph	20	student	27	here
L	Bannon Mary—†	20	housewife	24	"
M	Connolly Delia—†	20	"	57	"
N	Connolly Helen—†	20	clerk	22	
O	Hanley Mary E—†	20	housewife	57	"
P	Hanley William J	20	electrician	58	"
R	Greim George	20	retired	73	
S	Greim Margaret—†	20	housewife	71	"
T	Carten Christine—†	23	nurse	21	
U	Carten Della—†	23	housewife	50	"
V	Carten Leo	23	foreman	49	"
W	DeCoste Harold	23	U S M C	23	"
X	DeCoste Ruth—†	23	housewife	23	"
Y	Seguin Constance—†	24	clerk	20	
Z	Seguin Joseph A	24	laborer	44	

944

A	Seguin Mary L—†	24	housewife	45	"
B	Halmstrom Ethel—†	24	stenographer	37	"
C	Scheufele Irma R—†	26	housewife	36	"
D	Scheufele William R	26	guard	38	

Egleston Street—Continued

E	McDermott Evelyn—†	26	housewife	37	30 Montebello rd
F	McDermott Thomas L	26	brewer	38	30 "
H	Broderick Helene—†	27	winder	60	here
K	Giancola John	27	engineer	56	"
L	House Horatio E	27	machinist	63	"
M	Kelliher Anna—†	27	housewife	46	"
N	Kelliher Francis M	27	salesman	46	"
O	Matthei Bernhard	30	engineer	39	"
P	Matthei Evelyn R—†	30	housewife	34	"
R	Bacher Elizabeth—†	30	"	73	
S	Schleich Charles	30	machinist	47	"
T	Jefferds Susan B—†	30	housewife	76	"
U	Pforte Elizabeth H—†	34	clerk	26	
V	Pforte Helen E—†	34	housewife	61	"
W	Pforte Robert J	34	mixer	62	"
X	Burns Gladys—†	34	clerk	26	"
Y	Burns Lulu—†	34	housewife	58	"
Z	Burns Phyllis—†	34	clerk	23	

945

A	Somes Caroline—†	34	housewife	75	"
B	Tardiff Arthur O	34	machinist	55	"
C	Tardiff Eva M—†	34	housewife	57	"
D	Timmermon Joseph H	34	maintenance	33	"
E	Timmermon Rita L—†	34	housewife	27	"

Germania Street

F	Mahoney Frances—†	4	grinder	36	here
G	Ward Charles H	4	painter	32	"
H	Ward Eleanor B—†	4	housewife	29	"
K	Willwerth John C	4	shipfitter	22	27 Brookside av
L	Lynch Jean—†	4	storekeeper	57	here
M	Lynch Jean—†	4	clerk	20	"
N	Lynch William	4	metalworker	55	"
O	Nagoe Helen—†	6	housewife	49	Wash'n D C
P	Buckley Anne M—†	6	accountant	22	here
R	Buckley Edward F	6	checker	64	"
S	Buckley Frances L—†	6	housewife	50	"
T	Buckley William X	6	U S A	21	
V	Roy Janet—†	7	housewife	50	"
W	Kisby Ernest H	7	machinist	52	"

Germania Street—Continued

x	Kisby Ethel—†	7	housewife	48	here
y	Canavan Ann—†	8	bookkeeper	21	"
z	Canavan Joseph F	8	U S A	23	"

946

A	Canavan Mary—†	8	housewife	49	"
B	Canavan Mary F—†	8	operator	26	"
c	Canavan Thomas	8	clerk	60	
D	Barrett Margaret E—†	8	housewife	47	"
E	Barrett Patrick J	8	meatcutter	49	"
F	MacDonald Alexander W	8	laborer	48	
G	*MacDonald Catherine—†	8	domestic	73	"
H	MacDonald Gertrude—†	8	"	42	
K	MacDonald Gertrude—†	8	stenographer	20	"
L	MacDonald Mary—†	8	"	23	"
M	Messina Claire—†	9	factoryworker	23	"
N	Messina Dominic W	9	mechanic	26	"
o	Punchard Katherine M—†	9	clerk	27	1½ Cardington
P	Punchard William	9	janitor	67	1½ "
R	Punchard William G	9	chauffeur	22	1½ "
s	O'Neil Mary K—†	12	housewife	39	here
T	O'Neil Thomas	12	chauffeur	45	"
U	*Lynch Catherine—†	12	housewife	64	"
v	McManus Mary—†	12	at home	67	"
w	Tatro Clarence J	12	brewer	46	
x	Tatro Helen G—†	12	housewife	45	"
Y	Powers Mary M—†	14	"	33	
z	Powers Thomas J	14	brewer	36	

947

A	Rightmyer Blanche A—†	14	housewife	34	"
B	Rightmyer Edward C	14	machinist	41	"
c	Johnston Catherine J—†	14	housewife	55	"
D	Johnston John J	14	painter	49	
E	Johnston Joseph A	14	U S A	23	
F	Barnes Catherine—†	15	housewife	69	"
G	Barnes John	15	laborer	65	
H	Burke John F	15	operator	38	"
K	Burke Mary A—†	15	housewife	36	"
L	Burke Thomas P	15	electrician	40	"
M	Kloth Herman	15	seaman	42	
N	Thompson Frederick A	15	machinist	49	"
o	*Thompson Mary—†	15	housewife	50	"

29

Page.	Letter.	FULL NAME.	Residence, Jan. 1, 1946.	Occupation.	Supposed Age.	Reported Residence, Jan. 1, 1945. Street and Number.

Germania Street—Continued

	P	Hofnagel Alice—†	17	domestic	42	here
	R	Hofnagel Bridget—†	17	housewife	75	"
	s	Young Frederick W	17	bookbinder	47	"
	T	Young Miriam E—†	17	housewife	37	"
	U	Carney James G	17	clerk	58	
	v	Mills Nellie A—†	17	housekeeper	72	"
	w	Hickey Annie D—†	21	clerk	60	"
	x	Mahoney Hugh	21	shipper	63	"
	Y	O'Brien Lillian R—†	21	housewife	61	"
	z	Jacobs Emma F—†	21	"	40	"

948

| | A | Jacobs John J | 21 | plumber | 46 | " |

Haverford Street

	B	Spellman Ann—†	36	housewife	56	here
	c	Spellman James F	36	laborer	27	"
	D	Spellman Margaret R—†	36	stenographer	24	"
	E	Spellman Michael	36	laborer	58	"
	F	Spellman Catherine—†	38	housewife	56	"
	G	Spellman Edward F	38	motorman	46	"
	H	Spellman Mary W—†	38	bookkeeper	21	"
	K	Licciardi Annie—†	42	housewife	34	"
	L	Licciardi Vincent	42	machinist	37	"
	M	Tringali Guy	42	fisherman	27	24 Chilcott pl
	N	Tringali Mary—†	42	housewife	26	43 Minot
	o	Johnston Lillian—†	44	clerk	55	here
	P	Carter Dorothy—†	44	housewife	21	N Hampshire
	R	Carter Lloyd L	44	laborer	21	4 Lamartine pl
	s	Reagan Frances—†	46	housewife	41	here
	T	*Laffes Peter	46	pedler	69	"
	U	Winslow Claire—†	52	housewife	23	83 Atherton
	x	Winslow Raymond	52	machinist	28	83 "
	v	Camparella Eleanor—†	52	housewife	32	here
	w	Camparella Francis J	52	manager	34	"

949 ## Marmion Street

	B	Chalifoux Otis	44	foreman	47	here
	c	Chalifoux Yvonne—†	44	housewife	35	"
	D	Gorham Martin J	44	foreman	48	"

Marmion Street—Continued

E	Gorham Mary—†	44	housewife	38	here
F	Hufnagel Cecilia—†	51	florist	44	"
G	Hufnagel John J	51	steamfitter	44	"
H	Hufnagel Mary F—†	51	WAC	22	
K	Hussmaul Alfred	54	clerk	52	
L	Hussmaul Emily—†	54	housewife	47	"
M	Johanson Geraldine A—†	55	"	26	
N	Johanson John N	55	clerk	27	
O	Burke James	55	laborer	45	
P	Concannon John	55	clerk	22	
R	Concannon Nora—†	55	saleswoman	48	"
S	Concannon Paul	55	U S A	21	
T	Cady James A	55	clerk	35	
U	Cady Mary A—†	55	housewife	31	"

Porter Street

W	Hartz Forrest	6	electrician	54	129 Boylston
X	Hartz Gladys R—†	6	housewife	47	129 "
Y	*Lundstrom Hilda—†	6	"	53	here
Z	*Lundstrom John L	6	molder	57	"

950

A	Lundstrom Karl	6	repairman	36	"
B	Foster Ruth—†	6	housewife	45	"
C	*McAdams Amelia J—†	8	"	37	
D	McAdams William J	8	operator	38	"
E	Hicks Carrie—†	8	housewife	43	"
F	Hicks William	8	laborer	50	
G	Mullis Arthur E	8	U S A	23	
H	Mullis Harry	8	tailor	63	
K	Mullis Lillie—†	8	housewife	56	"
L	Chatterton Clifton	10	painter	70	
M	Chatterton Lillian M—†	10	housewife	60	"
O	Williams Mary A—†	12	"	71	
R	Mrosk Christina A—†	14	"	73	
U	Himmel Bertha E—†	18	"	64	
V	Himmel George F	18	U S N	21	
W	Himmel John A	18	electrician	28	"
X	Aspacher Arthur	18	printer	21	
Y	Aspacher Clara M—†	18	U S N	24	
Z	Aspacher Martha M—†	18	housewife	52	"

Page	Letter	FULL NAME.	Residence, Jan. 1, 1946.	Occupation.	Supposed Age.	Reported Residence, Jan. 1, 1945. Street and Number.

951
Porter Street—Continued

A	Aspacher William C	18	chauffeur	57	here
B	Green Martha—†	18	seamstress	28	"
C	Hofling Catherine—†	18	housewife	78	"
D	Rist Adolph F	20	foreman	43	"
E	Rist Dorothea—†	20	housewife	39	"
G	Schlotter Dorothea—†	20	storekeeper	65	"

School Street

K	Dennis Elizabeth M—†	104	librarian	27	here
L	Dennis Mary E—†	104	housewife	65	"
M	Green John T	104	clerk	41	"
N	Nixon Annette J—†	104	"	29	
O	Nixon Blanche M—†	104	"	26	
P	Nixon Diana M—†	104	housewife	53	"
R	Nixon John W	104	fireman	53	
S	Casey Matthew	106	retired	60	
T	Reiling Henry	106	realtor	60	
U	Reiling Henry, jr	106	inspector	21	"
V	Bastable Dagmar—†	108	housewife	60	"
W	Bastable John F	108	U S N	24	
X	Bastable Thomas	108	machinist	64	"
Y	Bastable Thomas A	108	technician	40	"
Z	Bastable Wilfred E	108	buffer	38	

952

A	Hurley Joseph J	110	engineer	70	"
B	Hurley Margaret A—†	110	housewife	58	"
C	Maguire Aloysius	110	U S A	25	
D	Towle Burton W	110	laborer	27	
E	Towle Helen M—†	110	clerk	29	
F	Livingston Catherine—†	110	nurse	37	
G	Livingston Robert	110	retired	70	
H	Doherty Francis S	110	clerk	29	
K	Doherty Mary—†	110	housewife	29	"
L	Gillespie Dorothy H—†	112	"	36	
M	Gillespie John J	112	technician	37	"
N	Gillespie Nora M—†	112	housewife	71	"
O	Heine Laurence F	112	U S C G	21	"
P	Weiler Anne V—†	112	housewife	38	"
R	Weiler Joseph F	112	laborer	39	

School Street—Continued

s	Aliberti Joseph	112	painter	36	here
t	Aliberti Vivian—†	112	housewife	31	"
u	Walsh Richard T	112	retired	61	88 Worcester
v	Gormley Henry L	114	merchant	52	here
w	Gormley Margaret F—†	114	housewife	48	"
x	McDonald Stephen	116	laborer	68	"
y	McGinnis John	116	retired	76	"
z	Pollitt Walter	116	"	75	

953

a	Quinlan Austin	116	chauffeur	42	"
b	Quinlan Helen—†	116	housewife	37	"
c	Jennetti Helen—†	120	checker	30	10 Amory ter
d	Jennetti John	120	buffer	36	10 "
e	Bugbee Agnes E—†	142	housewife	63	here
f	Bugbee June A—†	142	inspector	25	"
g	Anderson Elizabeth A—†	142	housewife	58	"
h	Anderson James W	142	hatter	59	
k	Anderson Robert P	142	U S N	20	"
l	Anderson Thomas F	142	brakeman	32	"
m	Danforth Marie—†	142	housewife	26	"
n	McCabe Annie—†	142	clerk	65	
o	Walsh Barbara—†,	142	"	24	
p	Walsh John J	142	"	25	
r	Gilmore William F	154	fireman	54	"
s	Hackett Mary—†	154	housewife	58	"
t	Kelley Katherine E—†	154	tel operator	54	"
u	Kelley James	154	retired	65	"
v	Kelley Joseph C	154	student	23	
w	Kelley Katherine—†	154	housewife	61	"
x	Shea Mary A—†	154	secretary	25	"
y	Shea Russell F	154	undertaker	25	512 Centre
z	Stier Christian J	157	agent	32	here

954

a	Stier Doris M—†	157	typist	27	"
b	Stier Joseph F	157	laborer	25	"
c	Stier Leo J	157	clerk	29	"
d	Stier Mary—†	157	housewife	50	"
e	Stier Rita—†	157	typist	21	
f	Stier William	157	laborer	23	"
g	Cusick James E	158	policeman	46	"
h	Cusick James E jr	158	U S M C	22	"

School Street—Continued

K	Cusick Sybil B—†	158	operator	42	here
L	Chamberlain Bertha—†	158	at home	67	"
M	Sawyer Ella G—†	158	housewife	76	"
N	Duggan Doris—†	165	secretary	21	"
O	Duggan Lorraine—†	165	clerk	20	"
P	Duggan Mary—†	165	"	40	
R	Bennett Dorothy B—†	167	"	23	
S	Bennett Kathleen—†	167	tel operator	24	"
T	Bennett Margaret T—†	167	operator	21	"
U	Walsh Edward J	167	custodian	27	"
V	Walsh Mary—†	167	housewife	29	"
W	Brash Duncan	169	machinist	67	"
X	Coughlin Elizabeth—†	169	clerk	20	
Y	Paschoff Bertha—†	169	at home	55	"
Z	Pauly Eloise—†	169	housewife	69	"

955

A	Provencher Raymond	169	supervisor	45	"
B	Randall Dixie—†	169	operator	40	"
C	Hartwig Eloise—†	171	housewife	38	"
D	Hartwig Kurt P	171	paperhanger	40	"
E	Fletcher Margaret E—†	171	inspector	25	"
F	Schaefer Hubert	171	machinist	63	"
G	Malone Harriet—†	173	waitress	39	"
H	Brown Richard A	173	carpenter	41	10 Westminster av
L	DeLong Ferdinand J	173	electrician	45	here
K	DeLong Margaret A—†	173	housewife	45	"
M	Gray Pauline F—†	173	secretary	21	"
N	Goddard Rae—†	175	housewife	36	"
O	Goddard Robert	175	clerk	36	
P	Glynn Sarah—†	175	laborer	30	"
R	Hambury Anna M—†	175	housewife	58	"
S	Hambury Helen—†	175	clerk	24	
T	Hambury Patrick B	175	machinist	59	"
U	Puleo Concetta—†	176	housewife	68	"
V	Puleo Dominic	176	laborer	28	
W	Puleo Leo	176	"	42	
X	Puleo Stephania—†	176	secretary	26	"
Y	*Hoffman Alfred	176	clerk	25	"
Z	*Hoffman C Aristel—†	176	secretary	23	"
¹Z	*Hoffman Emily—†	176	housewife	52	"

956
School Street—Continued

A	*Hoffman Max	176	retired	56	here
B	Scaletta Anna—†	177	clerk	44	"
C	Scaletta John	177	carpenter	54	"
D	Scaletta Margaret—†	177	clerk	20	
E	Buchta Emma—†	177	housewife	41	"
F	Buchta Max	177	machinist	40	"
G	Carroll Margaret G—†	177	at home	30	"
H	Carroll Mary A—†	177	housewife	78	"
K	Carroll Owen J	177	glazier	40	
L	Carroll Rhea L—†	177	clerk	35	
N	Hopkins Fred E	178	retired	84	"
O	Hopkins Ruth—†	178	wrapper	31	"
M	Miley Ethel—†	178	"	34	
P	Morrill Lillian—†	178	sorter	41	"
R	Schmidt Frederick	179	physician	72	"
S	Schmidt Jean	179	laborer	36	
T	Schmidt Marie C—†	179	housewife	70	"
U	Doerr Michael	179	retired	81	"
V	Doyle Arthur	179	fireman	40	8 Wallace pk
W	Lehman Martha—†	179	housewife	54	here
X	Stockton James	179	engineer	78	Brookline
Y	O'Brien Edward L	180	retired	76	here
Z	O'Brien Francis E	180	breweryworker	43	"

957

A	O'Brien Helen G—†	180	housewife	40	"
B	O'Brien Joseph L	180	brewer	41	"
C	Mitchell Katherine—†	180	secretary	45	"
D	Mitchell Roy E	180	salesman	45	"
E	Carroll Gussie—†	184	housewife	53	"
F	Carroll Leo V	184	operator	54	"
G	Downey Anna A—†	184	housewife	50	"
H	Downey John J	184	steamfitter	56	"
K	Downey John J, jr	184	U S N	22	"
L	Connolly Christopher	184	laborer	53	"
M	Connolly John	184	U S A	25	
N	Connolly Margaret—†	184	housewife	53	"
O	Connolly Mary—†	184	operator	29	"
R	Pickett Edna—†	188	housewife	65	"
S	*Pickett Frederick W	188	retired	71	

Page.	Letter.	FULL NAME.	Residence, Jan. 1, 1946.	Occupation.	Supposed Age.	Reported Residence, Jan. 1, 1945. Street and Number.

School Street—Continued

| | T | Pickett Helen W—† | 188 | secretary | 35 | here |
| | U | Pickett Robert S | 188 | student | 24 | " |

958 Washington Street

	F	Silver Clarence	3135A	janitor	59	here
	G	Silver Marian—†	3135A	housewife	53	"
	H	Terrill Ida—†	3135A	domestic	44	"
	K	Terrill Florence—†	3135A	dressmaker	70	"
	P	Martin Mary—†	3139	laundress	49	"
	R	Ferguson Anna—†	3139	housekeeper	76	"
	S	Ferguson John W	3139	laborer	42	"
	T	Ferguson Peter H	3139	"	43	"
	U	Giragosian John	3139	clerk	22	"
	V	Morris Benjamin	3139	U S A	25	"
	W	Morris Charles	3139	"	27	"
	X	Morris Edward	3139	"	23	"
	Y	Morris John	3139	laborer	29	"
	Z	Morris Josephine—†	3139	housewife	34	"

959

	A	Morris Margaret—†	3139	"	46	
	B	Morris Stanley J	3139	fireman	56	"
	D	Waters Harold	3141	laborer	24	35 School
	E	Waters Teresa—†	3141	housewife	23	35 "
	F	Aymond George L	3141	U S A	28	here
	G	Aymond Irene—†	3141	operator	28	"
	H	Rocha Louise M—†	3141	clerk	24	"
	K	Birnbaum Bessie—†	3141	bookkeeper	24	"
	L	*Birnbaum Fannie—†	3141	housewife	58	"
	M	*Birnbaum Joseph	3141	shoemaker	57	"
	S	Mailhot Dorothy—†	3145	housewife	34	"
	T	Mailhot Wilfred	3145	electrician	39	"
	U	Meehan Andrew	3145	laborer	65	
	V	Richter Edward	3145	foreman	40	"
	W	Richter Helen—†	3145	housewife	39	"
	Z	Drury Christine L—†	3147	"	32	

960

	A	Drury John W	3147	operator	38	"
	B	Williamson Dora E—†	3149	"	44	14 Kempton
	C	Cammack Gordon	3149	repairman	30	here
	D	Cammack Mabel—†	3149	housewife	50	"

Page.	Letter.	FULL NAME.	Residence, Jan. 1, 1946.	Occupation.	Supposed Age.	Reported Residence, Jan. 1, 1945. Street and Number.

Washington Street—Continued

	E	Cammack Philip	3149	painter	28	here
	F	Thompson Thelma—†	3149	clerk	21	3109 Wash'n
	G	Carty Edwina—†	3151	housewife	32	here
	H	Carty Paul L	3151	clerk	35	"
	K	Kavanagh Michael P	3151	mechanic	65	"
	L	Kavanagh Nellie M—†	3151	housewife	69	"
	M	Beninowski Theodore	3151	clerk	21	
	N	Naruszewicz Anna—†	3151	housewife	58	"
	O	Naruszewicz Stanley	3151	baker	69	"
	P	Denekamp Doris—†	3151	housewife	20	3307 Wash'n
	R	Denekamp Herman	3151	U S N	23	29 Kittredge
	S	Rhude Lena—†	3151	clerk	20	Indiana
	T	Kirk Esme A—†	3155	nurse	60	here
	U	Brophy Richard	3155	electrician	39	"
	V	Merrill Dwight F	3155	oiler	34	"
	W	Merrill Gloria C—†	3155	housewife	35	"
	X	McLaughlin Robert J	3157	laborer	41	"
	Y	Chubbuck Leslie M	3157	guard	50	3316 Wash'n
	Z	Chubbuck Leslie M, jr	3157	chauffeur	21	3316 "

961

	A	Chubbuck Marjorie—†	3157	housewife	50	3316 "
	B	Fields Eva M—†	3157	"	24	3316 "
	C	Fields Peter L	3157	welder	33	3316 "

12
1

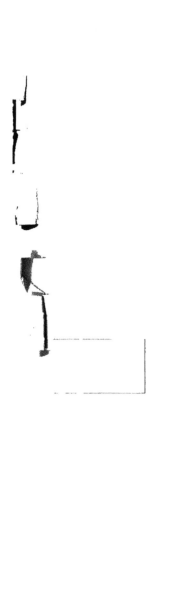

Ward 11–Precinct 10

CITY OF BOSTON

IST OF RESIDENTS
20 YEARS OF AGE AND OVER

(NON-CITIZENS INDICATED BY ASTERISK)
(FEMALES INDICATED BY DAGGER)

AS OF

JANUARY 1, 1946

THOMAS F. SULLIVAN, *Chairman*
FREDERIC E. DOWLING, *Secretary*
WILLIAM A. MOTLEY, JR.
ARTHUR V. COUGHLIN
EVERETT R. PROUT

Listing Board.

CITY OF BOSTON PRINTING DEPARTMENT

Page.	Letter.	Full Name.	Residence, Jan. 1, 1946.	Occupation.	Supposed Age.	Reported Residence, Jan. 1, 1945. Street and Number.

1000

Amory Street

	B	Hinder Frank	244	machinist	53	here
	c*	Hinder Paula—†	244	housewife	52	"
	D	Leidner Alfred	244	U S A	31	"
	E	Doerr Anna—†	246	housewife	54	"
	F	Doerr Elizabeth—†	246	packer	20	
	G	Doerr Ethel—†	246	clerk	20	
	H	Doerr John	246	brewer	55	
	K	Doerr Otto	246	laborer	30	
	L	Norman Barbara H—†	248	at home	52	
	M	Norman Clementine G—†	248	storekeeper	62	"
	N	Mitchell Edwin	248	janitor	74	"
	o	Mitchell Jessie—†	248	housewife	70	"
	P	Alber Gustav T	250	chauffeur	40	"
	R	Alber Marguerite E—†	250	bookkeeper	37	"
	s	Rist Edward B	250	checker	24	"
	T	Fink Ethel—†	252	housewife	22	"
	U	Fink Robert	252	U S N	23	
	v	Getz Charles	252	clerk	57	
	w	Getz Freda—†	252	housewife	56	"
	x	Cahill Frank	252	bottler	35	"
	Y	Cahill Ruth—†	252	housewife	32	"
	z	Hand Arthur	254	social worker	24	18 Egleston

1001

	A	Hand Marie—†	254	"	24	18 "
	B	Backman Edwin	254	machinist	25	70 School
	c	Backman Elizabeth—†	254	coilwinder	23	66 Boylston
	D	McLeod John	256	retired	75	here
	E	McLeod Julia—†	256	housewife	75	"
	F	Robshaw Margaret—†	256	domestic	49	"
	G	Ming Edith—†	258	housewife	65	"
	H	Lysle Almida—†	258	"	57	"
	K	Clark Fred	260	laborer	43	254 Amory
	L	MacNeill Annie—†	264	housewife	68	here
	M	MacNeill Mary—†	264	stenographer	33	"
	o	Raven Amanda—†	266	housewife	47	Brookline
	P	Raven Carl	266	filler	54	521 Mass av
	R	Danforth Clifford	266	machinist	52	here
	s	Danforth Elizabeth—†	266	housewife	83	"
	w	Treloar Esther—†	280	"	58	"
	x	Smith Harriet—†	280	"	40	

2

Amory Street—Continued

Y	Smith Warren E, jr	280	bricklayer	41	here
z	Smith Warren E, 3d	280	U S N	20	"

1002

A	Ouellette Mary C—†	282	housewife	59	"
B	Ouellette Omer	282	carpenter	62	"
c	Ouellette Omer J	282	U S N	22	"
D	Jones Albion	282	chauffeur	41	3150 Wash'n
E	Jones Gwendolyn—†	282	housewife	36	3150 "
F	Rankin Arthur	282	laborer	29	3150 "
G	Ellis Ernest	284	painter	47	here
H	Harding Bridie—†	286	housewife	51	"
K	Shea James D	286	dishwasher	38	56 Neponset av
L	Shea Nora—†	286	housewife	71	56 "
M	Turner Grace E—†	286	"	35	here
N	Willock Thomas	288	chauffeur	35	28 Sagamore
o	Willock Vanessa S—†	288	housewife	24	Beverly
P	Baker Helen R—†	288	"	35	10 Cable
R	Slyva Ruth J—†	288	inspector	26	here
s	Smith Antoinette—†	288	housewife	59	"
T	DeRosa Estelle—†	290	dressmaker	52	"
U	DeRosa John	290	seaman	28	
v	DeRosa Joseph	290	painter	54	
w	May Hubert A	292	clerk	40	
x	May Margaret—†	292	housewife	36	"
Y	May John	292	laborer	42	"
z	Brehm Natalie—†	296	checker	23	51 Rockvale Cir

1003

A	Burkhardt John	296	mover	49	here
B	Rankin Olive—†	296	housewife	30	"
c	Alberg Alice C—†	300	"	51	"
D	Alberg Frederick L	300	packer	56	"
E	VanPutten Alice—†	300	stenographer	25	"
F	VanPutten William	300	decorator	30	"
G	Leonard James	300	bottler	29	
H	Leonard Mary—†	300	housewife	28	"
K	Hanley Joseph M	304	shipper	32	
L	Hanley Virginia—†	304	housewife	30	"
M	Hanley Bridget—†	308	"	65	"
N	Hanley Mary—†	308	"	29	5 Marlowe
o	Hanley Matthew	308	U S N	37	here
P	Walsh Mary J—†	312	housewife	45	"

Amory Street—Continued

R	Walsh Michael F	312	chauffeur	44	here
S	Arensberg Lenore—†	314	secretary	21	"
T	Arensberg Nora—†	314	operator	41	"
U	Devaney Bridget—†	314	housewife	72	65 Averton
V	*Maher Angelina—†	314	waitress	41	here
W	Maher William	314	chauffeur	55	"
X	Burns Lavinia—†	314	housewife	69	"
Y	Joaquin Catherine—†	314	"	37	
Z	Joaquin Francis	314	chauffeur	43	"

1004

A	McDonough Edward	314	manager	24	"
B	Knapp Alice—†	320	housewife	43	"
C	*Almon Frances—†	320	"	53	
D	McDonald Bernard	320	laborer	30	
E	Hough Sarah—†	320	housewife	26	"
F	McKay Bernard	320	welder	31	
G	McKay Catherine—†	320	housewife	58	"
H	Donovan Mary—†	322	"	55	372 Amory
K	Donovan Timothy	322	inspector	34	372 "
L	Hardcastle James	322	laborer	46	here
M	Hardcastle John	322	"	39	"
N	Hardcastle Joseph	322	"	36	"
O	Hardcastle Margaret—†	322	housewife	69	"
P	Hardcastle Margaret F—†	322	operator	42	"
R	Duncan Murray	324	manager	72	"
S	*Haasis Margaret—†	332	folder	34	
T	Smithers Annie—†	332	housewife	73	"
U	Harrington Ella D—†	332	seamstress	47	5 Cazenove
V	Harrington Shirley A—†	332	operator	20	5 "
W	Manganis Marguerite—†	334	housewife	31	here
X	Manganis Peter	334	cook	54	"
Y	Flanagan Michael P	336	repairman	45	460 Parker
Z	Flanagan Rachel—†	336	housewife	56	460 "

1005

A	Gray Burton A	336	messenger	25	460 "
B	Tierney Jeannette—†	336	housewife	50	here
C	Merloughi Fortunata—†	342	"	30	"
D	Merloughi Frank	342	pipefitter	47	"
E	Carey Catherine—†	342	housewife	70	40 Brookside av
F	Finley Catherine—†	342	"	47	here
G	Finley Terrence L	342	laborer	48	"

Amory Street—Continued

H	Arnold Herbert W	342	mechanic	48	here
K	*Arnold Stella A—†	342	housewife	48	"
L	Tajima George S	350	mechanic	34	Milton
M	Tajima Hanako—†	350	housewife	28	Idaho
N	Topaski Olga—†	350	"	37	here
O	Topaski Theodore	350	watchman	37	"
P	Keegan James	350	carpenter	57	"
R	Keegan Mary—†	350	housewife	53	"
S	Foley Madeline—†	352	"	43	
T	Foley Maurice	352	fireman	44	"
U	Florek Floryan	352	molder	61	5 Mohawk
V	Florek Mary—†	352	housewife	59	here
W	Carey Helen—†	352	"	36	"
X	Carey John J	352	U S A	37	"
Y	Pecci Margaret—†	352	housewife	29	"
Z	Pecci Otillio	352	U S A	30	

1006

B	Mason George	384	molder	26	4 Jess
C	Mason Irving	384	carpenter	52	4 "
D	Mason Irving, jr	384	molder	24	4 "
E	Mason James	384	"	27	4 "
F	Mason Martha—†	384	housewife	50	4 "
G	Coyne Harry	384	painter	58	N Hampshire
H	Coyne Violet—†	384	housewife	48	"
K	Shuttleworth Ruth—†	384	"	24	112 Pleasant
L	Shuttleworth William	384	radio mechanic	25	112 "
M	*Barrett Catherine—†	384	housewife	35	17 Neponset av
N	Barrett Edward F	384	laborer	40	17 "
O	Fisher John	384	decorator	34	Dedham
P	Joyce Lillian—†	384	housewife	31	"
R	Tisot Constance—†	384	"	29	Brookline
S	Tisot John D	384	U S N	32	"
T	Summerhayes Dorothy—†	384	housewife	25	"
U	Summerhayes Robert	384	chauffeur	25	"
V	Arnold Caroline—†	384	housewife	32	Rhode Island
W	Arnold Henry F	384	machinist	40	"
X	Kucharski Catherine—†	384	housewife	37	11 Highland av
Y	Kucharski Joseph	384	machinist	39	11 "
Z	Cunniff Mary—†	384	housewife	26	Brookline

1007

A	Cunniff Michael	384	shipper	26	

Amory Street—Continued

B	Donlan Agnes M—†	384	housewife	22	34 Hall
C	Donlan Martin E, jr	384	laborer	22	34 "
D	Coffin George E	384	chauffeur	29	1A Haynes pk
E	Coffin Mary V—†	384	housewife	23	1A "
F	Schmoker Marjorie P—†	384	"	24	3 Woolsey sq
G	Schmoker Raymond A	384	electrotyper	25	3 "
H	Ellsworth James	384	conductor	49	Brookline
K	Gaylord Fredricka—†	384	housewife	27	85 Call
L	Gaylord Irving	384	clerk	42	85 "
M	Leonard Evelyn F—†	384	housewife	39	20 Ingleside
N	Leonard Thomas	384	chauffeur	36	20 "
O	Stanley Jessie—†	392	housewife	29	here
P	Stanley Joseph	392	mechanic	31	"
R	Stanley Bessie—†	392	housewife	42	"
S	Stanley Margaret—†	392	"	62	
T	Stanley William P	392	laborer	37	
W	Quinn David	394	printer	50	
X	Quinn Margaret T—†	394	operator	24	"
Y	Quinn Sarah A—†	394	housewife	45	"
Z	Stanley Mary—†	402	"	28	

1008

A	Stanley William V	402	laborer	32	"
B	Stanley Beatrice—†	402	housewife	38	"
C	Stanley Cornelius V	402	laborer	39	"
D	Stober Gertrude—†	404	operator	62	28 Mozart
E	*Buote Bertha A—†	404	housewife	43	here
F	*Buote George H	404	painter	42	"
G	Buote George L	404	U S N	20	"
H	Cauldwell Dorothy E—†	404	housewife	49	"
K	Cauldwell Dorothy E—†	404	operator	25	"
L	Coogen Ada—†	406	matron	50	
M	Cantoni Mary R—†	406	housewife	60	"
N	McGregor Barbara—†	408	"	31	85 Monument
O	McGregor David	408	molder	36	85 "
P	Gately Thomas	408	laborer	57	394 Amory
R	Rossborough Charles B	408	mechanic	42	here
S	Rossborough Josephine—†	408	housewife	41	"
T	Blake Marie H—†	408	"	50	"
U	DeMarco Harry	408	millwright	56	"
V	*Wagner Lawrence	412	painter	49	"
W	*Wagner Mabel—†	412	housewife	40	"

Page	Letter	Full Name.	Residence, Jan. 1, 1946.	Occupation.	Supposed Age.	Reported Residence, Jan. 1, 1945. Street and Number.

Amory Street—Continued

	z	Higgins James M	440	laborer	44	N Hampshire
1009						
	A	Higgins Mary E—†	440	housewife	41	"
	B	Schroeder Fred A	440	U S N	21	"

Brookside Avenue

	c	Anderson Charles A	21	brewer	50	here
	D	Anderson Hazel—†	21	housewife	49	"
	E	Anderson Pearl—†	21	waitress	25	"
	F	McCormick Catherine M–†	27	housewife	60	"
	G	McCormick John W	27	U S A	25	
	H	Riordan Agnes—†	27	stenographer	40	"
	K	Keane Mary—†	27	housewife	36	15 Elm Hill av
	L	*Keane Patrick	27	laborer	43	Maine
	M	Milliard Caroline W—†	29	housewife	68	here
	N	Milliard Joseph W	29	printer	59	"
	o	Reardon Mary B—†	29	housewife	39	"
	P	Bagley Elizabeth B—†	29	stenographer	22	"
	R	Bagley John T	29	motorman	28	"
	s	O'Brien Mary T—†	29	housewife	54	"
	T	O'Brien Thomas J	29	foreman	54	"
	U	Walraven Adrian D	29	metalsmith	24	"
	V	Walraven Rita M—†	29	housewife	21	"
	w	McCarthy Dennis J	33	supt	44	
	x	McCarthy Margaret M—†	33	housewife	43	"
	Y	Sullivan Delia M—†	33	"	52	
	z	Sullivan Elizabeth C—†	33	stenographer	22	"
1010						
	A	Sullivan Harry A	33	steamfitter	52	"
	B	Sullivan Harry P	33	U S A	26	
	c	Sullivan Rita M—†	33	stenographer	25	"
	D	Sullivan William E	33	U S A	24	"
	E	Egan Mabel D—†	33	seamstress	50	"
	F	Egan Paul G	33	U S A	27	
	G	Brenckle Ernest	53	laborer	27	
	H	Brenckle Mildred—†	53	housewife	26	"
	K	Mullen Frederick W	53	B F D	55	
	L	Reynolds Robert	53	U S A	25	
	M	Reynolds Rosa G—†	53	housekeeper	43	"
	N	Campbell Anthony A	56	chauffeur	34	"

Page.	Letter.	Full Name.	Residence, Jan. 1, 1946.	Occupation.	Supposed Age.	Reported Residence, Jan. 1, 1945. Street and Number.

Brookside Avenue—Continued

	o	Campbell Geraldine F—†	56	housewife	21	here
	p	Askowski Ann—†	56	"	65	"
	r	Askowski John	56	laborer	66	"
	s	Shubster Mary T—†	56	supervisor	32	"
	t	Corleto Eleanor—†	56	housewife	25	"
	u	Richard Agnes B—†	56	"	48	
	v	Richard Edmund J	56	laborer	48	
	w	Richard Mary C—†	56	operator	22	"
	x	Richard Theresa F—†	56	packer	21	
	y	Richard William J	56	U S N	20	

1011

	a	Alconada Dorothy—†	58	operator	37	"
	b	Alconada Joseph	58.	laborer	40	
	c	O'Brien Alma M—†	58	housewife	37	"
	d	O'Brien William F	58	guard	42	"
	e	Mangan Mary A—†	58	housewife	31	"
	f	Mangan William A	58	clerk	40	
	g	O'Connor Bridget M—†	60	housewife	46	"
	h	O'Connor Michael J	60	shipper	45	
	k	Benham Marion—†	60	stenographer	25	"
	l	Benham Richard	60	chauffeur	27	New York
	m	*Joyce Mary A—†	60	housewife	58	here
	n	Gotovich Marion J	60	operator	32	"
	o	Gotovich Mary A—†	60	housewife	37	"
	r	Diggins Joan—†	62	"	44	
	s	Diggins John J	62	policeman	43	"
	t	McLeod Anna J—†	62	housewife	55	"
	u	McLeod John E	62	baker	24	
	v	McLeod Malcolm R	·62	mechanic	56	"
	w	Doherty John J	62	policeman	41	2 Derne
	x	Doherty Margaret D—†	62	housewife	26	Belmont
	z	Clark Lillian—†	64	seamstress	27	here

1012

	a	Conners Joseph M	64	U S A	22	
	b	Conners Lillian—†	64	housewife	44	"
	c	Conners Robert J	64	U S N	20	
	d	Gauthier Dorothy E—†	64	housewife	25	"
	e	Gauthier Roland E	64	baker	26	
	f	*Hansen Annie—†	64	housewife	47	"
	g	Hansen John A	64	U S A	25	3235 Wash'n
	k	Carrabis James	66	chauffeur	27	18 Cooper

Brookside Avenue—Continued

	Letter	Full Name	Residence	Occupation	Age	Reported Residence
	L	Carrabis Margaret—†	66	housewife	24	18 Cooper
	M	Campbell Dorothea E—†	66	"	31	here
	N	Campbell Joseph D	66	chauffeur	42	"
	O	Grant Henry L	66	porter	60	"
	P	Grant James P	66	operator	25	"
	R	Grant Margaret C—†	66	clerk	22	
	S	Grant Nora J—†	66	housewife	50	"
	T	Canning Florence—†	68	"	45	
	U	Canning Walter H	68	laborer	49	
	V	Foley James D	68	janitor	63	
	W	Foley Mary E—†	68	housekeeper	21	"
	X	Foley Thomas W	68	U S N	21	"
	Y	Kelley Joseph	68	painter	38	
	Z	Kelley Mary—†	68	housewife	37	"
		1013				
	A	Gordon Pauline—†	70		32	29 Custer
	B	McLaughlin Mary—†	70	"	46	here
	C	McLaughlin Neil	70	checker	44	"
	D	Halder Catherine M—†	70	housewife	33	12 Marmion
	E	Halder George W	70	engineer	38	14 Gay Head
	F	Reilly Bernard F	79	electrician	48	here
	G	Reilly Bernard F, jr	79	U S A	22	"
	H	Reilly Cecelia J—†	79	housewife	50	"
	K	Reilly Rose C—†	79	storekeeper	38	"
	L	Reilly Virginia M—†	79	operator	21	"
	M	Murray Thomas E	81	instructor	55	"
	N	Stone Carl P	81	repairman	49	"
	O	Stone Helen R—†	81	housewife	49	"
	P	Stone Rose C—†	81	clerk	21	
	R	McGrath Ann E—†	87	housewife	56	"
	S	McGrath Dennis P	87	guard	56	
	T	McGrath John B	87	U S A	21	"
	U	Monahan Helen M—†	87	housewife	33	"
	V	Trowbridge Charlotte F—†	89	"	36	
	W	Trowbridge Frederick R	89	U S N	37	
	Y	Ferdinand Mary—†	91	housewife	36	"
	Z	Morgan Anthony T	91	clerk	31	
		1014				
	A	Morgan Dominick F	91	motorman	59	"
	B	Morgan Frank G	91	factoryworker	26	"
	C	Morgan Henrietta—†	91	housewife	59	"

9

Brookside Avenue—Continued

D	Morgan John G	91	clerk	22	here
E	Morgan Manuel G	91	U S A	28	"
F	Doyle John F	91	orderly	40	"
G	Tobin Mary E—†	91	housewife	47	"
H	Tobin Thomas M	91	engineer	52	"
K	Killion John F	93	U S M C	21	666 Metropolitan av
L	Killion Mary C—†	93	operator	42	666 "
M	Stewart Daniel	93	boilermaker	46	here
N	Stewart Lottie F—†	93	housewife	40	"
O	Latendorf Fred C	94	operator	51	"
P	Latendorf Frederick A	94	U S A	22	
R	Latendorf Valentine I—†	94	housewife	51	"
S	Huebner Kate E—†	94	"	49	54 Walnut av
T	Huebner Olga M—†	94	at home	77	here
U	Huebner William J	94	painter	50	54 Walnut av
V	Nemet Harriet A—†	95	packer	21	here
W	Nemet Henry	95	chauffeur	49	"
X	Nemet Henry G	95	"	23	"
Y	Nemet Mary A—†	95	housewife	46	"
Z	Nemet Russell W	95	U S A	20	

1015

A	Ahern Cornelius W	97	laborer	22	
B	Ahern Donald E	97	student	20	
C	Ahern Edward M	97	laborer	24	
D	Ahern John J	97	clerk	56	
E	Ahern John J, jr	97	U S A	26	
F	Ahern Margaret M—†	97	housewife	48	"
G	Gately Bertha L—†	rear 97	"	44	
H	Gately John F	" 97	laborer	52	
L	Peterson Harold F	98	machinist	24	"
M	Peterson Joseph E	98	diemaker	58	"
N	Peterson Leslie J	98	U S A	27	108 Brookside av
O	Peterson Marie A—†	98	housewife	52	here
R	Barth Henry W	99	mechanic	24	"
S	Barth Martha L—†	99	housewife	54	"
T	Barth Paul	99	painter	58	"
U	Martin Harold G, jr	99	chauffeur	23	"
V	Martin Louise A—†	99	inspector	24	"
W	McLaughlin Frank J	103	longshoreman	43	"
X	McLaughlin Valeria M—†	103	housewife	44	"
Y	Finnity Gerald J	103	laborer	46	

Page	Letter	Full Name.	Residence, Jan. 1, 1946.	Occupation.	Supposed Age.	Reported Residence, Jan. 1, 1945. Street and Number.

Brookside Avenue—Continued

	z	Finnity Lena M—†	103	bookkeeper	54	here
1016						
	A	Finnity Margaret E—†	103	housewife	83	"
	B	Nielsen Emma—†	105	"	49	
	C	Nielsen Paul A	105	U S N	22	"
	D	Tagliera Eliza—†	105	factoryworker	37	"
	E	Tagliera Gene	105	operator	35	"
	F	Wille Olga—†	105	housewife	76	"
	G	Bennett Helen W—†	108	"	48	
	H	Bennett Joseph I	108	machinist	43	"
	K	Philbrook Annie—†	108	inspector	63	"
	L	Kirchenbauer George	108	laborer	52	
	M	Crowell Kenneth	112	estimator	51	"
	N	Roy Joseph A	112	retired	69	
	O	Roy Marion A—†	112	housewife	72	"
	P	Townsend Dorothy M—†	112	"	49	
	R	Townsend Robert F	112	barber	60	
	U	Phillips Beatrice M—†	123	housewife	56	"
	V	Phillips Beatrice M—†	123	shipper	22	
	W	Phillips Etta M—†	123	"	24	
	X	Phillips George E	123	chauffeur	65	"
	Y	Phillips Norma V—†	123	clerk	26	"
1017						
	A*	Bennett Clarence J	125	fisherman	41	"
	B	Voucher Beatrice M—†	125	housewife	36	"
	G	McCann Edward J	130	proprietor	49	"

Cable Street

	K	Kilroy Thomas	2	machinist	39	84 Mt Pleasant av
	L	Cossitt Herbert N	2	mechanic	36	Brookline
	M	Varney Jennie—†	2	housewife	63	61 Everett
	N	Varney Walter S	2	laborer	30	61 "
	P	Degan Cecelia—†	4	housewife	73	here
	R	O'Brien George W	6	retired	56	"
	S	O'Brien Mary F—†	6	housewife	66	"
	T	Crowell Burpee G	6	chauffeur	30	"
	U	Crowell Lillian F—†	6	housewife	27	"
	V	Adams Eleanor—†	10	"	30	Maryland
	W	Adams Robert	10	chauffeur	37	"
	X	Dalton Nicholas	10	laborer	37	here
	Y	Dutiley Elizabeth—†	10	housewife	57	"
	Z	Hanley Michael	12	retired	76	"

1018
Cable Street—Continued

A	Young Arthur	14	machinist	22	here
B	Young Arthur W	14	"	46	"
C	Young Mary—†	14	housewife	44	"
D	Belleville Arthur	14	U S N	28	"
E	Belleville Irene—†	14	housewife	27	"
F	Damshkaln Anna—†	14	cashier	29	
G	Damshkaln Elizabeth—†	14	laundress	59	"
H	Eshenwald Anna—†	14	housewife	61	"
K	Eshenwald Ernest	14	draftsman	33	"
L	*Coy Beatrice—†	16	housewife	43	"
M	Coy Frank	16	clerk	41	"
N	Redmond Rose—†	16	housewife	49	Connecticut
O	Feeney Catherine—†	16	"	63	here
P	Feeney John	16	laborer	25	"

Cornwall Street

R	Lucier Ellen—†	8	housewife	45	here
S	Lucier Mary—†	8	stenographer	22	"
T	Lucier Walter	8	machinist	46	"
U	Lucier Walter	8	laborer	20	"
V	McLaughlin Bridget—†	9	housewife	41	4 Haverford
W	McLaughlin William	9	laborer	45	4 "
X	Quinn Charles	9	chauffeur	53	24 Newbern
Y	Quinn Marion—†	9	housewife	50	24 "
Z	Leonard Mary—†	9	"	48	11 Greeley pl

1019

A	Leonard Thomas	9	laborer	54	11 "
B	Moore Bridget—†	10	housewife	52	here
C	Moore Francis	10	U S N	23	"
D	Moore James	10	laborer	20	"
E	Moore Martin	10	electrician	25	"
F	White Dorothea—†	11	stenographer	26	"
G	White Edith—†	11	bookkeeper	20	"
H	White Edward	11	electroplater	58	"
K	White Frances M—†	11	housewife	61	"
L	White Frances T—†	11	stenographer	31	"
M	White Ruth—†	11	"	23	"
N	Mullins Timothy	15	fireman	55	
O	Sweeney Dennis	15	"	38	

Cornwall Street—Continued

P	Sweeney Helen—†	15	housewife	39	here
R	Hughes Mary E—†	18	teacher	51	"
S	Dolan Joseph	21	machinist	32	"
T	Dolan Margaret—†	21	housewife	23	"
U	VanDerSnoek Catherine-†	21	"	56	"
V	VanDerSnoek Paul	21	attendant	54	"
W	Graham Blanche—†	21	housewife	33	"
X	Graham Emery	21	chauffeur	35	"
Y	Carless Constance—†	25	operator	45	"
Z	Carless Francis	25	machinist	50	"

1020

A	Cummings Gertrude—†	25	housewife	35	"
B	Cummings James	25	chauffeur	43	"
C	Kruse Emil	28	blacksmith	63	"
D	Kruse Helena—†	28	housekeeper	58	"
E	Kruse Otto	28	shoecutter	60	"
F	Connolly Ann—†	28	housewife	40	"
G	Connolly Robert	28	carpenter	41	"
H	Lynch Henry	28	operator	36	"
K	Lynch Mary—†	28	housewife	32	"
L	Hachey Joseph	29	baker	41	80 Codman pk
M	Hachey Ronald	29	"	37	Michigan
N	Harris Josephine—†	29	housewife	66	80 Codman pk
O	May Margaret—†	29	"	43	141 Lamartine
P	Logan Raymond	29	U S N	38	Revere
R	Logan Rita—†	29	housewife	34	42 Brookside
S	Kenney Mary—†	33	"	41	here
T	Kenney William	33	electrician	33	"
U	Conroy Catherine—†	33	housewife	32	"
V	Conroy James	33	electrician	36	"
W	DuBois Victoria—†	33	housewife	65	"
X	Willis Arthur	41	welder	37	
Y	Willis Christine—†	41	inspector	37	"
Z	Hall Christina—†	41	laborer	37	"

1021

A	Hall Margaret—†	41	housewife	62	"
B	Hall William	41	manager	34	"
C	Cunningham Catherine—†	45	housewife	52	"
D	Cunningham Ellen—†	45	winder	21	
E	Cunningham George	45	carpenter	54	"
F	Cunningham George, jr	45	laborer	23	"

Cornwall Street—Continued

G	Cunningham John	45	electrician	48	here
H	Cunningham John	45	"	28	"
K	Ivers Edward J, jr	45	chauffeur	25	"
L	Ivers Helen U—†	45	inspector	23	"
M	Ivers Margaret—†	45	housewife	27	"
N	Ivers Mary A—†	45	"	52	"
O	Ford Alice L—†	47	"	45	
P	Ford Thomas F	47	pipefitter	47	"
R	Brennan Mary—†	47	housekeeper	48	"
S	Brennan William	47	plasterer	50	"
T	Stevens Albert	47	U S A	28	
U	Stevens Alice—†	47	housewife	26	"
V	Boyce Rita—†	51	" .	25	
W	Boyce William	51	painter	29	"
X	Dolan Hermina—†	51	housewife	35	"
Y	Dolan James	51	laborer	39	
Z	Kenny Elizabeth—†	51	housewife	53	"

1022

A	Kenny John	51	machinist	25	"
B	Smith Joshua	62	welder	35	N Carolina
C	Smith Sophie—†	62	housewife	33	"
D	Stanley James	62	chauffeur	30	Saugus
E	Stanley Jennie—†	62	housewife	29	"
F	Campbell Sarah—†	62	at home	65	78 Mozart
G	Russell Norman	62	busboy	21	78 "
H	List William	64	painter	74	here
K	Bevington Elizabeth—†	64	domestic	52	370 Amory
L	Daley Joseph	64	clerk	38	here
M	Daley Mary—†	64	housewife	55	"
N	Beaulieu Delina—†	66	"	40	"
O	Beaulieu Henry	66	plumber	43	"

Dolan's Court

P	*Fuller Florence—†	2	housewife	29	here
R	Fuller Louis	2	plumber	33	"
S	Belyea Evelyn—†	4	housewife	28	"
T	Belyea Robert	4	steamfitter	30	"
U	DeCoste Edward	6	ironworker	44	"
V	DeCoste Mary—†	6	housewife	42	"
W	Fuller Everett P	8	plumber	68	"

Dolan's Court—Continued

x	Fuller Everett P, jr	8	molder	27	here
y	Fuller Frank T	8	plumber	44	"
z	Fuller Harold E	8	U S A	24	"
	1023				
a	Fuller Mabel W—†	8	housewife	66	"

Forest Hills Street

b	Pezzulo Albert	37	pipefitter	46	here
c	Pezzulo Concetta—†	37	housewife	38	"
d	Crowley Kathleen—†	37	at home	23	3252 Wash'n
e	Crowley Patrick	37	machinist	29	3276 "
f	Berry Georgia—†	37	housewife	27	here
g	Berry Paul K	37	U S A	25	"
h	McGann Louise—†	39	housewife	51	"
k	McGann Patrick H	39	clerk	56	"
l	Feeney John	39	"	35	
m	Feeney Mary—†	39	housewife	68	"
n	Anderson Forsten S	39	laborer	62	"
o	Atton Augusta E—†	39	housewife	71	"
p	Johnson Axel S	39	engineer	50	"
r	Groves Charles C	43	carpenter	43	"
s	Groves Lillian—†	43	housewife	39	"
t	McCormick Alice—†	43	"	64	
u	McCormick Daniel J	43	laborer	64	
v	Meaney Esther—†	43	housewife	21	"
w	Meaney Thomas	43	mechanic	23	"
x	Meaney George	45	ironworker	23	"
y	Meaney Mary—†	45	housewife	21	"
z	Dixon Ada E—†	45	"	73	
	1024				
a	Dixon Ethel M—†	45	clerk	31	
b	Crane Alice—†	45	factoryworker	44	"
c	Crane Catherine—†	45	housewife	65	"
d	Crane Dennis E	45	motorman	67	"
e	Fuller Catherine F—†	47	housewife	38	53 Forest Hills
f	Fuller Walter T	47	pressman	49	53 "
g	McCauley Madeline—†	51	housewife	37	here
h	Guinan Doris—†	51	"	31	"
k	Guinan Francis V	51	guard	38	"
l	Perrello Evelyn—†	51	housewife	26	"

15

Forest Hills Street—Continued

	M	Perrello Ralph	51	polisher	31	here
	N	Keefe Dorothy F—†	53	housewife	44	7 Sylvia
	O	Keefe Raymond J	53	salesman	47	7 "
	P	Palmer Marshall	53	billposter	31	Cambridge
	R	Palmer Mary C—†	53	housewife	20	"
	S	*Allsop Esther M—†	53	"	46	here
	T	Allsop James	53	mechanic	60	"
	U	Allsop Louis J	53	U S M C	21	"
	V	DeLesdernier Bessie—†	55	at home	65	"
	W	Palmer Mary C—†	55	housewife	35	"
	X	Palmer Robert T	55	mechanic	40	"
	Y	Felton Evelyn—†	55	housewife	38	"
	Z	Felton John	55	laborer	45	"

1025

	A	Hinterleitner Anna—†	59	housewife	55	"
	B	Hinterleitner Jacob	59	machinist	58	"
	C	Catterson Anna—†	59	supervisor	34	127 Dana av
	D	Catterson Peter	59	steamfitter	38	127 "
	E	Ashmore Mary L—†	63	WAC	20	here
	F	Boyle Ann E—†	63	clerk	20	"
	G	Boyle Mary L—†	63	housewife	58	"
	H	Boyle Patrick J	63	agent	63	
	K	Boyle Robert J	63	U S A	22	
	L	Scott Elsie—†	63	housewife	39	"
	M	Scott John B	63	draftsman	38	"
	N	Frank Edna D—†	63	nurse	42	
	O	*Frank Harold M	63	salesman	49	"
	P	Frank Hilda D—†	63	cashier	51	
	R	Frank Marion E—†	63	at home	44	"
	S	Andrews James	71	inspector	42	"
	T	Andrews Mary—†	71	housewife	34	"
	U	Boutillette Edna—†	71	"	35	
	V	Boutillette Leo	71	metalworker	36	"
	W	Procum Mary—†	71	hairdresser	36	"
	X	Osol Eva—†	75	housewife	58	"
	Y	Osol Jacob E	75	machinist	59	"
	Z	Delorey Arthur H	75	optometrist	50	"

1026

	A	Delorey Doris C—†	75	housewife	40	"
	B	Fitzgerald Ella G—†	75	housekeeper	75	"

Page.	Letter.	Full Name.	Residence, Jan. 1, 1946.	Occupation.	Supposed Age.	Reported Residence, Jan. 1, 1945. Street and Number.

Green Street

N	Connor Mary V—†	190	operator	45	here
O	Flanagan Helen L—†	190	at home	77	"
P	Flanagan Madeline G—†	190	housewife	34	"
R	Flanagan Thomas W	190	clerk	42	'
S	McDonald Frank	194	bricklayer	49	"
T	McDonald Helen—†	194	housewife	46	"
U	McDonald James	194	laborer	20	
V	Thompson Leroy	194	"	65	
W	Devereaux Charles	196	retired	23	
X	Devereaux Ethel—†	196	housewife	52	"
Y	Devereaux George E	196	laborer	25	
Z	Devereaux John	196	"	21	

1027

A	Devereaux William C	196	operator	62	"
B	Devereaux William J	196	"	29	
C	Barrio Hubert T	198	painter	65	
D	Barrio Joseph J	198	meter reader	60	"
E	Barrio Thomas F	198	laborer	63	
F	O'Donnell Albert	198	U S A	26	
G	O'Donnell Rose L—†	198	housewife	63	"
H	O'Donnell William P	198	watchman	64	"
K	Harrington Helen—†	198	housewife	35	"
L	Harrington James	198	chauffeur	36	"

Greenley Place

O	Arsenault Alyre	5	machinist	45	3148 Wash'n
P	Arsenault Malvin	5	U S N	27	3148 "
R	Arsenault Marion—†	5	housewife	43	3148 "
S	Arsenault Rena—†	5	nurse	20	3148 "
T	Curran Bernard	5	retired	80	here
U	Curran Francis	5	clerk	35	"
V	Curran Letitia—†	5	at home	26	"
W	Curran Susan—†	5	"	46	
X	McLean Daniel	5	clerk	23	"
Y	Snow Cecelia E—†	5	housewife	56	"
Z	Snow Earl L	5	mechanic	66	"

1028

A	Snow Paul L	5	clerk	26	
B	Snow Robert E	5	chauffeur	22	"
C	Peterson Nicholas	7	mechanic	49	"

Greenley Place—Continued

D	Peterson Susan—†	7	housewife	53	here	
E	Goetze Christina—†	7	"	81	"	
F	Goetze Henry G	7	toolmaker	53	"	
G	Stotz Edith—†	rear 7	at home	25	137 School	
H	Hederson Florence—†	8	"	52	Chelsea	
K	Bauer Ruth—†	8	"	25	326 Tremont	
L	Remlinger Fred W	8	laborer	47	here	
M	Remlinger Marjorie K—†	8	housewife	45	"	
N	Proctor Eleanor—†	9	at home	26	"	
O	Yankowsky Joseph	9	laborer	48	"	
P	Zabczuk Janet—†	9	clerk	22	"	
R	Zabczuk Rosalie—†	9	housewife	49	"	
S	Zabczuk Vincent	9	cook	52		
T	Abberton Charles P	10	carpenter	22	"	
U	Abberton Marguerite C—†	10	stenographer	25	"	
V	Abberton Rose A—†	10	clerk	46	"	
W	Galeota Mary—†	10½	housewife	55	"	
X	Galeota Ralph	10½	storekeeper	65	"	
Y	Durfee Fred J	11	grinder	56	85 Lamartine	
Z	Durfee Lawrence A	11	U S A	23	here	

1029

A	Durfee Mary R—†	11	laundress	25	"	
B	Sheran Peter	11	shipper	31	30 Hyde Park a	
C	Sheran Winifred—†	11	housewife	28	30 "	
D	MacKenzie Maude—†	11	at home	40	here	
E	Atanasio Anna J—†	12	housewife	42	"	
F	Atanasio Dorothy—†	12	student	21	"	
G	Atanasio Salvatore	12	mechanic	45	"	
H	Johnson Victoria—†	12	housewife	45	"	
K	Reardon Michael	14	chauffeur	60	"	
L	Grover Edgar	14	retired	84		
M	Grover Gertrude—†	14	housewife	63	"	
N	Hofmann Violet M—†	14	"	49		
O	Hofmann William F	14	retired	75		
W	Good Irene—†	16	typist	22		
X	Good Isaac	16	laborer	71		
Y	Good John	16	U S A	24		
Z	Good Robert	16	machinist	26	"	

1030

A	Finn Arthur B	18	rigger	29	Rhode Island	
B	Finn Joan A—†	18	housewife	23	"	
C	Flynn Catherine A—†	18	at home	55	"	

18

Haverford Street

D	Kelly Arthur J	4	chauffeur	46	here
E	Kelly Margaret A—†	4	housewife	45	"
F	VanderSnoek Everett H	4	chauffeur	50	"
G	VanderSnoek Gertrude A—†	4	housewife	51	"
H	Cox Mae—†	5	"	44	
K	Cox William E	5	assembler	41	"
L	Conway Florence M—†	5	housewife	30	"
M	Conway Vincent D	5	inspector	35	"
N	Kruse Hugo	5	brewer	47	
O	Kruse Mary A—†	5	housewife	42	"
P	Murphy Cornelius M	6	pipefitter	45	157 Lamartine
R	Murphy Dorothy A—†	6	housewife	37	157 "
S	Carr Emery P	6	policeman	34	here
T	Carr Sarah W—†	6	at home	60	"
U	Carr Herbert G	6	chauffeur	35	"
V	Carr Lillian E—†	6	housewife	36	"
W	Mihans Ethel E—†	6	"	28	Texas
X	Nordman Abraham	6	packer	61	here
Y	Bohane Agnes B—†	7	housewife	36	"
Z	Bohane Francis J	7	tree surgeon	41	"

1031

A	Cheever Anna T—†	7	saleswoman	46	29 Montebello rd
B	Goode Gertrude M—†	7	housewife	36	here
C	Goode Thomas M	7	chauffeur	37	"
D	Hiltz Arthur E	7	"	21	"
E	Murphy Arthur D	7	inspector	54	29 Montebello rd
F	Whitehouse Agnes—†	7	at home	65	here
G	Hickey Daniel J	8	chauffeur	43	"
H	Hickey Delia—†	8	housewife	41	"
K	Crowley Joseph F	8	technician	27	"
L	Crowley Marie F—†	8	operator	21	"
M	Crowley Mary—†	8	housewife	57	"
N	Crowley Patrick	8	factoryworker	65	"
O	Lawless John J	8	attorney	34	"
P	Lawless Mary G—†	8	teacher	35	"
R	Corcoran Isabelle—†	9	housewife	37	"
S	Corcoran John F	9	salesman	38	"
T	Linse Francis X	9	U S N	35	
U	Linse Hirlanda—†	9	at home	68	"
V	Linse Joseph F	9	collector	39	"
W	Linse William J	9	U S A	27	

Haverford Street—Continued

x	Craven Delia M—†	10	clerk	22	here
y	Craven Thomas	10	laborer	63	"
z	Sauer Catherine I—†	10	housewife	43	"
	1032				
A	Sauer George J	10	woolhandler	45	"
B	Emerson Catherine—†	10	tel operator	48	"
c	Emerson John W	10	fireman	47	"
D	Broderick John J	11	bartender	32	26 Tower
E	Broderick Mary A—†	11	at home	65	26 "
F	Cannon Frederick P	11	maintenance	31	here
G	Cannon Margaret E—†	11	housewife	27	Cambridge
H	Cannon Patrick F	11	laborer	65	here
K	Feeney James F	11	rubberworker	36	"
L	Feeney Mary G—†	11	housewife	34	"
M	Jordan Dorothy T—†	12	"	36	
N	Jordan George S	12	seaman	35	'
o	Walsh Clement L	12	chauffeur	44	"
P	Walsh Elizabeth A—†	12	housewife	43	"
R	Walsh Thomas C	12	chauffeur	21	"
s	Prive Veda M—†	12	housewife	44	"
T	Prive Wallace A	12	chauffeur	45	"
U	Prive Wallace A, jr	12	U S N	22	
V	Callahan Alice F—†	14	housewife	37	"
w	Callahan William G	14	chauffeur	37	"
x	Lowe Teresa M—†	14	factoryworker	29	87 Atherton
Y	Gallagher Lawrence F	14	U S N	24	here
z	Gallagher Sarah E—†	14	housewife	48	"
	1033				
A	Gallagher William E	14	retired	54	"
B	Gallagher William T	14	U S N	25	
c	O'Connell Francis J	14	teller	63	
D	O'Connell Francis J, jr	14	chauffeur	25	"
E	O'Connell John T	14	"	20	
F	O'Connell Mary A—†	14	housewife	48	"
G	Spiegelhalter Joseph H	16	machinist	48	"
H	Spiegelhalter Mary J—†	16	housewife	38	"
K	*Nee Mary V—†	16	"	37	"
L	Nee Michael	16	laborer	37	
M	Nee John J	16	custodian	44	"
N	*Nee Margaret H—†	16	housewife	42	"
o	Dullea Edward J	18	U S N	25	

Haverford Street—Continued

Page.	Letter.	FULL NAME.	Residence, Jan. 1, 1946.	Occupation.	Supposed Age.	Reported Residence, Jan. 1, 1945. Street and Number.
	P	Dullea Julia J—†	18	at home	60	here
	R	Dullea Margaret M—†	18	stenographer	22	"
	S	McLaughlin Elizabeth—†	18	housewife	55	"
	T	McLaughlin Helen T—†	18	secretary	22	"
	U	McLaughlin John	18	machinist	55	"
	V	McLaughlin John J	18	U S A	20	
	W	Sikora Elizabeth R—†	18	housewife	28	"
	X	Sikora Walter A	18	U S N	29	"
	Y	McLaughlin Annette B—†	18	housewife	28	"
	Z	McLaughlin Cornelius V	18	U S N	30	
1034						
	A	Leary Cornelius M	19	chauffeur	67	"
	B	Leary Delia L—†	19	housewife	66	"
	C	Collins Mary—†	19	"	44	
	D	Collins Michael	19	salesman	43	"
	E	Manning John T	19	social worker	38	"
	F	Manning Margaret—†	19	at home	66	"
	G	Manning Mary M—†	19	teacher	34	"
	H	MacKenzie Christine L—†	21	housewife	31	"
	K	Stoddard Preston A	21	retired	57	
	L	Mullis Eunice M—†	21	housewife	26	"
	M	Mullis George J	21	auditor	29	"
	N	Hiltz Anna M—†	21	housewife	29	"
	O	Hiltz Philip G	21	assembler	32	"

Jackson Place

Page.	Letter.	FULL NAME.	Residence, Jan. 1, 1946.	Occupation.	Supposed Age.	Reported Residence, Jan. 1, 1945. Street and Number.
	P	Burke Paul N	7	foreman	36	137 Green
	R	Burke Yola—†	7	housewife	35	137 "
	S	MacLeod Eunice—†	9	"	60	here
	T	MacLeod Jennie—†	9	clerk	22	"
	U	Meulenaere Dorothy—†	11	housewife	27	4 Newland
	V	Meulenaere Joseph	11	mechanic	27	4 "
	W	McNally Jeremiah	11	starter	50	here
	X	Burke Claire P—†	16	cashier	32	"
	Y	Burke Leo M	16	laborer	38	"
	Z	Burke Mary J—†	16	housewife	58	"
1035						
	A	Burke Mary R—†	16	nurse	34	
	B	Mills Earl	19	chauffeur	24	"
	C	Mills Margaret F—†	19	housewife	23	"

Page.	Letter.	FULL NAME.	Residence, Jan. 1, 1946.	Occupation.	Supposed Age.	Reported Residence, Jan. 1, 1945. Street and Number.

Jackson Place—Continued

	D	Feeley Anna—†	19½	operator	37	here
	E	Meaney James	19½	bricklayer	49	"
	F	Barrows Thaddeus C	19½	projectionist	57	"
	G	Crowell Clifton	20	beltmaker	65	"
	H	Crowell Edna L—†	20	operator	22	"
	K	Crowell Edward	20	clerk	21	
	L	Crowell Esther—†	20	housewife	61	"

Jess Street

	N	Clancy Joseph	1	mechanic	50	here
	o*	Clancy Mary—†	1	housewife	47	"
	P	McKenney Mary—†	1	"	20	"
	R	McKenney Thearman	1	chauffeur	23	35 Rossmore rd
	S	Cavanaugh Leona G—†	2	clerk	22	here
	T	Cavanaugh Susan—†	2	at home	52	"
	U	Rafferty Margaret C—†	2	housewife	42	"
	V	Rafferty William C	2	plumber	50	"
	W	Naumann Herbert A	2	chauffeur	31	"
	X	Naumann Margaret E—†	2	at home	65	"
	Y	Crawford Bertille—†	3	housewife	51	"
	Z	Crawford James	3	shipfitter	51	"

1036

	A	Murphy John J	3	factoryworker	56	"
	B	Murphy John J, jr	3	poster	22	
	C	Murphy Mary—†	3	housewife	50	"
	D	Lemieux Rita—†	4	"	21	237 Amory
	E	Lemieux Roland	4	laborer	31	Rhode Island
	F	Gray Edward R, jr	4	chauffeur	22	22 Dorr
	G	Gray Ethel M—†	4	housewife	20	22 "
	H	Waselewsky Alexander	4	student	24	21 Barton
	K	Waselewsky Ann—†	4	secretary	23	S Hanson
	L	Sullivan Bridget—†	5	housewife	79	here
	M	Sullivan James E	5	shipper	39	"
	N	Sullivan John	5	retired	80	"
	o	Sullivan Joseph F	5	chauffeur	35	"
	P	Sullivan Mary E—†	5	housekeeper	43	"
	R	Moylan Margaret B—†	6	"	37	Winthrop
	S	Denning Bertha—†	6	housewife	33	246 Hyde Park a
	T	Denning Edward	6	chauffeur	34	246 "
	U	Beatty Celia—†	6	stenographer	30	7 Albemarle

Jess Street—Continued

v	Beatty George C	6	clerk	31	Malden
w	Flynn Mary J—†	7	at home	66	here
x	Halpin Dorothy—†	7	housewife	23	16 Whitney pk
y	Halpin Walter R	7	machinist	24	22 Valentine
z	Donovan Mary M—†	8	housewife	44	here

1037

A	Donovan Thomas J	8	fireman	53	"
B	Rancourt Irene—†	9	housewife	28	92 Worcester
c	Rancourt Norman	9	chauffeur	29	92 "
D	Peterson John	9	retired	73	here
E	Cosseboom Evelyn—†	10	waitress	36	"
F	Cosseboom Jefferson	10	blacksmith	40	"
G	Odabashian Barton	11	shoeworker	57	"
H	*Odabashian Mary—†	11	housewife	50	"
K	Odabashian Newman	11	mechanic	21	"
L	Corkum Raymond W	11	machinist	40	"
M	Corkum Sophie J—†	11	housewife	30	"
N	Everard Richard	11	clerk	39	49 Worcester
o	LaVoie Frances—†	15	housewife	21	217 Amory
P	LaVoie Victor R	15	chauffeur	21	217 "
R	Connolly James	15	messenger	64	here
s	Munzenmaier Olive—†	15	housewife	62	"

Marmion Street

T	Jordan Joseph	6	guard	49	here
U	Jordan Mary J—†	6	housewife	37	"
v	Liddell Helen M—†	8	tel operator	24	"
w	Liddell Jean M—†	8	waitress	42	"
x	Liddell Susan—†	8	housewife	67	"
z	Glennon Clara J—†	9	"	62	

1038

A	Glennon Frank J	9	retired	77	
B	McDevitt Francis J	10	manager	37	"
c	McDevitt Marjorie T—†	10	U S C G	26	"
D	Smith George L	10	salesman	33	"
E	Smith Marie A—†	10	housewife	35	"
F	Smith Eleanor F—†	11	"	62	
G	Smith George P	11	retired	70	
H	Teehan Eleanor F—†	11	at home	39	"
K	Thompson Catherine—†	12	clerk	33	

Marmion Street—Continued

L	Thompson Joseph	12	painter	70	here
M	Martin Margaret—†	12	waitress	39	"
N	Schatz Catherine—†	12	at home	73	"
O	Schatz Francis L	12	manager	31	"
P	Johnson Bertha—†	13	teacher	40	"
R	Johnson Ernest	13	patternmaker	76	"
S	Clarke Margaret—†	14	housewife	47	"
T	Clarke William S	14	clerk	49	"
U	Earl Mary—†	14	housekeeper	60	"
V	Hesselschwerdt Carl A	14	watchman	60	"
W	DeBassio Alexander	15	cabinetmaker	69	"
X	DeBassio Christina—†	15	housewife	67	"
Y	DeBassio Joseph	15	clerk	27	"
Z	Raftery Margaret—†	15	housewife	31	"

1039

A	Raftery William	15	steelworker	34	"
B	Harris George A	16	mechanic	40	"
C	Harris Gladys W—†	16	housewife	35	"
D	Johnson Charles F	16	mover	38	
E	Concannon Margaret G—†	20	housewife	49	"
F	Concannon Michael J	20	roofer	52	
G	Concannon Veronica—†	20	tel operator	21	"

Merriam Street

H	Arsenault Avis	1	carpenter	55	here
K	Arsenault Margaret—†	1	housewife	55	"
L	Pettipaw Harold	5	plumber	46	"
M	Pettipaw Lucy—†	5	housewife	45	"

Minton Street

O	Tierney Marion D—†	1	housewife	27	here
P	Dacey Clare M—†	1	"	33	"
R	Dacey Daniel A	1	cutter	36	"
S	Feeney Nora M—†	1A	clerk	28	
T	Feeney Thomas J	1A	retired	67	
U	Gilbert Anne—†	1A	stenographer	43	"
V	Gilbert Earl	1A	mechanic	46	"
W	Murphy Nora—†	2	housewife	63	"
X	Woernle Marie—†	2	"	74	

24

Page.	Letter.	FULL NAME.	Residence, Jan. 1, 1946.	Occupation.	Supposed Age.	Reported Residence, Jan. 1, 1945. Street and Number.

Minton Street—Continued

	Y	Daley Helen V—†	3	inspector	21	here
	z	Daley John J	3	laborer	58	"
1040						
	A	Daley Mary N—†.	3	operator	28	77 Litchfield
	B	O'Brien Francis R	3	electrician	26	here
	C	O'Brien Katherine J—†	3	housewife	26	"
	D	Perry Marion B—†	3	"	23	45 Cornwall
	E	Perry William S	3	laborer	26	45 "
	F	Traynor Helen—†	4	operator	47	here
	G	Gebhard Josephine—†	4	housewife	77	"
	H	Donovan Helen M—†	5	"	35	"
	K	Donovan Patrick J	5	clerk	39	

Montebello Road

	L	Breen Dorothy P—†	15	teacher	33	here
	M	Cronin Helen M—†	15	"	22	"
	N	Dolan Frances M—†	15	"	43	"
	O	Finlan Margaret B—†	15	"	32	
	P	Finneran Mary S—†	15	"	35	
	R	Fisher Mary E—†	15		63	
	S	Fitzgerald Mary W—†	15	"	36	"
	T	Goss Sarah A—†	15		30	Cambridge
	U	Hughes Eileen M—†	15		24	here
	V	Hurley Julia A—†	15	"	46	"
	W	McCarthy Mary E—†	15	"	34	"
	X	McInnis Kathleen P—†	15	"	28	"
	Y	McShane Catherine T—†	15	"	46	Arlington
	z	Regan Anna M—†	15	"	38	here
1041						
	A	Riccioli Anna R—†	15		39	
	B	Rourke Katherine—†	15	"	54	
	C	Sullivan Margaret E—†	15	"	52	"
	D	Thurston Mary E—†	15	laundress	31	Quincy
	E	Tobin Lillian R—†	15	teacher	45	here
	F	Toomey Catherine G—†	15	"	38	"
	G	Johnson Anne—†	27	housewife	61	"
	H	Johnson John A	27	retired	63	"
	K	Kelley Francis L	27	bartender	46	"
	L	Daly Edward J	27	chauffeur	60	"
	M	Daly Edward J, jr	27	U S A	24	

Montebello Road—Continued

	N	Daly Mary—†	27	housewife	56	here
	o	Daly Mary C—†	27	waitress	28	"
	P	Daly Patrick J	27	chauffeur	26	"
	R	Daly Rose A—†	27	stenographer	20	"
	s	Wilkinson Albert E	27	engineer	63	"
	T	Wilkinson Mary—†	27	housewife	60	"
	u	Wythe Thomas J	29	shipfitter	63	"
	v	Johnson Josephine—†	29	at home	80	"
	w	Mulhane Alice I—†	29	housewife	39	"
	x	Mulhane William	29	letter carrier	47	"
	Y	McCauley Catherine—†	29	at home	70	"
	z	O'Connor Elizabeth—†	29	housekeeper	46	"

1042   Ophir Street

	A	Lutz Cecil F	10	mechanic	43	here
	B	Lutz Esther A—†	10	housewife	40	"
	c	Perkins Frank C	10	chef	21	"
	D	Cameron Angela G—†	12	housewife	31	"
	E	Cameron Malcolm E	12	entertainer	41	"
	F	Murphy Bridget—†	16	at home	73	"
	G	McDonough James J	16	chauffeur	37	Waltham
	H	McDonough Rita—†	16	housewife	24	"
	K	McLaughlin Alice—†	18	at home	75	here
	L	McLaughlin Cecelia G—†	18	housewife	34	"
	M	McLaughlin Edward J	18	longshoreman	37	"
	N	Murphy Marjorie—†	18	housewife	31	"
	o	Murphy Paul E	18	baker	36	
	P	Lymneos Anastasia—†	30	stitcher	22	"
	R*	Lymneos Charles	30	chef	65	"
	s*	Lymneos Mary—†	30	housewife	54	"
	T	Varkas Anne—†	30	clerk	23	
	u	Varkas James	30	student	24	
	v	Varkas Michael	30	chef	50	
	w	Varkas Pelazia—†	30	housewife	49	"
	x	Varkas William	30	U S N	20	
	Y	Varkas George	30	barber	60	
	z	Varkas George	30	U S A	20	

1043

	A	Varkas Irene—†	30	housewife	48	"
	B	Lymneos Charles	30	draftsman	31	"

Ophir Street—Continued

	c	Lymneos Sally—†	30	housewife	24	here
	d	Hatch Mary—†	34	"	53	"
	e	Hatch William F	34	foreman	58	"
	f	MacLellan Rita M—†	34	secretary	30	"
	g	Ladue Alice—†	36	housewife	34	"
	h	Schmier Elizabeth—†	36	"	53	
	k	Schmier Otto	36	student	23	

Porter Street

	l	Sousa Irene—†	9	saleswoman	33	4 Jess
	m	*Sousa Virgil	9	painter	42	4 "
	n	Allen Angela—†	9	housewife	31	527 E Sixth
	o	Allen Thomas J	9	sign painter	29	527 "

Sylvia Street

	p	Calvi Isadore C	2	laborer	58	Maine
	r	Calvi Lottie C—†	2	housewife	58	"
	s	Anderson Etta J—†	2	"	67	here
	t	Anderson John W	2	electrician	50	"
	u	St Clair Arthur	2	"	24	"
	v	St Clair Cecelia—†	2	housewife	48	"
	w	St Clair Clement	2	laborer	26	"
	x	St Clair Maurice	2	chauffeur	50	"
	y	St Clair Peter	2	student	21	"
	z	Donlan Catherine—†	5	housewife	40	19 Forest Hills
1044						
	a	Donlan Peter	5	laborer	45	19 "
	b	Lynch Catherine—†	5	housewife	45	here
	c	Lynch Joseph	5	machinist	45	"
	d	Klopf Elizabeth—†	5	at home	59	"
	e	Duffy Leslie D	7	U S A	23	
	f	Noonan Mary B—†	7	housewife	64	"
	g	Noonan Patrick J	7	mechanic	65	"
	h	Harrison Jessie—†	7	housewife	30	"
	k	Harrison Noel	7	U S M C	28	"
	l	Hinds Daniel K	7	U S A	25	
	m	Hinds David H	7	laborer	24	
	n	Hinds Elsie—†	7	operator	21	"
	o	Hinds Flora—†	7	at home	61	"

Sylvia Street—Continued

R	Nolan John	8	retired	72	here
S	Nolan Nellie B—†	8	housewife	72	"
T	Fox Sarah—†	8	matron	65	24 Union av
U	Benoit Frederick	8	longshoreman	30	Everett
V	Benoit Muriel—†	8	housewife	27	"
W	Hatfield Ernest L	8	mechanic	48	here
X	Hatfield Joseph E	8	retired	21	"
Y	Hatfield Lucy—†	8	housewife	48	"
Z	Barrett Alvina—†	8	"	56	96 Thornton

1045

A	Barrett Frederick	8	chauffeur	57	96 "
B	Correnti Viola—†	8	housewife	32	here

Washington Street

H	Dep Leong	3209	laundryman	62	here
M	Manning James	3215	shipper	30	"
N	Manning Mildred—†	3215	housewife	29	"
O	O'Brien John	3215	chauffeur	26	"
P	O'Brien Margaret—†	3215	housekeeper	54	"
R	O'Brien Thomas	3215	chauffeur	32	"
S	O'Hannessian Mary—†	3215	housewife	25	"
T	O'Hannessian Robert	3215	chauffeur	27	"
V	Finneran Annie—†	3219	at home	85	"
W	Murphy Andrew	3219	shipwright	44	"
X	Murphy Marie—†	3219	housewife	40	"
Y	Nyhan Bridget E—†	3223	"	65	
Z	Nyhan James	3223	retired	68	

1046

A	Rossetti Mary E—†	3223	domestic	37	"
B	Nyhan Eileen—†	3223	housewife	42	"
C	Nyhan Timothy P	3223	estimator	40	"
D	Coffey Helen K—†	3227	housewife	28	"
E	Coffey Timothy	3227	policeman	35	"
F	Grenham Anna—†	3227.	bookkeeper	26	"
G	Grenham Francis	3227	inspector	36	"
H	Grenham John	3227	laborer	38	
K	Grenham Mary—†	3227	housewife	68	"
L	Grenham Michael	3227	retired	70	
M	McGlone Mary—†	3231	housekeeper	74	"
N	Thomas Helen—†	3231	operator	45	"

Washington Street—Continued

o	Romano Mario	3231	laborer	42	here
p	Romano Rose—†	3231	housewife	39	"
s	Kirwin John J	3235	toolmaker	69	"
t	Kirwin Raymond P	3235	U S N	24	
u	Kirwin Rose A—†	3235	housewife	38	"
w	Kubler Joseph	3239	chauffeur	32	"
x	Kubler Rita—†	3239	housewife	28	"
y	McLaughlin James	3239	bookkeeper	26	"
z	McLaughlin Mary—†	3239	housewife	22	"

1047

a	Hunt Alice—†	3239	"	22	"
b	Hunt Thomas	3239	salesman	22	8 Longwood ter
c	McGuire Marjorie—†	3239	clerk	20	here
d	McGuire Mary—†	3239	housewife	53	"
e	McGuire Patrick	3239	carpenter	66	"
f	McLaughlin John	3239	student	24	
g	McDermott Edward	3243	laborer	45	
h	McDermott Mary—†	3243	housekeeper	46	"
k	Steele George	3243	chauffeur	45	"
l	Steele Jessie—†	3243	housewife	46	"
o	Reilly Edith—†	3252	"	43	
p	English Mary H—†	3252	stenographer	23	"
r	English Robert E	3252	polisher	21	"
s	English Rose—†	3252	housekeeper	58	"
t	Goss Albert	3252	engraver	52	"
u	Goss Anna—†	3252	housewife	42	"
y	Duggan Celia H—†	3266	"	40	
z	Howe James W	3266	clerk	38	

1048

a	Howe Nora T—†	3266	housewife	32	"
b	Cappuccio Angelina—†	3266	"	34	
c	Cappuccio Antonio	3266	laborer	39	
f	Kelley Evelyn—†	3270	housewife	21	"
g	Kelley Joseph	3270	roofer	30	"
h	Sanchez Marie—†	3270	factoryworker	25	131 Hampden
k	Tower Harold	3270	roofer	50	here
l	Tower Harriet—†	3270	housewife	46	"
m	Goode Catherine C—†	3273	"	31	"
n	Goode Joseph	3273	clerk	36	
o	Howe Annie—†	3273	at home	58	"
p	Boettcher Frances C—†	3273	housewife	29	"

Page.	Letter.	FULL NAME.	Residence, Jan. 1, 1945.	Occupation.	Supposed Age.	Reported Residence, Jan. 1, 1945. Street and Number.

' Washington Street—Continued

	R	Boettcher Joseph	3273	chauffeur	31	here
	S	Darrow Thelma—†	3274	bookkeeper	41	425 Beacon
	T	Meade Christina—†	3274	housewife	48	745 Shawmut av
	U	Meade John C	3274	laborer	50	745 "
	W	Cody James I	3275	chauffeur	36	here
	X	Stober Herbert	3275	plasterer	35	"
	Y	Stober Rita—†	3275	housewife	31	"
	Z	Raftery Andrew J	3275	chauffeur	25	"
1049						
	A	Raftery Francis	3275	mechanic	24	"
	B	Raftery Margaret—†	3275	housewife	56	"
	C	Raftery Paul	3275	U S N	20	"
	D	Raftery Rosamond—†	3275	housewife	26	Newton
	E	Reynolds Alice—†	3275	"	38	here
	F	Reynolds William	3275	painter	35	"
	G	Phelps Robert	3276	laborer	37	"
	H	Dennett George S	3276	student	21	"
	K	Dennett George W	3276	laborer	49	
	L	Dennett Yvonne—†	3276	housewife	41	"
	M	Conte Anna—†	3276	housekeeper	37	5 W Park
	N	Conte Louis	3276	painter	42	5 "
	O	Keene Kathleen—†	3278	nurse	58	Malden
	P	Dorr John H	3278	carpenter	64	here
	R	Meredith Joseph	3278	porter	58	"
	S	Meredith Margaret—†	3278	housewife	42	"
	T	Gilliard Alfreda—†	3278	housekeeper	44	"
	U	Brown John	3282	laborer	35	Rockport
	V	Brown June—†	3282	housewife	27	"
	W	Gallagher Helen—†	3282	"	35	2 Burroughs pl
	X	Gallagher Joseph	3282	clerk	38	2 "
	Y	Gallant Charles	3282	U S N	22	here
	Z	Gallant Columbia—†	3282	housewife	53	"
1050						
	A	Gallant Joseph	3282	fireman	56	"
	D	Burns Roxie—†	3286	housewife	30	"
	E	Burns Thomas	3286	brakeman	31	"
	F	Davidson Clarence	3286	laborer	48	
	G	Davidson Margaret—†	3286	housewife	40	"
	H	Pollard James	3286	U S N	35	
	K	Pollard Mary—†	3286	housewife	32	"
	L	Sicari Louise—†	3294	nurse	31	"

Washington Street—Continued

M	Sicari Marie—†	3294	at home	57	here
N	Harrington Catherine—†	3294	housewife	37	"
O	Harrington Timothy	3294	laborer	40	"
P	Boyajian Richard	3294	"	51	"
R	Jerigan Lena—†	3296	laundress	41	4 Cable
S	*Trulson Nils	3296	stevedore	47	here
T	*Trulson Vera—†	3296	housewife	39	"
U	Webber Bertha—†	3296	"	46	"
V	Webber Edward	3296	clerk	49	
W	Ufheil Catherine—†	3298	domestic	52	"
X	Ufheil Joseph	3298	U S A	32	"
Y	D'Entremont Augustine	3298	cutter	45	3322 Wash'n
Z	D'Entremont Eileen—†	3298	housewife	28	3322 "
	1051				
A	Rapp Carlton	3298	fishcutter	41	here
B	Jones Clarence	3298	chauffeur	34	"
C	Jones Dorothy—†	3298	housewife	30	"
D	Horgan Michael J	3300	longshoreman	48	"
E	Horgan Sarah—†	3300	housewife	52	"
F	Long Arthur	3300	rigger	50	
G	Long Charlotte—†	3300	housewife	46	"
H	Long Helen—†	3300	saleswoman	20	"
K	Collins Evelyn—†	3300	housewife	39	"
L	Collins John	3300	welder	41	"
M	Hanlon Anna—†	3302	housewife	21	"
N	Hanlon James	3302	mechanic	25	"
O	Connolly Mary—†	3302	housewife	21	"
P	Connolly Michael	3302	machinist	26	"
R	Mullen Catherine—†	3302	housewife	25	"
S	Mullen George L	3302	mechanic	25	"
T	Tracy Helen—†	3302	housewife	48	"
U	Tracy Thomas	3302	U S A	23	
V	Kinlin Esther—†	3302	housewife	27	"
W	Kinlin Thomas	3302	chauffeur	32	"
X	Lomas Clarence B	3304	machinist	37	10 Wise
X¹	Lomas Louise M—†	3304	housewife	24	3313 Wash'n
Y	Gillis Charles L	3304	cutter	33	here
Z	Gillis John C	3304	chauffeur	45	"
	1052				
A	Gillis Sarah H—†	3304	at home	70	"
B	McKinney Ann—†	3304	housewife	47	"

Washington Street—Continued

c	McKinney James	3304	clerk	49	here
d	McKinney James D	3304	"	22	"
e	McDonough Claire H—†	3305	housewife	35	"
f	McDonough Peter J	3305	accountant	55	"
g	Porter Joseph I	3306	soapmaker	41	"
h	Porter Lillian K—†	3306	housewife	36	"
k	Solovicos Angelica—†	3306	"	50	"
l	Solovicos Constantine	3306	candymaker	61	"
m	Solovicos Katherine—†	3306	cashier	22	
n	Solovicos Rita—†	3306	dressmaker	24	"
o	Solovicos Thedora—†	3306	"	21	
p	DiRienzo Josephine—†	3306	housewife	58	"
r	Petrillo Albina—†	3306	forewoman	26	"
s	Petrillo Carmine	3306	laborer	31	
t	Anderson Alverne	3307	U S A	26	"
u	Anderson Grace—†	3307	housekeeper	51	"
v	Lowell Paul	3307	mechanic	33	"
w	Mountain Henry	3307	merchant	33	"
x	Mountain Rachel—†	3307	housewife	24	"
z	Bates Jeannette—†	3309	nurse	27	14 Dimock

1053

a	Lees Mary—†	3309	housekeeper	70	here
b	Murphy John F ·	3309	U S A	24	"
c	Westberg Anna M—†	3309	at home	72	"
d	Westberg Gustaf J	3309	manager	42	"
e	Kennedy Helen—†	3310	housewife	47	"
f	*Kennedy Hughina—†	3310	at home	76	"
g	Kennedy John W	3310	watchman	52	"
h	Burgess Doris—†	3310	operator	21	"
k	Burgess Mabel—†	3310	housewife	47	"
l	Salamy Abdou B	3312	merchant	34	"
m	Salamy Beshara S	3312	"	64	
n	Salamy Virginia H—†	3312	housewife	30	"
o	Chiampa Carolina—†	3312	"	42	
p	Chiampa Ralph	3312	barber	45	
r	Anastos Joseph	3313	machinist	58	"
s	Anastos Louise H—†	3313	housewife	43	"
u	Sheehan Moniea—†	3317	"	30	
v	Sheehan Ralph	3317	chauffeur	30	"
w	Norcross Theo M—†	3319	housewife	39	"
x	Norcross Theodore E	3319	electrician	53	"

1054
Woodside Avenue

H	Borden Etta—†	4	saleswoman	45	here
K	McKenzie Richard M	4	chauffeur	25	"
L	Defren Charles J	4	student	24	"
M	Defren Emily A—†	4	housewife	66	"
N	O'Malley Anthony	4	laborer	34	
O	O'Malley Gertrude—†	4	housewife	31	"
P	Cooney Patrick	4	baker	43	
R	Thornton Julia—†	4	housewife	65	"
S	Thornton Michael	4	laborer	63	
T	Connolly Hugh	6	painter	56	
U	*Connolly Lillian—†	6	housewife	55	"
V	Irgens Donald	6	baker	24	Montana
W	Irgens Lillian—†	6	housewife	24	here
X	*Giannelli Carmelia—†	6	"	48	70 Brookside av
Y	Giannelli Ettore	6	chef	50	70 "
Z	Cummings Marjorie—†	6	housewife	28	here

1055

A	Cummings Paul H	6	chauffeur	31	"
B	Welby Margaret—†	8	housewife	45	"
C	Welby Matthew	8	chauffeur	47	"
D	Hanley Helen—†	10	housewife	33	"
E	Hanley John	10	oilman	37	"
F	Hoffman Charles	10	chauffeur	50	"
G	Hoffman Charlotte—†	10	housewife	25	"
H	Hoffman Edward	10	tester	27	
K	Hoffman Frances—†	10	housewife	45	"
L	Petrocca Anthony T	10	chauffeur	26	"
M	Charyna Joseph	16	painter	32	
N	Charyna Mildred—†	16	housewife	32	"
O	Koresky Helen—†	16	"	51	
P	Koresky John	16	chef	54	"
R	*Messingill Olga—†	16	housewife	27	Connecticut
S	Wishnowsky John	16	painter	31	here
T	Wishnowsky Kornell	16	"	54	"
U	Wishnowsky Martin	16	factoryworker	29	"
V	Wishnowsky Mary—†	16	housewife	48	"
W	Wishnowsky Walter	16	printer	27	

1:
1

Ward 11—Precinct 11

CITY OF BOSTON

LIST OF RESIDENTS
20 YEARS OF AGE AND OVER

(NON-CITIZENS INDICATED BY ASTERISK)
(FEMALES INDICATED BY DAGGER)

AS OF

JANUARY 1, 1946

THOMAS F. SULLIVAN, *Chairman*
FREDERIC E. DOWLING, *Secretary*
WILLIAM A. MOTLEY, Jr.
ARTHUR V. COUGHLIN
EVERETT R. PROUT

Listing Board.

CITY OF BOSTON PRINTING DEPARTMENT

1100
Forest Hills Street

D	Mitchell Margaret—†	46–48	housewife	44	here	
E	Mitchell Patrick	46–48	storekeeper	47	"	
F	Koehler Doris—†	46–48	housewife	42	10 Olmstead	
G	Koehler Harold	46–48	inspector	44	10 "	
H	Linden Alice E—†	46–48	housewife	55	here	
K	Linden Patrick J	46–48	operator	61	"	
L	Linden Walter D	46–48	clerk	23	"	
M	McDermott Frank	50–52	"	38	"	
N	McDermott Mary—†	50–52	housewife	32	"	
O	*MacNamara Jessie—†	50–52	"	39		
P	MacNamara John W	50–52	fisherman	40	"	
R	McGillicuddy Elizabeth J—†	50–52	housewife	34	"	
S	McGillicuddy James C	50–52	librarian	34	"	
T	Goode Christopher	54–56	U S A	25	"	
U	Goode Delia—†	54–56	housewife	60	"	
V	Goode Francis	54–56	clerk	24		
W	Goode John	54–56	U S A	28		
X	Ross Elsie J—†	54–56	clerk	34	"	
Y	Ross Mary A—†	54–56	housewife	64	"	
Z	Ross Mary A—†	54–56	clerk	35		

1101

A	Ross Waldo C	54–56	machinist	60	"	
B	Griffin Ann—†	54–56	operator	23	"	
C	Griffin Julia—†	54–56	housewife	50	"	
D	Groswald A Wilma—†	58	"	31		
E	Groswald Alma R—†	58	at home	60		
F	Groswald Arrid J	58	breweryworker	32	"	
G	Nicholson Bridget T—†	58	housewife	60	"	
H	Nicholson John J	58	retired	64		
K	O'Connor Mary—†	58	secretary	26	"	
L	Abaghian Agavnie—†	58	at home	67	"	
M	DerAvedisian Agnes—†	58	housewife	47	"	
N	DerAvedisian Arthur	58	U S A	22		
O	DerAvedisian Magarditch	58	printer	47		
P	Timmons James	70	manager	40	"	
R	Timmons Louise M—†	70	inspector	39	"	
S	Doherty Catherine C—†	76	housewife	38	"	
T	Doherty Lester T	76	salesman	42	"	
U	Chronopoulos George A	76	manager	47	32 Iffley rd	
V	Chronopoulos George E	76	restaurateur	50	32 "	

2

Forest Hills Street—Continued

w	Chronopoulos Jerry	76	clerk	21	32 Iffley rd
x	Chronopoulos Theodora—†	76	housewife	48	32 "
y	Regan Frank M	78	supervisor	36	here
z	Regan Mary H—†	78	housewife	30	"
	1102				
a	Baldyga Evelyn A—†	78	"	30	
b	Baldyga Leo J	78	compositor	35	"
c	McGurk Arthur J	78	clerk	25	
d	McGurk Catherine G—†	78	housewife	57	"
e	McGurk Claire C—†	78	secretary	23	"
f	McGurk Frederick L	78	clerk	33	"
g	McGurk James F	78	U S N	35	
h	Sullivan George H	78	machinist	60	"
k	Tahaney Eleanor—†	82	teacher	27	
l	Tahaney James	82	retired	65	
m	Tahaney Mary—†	82	housewife	60	"
n	Coates Blanche E—†	82	"	50	
o	Coates William H	82	foreman	50	
p	Bowes Helen—†	82	housewife	36	"
r	Bowes John	82	surveyor	42	"
s	Salami Ruth—†	83	stenographer	21	17 Laconia
t	Salami Simon S	83	storekeeper	55	17 "
u	*Salami Zelpha—†	83	housewife	44	17 "
v	Dempsey Nora F—†	86	"	55	here
w	Dempsey William, jr	86	clerk	25	"
x	Dempsey William J	86	machinist	58	"
y	Hickey Mary—†	86	housewife	53	"
z	Hickey Michael	86	milkman	55	"
	1103				
a	Hickey William J	86	clerk	21	
b	Gendrolius Constance—†	86	housewife	64	"
c	Gendrolius Edward	86	U S A	29	"
d	Gendrolius Nicodemus	86	machinist	65	"
e	Gendrolius William	86	U S A	27	
f	Galvin James J	89	policeman	52	"
g	Galvin Mary A—†	89	housewife	43	"
h	McLaughlin Daniel P	89	clerk	41	
k	Eida Ernest	89	machinist	57	"
l	Eida Mary—†	89	housewife	55	"
m	Eida Virginia—†	89	bookkeeper	22	"
n	Gross Eric N	89	U S A	35	"

Page.	Letter.	FULL NAME.	Residence, Jan. 1, 1946.	Occupation.	Supposed Age.	Reported Residence, Jan. 1, 1945. Street and Number.

Forest Hills Street—Continued

o	Gross Robert	89	watchman	63	here
p	Gross Wilma M—†	89	clerk	29	"
r	Jordan Esther M—†	90	at home	34	Brookline
s	Jordan Frank V	90	U S A	34	"
t	Rogers John L	90	U S C G	40	here
u	Rogers Rosalind G—†	90	housewife	59	"
v	Brenz Anna—†	90	"	56	"
w	Brenz Edgar	90	lawyer	30	"
x	Brenz Peter A	90	printer	57	
y	Brenz Rita—†	90	student	20	
z	Nolan Agnes M—†	90	clerk	23	

1104

a	Nolan Anne V—†	90	secretary	32	"
b	Nolan John S	90	proprietor	30	"
c	Nolan Joseph F	90	U S A	21	"
d	Nolan Mary A—†	90	clerk	62	"
e	Geer Martha E—†	93	archivist	58	"
f	Geer Philip W	93	retired	62	
g	Harrington Catherine M–†	94	housewife	39	"
h	Harrington James G	94	social worker	42	"
k	McDonald James W	94	contractor	62	"
l	McDonald Mary W—†	94	housewife	58	"
m	Cadwell Catherine—†	94	at home	34	596 Parker
n	Cadwell Henry L	94	secretary	40	596 "
o	Cadwell Joseph F	94	retired	76	596 "
p	Cadwell Mary C—†	94	winder	37	596 "
r	Grant Margaret—†	98	housewife	67	here
s	McDermott Esther R—†	98	bookkeeper	54	"
t	McDermott Mary D—†	98	at home	58	"
u	McDermott Raymond A	98	clerk	48	
v	Carey Gertrude—†	98	teacher	35	
w	Palmer James A	101	realtor	57	
x	Palmer Julian J	101	U S A	24	
y	Palmer Sadie—†	101	housewife	47	"
z	Puccio David J	101	foreman	25	"

1105

a	Puccio Viola—†	101	housewife	23	"
b	Coffey Catherine—†	105	at home	85	"
c	Finn Katherine M—†	105	teacher	52	"
d	Finn Martin	105	salesman	51	"
e	Kelly Arthur J	105	treasurer	56	"

Forest Hills Street—Continued

F	Kelly Helen F—†	105	housewife	54	here
G	Kelly Sheila—†	105	secretary	24	"
H	Lange Adele—†	106	housekeeper	40	Rochdale
K	Pade Reinhold	106	laborer	36	here
L	Patz Clara R—†	106	housekeeper	67	"
M	Prendergast Gladys L—†	106	housewife	54	"
N	Shields Edward	106	molder	41	"
O	Yoe Eva R—†	106	clerk	21	59 Mozart
R	Austin August	139	toolmaker	63	here
S	Austin Matilda—†	139	housewife	58	"
T	Austin Molly—†	139	clerk	29	"
U	Farrell Catherine—†	139	maid	60	
V	Farrell Margaret—†	139	newsdealer	48	"
W	Leahan Frank E	139	operator	46	"
X	Leahan Margaret—†	139	housewife	39	"
Y	Ogg David T, jr	143–145	foreman	30	"
Z	Ogg Katherine—†	143–145	housewife	29	"

1106

A	McLaughlin Genevieve—†	143–145	"	39	"
B	McLaughlin John T	143–145	letter carrier	45	"
C	Vuozzo Arthur G	143–145	clerk	22	
D	Vuozzo Gary	143–145	cutter	50	
E	Vuozzo Louis G	143–145	agent	25	
F	Vuozzo Theresa—†	143–145	housewife	48	"
G	McCabe Annie—†	146	"	73	
H	McCabe John	146	caretaker	72	"
K	Josephs Annie M—†	147–149	housewife	45	"
L	Josephs Luke K	147–149	stockman	52	"
M	Curley Elizabeth E—†	147–149	teacher	65	"
N	Flynn Mildred—†	147–149	cashier	35	
O	Wildermuth Louise—†	147–149	housewife	53	"
P	Wildermuth Max	147–149	roaster	60	
R	Hunt John	151	watchman	43	"
S	Hunt Mary—†	151	housewife	32	"
T	Loughman Vera—†	151	stenographer	20	35 Peter Parley rd
U	Sullivan Rita M—†	151	housewife	28	here
V	Sullivan Robert F	151	manager	32	"
W	Gleason Dorothy W—†	151	stenographer	28	"
X	Gleason Francis J	151	clerk	32	"
Y	Gleason Irene C—†	151	at home	27	Colorado
Z	Gleason Mary C—†	151	housewife	59	here

1107
Forest Hills Street—Continued

A	Galeota Catherine—†	155	housewife	36	here
B	Galeota Joseph M	155	engineer	38	"
C	Hogarty George H	155	letter carrier	39	"
D	Hogarty Margaret—†	155	housewife	38	"
E	Ciccone Catherine T—†	155	forewoman	26	"
F	Ciccone John A	155	U S A	27	
G	Carew Michael F	156	fisherman	40	"
H	Redmond Chester	156	engineer	40	"
K	Redmond Ella—†	156	housewife	42	"
L	Carty Frances—†	159	cashier	32	
M	Carty Steven H, jr	159	laborer	50	
N	Harlow Elsa—†	159	housewife	63	"
O	Harlow Frederick	159	foreman	64	"
P	McCollum Joseph R	159	laborer	69	
R	Kearney Mary A—†	159	at home	73	"
S	Sullivan Catherine—†	159	housewife	25	"
T	Sullivan Thomas	159	chauffeur	30	"
U	Cunniff Dorothea E—†	167	stenographer	25	"
V	Cunniff Eleanor—†	167	"	23	"
W	Cunniff Mary P—†	167	clerk	24	
X	Kane Winifred—†	167	housewife	50	"
Y	Lammers Albert T	167	mechanic	64	"
Z	Lammers Mary—†	167	housewife	60	"

1108

A	Stanger John S	167	agent	54	
B	Stanger John W	167	student	22	
C	Stanger Leonora F—†	167	housewife	48	"
D	McCready Elizabeth A-†	171	"	30	
E	McCready Thomas F	171	broker	35	
F	Faurer Charles	171	retired	76	
G	Faurer Ida—†	171	at home	70	"
H	Faurer Martin	171	upholsterer	39	"
K	Faurer Ruth E—†	171	housewife	38	"
L	Collins Catherine M—†	171	"	25	
M	Collins Frank	171	U S N	26	
N	DeCarl Catherine—†	171	operator	48	"
O	Haddad Abraham N	174	retired	60	
P	Haddad Dabely—†	174	housewife	50	"
R	Haddad Lydia—†	174	saleswoman	21	"
S	Haddad Mabel W—†	174	housewife	26	"

Page.	Letter.	FULL NAME.	Residence, Jan. 1, 1946.	Occupation.	Supposed Age.	Reported Residence, Jan. 1, 1945. Street and Number.

Forest Hills Street—Continued

	T	Haddad Namey A	174	repairman	23	here
	U	Haddad William A	174	chauffeur	25	"
	V	Barney Louis E	175	machinist	52	"
	W	Shamon Josephine—†	175	housewife	48	"
	X	Boyle Eleanora—†	191	student	20	
	Y	Boyle Margaret M—†	191	teacher	25	"
	Z	Boyle Rose M—†	191	housewife	52	"

1109

	A	Boyle William E	191	manager	54	"
	B	Norton Margaret—†	191	at home	90	"
	C	Paul Jessie M—†	215	cook	59	"
	D	Squires H Louise—†	215	secretary	23	Vermont
	E	Stafford Fanny E—†	215	maid	74	here
	F	Wood Inez W—†	215	bookkeeper	62	"
	G	Donahue Douglas A	235	U S M C	23	"
	H	Donahue Isabel C—†	235	housewife	56	"
	K	Donahue Robert J	235	student	24	

Glade Avenue

	M	Fennessey Elizabeth—†	4	housewife	45	here
	N	Fennessey James	4	patrolman	46	"
	O	Fennessey Elizabeth—†	4	housewife	80	"
	P	Fennessey Francis	4	salesman	40	"
	R	Kenney John J	4	clerk	49	
	S	Kenney Mary G—†	4	housewife	42	"
	T	Kerrigan Mary—†	6	"	38	
	U	Kerrigan Paul	6	carpenter	45	"
	V	Gardner Alice—†	6	housewife	49	"
	W	Gardner Alice M—†	6	"	25	
	X	Gardner James A	6	maintenance	59	"
	Y	Gardner James F	6	clerk	26	"
	Z	Gardner Paul V	6	"	25	New Jersey

1110

	A	O'Neill Theresa—†	6	housewife	55	here
	B	O'Neill Thomas E	6	salesman	55	"
	C	Sullivan Ann—†	7	housewife	34	"
	D	Sullivan John	7	electrician	34	"
	E	Anderson Carl A	7	machinist	59	"
	F	Anderson Svea—†	7	housewife	55	"
	G	Hohleen Alice V—†	7	clerk	35	"

Glade Avenue—Continued

H	Zolon Charles	7	chef	29	here
K	Zolon Virginia—†	7	housewife	28	"
L	Anderson Dorothea M—†	8	"	27	19 Glade av
M	Anderson Henry L	8	clergyman	27	19 "
N	Valliere Oliver	8	U S N	25	here
O	Valliere Rachelle—†	8	housewife	20	"
P	Ging George W	8	letter carrier	47	"
R	Ging Mary G—†	8	housewife	39	"
T	McDermott Amy—†	11	"	53	
U	McDermott Arthur	11	foreman	60	"
V	McDermott Arthur, jr	11	electrician	29	"
W	McDermott John P	11	U S A	26	
X	McDermott Mary M—†	11	statistician	30	"
Y	McDermott Paul M	11	U S A	20	
Z	LaBrecque Henry J	12	mechanic	41	"

1111

A	LaBrecque Medora—†	12	housewife	38	"
B	Grisdale J Howard	12	engineer	50	"
C	Gridale Louise—†	12	housewife	75	"
D	Grisdale Thomas I	12	supervisor	51	"
E	Belliveau Joseph	12	machinist	65	"
F	Belliveau Margaret—†	12	housewife	56	"
G	Belliveau Marion—†	12	clerk	32	
H	Dreier John G	16	shoecutter	55	"
K	Dreier Mary T—†	16	housewife	54	"
L	Swanson Gottwill W	16	machinist	50	"
M	Swanson Karen—†	16	housewife	48	"
N	Pulster Edward	16	technician	56	"
O	Pulster Mary—†	16	housewife	54	"
P	Lyle Nellie—†	17	"	50	
R	Lyle Robert	17	shipfitter	48	"
S	Derzanski Chester	17	U S N	26	64 School
T	Derzanski Mary—†	17	housewife	26	64 "
U	MacInnis Katherine—†	17	forewoman	50	here
V	MacInnis Neil	17	chauffeur	59	"
W	MacInnis Thomas F	17	insulator	25	"
X	DeCosta Charles	17	painter	37	"
Y	DeCosta Mary—†	17	housewife	32	"
Z	Cavanaugh Hannah—†	19	"	48	

1112

A	Cavanaugh Michael T	19	patrolman	48	"

8

Glade Avenue—Continued

Letter	Full Name	Residence Jan. 1, 1946	Occupation	Supposed Age	Reported Residence Jan. 1, 1945 Street and Number
c	Houlsen Ann—†	19	at home	27	75 Glen rd
d	Houlsen Arnold	19	cook	37	75 "
e	Magnuson Edward B	20	inspector	37	Quincy
f	Magnuson Thelma—†	20	housewife	27	"
g	*Smith William	20	proprietor	48	here
h	Stewart Jean—†	20	housewife	50	"
k	Stewart William	20	salesman	52	"
l	Clevestrom Anna—†	20	housewife	67	"
m	Clevestrom Ewald	20	machinist	70	"
p	Osh Edward	21	U S A	33	"
n	Osh Howard	21	"	36	
o	Osh Lena—†	21	housewife	66	"
r	Tippo Anna—†	21	"	63	"
s	Tippo John	21	cabinetmaker	63	"
t	Sullivan Catherine—†	21	housewife	60	"
u	Sullivan Catherine—†	21	factoryworker	28	"
v	Sullivan May—†	21	clerk	30	

Glen Road

Letter	Full Name	Residence Jan. 1, 1946	Occupation	Supposed Age	Reported Residence Jan. 1, 1945 Street and Number
w	Dutczak Henry A	3	operator	33	here
x	Dutczak Julia M—†	3	housewife	55	"
y	Dutczak Michael	3	retired	65	"
z	Dutczak Michael, jr	3	metalworker	31	"
	1113				
a	Dutczak Robert R	3	U S A	27	
b	Dutczak William W	3	machinist	36	"
e	Dixon Jane—†	3	housekeeper	61	"
d	Jacobs Catherine—†	3	housewife	27	"
c	McDevitt Irene—†	3	assembler	27	Randolph
f	McCarren Dorothea E—†	3	secretary	27	here
h	McCarren Edward F	3	salesman	60	"
g	McCarren Edward F, jr	3	U S A	26	"
k	McCarren Mary E—†	3	housewife	55	"
l	Carr Ralph L, jr	5	machinist	28	"
m	Duprey Barbara M—†	5	WAC	24	
n	Duprey Helen E—†	5	housewife	49	"
o	Duprey Leslie M	5	machinist	53	"
p	Elliott Alfred	5	fireman	54	
r	Elliott Gladys—†	5	operator	21	"
s	Elliott Harold	5	mover	26	

Glen Road—Continued

	Letter.	FULL NAME.	Residence, Jan. 1, 1946.	Occupation.	Supposed Age.	Reported Residence, Jan. 1, 1945. Street and Number.
	T	George Julia—†	5	housewife	74	here
	U	George William	5	retired	67	"
	V	Hicks Gertrude—†	5	housekeeper	45	"
	W	Hicks Helen—†	5	housewife	22	Pennsylvania
	X	Dardano Nicholas	5	laborer	56	here
	Y	Dardano Pasquale	5	"	50	"
	Z	Dunne Mary E—†	5	housewife	45	"
		1114				
	A	Dunne Stephen G	5	carpenter	45	"
	B	Dunne Stephen J, jr	5	U S N	22	
	C	Forte Elizabeth—†	16–18	housewife	72	"
	D	Forte Frank	16–18	laborer	47	
	E	Forte Wilford	16–18	retired	75	
	F	McGinnis Daniel	16–18	expressman	32	"
	G	Carroll Catherine—†	16–18	housewife	42	"
	H	Carroll David	16–18	steamfitter	43	"
	K	Landry Alice—†	16–18	housewife	65	"
	L	Landry Amelia A—†	16–18	clerk	29	
	M	Landry Julian B	16–18	engineer	32	"
	N	Hanley Anna B—†	20–22	housewife	55	"
	O	Hanley James	20–22	draftsman	33	"
	P	Linnehan Mary C—†	20–22	housewife	44	"
	R	Linnehan William F	20–22	B F D	45	
	S	Linnehan William F, jr	20–22	U S A	21	
	T	O'Connell Mary—†	20–22	housewife	78	"
	U	McKay Catherine R—†	20–22	"	54	
	V	McKay William J	20–22	salesman	53	"
	W	McKay William J, jr	20–22	clerk	29	"
	X	MacDonald James S	26	engineer	36	Springfield
	Y	MacDonald Katherine B—†	26	housewife	34	
	Z	Donavon Margaret B—†	26	"	75	32 Yeoman
		1115				
	A	Kinley May E—†	26	bookkeeper	36	32 "
	B	Smith Edward	26	salesman	45	36 "
	C	French Margaret—†	26	clerk	25	Quincy
	D	French Richard	26	cook	27	"
	E	Gustavson George	28	mechanic	3S	here
	F	Gustavson Marion—†	28	housewife	37	"
	G	Burns Austin J	28	U S N	21	"
	M	Burns John	28	stableman	5S	"
	H	Burns John J	28	U S A	24	

Glen Road—Continued

	Letter	FULL NAME	Residence	Occupation	Age	Reported Residence
	K	Burns Mary K—†	28	housewife	58	here
	L	Burns Mary R—†	28	bookkeeper	26	"
	N	Burns Vincent	28	teacher	23	"
	P	Conaghan Charles	29A	repairman	37	"
	R	Conaghan Mary—†	29A	housewife	30	"
	S	Koen Frances D—†	29A	secretary	51	"
	T	Koen Francis X	29A	retired	63	"
	U	Huntington Elizabeth Q–†	31	housekeeper	65	"
	V	Dudley Catherine F—†	39	"	70	..
	W	Petraitis Albert	39	machinist	27	"
	X	Petraitis John	39	operator	54	"
	Y	Petraitis Olga—†	39	stenographer	21	"
	Z	Petraitis Rose—†	39	housewife	53	"
1116						
	A	Riley Mary—†	39	housekeeper	84	"
	B	Viles Helen C—†	39	clerk	34	''
	C	Viles Joseph M	39	chauffeur	33	"
	D	Salles Andre	42	electrician	29	"
	E	Salles Bernard	42	cook	62	
	F	Salles Edna—†	42	housewife	30	"
	G	Salles Melanie—†	42	"	52	
	H	Henning Edward F	42	manager	58	"
	K	Henning Theresa W—†	42	housewife	50	"
	L	McCusker Agnes—†	42	clerk	35	..
	M	McCusker Clement M	42	plumber	30	"
	N	McCusker Loretta—†	42	nurse	33	
	O	McCusker William	42	dispatcher	41	"
	P	Connaughton Delia M—†	43	housewife	64	"
	R	Connaughton John J	43	operator	38	"
	S	Connaughton Sarah L—†	43	housewife	38	"
	T	Higgins Catherine F—†	43	"	43	
	U	Higgins William F	43	commissioner	45	"
	V	Kelly Mary K—†	43	clerk	61	..
	W	Kelly Michael	43	chauffeur	49	"
	X	Brunner Herman	46	machinist	58	"
	Y	Brunner Minnie C—†	46	housewife	66	"
	Z	Mulvey John J	46	accountant	25	"
1117						
	A	Mulvey Ruth M—†	46	housewife	24	"
	B	Sullivan Emma—†	46	saleswoman	53	"
	C	Laffey Annie—†	46	at home	71	"

Glen Road—Continued

Letter	Full Name	Residence, Jan. 1, 1946.	Occupation	Supposed Age	Reported Residence, Jan. 1, 1945.
D	Laffey Catherine J—†	46	housewife	60	here
E	Laffey Katherine F—†	46	clerk	25	"
F	Laffey Michael F	46	toolkeeper	57	"
G	Laffey Rita M—†	46	cashier	22	"
H	Laffey Thomas F	46	U S A	29	
K	O'Brien Anna A—†	47	housewife	49	"
L	O'Brien John J	47	carpenter	51	"
M	O'Brien John J, jr	47	student	21	
N	O'Brien Regina F—†	47	clerk	22	
O	McCarthy Annie E—†	50	at home	80	"
P	McCarthy Catherine R—†	50	housewife	50	"
R	McCarthy Justin J	50	tel worker	52	"
S	Schilling Frances—†	50	operator	36	"
T	Schilling Henry	50	molder	34	
U	Schilling Johanna—†	50	housewife	56	"
V	Schilling Phillip	50	laborer	65	
W	Scollins Hugh J	50	clerk	53	
X	Scollins Veronica—†	50	collector	46	"
Y	Lake Agnes M—†	rear 53	housewife	38	"
Z	Lake Arthur F ,	" 53	chauffeur	38	"

1118

Letter	Full Name	Residence, Jan. 1, 1946.	Occupation	Supposed Age	Reported Residence, Jan. 1, 1945.
A	Doherty Bernard C	54	salesman	24	"
B	Doherty Eileen—†	54	housewife	24	"
C	Hankey Charles W	54	policeman	49	"
D	Hankey Mary R—†	54	housewife	50	"
E	Rich Catherine A—†	54	"	46	320 La Grange
F	Rich Frank P	54	teacher	53	320 "
G	Rich Paul	54	U S N	20	320 "
H	Dolan Delia—†	54	at home	60	here
K	Hogan Isabel M—†	54	tel operator	24	"
L	Taylor Elizabeth—†	54	packer	54	"
M	Taylor Elizabeth E—†	54	nurse	23	
N	Jason Helen A—†	58	housewife	40	"
O	Jason Peter P	58	student	43	"
P	Zabitis Antoinette—†	58	housewife	55	Cambridge
R	Zabitis Kazimienas	58	electrician	56	"
S	Anzalone Louis	58	U S N	36	here
T	Anzalone Martha—†	58	housekeeper	34	"
U	Connors Ann M—†	58	housewife	30	"
V	Connors John D	58	clerk	33	"
W	Cremin Dennis E	59	boxmaker	67	Arlington

Glen Road—Continued

X	Cremin Gertrude M—†	59	at home	38	Arlington
Y	O'Connell Kathleen M—†	59	housewife	37	here
Z	Seager Augustus	59	tester	38	"

1119

A	Seager Marie—†	59	milliner	38	
C	Heizmann Gladys—†	59	housewife	38	"
B	Heizmann Victor	59	waiter	36	
D	Lockerby Rosine—†	59	clerk	46	
E	Lockerby Walter M	59	molder	48	
F	Taylor Esther—†	59	housewife	27	"
G	Taylor Wallace	59	clerk	27	
H	Quigley Helen—†	59	boxmaker	64	"
K	Shaughnessy Alice T—†	59	housewife	42	"
L	Shaughnessy Arthur L	59	chauffeur	49	"
M	Anderson Hulda—†	65	stitcher	64	83 Glen rd
N	Balduc Flora M—†	65	housewife	53	here
O	Balduc Ludger J	65	mechanic	50	"
P	Balduc Rita T—†	65	clerk	23	"
R	Cousin Louis W	65	salesman	35	14 Woolsey sq
S	Dufault Beatrice K—†	65	housewife	34	New York
T	Dufault Ernest J	65	U S M C	43	Marlboro
U	Glover William O	65	millworker	23	1 Alfred
V	Hamilton Hollis	65	U S N	41	Rhode Island
W	Lynch William	65	machinist	45	4 Germania
X	McCarthy Edward J	65	laborer	37	38 Chandler
Y	McCarthy Mary—†	65	clerk	25	38 "
Z	McGill Anna—†	65	operator	40	Everett

1120

A	Newell Mozelle—†	65	housewife	27	Virginia
B	Newell Stanley	65	U S N	26	"
D	Ochs Frederick W	71	designer	50	here
E	Ochs Jane J—†	71	housewife	50	"
F	Kozlowski Amelia—†	71	"	53	"
G	*Kozlowski Kostontz	71	cook	52	
H	Kennedy Helen M—†	71	housewife	35	"
K	Kennedy James F	71	chauffeur	38	"
L	Tringalli Rosaria—†	75	housewife	35	"
M	Tringalli Sebastiano	75	fisherman	37	"
N	Hooley Dorothy—†	75	clerk	22	
O	Hooley James	75	chauffeur	47	"
P	Hooley Jeanette—†	75	clerk	21	

Glen Road—Continued

	R	Hooley Mary—†	75	housewife	44	here
	S	Hulbert George	75	mechanic	35	146 Boylston
	T	Hulbert Mary—†	75	housewife	28	146 "
	U	Buchanan George W	79	retired	70	here
	V	Hall Margaret A—†	79	manager	26	"
	X	Latter Cecil A	79	metalworker	45	"
	W	Latter Hazel—†	79	at home	42	..
	Y	Ring Evelyn—†	79	"	33	
	Z	Ring Samuel	79	salesman	42	"
		1121				
	A	Wilson Jane—†	82	hostess	50	
	B	Shire Abraham	82	technician	37	"
	C	Shire Anna—†	82	WAC	41	
	D	Shire Wadad R—†	82	housewife	37	"
	E	Raymo Arthur S	82	chauffeur	58	"
	F	Raymo Maude L—†	82	housewife	60	"
	G	Scharle Katherine—†	83	at home	66	"
	H	Keane Helen—†	83	housewife	48	"
	K	Keane Patrick	83	policeman	47	"
	L	Scharle Edwin	83	engineer	34	"
	M	Scharle Gladys—†	83	housewife	31	"
	N	Johnson Claire—†	85	"	27	
	O	Johnson Warren	85	clerk	27	
	P	Nesky Edward P	85	machinist	28	"
	R	Anderson Anna B—†	85	housewife	30	"
	S	Anderson Herbert	85	machinist	30	"
	T	Graveley James O	85	salesman	54	"
	U	Leonard Elsie—†	85	nurse	43	
	V	Wilbur Howard	86	teacher	56	
	W	Wilbur Mildred L—†	86	housewife	53	"
	Y	Davenport Myrtle—†	91	"	47	
	Z	Davenport Richard L	91	inspector	42	"
		1122				
	A	Brophy Ursula J—†	91	agent	24	
	B	Burnes Agnes G—†	91	housewife	58	"
	C	Burnes Henry A	91	inspector	59	"

Glenside Avenue

	D	Mason May M—†	6	housewife	45	here
	E	Mason Warren S	6	roofer	48	"

Page.	Letter.	Full Name.	Residence, Jan. 1, 1946.	Occupation.	Supposed Age.	Reported Residence, Jan. 1, 1945. Street and Number.

Glenside Avenue—Continued

	F	Breslin J Frank	6	compositor	57	here
	G	Breslin Margaret O—†	6	housewife	52	"
	H	Donovan Annie B—†	6	"	53	"
	K	Donovan Robert E	6	gardener	62	"
	L	Walsh Elizabeth A—†	8	housewife	65	"
	M	Walsh Patrick J	8	retired	69	
	N	Boyle Elizabeth M—†	8	housewife	42	"
	O	Boyle James F	8	clerk	52	
	P	Pink Catherine H—†	8	housewife	27	"
	R	Pink William P	8	accountant	30	"
	S	Parlon Lillian L—†	14	housewife	28	"
	T	Parlon William J	14	policeman	29	"
	U	Talbot Elizabeth A—†	14	housewife	56	"
	V	Talbot Felix F	14	guard	56	
	W	Drews Anne T—†	14	housewife	27	"
	X	Drews Carrie P—†	14	teacher	51	
	Y	Drews Gladys N—†	14	lawyer	30	
	Z	Drews John T	14	plumber	31	"
1123						
	A	Karcher Catherine D—†	14	housewife	35	"
	B	Karcher John C	14	clerk	37	
	C	Henry Dorothy—†	14	secretary	22	"
	D	Henry Walter	14	clerk	23	"
	E	Leonard Grace E—†	14	housewife	28	63 Bradfield av
	F	Leonard James M	14	salesman	36	25 Forest Hills
	G	Talbot John J	14	U S A	25	here
	H	Talbot Ruth E—†	14	housewife	26	63 Bradfield av
	K	Creighton Anna C—†	16	"	69	here
	L	Creighton Arthur J	16	retired	71	"
	M	Woods Grace—†	16	secretary	37	"
	N	Woods Robert E	16	engineer	43	"
	O	Waters Emily F—†	16	housewife	45	"
	P	Waters Robert A	16	U S N	21	
	R	Waters Thomas J	16	bank teller	47	"
	S	McPherson Joseph	16	chauffeur	48	"
	T	*McPherson Margaret—†	16	housewife	45	"
	U	Meehan Joseph F	16	yardman	52	"
	V	Meehan Julia A—†	16	clerk	48	
	W	Funcannon Edith M—†	16	housewife	42	"
	X	Funcannon Helen M—†	16	student	21	
	Y	Funcannon Ray	16	gardener	42	"

15

1124

Green Street

A	Arnott Mary A—†	151	stitcher	54	366 Amory
B	McGeggen Edna W—†	151	housewife	36	366 "
C	McGeggen Hugh	151	foreman	40	366 "
H	French Hazel—†	165	clerk	27	here
K	Ryan James	165	carpenter	55	"
L	Ryan Lydia—†	165	housewife	50	"
N	Donahue Cecelia P—†	171	"	24	
O	Donahue Francis H	171	retired	58	
P	Donahue Mary C—†	171	housewife	44	"
R	Kelly Kathleen—†	171	sorter	22	
S	Kelly Kathleen V—†	171	housewife	43	"
T	Kelly Louise M—†	171	sorter	23	..
U	Kelly Thomas F	171	chauffeur	45	"
V	Kelly Ellen—†	171	housewife	65	"
W	Cook Beatrice—†	171	"	64	
X	Cook Henry	171	yardman	66	"
Y	Donahue Dorothy M—†	171	housewife	42	"
Z	Donahue Thomas F	171	breweryworker	43	"

1125

C	Spellman Frederick K	177½	mechanic	41	Maine
D	Spellman Frederick K	177½	clerk	20	"
E	Spellman Mary A—†	177½	housewife	38	"
K	Ahl Edward F	185	U S A	21	here
L	Ahl John E	185	plumber	52	"
M	Ahl John R	185	machinist	23	"
N	Ahl Josephine V—†	185	housewife	52	"
O	Collins Anna—†	185	beautician	50	"
P	Collins Jacob	185	machinist	55	"
R	Collins Vito	185	"	25	
S	Abberton Priscilla—†	185	housewife	36	"
T	Abberton William	185	printer	42	..
U	Abberton Alfred G	185	chauffeur	36	"
V	Abberton John J	185	"	40	
W	Abberton Mary—†	185	housewife	70	"
Y	Macdonald Alexander S	185	laborer	52	
Z	O'Connell John J	185	clerk	22	

1126

C	Coolidge Charlotte—†	191	housewife	42	"
D	Coolidge Leslie A	191	mechanic	42	"
E	Morahan Alice—†	191	clerk	29	

Green Street—Continued

	F	Morahan Richard	191	laborer	64	here
	G	*Pittore Arthur	191	barber	49	"
	H	*Pittore Concerto—†	191	housewife	43	"
	K	Smith Edward A	191	packer	54	
	L	Smith Edward J	191	clerk	21	
	M	Smith Mary E—†	191	housewife	53	"
	N	Stronach Mary—†	191	at home	75	32 Amory
	O	Tosi Henry	191	pharmacist	38	32 "
	P	Tukey Helen H—†	191	clerk	30	N Hampshire
	R	Tukey Lillian M—†	191	"	20	here
	S	Tukey Robert D	191	mechanic	42	"
	V	Hobbs John W	197	butcher	45	137 W Concord
	W	Hobbs Lillian E—†	197	housewife	39	137 "

1127

	A	*Quen Jan	205	laundryman	44	here

Kenton Road

	E	Conlin Anna M—†	2	hairdresser	50	here
	F	Conlin Elizabeth D—†	2	nurse	43	"
	G	Timmons Emma L—†	2	at home	70	"
	H	Timmons Emma T—†	2	bookkeeper	35	"
	K	Mahoney Earlena F—†	18	housewife	28	"
	L	Mahoney Garrett	18	plumber	40	"
	M	Swanson Anna S—†	18	domestic	62	"
	N	Keating Dennis F	20	foreman	45	"
	O	Keating Margaret F—†	20	housewife	45	"
	P	Morris Catherine—†	20	at home	80	"
	R	Meehan Katherine V—†	20	housewife	55	"
	S	Meehan Margaret M—†	20	WAVE	30	
	T	Smith Anne F—†	20	housewife	29	"
	U	Smith Thomas G	20	U S N	35	"
	V	Barry Catherine B—†	20	stenographer	21	"
	W	Barry Frederick L	20	clerk	61	"
	X	Barry Mary E—†	20	housewife	56	"
	Y	Becker Emma C—†	24	at home	63	"
	Z	Johnson Curtis G	24	manager	43	"

1128

	A	Johnson Lena J—†	24	housewife	49	"
	B	Kelly Charles H	30	billposter	28	36 Cobden
	C	Regan Florence L—†	30	housewife	24	1865 Col av

Kenton Road—Continued

D	Sadoski Frank J	30	shoeworker	55	1865 Col av
E	Sadoski James G	30	U S M C	22	1865 "
F	Peterson Charles L	30	chauffeur	28	here
G	Peterson Josephine V—†	30	housewife	28	"
H	Davidson Cecil E	30	student	20	"
K	Davidson Clarence E	30	toolmaker	53	139 Hillside
L	McCarthy Louise—†	30	housewife	33	111 Smith
M	English Blanche M—†	34	"	26	here
N	English Richard	34	U S A	28	"
O	Mills Francis W	34	U S N	23	Maine
P	Mills Virginia M—†	34	housewife	21	here
R	O'Leary Arthur F	34	U S M C	24	"
S	O'Leary Clara E—†	34	housewife	44	"
T	O'Leary Eugene J	34	shipfitter	45	"
U	Strattard Grace E—†	34	housewife	25	"
V	Lunette Louis	40	student	23	4 Michelangelo
W	Lunette Mary L—†	40	seamstress	24	here
X	Pergola Phillippe—†	40	housewife	47	"
Y	Pergola Vincenzo	40	laborer	54	"
Z	Zuccola Rocco	40	"	44	

1129

A	Coppinger Bridget—†	40	housewife	39	"
B	Coppinger John J	40	laborer	43	
C	Hutchinson Nellie B—†	44	housewife	44	"
D	Hutchinson Patrick J	44	laborer	47	
E	Moynihan John	44	breweryworker	50	"
F	Smith Annie E—†	46	housewife	52	"
G	Smith James P	46	retired	76	
H	White Alice C—†	56	clerk	26	
K	White Eleanor T—†	56	stenographer	31	"
L	White Henry F	56	clerk	29	"
M	White Henry P	56	retired	67	
N	White Mary M—†	56	at home	77	"
O	White Robert J	56	U S N	22	
P	White William J	56	instructor	73	"
R	Cover Albert	63	student	22	21 Clarence
S	Cover Antonio	63	tileworker	46	21 "
T	Cover Mary—†	63	housewife	43	21 "
U	Miniutti Santinia—†	63	at home	71	240 Shirley
V	White Gertrude F—†	64	hairdresser	57	here
W	White Julia A—†	64	at home	51	"
X	White Mary H—†	64	hairdresser	59	"

18

Lourdes Avenue

Y	Berghaus Charles	6–8	polisher	25	here
z	Berghaus Mary E—†	6–8	housewife	50	"
1130						
A	Berghaus Mildred—†	6–8	clerk	22	"
B	Berghaus William C	6–8	chauffeur	55	"
c	Kelley Mary A—†	6–8	housewife	44	"
D	Kelley Martin E	6–8	steamfitter	44	"
E	Ward William J	6–8	shipper	48	'
G	Kopp Agnes B—†	6–8	housewife	38	"
H	Kopp William J	6–8	chauffeur	38	"
F	*Sharkey Catherine—†	6–8	housewife	58	"
K	Miller Eleanor M—†	7	stenographer	27	"
L	Miller Virginia R—†	7	student	21	"
M	Miller William J	7	manager	52	"
N	Sullivan Margaret A—†	7	tel operator	28	"
O	Freeman Mary L—†	7	at home	70	"
P	Wells Francis J	7	salesman	39	"
R	Wells Hilda M—†	7	housewife	38	"
S	Tosko Helen A—†	7	"	35	"
T	Tosko John	7	policeman	48	"
U	Regan Eugene P	10–12	student	20	"
V	Regan Peter T	10–12	machinist	55	"
W	Regan Rose R—†	10–12	housewife	41	"
X	Marinos Christine—†	10–12	"	34	"
Y	Marinos Peter	10–12	restaurateur	45	"
z	Charchut Annie—†	10–12	secretary	24	"
1131						
A	*Charchut Margaret—†	10–12	housewife	55	"
B	Charchut Theodore	10–12	cook	55	"
c	Huether Frank J	13	upholsterer	50	"
D	Huether Marion Y—†	13	clerk	23	"
E	Huether Yvonne M—†	13	housewife	47	"
F	Lindroth Esther G—†	13	stenographer	48	"
G	Lindroth John E	13	salesman	43	"
H	Lindroth Selma—†	13	housewife	71	"
K	Mulkeen Anna—†	13	"	52	
L	Mulkeen Catherine—†	13	secretary	23	"
M	Mulkeen Frank	13	U S A	27	"
N	Mulkeen Martin	13	chauffeur	53	"
O	Mulkeen William	13	U S N	22	"
P	Lehan James	16–18	chauffeur	52	"
R	Treacy Beatrice—†	16–18	housewife	35	"

Page.	Letter.	FULL NAME.	Residence, Jan. 1, 1946.	Occupation.	Supposed Age.	Reported Residence, Jan. 1, 1945. Street and Number.

Lourdes Avenue—Continued

	s	Treacy Michael F	16–18	policeman	38	here
	t	Treacy Thomas M	16–18	mechanic	39	"
	u	Aborjaily Edna H—†	16–18	housewife	32	"
	v	Aborjaily Frederick C	16–18	accountant	33	"
	w	Grey Elizabeth—†	17	at home	44	
	x	Grey Hester—†	17	"	88	
	y	Grey Joseph T	17	clerk	53	
	z	Rostron Ada—†	17	at home	68	..
		1132				
	a	Conroy Florence B—†	17	housewife	40	"
	b	Conroy James J	17	agent	47	
	c	Dow Mary E—†	17	housewife	50	"
	d	Dow Warren P	17	estimator	43	"
	e	Rileigh George S	19	dentist	42	
	f	Rileigh Mary—†	19	housewife	43	"
	g	Alward Eugene H	19	operator	49	"
	h	Alward Nellie I—†	19	housewife	48	"
	k	*Fallon Anna—†	19	"	39	
	l	Fallon Thomas J	19	chauffeur	39	"
	m	Welch David E	25	manager	32	"
	n	Welch Evelyn C—†	25	housewife	28	"
	o	Friberg Iris—†	25	at home	64	
	p	Friberg Karen—†	25	clerk	36	
	r	Gleason Edward J	25	U S N	32	
	s	Gleason Julia—†	25	housewife	34	"
	t	Coldwell Ruth—†	25	clerk	40	
	u	Coldwell William	25	blacksmith	52	"
	v	Hall Esther—†	25	clerk	35	"
	w	Rheault Mary A—†	25	housewife	32	Maine
	x	Rheault Noel L	25	pipefitter	33	"
	y	Mulloy Anna K—†	25	housewife	36	here
	z	Mulloy John P	25	clerk	42	"
		1133				
	a	White Hannah M—†	25	at home	67	
	b	Mee Georgia M—†	29	housewife	30	"
	c	Mee William H	29	chauffeur	36	"
	d	Hoban Irene E—†	29	housewife	29	"
	e	Hoban Walter J	29	U S N	30	"
	f	Martin Irene E—†	29	at home	48	Weymouth
	g	*Farrell Ellen L—†	29	housewife	33	here

Lourdes Avenue—Continued

H	Farrell Joseph C	29	baker	38	here
K	*Crawford Minnie—†	29	at home	89	"
L	Page Annie I—†	29	housewife	58	"
M	Page Charles E	29	conductor	61	"
N	Hurley Joseph R	29	chauffeur	26	368 Riverway
O	Hurley Margaret C—†	29	housewife	21	368 "
P	Burke Grace M—†	29	"	53	here
R	Burke Peter	29	steamfitter	66	"
S	Campbell Louise N—†	33	manager	38	"
T	Campbell Wendell P	33	U S A	38	
U	Dawson Barbara—†	33	housewife	38	"
V	Dawson Joseph W	33	chauffeur	37	"
W	Mullen Mary T—†	33	housewife	26	"
X	Mullen Robert F	33	color matcher	25	"
Y	O'Toole Mabel—†	33	housewife	31	"
Z	O'Toole William	33	manager	31	"

1134

A	Monticone Ann V—†	33	housewife	32	"
B	Monticone John B	33	teacher	37	
C	Chute Alfred E	33	steelworker	34	"
D	Chute Edith E—†	33	housewife	30	"
E	Crawford Della—†	33	at home	24	13 Adams
F	Elkind Maurice	42	demonstrator	36	here
G	Elkind Mollie—†	42	housewife	34	"
H	Vaughan Leonard E	42	machinist	47	"
K	Vaughan Mary O—†	42	housewife	47	"
L	O'Donnell Margaret M—†	42	"	35	213 Weld
M	O'Donnell Thomas G	42	chauffeur	37	213 "

Meehan Place

N	Mulcahy George J	1	bartender	40	9 Sunset
O	Mulcahy Lois M—†	1	housewife	32	9 "
P	Wagner Howard	1	laborer	35	here
R	Wagner Mary E—†	1	housewife	29	"
S	Dick Elizabeth—†	1	"	51	13 Union av
T	Dick William	1	waiter	57	13 "
U	Hynes Ellen E—†	1	clerk	50	here
V	Neill Francis J	1	U S N	27	19 Cedar rd
W	Neill Louise R—†	1	secretary	29	here

Meehan Place—Continued

	x	Graham William L	2	metalworker	53	here
	z	Burgess Esther—†	3	housewife	29	"
1135						
	A	Burgess Michael H	3	U S A	31	"

Peter Parley Road

	B	Drake John E	11	retired	76	here
	c	Drake Margaret C—†	11	housewife	69	"
	D	Brickley John P	15	supervisor	39	"
	E	Brickley Margaret—†	15	housewife	37	"
	F	Murphy Albert D	15	salesman	50	Newton
	G	Murphy Mary O—†	15	housewife	45	"
	H	Ormond Winifred T—†	15	teacher	40	here
	K	Thurston James H	19	manager	37	"
	L	Thurston Madelyn—†	19	housewife	33	"
	M	Byrnes Henry J	19	fireman	49	
	N	Byrnes Mary A—†	19	housewife	48	"
	o	McCarthy Daniel D	19	salesman	52	"
	P	McCarthy Margaret T—†	19	secretary	42	"
	R	Hurley Mary J—†	25	housewife	63	"
	s	Hurley Paul D	25	physician	32	"
	T	Hurley Rita M—†	25	housewife	27	"
	u	Hurley Thomas F	25	plumber	65	"
	v	Kelly Anastasia—†	25	teacher	47	
	w	Tobin Catherine A—†	33	at home	74	"
	x	Carlisle Elizabeth G—†	33	matron	53	
	Y	Nazzaro Edward M	33	clerk	55	
	z	Nazzaro Rose O—†	33	housewife	45	"
1136						
	B	Kenney Mary—†	35	"	56	
	c	Kenney Philip A	35	clerk	35	
	D	Kenney William	35	agent	59	
	E	McVeon Jeanette—†	35	clerk	31	
	F	Fay Arthur J	37	salesman	34	"
	G	Fay Catherine T—†	37	housewife	57	"
	H	Fay James G	37	electrician	23	"
	K	Fay John J	37	foreman	64	"
	L	Fay Ruth E—†	37	manager	28	"
	M	Connelly Bartley	37	motorman	52	"
	N	Connelly Mary—†	37	housewife	43	"

Peter Parley Road—Continued

o	Leary Annie—†	37	housewife	72	here
p	Goldwait Gladys—†	43	bookkeeper	36	"
r	McCabe Constance—†	43	housewife	26	"
s	McCabe Warren J	43	newspaper	28	"
t	Woods Rose—†	43	housewife	70	"
u	Dana Lester H	45	broker	44	"
v	Dana Rebecca—†	45	housewife	75	"
w	Dana Samuel	45	realtor	75	
x	Wilner Jacob S	49	broker	62	
y	Wilner Marvin J	49	engineer	31	"
z	Wilner Rose C—†	49	housewife	54	"

1137

a	Howatt Sadie W—†	53	"	58	
b	Howatt Welton M	53	salesman	71	"
c	Burke Gerard F	57	copywriter	32	"
d	Burke Grace S—†	57	nurse	25	"
e	Burke Margaret M—†	57	housewife	66	"
f	Bopp Charles W	63	fitter	29	8 Elmore
g	Bopp Patricia—†	63	housewife	25	here
h	Miller Agnes B—†	63	"	53	"
k	Miller Edward J	63	U S A	30	"
l	Miller Mary B—†	63	factoryworker	23	"
m	Miller Michael J	63	rigger	60	
n	Miller Rita A—†	63	clerk	20	"
o	Carty Ellen A—†	67	housewife	64	"
p	Carty John J	67	U S A	38	
r	Carty Rita A—†	67	stenographer	25	"
s	Carty Stephen H	67	retired	80	"
t	Crane Catherine A—†	67	stenographer	30	"
u	Crane Thomas A	67	"	30	"
v	Flynn John L	71	clerk	60	"
w	Flynn Leo L	71	student	25	"
x	Flynn Mary A—†	71	housewife	58	"
y	Flynn Regina M—†	71	at home	23	"
z	Flynn Rita M—†	71	secretary	29	"

1138

a	Sullivan James J	71	trimmer	60	"
k	Allen Jane—†	75	housewife	27	Texas
l	Allen Lloyd E, 3d	75	agent	26	"
b	Anderson Bernard	75	chauffeur	22	Fitchburg
c	Bolduc Lea—†	75	housewife	44	"

Page.	Letter.	Full Name.	Residence, Jan. 1, 1946.	Occupation.	Supposed Age.	Reported Residence, Jan. 1, 1945. Street and Number.

Peter Parley Road—Continued

D	Bolduc Louis	75	copywriter	47	Fitchburg
E	Daley Joseph	75	fireman	30	15 Bullard
F	Daley Mary—†	75	at home	28	15 "
M	Pruyn Mary—†	75	housewife	21	New Jersey
N	Pruyn William J	75	U S N	23	6 Hillview av
G	Sofrine Blanche—†	75	housewife	41	62 Alexander
H	Sofrine Manuel	75	mechanic	45	62 "

Robeson Street

O	Beatty Jeannette D—†	1	housewife	45	here
P	Beatty Patrick J	1	pharmacist	46	"
R	Doyle Alice M—†	1	housewife	44	"
S	Doyle Joseph P	1	clerk	43	
T	DesJardins Agnes L—†	4	housewife	63	"
U	DesJardins Alexander J	4	laster	62	
V	DesJardins Joseph G	4	foreman	34	"
W	Bode Martha—†	4	housekeeper	59	4 Carolina pl
X	Costello Blanche E—†	8	housewife	57	here
Y	Costello Coleman J	8	mechanic	58	"
Z	Gorman B Louise—†	8	operator	31	"
	1139				
A	Gorman Robert J	8	accountant	35	"
B	Sullivan Cornelius J	8	mechanic	63	"
C	Sullivan Joseph M	8	U S N	30	"
D	Sullivan Julia—†	8	housewife	54	"
E	Curley Peter M	11	inspector	57	"
F	Curley Robert P	11	commissioner	48	"
G	Kijewski Alice—†	12	clerk	20	168A Cedar
H	Kijewski Felix	12	storekeeper	51	168A "
K	Kijewski Helen—†	12	housewife	43	168A "
L	Kijewski William R	12	repairman	22	168A "
M	Harris Arthur F	12	U S A	33	here
N	Harris Dorothy M—†	12	secretary	21	"
O	Harris Sophia—†	12	housewife	50	"
P	Harris William J	12	printer	54	
R	Marshall Andrew	12	clerk	25	
S	Marshall Lillian—†	12	housewife	24	"
T	Greyser Gladys—†	16	"	37	
U	Greyser Morris	16	teacher	40	
V	Koven Lois—†	16	bookkeeper	25	"

24

Robeson Street—Continued

w	Jones Anna L—†	18	housewife	23	Texas
x	Jones Ralph J, jr	18	salesman	27	here
y	Jones Viola S—†	18	clerk	28	"
z	McGarry Bernard	18	proprietor	34	"

1140

A	McGarry Marie—†	18	housewife	31	"
B	Groves Byron	18	salesman	24	Connecticut
c	Groves Harriette—†	18	housewife	27	"
D	Irbin Erna—†	22	"	42	here
E	Irbin Paul	22	machinist	34	"
F	Munkens Antoinette—†	22	housewife	67	"
G	Daniel Margaret—†	22	"	25	Florida
H	Daniel Nathaniel	22	U S A	27	"
K	Crawford Alice—†	22	housewife	29	here
L	Crawford William	22	clergyman	30	"
M	Sheehan Esther B—†	26	housewife	46	"
N	Sheehan John J	26	supervisor	46	"
O	Douglas Herbert W	26	salesman	41	"
P	Douglas Madeline—†	26	housekeeper	68	"
R	Connolly Alice B—†	26	clerk	28	"
S	Connolly John P	26	U S A	38	
T	Connolly Margaret T—†	26	housewife	70	"
U	Connolly Mary R—†	26	forewoman	41	"
V	Fernandez Frank L	30	restaurateur	40	"
W	Fernandez Josephine K—†	30	housewife	37	"
x*	Kasetta Eva H—†	30	counterwoman	60	"
Y	Kasetta Vincent R	30	clerk	31	
z	Yurenas Gertrude—†	30	secretary	25	"

1141

A	Yurenas Irene—†	30	teacher	28	
e	Tumovicus Baltramejus	30	truckman	59	"
B	Tumovicus Jodviga—†	30	housewife	52	"
D	Higgins Charles F	30	foreman	48	"
E	Higgins Eleanor V—†	30	housewife	47	"
F	Murphy Thomas	30	retired	80	
G	Murphy Timothy J	30	stationmaster	40	"
H	Greany Arthur W	31	machinist	31	"
K	Greany Bridget M—†	31	housewife	36	"
L	Duffin Frank J	31	welder	22	
M	Duffin Kathleen B—†	31	stenographer	21	"
N	Duffin Mary A—†	31	housewife	56	"

Robeson Street—Continued

o	Duffin Michael J	31	molder	60	here
p	Hoey Mary A—†	31	housewife	51	"
r	Hoey Patrick G	31	chauffeur	53	"
s	Closson Frederick Q	34	U S N	30	California
t	Closson Margaret M—†	34	housewife	30	"
u	Roche James J	34	motorman	60	here
v	Roche James T	34	letter carrier	26	"
w	Craig Alice J—†	34	bookkeeper	20	"
x	Craig Mabel R—†	34	housewife	55	"
y	Craig Milton T	34	architect	58	"
z	Schneider Anna E—†	34	milliner	52	

1142

A	Schneider Maria M—†	34	at home	84	"
B	Doherty James E	38	baker	43	"
c	Doherty John E	38	mechanic	45	"
D	Doherty Mary—†	38	at home	28	"
E	Baldwin Edward J	38	shipper	31	
F	Baldwin Mary—†	38	housewife	31	"
G	Baldwin Richard M	38	U S N	21	
H	Reagan Catherine—†	38	at home	60	"
K	Reagan William	38	U S A	29	
L	Cunningham Arthur	38	meatcutter	42	"
M	Cunningham Catherine—†	38	housewife	43	"
N	Thomas Clifton H	39	machinist	39	"
o	Thomas Ruth M—†	39	housewife	33	"
P	Bowman Adelaide—†	39	"	45	"
R	Bowman Alexander	39	newspapers	43	"
S	Bowman Alexander	39	U S A	21	"
T	Riley Eugene A	39	clerk	49	
U	Riley Orryl F—†	39	housewife	50	"
v	Manning Dorothy D—†	39	"	45	
w	Manning Thomas	39	manager	55	"
x	Lombard Edward W	44	U S N	52	
y	MacDonald Bessie A—†	44	housekeeper	62	"
z	Walsh Hugh M	45	seaman	26	"

1143

A	Walsh Mary M—†	45	technician	28	"
B	Heffern Alice M—†	45	housewife	49	"
c	Heffern Evelyn F—†	45	"	34	Illinois
D	Heffern William H	45	retired	76	here
E	Heffern William M	45	inspector	47	Illinois

Robeson Street—Continued

F	Keenan Frank L	45	clerk	62	here
G	Barrett Catherine L—†	48	housewife	48	"
H	Barrett Edward F	48	teacher	26	"
K	Barrett John G	48	accountant	30	"
L	Barrett John V	48	teacher	57	
M	Barrett William L	48	U S A	28	"
N	Lepore Elena—†	53	forewoman	39	Winthrop
O	Lepore Matilda—†	53	"	42	"
P	Spano Alexander	53	U S A	29	"
R	Spano Anna—†	53	housewife	55	"
S	Spano Joseph	53	reporter	59	"
T	Spano Joseph, jr	53	student	25	
U	Spano Lillian—†	53	tel operator	26	"
V	Spano Rose—†	53	"	27	"
W	Jacobson Alan B	54	U S A	23	here
X	Jacobson Anna H—†	54	housewife	53	"
Y	Jacobson William	54	agent	55	"
Z	Levine Charlotte—†	54	secretary	30	"

1144

A	Swister Veronica A—†	54	maid	32	
B	Bortnick Philip A	54	teacher	40	
C	Bortnick Rose H—†	54	housewife	39	"
D	Cook Gertrude E—†	58	at home	75	"
E	Cook Laura G—†	58	housekeeper	50	"
F	Clemon Celia—†	63	housewife	34	"
G	Clemon Simon	63	manager	34	"
H	Wise Esther—†	63	housewife	38	"
K	Wise Isadore	63	attorney	40	"
L	Hark Alfred	63	U S A	21	"
M	*Hark Anna—†	63	housewife	41	"
N	Hark Jacob	63	merchant	41	"
O	Selib Gertrude—†	69	housewife	57	"
P	Selib Morris L	69	manufacturer	60	"
R	Buba Edmund	69	laborer	33	"
S	Buba Rose—†	69	housewife	30	"
T	Rothstein Anna B—†	71	"	36	"
U	Rothstein Morris	71	manufacturer	42	"

Rockvale Circle

V	McDonald Margaret—†	28	housewife	55	21 Plainfield
W	McDonald Margaret M—†	28	clerk	28	21 "

Rockvale Circle—Continued

x	McKenna Gertrude—†	28	clerk	20	21 Plainfield
y	Allaire Adele—†	28	housewife	34	here
z	Allaire Leon	28	welder	46	"
	1145				
a	Carr Edward	28	watchman	58	"
b	Carr Marguerite—†	28	housewife	42	"
c	Walsh Helen—†	32	"	27	"
d	Walsh Richard	32	buyer	28	
e	Coska Clara M—†	32	housewife	33	"
f	Coska John A	32	painter	36	
g	Cowart Dora I—†	32	at home	59	"
h	Weiand Joseph	32	U S N	27	
k	Weiand Millicent M—†	32	housewife	24	"
l	Finney Barbara—†	36	clerk	24	
m	Finney Helen—†	36	"	50	
n	Finney Kenneth	36	U S A	21	
o	Enos Charles A	36	printer	47	
p	Enos Marie I—†	36	clerk	49	
r	Frost Asa R	36	"	34	"
s	Frost Dorothy M—†	36	housewife	28	"
t	Bohane Catherine—†	36	"	80	
u	Bohane Cornelius J	36	retired	78	
v	Watt Margaret E—†	36	housewife	35	"
w	Watt William T	36	chauffeur	40	"
x	Roy Anna F—†	39	housewife	38	"
y	Roy George J	39	fireman	40	
z	Maguire James H	39	policeman	36	"
	1146				
a	Maguire Mary—†	39	housewife	31	"
b	John Delia—†	39	"	35	
c	John Walter	39	machinist	40	"
d	Crehan Kathleen—†	40	housewife	43	"
e	Crehan William J	40	retired	51	
f	Sarkis Abraham	40	polisher	32	
g	Sarkis Dorothy—†	40	housewife	27	"
h	McNulty George J, jr	40	fireman	35	"
k	McNulty Julia M—†	40	housewife	28	"
l	Murphy Christina—†	43	at home	69	
m	Tanner Alfred C	43	waiter	35	
n	Tanner Marjorie—†	43	housewife	35	"
o	Barteaux Edward	43	clerk	52	

28

Rockvale Circle—Continued

	P	Barteaux Mildred—†	43	clerk	51	here
	R	Souza Frank L	43	"	45	"
	S	Cunningham Helen—†	43	housewife	26	"
	T	Cunningham James	43	U S N	31	
	U	Kimball John	44	policeman	34	"
	V	Kimball Katherine—†	44	housewife	38	"
	W	Marecaux Claude	44	welder	31	"
	X	Marecaux Marjorie—†	44	housewife	24	"
	Y	Siebel Alice—†	44	"	33	
	Z	Siebel Karl	44	chef	39	

1147

	A	Hagan Ethel—†	47	housewife	25	"
	B	Hagan Timothy	47	clerk	27	
	C	Banks Charles W	47	photographer	37	"
	D	Banks Margaret C—†	47	housewife	32	"
	E	Condon John R	47	salesman	38	"
	F	Condon Theresa—†	47	housewife	31	"
	G	Gould Mary A—†	48	at home	67	"
	H	Whitten Antoinette—†	48	waitress	39	"
	K	Whitten Edward A	48	clerk	39	
	L	Foley Flora G—†	48	housewife	38	"
	M	Foley Timothy	48	clerk	47	"
	N	Nowell Nellie E—†	48	at home	67	"
	O	Martin Anna D—†	48	supervisor	32	"
	P	Martin Annie M—†	48	housewife	65	"
	R	Martin Mary T—†	48	teacher	35	"
	S	Allen Clara—†	51	tel. operator	52	12 Ophir
	T	Palumbo Frances—†	51	housewife	36	here
	U	Palumbo Joseph	51	policeman	43	"
	V	Runge John	51	shipfitter	30	"
	W	Runge Rita—†	51	housewife	27	"

Rocky Nook Terrace

	X	Kelley John G	6–8	supt	48	here
	Y	Kelley Mary J—†	6–8	housewife	45	"
	Z	Whalen Helen J—†	6–8	clerk	50	"

1148

	A	Carr Mary E—†	6–8	housewife	45	"
	B	Carr Thomas H	6–8	examiner	46	"
	C	Greenwood Ernest J	10–12	waiter	57	

Rocky Nook Terrace—Continued

D	*Greenwood Pauline V–†	10–12	housewife	51	here
E	Greenwood Richard P	10–12	U S A	31	"
F	Cestoni Diva—†	10–12	housewife	48	"
G	Cestoni Frances E—†	10–12	secretary	22	"
H	Cestoni Settimio	10–12	retired	58	"
K	Luff Abraham	11	manager	66	"
L	Luff Anna—†	11	housewife	65	"
M	Freedman John M	11	telegrapher	52	1663 Com av
M¹	Carter Joseph F	11	engraver	25	185 Boylston
N	Carter Patricia P—†	11	housewife	20	34 Hall
O	Dowling Thomas F	11	chauffeur	49	34 "
P	Clougher Eleanor—†	11	stenographer	27	here
R	Clougher Gerald P	11	U S M C	21	"
S	Clougher Marie A—†	11	operator	25	"
T	Clougher Mary A—†	11	housewife	46	"
U	Clougher Timothy F	11	U S N	22	"
V	Otto Frank M	11	mechanic	34	"
W	Otto Louise B—†	11	housewife	31	"
X	Erickson Herbert	11	decorator	21	Templeton
Y	Fay Clifford L	14–16	chauffeur	32	here
Z	Fay Rose A—†	14–16	housewife	28	"
	1149				
A	Kelley Lillian—†	14–16	"	48	
B	Hunter Alfred	15	chauffeur	60	"
C	Hunter Mary P—†	15	housewife	45	"
D	McPherson Arthur P	15	builder	48	
E	McPherson Robert T	15	U S A	20	"
F	McPherson Victoria B—†	15	nurse	48	
G	Masaschi Joseph	17	printer	48	
H	Masaschi Joseph, jr	17	U S N	24	
K	Masaschi Winifred—†	17	housewife	51	"
L	Peterson Carl A	17	mechanic	63	"
M	Peterson Carl R	17	"	29	
N	Peterson Matilda—†	17	housewife	66	"

Rowen Court

O	Kane Edward	1	retired	83	here
P	Kane Mary—†	1	housewife	65	"
R	Seward Fred	3	printer	37	"
S	MacDonald Rita M—†	3	housewife	31	"

Rowen Court—Continued

T	Mood Howard K	3	toolmaker	32	Medford	
U	Fuller Mary E—†	5	housewife	29	here	
V	Fuller Warren E	5	operator	40	"	
W	Belmont Marion A—†	5	housewife	26	"	
X	Carmichael Annie—†	5	at home	78	"	
Y	Carmichael Francis X	5	U S N	22	"	
Z	Carmichael Joseph A	5	laborer	49	··	

1150

A	McGarrell Edward D	5	"	39		
B	McGarrell Helen E—†	5	housewife	38	"	

Sigourney Street

C	Bardzilowski Alfred	12	U S N	20	here	
D	Bardzilowski John	12	"	25	"	
E	Bardzilowski Sophie—†	12	benchworker	21	"	
F	Bardzilowski Stanley	12	U S A	27	"	
G	Bardzilowski Stephanie—†	12	housewife	48	"	
H	Bardzilowski Walter	12	foreman	61	"	
K	Carriere Alphonse	12	salesman	34	"	
L	Carriere Mafalda—†	12	housewife	33	"	
M	Kwiatkowski John	12	machinist	26	"	
N	Kwiatkowski Sophie—†	12	housewife	24	"	
O	Day Horace T	24	agent	67		
P	Hubley James C	24	radioman	62	"	
R	Hubley Mary T—†	24	housewife	62	"	
S	English Mary E—†	25	at home	74	··	
T	Paris William H	25	caretaker	72	"	
U	Diab Rose—†	26	housewife	52	"	
V	Gibran Horace	26	chemist	26		
W	Gibran Kahlil	26	artist	24		
X	Gibran Nicholas	26	carpenter	65	"	
Y	Gibran Rose—†	26	housewife	51	"	
Z	Girala Jose	26	exporter	48	··	

1151

A	Cohen David	32	musician	30	"	
B	Cohen Esther—†	32	teacher	30	"	
C	Rubin Anna M—†	32	housewife	57	"	
D	Rubin Arnold J	32	student	22		
E	Rubin Israel G	32	merchant	58	"	
F	Rubin James	32	manager	38	"	

31

Sigourney Street—Continued

G	Rubin Samuel	32	musician	29	here
H	Barr Anna—†	56	at home	80	"
K	Barr Mildred—†	56	housewife	27	"
L	Barr Sally—†	56	bookkeeper	42	"
M	Barr Sidney	56	attorney	35	"
N	Lofchie Harry	56	conveyor	51	"
O	Lofchie Lena—†	56	housewife	40	"

Union Avenue

R	Rofe Arthur	4	student	21	here
S	Rofe Henry	4	mechanic	22	"
T	Rofe Herbert	4	coremaker	22	"
U	Rofe Margaret—†	4	housewife	57	"
V	Rofe Marie E—†	4	benchworker	23	"
W	Rofe William	4	shipper	57	
X	Ellsworth Elizabeth—†	4	housewife	72	"
Y	Ellsworth Russell C	4	mason	38	
Z	Ellsworth Thomas	4	carpenter	71	"
	1152				
A	Petersen Madeline—†	4	maid	59	
B	Bagley Mary—†	5	housewife	52	"
C	Nordling Alfreda—†	5	"	80	46 Westland av
D	Nordling Elsa—†	5	at home	28	46 "
E	Kolf Helen—†	5	waitress	36	here
F	Reardon Helen—†	5	housewife	44	"
G	Reardon Thomas J	5	porter	48	"
H	Franck Emma—†	5	housewife	79	"
K	*Stott Susan—†	5	"	53	"
L	Moore Frank L	5	salesman	55	414 E Third
M	Morton Douglas	5	engineer	50	Randolph
N	*Morton Elmira—†	5	housewife	48	"
O	Morton Robert J	5	U S N	21	"
P	Powell Benjamin	5	"	26	
R	Powell Olive—†	5	clerk	22	"
S	Burton Jane—†	6	housewife	27	153A Centre
T	Burton John A	6	driller	28	153A "
U	Ellsworth Alban F	6	carpenter	43	here
V	Ellsworth Thomas	6	U S N	22	"
W	Marden Mary E—†	6	housewife	70	"
X	Marden Robert E	6	laborer	68	

Union Avenue—Continued

	Y	O'Quinn Catherine—†	8	housewife	48	here
	Z	O'Quinn Isaac	8	leatherworker	53	"
1153						
	A	O'Quinn Wallace	8	retired	21	"
	B	Jackimowicz Helen G—†	8	housewife	38	"
	C	Jackimowicz Joseph	8	laborer	40	
	D	Pierce Anne—†	8	housewife	32	"
	E	Pierce Arnold	8	pipefitter	38	"
	F	Olmsted Henry	9	cook	31	Revere
	G	Olmsted Margaret—†	9	housewife	27	"
	K	Johnson Herbert	9	technician	45	180 Dorchester
	L	Zaldoks Alfred J	9	U S N	24	here
	M	Zaldoks John L	9	painter	28	"
	N	Buckley Catherine A—†	10	at home	81	"
	O	Flate Nicholas	10	retired	70	
	R	Foye Edward W	2d r 10	"	24	
	S	Foye Elizabeth—†	" 10	housewife	49	"
	T	Foye Leo	" 10	porter	63	
	U	Ryan Helen—†	" 10	forewoman	30	"
	V	Parlon Catherine A—†	12	at home	68	"
	W	Parlou Mary E—†	12	housewife	72	"
	X	Donovan Beatrice—†	12	domestic	38	"
	Y	Trotter Edmund F	12	foreman	33	"
	Z	Trotter Matilda—†	12	housewife	36	"
1154						
	A	Lemay George	13	clerk	43	
	B	Lemay Margaret—†	13	housewife	42	"
	C	Simms Dorothy—†	13	"	27	Worcester
	D	Simms Jacob	13	factoryworker	27	"
	E	Desharnis Juliette—†	13	housewife	39	here
	F	Desharnis Wilfred	13	pipefitter	45	"
	G	Strickland Barbara—†	14	housewife	29	21 Union av
	H	Strickland Harry	14	inspector	33	21 "
	K	Lagsdin Bertha M—†	14	housewife	32	here
	L	Lagsdin John E	14	painter	32	"
	M	Keaveney Henry M	17	printer	42	"
	N	Keaveney Margaret—†	17	housewife	45	"
	O	Leonard Mary—†	17	at home	55	
	P	Madeno Ellen—†	17	housekeeper	69	"
	R	Fleming Ann—†	19	housewife	37	"
	S	*Fleming Michael	19	laborer	43	

Union Avenue—Continued

т	Bryant George	19	factoryworker	61	here
u	White Ella—†	19	housewife	63	"
v	Petrillo Albert	19	molder	33	"
w	Petrillo Helen—†	19	housewife	28	"
x	Mahoney John	19A	breweryworker	27	"
y	Paige Daniel F	19A	mechanic	40	"
z	Paige Margaret—†	19A	housewife	46	"

1155

в	Schofield Edna—†	19A	clerk	35	
c	Donnelly Mary—†	19A	housekeeper	65	"
d	Kennedy Viola—†	20	at home	25	"
e	*Zazzaretti Angelina—†	20	housewife	53	"
f	Zazzaretti Catherine—†	20	operator	27	"
g	Zazzaretti Frances—†	20	"	21	"
н	Zazzaretti Joseph	20	cook	57	
к	Zazzaretti Mary—†	20	assembler	23	"
l	*Belanger Norma—†	21	waitress	35	3 Rowan ct
м	Belanger Victor	21	chauffeur	34	3 "
n	Small Eva J—†	21	housewife	42	here
o	Small Solon	21	cabinetmaker	40	"
p	Fabi Constantino	22	laborer	53	"
r	Fabi Rosina—†	22	housewife	58	"
s	Bowen Daniel	22A	retired	81	
т	Bowen Hannah—†	22A	housewife	81	"
u	Bowen Margaret—†	22A	bookbinder	39	"
v	Bowen Michael	22A	machinist	35	"
w	DiJiacomo Albert	22A	molder	36	
x	DiJiacomo Nellie—†	22A	housewife	36	"
y	Hart Mary—†	22A	"	45	83 Call
z	Hart Thomas	22A	laborer	45	83 "

1156

a	Langlois Alice M—†	23	housewife	69	35 Union av
b	Quigley Dorothea—†	23	"	29	35½ Wash'n
c	Quigley John F	23	boilermaker	65	35½ "
d	Smiddy Anna—†	24	housewife	32	here
e	Smiddy William	24	checker	42	"
f	Foley Mary—†	25	housewife	65	Quincy
g	Simms Alexander	25	piledriver	38	20 Oakland
н	Simms Elizabeth—†	25	housewife	35	20 "
к	Bosse Arthur	26	salesman	40	here
l	Bosse Marguerite—†	26	housewife	29	"

Union Avenue—Continued

		FULL NAME.	Res.	Occupation.	Age.	Reported Residence
	M	Kossey Leonora—†	26	housewife	56	here
	N	Kossey Stanley	26	painter	59	"
	O	Hernon Ann—†	27	teacher	28	"
	P	Hernon Mary—†	27	"	29	
	R	Hernon Thomas J	27	mechanic	61	"
	S	Estabrook Leslie	28	laborer	31	
	T	Estabrook Margaret—†	28	operator	32	"
	U	Estabrook Perley	28	U S A	36	
	V	Corbett Catherine F–† rear	30	operator	22	"
	W	Corbett Domenic "	30	guard	53	
	X	Corbett Margaret—† "	30	housewife	50	"
	Y	Corbett Mary E—† "	30	operator	23	"
	Z	Hughes Norma K—†	32	clerk	22	
1157						
	A	*Hughes William	32	retired	65	"
	B	Lovett Elinor—†	33	housewife	22	Virginia
	C	Lovett Frederick	33	laborer	25	"
	D	Brinkman John E	33	U S A	32	here
	E	Brinkman Mary—†	33	housewife	30	"
	F	Keough Charles	33	U S N	22	"
	G	*Keough William R	33	mover	68	"
	H	Gillespie James	35	steelworker	50	123 Brookside av
	K	Gillespie Margaret—†	35	housewife	35	123 "
	L	Cutini Peter	37	custodian	48	here
	M	Cutini Prudence—†	37	housewife	31	"
	N	Barnaby Anecito	40	custodian	61	"
	O	*Barnaby Mary—†	40	housewife	60	"
	P	Barnaby Rita M—†	40	factoryworker	29	"
	R	Sinacola Margaret—†	41	"	48	
	S	Sinacola Michael	41	attendant	40	"
	T	Robbs Albert	42	manager	36	"
	U	Robbs Helena N—†	42	housewife	31	"
	V	Connolly Joseph	43	U S N	32	
	W	Connolly Rose—†	43	housewife	30	"
	X	Nye George L	43	retired	64	
	Y	Nye Ralph	43	salesman	33	"
	Z	Bennett Alfred	43	carpenter	54	"
1158						
	A	Crawford Anna—†	43	housewife	26	"
	B	Crawford Walter	43	chauffeur	25	"
	C	Weschrob Margaret–† rear	43	factoryworker	22	"

Union Avenue—Continued

D	*Weschrob Mary—†	rear 43	housewife	47	here
E	Weschrob Richard	" 43	painter	50	"
F	Maguire Daniel	" 43	factoryworker	40	"
G	*Maguire Sheila—†	" 43	housewife	40	"
H	Maloney George	" 43	chauffeur	22	"
K	Maloney Helen—†	" 43	housewife	20	"
L	Maloney Delia—†	46	"	50	
M	Maloney Thomas	46	chauffeur	27	"
N	Doran Mae—†	48	stitcher	50	
O	Doran Stanley	48	retired	53	
P	Martin Catherine—†	48	boxmaker	63	"
R	Maloney Francis	48	mechanic	33	"
S	Maloney Richard	48	U S A	21	"
T	Walsh John L	48	stockman	22	Needham
U	Kelly Florence—†	49	housewife	39	here
V	Kelly James J	49	guard	42	"
W	Kelly James J, jr	49	U S A	20	"
X	Larkin Catherine—†	49	waitress	27	"
Y	Page Anna A—†	58	housewife	38	"
Z	Page George D	58	stoker	41	

1159

A	Ledermann Barbara—†	60	laundress	77	"
B	Wimbauer Anthony	60	cooper	65	
C	Wimbauer Antonia M—†	60	nurse	42	
D	Wimbauer Charles	60	cooper	28	
E	Wimbauer Theresa—†	60	housewife	64	"
F	Manning Annie F—†	62	"	52	
G	Manning Edward F	62	laborer	56	
H	Manning Mary F—†	62	benchworker	25	"
K	Rauscher George	63	carpenter	36	"
L	Rauscher Katherine—†	63	housewife	43	"
M	Prue Albert	64	chauffeur	34	"
N	Prue Vivian—†	64	housewife	35	"
O	Cogan Anna—†	64	"	28	
P	Cogan Joseph	64	chauffeur	30	"

Washington Street

R	Burke Charles	3316	supt	32	131 Zeigler
S	Burke Frances—†	3316	housewife	33	131 "
T	Kuattrochi Anna M—†	3316	stenographer	20	here

Washington Street—Continued

U	Kuattrochi Frances J—†	3316	housewife	50	here
V	Samuel Catherine—†	3316	domestic	23	"
W	Samuel Charles	3316	radarman	31	"
X	Samuel Edward	3316	guard	64	"
Y	Samuel Elizabeth—†	3316	housewife	20	2888 Wash'n
Z	Samuel Marion—†	3316	domestic	27	here

1160

A	Samuel Mary—†	3316	housewife	63	"
B	Rockwell Elliot	3318	shipper	28	10 Epping
C	Rockwell Marion—†	3318	housewife	24	229 Metropolitan av
D	Ladd Ida M—†	3318	"	66	here
E	Rumsey Charles L	3318	baker	37	"
F	*Rumsey Mary—†	3318	housewife	37	"
G	Lemoine Emile	3320	coremaker	30	"
H	Lemoine Jeanne M—†	3320	housewife	25	"
K	Doiron Francis O	3320	fireman	33	
L	Doiron Mary A—†	3320	housewife	28	"
M	Hough Harold	3320	operator	44	"
N	Hough Harold J	3320	U S A	26	
O	Hough Joseph	3320	"	24	
P	Hough Mary—†	3320	assembler	22	"
R	Hough Philomena—†	3320	housewife	42	"
S	Hough Rita—†	3320	assembler	20	"
T	Connelly Catherine F—†	3322	housewife	27	50 Green
U	Connelly James P	3322	laborer	31	50 "
V	Kuegel Ernest S	3322	operator	21	here
W	Kuegel Florence L—†	3322	housewife	43	"
X	Kuegel Walter A	3322	U S A	23	"
Y	Healey Evelyn—†	3322	housewife	36	"
Z	Healey Timothy	3322	molder	37	..

1161

B	White Herbert T	3326	fireman	22	33 Hale
C	White Patricia C—†	3326	housewife	21	33 "
D	Adams Richard	3328	seaman	20	here
E	Mycroft Florence—†	3328	housewife	40	"
F	Mycroft Frederick	3328	soapmaker	46	"
U	Magliarditi Emma—†	3377	housewife	55	"
V	Magliarditi Joseph	3377	storekeeper	64	"
W	Magliarditi Lena M—†	rear 3377	housewife	34	"
X	Magliarditi Peter	" 3377	shipper	38	
Y	Glennon John A	3379	plumber	56	"

Washington Street—Continued

	z	Glennon Mary J—†	3379	housewife	52	here
1162						
	A	Slovitky Joseph J	3379	fireman	50	3387 Wash'n
	B	Slovitky Madeline M—†	3379	housewife	32	3387 "
	C	Davis Mary A—†	3379	"	44	here
	F	Robinson Anna—†	3381A	housewife	38	"
	G	Robinson James	3381A	mechanic	36	"
	L	Sheedy Ruth A—†	rear 3383	housewife	38	835 Albany
	M	Sheedy Thomas A	" 3383	chauffeur	41	835 "
	N	Swanson Annie C—†	3385	housewife	76	here
	O	Swanson Ernest T	3385	retired	83	"
	P	Swanson Ernest T	3385	machinist	32	52 Montebello r'd
	R	Keenan John	3385	"	45	here
	T	Egan Gladys M—†	3387	housewife	35	4 Hoffman
	U	Egan James E	3387	chauffeur	38	4 "
	W	Chesterfield John	rear 3387	mechanic	45	here
	X	Salzgeber Alma H—†	" 3387	housewife	66	"
	Y	Ferris Dorothy E—†	" 3387	clerk	34	" .
	z	Ferris Frank	" 3387	watchman	45	"
1163						
	B	*MacDougall Catherine—†	3389	housewife	41	"
	C	*MacDougall John A	3389	roofer	47	"
	D	Hathaway Dorothy E—†	3389	housewife	31	9 Delle av
	E	Hathaway Francis	3389	chauffeur	34	9 "
	F	Parks Evelyn E—†	3389	machinist	29	Tennessee
	S	Collyer Frank	3401	shoeworker	54	here
	T	Collyer Mabel—†	3401	housewife	49	"
	U	Reposa Loretta—†	3411	"	33	201 Harrison av
	V	Reposa Mackey	3411	syrupmaker	38	201 "
	W	Costa Amelia R—†	3411	housewife	38	here
	X	Costa Clifford C	3411	operator	39	"
	Y	White Leo A	3411	welder	23	"
	z	Longuemare Alfred R	3415	cablemaker	38	"
1164						
	A	Longuemare Florence M—†	3415	housewife	35	"
	B	Groves Blanche K—†	3415	"	47	
	C	*Groves George H	3415	carpenter	50	"
	D	Groves George R	3415	laborer	27	
	E	Groves Nilda J—†	3415	clerk	26	
	F	Hoyte Laura—†	3417	operator	61	"
	G	Hoyte Thelma—†	3417	"	23	

Washington Street—Continued

H	Starr Georgina—†	3417	housewife	37	29 Whitney
K	Noble James E	3417	mechanic	50	3411 Wash'n
L	Noble Mary—†	3417	housewife	45	3411 "
M	Rhodes Anna M—†	3421	"	38	here
N	Rhodes Theodore E	3421	chauffeur	46	"
o	*Piatelli Concetta—†	3425	stitcher	46	"
P	*Piatelli Rosa—†	3425	housewife	81	"
R	Timperi Julio	3425	pipefitter	29	"
s	Timperi Rose—†	3425	housewife	23	"
T	Webster Virginia—† rear	3425	"	36	
U	Golden Hildegarde—† "	3425	"	30	
V	Piatelli Antoinette—† "	3425	"	38	
W	Piatelli Thomas "	3425	sandblaster	42	"
Y	Browne Burton L	3451	shoecutter	65	"
z	Browne Burton L, jr	3451	U S A	22	

1165

A	Browne Edith G—†	3451	housewife	57	"
B	Browne Robert W	3451	stockman	20	"
C	Griffin Lila A—†	3451	housewife	66	"

Williams Street

E	Calkins Alfred W	102	operator	26	here
F	Calkins Jane—†	102	housewife	22	"
G	Lane Henry	102	operator	36	"
H	*Landry Claudia—†	102	housewife	34	"
K	Landry William	102	painter	34	
L	Grinnell Charles R	102	leatherworker	32	"
M	Grinnell Rose E—†	102	housewife	31	"
o	Smith Francis C	104	U S N	32	Lexington
P	Smith Isolena—†	104	housewife	33	"
R	*O'Brien Helen—†	104	"	45	here
s	O'Brien Helen—†	104	stitcher	23	"
T	O'Brien John	104	U S A	26	"
U	O'Brien Mary—†	104	wrapper	22	"
V	Birkbeck Dorothy—†	104	housewife	27	"
W	Birkbeck Lawrence	104	U S A	27	
Y	Gerlardi Mary—†	116	housewife	49	"
z	Gerlardi Ralph	116	welder	51	

1166

A	Gerlardi Sara—†	116	student	21	

Williams Street—Continued

B	Sexton Leo	116	policeman	44	here
C	Sexton Mary—†	116	housewife	41	"
D	Thomas Frederick	116	ropemaker	31	"
E	Thomas Mary—†	116	housewife	30	"
F	Reis Charlotte—†	120	"	65	"
G	Sawbridge Annie—†	120	at home	69	Hingham
H	Lynds Annie—†	120	housewife	52	here
K	Lynds Charles	120	U S A	26	"
L	Lynds Louis	120	garageman	52	"
M	Klees August O	120	laborer	48	"
N	Klees Martha—†	120	housewife	47	"
O	Dooley Mary—†	124	"	36	
P	Dooley Thomas J	124	contractor	41	"
R	Strange Bertha—†	124	housewife	45	"
S	Strange Doris M—†	124	clerk	22	
T	Strange Martin	124	upholsterer	45	"
U	Daly Lawrence P	124	policeman	37	"
V	Daly Mary—†	124	housewife	29	"
W	Bartolo Anthony	128	laborer	59	New York
X	Weed John	128	mason	77	here
Y	*Weed Maria—†	128	housewife	62	"
Z	*Ficarra Josephine—†	128	"	62	"

1167

A	Pagnotto Anthony	128	shipfitter	39	"
B	Pagnotto Santina—†	128	housewife	32	"
C	Gallant Fred J	128	draftsman	27	75 Rossmore rd
D	Gallant Mildred—†	128	housewife	23	75 "
E	Conway Agnes—†	132	"	35	here
F	Conway John	132	warehouse	35	"
G	Hasson George	132	operator	59	"
H	Hasson Theresa—†	132	housewife	55	"
K	Kiddy Frederick	132	electrician	23	"
L	Kiddy Frederick W	132	auditor	49	
M	Kiddy Rosetta A—†	132	housewife	78	"
N	Earl Oscar	136	retired	89	Medford
O	McAleer Gladys—†	136	housewife	40	"
P	McAleer James E	136	chauffeur	49	"
R	Barthiewicz Florence—†	136	housewife	47	5 Eldridge rd
S	Barthiewicz Pearl S—†	136	typist	25	5 "
T	Mirabello John	136	laborer	53	here
U	Mirabello Nancy—†	136	dressmaker	36	"
V	O'Sullivan Barbara—†	140	housewife	35	"

Williams Street—Continued

w	O'Sullivan John U	140	policeman	35	here
x	Pepper Mary—†	140	housewife	27	"
y	Pepper Norman	140	chauffeur	30	"
'y	*Quinzani Joseph	140	retired	80	
z	Salvi Angelo L	140	"	56	

1168

A	Salvi Rose—†	140	housewife	46	"
c	Spencer Dorothy—†	144	"	29	
D	Spencer John	144	leatherworker	37	"
E	Suplee Catherine—†	144	housewife	60	"
F	Struzziero Anna—†	144	"	32	
G	Struzziero Joseph	144	machinist	35	"
H	Masules Anna—†	144	housewife	27	392 Athens
K	Masules Paul	144	welder	33	392 "
L	*Geaney Bridie—†	148	housewife	40	here
M	Geaney James	148	metalworker	41	"
N	Sciaba Anthony	148	barber	47	"
O	Sciaba Victoria—†	148	housewife	39	"
P	Gately Alice—†	148	"	55	"
R	Gately John L	148	U S A	21	
S	Race Ernest C	148	rigger	59	
T	Rehill Edward W	152–154	clerk	44	
U	Rehill Margaret M—†	152–154	housewife	44	"
V	Judge Anna V—†	152–154	"	32	
w	Judge Henry M	152–154	chauffeur	32	"
x	Wilson Arthur J	152–154	foreman	38	"
Y	Wilson Josephine—†	152–154	housewife	36	"
z	Kenyon Elgie—†	156	"	38	

1169

A	Kenyon Robert	156	carpenter	49	"
B	*Barnett Ellen—†	156	housewife	58	"
c	Barnett Herbert	156	letter carrier	32	"
D	O'Connell Margaret—†	160–162	clerk	31	
E	Lyon John	160–162	electrician	35	"
F	Lyon Rita—†	160–162	housewife	31	"
G	Rodrigue Emiline—†	160–162	"	47	
H	Rodrigue Joseph F	160–162	salesman	47	"

Woodside Avenue

K	McCarthy Florence—†	5	housewife	43	here
L	Doiron Clarence	5	painter	42	"

Page.	Letter.	FULL NAME.	Residence, Jan. 1, 1946.	Occupation.	Supposed Age.	Reported Residence, Jan. 1, 1945. Street and Number.

Woodside Avenue—Continued

	M	Doiron Jessie—†	5	housewife	41	here
	N	Ennis Arlene—†	5	nurse	36	"
	O	Ennis Dorothy—†	5	at home	23	"
	P	Ennis Eva—†	5	housewife	24	"
	R	Ennis Joseph	5	guard	59	
	S	Ennis Lawrence	5	U S A	24	
	T	Ennis Mary—†	5	housewife	61	"
	U	Ennis Virginia—†	5	at home	21	"
	V	Reidy Martha—†	7	housewife	46	47 Forest Hills
	W	Reidy William	7	machinist	50	47 "
.	X	Mulvey Bridget T—†	7	housewife	72	here
	Y	Mulvey James F	7	mason	38	55 Yeoman
	Z	Mulvey Nora—†	7	housewife	35	55 "
		1170				
	A	Mulvey Patrick T	7	builder	70	here
	B	Auclair Mary—†	7	housewife	39	"
	C	Auclair Oscar	7	rigger	40	"
	D	Nestor William P	7	retired	40	"
	E	Dorrwachter Anna—†	9	housewife	45	"
	F	Dorrwachter Paul	9	mechanic	47	"
	G	Cecconi Carl	11	U S A	26	
	H	Cecconi Claudia—†	11	clerk	29	
	K*	Cecconi Paulina—†	11	housewife	62	"
	L	Connor Catherine—†	13	clerk	52	
	M	Connor Thomas	13	retired	48	
	N	Herlihy Mary—†	13	operator	30	"
	O	Redden Margaret—†	13	matron	51	
	P	Connor Helen L—†	15	housewife	43	"
	R	Connor Martin J	15	milkman	45	"
	S	Ozol Anna—†	17	housewife	58	"
	T	Ozol John	17	machinist	65	"
	U	Doyle Francis X	17	shipper	34	
	V	Doyle Mary E—†	17	housewife	47	"
	W	Nickerson A Eda—†	17	clerk	27	93 Revere
	X	Nickerson James K	17	surveyor	35	65 Glen rd
	Y	Shulz Anne—†	17	housewife	47	36 Ophir
	Z	Shulz Gunther	17	U S A	34	New York
		1171				
	A	Schulz Rudolph	17	waiter	63	36 Ophir
	B	Aitken Alfred	19–21	manager	52	here
	C	Aitken Sylvia—†	19–21	housewife	48	"

42

Woodside Avenue—Continued

D	Emerson Irene—†	19–21	operator	40	here
E	Sullivan John J	19–21	policeman	46	"
F	Sullivan Mary E—†	19–21	housewife	43	"
G	Barca Nora—†	19–21	"	33	
H	Barca Michael	19–21	technician	33	"
K	Carney Catherine—†	19–21	at home	79	
L	Carney Margaret—†	19–21	housewife	23	"
M	Carney Martin	19–21	fireman	36	
N	Benson Caroline—†	19–21	at home	72	

Ward 11—Precinct 12

CITY OF BOSTON

LIST OF RESIDENTS
20 YEARS OF AGE AND OVER

(NON-CITIZENS INDICATED BY ASTERISK)
(FEMALES INDICATED BY DAGGER)

AS OF

JANUARY 1, 1946

THOMAS F. SULLIVAN, *Chairman*
FREDERIC E. DOWLING, *Secretary*
WILLIAM A. MOTLEY, JR.
ARTHUR V. COUGHLIN
EVERETT R. PROUT

Listing Board.

CITY OF BOSTON ⬦ PRINTING DEPARTMENT

1200

Arborway

A	Ryan John B	194	laborer	76	here
B	Ryan Margaret M—†	194	housewife	48	"
C	Ryan Martha L—†	194	clerk	27	"
D	Ryan Thomas E	194	"	51	
E	McElaney Jessie—†	194	at home	75	..
F	McElaney Robert S	194	investigator	40	"
G	Donahue Eleanor F—†	194	secretary	27	"
H	Donahue John I	194	clerk	24	"
K	Donahue Patrick J	194	operator	66	"
L	O'Brien Frank J	194	U S A	32	
M	O'Brien Margaret M—†	194	secretary	30	..
N	Walsh Rosemary E—†	198	housewife	32	"
O	Walsh Thomas P	198	teacher	38	"
P	Gately Frank J	198	laborer	54	
R	Gately Margaret M—†	198	typist	23	
S	Gately Mary J—†	198	housewife	54	"
T	Gately Sally F—†	198	bookkeeper	21	"
U	Lundgren Charles C	198	electrician	37	"
V	Lundgren Charles W	198	shipper	64	
W	Lundgren Ellen C—†	198	secretary	35	"
X	Lundgren Sarah—†	198	housewife	60	"
Y	O'Donnell Irene—†	198	"	34	"
Z	O'Donnell Joseph	198	cashier	35	Winthrop

1201

A	Binkley Ethel M—†	202	housewife	65	here
B	Binkley Russell A	202	auditor	65	"
C	Keith Jane M—†	202	at home	83	"
D	Nowlin Betty B—†	202	housewife	26	"
E	Nowlin William G	202	buyer	23	
F	Barnes Mildred W—†	202	bacteriologist	40	"
G	McDonough Mary C—†	202	housewife	56	"
H	McCann John J	206	manager	32	"
K	McCann Katherine—†	206	teacher	28	
L	McCann Marie—†	206	housewife	57	"
M	Cronan William H	206	instructor	59	..
N	O'Leary Arthur A	206	realtor	67	
O	O'Leary Gwendolyn C—†	206	housekeeper	46	"
P	O'Leary John E	206	policeman	41	"
R	Jones Alice J—†	218	housewife	59	"
S	Jones Ellen S—†	218	secretary	22	"

Arborway—Continued

T	Jones Francis J	218	clerk	62	here
U	Jones Joseph F	218	U S A	29	"
V	Jones Paul B	218	U S N	24	"
W	Smith James P	218	clerk	64	
X	Dufault Lorraine L—†	224	operator	22	"
Y	Dufault Winifred—†	224	"	63	
Z	Dwyer Amelia W—†	224	housewife	34	"
	1202				
A	Dwyer Richard C	224	U S A	34	
B	Lane Fred C	240	U S C G	48	"
C	Lane Mary F—†	240	housewife	49	"
D	LaRonde Elizabeth—†	240	"	55	
E	LaRonde Romeo	240	milkman	56	"
F	Rogers Mary E—†	240	clerk	63	
G	Kilduff Agnes G—†	242	housewife	55	"
H	Kilduff Janet M—†	242	typist	22	
K	Kilduff Maria—†	242	at home	81	"
L	Kilduff William F	242	broker	57	
M	Rooney Augustine J	248	clerk	53	
N	Rooney Katherine J—†	248	housewife	50	"
O	Rooney Margaret L—†	248	clerk	27	
P	Cleary Elizabeth H—†	248	housewife	52	"
R	Cleary John H	248	instructor	60	"
S	Dillon Agnes—†	248	waitress	32	"
T	Dillon Elizabeth—†	248	housewife	55	"
U	Dillon James J	248	compositor	58	"
V	Forrest Catherine E—†	250	housewife	42	"
W	Forrest Edward J	250	machinist	45	"
X	O'Brien Mary E—†	250	housewife	45	"
Y	O'Brien Mary E—†	250	clerk	22	
Z	O'Brien Michael J	250	policeman	46	"
	1203				
	Sullivan Ellen—†	250	housewife	47	"
	Sullivan Joseph T	250	operator	54	"
	Sullivan Mary A—†	250	clerk	21	
A B	Kelleher John J	254	fireman	24	"
	Kelleher Mary H—†	254	operator	22	"
	Kelleher Nora A—†	254	housewife	52	"
G	Kelleher Patrick	254	laborer	55	
H	Kelleher William F	254	U S N	20	"
K	Dolan Anastasia—†	254	housewife	65	"

3

Page	Letter	FULL NAME.	Residence, Jan. 1, 1946.	Occupation.	Supposed Age.	Reported Residence, Jan. 1, 1945. Street and Number.

Arborway—Continued

L	Dolan Joseph E	254	factoryworker	31	here
M	Dolan Thomas J	254	retired	75	"
N	Bulman Cornelius J	258	U S A	21	"
O	Bulman Francis D	258	architect	62	"
P	Bulman John B	258	U S N	25	
R	Bulman Margaret B—†	258	housewife	56	"
S	Bulman Mary C—†	258	typist	27	
T	Barry Lillian M—†	258	housewife	48	"
U	Barry Thomas A	258	salesman	48	"
V	Rodgers Thomas M	258	retired	79	"
W	Kelley Helen M—†	266	housewife	35	"
X	Kelley Joseph F	266	supt	39	
Y	Andrias James	266	engineer	27	"
Z	Andrias Katherine—†	266	housewife	60	"

1204

A	Kutrubes Anna—†	266	"	39	
B	Kutrubes Stephen P	266	salesman	49	"
C	Engewald Martha K—†	270	at home	68	"
D	McKinnon John A, jr	270	architect	51	"
E	McKinnon Martha—†	270	clerk	32	
F	Halloran Joseph A	270	forester	52	
G	Clark John P	270	teacher	27	"
H	Clark Margaret F—†	270	housewife	25	"
K	Wall Ann M—†	274	clerk	40	
L	Wall Jane—†	274	housewife	70	"
M	Wall Jean—†	274	bookkeeper	37	"
N	Wall Mary—†	274	clerk	35	
O	Lavery Alice D—†	274	"	52	
P	Lavery Frank J, jr	274	collector	58	"
R	McKinnon Catherine A—†	278	clerk	36	
S	McKinnon Clara N—†	278	"	39	
T	McKinnon Earl R	278	salesman	41	"
U	McKinnon John A	278	retired	73	
V	Remsen Leard D	278	electrician	46	"
W	Remsen Viola M—†	278	housewife	45	"

Atwood Square

X	Becon Louis	9	machinist	45	here
Y	Reilly Fergus	9	mechanic	65	"
Z	Reilly Mary—†	9	housewife	65	"

1205
Atwood Square—Continued

A	McDonald Mary—†	9	cook	55	here
B	Kirrane John L	11	U S C G	24	"
C	Kirrane Joseph	11	machinist	22	"
D	Kirrane William	11	carpenter	56	"
E	Kirrane William J	11	U S N	27	
F	Donahue John J	11	retired	68	
G	Donahue Mary—†	11	housewife	43	"
H	Donahue Paul J	11	electrician	32	"
K	O'Brien John	11	clerk	50	
L	O'Brien Mary—†	11	housewife	42	"
M	King Frederick V	15	U S N	28	
N	King Ruth E—†	15	housewife	25	"
O	O'Rourke Margaret—†	15	"	37	
P	O'Rourke Thomas	15	milkman	41	"
R	Eldridge Bernard F	15	woolhandler	40	"
S	Eldridge Mary—†	15	housewife	33	"
T	Rourke Cecelia—†	15	"	40	4 Merton pl
U	Rourke Thomas B	15	supervisor	35	4 "
V	Hilson Melida—†	18	housewife	71	here
W	Campbell Margaret—†	18	"	70	20 Marcella
X	Cabana Pauline—†	18	clerk	50	here
Y	Bragger Adelaide—†	19	housewife	37	"
Z	Bragger William	19	butcher	39	"

1206

A	LeBlanc Edward	19	painter	42	
B	LeBlanc Frederick	19	electrician	37	"
C	Greenwood Lillian—†	19	housewife	71	"
D	Mulkern Alma—†	19	clerk	34	"
E	Taylor Hannah—†	20	housewife	72	339 Wash'n
G	Kendall Alfred	20	U S A	30	12 Jamaica
H	Kendall Helen—†	20	housewife	25	12 "
K	Mathews Elizabeth—†	20	"	64	here
L	O'Rourke Patrick	20	janitor	72	"
M	Frazier Mary—†	20	housewife	30	"
N	Frazier Ralph	20	repairman	34	"
O	Lawson Alma—†	20	housewife	29	19 Dunster rd
P	Lawson Joseph	20	chauffeur	30	19 "
R	Cahill Catherine—†	21	housewife	24	here
S	Cahill Martin	21	operator	28	"
T	Mayo Audrey L—†	21	housewife	26	"

Atwood Square—Continued

U	Mayo Frank G	21	U S M C	25	here
V	Quinn Charles E	21	packer	32	"
W	Quinn Helen—†	21	housewife	25	"

Ballard Way

X	Wood Amanda—†	2	housewife	58	here
Y	Wood Fred	2	retired	76	"
Z	Lee Dorothy C—†	2	clerk	36	"
	1207				
A	McCarthy Mary H—†	2	waitress	68	"

Bower Terrace

B	Perkins George H	1	U S A	21	here
C	Perkins Lillian S—†	1	housewife	46	"
D	Werner Henry E	2	clerk	20	"
E	Werner Marie M—†	2	housewife	49	"
F	Francis Eunice M—†	3	"	32	
G	Francis Howard J	3	freighthandler	37	"
H	Hamman Edward E	3	laborer	27	

Call Street

K	Vyth Carl J	71	engineer	65	here
O	Cregg Francis T	77	cutter	26	20 Richmond
P	Cregg Louise J—†	77	housewife	24	20 "
R	Cunningham Catherine—†	77	"	.34	here
S*	Cunningham James J	77	porter	42	"
T	McNulty Adeline R—†	77	factoryworker	32	"
U	McNulty William C	77	laborer	35	
V	Roody Ellen—†	79	hostess	36	
W	Ryder Patrick J	79	gardener	60	"
X	Duncan Frances—†	79	laundress	45	"
Y	Henthorne Albert L	79	U S N	26	Kansas
Z	Henthorne Eleanor—†	79	housewife	26	here
	1208				
A	Folkins Laura—†	79	housekeeper	74	"
B	Cross Dorothy A—†	81	housewife	22	107 Hooker
C	Cross Paul E	81	welder	37	107 "
D	Oster Mary—†	81	retired	62	50 Newton

Call Street—Continued

E	Sheehan Dennis	81	clerk	30	here
F	Sheehan Sandra—†	81	housewife	35	"
G	Hedberg Ivar	81	contractor	54	"
H	Hedberg Martha M—†	81	housewife	54	"
K	Hedberg Violet—†	81	"	28	"
M	Marsinelli Dorothy G—†	83	"	22	61 Robinwood av
N	Marsinelli Gasparino	83	warehouseman	24	61 "
O*	Moroney Christina—†	83	housewife	40	here
P	Moroney John J	83	foreman	41	"
R	Flaherty Edna K—†	85	housewife	39	Hingham
S	Flaherty Morgan P	85	sexton	35	"
T	Hurley James M	85	chauffeur	34	826 Hunt'n av
U	Hurley Ruth M—†	85	housewife	29	826 "
V	O'Brien Margaret E—†	85	"	33	here
W	O'Brien Patrick	85	retired	38	"
X	Mannion Anna T—†	89	clerk	27	"
Y	Mannion Bartholomew	89	laborer	58	
Z	Mannion Nora A—†	89	housewife	58	"

1209

A	Getz Mary E—†	89		26	81 Polk
B	Kerle Mary A—†	89	"	57	75 Call
C	Kerle Virginia M—†	89	factoryworker	25	75 "

Carolina Avenue

D	Cadigan Eileen M—†	7	clerk	23	here
E	Cadigan Laura M—†	7	housewife	53	"
F	Berry Francis E	7	U S A	43	220 South
G	Berry Ursula L—†	7	housewife	33	220 "
H	Hucksam Mary F—†	7	tel operator	21	here
K	Hucksam Rose K—†	7	at home	62	"
L*	Kechejian Andrew	7	storekeeper	55	"
M	Kechejian Hazel—†	7	fitter	22	"
N	Kechejian Lillian—†	7	clerk	23	"
O	Kechejian Margaret—†	7	housewife	43	"
P	Kechejian Stella—†	7	clerk	20	"
R	Bowes Bryan	9	salesman	27	"
S	Bowes Catherine—†	9	housewife	55	"
T	Bowes Claire—†	9	clerk	21	
U	Bowes Michael	9	cook	62	
V	Bowes Robert	9	U S A	24	

Carolina Avenue—Continued

w	Bowes Ruth—†	9	housewife	25	here
x	Boyce John F	11	inspector	56	"
y	Boyce Mary A—†	11	domestic	60	"
z	Boyce Mary E—†	11	housewife	49	"

1210

a	Boyce Mary E—†	11	clerk	24	
b	Boyce Robert E	11	U S A	20	
c	Sullivan Daniel J	75	operator	65	"
d	Sullivan Mary A—†	75	stenographer	36	"
e	Sullivan Mary J—†	75	housewife	65	"
f	Sullivan Daniel J, jr	75	instructor	40	"
g	Sullivan Mary M—†	75	housewife	40	"
h	Sullivan James F	75	machinist	32	15 Woodman
k	Sullivan Madeline M—†	75	housewife	28	15 "
l	Naughton Catherine—†	79	"	40	here
m	Naughton John	79	chauffeur	40	"
n	Finneran Genevieve V–†	79	saleswoman	22	"
o	Finneran John J	79	retired	75	
p	Finneran John M	79	chauffeur	38	"
r	Finneran Joseph H	79	packer	43	
s	Finneran Margaret M—†	79	housewife	68	"
t	Gray Harvey L	79	shipfitter	47	"
u	Gray Mary M—†	79	secretary	39	"
v	Crowley Bridget—†	79	housewife	50	"
w	Crowley John	79	operator	60	"
x	Crowley John P	79	U S A	29	"
y	Crowley Mary J—†	79	stenographer	26	"
z	Donahue Anna—†	89	clerk	61	"

1211

a	Leland William	89	"	71	
b	Kennedy Arthur	89	laborer	38	
c	Kennedy Elizabeth—†	89	at home	50	"
d	Kennedy Helen—†	89	clerk	46	
e	Cunniff Anne—†	95	housewife	40	"
f	Cunniff William F	95	janitor	46	
g	Kay James	95	machinist	34	"
h	Kay Marjorie—†	95	housewife	34	"
k	Pilibosian Pessant J	95	manager	33	"
l	Pilibosian Rose E—†	95	housewife	25	"
m	Brown Eugene M	101	contractor	42	"
n	Brown Madeline T—†	101	housewife	42	"

Carolina Avenue—Continued

o	Gibson Ann P—†	101	housewife	29	here
p	Gibson James A	101	chauffeur	34	"
r	O'Hara Delia—†	105	housewife	43	"
s	O'Hara Hugh	105	mechanic	40	"
t	Nicholson Evelyn—†	105	housewife	55	"
u	Nicholson Robert	105	bartender	56	"
v	Lavin Grace—†	107	nurse	33	
w	Lavin Harold	107	chauffeur	40	"
x	Lunn Charles B	107	shipper	65	"
y	Lunn Effie R—†	107	housewife	64	"
z	Stone Mary E—†	107	proofreader	36	"
	1212					
a	Smith Mary A—†	109	housewife	43	"
b	Shook Adelaide—†	111	"	43	
c	Shook Earl L	111	chauffeur	41	"
d	Buckley Helen F—†	111	at home	71	"
e	Doonan Catherine T—†	111	clerk	60	
f	Doonan S Gertrude—†	111	"	60	
g	Gaides Hilda—†	113	housewife	35	"
h	Gaides William	113	clerk	48	"
k	Birch Andrew J	113	supervisor	64	"
l	Birch Annie M—†	113	housewife	52	"
m	McDonough John	127	machinist	45	"
n	McDonough Margaret—†	127	housewife	45	"
o	Murphy James F	131	laborer	53	
p	Murphy Nora—†	131	housewife	52	"
r	McCalder Jessie—†	131	at home	78	"
s	*McParland Anna—†	135	housewife	35	"
t	McParland James	135	waiter	32	
u	Dolan Gertrude—†	135	interviewer	46	"
v	Donahue Catherine—†	137	at home	80	"
w	Scafati Florence—†	137	clerk	45	
x	Scafati Palmer	137	guard	45	

Carolina Place

y	Ginty Anthony	1	laborer	52	here
z	*Ginty Margaret—†	1	housewife	45	"
	1213					
a	Bachofner Catherine—†	1	"	40	
b	Bachofner Frederick M	1	guard	46	

Carolina Place—Continued

c	Devaney Dorothy—†	1	operator	22	here
d	Devaney Rita—†	1	housewife	27	"
e	Devaney Thomas	1	chauffeur	30.	"
f	Feeney John	2	bookkeeper	27	Revere
g	Feeney Patrician—†	2	housewife	22	"
h	Cady Rita—†	2	"	23	58 Jamaica
k	Cady Robert	2	chauffeur	23	58 "

Child Street

n	Beath John F	8	mechanic	41	here
o	Beath Winifred—†	8	housewife	41	"
p	Breen John	8	laborer	60	"
r	Breen Mary—†	8	housewife	58	"
s	Gamricki Helen—†	10	stenographer	20	"
t	Gamricki John T	10	U S A	23	"
u	Gamricki Mary R—†	10	housewife	53	"
v	Tracy Alice M—†	10	"	45	27 South
w	Tracy Warren B	10	carpenter	49	27 "
x	Tirrill Adeline R—†	10	housewife	32	here
y	Tirrill James J	10	guard	46	"
z	Tirrill John F	10	attorney	42	"

1214

a	Tirrill Thomas F	10	manager	44	"
b	Costello James P	72	bartender	45	"
c	Costello Mary—†	72	housewife	38	"
d	McDonnell John	72	waiter	32	
e	Dunnett James W	76	carpenter	46	"
f	Dunnett Margaret—†	76	clerk	20	
g	Dunnett Sarah—†	76	housewife	41	"
h	Ruddell George	78	finisher	50	
k	Ruddell Isabelle—†	78	stenographer	50	"
l	Burkhardt Margaret—†	80	nurse	62	"
m	Cowie Elizabeth H—†	80	housewife	67	"
n	Cowie Samuel	80	mason	72	"
o	Devaney Dorothy—†	80	operator	24	90 Call
p	McLaughlin Catherine—†	80	at home	82	here
r	Biggs Christine M—†	82	housewife	54	"
s	Biggs Herbert	82	butcher	50	"
u	Madden Andrew F	106	painter	57	4 Robeson
v	Madden Lillian—†	106	inspector	61	4 "

Child Street—Continued

w	Miller Charles W	108	pipefitter	35	here
x	Miller Lena—†	108	at home	70	"
y	Miller Virginia D—†	108	housewife	31	"
z	Hawkins Catherine—†	110	"	49	

1215

A	Hawkins Charles W	110	electrician	46	"
B	Glennon Edith E—†	116	housewife	55	"
c	Glennon John H	116	clerk	52	
D	Smith James H	120	"	39	
E	Smith Walter A	120	letter carrier	67	"

Custer Street

F	DeMark Sarah T—†	8	clerk	45	here
G	*Grady Mary K—†	8	housewife	36	"
H	Grady Patrick J	8	inspector	38	"
K	*Larkin Ann B—†	8	waitress	38	Brookline
L	Lydon Ruth M—†	8	housekeeper	24	here
M	Norton Helen V—†	8	matron	47	"
N	Marshall Gordon V	10	salesman	30	"
o	*Marshall Ida M—†	10	housewife	28	"
P	McBride Bernard T	10	salesman	22	"
R	McBride John J	10	U S N	20	
s	McBride Katherine L—†	10	housewife	40	"
T	McBride Peter T	10	stonecutter	45	"
U	Hamilton John F	10	machinist	52	82 Chestnut av
v	Hamilton June M—†	10	operator	20	82 "
w	Hamilton Margaret A—†	10	housewife	50	82 "
x	Hamilton Margaret A—†	10	operator	28	82 "
y	Carmichael Blowers A	12	fireman	75	here
z	Carmichael Katherine—†	12	housewife	78	"

1216

A	Mooers Maurice C	12	waiter	34	
B	Mooers Rachel A—†	12	housewife	34	"
c	Lee Edward J	14	janitor	57	"
D	Lee Margaret M—†	14	housewife	47	"
E	Lee Martha T—†	14	housekeeper	20	"
F	Sweeney James M	14	photographer	21	"
G	Sweeney John J	14	bartender	25	"
H	Sweeney Michael	14	fireman	54	
K	Jakas Joseph R	16	steelworker	42	"

Custer Street—Continued

L	Jakas Mary J—†	16	housewife	40	here	
M	Bertrand Anne A—†	16	"	26	"	
N	Bertrand Francis J	16	clerk	31	"	
O	O'Shea James P	16	watchman	70	"	
P	Hagar Annie M—†	18	housewife	22	Maine	
R	Hagar Edward W	18	clerk	28	39 Chestnut av	
S	Ryan John H	18	metalworker	44	here	
T	Ryan John H, jr	18	U S A	21	"	
U	Ryan Nora C—†	18	housewife	42	"	
V	McCarthy Anna E—†	18	"	50		
W	McCarthy Maurice J	18	laborer	52		
X	Campbell Francis	22	"	52		
Y	Campbell Theresa E—†	22	housewife	47	"	
Z	Easco Loretta A—†	24	"	27	28 Wyman	

1217

A	Easco Michael J	24	machinist	29	28 "	
B	Connelly Alice E—†	26	clerk	40	here	
C	Connelly Josephine A—†	26	"	41	"	
D*	Bittrolf Kathleen M—†	28	housewife	35	"	
E	Bittrolf Ralph J	28	salesman	36	"	
F	Reardon Mary E—†	28	housewife	53	"	
G	Reardon Stephen F	28	rubberworker	56	"	
H	Reardon Stephen P	28	clerk	23		
K	Reardon Thomas C	28	U S A	20		
L	Carroll Edward J	32	guard	52		
M	Carroll Mary A—†	32	housewife	47	"	
N	Horan Francis J	32	chauffeur	39	"	
O	Horan Margaret M—†	32	housewife	35	"	
P	Manning John J	32	U S N	27		
R	Manning Katherine V—†	32	assembler	22	"	
S	McCluskey Joseph V	32	teamster	49	"	
T	McCluskey Mary A—†	32	housewife	51	"	
U	McCluskey Mary V—†	32	operator	24	"	
V	DeLappe John J	34	clerk	24		
W	Duff Annie—†	34	social worker	55	"	
X	Duplain Leon B	34	clerk	44		
Y	Glennon Benjamin G	34	laborer	60		
Z	Gavin John J, jr	38	foreman	25	"	

1218

A	Gavin Phyllis—†	38	housewife	33	"	
B	Gavin Catherine M—†	38	"	66		

Page.	Letter.	FULL NAME.	Residence, Jan. 1, 1946.	Occupation.	Supposed Age.	Reported Residence, Jan. 1, 1945. Street and Number.

Custer Street—Continued

	c	Gavin John G	38	operator	68	here
	d	Gavin William L	38	policeman	34	"
	e	Florentino Doris M—†	38	housewife	25	47 Woodlawn
	f	Florentino James C	38	butcher	23	360 Bennington
	g	Griffin John V	40	starter	35	here
	h	Griffin Loretta C—†	40	housewife	36	"
	k	Griffin Daniel J	40	clerk	62	"
	l	Griffin Mary—†	40	housewife	62	"
	m	Griffin Mary P—†	40	clerk	37	
	n	Griffin Mildred J—†	40	secretary	30	"
	o	Griffin Narro V—†	40	"	22	"
	p	O'Brien Johanna—†	40	at home	84	"
	r	Robichaud Anne G—†	52	housewife	44	"
	s	Robichaud James A	52	chauffeur	44	"
	t	Broderick Alice C—†	52	housewife	40	624 Cummins H'way
	u	Broderick Fred E	52	engineer	45	624 "
	v	Montana Richard F	52	salesman	34	here
	w	Montana Winifred F—†	52	housewife	32	"
	x	Burdell Anne R—†	52	"	25	"
	y	Burdell James A	52	mechanic	32	"

Goldsmith Street

	z	Spellman Margaret B—†	48	housewife	66	here
1219						
	a	Spellman Mary K—†	48	secretary	36	"
	b	Ellison Constance—†	48	housekeeper	50	"
	c	Souza Catherine M—†	48	manager	42	"
	d	MacLean Earl D	48	mechanic	43	"
	e	MacLean Rose E—†	48	housewife	41	"
	f	Adams Florence—†	48	clerk	60	
	g	Doherty Agnes—†	48	waitress	58	"
	h	McLaughlin Marie—†	48	secretary	38	"

Jamaica Place

	k	Scoledge John G	1	mechanic	48	here
	l	Scoledge Rose E—†	1	housewife	47	"
	m	Lyons Elizabeth—†	2	"	73	"
	n	Lyons William J	2	retired	76	"
	o	Connolly Cornelius J	7	painter	37	91 Belgrade av

13

Jamaica Place—Continued

P	Connolly Ethel M—†	7	housewife	21	91 Belgrade av
R	Shanney Elizabeth A—†	7	bookkeeper	52	here
S	Shanney Gertrude E—†	7	housekeeper	60	"
T	Caldwell Owen	8	carpenter	40	"
U	Casey Lillian—†	8	housewife	32	"
V	Casey Stephen	8	operator	32	"

Jamaica Street

X	Broderick Catherine T—†	24	housekeeper	73	here
Y	Morton Mabel E—†	24	at home	68	"
Z	Quilty Anna T—†	26	housewife	39	"
	1220				
A	Quilty Michael	26	shipper	50	
B	Fossa Charles F	28	electrician	69	"
C	Fossa Frank J	28	laborer	61	
D	Dolan Catherine A—†	30	packer	67	
E	Dolan James J	30	retired	73	
F	Dolan Mary E—†	30	housekeeper	71	"
G	McDermott Mary E—† rear	30	stenographer	36	"
H	Brown Agnes—† "	30	clerk	21	..
K	Brown Flora—† "	30	housewife	52	"
L	Doherty Esther—†	31	"	27	1 Elm
M	Doherty John S	31	clerk	27	1 "
N	Hinckley Elizabeth—†	31	housewife	65	here
O	Richards Bertha—†	31	"	49	"
P	Richards Ruth—	31	bookkeeper	21	"
R	Richards Stanley	31	carpenter	51	"
S	Connolley Sarah J—†	32	housewife	39	"
T	Connolley Thomas M	32	chauffeur	40	"
U	Cutcliffe Elinor—†	33	housewife	27	24 Maynard
V	Cutcliffe Paul	33	operator	27	24 "
W	Floyd Leo H	33	U S A	36	59 Brookley rd
X	Floyd Mary—†	33	housewife	37	59 "
Y	Johnson David E	34	engineer	50	here
Z	Johnson David E, jr	34	U S N	21	"
	1221				
A	Johnson Mary A—†	34	housewife	41	"
B	LaBay Catherine—†	35	"	70	
C	Riette John C	35	painter	40	"
D	Riette Nora—†	35	housewife	38	"

14

Jamaica Street—Continued

		Residence Jan. 1 1946	Occupation	Age	Reported Residence
E	McLaughlin Daniel J	35	repairman	33	here
F	McLaughlin Mary A—†	35	housewife	30	"
G	Anthony Francis M	36	laborer	57	"
H	Glynn Catherine—†	36	at home	50	"
K	Glynn Daniel M	36	clerk	31	
L	Glynn John J	36	laborer	33	..
M	Glynn Joseph A	36	clerk	21	
N	Glynn Martin D	36	U S A	23	"
O	McDonald Eleanor—†	36	waitress	25	26 Macdonald
P	McGeehan Mary—†	37	at home	60	Revere
R	Flemming Agnes—†	37	housewife	36	here
S	Flemming John	37	laborer	35	"
T	McNulty Catherine—†	37	housewife	59	"
U	McNulty Michael J	37	fireman	62	..
V	Fidler Janet E—†	38	waitress	41	"
W	Kelley Delia M—†	38	checker	52	15 Asticou rd
X	Publicover James	39	U S A	30	here
Y	Publicover Mary—†	39	housewife	26	"
Z	Sadowski John	39	U S N	23	"
	1222				
A	Twohig Annie—†	40	housewife	38	"
B	Twohig Francis J	40	clerk	38	
C	Balabanis Doris—†	41	housewife	38	"
D	Balabanis Ernest	41	cook	48	
E	English Alfred J	43	metalworker	42	"
F	English Caroline G	43	housekeeper	46	..
G	English Mary M—†	43	bookkeeper	48	"
H	English William J	43	clerk	44	..
K	Bingle Adolph P	44	manager	30	..
L	Bingle Grace A—†	44	housewife	27	"
M	Caulfield Catherine J—†	45	at home	47	156A South
N	Kelly Eileen M—†	45	clerk	21	here
O	Kelly Mary T—†	45	housewife	48	"
P	Kelly Michael J	45	laborer	50	"
R	Fitzgerald Gertrude—†	47	housewife	26	"
S	Fitzgerald John	47	U S A	25	53 Summit
T	Daley Catherine—†	47	saleswoman	52	here
U	O'Brien Annie—†	rear 47	housekeeper	73	"
V	Gallagher Bridget—†	" 47	at home	70	"
W	Angelick August A	" 47	student	21	..
X	*Angelick Joseph H	" 47	tailor	56	

15

Page.	Letter.	Full Name.	Residence, Jan. 1, 1946.	Occupation.	Supposed Age.	Reported Residence, Jan. 1, 1945. Street and Number.
	Y	*Angelick Louise—†	rear 47	housewife	56	here
	Z	'Angelick Raymond M	" 47	U S M C	22	"
1223						
	A	Bosse Adele—†	48	clerk	42	
	B	*Gordon Bridget—†	48	housewife	42	"
	C	Gordon John J	48	chauffeur	45	"
	D	Scully Elizabeth—†	48	housewife	30	"
	E	Scully Joseph	48	painter	38	"
	F	Hinckley Harold E	49	plumber	41	"
	G	Hinckley Mildred E—†	49	housewife	39	"
	H	Shone Catherine E—†	53	"	62	
	K	Shone John W	53	policeman	70	"
	L	Shone John W, jr	53	U S N	21	
	M	Feeley Martin J	56	mechanic	48	"
	N	*Keane Ellen—†	56	housewife	45	"
	O	Keane Patrick J	56	retired	55	
	P	Cady John J	58	chauffeur	50	"
	R	Cady Rose M—†	58	housewife	44	"
	S	McGoldrick James J	59	fireman	50	
	T	McGoldrick Louise M—†	59	housewife	49	"
	U	Fay James R	59	engineer	40	"
	V	Fay Kathleen M—†	59	housewife	33	"
	W	Keane Julia A—†	59	clerk	53	
	X	Keane Lenore B—†	59	"	39	"
	Y	Fennessey Joseph	61	chauffeur	39	Brookline
	Z	Keane Helen F—†	61	housewife	36	here
1224						
	A	Keane William T	61	foreman	40	"
	B	Doyle Kathleen—†	62	housewife	34	15 Asticou rd
	C	Doyle Patrick C	62	fireman	37	15 "
	D	Hackett Cornelia—†	62	saleswoman	42	here
	E	Hackett Dora G—†	62	beautician,	34	"
	F	Mitchell Mary D—†	62	clerk	44	"
	G	Murphy John C	62	student	25	
	H	Murphy Phyllis—†	62	saleswoman	23	"
	K	Connelly Mary—†	62	housewife	57	"
	L	Connelly Patrick J	62	laborer	60	
	M	Carney Annie F—†	63	at home	76	"
	N	Kendall Mary E—†	63	teacher	4*	"
	O	Kendall Rose L—†	63	housekeeper	72	"
	P	McDonough Catherine—†	64	housewife	37	"

Jamaica Street—Continued

R	McDonough Thomas J	64	bartender	45	here
T	Sullivan M Louise—†	65	stewardess	26	"
S	Sullivan Margaret—†	65	housewife	51	"
U	Lanagan Anna G—†	67–69	"	46	"
V	Lanagan William J	67–69	mechanic	54	"
W	Linehan Bartholomew J	67–69	agent	50	
X	Linehan Margaret L—†	67–69	housewife	51	"
Y	Murphy Jane L—†	67–69	operator	22	"
Z	Murphy John B	67–69	U S N	21	
	1225				
A	Murphy Katherine V-†	67–69	housewife	49	"
B	Murphy Morgen C	67–69	policeman	53	"
C	McDonald John L	68	student	21	
D*	McDonald Mary J—†	68	housewife	51	"
E	McDonald William F	68	steamfitter	53	"
F	Quilty Catherine—†	68	housewife	73	"
G	Quilty Morton W	68	clerk	40	
K	Quilty Thomas H	68	retired	82	"
H	Quilty Thomas L	68	clerk	42	
L	Gleason M Louise—†	68	housewife	80	"
M	Shaab Henrietta—†	68	"	73	
N	Healy Catherine—†	70	"	40	
O	Healy John M	70	clerk	40	
P	Healy Florence T—†	70	stenographer	35	"
R	Healy Joseph E	70	clerk	46	"
S	Healy Mary A—†	70	housewife	78	"
T	Healy Ruth E—†	70	stenographer	38	"
U	Goddette Marion G—†	71	journalist	52	"
V	Sullivan John	71	mechanic	30	16 Rosemary
W	Sullivan Marie—†	71	housewife	34	288 Amory
X	Lee Annie F—†	72	housekeeper	82	here
Y	Lee Thomas F	72	laborer	61	"
Z	Hannon Kathleen P—†	73	housewife	25	Florida
	1226				
A	Hannon William, jr	73	agent	30	"
B	Peyton Catherine—†	73	housewife	58	here
C	Peyton Eugene F	73	U S N	22	"
D	Peyton John J	73	foreman	58	"
E	Peyton John T	73	U S A	27	
F	Birkbeck Lillian K—†	73	housewife	25	"
G	Birkbeck William L	73	machinist	30	"

11—12   17

Jamaica Street—Continued

H	Chioccola Armond	73	U S A	35	here
K	Chioccola John	73	shoemaker	65	"
L	Chioccola Louis	73	U S A	38	"
M	Harkins John J	rear 74	policeman	43	"
N	Harkins Julia—†	" 74	housewife	69	"
O	Harkins Michael	" 74	retired	77	"
P	Glynn John J	" 74	clerk	55	"
R	Glynn Lillian E—†	" 74	housewife	54	"
S	Downey Dorothy—†	" 74	"	38	
T	Shaw Helen G—†	75	clerk	45	
U	McGrath Catherine J—†	75	housewife	35	"
V	McGrath John F	75	clerk	42	
W	Gately Mary F—†	77	housewife	43	"
X	Gately William H	77	clerk	58	
Y	Madden Catherine L—†	79	housewife	74	"
Z	Madden Vincent P	79	U S A	33	
	1227				
A	Lane Doris A—†	80	housewife	43	"
B	Lane John C	80	operator	48	"
C	Rowan Catherine—†	80	housekeeper	52	"
D	McDonough Frank P	81	clerk	38	"
E	McDonough Victoria—†	81	housewife	33	"
F	Martell Anastasia—†	81	"	47	
G	Martell Gordon	81	mechanic	44	"
H	Martell John T	81	U S N	20	"
K	Lake Albert	81	foreman	33	"
L	Lake Mildred—†	81	housewife	30	"
M	Sullivan Freida—†	82	"	42	"
N	Armstrong David J	83	laborer	57	"
O	Corscadden Eileen F—†	83	operator	36	Texas
P	McGarry Lillian—†	83	clerk	38	here
R	McGarry Margaret—†	83	beautician	37	"
S	Duffy Catherine—†	83	housewife	48	"
T	Duffy Edward	83	inspector	48	"
U	Buckley Catherine—†	85	housewife	36	"
V	Buckley Stephen	85	carpenter	40	"
W	O'Connell Bertha—†	85	clerk	35	
X	O'Connell Edward	85	collector	40	"
Y	Fallon James H	85	motorman	31	"
Z	Fallon Thomas E	85	clerk	27	

1228
Jamaica Street—Continued

A	Bell Everett	86	U S N	30	here
B	Bell Gertrude A—†	86	housewife	24	"
C	Bell Josephine B—†	86	at home	50	"
D	Gebhard Kathleen R—†	86	waitress	28	"
E	Kopp Albert T	86	plater	58	
F	Kopp Ellen G—†	86	housewife	52	"
G	Kopp Josephine A—†	86	student	22	
H	White Elizabeth E—†	87	housewife	39	"
K	White John J	87	carpenter	39	"
L	Kenney Doris E—†	87	housewife	34	"
M	Kenney Herbert	87	painter	37	
N	Carroll John E	87	laborer	38	
O	Carroll Pauline—†	87	housewife	35	"
P	Sabadini Louis F	88	salesman	39	"
R	Sabadini Mary E—†	88	housewife	40	"
S	Carey Francis M	90	inspector	39	4 Malcolm rd
T	Carey Margaret V—†	90	housewife	39	4 "
U	Martin Anna—†	91	"	43	here
V	Martin Joseph	91	shipwright	49	"
W	Cavanaugh Agnes V—†	91	laundress	33	"
X	Cavanaugh Bartholomew	91	laundryman	39	"
Y	Butler Elizabeth M—†	91	secretary	32	"
Z	Butler Martin B	91	clerk	31	"

1229

A	Evans Bridget D—†	91	cleaner	64	"
C	Cunha Agnes W—†	94	packer	47	Cambridge
D	Cunha James A	94	clerk	22	"
E	Strecker Louis	94	retired	72	here
F	Strecker Mary E—†	94	housewife	69	"
G	Kelley Joseph M	95	longshoreman	58	"
H	Moore Anna M—†	95	housewife	45	"
K	Gallagher Mary—†	95	"	28	"
L	Gallagher William J	95	salesman	37	Quincy
M	Sutherland Ann S—†	95	clerk	32	here
N	Sutherland Elizabeth—†	95	beautician	23	"
O	Sutherland William E	95	laborer	57	"
P	Swaine Hedley	95	supt	46	
R	Swaine Mary—†	95	housewife	44	"
S	Donahue Helen—†	96	"	47	

Jamaica Street—Continued

T	Powers Margaret M—†	96	bookkeeper	21	here	
U	Powers Mary B—†	96	housewife	58	"	
V	Doyle Cecelia B—†	96	collector	64	"	
W	Doyle Katherine M—†	96	housekeeper	70	"	
X	MacDonald Catherine M—†	100	housewife	46	"	
Y	Sevigny Ernest E	100	carpenter	41	"	
Z	Sevigny Margaret M—†	100	housewife	44	"	
	1230					
A	Hogan John A	rear 100	machinist	44	"	
B	Curley Marion—†	102	housewife	23	"	
C	Giller Margaret M—†	102	packer	38	"	
D	Giller Margaret V—†	102	housewife	59	"	
E	Hartnett Florence—†	102	"	25		
F	Dempsey Clare L—†	104	clerk	21		
G	Dempsey John T	104	lineman	23		
H	Dempsey Sadie G—†	104	housewife	47	"	
K	Curley Chester W	104	chauffeur	33	"	
L	Curley Grace A—†	104	housewife	32	"	
M	Curley Robert W	104	packer	24		

Lee Street

N	Clifford Augustus	15	gardener	39	here	
O	Clifford Julia—†	15	housewife	37	"	
P	Steele Helen B—†	15	"	33	"	
R	Steele Wilfred J	15	chauffeur	38	"	
S	Hayer Doris G—†	15	housewife	35	"	
T	Hayes John E	15	attorney	35	"	
U	Polo Angelo	15	shoeworker	28	"	
V	Polo Mary R—†	15	housewife	26	"	
W	O'Connor Daniel	15	guard	51		
X	O'Connor Dora A—†	15	housewife	52	"	
Y	Sullivan John J	15	operator	36	"	
Z	Sullivan Mary—†	15	stitcher	49	"	
	1231					
A	Sullivan Mary—†	15	housewife	79	"	
B	McAvoy Francis A	17	U S A	28		
C	McAvoy Kevin J	17	"	33		
D	McAvoy Pauline—†	17	housewife	68	"	
E	*McAvoy William P	17	retired	76		
F	Fitzgerald Edward N	19	checker	35	"	

Lee Street—Continued

G	Fitzgerald Josephine—†	19	housewife	32	here
H	Matthes George H	20	retired	70	"
K	Matthes Joanna E—†	20	housewife	71	"
L	Matthes Joseph D	20	teacher	35	"
M	Fitzgerald Mary E—†	21	stenographer	30	75 Carolina av
N	Fitzgerald Mary E—†	21	housewife	50	75 "
O	Ward Mary T—†	23	clerk	38	here
P	McGlame Eleanor J—†	25	housewife	28	"
R	McGlame John J	25	plumber	29	"
S	Fitzgerald Catherine G—†	26	housewife	45	"
T	Fitzgerald Raymond H	26	laborer	45	"
U	Coelsch Catherine B—†	27	housewife	52	"
V*	Coelsch Otto L	27	shoecutter	54	"
W	Coelsch Ruth D—†	27	secretary	27	"

Saint Joseph Street

Y	Alves Mary A—†	20	teacher	22	here
Z	Beaton Margaret—†	20	domestic	58	"
	1232					
A	Burke Mary A—†	20	teacher	42	"
B	Carson Almin C—†	20	"	38	
C	Conway Elizabeth D—†	20	"	64	
D	Corcoran Mary E—†	20	"	32	
E	Crowley Gertrude—†	20	"	55	"
F	Cullen Catherine R—†	20	"	41	295 Adams
G	Curtin Hannah—†	20	housekeeper	59	here
H	Davidson Lois W—†	20	teacher	22	"
K	Donohue Marion J—†	20	"	45	"
L	Donovan Mary V—†	20	"	53	
M	Duffy Irene C—†	20	"	36	
N	Fagan Grace A—†	20	"	34	'
O	Fitzgerald Helen M—†	20	"	34	'
P	Galvin Julia A—†	20	"	52	"
R	Horgan Gertrude A—†	20	"	20	Framingham
S	Joyce Elizabeth V—†	20	"	54	here
T	Keefe Margaret A—†	20	"	57	"
U	Kelleher Margaret L—†	20	"	55	"
V	Kelley Alice G—†	20	"	70	"
W	Kelley Kathleen E—†	20	"	25	"
X	LeSage Gladys M—†	20	"	42	Cambridge

Saint Joseph Street—Continued

Y	Lonergan Margaret M—†	20	teacher	41	here
z	Long Catherine G—†	20	"	53	"

1233

A	MacInnes Rose E—†	20	"	43	
B	Mahoney Mary F—†	20	"	30	
C	McCarthy Catherine M—†	20	"	34	
D	McGough Agnes—†	20		51	"
E	O'Leary Margaret M—†	20	"	29	"
F	Shinnick Helen—†	20	"	52	Lynn
G	Sullivan Bridget—†	20	laundress	41	here
H	Sweeney Anna R—†	20	teacher	24	"
K	Wilkie Katherine C—†	20	"	42	"
L	Finerty Anne E—†	30	housewife	48	"
M	Finerty Edward L	30	policeman	48	"
N	Finerty Edward L, jr	30	clerk	23	
O	Perry William	30	retired	85	
P	Finerty James M	30	porter	55	
R	Finerty Katherine—†	30	housekeeper	53	"
S	Nolan Annie V—†	36	housewife	48	"
T	Nolan Helen S—†	36	tel operator	20	"
U	Nolan Mary V—†	36	secretary	22	"
V	Nolan Peter F	36	motorman	62	"
W	Ahlstrom Joanne—†	38	housewife	46	"
X	Ahlstrom Oscar R	38	U S N	49	
Y	Wells Cora G—†	38	at home	48	
z	Ghazarian Hagop	38	shoeworker	56	"

1234

A	Ghazarian Suran—†	38	forewoman	41	"
B	Hayes Benjamin I	39	mechanic	57	"
C	Hayes Doris—†	39	operator	23	"
D	Hayes Florence—†	39	housewife	52	"
E	Ryan Alice—†	39	"	44	23 Woodman
F	Ryan Peter J	39	maintenance	46	23 "
G	Connaughton Bernard	39	gardener	60	here
H	Connaughton Louise—†	39	clerk	25	"
K	Lyon Bessie—†	39	housewife	26	92 W Walnut pk
L	Lyon Marie—†	39	domestic	49	here
M	Lyon Paul	39	U S A	26	92 W Walnut pk
N	Fimburgh Louis	39	salesman	56	here
O	Fimburgh Mary—†	39	housewife	60	"
P	Fleming John	39	U S A	30	"

Saint Joseph Street—Continued

R	Sullivan Catherine A—†	39	housewife	34	here
S	Sullivan Thomas A	39	operator	38	"
T	Haskell George C	40	clerk	40	"
U	Haskell Julia A—†	40	housewife	42	"
V	MacDonald Katherine A-†	42	"	42	
W	MacDonald William J	42	broker	50	
X	McCarthy John J	42	laborer	49	"
Y	Duffy Arthur	43	agent	37	
Z	Duffy Edith V—†	43	housewife	35	"

1235

A	Norton Thomas M	43	retired	67	Hopkinton
B	Norton Winifred E—†	43	housewife	65	"
C	Kelly Bridget A—†	43	waitress	51	"
D	Maynes Katherine J—†	43	at home	70	"
E	Jex James	43	retired	85	
F	Jex Rita—†	43	housewife	60	"
G	L'Heureux William L	43	retired	80	"
H	Jordan Frances L—†	43	stenographer	46	"
K	Jordan Nellie—†	43	housewife	69	"
L	Grady Frances—†	43	"	30	
M	Grady William	43	fireman	31	"
N	Wencus Adeline B—†	43	housewife	26	"
O	Wencus Joseph J	43	mechanic	29	"
P	Ford Catherine—†	47	housewife	45	17 Ballard
R	Ford John J	47	machinist	49	17 "
S	O'Gorman John J	47	social worker	36	here
T	O'Gorman Joseph B	47	U S A	27	"
V	O'Gorman Mary—†	47	housewife	26	"
U	O'Gorman Mary J—†.	47	social worker	33	"
W	McDonald Catherine—†	49	housewife	43	"
X	McDonald Mary—†	49	clerk	21	
Y	McDonald William J	49	operator	50	"

Saint Rose Street

Z	Collins Helen A—†	47–49	tel operator	29	here

1236

A	Collins John	47 49	laborer	74	"
B	Collins John P	47 49	letter carrier	38	"
C	Collins Josephine—†	47 49	housewife	69	"
D	Collins Meda—†	47–49	"	26	New Jersey

Saint Rose Street—Continued

E	Collins William F	47–49	instructor	40	New Jersey
F	Murphy George J	47–49	machinist	38	90 Jamaica
G	Murphy Mary F—†	47–49	tel operator	37	90 "
H	O'Brien Alice M—†	51	housewife	27	here
K	O'Brien Stanley	51	chauffeur	29	"
L	Connaughton Mary—†	53	housewife	37	"
M	Connaughton William	53	clerk	44	"
N	Peak Constance—†	53	housewife	25	"
O	Peak Philip G	53	U S A	27	
P	Fogarty Frederick	55	draftsman	60	"
R	Fogarty Mary A—†	55	housewife	58	"
S	Tulk Carolina—†	55	"	63	"
T	Tulk Edwin	55	retired	78	
U	Tulk Phyllis B—†	55	saleswoman	41	"
V	Sheeran Margaret—†	55	clerk	45	"
W	Long Margaret—†	59	housewife	37	"
X	Long William	59	lineman	38	"
Y	McFarland Alexander	59	chauffeur	27	"
Z	McFarland Jessie—†	59	housewife	28	"
	1237				
A	McLean Mary E—†	59	"	52	
B	McLean Neil	59	carpenter	55	"
C	Basler Albert M	59	chauffeur	26	Cambridge
D	Basler Mary C—†	59	housewife	24	here
E	Reed Mary—†	63	"	22	"
F	Reed Melvin	63	U S N	29	"
G	O'Brien Alta—†	65	housewife	53	"
H	O'Brien Frank J	65	laborer	63	"
K	O'Brien Barbara A—†	65	tel operator	25	Milton
L	O'Brien Robert J	65	U S A	25	"
M	Donaghy Ann—†	69	housewife	44	here
N	Donaghy Hugh	69	laborer	59	"
O	Dolan Mary—†	69	housewife	75	"
P	Dolan William	69	retired	76	
R	Rowen Catherine D—†	69	housewife	33	"
S	Rowen Joseph E	69	letter carrier	37	"
T	Farrenden Margaret—†	71	housekeeper	32	"
U	Fitzgerald James	71	laborer	28	34 Cobden
V	Fitzgerald Mary—†	71	housewife	58	here
W	Fitzgerald Raymond	71	U S N	24	"
X	Regan Richard	71	cleaner	65	"

Page.	Letter.	FULL NAME.	Residence, Jan. 1, 1946.	Occupation.	Supposed Age.	Reported Residence, Jan. 1, 1945. Street and Number.

Saint Rose Street—Continued

Y	McGinn Ellen J—†	71	retired	72	here
z	Sullivan Edith C—†	71	tel operator	20	"
	1238				
A	Sullivan Ellen J—†	71	housewife	46	"
B	Sullivan John J	71	retired	50	
c	Sullivan Mary E—†	71	stenographer	25	"
D	Cahill John M	71	assembler	47	"
E	Cahill John M, jr	71	U S N	23	
F	Cahill Robert F	71	"	22	
G	Cahill Rose B—†	71	housewife	44	"
H	Ryan Eleanor—†	75	"	28	
K	Ryan James S	75	foreman	31	"
L	Campanello Matthew	75	U S A	28	
M	Campanello Mildred—†	75	housewife	28	"
N	Hutchinson Mary—†	75	"	37	
o	Hutchinson Thomas	75	operator	33	"
P	Manderville Arlene—†	79	housewife	33	"
R	Manderville Lyman	79	salesman	40	"
s	Michaud Evelyn—†	79	housewife	25	"
T	Michaud Paul	79	chauffeur	26	"
U	Sullivan Mary—†	79	seamstress	53	"
V	Twiss Evelyn—†	79	housewife	50	"
w	Twiss George	79	clerk	23	
x	Wright Helen—†	83	housewife	50	"
Y	Wright Thomas	83	U S A	21	
z	Wright William	83	student	22	"
	1239				
A	Deery Catherine—†	83	housewife	54	"
B	Deery Joseph H	83	accountant	23	"
c	Deery Joseph T	83	engineer	58	"
D	Deery William J	83	U S N	21	
E	Cooper Laura A—†	83	housewife	24	"
F	Cooper Philip P	83	musician	28	"
G	Wright Beatrice—†	83	secretary	24	"
H	Murphy Elizabeth—†	87	housewife	50	"
K	Murphy James A	87	checker	36	"
L	Miller Frederick S	87	retired	73	
M	Sanning Herman J	87	"	73	
N	Maguire Fred E	91	policeman	36	"
o	Maguire Mary E—†	91	housewife	30	"
P	Harrington James P	91	painter	47	"

Page.	Letter	FULL NAME.	Residence, Jan. 1, 1946.	Occupation.	Supposed Age.	Reported Residence, Jan. 1, 1945. Street and Number.

Saint Rose Street—Continued

R	McAvoy Anna—†	91	housewife	53	here
s	McAvoy Francis T	91	engineer	57	"
T	McAvoy Francis T	91	U S N	29	"
U	McAvoy James H	91	U S A	26	
v	Reidl Olga—†	95	housewife	34	"
w	Reidl Robert F	95	clerk	35	
x	Hucksam Helen—†	95	housewife	24	"
y	Hucksam John	95	U S A	24	7 Carolina av
z	O'Donnell Charles E	95	clerk	37	here
	1240				
A	O'Donnell Florence M—†	95	housewife	38	"
B	O'Connor Mary S—†	99	"	45	
c	O'Connor Michael J	99	policeman	55	"
D	Dowd Ella G—†	99	housewife	54	"
E	Dowd Patrick J	99	operator	57	"
F	MacEachern Margaret—†	103	housewife	41	"
G	MacEachern Robert	103	electrician	41	"
H	Burnside Metta—†	103	housewife	49	"
K	Burnside Nelson E	103	teacher	49	"
L	Tobin Dorothy—†	107	housewife	34	"
M	Tobin John E	107	clerk	37	
N	Gillooly Catherine—†	107	housewife	53	"
O	Gillooly Margery C—†	107	clerk	27	
P	Gillooly Peter J	107	salesman	53	"
R	Gillooly Robert P	107	repairman	23	"
s	Carney Lucille—†	109	housewife	39	"
T	Carney Walter	109	manager	45	"
U	Baatz Anna C—†	109	housewife	49	"
v	Baatz Carl J	109	salesman	58	"
w	Baatz David C	109	U S A	24	
x	Walsh Barbara—†	111	housewife	52	"
y	Walsh Thomas C	111	instructor	54	"
z	Morton Charles	111	guard	56	"
	1241				
A	Morton May—†	111	housewife	54	"
B	Malone Anna M—†	115	"	42	
c	Malone Lawrence	115	mechanic	42	"
D	Lang Donald C	121-123	"	46	
E	Lang Gladys—†	121-123	housewife	44	"
F	Lang Phyllis—†	121-123	secretary	21	"
G	Ray Joseph	121-123	chauffeur	34	"

Saint Rose Street—Continued

H	Ray Rose—†	121–123	housewife	33	here	
K	Bailey Abigail R—†	131	teacher	50	"	
L	Carroll Margaret—†	131	social worker	45	"	
M	Cronin Mary A—†	131	housekeeper	60	"	

South Street

s	Olson Charles	67	U S A	29	here	
T	*Olson Norma—†	67	housewife	21	"	
U	*Snow Douglas	67	longshoreman	20	"	
v	*Snow Ira	67	fishcutter	46	"	
w	*Snow Rhoda—†	67	housewife	43	"	
z	Kearney Florence M—†	70	"	51		
	1242					
A	Kearney John P	70	foreman	49	"	
B	Kelly John P	rear 70	U S A	24		
c	Kelly Leo M	" 70	student	20	"	
D	Kelly Mary A—†	" 70	at home	62	Southbridge	
E	Kelly Rose A—†	" 70	housewife	60	here	
F	Kelly Thomas J	" 70	policeman	59	"	
G	McKenna Catherine—†	" 70	technician	57	"	
H	Connolly Annie F—†	71	housewife	67	58 Carolina av	
K	Cooney Audrey F—†	71	waitress	23	58 "	
L	Cooney John F	71	U S M C	26	58 "	
M	Lynch Mary J—†	71	at home	65	58 "	
N	Donahue John J	71	electrician	61	here	
O	Donahue Mildred E—†	71	housewife	45	"	
P	Donahue Pearl M—†	71	inspector	25	"	
R	McCall Ellen—†	72	housewife	75	"	
s	McCall Joseph P	72	clergyman	39	"	
T	McCall Mary E—†	72	at home	53	"	
U	Majeski John B	74	U S N	34	"	
v	Majeski Katherine—†	74	housewife	32	"	
w	McCauley Helen—†	74	clerk	27		
x	Murdock Edith—†	74	housewife	37	"	
Y	Murdock Thomas J	74	electrician	44	"	
z	Beatty Eileen—†	74	housewife	38	83 Call	
	1243					
A	Beatty John J	74	laborer	39	83 "	
B	Fenerty Margaret H—†	75	housewife	56	here	
c	Fenerty Mary C—†	75	clerk	26	"	

1

South Street—Continued

D	Fenerty William	75	mechanic	56	here	
E	McCarthy Annie—†	75	at home	74	"	
F	McCarthy Catherine—†	75	housewife	74	"	
G	Billingham Bridget—† rear	75	"	33		
H	Billingham James P "	75	salesman	38	"	
K	Lynch Ellen F—† "	75	at home	75	"	
L	Gaffney Francis J	76	U S A	21		
M	Gaffney Mary E—†	76	housewife	49	"	
N	Gaffney Thomas F	76	fireman	52		
O	Holland Ellen M—†	76	at home	71	"	
P	King Hannah M—†	76	"	69		
R	King Margaret R—†	76	teacher	34	"	
S	Flaherty John F	76	checker	48	"	
T	Flaherty Margaret E—†	76	housewife	56	"	
V	Gately Evelyn—†	78	"	28	48 Wenham	
W	Ritchie Pearl—†	78	manager	26	48 "	
X	Scott Evelyn—†	78	housewife	26	here	
Y	Scott Walter F	78	shipworker	29	"	
	1244					
B	Murdock Edward	80	chauffeur	47	"	
C	Murdock Margaret—†	80	housewife	48	"	
D	Bradley Edward J	80	pipefitter	44	"	
E	*Bradley Mary—†	80	housewife	40	"	
G	Chaoing Peter	81	laundryworker	49	"	
H	Burke Mary—†	82	housewife	57	"	
K	Burke Mary—†	82	stenographer	26	"	
L	Burke Thomas	82	U S N	21	"	
M	Burke William F	82	"	20		
P	Johnson Marie D—†	84	housewife	40	"	
R	Johnson Marie D—†	84	typist	21		
U	Higgins Marie T—†	86	student	20	"	
V	Lennon Frank V	86	salesman	60	"	
W	Lennon Grace D—†	86	teacher	50		
X	Harrington Frederick R	86	factoryworker	62	"	
Y	Harrington Maude E—†	86	housewife	72	"	
	1245					
D	Casey William J	97	clergyman	72	"	
E	Foley Abbie F—†	97	domestic	28	28 Rawson	
F	Magner Eliza M—†	97	housekeeper	61	here	
G	Parsons John L	97	clergyman	43	"	
H	Riordan Daniel F	97	"	43	"	
K	Ryan Lawrence M	97	"	39		

Verona Street

L	Cohen Matthew	12	salesman	28	here
M	Cohen Mildred—†	12	housewife	30	"
N	Driscoll Julia A—†	12	"	41	"
O	Driscoll Thomas S	12	laborer	45	"
P	Mann Elinor C—†	12	housewife	25	"
R	Mann Ralph E	12	teacher	29	"
S	Niland Marie C—†	12	housewife	51	"
T	Niland William J	12	operator	55	"
U	Niland William J, jr	12	draftsman	20	"
V	Foley Delia M—†	12	housewife	35	"
W	Foley Martin J	12	repairman	45	"
X	Murphy Frank G	12	guard	26	"
Y	Murphy Mary A—†	12	housewife	23	"
Z	Kawana John L	16	custodian	44	"

1246

A	Rose Marion—†	16	bookkeeper	37	"
B	Shaw Loretta—†	16	housewife	75	"
C	Erickson Anna—†	16	at home	69	"
D	Rankin Bertha G—†	16	housewife	37	"
E	Rankin James H	16	collector	38	"
F	Shea Daniel	16	laborer	58	"
G	Shea Julia A—†	16	housewife	68	"
H	Ladd Florence K—†	16	"	37	
K	Ladd John T	16	teamster	39	"
L	McConville Mary C—†	16	housewife	30	"
M	McConville Matthew J	16	electrician	34	"

Woodman Street

N	Coffey Catherine L—†	3	housewife	31	here
O	Coffey James E	3	machinist	37	"
P	Owens Katherine M—†	3	stenographer	40	"
R	Owens Susan A—†	3	housewife	77	"
S	Aldred Margaret—†	5	"	37	
T	Aldred William D	5	messenger	37	"
U	Brennick Mary C—†	5	housewife	28	"
V	Brennick Robert E	5	chauffeur	35	"
W	Boucher Joseph D	8	foreman	38	"
X	Boucher Josephine—†	8	housewife	30	"
Y	Reilly Elizabeth J—†	8	typist	27	"
Z	Reilly Francis W	8	U S N	30	Milton

1247
Woodman Street—Continued

A	Walsh Francis J	8	U S A	29	here
B	Walsh Rose F—†	8	housewife	64	"
C	Walsh Thomas E	8	policeman	24	"
D	Powers Gerard H	9	agent	24	
E	Powers Laurence J	9	retired	70	
F	Powers Teresa—†	9	housewife	62	"
G	Kirwan Helen—†	9	"	28	95 Montclair av
H	Kirwan Thomas	9	checker	29	95 "
K	Longo Anna—†	9	housewife	36	252 Chambers
L	Longo Nicholas	9	bartender	40	252 "
M	Barrett Helen L—†	10	welder	29	here
N	Barrett James L	10	U S A	34	"
O	Barrett Margaret E—†	10	stenographer	37	"
P	Lamond Archibald	10	mechanic	43	"
R	Lamond Theresa—†	10	at home	35	"
S	Hounsell James W	11	U S A	30	
T	Hounsell Marguerite—†	11	housewife	30	"
U	Strecker Frank A	11	machinist	35	"
V	Strecker Mary—†	11	housewife	34	"
W	Houlihan Barbara—†	11	"	52	
X	Houlihan William J	11	porter	52	
Y	Kane Abbie—†	11	laundress	71	"
Z	Lavin Mary—†	11	at home	58	

1248

A	Bohmbach Marie—†	15	housewife	40	"
B	Keady John P	15	chauffeur	60	"
C	Keady Martha J—†	15	housewife	50	"
D	Keady Martha J—†	15	stenographer	20	"
E	Connelly Helen—†	15	housewife	30	6 Germania
F	Connelly Laurence J	15	policeman	28	6 "
G	McDowell Eva F—†	21	housewife	57	here
H	McDowell John M	21	clerk	57	"
K	McDowell Margaret E—†	21	WAVE	21	"
L	Smith Claire M—†	21	clerk	30	
M	Smith Emily—†	21	"	23	
N	Higgins Helen—†	21	housewife	41	"
O	Higgins Patrick J	21	bartender	38	"
P	O'Donnell Frank	21	clerk	30	
R	O'Donnell Mary—†	21	housewife	31	"
S	Reed Bernadine—†	21	"	29	

Woodman Street—Continued

T	Reed Warren J	21	machinist	35	here
U	Rosco Charles	21	clerk	30	"
V	Rosco Mary—†	21	housewife	30	"
W	Glennon Joseph M	21	foreman	38	"
X	Glennon Mildred—†	21	housewife	35	"
Y	MacNeil Sarah J—†	23	stitcher	37	13 Sunnyside
Z	McDevitt Elizabeth—†	23	housewife	68	13 "

1249

A	Mellett Coleman	23	painter	42	35 Ballard
B	Mellett Nora—†	23	housewife	40	35 "
C	Euscher Fred	27	chauffeur	37	here
D	Euscher Rachael—†	27	housewife	35	"
E	Cullen Hugh	27	mechanic	49	"
F	Cullen Margaret—†	27	housewife	37	"
G	Barry William J	31	guard	60	
H	Hughes Martin	31	retired	74	"
K	O'Connor Catherine—†	31	housewife	53	"
L	O'Connor James J	31	U S N	25	
M	O'Connor Patrick J	31	porter	55	
N	O'Connor Patrick J, jr	31	clerk	21	"
O	Raftery Richard	33	mechanic	29	"
P	Raftery Sarah—†	33	housewife	29	"
R	Tierney Joseph	33	chauffeur	35	"
S	Tierney Margaret—†	33	housewife	31	"
T	*Letourneau Henry	33	carpenter	46	"
U	*Letourneau Sadie—†	33	housewife	43	"
V	Roden Bridget A—†	33	"	64	
W	Cawley Bridget—†	35	"	60	
X	Cawley James J	35	laborer	64	"
Y	Brady Andrew J	35	fireman	31	175 Florence
Z	Brady Eleanor M—†	35	housewife	29	175 "

Ward 11–Precinct 13

CITY OF BOSTON

LIST OF RESIDENTS
20 YEARS OF AGE AND OVER

(NON-CITIZENS INDICATED BY ASTERISK)
(FEMALES INDICATED BY DAGGER)

AS OF

JANUARY 1, 1946

THOMAS F. SULLIVAN, *Chairman*
FREDERIC E. DOWLING, *Secretary*
WILLIAM A. MOTLEY, Jr.
ARTHUR V. COUGHLIN
EVERETT R. PROUT

Listing Board.

1300

Boynton Street

A	Hebert Elizabeth—†	5	housewife	48	here
B	Hebert Leon J	5	guard	45	"
C	Welch Mary—†	5	stenographer	27	"
D	Welch Thomas	5	laborer	55	"
E	Sullivan Daniel L	5	engineer	44	"
F	Sullivan Susan—†	5	housewife	44	"
G	Martin Dora—†	9	"	40	
H	Martin Thomas F	9	salesman	40	"
K	Hilton Eleanor G—†	10	housewife	41	"
L	Hilton Lewis J	10	inspector	41	"
M	White Mary A—†.	10	typist	37	"
N	*Cullen Sarah—†	10	housekeeper	56	Florida
O	Lynch Helen—†	10	tel operator	40	here
P	Lynch Rose—†	10	housekeeper	35	"
R	Boyd Charles F	11	chauffeur	55	"
S	Boyd Mary D—†	11	housewife	51	"
T	Arnold Alvin	11	U S N	22	"
U	Arnold Emile J	11	laborer	44	
V	Arnold Lilly B—†	11	housewife	44	"
W	Connell John V	14	U S A	31	
X	Connell Mary J—†	14	housewife	55	"
Y	Connell Michael J	14	laborer	56	
Z	Connell Michael J, jr	14	U S A	25	

1301

A	Reilly John	14	clerk	24	
B	Reilly Joseph P	14	"	25	
C	Reilly Margaret P—†	14	typist	27	
D	Reilly Mary J—†	14	housewife	56	"
E	Marshall Chester G	14	printer	56	
F	Marshall Hattie W—†	14	housewife	47	"
G	Davin Anne—†	15	"	60	
H	Davin Edward	15	gardener	55	"
K	*Stanlaske Anne—†	15	housewife	41	"
L	Dec Doris—†	15A	"	25	
M	Dec Joseph	15A	bartender	35	"
N	Kearns Angelina—†	15A	at home	73	"
O	Hogarty Michael	17	breweryworker	46	"
P	Hogarty Nellie—†	17	housewife	41	"
R	Slafer Helen—†	17	"	37	
S	Slafer Nelson	17	dairyman	39	"

Boynton Street—Continued

T	Cahill Mary F—†	17	operator	59	here
U	Fallon Jane M—†	17	"	54	"
V	Fallon William F	17	laborer	64	"
X	*O'Brien Catherine—†	18	housewife	30	"
Y	*O'Brien William P	18	shipper	35	"
Z	Galvin Paul	18	engineer	45	"

1302

A	Galvin Winifred—†	18	housewife	34	"
B	Grant Edward R	18	foreman	30	86 Jamaica
C	Grant Mary—†	18	housewife	27	86 "
D	Donahue Daniel	20	U S N	23	here
E	Donahue Ellen—†	20	packer	48	"
F	Murphy Catherine A—†	20	housewife	40	"
G	Murphy Charles F	20	chauffeur	41	"
H	Rock Anthony	20	carpenter	61	"
K	Rock Edward	20	mechanic	31	"
L	Rock Eileen—†	20	clerk	21	"
M	Rock Margaret—†	20	housewife	57	"
N	Rock Mary—†	20	saleswoman	25	"
O	Dailey Edward G	21	bricklayer	37	"
P	Dailey Mary J—†	21	housewife	34	"
R	Murphy Charles L	21	U S N	47	"
S	Murphy Mary F—†	21	housewife	50	"
T	Pulaski Joseph	21	chauffeur	41	"
U	Pulaski Margaret F—†	21	operator	39	"
V	Reilly Agnes E—†	21	waitress	41	"
W	Reilly Margaret—†	21	at home	80	"
X	Gates Dorothy—†	22	housewife	35	"
Y	Gates John W	22	agent	36	
Z	Berg Beatrice—†	22	housewife	43	"

1303

A	Davis Florence M—†	22	"	47	"
B	Davis Frank H	22	clerk	55	
C	Delaney Anna—†	23	housewife	58	"
D	Delaney Charles	23	salesman	29	"
E	Delaney Dorothy—†	23	saleswoman	25	"
F	Delaney George	23	mechanic	28	"
G	Delaney William	23	machinist	57	"
H	*Struzzieri Carmela—†	23	housewife	66	"
K	Struzzieri Domenico	23	laborer	66	"
L	Struzzieri Eugene	23	chauffeur	38	"

Page.	Letter.	FULL NAME.	Residence, Jan. 1, 1946.	Occupation.	Supposed Age.	Reported Residence, Jan. 1, 1945. Street and Number.

Boynton Street—Continued

	M	Sargent Albert F	23	U S N	32	here
	N	Sargent Clifford L	23	salesman	34	"
	O	Sargent Mary—†	23	housewife	66	"
	P	Kilrow Walter G	25	machinist	36	"
	R	McAteer Bertha—†	25	shoeworker	39	"
	S	McAteer Thomas A	25	"	39	
	T	Sweeney Martha A—†	25	"	30	
	U	Sweeney William F	25	custodian	29	"
	W	Moylan Elizabeth—†	25	housewife	49	"
	X	Moylan Kathleen—†	25	stenographer	22	"
	Y	Moylan Thomas	25	letter carrier	54	"
	Z	Duggan Annie T—†	26	housewife	48	25 Boynton
1304						
	A	Duggan Marion F—†	26	typist	20	25 "
	B	Duggan Michael F	26	engineer	48	25 "
	C	Toolin Elizabeth—†	29	housewife	37	here
	D	Toolin Patrick	29	fireman	38	"
	E	Matthews Donald S	29	U S C G	20	"
	F	Matthews Marion—†	29	housewife	42	"
	G	Matthews Owen J	29	watchman	49	"
	H	McGonigle Jennie—†	29	housewife	33	"
	K	McGonigle William	29	chauffeur	37	"
	L	Reardon John	30	fireman	60	
	M	Reardon Mary—†	30	housewife	50	"
	N	Kelly James T	30	chauffeur	26	109 Sheridan
	O	Kelly Margaret—†	30	housewife	24	109 "
	P	Koney John	30	barber	50	109 "
	R	Koney Margaret—†	30	housewife	48	109 "
	S	Craven Bridget—†	30	"	61	21 Plainfield
	T	Craven Malachi	30	laborer	24	21 "
	U	Craven Rita—†	30	typist	20	21 "
	V	Sargent Julia—†	31	waitress	38	here
	W	Atkinson Eva—†	31	housewife	54	"
	X	Leach Mildred—†	31	saleswoman	27	"
	Y	Hunt Agnes M—†	33	housewife	43	"
	Z	Hunt Thomas F	33	inspector	57	"
1305						
	A	Cuddy Agnes—†	33	housewife	46	"
	B	Cuddy Joseph	33	fireman	50	"
	C	Smythe Joseph	34	cook	46	79 Fort av
	D	Smythe Rosella—†	34	housewife	44	79 "

Page.	Letter.	Full Name.	Residence, Jan. 1, 1946.	Occupation.	Supposed Age.	Reported Residence, Jan. 1, 1945. Street and Number.

Boynton Street—Continued

	E	Monahan Margaret—†	34	housewife	51	here
	F	Monahan Mary—†	34	clerk	24	"
	G	Monahan Michael	34	custodian	54	"
	H	Gunaris Rheta—†	34	clerk	33	721 La Grange
	K	Gunaris Theodore	34	"	**36**	**721** "
	L	Cronin Bridie—†	35	housewife	35	here
	M	Cronin Timothy	35	pipefitter	49	"
	N	Manning Walter	35	laborer	50	"
	O	Lundsgaard Pauline—†	37	housewife	28	"
	P	Lundsgaard Victor T	37	packer	29	
	S	Barr Florence—†	38	housewife	27	"
	T	Barr Harold	38	electrician	34	"
	U	Murray Evelyn—†	38	housewife	26	"
	V	Murray William M	38	chauffeur	36	"
	W	Ledwith Evelyn M—†	38	housewife	39	"
	X	Ledwith Thomas J	38	letter carrier	40	"
	Y	Sullivan John J	38	retired	61	
	Z	Sullivan Margaret M—†	38	housewife	62	"

1306

	A	Gill Alice E—†	38	"	32	
	B	Gill John J, jr	38	chipper	35	"
	C	Ulrich Florence—†	38	nurse	42	
	D	Ulrich William	38	retired	49	
	E	McDonald Gordon	39	mechanic	33	"
	F	McDonald Mildred—†	39	housewife	28	"
	G	Deneault Angeline—†	39	stitcher	47	"
	H	Deneault Herve	39	plasterer	50	"
	K	*Flanagan Bridget—†	39	housewife	39	"
	L	Flanagan Edward	39	operator	45	"
	M	Foley Patrick	39	pressman	32	"
	N	Foley Stella—†	39	housewife	30	"
	O	Flynn Daniel	39	foreman	42	"
	P	Flynn Marguerite—†	39	clerk	38	
	R	McElhinney Bernard C	39	accountant	32	"
	S	McElhinney Mary V—†	39	housewife	32	"
	T	Boris Vincent	42–44	U S A	25	
	U	Boris William	42–44	laborer	67	
	V	Carmody Margaret—†	42–44	housewife	52	"
	W	Costello James	42–44	fireman	41	"
	X	Gilmore Frank	42–44	laborer	46	
	Y	Bowen Elizabeth—†	42–44	packer	39	"

Page.	Letter	FULL NAME.	Residence, Jan. 1, 1946.	Occupation.	Supposed Age.	Reported Residence, Jan. 1, 1945. Street and Number.

Boynton Street—Continued

	z	Bowen Martin	42–44	chauffeur	42	here
1307						
	A	Denaro Angelina C—†	43	machinist	21	"
	B	Denaro Rose—-†	43	housewife	59	"
	C	Carrigan Mary B—†	43	"	29	
	D	Carrigan William J	43	fireman	30	
	E	Conway Frank	43	laborer	45	
	F	Conway Mary—†	43	housewife	35	"
	G	Smith Howard J	43	shoeworker	51	"
	H	Smith Olive S—†	43	housewife	47	"
	K	Denaro Agnes—†	43	"	31	
	L	Denaro Frank	43	coppersmith	32	"
	M	Denaro James J	43	mechanic	27	"
	N	Denaro Josephine P—†	43	housewife	22	"
	O	Donahue William	43	mechanic	23	S Carolina
	P	Vellaca Nicholas	53	laborer	65	here
	R	Marshall Angie—†	53	nurse	56	"
	S	Pennington Ulysses	53	retired	75	"
	T	Skelly Hugh	53	plumber	69	"
	U	Skelly Rose—†	53	housewife	73	"
	V	Parks John S	rear 53	shipper	42	
	W	Parks Mary A—†	" 53	housewife	37	"
	X	Parks Herbert A	" 53	dairyman	63	"
	Y	Parks Mary H—†	" 53	housewife	62	"
	Z	Killion John J	54	chauffeur	44	"
1308						
	A	Killion Joseph J	54	U S N	22	
	B	Killion Ruth G—†	54	housewife	39	"
	C	Taber Eldon D	54	mechanic	43	"
	D	Taber Helen I—†	54	housewife	47	"
	E	Arkmejian Emust—†	54	housekeeper	52	"
	F	Arkmejian Sarkis	54	shoemaker	51	"
	G	Sharbetian Byron	54	carpenter	31	"
	H	Meader Marjorie—†	58	housewife	28	"
	K	Meader Quincy A	58	assembler	28	"
	L	Thompson Clifton W	58	chauffeur	30	"
	M	Thompson Mary—†	58	housewife	56	"
	N	Palmer Alice G—†	58	"	41	"
	O	Palmer Anthony J	58	bartender	47	"
	P	Carroll John	58	druggist	37	"
	R	Carroll Winifred R—†	58	housewife	30	"

Boynton Street—Continued

s	Sullivan Adeline—†	58	housewife	33	here
t	Sullivan Joseph	58	electrician	32	"
u	Snow Effie M—†	58	housewife	44	"
v	Snow John T	58	guard	43	"
w*	Cohen Ella R—†	66	housewife	65	"
x	Cohen Tela—†	66	typist	'32	
y	Klass Helen—†	66	housewife	35	"
z	Klass Simon	66	shoemaker	37	"

1309

a	Bemis Charles E	66	supt	38	"
b	Bemis Margaret—†	66	housewife	36	"
c	Kerr Robert	66	laborer	49	
d	Rakoski Marjorie E—†	66	housewife	32	"
e	Rakoski William J	66	baker	31	"
f	Hall Geraldine—†	66	housewife	34	"
g	Hall John H	66	mechanic	40	"
h	Anzelmo Alfred	66	presser	37	"
k	Anzelmo Violette—†	66	housewife	27	"
l	Hough Albert H	68	painter	50	
m	Hough Mary A—†	68	housewife	50	"
n	McCarthy Timothy J	68	watchman	52	"
o	Cotugno Anthony	72	chauffeur	24	"
p	Cotugno Jennie—†	72	housewife	49	"
r	Cotugno Jose—†	72	clerk	20	
s	Cotugno Joseph	72	laborer	53	
t	Cotugno Matthew	72	U S A	27	"

Call Street

u	O'Donnell Julia A—†	74	housewife	40	here
v	O'Donnell Michael J	74	laborer	40	"
w	DesChamps Herman A	74	chauffeur	41	"
x	Gilmore Anna B—†	74	housewife	42	"
y	Gilmore Howard A	74	supt	42	
z	Nolan Mary A—†	78	at home	80	"

1310

a	Connare Julia A—†	78	housewife	59	"
b	Connare Julia A—†	78	clerk	38	5 Arcadia
c	Connare Vincent M	78	U S A	22	here
d	Godet Amedee R	80	carpenter	58	16 Auburn
e	Christo George	80	operator	21	Somerville

Call Street—Continued

F	Christo Hazel—†	80	housewife	22	Somerville
G	Mulhern Isabella—†	rear 80	"	49	here
H	Mulhern Matthew	" 80	carpenter	50	"
K	Grenon Edgar R	82	rigger	30	"
L	Grenon Mary L—†	82	housewife	29	"
M	MacKay Betty—†	86	"	25	Illinois
N	MacKay Francis	86	student	22	here
O	MacKay H Edna—†	86	housewife	50	"
P	MacKay Joseph A	86	operator	52	"
R	MacKay Josephine—†	86	housewife	23	Pennsylvania
S	MacKay Richard H	86	U S N	24	here
T	MacKay Robert S	86	shipper	20	"
U	MacKay Theodore	86	machinist	28	"
V	Maeser Bert	rear 88	toolmaker	40	"
W	Maeser Floreda—†	" 88	housewife	39	"
X	Walthour Robert	" 88	salesman	58	95 Union Park
Y	Sullivan Harold F	90	laborer	47	here
Z	Sullivan Mary E—†	90	housewife	45	"
	1311				
A	Gormley Joseph E	90	chauffeur	42	"
B	Gormley Muriel—†	90	housewife	34	"
C	Cahalane Anna—†	90	presser	39	
D	Cahalane Dennis	90	clerk	45	"
F	Keavy Michael F	rear 94	longshoreman	49	2792 Wash'n
G	Keavy Mildred—†	" 94	housewife	40	2792 "
H	Beattie Mary—†	" 94	"	45	59 Chestnut av
K	Beattie William	" 94	laborer	49	59 "
M	O'Donnell Bridget—†	96	housewife	73	here
N	O'Donnell William	96	retired	86	"
O	Reneau Marie R—†	96	housewife	70	"
P	Smith Ada—†	98	stitcher	60	
R	*Duffy Mary—†	98	housewife	63	"
S	Groover Howard	98	U S N	35	
T	Groover Mary—†	98	housewife	35	"
U	Mulvey Dorothy F—†	99	"	30	
V	Mulvey James K	99	operator	29	"
W	Gill Delia R—†	99	"	42	
X	Gill Ellen—†	99	housewife	82	"
Y	MacGillivray James	102	engineer	40	11 Copeland
Z	MacGillivray Thelma—†	102	housewife	35	11 "

Call Street—Continued

A	Sousa Frank	102	chauffeur	55	here
B	Westcott Mary—†	102	operator	46	"
C	Westcott Muriel—†	102	"	24	"
D	Traficanti Antoinette—†	104	housewife	27	"
E	Traficanti Nicholas	104	brakeman	37	"
F	Connerty Clementina—†	104	housewife	26	Maynard
G	Connerty Thomas	104	chauffeur	32	here
K	Conrad Annie—†	110	sorter	52	"
L	Conrad Catherine—†	110	photographer	25	"
M	Conrad James W	110	U S N	21	"
N	Ortendahl Ethel D—†	110	housewife	28	"
O	Ortendahl Jens A	110	machinist	46	"
P	Mahoney Michael J	111	retired	68	
R	Martin George	111	policeman	30	"
S	Martin Margaret J—†	111	housewife	29	"
T	Glennon Sadie E—†	111	"	67	
U	Teehan John F	111	chauffeur	27	"
W	Volpe Arthur D	133	"	43	
X	Volpe Rose D—†	133	operator	39	

1313   Child Street

A	Flynn Anthony	21	caterer	45	here
B	Flynn Mary—†	21	housewife	35	"
C	McIsaac Margaret F—†	21	"	62	"
D	Reilly James P	21	U S N	26	
E	Shewan Margaret—†	21	housewife	64	"
F	Purin Louise—†	25	"	38	
G	Purin William	25	pressman	39	"
H	Hanley Annie—†	25	housewife	54	"
K	Hanley John J	25	laborer	56	
L	Hanley Mary—†	25	clerk	22	
M	Hanley Thomas J	25	U S A	27	"
N	Flaherty Delia—†	25	housewife	52	"
O	Flaherty Patrick	25	manager	56	
P	Sullivan Patrick	25	clerk	32	
R	Sullivan Theresa—†	25	housewife	24	"
S	Foley Patrick W	29	U S A	21	
T	Stevens David A	29	custodian	69	"

Child Street—Continued

u	*Stevens Mary A—†	29	housewife	65	here
v	Galvin Catherine A—†	29	"	69	"
w	Galvin Thomas	29	retired	70	"
x	Galvin Thomas J, jr	29	U S N	32	
y	Corney George	29	operator	60	"
z	Corney Rose—†	29	housewife	62	"

1314

a	Garabedian Armenog	33	mechanic	24	Whitinsville
b	Mouradian Abraham	33	clerk	55	here
c	Mouradian Alice—†	33	housewife	40	"
d	Downey Margaret—†	33	"	65	"
e	Downey William	33	operator	64	"
f	Duffy Ann J—†	33	at home	71	"
g	Panenondas George	33	baker	43	
h	Panenondas Mary—†	33	housewife	35	"
k	Sullivan Elizabeth—†	37	"	32	
l	Sullivan Humphrey	37	dispatcher	31	"
m	Dolan Mary—†	37	housewife	41	"
n	Dolan Thomas	37	welder	39	
o	Campbell James	37	shipper	42	
p	Campbell Mary—†	37	housewife	41	"
r	Dean Andrew	41	student	24	Arizona
s	Dean Helen—†	41	housewife	24	here
t	Murray Mary—†	41	"	49	"
u	Ring Elizabeth—†	41	secretary	22	"
v	Ring Ellen E—†	41	housewife	64	"
w	Ring William	41	U S A	37	
x	Ring William B	41	retired	71	
y	Ring Thomas	41	carpenter	30	"
z	Ring Virginia—†	41	housewife	26	"

1315

a	Keohane John	41	engineer	42	"
b	Keohane Mary K—†	41	housewife	40	"
c	Kelledy Lawrence	45	operator	52	"
d	Kelledy Mary—†	45	housewife	47	"
e	Walsh Hazel F—†	45	"	50	
f	Walsh James M	45	laborer	47	
g	Walsh Patrick J	45	"	50	
h	McDougall Mary—†	45	housewife	36	"
k	McDougall Timothy	45	printer	38	
l	Welsh Florence—†	49	housewife	41	"

Child Street—Continued

M	Welsh William	49	chauffeur	41	here
N	Toland Michael	49	operator	66	"
O	Flynn Margaret—†	49	housewife	55	"
P	Flynn Patrick J	49	laborer	55	"
R	Hampton Leroy	53	roofer	24	Texas
S	Hampton Marie C—†	53	housewife	21	here
T	Kearney Harriet—†	53	typist	27	"
U	Kearney Margaret—†	53	housewife	60	"
V	Gately Catherine—†	53	"	74	
W	Gately John	53	electrician	37	"
X	Gately Louise—†	53	bookkeeper	38	"
Y	Mulry Annie A—†	53	housewife	56	"
Z	Mulry James J	53	U S A	23	

1316

A	Mulry John T	53	operator	56	"
B	Mulry Leo	53	printer	21	"
C	Ericksen Catherine—†	57	housewife	37	"
D	Ericksen Conrad	57	electrician	34	"
E	McCann Elizabeth—†	57	housewife	50	"
F	McCann Mary—†	57	clerk	20	
G	McCann William	57	"	23	"
H	Dolan Alice V—†	57	housewife	42	344 Hyde Park av
K	Dolan Thomas C	57	salesman	45	344 "
L	Lehane Beatrice—†	61	housewife	32	here
M	Lehane John J	61	boilermaker	37	"
N	Gallagher Kathleen—†	61	housewife	32	"
O	Gallagher William J	61	fireman	36	
P	Hart John	61	U S A	35	"
R	McPhee Annie M—†	61	housewife	52	10 Fort av
S	McPhee Claire M—†	61	clerk	24	10 "
T	McPhee James A	61	"	52	10 "
U	McPhee Robert J	61	U S N	20	10 "
V	McPhee William J	61	baker	29	10 "
W	McGann Edward	65	clerk	39	here
X	McGann Florence R—†	65	housewife	38	"
Y	Perrin Donald P	65	plasterer	39	"
Z	Perrin Dorina—†	65	housewife	41	"

1317

A	O'Hara John	65	laborer	43	
B	O'Hara Rose—†	65	housewife	43	"
C	Kiernan Kathleen—†	69	stenographer	22	"

11

Child Street—Continued

D	Kiernan Margaret—†	69	housewife	51	here
E	Kiernan Patrick F	69	clerk	51	"
F	Kent Chester	69	U S A	38	"
G	Kent Rose—†	69	housewife	42	"
H	Korman Agnes—†	69	clerk	33	
K	Korman Francis	69	U S A	45	
L	Korman Ignatius	69	mechanic	53	"
M	Korman Martin	69	U S A	21	
N	Davis Ethel L—†	69	at home	46	"
O	Scheele Frederick C	69	salesman	29	"
P	Scheele Gertrude—†	69	housewife	28	"
R	Bury Agnes—†	73	"	66	
S	LaFleur Eileen—†	73	"	22	
T	LaFleur Romeo	73	U S A	22	
U	Madden Joseph V	73	retired	47	
V	Madden Mary —†	73	housewife	46	"
W	Kukla Helen—†	73	"	32	31 Jamaica
X	Sadowski Joan—†	73	coppersmith	23	here
Y	Hynes Mary—†	77	housewife	37	"
Z	Hynes Michael	77	bartender	44	"

1318

A	Sexton Alice—†	77	secretary	26	"
B	Sexton Ann—†	77	hairdresser	27	"
C	Sexton John	77	milkman	34	Weymouth
D	Sexton Mary—†	77	housewife	34	"
E	Riley Charles A	77	plumber	70	here
F	Riley Eleanor J—†	77	housewife	57	"
G	Glynn Delia—†	81	"	52	"
H	Glynn Joseph	81	U S A	27	
K	Glynn Michael F	81	operator	54	"
L	*Mee Delia—†	81	housewife	32	"
M	Mee Michael	81	operator	38	"
N	Greene Joseph	81	molder	41	
O	Keaney Bartley	81	laborer	51	
P	Keaney Bridget—†	81	housewife	48	"
R	Ballard Boyd	85	student	28	N Hampshire
S	Ballard Ruth—†	85	housewife	24	"
T	Jones Alfred	85	U S N	20	"
U	Jones Margaret—†	85	clerk	26	162 Boylston
V	Jones Sara—†	85	housewife	58	here
W	Jones William	85	machinist	62	"

Child Street—Continued

x	Dunning Margaret—†	85	housewife	42	here
y	*MacKenney Douglas	85	carpenter	43	"
z	Doyle Sara—†	95	housewife	55	117 Williams
	1319				
a	Coleman Alice—†	95	"	30	62 Brookside av
b	O'Neill Edmund J	95	metalworker	44	here
c	*O'Neill Mary E—†	95	housewife	44	"
d	Methot Mildred—†	97	"	37	"
e	Methot Wilbrod	97	steelworker	44	"
f	Mathews Elsie—† rear	103	housewife	45	New York
g	Osso Stella—† "	103	"	29	here
h	*Tarucewitch Constance "	103	"	53	"
k	Tarucewitch Josephine "	103	clerk	21	"
l	Tarucewitch Phyllis—† "	103	"	21	"
m	Petruzis Benjamin	105	machinist	33	103 Child
n	Petruzis Florence—†	105	housewife	30	103 "
o	Driscoll Catherine—†	105	"	66	here
p	Driscoll Edmund F	105	U S A	34	"
r	Driscoll Frederick J	105	"	36	"
s	Driscoll Gerald T	105	painter	27	"
t	Driscoll John J	105	retired	77	"
u	Driscoll John J, jr	105	bellboy	39	
v	Driscoll Paul	105	clerk	38	
w	Noonan David B	109	attorney	45	"
x	Noonan Ellen—†	109	housewife	80	"
y	Noonan Stella—†	109	"	34	"
z	Carey Rita—†	113	"	24	37 Cobden
	1320				
a	Carey William M	113	U S A	30	37 "
b	Cronan Agnes—†	113	janitor	49	37 "
c	Bensaia Bertha—†	115	housewife	39	here
d	Bensaia Frank	115	bookkeeper	49	"
e	Fellows Albert E	115	electrician	57	"
f	Fellows Charles H	115	U S A	30	
g	Fellows Mary—†	115	housewife	57	"

Hall Street

o	Foley Daniel J	8	clerk	39	here
p	Foley Dorothy M—†	8	housewife	39	"
r	Russo Edith E—†	8	"	38	"

Page.	Letter.	FULL NAME.	Residence, Jan. 1, 1946.	Occupation.	Supposed Age.	Reported Residence, Jan. 1, 1945. Street and Number.

Hall Street—Continued

	s	Russo Phillip	8	mechanic	36	here
	t	Woodward Alvin M	8	chauffeur	52	"
	u	Woodward Horace W	8	policeman	24	"
	v	Woodward Virginia J—†	8	clerk	23	
	w	Woodward Winifred M—†	8	housewife	62	"
	y	Fennessey Cecelia—†	9	"	39	32 Gay Head
	x	Fennessey George P	9	mechanic	39	32 "
	z	Jens Karl T	9	U S C G	25	Virginia
		1321				
	a	Jens Margaret K—†	9	housewife	24	"
	b	Shields Catherine V—†	9	"	47	here
	c	Shields Columbus M	9	shipper	46	"
	d	Watson Elizabeth V—†	12	housewife	72	"
	e	Watson Mary J—†	12	at home	78	"
	f	Sprague Ann B—†	12	housewife	22	"
	g	Sprague Arthur B	12	operator	26	
	h	Squarebridge George H	13	carpenter	70	Brookline
	k	Squarebridge Katherine-†	13	housewife	55	"
	l	Williams Cora E—†	13	"	42	here
	m	Williams George R	13	supervisor	43	"
	n	Winchenbach Katherine-†	13	at home	70	"
	o	Wood Francis A	15	treasurer	48	"
	p	Wood Theresa D—†	15	housewife	48	"
	r	Bell Mary J—†	16	housekeeper	61	"
	s	Salmon Lawrence M	16	metalworker	34	"
	t	Allen Ann—†	16	housewife	32	"
	u	Allen Frank	16	grinder	29	
	v	Bennett Mary—†	16	waitress	27	"
	w	Mealey Margaret—†	16	assembler	41	"
	x	Brennan Helen E—†	17	nurse	23	
	y	Brennan Joseph F	17	cable splicer	50	"
	z	Brennan Marie F—†	17	housewife	50	"
		1322				
	a	Cronin Andrew L	17	salesman	45	"
	b	Cronin Winifred A—†	17	housewife	45	"
	c	McKenzie Theresa—†	17	at home	75	"
	d	Welsh Cleona—†	19	housewife	40	214 South
	e	Welsh James	19	machinist	45	214 "
	f	Keogh Winifred—†	19	housekeeper	65	here
	g	Staryk Elizabeth A—†	19	housewife	31	17 Bonad rd
	h	Staryk William F	19	oiler	31	272 Itasca

14

Page.	Letter.	Full Name.	Residence, Jan. 1, 1946.	Occupation.	Supposed Age.	Reported Residence, Jan. 1, 1945. Street and Number.

Hall Street—Continued

K	*Little Eileen—†	21	housewife	25	here
L	Little James A	21	splicer	28	"
M	Hatch Dennis	21	electrician	44	"
N	Hatch Theresa—†	21	housewife	33	"
O	Shea John	21	retired	75	
P	Shea Mary—†	21	housewife	75	"
R	Russo Bruno	22	expressman	37	"
S	Russo Camile—†	22	housewife	29	"
T	Durant Beatrice—†	22	saleswoman	25	"
U	Durant Emil	22	shoeworker	65	"
V	Durant Georgina—†	22	stitcher	56	
W	Harkins Catherine—†	22	librarian	25	"
X	Walsh Mary—†	22	housewife	56	"
Y	Walsh Patrick J	22	laborer	56	
Z	Russo Saverio	24	pipefitter	39	"

1323

A	Russo Victoria—†	24	housewife	31	"
B	Ratta Frank	24	laborer	49	"
C	Ratta Saveria—†	24	housewife	41	"
D	Russo Joseph	24	retired	74	"
E	Campana Edmund	24	electrician	26	Wellesley
F	Campana Marion—†	24	bookkeeper	26	here
G	Prestera Antonio	24	laborer	50	"
H	Prestera Catherine—†	24	bookkeeper	24	"
K	Prestera Frances—†	24	housewife	46	"
L	Burke Eleanor—†	25	"	45	9 Hall
N	Means Curtis	28	chauffeur	31	here
O	Means Marjorie—†	28	housewife	28	"
P	Murphy George	28	chauffeur	26	"
R	Guarino Concetta—†	30	housewife	39	"
S	Guarino Pasquale	30	laborer	53	"
T	Hogan Delia—†	31	housewife	67	"
U	Hogan Joseph	31	laborer	32	
V	Shurety Francis	31	laundryman	50	"
W	Shurety Mary—†	31	factoryworker	48	"
X	Evans Mary—†	32	housewife	37	"
Y	Evans William	32	assembler	37	"
Z	Fitzgerald John	32	trackman	38	"

1324

A	Fitzgerald Mary E—†	32	housewife	38	"
B	Delaney Anna—†	32	"	32	

Page.	Letter.	FULL NAME.	Residence, Jan. 1, 1946.	Occupation.	Supposed Age.	Reported Residence, Jan. 1, 1945. Street and Number.

Hall Street—Continued

c	Delaney Joseph E	32	chemist	32	here
d	Barry Edgar J	33	laborer	50	"
e	Barry Kathleen V—†	33	housewife	49	"
f	McCallum Agnes C—†	33	typist	20	
g*	McCallum Ann G—†	33	packer	48	
h	Sayers Edward A	33	driller	39	
k	Sayers Mary A—†	33	housewife	37	"
l	Nicholson Harriett—†	34	"	26	67 Call
m	Poole Edward	34	janitor	70	here
n	Poole Mary—†	34	saleswoman	68	"
o	Hewitt Helen—†	34	housewife	35	"
p	Davis Bertha C—†	35	"	36	"
r	Davis Emil A	35	machinist	39	"
s*	Keough Mary A—†·	35	housewife	46	"
t	Keough Mary T—†	35	stenographer	20	"
u	Keough Patrick F	35	watchman	45	"
v	Norton John J	35	foreman	39	"
w	Norton Mary J—†	35	housewife	35	"
x	Norton William J	35	shipper	40	
y	Mulvey Alice—†	36	at home	81	"
z	Mulvey Anne E—†	36	"	83	

1325

a	Glennon John T	36	guard	59	
b	Glennon Margaret—†	36	dressmaker	63	"
c	Glennon William H	36	custodian	59	"
d	McDonald Elizabeth—†	36	housewife	56	"
e	McDonald Joseph	36	teacher	27	"
f	Groarke Margaret—†	40	housewife	37	65 Lawn
g	Splaine Mary—†	40	"	40	here
h	Crowley Ellen M—†	40	"	59	"
k	Crowley John J	40	U S M C	20	"
l	Crowley Mary—†	40	assembler	21	"
m	Crowley Patrick	40	laborer	62	
n	Healey Laurel E—†	41	housekeeper	38	"
o	Gill Christine M—†	42	housewife	35	"
p	Gill Thomas	42	laborer	39	
r	Strecker Louis E	42	inspector	43	"
s	Strecker Sarah S—†	42	housewife	40	"
t	Nelson Harold J	42	fireman	34	
u	Nelson Helen A—†	42	housewife	25	"
w	Feeley Helen S—†	45	"	50	

16

Hall Street—Continued

	x	Feeley James E	45	plumber	50	here
	y	Maguire Edward B	45	laborer	21	Burlington
	z	Maguire Mary H—†	45	tel operator	21	here
1326						
	a	Ordway Clara M—†	45	housewife	61	"
	b	Ordway George A	45	chauffeur	60	"
	c	Slater Gertrude M—†	45	typist	30	
	d	Slater Robert C	45	chauffeur	39	"
	e	*Kelly Mary A—†	45	domestic	51	"
	f	*Kelly Thomas F	45	laborer	52	"
	g	Branley Catherine—†	47	housewife	43	"
	h	Branley Joseph	47	operator	52	"
	k	*Crocker Florence—†	47	housewife	41	"
	l	Keegan Bridget—†	47	domestic	46	"
	m	Kelly Anna—†	48	at home	28	"
	n	Kelly John	48	laborer	55	
	o	Kelly Joseph	48	U S A	24	
	p	O'Hare Catherine—†	48	at home	50	"
	r	Keaney Coleman	48	chauffeur	53	"
	s	Keaney Ellen—†	48	housewife	49	"
	t	Fennelly Rita M—†	49	"	32	
	u	Fennelly William C	49	fireman	32	
	v	O'Connor Mary—†	49	housewife	75	"
	w	O'Connor Michael	49	retired	75	"
	x	O'Connor Thomas M	49	laborer	39	
	y	Padgett John M, jr	49	U S N	22	"
	z	Padgett Mary A—†	49	housewife	20	"
1327						
	a	Short Anna—†	49	"	41	
	b	Short George T	49	pipefitter	42	"
	c	Barrett Ann F—†	50	housewife	36	"
	d	Barrett Joseph S	50	shipper	39	"
	e	Holland Annie T—†	50	housewife	55	"
	f	Holland Bernard A	50	machinist	63	"
	g	Holland Edward J	50	U S A	24	
	h	Holland Paul H	50	assembler	23	"
	k	Glennon James J	50	clerk	25	
	l	Glennon Margaret—†	50	housewife	56	"
	m	Glennon Thomas I	50	fireman	58	"
	n	Placido Mary E—†	54	housewife	46	"
	o	Placido Terrence S	54	chauffeur	49	"

11—13

17

Hall Street—Continued

P	Coffee Jennie—†	54	housewife	64	here
R	Coffee Walter	54	watchman	68	"
S	Mason John	54	laborer	42	"

Lee Street

U*	Dever Fannie—†	32	housewife	67	here
V	Dever James P	32	steamfitter	35	"
W	Dever John A	32	U S A	37	"
X	Dever Philip J	32	"	31	
Y	Dever Susan T—†	32	clerk	25	
Z	Blye John T	34	retired	68	

1328

A	McLaughlan Mary B—†	34	housekeeper	70	"
B	Dickie Ellen A—†	rear 34	housewife	65	"
C	Dickie Norman L	" 34	plumber	63	"
D	Flynn Ann E—†	37	housewife	29	"
E	Flynn Frederick C	37	U S A	28	
F	McManus Michael J	37	watchman	67	"
G	McCabe Elizabeth G—†	37	housewife	22	4 Adams
H	McCabe William G	37	guard	25	Winthrop
K	Connolly Barbara—†	37	housewife	67	here
L	Maloney John T	38	engineer	54	"
M	Maloney John T	38	U S N	21	"
N	Maloney Kathleen H—†	38	housewife	47	"
O	Curwen William C	41	seaman	22	..
P	Maloney John M	41	letter carrier	47	"
R	Maloney Marie M—†	41	housewife	35	"
S	Packenham Agnes—†	42	"	48	
T	Packenham Daniel	42	electrician	58	"
U	Packenham Daniel P	42	U S A	24	
V	Packenham James J	42	"	27	
W	Packenham John R	42	"	24	

1329   McBride Street

B	Lydon Clifford	9	chauffeur	26	246 Hyde Park av
C	Lydon Theresa—†	9	housewife	26	246 "
D	Whitney Charles	9	laborer	26	Maine
E	Whitney Marguerite—†	9	housewife	27	"
H	Leuppold Frances D—†	17	secretary	40	here

McBride Street—Continued

	k	Tarpey Annie G—†	17	housewife	65	here
	l	Goldrick Ellen—†	22	"	71	"
	m	Goldrick Helen T—†	22	clerk	34	"
	n	Goldrick Hugh C	22	inspector	27	"
	o	Goldrick Margaret H—†	22	stenographer	23	"
	p	Goldrick Martha M—†	22	clerk	32	"
	r	Goldrick Thomas F	22	chauffeur	31	"
	t	Godvin James J	25	watchman	64	"
	u	Godvin Julia A—†	25	at home	77	"
	v	Godvin Martin L	25	retired	71	
	w	Godvin Mary V—†	25	at home	67	"
	x	Ward Madeline B—†	27	housewife	28	37 Chestnut av
	y	Campbell Agnes M—†	27	"	33	here
	z	Campbell Lawrence J	27	shipper	33	"
1330						
	a	Murray Elizabeth—†	27	at home	71	"
	b	Hurd Glennie I—†	29	housewife	26	"
	c	Hurd Vernon W	29	chauffeur	31	"
	d	McCormack Michael F	30	machinist	46	"
	e	Murray John J	30	clerk	22	
	f	Murray Mary A—†	30	housewife	53	"
	g	Lyons William A	34	cutter	65	
	h	Vachon Melanie M—†	37	housewife	45	"
	k	Vachon Noella F—†	37	waitress	21	"
	l	Vachon Norbert G	37	janitor	51	"
	m	Phillips Albert E	39	chauffeur	51	"
	n	Phillips Dorothy F—†	39	stenographer	20	"
	o	Phillips Lillian C—†	39	housewife	48	"
	p	Phillips Walter A	39	metalworker	23	"
	r	Daly Eugene J	40	longshoreman	42	"
	s	Daly Frances—†	40	housewife	42	"
	t	Lennon Catherine C—†	46	"	51	"
	u	Lennon Joseph F	46	carpenter	60	"
	v*	Lennon Margaret R—†	46	housewife	50	"
	w	Donovan James A	46	clerk	23	
	x	Donovan Joseph P	46	rigger	47	
	y	Donovan Julia J—†	46	housewife	55	"
	z	Coffey James	46	electrician	41	"
1331						
	a	Coffey Joseph	46	bricklayer	53	"
	b*	Coffey Margaret—†	46	housewife	76	"

McBride Street—Continued

c	*Coffey Margaret—†	46	factoryworker	51	here
d	*Coffey Mary A—†	46	housewife	54	"
e	Harvey Catherine M—†	47	"	33	"
e¹	Harvey Frederick R	47	foreman	38	
f	Rumpf Carl	49	carpenter	35	"
g	Rumpf Ethel—†	49	housewife	33	"
h	Boughter Catherine—†	50	"	36	
k	Boughter Edwin E	50	mechanic	35	"
l	Hurley Katherine E—†	50	packer	52	
m	Larson Charlotte—†	54	housekeeper	77	"
n	Carney Dorothy M—†	54	nurse	31	"
o	Cavalier Charles	54	foreman	45	"
p	Cavalier Gertrude A—†	54	housewife	37	"
r	Baker Edna K—†	rear 54	sorter	28	1 Sterling sq
s	Baker Herbert E	" 54	U S A	27	1 "
t	MacMillan James A	55	operator	69	here
u	MacMillan Mary A—†	55	housewife	61	"
w	Lunn Burpee L	60	engineer	37	"
x	Lunn Mary —†	60	housewife	31	"
z	Hanson Mary A—†	63	"	41	
	1332				
a	Hanson Walter L	63	painter	42	
b	Kellett Mary J—†	rear 64	housewife	43	"
c	Kellett Owen	" 64	laborer	44	"
d	Andrews Charles E	68	chauffeur	32	California
e	McCormack Dorothy E—†	68	housewife	27	Maryland
f	McCormack Patrick T	68	pipefitter	48	169 Poplar
g	Fowler Florence E—†	68	clerk	41	here
h	Fowler Mabel—†	68	at home	91	"
k	Cunningham Henry T	69	repairman	52	"
l	Doody Edward P	69	retired	80	"
m	Doody Mary A—†	69	secretary	40	"
n	Doody Mary C—†	69	housewife	68	"
o	Thornton Marie A—†	71	supervisor	35	"
p	Thornton Mary A—†	71	housewife	80	"
r	Dunning Catherine P—†	71	clerk	23	
s	Dunning Delia A—†	71	housewife	53	"
t	Dunning John F	71	watchman	53	"
u	*McKinnon Thomas S	74	laborer	72	
v	Cleary Edward E	75	metalworker	37	"
w	Cleary Mary V—†	75	housewife	35	"

McBride Street—Continued

x	Dockray Rose A—†	76	housewife	75	here
y	Dockray Thomas F	76	barber	76	"
z	Cunniff Annie—†	79	housewife	56	"
	1333				
A	Cunniff Esther A—†	79	nurse	27	
B	Cunniff James H	79	laborer	24	
c	Cunniff John J	79	"	64	
D	Cunniff Morris W	79	mechanic	22	"
E	Hamilton Gertrude—†	80	housewife	28	"
F	Hamilton John	80	repairman	30	"
G	Karas Peter	80	cleaner	59	
H	Daley Charles M	82	bartender	63	"
K	Daley Lillian M—†	82	housewife	67	"
L	Cameron Frank F	82	inspector	63	"
M	Cameron Mary A—†	82	housewife	61	"
N	Flynn Mary E—†	85	"	31	"
o	Flynn Patrick C	85	chauffeur	37	"
P	Peterson Robert C	85	machinist	28	Belmont
R	Peterson Sophie—†	85	clerk	21	here
s	Wencus Anna—†	85	housewife	50	"
T	Wencus Jennie J—†	85	clerk	24	"
U	Wencus Joseph W	85	machinist	59	"
v	Rice Warren L	rear 85	steamfitter	28	"
w	Rice Yvonne F—†	" 85	housewife	26	"
x	Plansky Helen S—†	" 85	"	27	
y	Plansky Norman C	" 85	repairman	30	"
z	Drake Elsie F—†	" 87	housewife	35	"
	1334				
A	Drake Freeman S	" 87	mechanic	37	"
B	Dolan Pauline F—†	88	housewife	28	"
c	Dolan Robert L	88	shipper	34	
D	Smith George A	89	salesman	38	"
E	Smith Matilda C—†	89	housewife	62	"
F	Bueker Evelyn M—†	92	"	23	
G	Bueker Richard W	92	U S A	30	
H	Lehrer Anna M—†	92	housewife	40	"
K	Lehrer Esther E—†	92	saleswoman	21	"
L	Lehrer William R	92	engineer	52	"
M	Lawler Alice L—†	95–97	housewife	48	"
N	Lawler Henry J	95–97	clerk	56	
o	Sizer Annie G—†	95–97	nurse	50	

McBride Street—Continued

P	Kyle Helena—†	96	housekeeper	58	here
R	Walsh Julia—†	96	fitter	60	"
S	Daley Francis D	101	chauffeur	33	"
T	Daley Kathleen—†	101	nurse	34	"
U	Voice Gerald	103	garageman	40	82 Chestnut av
V	Voice Marie—†	103	housewife	34	82 "
W	Bower Grace M—†	107–109	"	38	here
X	Bower Henry A	107–109	laborer	39	Canada
Y	Regan Arthur L	107–109	mechanic	40	here
Z	Barbour Charles E	110	U S A	29	"
	1335				
A	Barbour Elizabeth—†	110	housewife	66	"
B	Barbour Robert	110	painter	73	
C	Barbour Woodrow W	110	U S A	25	"
D	Fuller Edward	110	clerk	30	California
E	Fuller Ruth B—†	110	housewife	29	here
F	Pepe Michael W	116	carpenter	39	"
G	Pepe Trudie M—†	116	housewife	21	"
H	Vardaro Angelina—†	116	"	52	
K	Vardaro Anthony P	116	U S A	21	
L	Vardaro Gaetano	116	"	23	
M	Vardaro Liberatore	116	laborer	55	
N	Walsh David I	117	inspector	28	"
O	Walsh Katherine L—†	117	clerk	45	
P	Walsh Mary G—†	117	secretary	42	"
R	Donovan Albert	120	accountant	39	"
S	Donovan Anne M—†	120	housewife	40	"
T	Ryan Mary E—†	120	"	68	
U	Mulkern Martin	120	laborer	57	
V	Falconetti Susan—†	123	clerk	43	"

Rosemary Street

W	Horton John F	8	inspector	58	here
X	Horton Katherine F—†	8	housewife	48	"
Y	Anderson Harry I	8	manager	40	"
Z	Anderson Isabelle—†	8	housewife	41	"
	1336				
A	Anderson Nora T—†	8	at home	80	"
B	Gibbons Mary F—†	8	housewife	75	"
C	Gibbons Richard	8	retired	75	

Rosemary Street—Continued

D	Shea Dorothy J—†	8	housewife	36	here
E	Shea Michael J	8	policeman	35	"
F	Mahoney Dennis J	8	metalworker	51	"
G	Mahoney Ellen E—†	8	housewife	48	"
H	Johnston Helen G—†	8	at home	70	"
K	Johnston Thomas F	8	photographer	40	"
L	Barrett Thomas J	12	retired	58	"
M	Fahey Mary—†	12	at home	65	"
N	Leonard Bridget D—†	12	"	70	
O	Murch Gertrude C—†	12	"	66	
P	Galvin Arthur	12	machinist	49	"
R	Galvin Mary—†	12	housewife	46	"
S	Sullivan Edward	16	laborer	25	
T	Sullivan Margaret J—†	16	housewife	52	"
U	Sullivan Margaret J—†	16	typist	23	
V	Sullivan Patrick J	16	boilermaker	57	"
W	McCarthy John J	16A	operator	55	"
X	McCarthy Mary—†	16A	housewife	55	"
Y	*Hackett Della—†	16A	"	46	"
Z	Hackett James	16A	custodian	45	"
	1337				
A	McDonagh Edward C	20	U S N	34	
B	McDonagh Julia P—†	20	housewife	30	"
C	Dolan Michael	20	storekeeper	79	"
D	Dolan Nellie E—†	20	housewife	72	"
E	Henehan Mary E—†	20	at home	74	"
F	McDonagh Frank T	20	operator	40	"
G	McDonagh Loretta G—†	20	housewife	40	"
H	Costello Jennie A—†	22	"	46	"
K	Costello John J	22	operator	48	"
L	Costello Mary T—†	22	bookkeeper	21	"
M	Mitchell Delia M—†	22	housewife	39	"
N	Mitchell John J	22	foreman	49	"
O	Hudson Harriet M—†	22	operator	46	"
P	Robertson Edna M—†	22	housewife	24	"
R	Coleman Anna M—†	26	"	45	
S	Coleman Martin J	26	policeman	49	"
T	Fennessy Elizabeth M—†	26	assembler	43	"
U	Mullins Dennis	26	rigger	46	
V	Mullins Ella—†	26	housewife	43	"
W	Nagle Alice—†	26	factoryworker	56	"

Page.	Letter.	FULL NAME.	Residence, Jan. 1, 1946.	Occupation.	Supposed Age.	Reported Residence, Jan. 1, 1945. Street and Number.

South Street

	z	Noonan Lillian M—†	rear 110	hairdresser	46	here
1338						
	A	Gavin Martin F	112	operator	39	26 Boynton
	B	Gavin Mary C—†	112	housewife	38	26 "
	c	Morris John J	112	retired	67	26 "
	D	Morris Thomas P	112	U S A	28	26 "
	G	Clark Arthur G	120	salesman	39	42 Burnett
	H	Clark Ruth V—†	120	housewife	37	42 "
	K	Crowley Adelaide E—†	120	"	48	30 Adelaide
	L	Crowley Adelaide M—†	120	student	20	30 "
	M	Crowley John E	120	draftsman	50	30 "
	X	Bow Wong	140A	laundryman	62	here
1339						
	G	Sexton Katherine E—†	150	housewife	32	199 South
	H	Sexton Leo M	150	machinist	38	199 "
	K	Kasparian Garabed	150	storekeeper	48	here
	L	Kasparian Veronica—†	150	housewife	38	"
	M	Ehrgott John J	150	U S A	28	"
	N	Hovestadt Bernard E	150	chauffeur	21	17 Anson
	o	Hovestadt Caroline E—†	150	housewife	51	17 "
	R	Self Muriel P—†	156	"	24	here
	s	Self Rufus P, jr	156	fireman	28	"
	T	Murphy Annie—†	156	at home	68	"
	U	Shedden Ernest V	156	bottler	45	1 Alfred
	V	Shedden Evelyn M—†	156	housewife	32	1 "
	W	Singer Anna J—†	156	"	39	here
	X	Singer Thomas	156	painter	38	"
	Y	Maloney Bessie V—†	156A	housewife	63	"
	z	Maloney Jessie C—†	156A	stenographer	37	"
1340						
	A	Pappas Stephen	156A	manager	58	"
	B	Pappas Virginia—†	156A	housewife	41	"
	c	Manning Kathleen B—†	156A	"	30	75 Marcella
	D	Manning Thomas J	156A	storekeeper	38	75 "
	E	Flynn Catherine A—†	156A	housewife	77	here
	F	Flynn Margaret R—†	156A	clerk	35	"
	G	Flynn Mary A—†	156A	tel operator	35	"
	H	Carter Henry W	156A	operator	61	"
	K	Carter Mary E—†	156A	housewife	58	"
	L	Daigneault Eugene H	156A	gardener	38	Acushnet
	M	Daigneault Harvey G	156A	agent	36	here

South Street—Continued

N	Daigneault Mary M—†	156A	housewife	32	here
O	Conway Mary A—†	158	at home	67	"
P	Walker Leo J	158	fireman	32	"
R	Walker Mary E—†	158	housewife	32	"
S	McGovern Helen J—†	158	"	65	
T	McGovern James J	158	clerk	33	
U	McGovern Peter T	158	"	37	"
V	Foley Catherine A—†	158	WAC	34	
W	Foley Delia T—†	158	at home	35	"
X	Fricka Amelia M—†	158	housewife	22	"
Y	Fricka Frederick H	158	engineer	26	"
Z	Landenberger Mary—†	158	housewife	62	"

1341

A	Landenberger William H	158	metalworker	24	"
B	Feeley Catherine M—†	158	at home	71	"
C	Grady Peter F	158	guard	65	
D	Jackley Mary—†	158	housewife	50	"
E	Jackley Mary T—†	158	clerk	25	
F	Jackley Theodore	158	chauffeur	51	"
G	Dillon Helen M—†	158	saleswoman	43	"
H	Dillon Mary T—†	158	housewife	69	"

Williams Street

K	Madden Dennis C		laborer	28	here
L	Madden Helen L—†		saleswoman	46	"
M	Madden James R		pharmacist	38	"
N	Madden Johanna M—†		housewife	72	"
O	Madden William M	5	clerk	31	

Ward 11–Precinct 14

CITY OF BOSTON

LIST OF RESIDENTS
20 YEARS OF AGE AND OVER

(NON-CITIZENS INDICATED BY ASTERISK)
(FEMALES INDICATED BY DAGGER)

AS OF

JANUARY 1, 1946

THOMAS F. SULLIVAN, *Chairman*
FREDERIC E. DOWLING, *Secretary*
WILLIAM A. MOTLEY, JR.
ARTHUR V. COUGHLIN
EVERETT R. PROUT

Listing Board.

CITY OF BOSTON PRINTING DEPARTMENT

1400

Brookley Road

A	Curtis Florence—†	2	at home	51	here	
B	Kelly Ellen—†	2	machinist	45	270 Quincy	
D	Jay Julia—†	4	housewife	67	here	
E	Hennessey Jeremiah J	41	mechanic	35	"	
F	*Hennessey Mary—†	41	housewife	34	"	
G	*Kolanski Anna—†	41	"	60		
H	Kolanski Anthony	41	laborer	63		
K	Kahler Anna—†	41	housewife	28	"	
L	Kahler George	41	salesman	27	"	
M	Coleman Mary—†	42	housewife	45	"	
N	Coleman Peter	42	warehouse	42	"	
O	Hogan Emily—†	42	housewife	39	"	
P	Hogan William	42	trackman	42	"	
R	*Dumont Armand	42	plasterer	42	34 Burnett	
S	*Dumont Jeanne—†	42	housewife	36	34 "	
T	Gulish George	46	U S N	37	here	
U	Gulish Margaret—†	46	housewife	35	"	
V	Maisey Maude C—†	46	"	64	"	
W	McLeod Alice—†	46	operator	38	"	
X	McLeod Donald	46	polisher	46	"	
Y	Peavey George	46	messenger	66	"	
Z	Murphy Arthur D	46	pressman	34	"	

1401

A	Murphy Louise—†	46	housewife	29	"	
B	Alford James	48	U S N	28		
C	Alford Veronica F—†	48	stenographer	23	"	
D	Kelley John J	48	U S N	31	"	
E	Kelley Marie G—†	48	instructor	31	"	
F	Stier Charles J	48	painter	55		
G	Stier Charles J	48	U S N	28		
H	Stier Marie G—†	48	housewife	58	"	
K	Stier Robert J	48	U S A	21		
L	Bohan Helen R—†	48	housewife	25	"	
M	Bohan John J	48	chauffeur	28	"	
N	Kropoff Marion—†	50	housewife	21	"	
O	Kropoff Peter	50	coppersmith	33	"	
P	Finn Frederick W	50	shipfitter	40	"	
R	Finn Rose M—†	50	housewife	36	"	
S	Wilkinson Annie—†	50	"	65		
T	Wilkinson Arthur	50	bellboy	36		

Page.	Letter.	FULL NAME.	Residence, Jan. 1, 1946.	Occupation.	Supposed Age.	Reported Residence, Jan. 1, 1945. Street and Number.

Brookley Road—Continued

	U	Wilkinson John	50	clerk	29	here
	V	Wilkinson Robert	50	"	31	"
	W	Wilkinson William	50	"	38	"
	X	Glennon John M	52	"	41	
	Y	*Glennon Mary—†	52	housewife	42	"
	Z	Lutz Louis	52	U S A	21	
1402						
	A	Lutz Walter	52	policeman	55	"
	B	Talanion Charles	52	storekeeper	40	"
	C	Talanion Mary—†	52	housewife	39	"
	D	Haskins Benjamin	55	chauffeur	53	"
	E	Haskins Edith—†	55	checker	22	"
	F	Carney Dorothy—†	55	housewife	22	166 Boylston
	G	Carney Eugene	55	clerk	28	7 Bardwell
	H	Vanstry Catherine—†	55	housewife	37	here
	K	Vanstry Leonard	55	clerk	36	"
	L	Venanzi Marie—†	55	housewife	28	"
	M	Venanzi Ralph	55	ironworker	32	"
	N	Mohan Charlotte—†	55	housewife	27	"
	O	Mohan Joseph W	55	engineer	30	"
	P	*Mankiewicz Anna—†	59–61	housewife	52	"
	R	Mankiewicz Edwin	59–61	salesman	28	"
	S	Mankiewicz William	59–61	mechanic	55	"
	U	Moynihan Daniel	59–61	U S N	32	
	V	Moynihan Lila—†	59–61	instructor	32	"
	W	Tierney Alvina—†	62–64	housewife	36	"
	X	*Tierney Joseph E	62–64	shipper	40	
	Y	Irvine George	62–64	mechanic	45	"
	Z	Irvine Lillian H—†	62–64	housewife	43	"
1403						
	A	O'Connell Helen—†	62–64	"	38	
	B	O'Connell John P	62–64	shipper	39	
	C	Murphy Margaret M-†	63–65	housewife	46	"
	D	Murphy Miles V	63–65	B F D	50	
	E	Oldfield Mary E—†	63–65	housewife	68	"
	F	Oldfield Nellie—†	63–65	cashier	29	"
	G	Oldfield William	63–65	machinist	67	"
	H	Russo Bernard L	63–65	welder	25	
	K	Russo Felix J	63–65	retired	50	"
	L	Russo Jennie L—†	63–65	housewife	45	"
	M	Pohlker Betty R—†	67–69	clerk	23	Minnesota

Brookley Road—Continued

N	Stewart Dorothy F—†	67–69	bookkeeper	22	here
O	Stewart Falba—†	67–69	housewife	45	"
P	Stewart Frank E	67–69	foreman	53	"
R	Stewart Roy D	67–69	seaman	21	"
S	Broderick Anna T—†	67–69	housewife	42	"
T	Broderick Joseph P	67–69	mechanic	20	"
U	Broderick Patrick J	67–69	"	45	
V	Boates Mary T—†	67–69	at home	78	"
W	Oberlander Mildred A–†	67–69	housewife	38	"
X	Oberlander Milton E	67–69	mechanic	41	"
Y	Thomas Andrew	71–73	chauffeur	34	"
Z	Thomas Louise—†	71–73	housewife	24	"
	1404				
A	Munafo Ida—†	71–73	"	32	
B	Munafo Leo	71–73	mechanic	32	"
C	Barron Evelyn—†	71–73	housewife	30	"
D	Butts Mary—†	71–73	"	52	
E	Butts Mildred J—†	71–73	bookkeeper	21	"
F	Butts Robert J	71–73	U S N	20	"
G	Butts Thomas J	71–73	chauffeur	52	"
H	Powers Charles J	76–78	student	23	
K	Powers Margaret—†	76–78	housewife	50	"
L	Powers William H	76–78	clerk	52	"
M	Powers William H	76–78	student	20	
N	Hobin Joseph	76–78	steamfitter	50	"
O	Kerr Catherine F—†	76–78	housewife	45	"
P	Kerr Thomas J	76–78	steamfitter	47	"
R	Webber Rita—†	76–78	housewife	25	"
S	Webber Russell W	76–78	coal dealer	26	"
T	Boucher Gertrude—†	79–81	housewife	31	"
U	Galvin Mary—†	79–81	"	36	
V	Galvin Maurice	79–81	machinist	36	"
W	Shevory Roselle—†	79–81	housewife	34	"
X	Shevory William B	79–81	attorney	38	"
Y	*Puzo Joseph	80–82	retired	74	"
Z	*Scipione Anthony	80–82	salesman	46	"
	1405				
A	*Scipione Lucy—†	80–82	housewife	43	"
B	Damato Antonio	80–82	U S A	25	
C	Damato George	80–82	"	23	
D	Damato James	80–82	salesman	59	"

Brookley Road—Continued

E	Damato John	80–82	factoryworker	21	here	
F	Lopez Carmen—†	80–82	housewife	60	"	
G	Lopez Celia—†	80–82	factoryworker	27	"	
H	Lopez Henry	80–82	seaman	26		
K	Lopez Mary—†	80–82	tel operator	22	"	
L	Devlin George	84–86	watchman	61	"	
M	Devlin Margaret J—†	84–86	secretary	22	"	
N	Devlin Nora—†	84–86	housewife	48	"	
O	Devlin Nora E—†	84–86	secretary	21	"	
P	Madsen Frances M—†	84–86	housewife	29	"	
R	Madsen George P	84–86	mechanic	30	"	
S	Alther Margaret—†	84–86	waitress	38	"	
T	Alther Robert	84–86	U S M C	20	"	
U	Fox Catherine—†	92–94	housewife	33	"	
V	Fox Michael J	92–94	carpenter	42	"	
W	Kelly Ann M—†	92–94	housewife	32	"	
X	Kelly Patrick	92–94	engineer	41	"	
Y	DerGarabedian Elizabeth—†	92–94	housewife	42	"	
Z	DerGarabedian Gary	92–94	artist	52		
	1406					
A	Conway Helen—†	96–98	housewife	47	"	
B	Conway John	96–98	mechanic	47	"	
C	Curtin Rose J—†	96–98	housewife	42	"	
D	Curtin William L	96–98	salesman	47	"	
E	Coelho Antero D	96–98	student	26	80 Blue Hill av	
F	Coelho Mildred R—†	96–98	housewife	33	80 "	

Burnett Street

H	Cheney Clifton	8	inspector	52	here	
K	Cheney Clifton L	8	clerk	20	"	
L	Bonner Elmer	8	U S A	27	Revere	
M	Bonner Margaret—†	8	housewife	26	"	
N	McNulty Francis J	10	insulator	42	here	
O	McNulty James P	10	clerk	40	"	
P	McNulty Mary—†	10	housewife	74	"	
R	Dinan John W	10	pumpman	37	48 Union Park	
S	Dinan Margaret—†	10	waitress	38	48 "	
T	LaBonta Helen—†	10	housewife	53	here	
U	LaBonta Paris J	10	chauffeur	49	"	
V	Prendergast Chester	10	"	35	"	

Burnett Street—Continued

w	French Edna—†	14	housewife	26	here
x	French Walter D	14	grinder	28	"
y	Nelson Violet—†	14	housewife	34	"
z	McGovern James J	18	mechanic	24	11 Durant
	1407				
A	McGovern Olive L—†	18	housewife	26	11 "
B	Costello Catherine—†	18	"	37	here
C	Costello John	18	laborer	42	"
D	Hansbury Mary—†	18	domestic	40	"
E	Major George	18	laborer	41	"
F	McGrory Mary E—†	20	housewife	60	Cambridge
G	McGrory Patrick	20	conductor	56	"
H	Kane Gertrude L—†	20	housewife	37	here
K	Haddad Florence C—†	20	"	28	35 Murray Hill r
L	Haddad Richard E	20	U S M C	27	650 Harrison av
M	Jay Allen J	32	sign painter	34	Connecticut
N	Jay Mary N—†	32	housewife	34	"
O	Cook Louis	32	chauffeur	38	here
P	Cook Mary—†	32	housewife	38	"
R	Pike Albert	32	clerk	45	"
S	Pike David	32	chauffeur	21	"
T	Pike Margaret—†	32	housewife	42	"
U	Vasil Bruno	34	guard	31	42 Frazer
V	Vasil Sophie—†	34	housewife	22	42 "
W	Devaney Elizabeth—†	34	"	48	176 Hyde Park av
X	Devaney James	34	U S N	20	here
Y	Devaney John	34	chauffeur	25	"
Z	Devaney Joseph	34	iceman	52	176 Hyde Park av
	1408				
A	McMahon Andrew	34	coremaker	40	68 McBride
B	McMahon Lillian—†	34	housewife	34	68 "
C	Galvin Almina—†	36	"	37	here
D	Galvin Francis J	36	chauffeur	44	"
E	Merrill Margaret—†	36	at home	75	"
F	*Connors Mary—†	36	housewife	81	"
G	Walsh John	36	laborer	63	
H	Crosby Alice—†	36	housewife	63	"
K	Crosby Frederick W	36	fireman	62	
L	Thompson Richard C	38	meatcutter	31	"
M	Thompson Winifred—†	38	housewife	28	"
N	Landry Clara M—†	38	"	25	68 Forbes

Burnett Street—Continued

Page.	Letter.	FULL NAME.	Residence, Jan. 1, 1946.	Occupation.	Supposed Age.	Reported Residence, Jan. 1, 1945. Street and Number.
	o	Landry Patrick	38	mechanic	29	68 Forbes
	p	Westerlund Alden F	42	U S N	24	30 Kenton rd
	R	Westerlund Virginia A—†	42	housewife	30	30 "
	s	Mandeville Caroline J—†	44	"	36	here
	T	Mandeville Edward R	44	chauffeur	42	"
	u	O'Brien Joseph E	50	painter	28	"
	v	O'Brien Mary E—†	50	housewife	27	"
	w	Ryan Theresa—†	51–51A	"	35	336 Amory
	x	Travers Blanche—†	51–51A	"	32	here
	Y	Travers Edward	51–51A	chauffeur	34	"
	z	Peterson Beatrice M—†	55	housewife	52	"
1409						
	! A	Peterson Charles L	55	retired	66	
	B	Callahan John	56	"	70	
	c	Callahan Patrick	56	fireman	40	
	D	Callahan Timothy	56	clerk	38	
	E	O'Brien Annie—†	56	housewife	65	"
	F	O'Brien Catherine—†	56	"	30	
	G	O'Brien Charles	56	factoryworker	32	"
	H	O'Brien John	56	mechanic	30	"
	K	Lundsgaard Borghild M—†	57	housewife	58	"
	L	Lundsgaard Emil P	57	janitor	65	
	M	Lundsgaard John E	57	U S M C	36	"
	N	Doyle Frederick J	58–60	electrician	21	"
	o	Doyle Julia—†	58–60	housewife	58	"
	P	Doyle Louis J	58–60	laborer	23	
	R	Doyle William B	58–60	clerk	24	
	s	Doyle William G	58–60	dairyman	58	"
	T	Gallagher James J	58–60	student	20	40 Mozart
	u	Mattie Edward J	58–60	U S A	33	here
	v	Mattie Mary H—†	58–60	housewife	31	"
	w	Mattie William H	58–60	agent	40	"
	x	Amicangelo Julio	58–60	packer	29	
	Y	Amicangelo Marie—†	58 60	housewife	34	"
	z	Schaffner Corinne—†	59	"	66	
1410						
	l A	Schaffner George H	59	retired	79	"
	B*	Johnson Anna T—†	59	housewife	39	62 Burnett
	c	Johnson Paul W	59	painter	39	62 "
	D	Middleton Harold J	61	U S A	27	here
	E	Rath John E	61	merchant	24	"

Burnett Street—Continued

F	Rath Rose A—†	61	housewife	52	here
G	Hawes Alice M—†	61A	"	45	"
H	Hawes Richard J	61A	shipper	44	"
K	Bloedt Catherine F—†	62	shoeworker	55	"
L	Bloedt John H	62	woodworker	48	"
M	Orrall Marie M—†	62	housewife	45	"
N	Kelly Charles J	62	U S A	32	
O	Kelly Edward V	62	U S N	21	
P	*Kelly John	62	gardener	58	"
R	*Kelly Mary E—†	62	housewife	55	"
S	Boute Elizabeth A—†	62	"	28	
T	Boute Harold	62	factoryworker	28	"
U	McLeod Alice—†	63	housewife	42	"
V	McLeod Roderick W	63	clerk	47	
W	Burke Mary—†	65	housewife	70	"
X	Gaetani Frank S	65	chauffeur	36	"
Y	Gaetani Loretta—†	65	tel operator	37	"
Z	Roche William	65	welder	37	

1411

A	Burke Helen—†	65	housewife	37	"
B	Burke John P	65	machinist	38	"

Forest Hills Street

D	Dempsey Ruth—†	269	clerk	25	here
E	Dempsey Welman	269	laborer	26	"
F	Styles Glenn	269	"	26	"
G	Styles Mildred—†	269	clerk	24	
H	Connell Margaret G—†	269	at home	73	"
K	Mahoney Alice R—†	269	housewife	54	"
L	Mahoney John F	269	custodian	55	"
M	Mahoney John G	269	laborer	24	
N	Killerby Clarence P	269	millwright	53	"
O	Killerby Irene—†	269	housewife	43	"
P	Parent Amelia D—†	269	"	52	
R	Parent Victor R	269	retired	53	
S	Cemach Benjamin	269	storekeeper	42	"
T	*Cemach Sarah—†	269	housewife	41	"
U	Gunn Charles E	269	engineer	64	Danvers
V	Gunn Margaret M—†	269	housewife	64	"
W	Keller George	269	mechanic	37	here

Page	Letter	Full Name.	Residence, Jan. 1, 1946.	Occupation.	Supposed Age.	Reported Residence, Jan. 1, 1945. Street and Number.

Forest Hills Street—Continued

	x	Keller Rose—†	269	housewife	32	here
	y	Corboy Carrie—†	277	"	35	"
	z	Corboy Philip	277	machinist	38	"
1412						
	a	Carney Anna—†	277	housewife	27	"
	b	Carney Thomas	277	clerk	30	
	c	Duffy Catherine—†	277	stitcher	37	
	d	McCollum Otis	277	laborer	74	
	e	Byrd John H	277	proofreader	48	"
	f	Byrd Sarah—†	277	housewife	48	"
	g	Brooks Augusta—†	281	"	43	
	h	Brooks John J	281	chauffeur	49	"
	k*	Gibran Mary—†	281	housewife	60	"
	l	Ray Eileen F—†	281	"	45	
	m	Ray Joseph F	281	clerk	25	
	n	Ray Margaret L—†	281	"	24	
	o	Ray Thomas N	281	manager	49	"
	p	Kelley Anne—†	285–87	housewife	42	"
	r	Kelley Joseph	285–87	laborer	48	
	s	Glenn Adeline E—†	285–87	housewife	49	"
	t	Glenn Albert E	285–87	carpenter	53	"
	u	Glenn Doris B—†	285–87	secretary	23	"
	v	Vaughan Michael D	285–87	bartender	48	"
	w	Vaughan Nellie A—†	285–87	housewife	45	"
	x	Johanson Carl P	289	carpenter	38	"
	y	Johanson Ruth C—†	289	housewife	38	"
	z	Zambella Harriette—†	289	"	30	15 Sagamore
1413						
	a	Zambella Theodore	289	machinist	28	15 "
	b	Doocey Edward A	289	laborer	30	Ohio
	c	Doocey Frances—†	289	housewife	27	"
	d	Doocey John P	289	gardener	23	here
	e	Doocey Mary V—†	289	secretary	26	"
	f	Doocey Michael	289	bartender	62	"
	g	Doocey Nora A—†	289	housewife	58	"
	h	Petersen Adeline—†	295	"	86	
	k	Petersen Martin	295	machinist	49	"
	l	Terkelsen Sophie—†	295	at home	82	"
	m	Tivnan Martin F	295	manager	54	"
	n	Tivnan Mary A—†	295	at home	25	"
	o	Tivnan Winifred N—†	295	housewife	57	"

Forest Hills Street—Continued

P	*Dalton Frederick J	295	laborer	34	here
R	*Dalton Josephine—†	295	housewife	77	"
S	McCarrick Eileen—†	297	clerk	20	"
T	McCarrick Margaret—†	297	waitress	41	"
U	McCarrick Thomas	297	chauffeur	43	"
V	McCarrick Thomas	297	clerk	22	
W	Coyne Henrietta—†	299	housewife	42	"
X	Coyné Michael	299	agent	44	
Y	Waddington Lillian—†	299	housewife	31	"
Z	Waddington Thomas	299	supervisor	33	"

1414

A	Leontie Helen L—†	301–03	housewife	24	"
B	Leontie William R	301–03	mechanic	26	"
C	Gatulis Frank	301–03	carpenter	27	Dedham
D	Gatulis Mary—†	301–03	housewife	29	"
E	Rosso Marie C—†	301–03	secretary	36	here
F	Rosso Mary G—†	301–03	housewife	61	"
G	Rosso Natalie—†	301–03	clerk	34	"
H	Gilday Frank	307	mechanic	60	"
K	Gilday Lucy—†	307	hostess	48	
L	Golden Joseph	307	laborer	60	
M	Galvin Helen—†	307	housewife	30	"
N	Galvin William	307	repairman	34	"
O	Tyo Agnes—†	307	housewife	57	"
P	Tyo Doris—†	307	at home	33	"
R	Tyo Walter	307	salesman	24	"
S	Fleming John J	311–13	foreman	37	"
T	Fleming Sarah—†	311–13	housewife	40	"
U	Canales Manuel J	311–13	manager	48	"
V	Canales Mary—†	311–13	housewife	36	"
W	Church Lucy—†	311–13	clerk	60	73 Elm
X	Harrington Helen—†	315	housewife	39	here
Y	Harrington James J	315	shipper	46	"
Z	Harrington Thomas	315	stockman	41	"

1415

A	Dykes Bernice—†	315	housewife	27	"
B	Dykes Geoffrey L	315	milkman	27	"
C	Engler Carl F	315	policeman	38	"
D	Engler Mary D—†	315	housewife	33	"
E	Baltusis Elizabeth—†	319	"	38	
F	Baltusis Joseph	319	maintenance	38	"

Forest Hills Street—Continued

	G	Geoghegan Alice—†	319	housewife	32	here
	H	Geoghegan Thomas	319	guard	32	"
	K	Baltusis Charles	319	fireman	38	"
	L	Baltusis Verna—†	319	stenographer	36	"

Gartland Street

	M	Dewey Arthur L	5–7	chauffeur	47	here
	N	Dewey Margaret T—†	5–7	housewife	42	"
	O	Coulman Dorothy C—†	5–7	coil winder	31	"
	P	Coulman Frederic E	5–7	electrician	37	"
	R	Foster Edward J	5–7	manager	32	"
	S	Foster Ilene T—†	5–7	housewife	30	"
	T	Brooks Catherine—†	8	"	34	"
	U	Brooks Thomas F	8	operator	35	"
	V	Foye Mary A—†	8	at home	65	"
	W	Foye Richard A	8	U S A	23	"
	X	Pace Alfred C	8	U S N	25	"
	Y*	Pace Mary—†	8	housewife	59	"
	Z	Pace Thomas J	8	metalworker	29	"
		1416				
	A	Gatturna Eileen F—†	9–11	stenographer	20	"
	B	Gatturna Frances V—†	9–11	housewife	54	"
	C	Gatturna John H	9–11	clerk	23	
	D	Morris Albert J	9–11	operator	31	"
	E	Morris Ann M—†	9–11	housewife	29	"
	F	Casale Anthony B	9–11	manager	55	"
	G	Casale Anthony C	9–11	machinist	24	"
	H	Casale Helen J—†	9–11	stenographer	20	"
	K	Casale Josephine J—†	9–11	housewife	48	"
	L	Cassale Walter J	9–11	tinsmith	22	"
	M	Suplee Catherine F—†	9–11	housewife	27	"
	N	Suplee Frederick W	9–11	clerk	29	
	O	Mahood Elizabeth M—†	9–11	housewife	31	"
	P	Mahood Wilham J	9–11	prison officer	36	"
	R	O'Neill John J	9–11	chauffeur	32	1142 Harrison av
	S	Spinazzolo Antoinette—†	10	housewife	41	here
	T	Spinazzolo Daniel	10	retired	51	"
	U	Fitzgerald Alice A—†	12	stitcher	49	"
	V	Fitzgerald John J	12	seaman	21	"
	W	Fitzgerald Richard E	12	retired	71	

Page.	Letter.	Full Name.	Residence, Jan. 1, 1946.	Occupation.	Supposed Age.	Reported Residence, Jan. 1, 1945. Street and Number.

Gartland Street—Continued

x	Fitzgerald Robert J	12	U S A	23	here
y	Fitzgerald William F	12	meatcutter	25	"
z	Stirling Margaret M—†	14	housewife	64	"
	1417				
a	Stirling Richard F	14	machinist	60	"
b	Stirling Richard F	14	operator	25	"
c	Bingham Harry S	14	carpenter	72	"
d	Bingham Julia—†	14	housewife	59	"
e	Lamont Alexander J	14	baker	63	
f	Lamont Mary P—†	14	housewife	57	"
g	Irvine Ruth B—†	17	"	38	
h	Irvine Thomas L	17	chauffeur	36	"
k	Haddock Christina M—†	17	housewife	40	"
l	Haddock Harry B	17	U S N	21	
m	Haddock Leroy G	17	manager	47	"
n	Haddock Leroy G	17	U S N	20	
o	Fatersek Anna—†	17	housewife	54	"
p*	Fatersek Dora—†	17	at home	88	"
r	Fatersek John R	17	U S A	30	
s	Fatersek Mary A—†	17	bookkeeper	34	"
t	Fatersek Rita V—†	17	housewife	30	"
u	Morrissey Emily C—†	20	housekeeper	52	"
v	Getz Henry J	21	metalworker	49	"
w	Getz Sally E—†	21	housewife	46	"
x	Getz William C	21	electrician	25	"
y	Ferreira Anna J—†	21	housewife	54	"
z	Ferreira George E	21	clerk	54	
	1418				
a	Keegan Mary R—†	21	housewife	31	"
b	Keegan William C	21	clerk	30	51 Sedgwick
c	Lovett Ann T—†	21	tel operator	21	here
d	Lovett Sarah A—†	21	housewife	60	"
e	Smith Lillian I—†	25	"	60	"
f	Smith William W	25	retired	74	
g	Mullen Gladys M—†	25	packer	42	
h	Mullen Thomas J	25	gardener	45	"
k*	Long Ernest W	25	machinist	25	"
l	Long Mary E—†	25	housewife	23	"
m	Donaldson James J	27–29	pipefitter	47	"
n	Donaldson Katherine M—†	27–29	housewife	45	"
o	Victor Jessie M—†	27–29	"	39	

Gartland Street—Continued

P	Victor John J	27–29	mechanic	39	here
R	Gannon Patrick J	27–29	clerk	20	"
S	Horgan Katherine M—†	27–29	housewife	57	"
T	Reed Ruth C—†	27–29	folder	23	"
U	Bishop Alice V—†	32	housewife	37	"
V	Bishop Arthur J	32	electrician	37	"
W	Tomasello Natalie—†	32	housewife	32	"
X	Tomasello Ross	32	clerk	35	
Y	Pagano Antonio	32	retired	67	"
Z	Pagano Augustine A	32	welder	39	

1419

A	Pagano Mary—†	32	housewife	59	"
B	McGorty Florence—†	33	hairdresser	31	"
C	McGorty Peter F	33	clerk	46	
D	Powers Christian A, jr	33	operator	30	"
E	Powers Dorothy C—†	33	housewife	29	"
F	Stoll Susannah—†	33	clerk	50	
G	Stoll Walter C	33	carpenter	52	"
H	Moreau Alfred N	33	salesman	25	"
K	Moreau Doris P—†	33	housewife	23	"
L	Moreau Louise E—†	33	"	64	
M	Moreau Robert J	33	toolmaker	22	"
N	Kelly Joseph	35–37	mechanic	43	"
O	Kelly Margaret—†	35–37	housewife	41	"
P	Langevin Amelia—†	35–37	seamstress	60	"
R	Langevin Edmond	35–37	carpenter	46	"
S	Bond Charles L	35–37	engineer	52	"
T	O'Neill Eileen L—†	35–37	housewife	22	"
U	O'Neill Francis A	35–37	clerk	24	
V	Thistle Frank C	36	laborer	50	
W	Thistle Helen—†	36	housewife	32	"
X	Fitzgibbons Jeremiah W	36	repairman	36	"
Y	Fitzgibbons Margaret A—†	36	housewife	36	"
Z	Cotter Adele R—†	36	"	46	

1420

A	Cotter Jeremiah J	36	chauffeur	49	"
B	Cotter Jeremiah J	36	U S A	22	
C	O'Donoghue Denis R	40	steamfitter	59	"
D	O'Donoghue Nora R—†	40	housewife	61	"
E	Kelly Michael J	40	porter	58	
F	McCormack Dorothy E—†	40	secretary	25	"

Gartland Street—Continued

G	McCormack Leo F	40	manager	23	here
H	McCormack Lillian—†	40	housewife	48	"
K	Hilland Elizabeth—†	40	"	59	"
L	Hilland Thomas J	40	machinist	62	"
M	Schlosky Margaret—†	40	clerk	23	
N	Schlosky Robert E	40	printer	25	
O	*Kairis Nellie A—†	43	housewife	59	"
P	O'Toole Joseph J	43	wireman	37	"
R	O'Toole Mary A—†	43	housewife	35	"
S	Saltis Albert A	43	leadman	29	"
T	Saltis Lillian G—†	43	housewife	27	"
U	Weeman Anna M—†	43	"	51	
V	Weeman Edward M	43	guard	51	
W	Weeman Edward M	43	clerk	28	
X	Weeman Walter H	43	machinist	26	"
Y	*Lynch Ellen—†	44	housewife	39	"
Z	Lynch John A	44	shipper	44	

1421

A	Sarkisian Hachig	44	machinist	59	"
B	Sarkisian Louisa—†	44	housewife	47	"
C	*Stanley Harold J	44	machinist	33	"
D	Stanley Lillian G—†	44	housewife	32	"

Kenton Road

E	Cayes Frances—†	7	operator	33	here
F	Holmes James	7	manager	29	"
G	Holmes Rita—†	7	housewife	30	"
H	McGrath Anne—†	7	at home	66	"
K	McGrath Lawrence—†	7	clerk	25	
L	Corscadden John J	9	retired	63	
M	Corscadden Mary F—†	9	housewife	63	"
N	Feeney James A	9	U S A	33	
O	Feeney Mary E—†	9	housewife	30	"
P	Nihill Anna L—†	11	tel operator	42	"
R	Nihill Eileen M—†	11	clerk	21	
S	Nihill Eugene M	11	operator	27	"
T	Nihill John M	11	U S A	31	
U	Nihill Josephine—†	11	housewife	62	"
V	Nihill Mary M—†	11	clerk	25	

Page.	Letter.	FULL NAME.	Residence, Jan. 1, 1946.	Occupation.	Supposed Age.	Reported Residence, Jan. 1, 1945. Street and Number.

Kenton Road—Continued

	w	Menjin Veronica—†	19	operator	46	624 E Second
	x	*Cammarata Anna—†	19	housewife	46	here
	y	Cammarata Michael	19	clerk	21	"
	z	Cammarata Rocco	19	shoemaker	26	"
		1422				
	a	Cammarata Vincent	19	operator	51	"
	b	Donnato Dominic	19	mechanic	29	"
	c	Donnato Theresa—†	19	housewife	28	"
	d	Gill Catherine—†	23	domestic	44	"
	e	Walsh Elizabeth—†	23	housewife	43	"
	f	Walsh John T	23	plumber	45	"
	g	Johnston George	31	pipefitter	45	"
	h	Johnston Mary—†	31	housewife	40	"
	k	Hartnett Edith R—†	35	"	44	
	l	Hartnett John W	35	buffer	52	
	m	Curley Arthur E	35	accountant	46	"
	n	O'Meara Irene—†	35	housewife	42	"
	o	O'Meara Stephen H	35	policeman	49	"
	p	Glennon Mary A—†	39	housewife	84	"
	r	Glennon William M	39	U S N	41	"
	s	Glennon William P	39	retired	81	

Lotus Street

	t	*Kelley Anne—†	19	housewife	58	here
	u	Kelley Thomas	19	mechanic	33	"
	v	Gillen Georgiana—†	19	housewife	21	"
	w	Edstrom Rose—†	33	"	29	"
	x	Edstrom William F	33	chauffeur	31	"
	y	Randon Elsie—†	33	nurse	26	
	z	Randon Isadore F	33	laborer	27	
		1423				
	a	Randon Peter	33		61	
	b	Pignant Alfred	33		21	
	c	Pipnant Anthony	33		63	
	d	Pignant Gino	33	"	22	
	e	Pignant Ida—†	33	housewife	50	"
	f	Pignant Joseph	33	retired	66	
	g	Pignant Yolànda—†	33	bookkeeper	25	"
	h	Vincenzi John	33	foreman	61	"

15

Page.	Letter.	FULL NAME.	Residence, Jan. 1, 1946.	Occupation.	Supposed Age.	Reported Residence, Jan. 1. 1945. Street and Number.

Meehan Street

M	Ryan Margaret M—†	11	housewife	48	here
N	Ryan Patrick J	11	chauffeur	48	"
O	Strachan Edward	11	U S A	26	"
P	Strachan Mary M—†	11	clerk	26	
R	Puleo Dominic	11	carpenter	49	"
S	Puleo Marie—†	11	housewife	48	"
T	Gravena Anthony	11	barber	36	
U	Gravena Katherine—†	11	dressmaker	36	"
V	Uminski Henry	13	chauffeur	26	"
W	Uminski John	13	machinist	54	"
X	*Uminski Josephine—†	13	housewife	49	"
Y	Uminski William	13	mechanic	22	"
Z	Treanni Carl	13	shipwright	36	"
	1424					
A	Treanni Johanna—†	13	housewife	20	"
B	Ryan Helena—†	13	"	26	
C	Ryan James	13	chauffeur	30	"
D	Leveroni Louise—†	15	housekeeper	65	"
E	DeSalvatori Dominic	15	shoemaker	74	"
F	*DeSalvatori Josephine—†	15	housewife	73	"
G	DeSalvatori Louis	15	laborer	40	
H	DeSalvatori Pasquale	15	retired	35	

Plainfield Street

L	Ogletree Frances—†	9	nurse	41	here
M	Ogletree Raymond	9	janitor	52	"
N	*Peterson Esther—†	10	housewife	60	"
O	*Peterson Thomas	10	engineer	55	"
P	Morrison Juha—†	10	housewife	43	"
R	Morrison Vincent	10	janitor	43	
S	Collyer Ruth—†	10	housewife	25	"
T	Collyer Walter J	10	U S N	27	
U	Collins Mary C—†	11	operator	46	"
V	Collins Raymond	11	diesetter	39	"
W	Harkins Gertrude—†	11	clerk	21	
X	Harkins Lena—†	11	housewife	56	"
Y	Murphy Agnes—†	11	"	26	"
Z	Murphy John J	11	clerk	28	Brookline
	1425					
B	Deveau Evelyn B—†	19	housewife	34	159 Calumet

16

Page.	Letter.	Full Name.	Residence, Jan. 1, 1946.	Occupation.	Supposed Age.	Reported Residence, Jan. 1, 1945. Street and Number.

Plainfield Street—Continued

	c	Deveau Simon C	19	manager	43	159 Calumet
	d	Coleman Patrick	21	retired	74	here
	e	Shuckrowe Margaret E—†	21	housewife	71	"
	f	Shuckrowe Timothy C	21	retired	63	"
	g	Morris Margaret—†	21	housewife	46	"
	h	Morris Mary—†	21	clerk	26	
	k	Morris Patrick J	21	engineer	48	"
	l	McLaughlin Fred G	21	butcher	28	9 Emrose ter
	m	McLaughlin Fred G	21	secretary	29	291 Forest Hills
	o	Marino Mary—†	29	housewife	28	here
	p	Marino Michael	29	clerk	31	"
	r	Lindholm Karl	29	manager	48	"
	s	Lindholm Mary—†	29	"	48	
	t	Werner Frances—†	29	bookkeeper	52	"
	u	Siblo Mildred—†	31	housewife	35	"
	v	Walsh Annie A—†	31	"	58	
	w	Walsh Chester R	31	U S N	33	
	x	Walsh John A	31	chauffeur	59	"
	y	Widing Pauline—†	31	housewife	28	"
	z	Widing Robert	31	welder	30	

1426

	a	MacPherson Annie M—†	33	housewife	55	"
	b	MacPherson Duncan	33	carpenter	54	"
	c	MacPherson John B	33	shipper	21	
	d	Horgan Catherine A—†	33	housewife	44	"
	e	Horgan James F	33	shipper	46	
	f	Murphy Elizabeth B—†	33	housewife	50	"
	g	Magee Francis	33	mechanic	21	"
	h	Magee Margaret—†	33	bookkeeper	22	"
	k	Magee Rose—†	33	housewife	57	"

Rossmore Road

	l	Hucksam Mary C—†	2	housewife	34	here
	m	Hucksam Paul F	2	clerk	38	"
	n	King Harriet—†	2	at home	73	"
	o	Lasko Alice G—†	2	housewife	26	"
	p	Lasko Stanley	2	electrician	31	"
	s	Fay John H	9	operator	70	18 Beethoven
	t	Fay Sarah F—†	9	housewife	68	18 "
	u	Spring Norman L	9	mechanic	32	here

11—14

17

Rossmore Road—Continued

v	Spring Rita—†	9	housewife	25	here
w	Gaynor Catherine C—†	9	"	22	"
x	Gaynor Richard J	9	welder	38	"
y	Drake Gertrude R—†	10	housewife	37	"
z	Drake James	10	patternmaker	39	"

1427

A	DiPietro Grace—†	10	housewife	31	"
B	DiPietro Louis	10	warehouse	30	"
c	Desto Joseph	10	barber	40	
D	Desto Martha—†	10	housewife	35	"
E	Burke Cornelius J	11	porter	50	
F	Burke Mildred G—†	11	housewife	38	"
G	Curtis Ellen M—†	11	operator	32	"
H	Curtis Hilda T—†	11	housewife	59	"
K	Curtis William C	11	watchman	68	"
L	McGonagle Cecelia—†	11	at home	50	"
M	McGonagle Edward M	11	U S A	27	
N	McGonagle H·Daniel	11	U S N	20	
o	McGonagle John A	11	painter	29	"
R	Bowen Doris—†	12	housewife	28	"
s	Bowen Michael	12	laborer	40	"
T	Bowen Peter	12	bricklayer	35	"
u	Murphy Frank	12	chauffeur	58	32 Hall
v	Murphy Frank, jr	12	laborer	31	32 "
w	Murphy Mary—†	12	housewife	24	32 "
x	Brodeur Rose—†	14	factoryworker	32	32 Gartland
y	DiGiovine Adeline—†	14	housewife	43	here
z	DiGiovine Daniel	14	student	21	"

1428

A	DiGiovine Robert	14	painter	48	
B	Copponi Anthony J	16	mechanic	35	"
c	Copponi Phoebe—†	16	housewife	34	"
D	Copponi Joseph	16	laborer	37	
E	Copponi Luigi	16	retired	68	
F	Copponi Virginia—†	16	housewife	68	"
G	DeAngelis Hugo	16	U S A	28	
H	DeAngelis Maria—†	16	housewife	54	"
K	Lattanzio Armand A—†	16	butcher	30	"
L	Lattanzio Eda—†	16	housewife	26	"
M	Kelley Edward J	19	shipper	29	
N	Kelley Marguerite M—†	19	operator	27	"

Rossmore Road—Continued

o	Kelley Mary—†	19	at home	69	here
p	Salvi John	19	U S A	20	"
r	Salvi Louise—†	19	housewife	59	"
s	Salvi Luigi	19	proprietor	55	"
t	Salvi Peter	19	U S A	28	
u	Salvi Victor	19	clerk	22	
v	Menchi Alice J—†	19	housewife	31	"
w	Menchi John	19	proprietor	30	"
x	Sarno Frederick J	21	mechanic	30	"
y	Sarno Muriel M—†	21	housewife	30	"
z	Ray Eleanor V—†	21	"	29	

1429

a	Ray Sylvester A	21	proprietor	28	"
b	LaGuardia Anthony	21	barber	45	
c*	LaGuardia Cesare	21	retired	72	
d	LaGuardia Eleanor A—†	21	housewife	29	"
e	Moffitt Florence—†	26	"	52	
f	Moffitt James	26	supervisor	57	"
g	DiBenedetto Anthony	26	blacksmith	45	"
h	DiBenedetto Rose—†	26	housewife	34	"
k	Scipione Domenic	27	laborer	37	
l	Scipione Helen—†	27	factoryworker	33	"
m	Scipione Vincenzo	27	"	66	
n	Capaldo Angelo	27	clerk	23	
o*	Capaldo Anna—†	27	housewife	48	"
p	Capaldo Luigi	27	laborer	49	
r	Haddad Elias	28–30	barber	58	
s	Haddad Lilly—†	28–30	housewife	56	"
t	Halligan Henry	28–30	machinist	27	"
u	Halligan Mary—†	28–30	housewife	25	"
v*	Rutledge Grace L—†	28–30	"	37	
w	Rutledge Peter	28–30	ironworker	42	"
x	Petrillo Lena—†	34	housewife	23	61 Rossmore rd
y	Petrillo Salvatore	34	chauffeur	29	61 "
z	Vitiello Adeline—†	34	housewife	35	here

1430

a	Vitiello Dominic	34	laborer	49	
b	Waring Bessie—†	35	housewife	51	"
c	Waring Hazen F	35	machinist	53	"
d	Waring Waldo	35	U S A	28	
e	Currier Adelard F	35	operator	43	

19

Page.	Letter.	FULL NAME.	Residence, Jan. 1, 1946.	Occupation.	Supposed Age.	Reported Residence, Jan. 1, 1945. Street and Number.

Rossmore Road—Continued

F	Currier Armand	35	welder	23	N Hampshire
G	Currier Freda A—†	35	operator	40	here
H	Kuczin Anna B—†	35	housewife	51	"
K	Kuczin Vincent	35	U S A	22	"
L	Kuczin Walter	35	mechanic	51	"
M	Kuczin Walter W	35	U S N	24	
N	*Koenig Bridget A—†	41	housewife	32	"
O	Koenig Otto	41	cabinetmaker	76	"
P	Koenig Robert L	41	cutter	32	
R	Armstrong Agnes—†	41	housewife	35	"
S	Armstrong David	41	checker	39	"
T	Davis Mary C—†	41	housewife	33	"
U	Davis Walter H	41	machinist	30	"
V	Burke Joseph J	41	clerk	32	
W	Burke Mildred R—†	41	housewife	29	"
X	Maloney Mabel—†	41	clerk	34	Belmont
Y	Maloney Thomas F	41	ironworker	38	81 Brookley rd
	1431				
A	Maxwell Sarah—†	41	stitcher	54	here
A¹	Williamson Peter	41	factoryworker	43	"
B	Lennon Bartholomew	46	guard	65	"
C	Lennon Bartholomew	46	U S A	26	
D	Lennon Margaret—†	46	housewife	70	"
E	Lennon Martin J	46	laborer	28	
F	Lennon Mary—†	46	secretary	31	"
G	Woods Margaret—†	46	operator	30	"
H	Crowley Joseph M	46	bartender	43	"
K	Crowley Winifred B—†	46	saleswoman	30	"
L	MacBeth Mary C—†	46	housekeeper	54	"
M	Brown Frances R—†	46	housewife	26	153 Centre
N	Brown George F	46	chauffeur	25	374 Dor av
O	Cavanagh James T	47	retired	59	here
P	Cavanagh Nora A—†	47	housewife	59	"
R	Crowley Julia F—†	47	matron	49	"
S	McCormack Elizabeth—†	47	clerk	60	
T	Feeley Mary—†	49–51	housewife	48	"
U	Feeley Patrick J	49–51	longshoreman	50	"
V	Brown George E	49–51	checker	34	"
W	Chislett Frank	49–51	"	43	'
X	Chislett Mabel—†	49–51	housewife	63	"
Y	MacLellan Donald J	49–51	papermaker	24	,"

20

Page	Letter	Full Name.	Residence, Jan. 1, 1946.	Occupation.	Supposed Age.	Reported Residence, Jan. 1, 1945. Street and Number.

Rossmore Road—Continued

	z	MacLellan Sabina—†	49–51	housewife	23	here
1432						
	A	McCormack William T	50	fireman	63	
	B	Potter Catherine A—†	50	housewife	60	"
	C	Potter George H	50	machinist	38	"
	D	May Bessie M—†	50	housewife	47	"
	E	May Daniel H	50	carpenter	48	"
	F	Casey Mary—†	50	cashier	55	
	G	Shields Cornelius M—†	53–55	laborer	40	
	H	Shields Elizabeth M—†	53–55	housewife	34	"
	K	Shields Lawrence H	53–55	shipper	44	
	L	McDonough Catherine E—†	53–55	housewife	33	"
	M	McDonough George J	53–55	prison officer	37	"
	N	Griffin Dorothea—†	54	housewife	28	"
	O	Griffin Kerrel	54	clerk	32	"
	P	Reardon Anna M—†	54	collector	51	163 Hemenway
	R	Sullivan Mary E—†	54	saleswoman	60	here
	S	Sidlauskas Petronella—†	58	domestic	49	Cambridge
	T	Valas Florence—†	58	housewife	20	N Hampshire
	U	Valas Frank	58	U S A	22	"
	V	Fallon Mary—†	58	housewife	38	here
	W	Fallon Timothy J	58	foreman	42	"
	X	Koziewicz Alice—†	58	secretary	31	"
	Y	Koziewicz Helen—†	58	housewife	56	"
	z	Koziewicz Jane M—†	58	secretary	29	"
1433						
	A	Koziewicz Michael	58	shoemaker	65	"
	B	Monk Josephine	58	secretary	33	"
	C	Welch James F	59	operator	36	"
	D	Welch Margaret A—†	59	housewife	34	"
	E	Cash Gertrude K—†	59	"	39	
	F	Cash Margaret—†	59	nurse	51	
	G	Cash Thomas L	59	chauffeur	45	"
	H	Brown Ethel M—†	59	housewife	30	"
	K	Brown Frank	59	repairman	33	"
	L	Boyd Rena M—†	61	stitcher	41	130 Rosseter
	M	Boyd Thompson	61	laborer	40	130 "
	N	Sheedy Albert M	61	brewer	38	here
	O	Sheedy Mary E—†	41	housewife	37	"
	P	Stanton Joseph F	61	grinder	39	"
	R	Stanton Ruth L—†	61	housewife	32	"

Rossmore Road—Continued

s	Graham Frank	61	checker	32	here
t	Graham Marie—†	61	housewife	28	"
u	Donovan Charles E	61	contractor	38	"
v	Donovan Esther E—†	61	clerk	43	
w	Harris Effie C—†	61	at home	45	..
x	Harris James B	61	machinist	76	"
y	Alward Daniel H	65	"	32	
z	Alward Dorothy F—†	65	operator	38	"

1434

a	Driscoll Elizabeth E—†	65	housewife	28	"
b	Driscoll Francis J	65	policeman	31	"
c	Foote Edward R	65	roofer	30	
d	Foote Jennie G—†	65	housewife	28	"
e	Spellman Bernard T	65	operator	30	"
f	Spellman Edith I—†	65	housewife	32	"
g	Jamieson Beatrice—†	65	"	31	
h	Jamieson Charles P	63	U S A	38	"
k	Shea John J	65	machinist	32	"
l	Shea Mary E—†	65	housewife	33	"
m	Heffernan Catherine T—†	66–68	"	51	
n	Heffernan James C	66–68	U S N	21	"
o	Heffernan James H	66–68	carpenter	51	"
p	Kayajanian Helen—†	66–68	housewife	39	"
r	Kayajanian John	66–68	tailor	55	
s	D'Agostino Antoinette—†	71	housewife	35	"
t	D'Agostino Francesco	71	barber	40	
u	O'Donnell Mary M—†	71	housewife	39	"
v	O'Donnell William G	71	fireman	38	
w	Morelli Angelo G	71	welder	35	..
x	Morelli Mary J—†	71	housewife	33	"
y	Lister John W	71	plasterer	34	"
z	Lister Lillian A—†	71	housewife	34	"

1435

a	White Alice M—†	71	"	28	
b	White Robert	71	carpenter	36	"
c	Duggie Ellen F—†	71	housewife	32	"
d	Duggie Roy B	71	foreman	35	"
e	LeTourneau Clifton D	75	proprietor	29	"
f	LeTourneau Dorothy T—†	75	housewife	26	"
g	Goldberg Alexander	75	proprietor	39	"
h	Goldberg Sima—†	75	housewife	38	"

Page.	Letter.	Full Name.	Residence, Jan. 1, 1946.	Occupation.	Supposed Age.	Reported Residence, Jan. 1, 1945. Street and Number.

Rossmore Road—Continued

	Letter.	Full Name.	Residence, Jan. 1, 1946.	Occupation.	Supposed Age.	Reported Residence.
	K	Fiorenza Christine—†	75	housewife	35	here
	L	Fiorenza Leo A	75	factoryworker	30	"
	M	Curran John J	75	supervisor	38	"
	N	Curran Sarah—†	75	housewife	35	"
	O	DiBella Frank	75	machinist	30	"
	P	DiBella Mary J—†	75	housewife	27	"
	R	Cummings Eldora A—†	75	"	22	
	S	Cummings Francis J	75	dyer	26	
	T	Bradley Florence G—†	78	housewife	43	"
	U	Bradley Joseph L	78	machinist	55	"
	V	Higgins Catherine M—†	78	housewife	43	19 Plainfield
	W	Higgins Michael A	78	chauffeur	46	19 "
	X	Higgins Rose—†	78	at home	73	19 "
	Y	O'Mara Edward R	78	laborer	25	here
	Z	O'Mara John	78	clerk	60	"

1436

	Letter.	Full Name.	Residence, Jan. 1, 1946.	Occupation.	Supposed Age.	Reported Residence.
	A	O'Mara Julia—†	78	housewife	48	"
	B	Ford Anna M—†	79–81	clerk	26	
	C	Ford Delia—†	79–81	housewife	60	"
	D	Ford John H	79–81	clerk	32	
	E	Ford Patrick J	79–81	operator	66	"
	F	Gardner George W	76–81	policeman	48	"
	G	Gardner Naomi M—†	79–81	housewife	51	"
	H	Hanson Dorothy N—†	79–81	stenographer	25	"
	K	Hanson Robert E	79–81	mechanic	25	"
	L	Ewaska Boleslow	79–81	"	50	
	M	Petkus Joseph	79 81	chauffeur	51	"
	N	Petkus Pauline—†	79–81	housewife	42	"
	O	Fitzgerald Helena J—†	82	"	47	
	P	Fitzgerald William F	82	foreman	38	"
	R	Wazen Catherine—†	82	housewife	27	"
	S	Wazen George	82	machinist	35	"
	T	Kroll Leonard A	82	steamfitter	27	"
	U	Kroll Marie M—†	82	housewife	27	"
	V	Gavin Bridget—†	83 85	"	31	
	W	Gavin Matthew	83–85	fireman	36	"
	X	Dennis David	83–85	draftsman	36	"
	Y	Dennis George W	83–85	"	26	"
	Z	Dennis Molly—†	83–85	clerk	22	

1437

	Letter.	Full Name.	Residence, Jan. 1, 1946.	Occupation.	Supposed Age.	Reported Residence.
	A	Dennis Rose—†	83–85	at home	62	"

Rossmore Road—Continued

	B	Winship Mary—†	83–85	housewife	26	here
	C	Winship Parker	83–85	U S N	28	"
	D	Sprague Robert G	86	welder	27	"
	E	Sprague Sophie—†	86	housewife	26	"
	F	Benner Mildred—†	86	waitress	43	"
	G	Neagle Dorothy—†	86	secretary	·23	"
	H	Lynch Mary—†	86	housewife	35	"
	K	Lynch Thomas	86	laborer	36	
	L	Suderis Genevieve—†	87–89	stenographer	23	"
	M	Suderis Marcella—†	87–89	factoryworker	49	"
	N	MacMillan Arthur H	87–89	guard	35	
	O	MacMillan Geraldine–†	87–89	housewife	34	"
	P	Haddad Jeanette—†	87–89	"	33	
	R	Haddad Michael E	87–89	chauffeur	35	"
	S	Kukstis Algirdia A	90	U S A	26	
	T*	Kukstis Anthony	90	butcher	51	"
	U*	Kukstis Diana—†	90	housewife	51	"
	V	Kukstis Edward	90	U S A	20	
	W	Wilson Harry T	90	mechanic	54	"
	X	Wilson Harry T, jr	90	U S A	21	
	Y	Wilson Julia E—†	90	housewife	47	"
	Z	Remick Allen T	90	U S A	22	

1438

	A	Remick Florence E—†	90	waitress	45	11 Dalrymple
	B	Remick Florine E—†	90	stenographer	20	here
	C	Barrett Anna M—†	91–93	housewife	42	"
	D	Barrett James F	91–93	brewer	42	"
	E	Ryan Thelma G—†	91–93	housewife	29	"
	F	Ryan Thomas P	91–93	policeman	30	"
	G	Smith Robert E	91–93	welder	28	
	H	Smith Thelma L—†	91–94	housewife	25	"
	K	Wiencus John	94	machinist	47	"
	L	Wiencus Josephine—†	94	housewife	45	"
	M	Wiencus Stanley	94	U S N	31	
	N	Lewis Elizabeth—†	94	housewife	53	"
	O	Lewis Mildred K—	94	factoryworker	33	"
	P	Vasilakas James	94	chef	50	
	R	Callanan Joseph F	94	photographer	34	"
	S	Callanan Kathleen A—†	94	housewife	34	"
	T	Green Anna—†	94	nurse	35	
	U	Whitson Patrick J	95–97	supervisor	41	"

Rossmore Road—Continued

v	Whitson Rita C—†	95–97	housewife	32	here
w	Kroll Katherine J—†	95–97	"	32	"
x	Kroll Victor J	95–97	supervisor	30	"
y	Burke Anna R—†	95–97	messenger	20	"
z	Burke Margaret I—†	95–97	housewife	32	"
	1439				
a	Burke Thomas F	95–97	bartender	40	"
b	Dantas Alfred M	98	manager	39	55 W Walnut pk
c	Dantas Mae—†	98	housewife	36	55 "
d	Hardiman Della A—†	98	"	39	here
e	Hardiman Kieren	98	chef	40	"
f	Donahue James	98	welder	61	"
g	Donahue Mary A—†	98	housewife	54	"
h	Donahue Mary T—†	98	bookkeeper	21	"
k	Welch Catherine—†	99–101	typist	44	"
l	Welch John J	99–101	meter reader	45	"
m	Mulryan Nora K—†	99–101	housewife	48	Medford
n	Mulryan Thomas	99–101	laborer	48	122 Parker Hill av
o	Kelley Michael	99–101	watchman	38	here
p	Mitchell Mary A—†	99–101	housewife	49	"
r	Mitchell Thomas J	99–101	laborer	48	"
s	Doherty Alice—†	102–104	at home	75	"
t	Hynes John J	102–104	policeman	41	"
u	Hynes Mary F—†	102–104	at home	40	"
v	Tosti Amelio J	102–104	student	23	Florida
w	Povilaitis Frances—†	102–104	housewife	29	here
x	Povilaitis Frank A	102–104	printer	29	"
y	Povilaitis Adele—†	102–104	housewife	58	"
z	Povilaitis Frank	102–104	molder	60	
	1440				
a	Burke John E	103–105	teacher	33	
b	Burke Rose—†	103–105	at home	70	"
c	Carey Margaret M-†	103–105	housewife	34	"
d	Carey Thomas J	103–105	carpenter	34	"
e	Kilduff Mary A—†	103–105	housewife	46	"
f	Kilduff Thomas J	103–105	foreman	53	"
g	Malloy Josephine—†	106–108	housewife	40	"
h	Malloy Thomas	106–108	foreman	39	"
k	Berry Mary F—†	106–108	housewife	32	"
l	Berry Robert H	106–108	chauffeur	35	"
m	Walsh Albert	106 108	checker	60	"

Rossmore Road—Continued

N	Walsh Eleanore—†	106–108	executive	37	here
o	Walsh Josephine—†	106–108	housewife	64	"
P	Ahern Charles F	107–109	checker	37	"
R	Ahern Irene A—†	107–109	housewife	36	"
s	*Daley Ellen J—†	107–109	"	36	
T	Daley James H	107–109	wool grader	32	"
U	Anglin Helen K—†	107–109	housewife	31	"
v	Anglin John F	107–109	clerk	38	

Shurland Street

w	Dorrer May—†	6	housewife	51	here
x	Dorrer Otto	6	collector	54	"

Stedman Street

Y	Edstrom Bernard	9	timekeeper	30	here
z	Edstrom Mary—†	9	housewife	30	"
	1441				
A	Feeley John H	9	machinist	61	"
B	Feeley Mary—†	9	housewife	51	"
c	O'Connell Gerard J	9	repairman	24	"
D	Colafrancesco Daphne—†	9	housewife	34	"
E	Colafrancesco Paul	9	machinist	36	"
F	Pierantoni Mabel—†	9	bookkeeper	28	"
G	Pierantoni Margaret—†	9	seamstress	56	"
H	Skenderian Alice—†	11	housewife	30	"
K	Skenderian Emil E	11	trackman	35	"
L	Neary Frances—†	11	clerk	24	
M	Neary Vincent	11	electrician	27	"
N	Sharks Annie—†	11	housewife	56	"
o	Sharks Leonard C	11	watchman	60	"
P	Krusz Eileen U—†	11	housewife	36	"
R	Krusz Stephen J	11	bartender	36	"
s	Stuart James	40	clerk	46	
T	*Stuart Kathleen—†	40	housewife	36	"
U	Keller Harriet—†	40	"	30	2 Brookley rd
v	Keller John	40	clerk	35	2 "

Washington Street

x	Campbell Emily—†	3464	housewife	58	here
y	Campbell James	3464	U S N	20	"
z	Campbell Patrick	3464	mason	62	"
	1442					
A	Duerden Albert H	3466	seaman	53	
B	Duerden Annie—†	3466	housewife	39	"
C	Duerden Edward F	3466	U S A	21	
D	Hagan Anna—†	3474	housewife	50	"
E	Hagan Daniel	3474	clerk	50	
F	Hagan Eleanor—†	3474	"	20	
G	Hagan Joseph	3474	policeman	28	"
H	Hagan Rita—†	3474	housewife	27	"
K	Hagan Ruth—†	3474	clerk	22	"
L	LaVie Anna—†	3476	"	26	"
M	LaVie Anne—†	3476	housewife	49	"
N	LaVie Francis J	3476	machinist	27	"
O	LaVie John J	3476	electrician	53	"
P	LaVie John J, jr	3476	clerk	28	
R	LaVie Philip	3476	U S A	23	
	1443					
B	Puleo Doris—†	3500	housewife	40	"
C	Puleo Vincent	3500	chauffeur	55	"
D	Casali Mary—†	3502	dipper	59	
E	Scagnoli Helena—†	3502	housewife	49	"
F	Scagnoli Henry	3502	bartender	62	"
G	Scagnoli Henry A	3502	U S N	23	
H	Scagnoli Joseph F	3502	U S M C	20	"
L	Scagnoli Gertrude—†	3504	at home	22	"
M	Mahoney Frank J	3504	installer	62	"
N	Mahoney Robert	3504	U S A	22	
R	VanTassell Florence—†	3508	stenographer	53	"
S	VanTassell Hilda—†	3508	matron	51	"
U	McArthur Florence—†	3510	housewife	66	"
V	McArthur Walter H	3510	welder	42	
W	Mercer William L	3510	porter	64	"
X	Morgan Catherine—†	3510	housewife	41	Beverly
Y	Shea Mary—†	3510	"	34	here
Z	Moran Mary T—†	3512	nurse	49	"
	1444					
A	*Blomquist Alma—†	3512	housewife	61	"

27

Washington Street—Continued

Page.	Letter.	FULL NAME.	Residence, Jan. 1, 1946.	Occupation.	Supposed Age.	Reported Residence, Jan. 1, 1945. Street and Number.
	B	*Blomquist Carl S	3512	laborer	60	here
	D	Francis Florence M—†	rear 3514	housewife	36	"
	E	Francis John W	" 3514	foreman	34	"
	F	Hubbard Freda—†	3516	housewife	28	Woburn
	G	Hubbard Leroy	3516	laborer	53	here
	H	Hubbard Leroy	3516	chauffeur	28	"
	K	Hubbard Marion—†	3516	housewife	59	"
	L	Dolan Alfred	3516	shipfitter	41	"
	M	Dolan Freda—†	3516	housewife	39	"
	P	Saverse Ethel—†	3526	"	42	
	R	Reed Hilda M—†	3526	"	26	"
	S	Reed Maurice, jr	3526	toolmaker	40	"
	T	O'Connor John C	3528	U S A	22	
	U	O'Connor Mary A—†	3528	housewife	48	"
	V	O'Connor Thomas J	3528	patternmaker	21	"
	W	Rhode Caroline—†	3528	housewife	21	12 Rossmore rd
	X	Rhode Charles	3528	fireman	26	12 "
		1445				
	A	Best Clifford S	3532	plumber	43	here
	B	Best Stella—†	3532	housewife	40	"
	C	Donnelly Eleanor—†	3532	clerk	20	"
	D	Donnelly John F	3532	U S A	21	..
	E	Donnelly Joseph P	3532	chauffeur	48	",
	F	Donnelly Joseph P	3532	shipfitter	25	"
	G	Donnelly Mary E—†	3532	housewife	47	"
	H	Allen Helen—†	3534	"	40	52 Dwight
	K	Allen Wesley	3534	machinist	50	here
	L	Quintaglie Mary—†	3534	housewife	36	"
	M	Quintaglie Peter	3534	cleaner	49	"
	N	Pilger Catherine—†	3536	housewife	36	"
	O	McGonagle John	3536	carpenter	40	"
	P	*McGonagle Katherine-†	3536	housewife	43	"
	R	Matthews Irene M—†	3536	"	47	
	S	Matthews William C	3536	U S N	20	"
	T	Hovestadt Fred	3540	U S A	26	38 Wensley
	U	Hovestadt Mary—†	3540	housewife	25	38 "
	V	Tully Elizabeth—†	3540	saleswoman	30	3 Morton pl
	W	Tully Frank	3540	welder	26	3 "
	X	Tully Margaret—†	3540	saleswoman	22	3 "
	Y	Tully Mary—†	3540	operator	29	3 "
	Z	Tully Phillip	3540	manager	28	3 "

1446
Washington Street—Continued

A	Tully Susan—†	3540	housewife	56	3 Morton pl
B	Tully Thomas	3540	welder	27	3 "
E	Smith James	3542	laborer	64	here
F	Smith Sarah—†	3542	housewife	62	"
G	Petruzzelli Frank A	3542	welder	44	564 Hyde Park av
H	Petruzzelli Sabatina—†	3542	housewife	25	564 "
K	West Florence—†	3542½	"	42	here
L	West Herbert A	3542½	machinist	40	"
N	Sullivan Daniel	3544	"	61	"
O	White Ann H—†	3544½	clerk	45	56 Whittier
R	Forbes Lawrence	3544½	operator	27	8 Rector rd
S	Sullivan Daniel J	3544½	machinist	61	here
T	Dolan Margaret—†	3546	housewife	28	"
U	Dolan William H	3546	machinist	31	"
V	White Judith—†	3546	saleswoman	23	"
W	Glendye Helen—†	3546	housewife	33	"
X	Ciavattieri Dominic	3546	laborer	59	"
Y	Kovar Clarence A	3546	U S N	26	202 South
Z	Kovar Margaret F—†	3546	saleswoman	23	202 "
	1447				
A	Connolly Alice—†	3546½	housewife	40	9 Jess
B	Connolly John	3546½	chauffeur	59	9 "
F	Downey Lloyd J	3555	plumber	26	608 Beech
G	Yeadon Carl H	3555	painter	46	608 "
K	Conway Charles E	3557	welder	45	here
L	Conway Johanna—†	3557	housewife	44	"
M	Conway John P	3557	clerk	21	"
N	Cicavi Josephine—†	3557	housewife	58	"
R	Russo Anthony F	3559	barber	52	
S	Russo Camilla—†	3559	clerk	24	
T	Russo Mary—†	3559	"	28	
U	Russo Rose—†	3559	"	23	
V	Bohan Mary B—†	3563	"	24	"
W	Bohan William P	3563	U S A	24	
X	Casey James T	3563	clerk	27	
Y	Casey John J	3563	chauffeur	58	"
Z	Casey John J, jr	3563	clerk	21	
	1448				
A	Casey Juha V—†	3563	housewife	53	"
B	Casey Louise—†	3563	secretary	23	"

Washington Street—Continued

c	Casey James J	3567	chauffeur	55	here
d	Casey Timothy P	3567	clerk	60	"
e	Connelly Esther C—†	3571	housewife	36	"
f	Connelly James B	3571	prison officer	42	"
g	McGinley Alexander J	3571	retired	50	
h	McGinley Caroline B—†	3571	laundress	57	"
k	Ingraham Frank T	3573	mechanic	58	"
l	Ingraham Helen E—†	3573	housewife	54	"
m	O'Malley Frances M—†	3573	clerk	33	
n	Daly Eugene F	3573	U S N	26	
o	Daly Mary C—†	3573	housewife	27	"
p	Hamill Margaret—†	3573	at home	81	"
r	Owen Margaret E—†	3573	clerk	47	
s	Fountain Errold H	3585	"	39	
t	Fountain Evelyn P—†	3585	housewife	41	"
u	Peterson George	3587	clerk	52	
v	Shurety Mary—†	3587	housewife	68	"

1449   Williams Street

f	McCreery Joseph D	62	mechanic	41	here
g	McCreery Matilda M—†	62	housewife	39	"
h	Bonsanti Dominic	62	shoemaker	61	"
k	Bonsanti Madeline—†	62	housewife	58	"
l	Bonsanti Marie—†	62	clerk	22	
m	Daly Helena—†	62	housewife	31	"
n	Daly James E	62	painter	34	
o	Burke Nora—†	64	housewife	44	"
p	Burke Stephen F	64	painter	45	
r	Denterio Anna M—†	64	housewife	64	"
s	Deuterio Joseph	64	pipefitter	61	"
t	McKeon Bartholomew	64	clerk	29	162 Lamartine
u	McKeon Dorothy—†	64	housewife	25	162 "
v	Sahagian Edward T	66	clerk	46	here
w	Sahagian Marguerite L—†	66	housewife	36	"
x	*Carrigg Catherine—†	66	"	70	"
y	Curry Arthur	66	cutter	35	
z	Curry Catherine—†	66	housewife	35	"

1450

a	Hession Catherine—†	66	"	42	
b	Hession John	66	freighthandler	59	"

Williams Street—Continued

c	Davin Catherine—†	68	housewife	54	here
d	Davin Catherine V—†	68	stenographer	21	"
e	Shields Joseph F	68	machinist	46	"
f	*Shields Nora—†	68	housewife	42	"
g	White Bridget—†	68	"	43	
h	White James J	68	soap mixer	49	"
k	*Caswell Helen—†	69	housewife	36	"
l	Caswell Wesley	69	chauffeur	38	"
m	Hurley Mary E—†	70	housewife	40	"
n	Hurley Michael	70	pipefitter	46	"
o	McCarthy Anne M—†	70	secretary	22	"
p	McCarthy Hannah—†	70	housewife	53	"
r	Burke Catherine—†	70	"	33	
s	Burke Patrick	70	longshoreman	38	"
t	Conroy Mary—†	70	factoryworker	36	14 Aldworth
u	Dillon Edith I—†	71	matron	48	here
v	Hulme John P	71	chauffeur	46	"
w	Grady Doris—†	71	housewife	31	"
x	Grady Joseph	71	letter carrier	31	"
y	Kachele Charles	71	salesman	59	"
z	Kachele Grace—†	71	housewife	57	"

1451

a	McLaughlin Anna—†	71	"	31	
b	McLaughlin Lawrence J	71	policeman	35	"
c	McGilvray Albert J	72	electrician	31	"
d	McGilvray Catherine—†	72	housewife	71	"
e	McGilvray Edward	72	laundryman	60	"
f	McGilvray Isabelle—†	72	typist	42	
g	*Hay Adele—†	72	housewife	44	"
h	Hay Kenneth	72	fireman	46	
k	Hayes Catherine A—†	72	housewife	65	"
l	Kelly Margaret M—†	72	"	39	
m	Kelly Patrick	72	laborer	43	
n	McDermott John J	74	gardener	40	"
o	McDermott Patrick	74	retired	85	
p	McDermott Rose A—†	74	auditor	38	
r	McDermott Susan A—†	74	housewife	80	"
s	Regan Ethel—†	74	"	50	
t	Regan William	74	inspector	45	"
u	Dunbar James M	74	plumber	70	"
v	Dunbar Janet—†	74	housewife	93	"

Williams Street—Continued

w	Dunbar Mary E—†	74	leatherworker	57	here
x	Fraser Jessie W—†	74	housewife	29	"
y	Fraser Paul W	74	shipper	30	"
z	Stuart George J	74	molder	27	..
	1452				
A	Stuart Jessie—†	74	housewife	66	"
B	Doyle Dorothy B—†	75	"	32	
C	Doyle William F	75	retired	43	"
D	Garren Arthur L	75	laborer	24	California
E	Garren Margaret—†	75	housewife	23	31 Duncan
F	Good Mary—†	75	at home	87	31 "
G	Molineaux John L	75	dispatcher	57	31 "
H	Molineaux John L	75	machinist	22	31 "
K	Molineaux Rose—†	75	housewife	51	31 "
L	Kachele Antoinette—†	75	"	36	here
M	Kachele Charles E	75	U S N	37	"
N	Allegra Mella—†	91	tel operator	38	Medford
O	Pasquale Santa—†	91	housewife	58	here
P	MacEwan Alfred	91	plumber	44	"
R	MacEwan Ruby J—†	91	housewife	28	"
S	Catogge Anna L—†	91	stitcher	45	
T	Catogge Camella—†	91	at home	30	..
U	Catogge Joseph E	91	draftsman	50	"
V	Catogge N Mary—†	91	stenographer	40	"
w*	McMackin Mary—†	97	housewife	57	"
x	McMackin William J	97	laborer	57	..
Y	Harvey David L	97	operator	35	..
z	Reil Jennie—†	97	inspector	35	..
	1453				
A	McFarlin Frank E	97	lawyer	47	
B	McFarlin Katherine—†	97	housewife	47	..
D	D'Entremont Agnes—†	109	"	32	
E	D'Entremont Bernard	109	pipefitter	34	..
G	Quigley Frances V—†	109	housewife	40	..
F	Quigley Francis J	109	cablemaker	45	..
H	Whitson Ann—†	109	housewife	32	..
K	Whitston William	109	maintenance	37	..
L*	Kelliher Nora—†	109	housewife	62	..
M	Kelliher William	109	chauffeur	60	"
N	English Mary L—†	109	at home	83	..
o*	Coyne Agnes—†	109	housewife	40	"

Williams Street—Continued

P	*Coyne Barbara—†	109	domestic	42	here	
R	Coyne Patrick	109	clerk	38	"	
S	Kirsis Arthur R	111	U S A	23	"	
T	Kirsis Margaret T—†	111	housewife	22	"	
U	Nash Ann P—†	111	clerk	20		
V	*Nash Elizabeth—†	111	housewife	53	"	
W	Nash Michael J	111	laborer	58	"	
X	Wilson Beatrice—†	111	stitcher	59		
Y	Wilson James P	111	paperhanger	72	"	
Z	Reiser Irene—†	111	housewife	29	"	

1454

A	Reiser Joseph	111	chauffeur	40	"	
B	Reiser Mary—†	111	at home	67	..	
C	Murphy Alice—†	113	stenographer	20	"	
D	Murphy David	113	custodian	64	"	
E	Murphy David F	113	supervisor	35	"	
F	Murphy John J	113	U S A	33	"	
G	Murphy Mary C—†	113	nurse	30		
H	Murphy Rita E—†	113	stenographer	24	"	
K	Cawley Abbie—†	115	housewife	47	"	
L	Cawley John F	115	operator	47	"	
M	Cawley John F, jr	115	U S M C	21	"	
N	Keith Catherine—†	115	housewife	28	"	
O	Keith Charles	115	U S A	29		
P	Harrington Julia—†	117	waitress	47	..	
R	Keegan Joseph	117	carpenter	45	"	
S	Keegan Nancy—†	117	housewife	45	"	
T	Ducey Francis	117	mechanic	30	14 Buswell	
U	Ducey Mary—†	117	housewife	30	14 "	
V	Barry David	117	U S A	25	here	
W	Barry Rita—†	117	housewife	22	"	
X	Calloe Irene M—†	121	"	43	"	
Y	Foran Michael J	121	packer	55		
Z	Foran Nellie—†	121	housewife	55	"	

1455

A	Carroll Helen—†	121	"	36	"	
B	Carroll Peter H	121	metalworker	36	"	
C	Feeney Bridget—†	123–25	housewife	40	58 Rossmore rd	
D	Feeney James	123–25	chauffeur	40	58 "	
E	Hergt Louisa—†	123–25	housewife	44	here	
F	Hergt Raymond W	123–25	operator	50	"	

Page.	Letter.	FULL NAME.	Residence. Jan. 1, 1946.	Occupation.	Supposed Age.	Reported Residence, Jan. 1, 1945. Street and Number.

Williams Street—Continued

	G	Hergt William	123–25	operator	62	here
	H	Ricker Helen—†	123–25	at home	22	"
	K	Ricker Robert	123–25	U S A	24	"
	L	Touhy Margaret—†	123–25	housewife	40	"
	M	Touhy Patrick	123–25	rubberworker	45	"
	N	Mitchell Margaret—†	127	housewife	40	"
	O	Mitchell Thomas	127	butcher	38	"
	P	Hanney Esther—†	127	teacher	39	
	R	Hanney Joseph	127	butcher	69	"
	S	Hanney Mary A—†	127	housewife	66	"
	T	Pihl Elna—†	127	"	49	
	U	Pihl Sophus	127	painter	50	
	V	O'Malley John	131	laborer	39	
	W	O'Malley Margaret—†	131	housewife	33	"
	X	Iskra Anthony	131	policeman	49	"
	Y	Iskra Anthony A	131	clerk	28	
	Z	Iskra Eleanore—†	131	at home	22	"
		1456				
	A	Iskra Nora G—†	131	housewife	48	"
	B	Bryan Arthur G	131	electrician	35	"
	C	Bryan Pauline—†	131	housewife	29	"
	D	Graynor James	135	bookbinder	50	"
	E	*Graynor Nora—†	135	housewife	47	"
	F	Labrie Elizabeth C—†	135	"	33	
	G	Labrie Leon	135	manager	35	"
	H	Stowell Frederick H	135	"	49	
	K	Stowell Ruth V—†	135	housewife	46	"
	L	Edwards Alexander W	139	letter carrier	41	"
	M	Edwards Elizabeth C—†	139	housewife	31	"
	N	*Lester Agnes—†	139	"	43	
	O	Lester James J	139	polisher	43	"
	P	Quinn Flora—†	139	housewife	39	"
	R	Quinn Joseph M	139	ironworker	42	"
	S	Quinn Michael	139	retired	70	
	T	Donahue Margaret—†	143–45	housewife	44	"
	U	Donahue Mary—†	143–45	secretary	20	"
	V	Donahue Patrick J	143–45	policeman	49	"
	W	Bailey Helen—†	143–45	housewife	37	"
	X	Bailey Joseph C	143–45	policeman	41	"
	Y	Schwelm Frederick	143–45	U S N	30	
	Z	Schwelm Mary—†	143–45	housewife	28	"

Ward 11–Precinct 15

CITY OF BOSTON

LIST OF RESIDENTS
20 YEARS OF AGE AND OVER

(NON-CITIZENS INDICATED BY ASTERISK)
(FEMALES INDICATED BY DAGGER)

AS OF

JANUARY 1, 1946

THOMAS F. SULLIVAN, *Chairman*
FREDERIC E. DOWLING, *Secretary*
WILLIAM A. MOTLEY, JR.
ARTHUR V. COUGHLIN
EVERETT R. PROUT

Listing Board.

CITY OF BOSTON PRINTING DEPARTMENT

Page.	Letter.	FULL NAME.	Residence, Jan. 1, 1946.	Occupation.	Supposed Age.	Reported Residence, Jan. 1, 1945. Street and Number.

1500
Bremen Terrace

A	*Cappuccio Mary—†	3	housekeeper	60	here
B	Cerrato Jane—†	3	housewife	41	"
C	Cerrato Louis	3	tailor	51	"
D	DiGregorio Alesio	5	plasterer	45	"
E	DiGregorio Christina—†	5	housewife	45	"
F	Burke Margaret L—†	6	"	53	
G	Burke Thomas F	6	repairman	54	"
H	Flynn Arthur T	7	instructor	53	"
K	Flynn Frances C—†	7	housewife	50	"
L	Flynn Walter J	7	clerk	23	
M	Flynn William A	7	cable splicer	24	"

Forest Hills Avenue

N	Hargroves Clarice—†	1	housewife	43	Westwood
O	Hargroves Fred E	1	foreman	49	"

Hyde Park Avenue

U	Barrett Daniel F	8A	laborer	49	here
V	Barrett Daniel F, jr	8A	bellboy	23	"
W	Barrett Hazel K—†	8A	housewife	43	"
X	Volk Laura E—†	8A	saleswoman	37	"
Y	Sullivan Albert F	10	U S A	22	
Z	Sullivan Elizabeth M—†	10	housewife	53	"

1501

A	Sullivan John E	10	laborer	26	
B	Sullivan Richard C	10	painter	60	
C	Sullivan Richard C, jr	10	clerk	28	
D	Sullivan Rita E—†	10	"	23	
E	Lyons Laura A—†	10	housewife	37	"
F	Lyons Martin P	10	checker	47	"
K	Delaney Ellen F—†	14A	housewife	66	"
L	Delaney Joseph A	14A	retired	78	
M	Nash Harold E	14A	dentist	53	
N	Sullivan John J	14A	laborer	51	
O	Sullivan Mary E—†	14A	housewife	51	"
P	Brownlow Genevieve—†	14½	"	56	
R	Brownlow Louis A	14½	packer	54	
S	Eudey Beatrice A—†	14½	housewife	34	"

Hyde Park Avenue—Continued

T	Eudey Francis E	14½	machinist	37	here
W	Christian Adrian E	20	"	40	"
X	Christian Amanda R—†	20	housewife	65	"
Y	Christian Emil H	20	laborer	42	
Z	Christian Ernest J	20	student	31	"

1502

A	Christian George E	20	mechanic	37	"
B	Doyle Alice T—†	20	housewife	35	2 Walk Hill
C	Doyle John J	20	rigger	39	2 "
D	Ryan Frank J	22	mechanic	56	here
E	Ryan Nora—†	22	housewife	46	"
F	Lawlor Margaret M—†	22	"	45	16 Tower
G	Lawlor Thomas G	22	carpenter	44	16 "
L	Rooney Marion E—†	28	housewife	47	here
M	Rooney Norma R—†	28	operator	20	"
N	Rooney Robert G	28	laborer	51	"
O	Allen Bernice B—†	28	housewife	51	"
P	Allen Richard W	28	technician	20	"
R	Lewis Annie M—†	30	housewife	38	"
S	Lewis Eleanor H—†	30	clerk	21	"
T	Cody Bernice M—†	30	housewife	28	Quincy
U	Cody Matthew J	30	bartender	33	"
W	Beineke Otto F	34	baker	40	here
X	Beineke Sophie G—†	34	housewife	30	"
Y	Bertelsen Albert A	34	U S N	23	"
Z	Harson Grace K—†	34	housewife	59	"

1503 Lennoco Road

B	Brannelly John J	1	bartender	47	here
C	Brannelly Margaret M—†	1	housewife	42	"
D	Leahy Anna—†	5	at home	70	"
E	Leahy Mabel—†	5	housewife	58	"
F	Meade David D	6	salesman	33	"
G	Meade Mary H—†	6	housewife	37	Missouri
H	Meade William F	6	clerk	39	here
K	O'Donnell Mary E—†	6	housewife	60	"
L	O'Donnell William J	6	clerk	67	"
M	Francis Anna W—†	9	housewife	36	"
N	Francis Richard T	9	electrician	41	"

3

Page.	Letter.	FULL NAME.	Residence, Jan. 1, 1946.	Occupation.	Supposed Age.	Reported Residence, Jan. 1, 1945. Street and Number.

Lennoco Road—Continued

| | o | Kohler Mary B—† | 9 | waitress | 40 | here |
| | p | Leonard Mary N—† | 9 | secretary | 26 | " |

Morton Street

	s	Baker Lillian W—†	29	dietitian	48	here
	t	Bowes Gertrude E—†	29	seamstress	64	"
	u	Bradley Cecelia V—†	29	nurse	43	"
	v	Brewer Edith H—†	29	bookkeeper	30	Maine
	w	Brown Martha—†	29	nurse	26	here
	x	Burns Helen G—†	29	"	36	"
	y	Carpenter Mary—†	29	domestic	50	"
	z	Cole Gladys O—†	29	supt	50	
		1504				
	a	Flannery Mary K—†	29	nurse	38	
	b	Johnson Myrtle—†	29	"	36	
	c	Kennedy Anne—†	29	"	30	
	d	LaPierre Delia A—†	29	"	30	
	e	Lomasney Helen—†	29	"	27	
	f	*Lynch Edward J	29	laborer	73	
	g	MacDonald Clara—†	29	nurse	41	
	h	*McConnell Norma—†	29	"	33	
	k	*McGuirk Elizabeth T—†	29	"	32	"
	l	Metivier Sophie—†	29	"	58	Watertown
	m	*O'Connor Mary—†	29	domestic	59	here
	n	*Polito John	29	fireman	58	"
	o	Schofield Virginia E—†	29	nurse	35	"
	p	Ward Alice L—†	29	"	31	
	r	Wedge Sarah H—†	29	"	50	
	s	White Lillian—†	29	"	45	
	t	Williamson Edith—†	29	"	49	
	u	Parker Herbert N	41	laborer	62	
	v	Shadman Alonzo J	rear 41	physician	67	"
	w	Carroll Anna C—†	81	housewife	43	"
	x	Carroll John F	81	operator	50	"
	y	Sullivan John J	81	retired	66	
	z	Sullivan Margaret V—†	81	housewife	60	"
		1505				
	a	McGinley Evelyn G—†	83	at home	75	"
	b	Starvish John J	97	jeweler	38	
	c	Starvish Theresa—†	97	housewife	29	"

4

Page.	Letter.	FULL NAME.	Residence, Jan. 1, 1946.	Occupation.	Supposed Age.	Reported Residence, Jan. 1, 1945. Street and Number.

Morton Street—Continued

	E	Coluccino Michael	rear 109	mechanic	52	here
	F	Driscoll Gerald T	113	investigator	44	"
	G	Monroe Mary—†	113	at home	73	"

Orchardhill Road

	K	McDonald Elizabeth M—†	40	social worker	32	here
	L	McDonald John F	40	"	28	"
	M	McDonald Mary E—†	40	housewife	71	"
	N	Greene Mary—†	41	"	48	..
	O	Greene William	41	laborer	57	
	P	Handy Frank	41	custodian	76	"
	R	McGlynn Mary D—†	41	supervisor	40	"
	S	Hoobin Helen J—†	41	housewife	37	"
	T	Hoobin James P	41	chauffeur	37	"
	U	Minton Anna I—†	45	housewife	74	"
	V	Minton Gertrude M—†	45	"	34	
	W	Minton John M	45	realtor	35	
	X	Minton Thomas M	45	teacher	37	..
	Y	Killion Edward J	50	florist	48	
	Z	Killion Josephine—†	50	housewife	75	"
		1506				
	A	Hannon Anna T—†	55	secretary	40	"
	B	Jordan Andrew R	55	inspector	50	"
	C	Jordan Donald F	55	student	20	..
	D	Jordan Dorothy M—†	55	secretary	21	"
	E	Jordan Helen G—†	55	housewife	45	"
	F	Murphy Edward F	59	clerk	43	
	G	Murphy Helen M—†	59	housewife	43	"
	H	Tracy John F	59	mason	48	
	K	Tracy Margaret—†	59	housewife	70	"
	L	Tracy Michael	59	retired	75	
	M	Tracy Thomas J	59	operator	50	"
	N	Day Alma—†	62	housewife	32	Ohio
	O	Day Donald S	62	agent	31	"
	P	Lewis Arthur J	63	broker	45	here
	R	Lewis Margaret C—†	63	housewife	42	"
	S	Tansey Anne—†	63	secretary	36	"
	T	Tansey Joseph L	63	physician	35	"
	U	Tansey Mary J—†	63	secretary	44	"
	V	MacDonald Helen—†	64	tel operator	48	"

Orchardhill Road—Continued

w	MacDonald John	64	clerk	35	here
x	MacDonald Margaret—†	64	saleswoman	42	"
y	MacDonald Mary—†	64	teacher	40	"
z	MacDonald Raymond	64	clerk	45	

1507

A	MacKay Charlotte M—†	66	hostess	36	
B	MacQueen John	66	salesman	46	"
c	MacQueen Laura—†	66	housewife	37	"
D	Traverse Ellen M—†	67	"	48	"
E	Traverse Helen R—†	67	stenographer	25	"
F	Traverse Joseph E	67	chemist	50	"
G	Traverse Joseph E, jr	67	U S M C	20	"
H	Traverse Margaret D—†	67	chemist	23	
K	Corrigan Delia M—†	68	housewife	73	"
L	Corrigan Peter J	68	retired	73	
M	Keelan Harry S	71	chemist	53	
N	Keelan Vera R—†	71	housewife	37	"
o	Looney Dennis J	72	supt	38	
P	Looney Rosalie A—†	72	housewife	38	"
R	Ford Frances H—†	74	social worker	22	"
s	Ford Marie L—†	74	secretary	23	"
T	Ford Mary M—†	74	housewife	50	"
U	Ford William J	74	manager	62	"
v	Adamski Dorothy C—†	75	housewife	24	"
w	Adamski Francis J	75	cable splicer	25	"
x	Henderson Mary F—†	75	stenographer	28	"
Y	Lang John H	75	testman	51	"
z	Lang Mary E—†	75	housewife	52	"

1508 Tower Street

E	Corrigan Paul	11	clerk	23	here
F	Doherty Dorothy—†	11	secretary	25	"
G	Doherty Thomas	11	bookkeeper	27	"
H	Sentance Agnes—†	11	housewife	55	"
K	Sentance Evelyn C—†	11	clerk	25	
L	Sentance Joseph W	11	blacksmith	57	"
M	Sentance Joseph W, jr	11	clerk	22	
N	Stanton Joseph G	11	U S N	24	
o	Stanton Mildred—†	11	housewife	46	"
P	Stanton Mildred M—†	11	bookkeeper	25	"

Tower Street—Continued

	Letter	FULL NAME	Residence	Occupation	Age	Reported Residence
	R	Stanton Thomas J	11	salesman	48	here
	S	Stanton Thomas J, jr	11	clerk	27	"
	T	Elfving Harry A	15	welder	38	"
	U	Elfving Theresa F—†	15	housewife	32	"
	V	Murray Catherine C—†	15	stenographer	33	"
	W	Murray Catherine F—†	15	housewife	65	"
	X	Murray Ruth M—†	15	clerk	25	"
	Y	Barrett Ellen H—†	15	housewife	34	77 Walk Hill
	Z	Barrett John	15	proprietor	36	77 "

1509

	Letter	FULL NAME	Residence	Occupation	Age	Reported Residence
	A	Ross Elizabeth F—†	16	clerk	50	Palmer
	B	Wipperman Mary—†	16	"	67	here
	C	Wipperman Victoria—†	16	at home	54	"
	D	Leonard Mary—†	16	"	96	"
	E	Leonard Mary A—†	16	housekeeper	59	"
	F	Leonard Thomas J	16	supervisor	54	"
	G	Healy Katherine—†	16	housewife	40	Cambridge
	H	Healy Patrick	16	fireman	43	"
	K	Young Ralph	17	agent	35	here
	L	Young Wilhelmina—†	17	housewife	30	"
	M	Young Dorothea C—†	17	tel operator	28	"
	N	Young Irene M—†	17	secretary	34	"
	O	Young John J	17	retired	72	"
	P	Young Maria G—†	17	housewife	66	"
	R	Young Marie G—†	17	secretary	32	"
	S	Sullivan Ada—†	17	housewife	33	"
	T	Sullivan Agnes—†	17	"	59	
	U	Sullivan Robert H	17	operator	34	"
	V	Delaney Phyllis A—†	18	housewife	29	"
	W	Delaney William E	18	supt	40	
	X	Kelley James E	18	clerk	55	
	Y	Kelley John J	18	laborer	53	
	Z	Kelley Mary E—†	18	tel operator	42	"

1510

	Letter	FULL NAME	Residence	Occupation	Age	Reported Residence
	A	Mahler Laura E—†	18	housewife	36	"
	B	Mahler Warrén A	18	manager	39	"
	C	Knightly Abbie—†	20	housewife	38	"
	D	Knightly Thomas	20	chef	39	
	E	Coyne Margaret—†	20	at home	79	"
	F	McGreehan James	20	motorman	53	20 Woodlawn
	G	Leslie Albert	20	shipper	48	here

Page.	Letter.	FULL NAME.	Residence, Jan. 1, 1946.	Occupation.	Supposed Age.	Reported Residence, Jan. 1, 1945. Street and Number.

Tower Street—Continued

	H	Leslie Rosemary—†	20	housewife	52	here
	K	Fiske Ann—†	23	"	40	"
	L	Fiske Betty G—†	23	stenographer	22	"
	M	Fiske Robert	23	auditor	50	"
	N	Kaine Elizabeth—†	23	operator	50	"
	O	Kaine Margaret E—†	23	stenographer	22	"
	P	Kaine Mary L—†	23	secretary	24	"
	R	Kaine Paul E	23	electrician	35	"
	S	Kaine Richard A	23	"	33	
	T	King Hugh	23	"	60	
	U	King James P	23	laborer	50	
	V	King John J	23	foreman	56	"
	W	McGillicuddy Daniel F	23	inspector	60	"
	X	McGillicuddy Daniel F, jr	23	student	29	
	Y	McGillicuddy Helen G—†	23	stenographer	30	"
	Z	McGillicuddy Leo X	23	U S C G	24	"
		1511				
	A	McGillicuddy Mary E—†	23	housewife	53	"
	B	Brauner Anna C—†	24	"	59	"
	C	Brauner Austin W	24	U S A	28	"
	D	Brauner Gustave J	24	manager	58	"
	E	Clark Clarence J	24	chauffeur	38	"
	F	Marsh Leora—†	24	cook	29	
	G	McLellan Frederick L	24	manager	24	"
	H	Cody Arthur L	24	machinist	27	"
	K	Cody Theresa J—†	24	housewife	26	"
	L	O'Donnell Hugh	24	operator	33	"
	M	O'Donnell Muriel—†	24	housewife	23	"
	N	Roberts Ethel M—†	25	"	41	Waltham
	O	Roberts Thomas J	25	chauffeur	48	"
	P	Doidge Clara M—†	25	housewife	73	here
	R	Lidell William	25	retired	75	"
	S	Garrity Katherine J—†	26	clerk	38	"
	T	Garrity Mary A—†	26	at home	39	"
	U	Laffey Grace A—†	26	housewife	27	71 Peter Parley rd
	V	Laffey John J	26	draftsman	28	74 Montebello rd
	W	Splaine Margaret J—†	26	inspector	38	here
	X	Splaine Nellie A—†	26	at home	44	"
	Y	Hagstrom Marie—†	27	domestic	66	"
	Z	Selig Albert E	27	chauffeur	50	"

8

1512
Tower Street—Continued

A	Selig Ann M—†	27	housewife	55	here
B	Rowen Mary G—†	27	"	58	"
C	Rowen Thomas J	27	plumber	52	"
D	Rowen Catherine E—†	27	stenographer	55	"
E	Cooper Gertrude—†	31	nurse	70	Brookline
F	Simmons Letha—†	31	at home	90	here
G	Tosi Alfreda—†	31	clerk	50	"
H	Guay Annie—†	31	housewife	67	"
K	Guay Henry J	31	watchman	65	"
L	Guay Joseph P	31	clerk	27	
M	Bird Harriet A—†	32	housewife	59	"
N	Bird William J	32	maintenance	59	"
O	Vierra Everett F	32	accountant	48	"
P	Vierra Kathryn—†	32	housewife	43	"
R	Waters Ann—†	32	"	24	23 East
S	Waters John	32	salesman	26	83 Tower
T	Kiely Eugene	33	checker	46	here
U	Kiely Marguerite—†	33	housewife	38	"
V	Bird Alfred J	33	clerk	26	"
W	Bird Edwin W	33	"	21	"
X	Bird Frances M—†	33	secretary	30	"
Y	Bird Louis A	33	chauffeur	62	"
Z	Bird Olla M—†	33	housewife	56	"

1513

A	Bird Rita G—†	33	tel operator	24	"
B	Bird Rose C—†	33	saleswoman	28	"
C	Feeney Edward T	33	proprietor	30	"
D	Feeney Mary A—†	33	housewife	32	"
E	McCann Edward	37	retired	77	
F	McCann Joseph P	37	painter	34	"
G	McCann Mary—†	37	waitress	41	"
H	McCann Mary—†	37	housewife	35	"
K	McCann William T	37	foreman	44	"
L	Martin Eleanor T—†	37	waitress	45	"
M	Muldoon Delia—†	37	domestic	48	"
N	Jacobs Frances L—†	38	clerk	28	
O	Jacobs Frank C	38	fireman	51	
P	Jacobs Grace M—†	38	dietitian	25	"
R	Jacobs Hazel M—†	38	housewife	53	"

Page.	Letter.	Full Name.	Residence, Jan. 1, 1946.	Occupation.	Supposed Age.	Reported Residence, Jan. 1, 1945. Street and Number.

Tower Street—Continued

s	Jacobs Robert D	38	U S A	23	here
t	Jacobs Eleanor H—†	38	secretary	21	"
u	Jacobs Harriet H—†	38	housewife	45	"
v	Jacobs Henry I	38	inspector	50	"
w	McMorrow Anna L—†	39	housewife	66	"
x	McMorrow Joseph M	39	shipper	35	
y	Field Anita G—†	39	tel operator	30	"
z	Field Bernadette M—†	39	clerk	30	

1514

! a	Field Susan A—†	39	housewife	73	"
b	Towle Thomas M	39	retired	75	
c	Murray Henry E	40	cutter	66	
d	Murray Henry E, jr	40	agent	21	
e	Murray Martha S—†	40	nurse	56	
f	Bowie Charlotte—†	40	at home	63	"
g	Bowie Macy E—†	40	beautician	25	"
h	Prebble Carrie—†	40	at home	80	Newton
k	Johnson Eleanor C—†	41	saleswoman	24	here
l	Johnson Esther L—†	41	housewife	51	"
m	Johnson John I	41	ironworker	58	"
n	Dunn John J	41	student	24	
o	Dunn Margaret M—†	41	housewife	51	"
p	Dunn Michael J	41	chauffeur	60	"
r	Dunn Roger M	41	shipper	21	
s	Finnegan Patrick J	41	retired	72	
! t	Peyton Mary A—†	43	housewife	43	"
u	Peyton William W	43	baker	46	
v	May Alice M—†	43	housewife	47	"
w*	O'Brien Jemima—†	43	"	29	
x	O'Brien Patrick F	43	boilermaker	36	"
y	Long Isabelle M—†	44	housewife	70	"
z	Long Leo R	44	teacher	37	"

1515

' a	Long William P	44	executive	70	"
b	Madden Anna—†	46	teacher	37	"
c	Madden Margaret E—†	46	housewife	63	"
d	Fitzpatrick Julia N—†	47	teacher	55	"
e	Rock Margaret T—†	47	housewife	50	"
f	Rock Thaddeus F	47	retired	70	
g	Geary Ann—†	47	housewife	40	"
h	Geary Robert F	47	caretaker	46	"

Tower Street—Continued

Page.	Letter.	FULL NAME.	Residence, Jan. 1, 1946.	Occupation.	Supposed Age.	Reported Residence, Jan. 1, 1945.
	K	Geehan John J	48	cutter	42	here
	L	Geehan Madeline—†	48	housewife	42	"
	M	O'Brien Elizabeth C—†	48	at home	69	"
	N	O'Brien Helen—†	48	teacher	41	..
	O	Walsh Martin	49	packer	51	
	P*	Walsh Mary—†	49	housewife	49	"
	R	Shea Catherine—†	49	"	37	Needham
	S	Shea Michael	49	laborer	35	"
	T	Ryan James J	49	"	58	here
	U	Ryan Nora—†	49	housewife	45	"
	V	Lewis Florence—†	52	"	69	"
	W	Lewis George	52	U S A	42	
	X	Cassidy Annie A—†	52	housewife	54	"
	Y	Cassidy Michael	52	U S N	70	
	Z	Donegan Catherine—†	55	housewife	60	"
1516						
	A	Donegan Robert	55	laborer	35	
	B	Clements Esther—†	57	housewife	50	"
	C	Downey John M	57	operator	52	"
	D	MacDonald Ann—†	57	nurse	48	
	E	Dinsmore Clayton	57	laborer	42	
	F	Dinsmore Lillian—†	57	housewife	37	"
	G	McIntyre Mary E—†	59	seamstress	50	"
	H	McIntyre Robert	59	student	27	..
	K	McIntyre Theresa E—†	59	clerk	23	
	L	Lowry David	61	chauffeur	56	"
	M	Lowry David F	61	clerk	29	
	N	Lowry Helen D—†	61	housewife	26	"
	O	Lowry Margaret M—†	61	"	55	
	P	Knowlton Aaron	62	chauffeur	59	"
	R	Knowlton Cora—†	62	housewife	58	"
	S	Knowlton Jessie—†	62	secretary	35	"
	T	Sybertz Lillian—†	62	housewife	26	"
	U	Sybertz Paul	62	U S N	27	"
	V	O'Leary Catherine—†	62	at home	60	"
	W	Connors Ellen—†	63	housewife	50	"
	X	Connors John J	63	foreman	50	"
	Y	Connors Mary E—†	63	bookkeeper	21	"
	Z	Rogers George	63	machinist	46	"
1517						
	A	Rogers Sadie—†	63	waitress	45	"

Tower Street—Continued

B	Corcoran Charles	63	retired	67	here
C	Corcoran Grace—†	63	domestic	55	"
D	Rose Alfred	66	letter carrier	60	"
E	Rose Joseph	66	U S A	23	..
F	Rose Mae—†	66	stenographer	21	"
G	Rose Virginia—†	66	"	35	..
H	Harrison Jennie G—†	66	housewife	52	"
K	Harrison Lillian F—†	66	secretary	21	"
L	Harrison Mary—†	66	housewife	25	"
M	Harrison Reginald B	66	mechanic	57	"
N	Harrison William B	66	engineer	28	"
O	Beyer Agnes—†	66	housewife	55	"
P	Beyer John L	66	clerk	55	"
R	Kerr George	66	mechanic	37	Medford
S	Kerr Hazel—†	66	housewife	38	"
T	Pazaree Charles	66	U S N	29	here
U	Pazaree Doris M—†	66	housewife	27	"
V	Toohy Anna—†	67	"	67	"
W	Toohy Thomas M	67	printer	68	
X	McCann Edward F	69	custodian	39	"
Y	McCann Mary A—†	69	housewife	37	"
Z	Leonard Ann N—†	69	"	30	
	1518				
A	Leonard Francis J	69	machinist	29	"
B	Vena Anna T—†	70	housewife	38	"
C	Vena Luigi S	70	clerk	38	
D	Page Laura—†	70	housewife	51	"
E	Page Wilfred	70	jeweler	52	..
F	Hildebrand Louise—†	70	operator	53	"
G	Hildebrand Richard	70	shipper	55	"
H	Mitchell John J	71	porter	45	194 Highland
K	*Mitchell Margaret T—†	71	housewife	34	194 "
L	Scanlon Elizabeth M—†	71	"	42	here
M	Scanlon William F	71	mechanic	47	"
N	Connolly John F	71	policeman	49	"
O	Connolly Margaret A—†	71	housewife	46	"
P	Dolan Dorothy M—†	73	tel operator	21	"
R	Dolan Frank J	73	chauffeur	51	..
S	Dolan Julia A—†	73	housewife	51	"
T	Herrick Daniel M	73A	chauffeur	64	..
U	Herrick Ora E—†	73A	housewife	65	"

Tower Street—Continued

v	Greene James	73A	proprietor	53	here
w	Greene Mary W—†	73A	clerk	45	"
x	Simpson Chester	75	pedler	48	"
y	Simpson Doris—†	75	bookkeeper	22	"
z	Simpson Elizabeth—†	75	housewife	46	"
1519					
A	Simpson James	75	clerk	24	"
B	Connolly Thomas H	75	guide	66	"
c	Sutherland Anna M—†	75	housewife	32	"
D	Sutherland John E	75	agent	30	
E	*Nicholson Catherine M—†	75	housewife	53	"
F	Nicholson Dolina—†	75	draftsman	23	"
G	*Nicholson John	75	baker	51	"
H	*Nicholson John M	75	U S A	27	"
K	Dolan Daniel M	76	pipecoverer	50	"
L	Dolan Mary E—†	76	housewife	50	"
M	Kelly Frances E—†	77	"	38	
N	Kelly William L	77	instructor	36	"
O	Ross Elizabeth—†	77	housewife	69	"
P	Murphy Agnes T—†	78	"	45	
R	Murphy John	78	plumber	45	"
S	Walsh Marie—†	78	operator	32	"
T	Connelly Thomas J	78	laborer	42	
U	Flynn Delia—†	78	housewife	50	"
v	Flynn Dennis M	78	laborer	52	
w	O'Brien Ellen A—†	79	clerk	42	"
x	O'Brien Mary—†	79	housewife	72	"
Y	Abbott Rose G—†	81	"	48	
z	Abbott Walter P	81	clerk	48	
1520					
A	Conaty Rose—†	83	checker	53	"
B	Timmins Margaret—†	83	cook	58	"
c	Waters Catherine—†	83	housewife	60	"
D	Waters Mary C—†	83	stenographer	20	"
E	Reilly Catherine—†	83	housewife	45	"
F	Reilly Edward	83	clerk	50	
G	Davey Colin L	84	guard	46	
H	Davey Helen—†	84	housewife	46	"
K	Procter Dorothy—†	84	teacher	20	
L	Procter Susie—†	84	housewife	42	"
M	Procter Willard	84	manager	42	"

13

Tower Street—Continued

N	Glynn Frederick J	85	U S A	30	here
o	Glynn Gertrude A—†	85	housewife	57	"
P	Glynn Mary—†	85	"	25	Brookline
R	Glynn William A	85	U S A	32	here
s	Glynn William J	85	guard	58	"
T	Lord Kathleen—†	86	housewife	41	"
U	Lord Robert A	86	machinist	43	"
v	Dimick Nelson	87	salesman	52	"
w	Dimick Phyllis—†	87	housewife	51	"

Union Terrace

Y	Carroll Charles C	18	student	31	Holliston
z	Carroll Maryanna—†	18	housewife	22	N Hampshire
	1521				
A	Levy Jean—†	18	housewife	42	here
B	Levy Morris E	18	carpenter	50	"
D	Flaherty Anna L—†	21	buyer	53	"
E	Flaherty James F	21	policeman	49	"
F	Flaherty John M	21	plumber	50	"
G	*Saulite Caroline—†	22	housewife	81	"
H	*Saulite Jacob	22	retired	78	
K	Centorino Joseph	22	clerk	40	
M	Byrne Daniel J	29	engineer	48	"
N	Byrne Daniel J	29	clerk	23	
o	Byrne Mabel B—†	29	stenographer	20	"
P	Byrne Nellie B—†	29	housewife	45	"
R	Thomas Grace M—†	29	"	21	"
s	DellaSala Emilio	29	manager	54	"
T	DellaSala Emma—†	29	housewife	53	"
U	DellaSala Justine—†	29	attorney	48	"
v	DellaSala Justine—†	29	teacher	27	"
w	*DellaSala Theresa—†	29	housewife	84	"
x	Patterson Lorraine—†	29	"	23	
Y	Patterson Malcolm	29	chauffeur	29	"
	1522				
A	Sharpe William W	60	auditor	58	

Weld Hill Street

v	Donaghy George	6	engineer	48	here
w	Donaghy Sarah J—†	6	housewife	41	"

14

Weld Hill Street—Continued

x	O'Dowd Patrick J	6	guard	40	here
y	Williamson Anna—†	8	housewife	43	"
z	Williamson Archibald	8	guard	45	"
	1523					
a	Williamson William	8	clerk	21	
b	Bonito Frances M—†	12	housewife	27	"
c	Bonito Ralph J	12	welder	25	
d	Polcari Margaret—†	12	assembler	30	"
e	Cocozza Julia—†	12	housewife	27	"
f	Cocozza William B	12	fireman	29	
g	Romano Mary—†	12	clerk	31	
h	Murray Mary C—†	14	housewife	28	"
k	Murray William G	14	fireman	28	
l	Shea Flora M—†	14	social worker	34	"
m	Shea John F	14	clerk	33	
n	Shea Mary A—†	14	"	29	
o	Thompson Eleanor A—†	14	housewife	34	"
p	Thompson Thomas G	14	dentist	32	
r	Downey Alice C—†	16	housewife	65	"
s	Downey John J	16	retired	64	
t	Long Dorothy A—†	16	seamstress	35	"
u	Long Mary A—†	16	housewife	62	"
v	LaPenna Anthony	16	ironworker	30	"
w	LaPenna Lucy—†	16	housewife	28	"
x	Meyer Helen—†	18	"	44	
y	Meyer Paul	18	laborer	43	
z	Dicey Emery B	18	technician	24	"
	1524					
a	Schluter Henry J	18	starter	49	
b	Schluter Irene F—†	18	secretary	24	"
c	Schluter Marie—†	18	housewife	40	"
d	Sherlock Elizabeth—†	18	"	24	Nahant
e	Sherlock James F	18	laborer	24	Somerville
f	Brown Bradford A	20	retired	66	here
g	Brown Elizabeth G—†	20	housewife	64	"
h	Collings Edna—†	20	at home	44	"
k	Driscoll Ellen—†	20	housewife	72	"
l	Driscoll Michael J	20	engineer	40	"
m	Smith Bertha—†	20	clerk	52	
n	Smith Florence—†	20	at home	71	"
o	Zorn Grace M—†	24	housewife	23	92 Wenham
p	Zorn Melvin G	24	mechanic	26	92 "

15

Weld Hill Street—Continued

R	Brady Edward J	24	chauffeur	40	here
S	Brady Helen C—†	24	housewife	36	"
T	Donnelly Elizabeth—†	24	at home	79	"
U	Gorham Hamilton	26	operator	37	"
V	Gorham Helen M—†	26	housewife	32	"
W	Gillis Catherine E—†	26	"	34	
X	Gillis Frank R	26	engineer	38	"
Y	Hall Madeline N—†	26	beautician	30	Newton
Z	Rooney Alfred A	26	pipefitter	24	"
	1525				
A	Rooney Philip R	26	laborer	21	"
B	Benedetti John C	28	chauffeur	35	here
C	Benedetti Margaret—†	28	housewife	32	"
D	Butler Alice E—†	28	"	47	"
E	Butler Raymond	28	storekeeper	46	"
F	Battite Madeline—†	28	housewife	33	"
G	Battite Nicholas J	28	diemaker	35	"
H	LaRonde James S	28	accountant	35	"
K	LaRonde Jean—†	28	housewife	35	"
L	Bray James F	36	chef	37	33 Cobden
M	Bray Mary J—†	36	housewife	35	33 "
N	Kelly Eileen A—†	36	"	39	here
O	Kelly John F	36	engineer	44	"
P	Faulkner Annie—†	36	housewife	75	"
R	Faulkner Clarence A	36	metalworker	76	"
S	Pemberton Florence G—†	38	housewife	42	"
T	Pemberton Theodore	38	metalworker	43	"
U	Tanner Mauretta—†	38	housewife	32	"
V	Tanner Randolph H	38	carpenter	37	"
W	Callahan Ann L—†	38	housewife	28	"
X	Callahan George J	38	metalworker	32	"
Y	Adams Dorothy D—†	40	housewife	32	"
Z	Adams Frank B	40	operator	32	"
	1526				
A	Downey James G	40	student	21	"
B	Downey James J	40	merchant	51	"
C	Downey Katherine M—†	40	housewife	50	"
D	Sutton Mary E—†	40	stenographer	22	"
E	MacDonald Sarah—†	40	inspector	32	"
F	MacKay Frank	40	electrician	37	"
G	MacKay Hannah C—†	40	housewife	35	"
N	Stanton Margaret—†	44	at home	84	"

Weld Hill Street—Continued

H	Waters John H	44	laborer	54	here
K	Waters Marion R—†	44	secretary	20	"
L	Waters Mary E—†	44	housewife	54	"
M	Waters Richard J	44	student	23	
O	Cunningham Maude—†	44	housewife	38	"
P	Cunningham Myles L	44	policeman	44	"
R	Hassett Josephine H—†	44	stenographer	45	"
S	Hassett Walter R	44	salesman	45	"
T	Barnicle Mary A—†	48	housewife	64	"
U	Barnicle Peter	48	carpenter	66	"
V	Birmingham Katherine—†	48	at home	91	"
W	Neary Mary A—†	48	"	81	
X	Corcoran Bridget—†	48	housewife	64	"
Y	Corcoran John J	48	machinist	63	"
Z	Johnson Mary—†	48	bookkeeper	28	"
	1527				
A	Moynihan James J	50	operator	43	"
B	Moynihan Julia M—†	50	housewife	43	"
C	McGrath Joseph M	50	clerk	56	"
D	McGrath Margaret J—†	50	housewife	55	"
E	McGrath Thomas	50	laborer	26	"
F	Folsom Agnes—†	50	at home	77	
G	Kearin Harold J	50	machinist	52	"
H	Kearin Luella J—†	50	housewife	50	"
K	Farr Eva M—†	52	"	43	
L	Farr Glenn W	52	machinist	45	"
M	Dawson Sterling	52	laborer	48	New York
N	McNeil Christine S—†	52	housewife	45	here
O	McNeil Michael R	52	carpenter	45	"
P	Corcoran Helen—†	52	operator	56	"
R	Lang Charles	54	retired	91	"
S	Wisholm Gustava—†	54	housewife	79	"
U	Svenson Frances M—†	54	"	39	
T	Svenson George J	54	auditor	43	
V	McCarthy Lawrence J	54	chauffeur	30	"
W	Ferrie Daniel J	60	mechanic	57	"
X	Ferrie Mary A—†	60	housewife	55	"
Y	Ferrie Rita I—†	60	secretary	25	"
Z	Fallon Edward F	60	clerk	27	"
	1528				
A	Fallon John L	60	U S A	24	
B	Fallon Mary I—†	60	housewife	54	"

Weld Hill Street—Continued

c	Fallon William F	60	U S A	26	here
d	Dorman Rosemond—†	64	operator	55	"
e	Doyle Irene M—†	64	housewife	35	"
f	Doyle Maurice F	64	salesman	38	"
g	Glynn Muriel V—†	64	housewife	26	"
h	Glynn Paul E	64	manager	27	"
k	Perry Bertha—†	66	housewife	48	"
l	Perry Mabel A—†	66	welder	24	"
m	Perry Mary G—†	66	clerk	23	"
n	Perry Thomas	66	laborer	24	
o	Sheehan Anna—†	66	housewife	74	"
p	Sheehan Bartholomew	66	mechanic	37	"
r	Sheehan Jeremiah	66	retired	75	
s	Sheehan Margaret—†	66	housewife	35	"
t	Sayers Stanley P	68	blacksmith	57	"
u	Sayers Susan—†	68	housewife	49	"
w	Joyce Mary F—†	68	"	35	"
v	Joyce Thomas	68	shipfitter	38	"
x	Mahoney Bridie T—†	70	housewife	36	"
y	Mahoney Peter P	70	mechanic	42	"
z	Brown Catherine—†	70	housewife	37	"

1529

a	Brown Daniel	70	clerk	36	
b	Doherty Mary A—†	70	housewife	38	"
c	Doherty Phillip	70	operator	38	"
d	Kohler Anna M—†	74	housewife	27	"
e	Kohler John L	74	operator	36	"
f	Gerety Gertrude—†	74	housewife	29	"
g	Gerety John F	74	trainman	33	"
h	Russell Catherine—†	74	housewife	52	"
k	Hickey Barbara R—†	76	"	33	"
l	Hickey Roger J	76	buyer	40	
m	Brauneis Henry	76	shipfitter	43	"
n	Brauneis Lillian K—†	76	housewife	41	"

Woodlawn Street

o	Flint Frank	3	mechanic	22	here
p	Flint Helen—†	3	housewife	20	"
r	Meiggs Anna—†	3	"	46	"
s	Meiggs Edward	3	painter	58	

Woodlawn Street—Continued

Page.	Letter.	FULL NAME.	Residence, Jan. 1, 1946.	Occupation.	Supposed Age.	Reported Residence, Jan. 1, 1945. Street and Number.
	t	Deagle Charles	3	chauffeur	45	51 Woodlawn
	u	Deagle John		laborer	21	51 "
	v	Deagle Margaret—†		housewife	38	51 "
	w	Russell Evangeline—†		"	35	32 Bataan ct
	x	Russell Joseph A		shipper	48	32 "
	y	Donahue Bridget—†		housewife	53	here
	z	Donahue Francis	3	clerk	26	"
1530						
	a	*Nelson Martha—†	6	housewife	42	"
	b	Nelson Walter	6	shipfitter	44	"
	c	Dosch Albert E	6A	mechanic	49	"
	d	O'Neill Dennis	7	laborer	45	
	e	O'Neill Eleanor—†	7	housewife	37	"
	f	Ahern James F	8	meatcutter	50	"
	g	Ahern Nora—†	8	housewife	49	"
	h	Stevens Clyde	8	supervisor	30	65 Seymour
	k	Stevens Dorothy—†	8	housewife	21	here
	l	Arthur Frank E	8A	clerk	34	"
	m	Arthur Sarah M—†	8A	housewife	33	"
	n	Burke Joseph	8A	retired	73	"
	o	*Nelson Elsie A—†	8A	housewife	45	"
	p	Nelson Gustave A	8A	mechanic	46	"
	r	Bellew Agnes—†	9	at home	69	
	s	Callahan Evelyn—†	9	housekeeper	42	"
	t	Carmichael Mary—†	9	housewife	56	"
	u	Geoghegan Delia—†	9	domestic	55	"
	v	Kerle George	9	electrician	35	"
	w	Kerle Mary—†	9	housewife	29	"
	x	McNaught George W	11	policeman	47	"
	y	McNaught Marjorie—†	11	housewife	36	"
	z	Ollen Helen—†	11	"	61	
1531						
	a	Ollen Stanley	11	machinist	28	"
	b	Leary Esther—†	11½	housewife	44	Cambridge
	c	Leary John	11½	painter	48	"
	d	Leary Thomas	11½	laborer	21	"
	e	O'Leary Arthur J	12	"	35	here
	f	O'Leary Charles M	12	mechanic	71	"
	g	O'Leary Edward F	12	"	26	"
	h	O'Leary Mary A—†	12	housewife	59	"
	k	Bradley Sarah—†	12	domestic	56	"

Woodlawn Street—Continued

L	Saldwalk Elsie—†	12	secretary	35	here
M	Saldwalk Ernest	12	clerk	45	"
N	English Joseph E	14	calker	47	18 Weld Hill
O	English Margaret—†	14	housewife	80	18 "
P	English Mary M—†	14	operator	42	18 "
R	English William T	14	packer	34	18 "
S	Goode E Regina—†	14	nurse	23	here
T	Goode Gerard J	14	salesman	26	"
U	Goode James M	14	clerk	32	"
V	Goode Mary—†	14	housewife	66	"
W	Goode Owen	14	laborer	71	
X	Paul Rita K—†	14	WAC	28	
Y	Walsh Anna T—†	14	clerk	35	
Z	Walsh Ellen—†	14	housewife	70	"
	1532				
A	Walsh Mary K—†	14	stenographer	38	"
B	Driscoll Francis	15	bookkeeper	20	"
C	Driscoll John J	15	clerk	53	"
D	Driscoll Theresa M—†	15	housewife	53	"
E	Doucette Anne M—†	16	"	51	
F	Doucette George R	16	machinist	43	"
G	Hurley Elizabeth—†	16	housewife	46	"
H	Hurley Timothy	16	operator	48	"
K	Faul Elizabeth—†	16	at home	71	"
L	Megerditchian Anne—†	16	housewife	52	"
M	Megerditchian Ervant D	16	manager	53	"
N	Clarke Elizabeth—†	17	housewife	45	"
O	Clarke Thomas	17	mechanic	50	"
P	Corcoran Anna C—†	17	agent	41	
R	Corcoran Joseph	17	musician	21	"
S	Fleury Celestine	19	cook	62	
T	Fleury Elizabeth—†	19	stenographer	22	"
U	Fleury Joseph G	19	shipfitter	23	"
V	Fleury Julia A—†	19	housewife	56	"
W	Fleury Paul C	19	assembler	24	"
X	Fleury Robert M	19	student	20	
Y	Connors Catherine—†	19	housewife	43	"
Z	Connors James E	19	carpenter	45	"
	1533				
A	Connors James J	19	mechanic	20	"
B	Grenda Adele—†	19	housewife	27	"

Woödlawn Street—Continued

c	Grenda Adolf	19	fireman	29	here
d	Bradley Anna M—†	20	housewife	49	"
e	Bradley Lawrence H	20	policeman	52	"
f	Morris Ruth B—†	20	housewife	31	"
g	Morris Thomas F	20	operator	37	"
h	Irvine Clara—†	20	housewife	30	"
k	Irvine William J	20	operator	33	"
l	Delaney Mary C—†	25	housewife	35	"
m	Delaney Patrick J	25	custodian	39	"
n	Broderick Catherine—†	25	housewife	28	11 Bertson av
o	Broderick James E	25	U S N	22	here
p	Broderick Theresa—†	25	housewife	60	"
r	Broderick Theresa M—†	25	clerk	24	"
s	Broderick Thomas	25	metalworker	61	"
t	Broderick Thomas	25	policeman	37	11 Bertson av
u	Dunn Benedict	25	retired	90	here
v	Smith Bernice—†	25	housewife	43	"
w	Smith Ernest	25	custodian	44	"
x	Gourley Christine—†	27	housewife	47	"
y	Gourley John S	27	chauffeur	43	"
z	Dolan Ellen E—†	27	housewife	34	"
	1534				
a	Dolan Peter F	27	salesman	41	"
b	Dolan William	27	operator	36	"
c	Gilleo Catherine F—†	27	housewife	35	"
d	Gilleo John F	27	brakeman	39	"
e	Murray Eleanor N—†	29	clerk	37	
f	Murray Francis	29	student	21	"
g	Murray Mary—†	29	housewife	63	"
h	Murray Patrick	29	operator	59	"
k	Murray Ruth—†	29	nurse	25	
l	Regan Francis J	29	clerk	51	
m	Regan Julia—†	29	housewife	51	"
n	Allen Alexander	29	welder	22	
o	Allen Edith—†	29	housewife	56	"
p	Allen Elaine—†	29	bookkeeper	24	"
r	Fitzpatrick Blanche E—†	30	housewife	42	"
s	Fitzpatrick George A	30	salesman	50	"
t	Lonergan Susan E—†	30	at home	70	"
u	Noble Nellie—†	30	agent	46	
v	Backoff Doris N—†	30	housewife	32	"

Woodlawn Street—Continued

w	Backoff William E	30	electrician	38	here
x	Maloof Anna—†	31	housewife	50	"
y	Maloof Edward G	31	clerk	22	"
z	Maloof George	31	"	51	

1535

' A	Maloof Mary F—†	31	stenographer	25	"
B	Perry Sarah—†	31	housewife	23	"
c	Boudreau Frances—†	31	WAVE	21	..
D	Desmond Gerald F	31	U S N	20	
E	Desmond Jerome	31	janitor	55	"
F	Desmond John B	31	U S A	24	
G	Desmond Josephine—†	31	housewife	53	"
H	Desmond William	31	clerk	25	
K	Short John	31	U S A	29	
L	Short Lillian D—†	31	housewife	27	"
M	McCarthy Anne—†	32	"	34	
N	Pazeree Barbara—†	32	housekeeper	59	"
O	Pazeree Charles A	32	machinist	61	"
P	Ambrose Anna M—†	32	housewife	35	"
R	Ambrose Frank A	32	operator	35	"
s	Laverdiere Arthur	32	painter	25	
T	Strokes Sylvester S	32	meatcutter	40	"
U	McKennedy Cecelia—†	32	housewife	48	"
V	McKennedy John F	32	manager	45	"
w	McKennedy John F	32	clerk	23	
x	McKennedy June A—†	32	housewife	23	"
Y	O'Halloran Marion—†	34	"	29	
z	O'Halloran Michael	34	operator	31	"

1536

' A	Burke Elizabeth—†	34	housewife	26	"
B	Burke Joseph	34	tel worker	30	"
c	McCraw Henry	34	U S A	26	
D	McCraw Marie—†	34	clerk	24	
E	Nilson Annette—†	34	housewife	73	"
F	Nilson Ruth—†	34	secretary	35	"
G	Hernan Anna N—†	35	housewife	47	"
H	Hernan Elizabeth K—†	35	clerk	21	
K	Hernan James C	35	electrician	23	"
L	Hernan Mary V—†	35	packer	20	
M	Mullins Mary—†	37	housekeeper	50	"
N	Burke Anna—†	37	cashier	22	"

o	Burke Annie G—†	37	housewife	50	here
p	Burke Thomas	37	bellboy	24	"
r	Burke William	37	U S N	26	"
s	Mintz Elizabeth—†	38	housewife	35	"
t	Mintz Julius	38	operator	43	
v	Hough Everett F	38	painter	41	
w	Hough Mary F—†	38	housewife	35	"
x	Backman Ida—†	39	operator	46	"
y	Bayers Sophia—†	39	housewife	56	"
z	Fay Nellie—†	39	"	36	

1537

a	Fay Robert	39	attendant	35	"
b	Casey Helen A—†	40	housewife	75	"
c	Casey John	40	operator	37	
d	Casey Thomas	40	salesman	37	
e	Milton Sanfred	40	painter	43	
f	Milton Svea—†	40	housewife	38	"
g	Faustrum Fred	40	checker	46	
h	Faustrum Marie—†	40	housewife	46	"
k	Kelley Annie T—†	41	clerk	42	
l	Kelley James E	41	steamfitter	46	"
m	McCarthy Gertrude—†	42	housewife	20	"
n	Priesing Edwin	42	clerk	44	
o	Delbou Alfonso	44	guard	79	
p	Hoey Anne—†	44	housewife	32	"
r	Hoey Paul	44	packer	36	
s	Norton Catherine—†	44	housewife	39	"
t	Norton John	44	mechanic	43	"
u	Spears Eric	46	fireman	43	
v	Spears Nora—†	46	housewife	37	"
w	Malloy Dorothy E—†	46	"	40	
x	Malloy James P	46	plumber	50	
y	Gorman Ella M—†	47	housewife	64	"
z	Gorman James L	47	optician	22	

1538

a	Gorman Richard E	47	U S A	27	
b	Graney Carmen—†	47	housewife	31	"
c	Graney John	47	printer	35	
d	Collins Bridget—†	47	housewife	73	"
e	Collins Timothy A	47	mechanic	73	"
f	Collins William E	47	chauffeur	44	"

Woodlawn Street—Continued

G	Princiotta James	48	assembler	45	here
H	Princiotta Margaret—†	48	housewife	34	"
K	Wythe Margaret—†	48	housekeeper	56	"
L	Barkley Herbert	49	steward	47	"
M	Barkley Rosina—†	49	housewife	37	"
N	Buote Bertha—†	49	housekeeper	57	"
O	VanWart Leslie	49	machinist	46	"
P	Doherty Catherine—†	49	saleswoman	20	"
R	Doherty Charles	49	fireman	58	
S	Doherty Eleanor—†	49	clerk	29	"
T	Doherty Margaret—†	49	housewife	25	15 Perth
U	Doherty Michael	49	U S A	22	here
V	Doherty Owen	49	student	26	"
W	Doherty Roger	49	mechanic	27	"
X	Doherty Sarah—†	49	housewife	37	"
Y	Doherty Catherine F—†	49	clerk	24	
Z	Doherty John T	49	laborer	28	

1539

A	McLaughlin Mary—†	49	housewife	37	"
B	McLaughlin Patrick	49	chauffeur	41	"
C	Thuftedal Julia—†	51	housewife	31	32 Woodlawn
D	Thuftedal Ralph	51	laborer	25	32 "
E	O'Rourke Catherine—†	51	saleswoman	26	here
F	O'Rourke Charles	51	meter reader	28	"
G	Davis Jessie G—†	51	operator	48	25 Juniper
H	Davis Lillian—†	51	housewife	31	here
K	Davis Ralph W	51	chauffeur	30	"
L	Julius Glenda—†	52	housewife	20	2894 Wash'n
M	Julius Irene—†	52	"	38	2894 "
N	Julius Joseph C	52	painter	41	2894 "
O	Cawley Patrick	52	fireman	41	here
P	Cawley Winifred J—†	52	housewife	43	"
R	Gorman Ellen—†	52	"	35	2 Fountain sq
S	Atkins Kenneth	54	printer	35	here
T	*Atkins Sally—†	54	housewife	33	"
U	Hanney Joseph	54	meter reader	35	"
V	Hanney Margaret—†	54	housewife	41	"
W	Walsh George	54	U S A	21	
X	Murray George	54	salesman	41	"
Y	Murray Helen—†	54	housewife	39	"
Z	Nihill John	55	retired	65	

1540
Woodlawn Street—Continued

A	Nihill Margaret—†	55	housewife	60	here
B	Walsh Evelyn M—†	55	"	29	"
C	Walsh Michael F	55	clerk	29	Cambridge
D	Cunningham Harriet A—†	55	housewife	41	here
E	Cunningham Thomas F	55	shipper	40	"
F	McIntyre Albert V	55	guard	33	"
G	McIntyre Mary—†.	55	housewife	61	"
H	Sloane Mary E—†	55	operator	41	"
K	Steponkus Anna—†	56	housewife	53	"
L	Steponkus William P	56	machinist	25	"
M	Carney Charles W	56	laborer	42	
N	Carney Rose M—†	56	housewife	38	"
O	Dufour Alfred	56	retired	66	"
P	DiNapoli John F	56	shipfitter	36	"
R	DiNapoli Philomena M—†	56	housewife	36	"
S	O'Brien Margaret—†	59	housekeeper	66	"
T	Spruin William F	59	electrician	57	"
U	Wenners Edward B	59	salesman	29	47 Cohasset
V	Wenners Helen E—†	59	housewife	27	47 "
W	Noonan Clyde	59	usher	26	here
X	Noonan James B	59	clerk	62	"
Y	*Noonan Loretta—†	59	housewife	60	"
Z	Kerrigan Anna—†	59	"	38	

1541

A	Kerrigan Daniel	59	chauffeur	46	"
B	Callahan Bertha—†	60	housekeeper	38	"
C	Skrzyszowski Bernard	60	clerk	34	"
D	Skrzyszowski Frank	60	U S A	27	
E	Skrzyszowski Helen—†	60	shipfitter	23	"
F	Skrzyszowski Nellie—†	60	housewife	55	"
G	Skrzyszowski Stanley	60	operator	57	"
H	Collins Dorothy F—†	60	housewife	32	"
K	Farrell Carrie E—†	60	"	60	
L	Farrell Charles	60	printer	28	
M	Farrell Joseph	60	salesman	21	"
N	Farrell Raymond	60	U S A	23	
O	Farrell William A	60	attendant	59	"
P	Lavin Agnes—†	63	housewife	32	"
R	Lavin John P	63	operator .	36	"
S	O'Brien Helen C—†	63	housewife	28	"

Woodlawn Street—Continued

T	O'Brien William W	63	manager	33	here
U	Kearney Catherine—†	63	at home	66	"
V	Freiberger Lyle	64	rigger	30	12 Brookdale
W	Freiberger Mary—†	64	housewife	25	12 "
X	Maloney Joseph	64	operator	48	here
Y	Maloney Mary—†	64	housewife	46	"
Z	McDonald George	64	student	23	"

1542

A	Laing George	65	machinist	48	"
B	Laing Isabel J—†	65	housewife	47	"
C	Walsh Delia—†	65	"	55	
D	Walsh Francis	65	operator	30	"
E	Walsh Mary—†	65	housewife	23	"
F	Hourigan James	66	mechanic	38	"
G	Hourigan Margaret M—†	66	housewife	32	"
H	MacDonald Archie A	66	metalworker	58	"
K	Molloy Bessie—†	68	housewife	53	"
L	Molloy Mary—†	68	operator	32	"
M	Molloy Michael	68	fireman	68	
O	Engler Elizabeth E—†	69	housewife	69	"
P	Engler Mildred—†	69	nurse	36	"
R	Siegmund Dorothy—†	69	housewife	41	57 Wachusett
S	Siegmund Waldo O	69	painter	51	57 "
T	Cronin Catherine—†	69	housewife	64	here
U	Cronin William F	69	porter	60	"
V	Kirby Hannah M—†	70	housewife	68	"
W	Kirby Kathleen H—†	70	secretary	31	"
X	Garvey Helen T—†	72	housewife	46	"
Y	Garvey Patrick J	72	machinist	52	"
Z	Cashman Mildred—†	72	clerk	24	

1543

A	Kearney Daniel H	72	carpenter	54	"
B	Kearney Johanna T—†	72	housewife	54	"
C	Cunniff John T	74	U S A	23	
D	Cunniff Martin J	74	"	21	
E	Cunniff Mary E—†	74	housewife	50	"
F	Cunniff Michael	74	chauffeur	59	"
G	McLaughlin Catherine—†	76	housewife	44	"
H	McLaughlin Joseph	76	mechanic	48	"
K	Connolly Mary E—†	76	housewife	49	"
L	Connolly Mary E—†	76	stenographer	20	"

M	Connolly William J	76	U S A	22	here
N	Kirby Anna B—†	77	housewife	38	"
O	Kirby William	77	foreman	41	"
P	Birmingham Agnes—†	77	stenographer	48	"
R	Birmingham Phillip	77	U S A	24	::
S	Mehroff George	77	operator	28	
T	Mehroff Mary—†	77	housewife	30	"
U	Greene James F	78	laborer	24	
V	Greene John P	78	gardener	55	"
W	Greene Joseph W	78	chauffeur	25	"
X	Greene Mary—†	78	housewife	53	"
Y	Kilday Dennis	78	plumber	45	'
Z	Wagner Elsie V—†	78	housewife	55	"

1544

A	Wagner Helene—†	78	clerk	21	
B	Wagner William J	78	operator	54	
C	Kirkpatrick Doris E—†	78	housewife	33	"
D	Kirkpatrick Lemuel A	78	machinist	43	"
E	Brennan Claire F—†	80	WAVE	35	
F	Brennan Margaret J—†	80	secretary	42	
G	Conway Maurice B	83	retired	76	
H	Flynn Winifred S—†	83	housekeeper	54	"
K	Harrington James P	83	U S N	20	"
L	Harrington Mildred L—†	83	secretary	40	
M	Murphy Josephine—†	83	"	40	

Ward 11—Precinct 16

CITY OF BOSTON

LIST OF RESIDENTS
20 YEARS OF AGE AND OVER

(NON-CITIZENS INDICATED BY ASTERISK)
(FEMALES INDICATED BY DAGGER)

AS OF

JANUARY 1, 1946

THOMAS F. SULLIVAN, *Chairman*
FREDERIC E. DOWLING, *Secretary*
WILLIAM A. MOTLEY, JR.
ARTHUR V. COUGHLIN
EVERETT R. PROUT

Listing Board.

CITY OF BOSTON PRINTING DEPARTMENT

1600

Anson Street

Letter	Full Name	Residence	Occupation	Age	
A	Cunningham Loretta C—†	9	housewife	41	here
B	Cunningham William F	9	checker	45	"
C	Cain Patrick E	9	retired	80	"
D	Cunningham Catherine J—†	9	clerk	45	..
E	Cunningham Maria A—†	9	housewife	74	"
F	Cunningham Mary E—†	9	inspector	43	"
G	Wright Evelyn F—†	11–11A	housewife	33	. "
H	Wright John S	11–11A	checker	38	"
K	Miller Henry	11–11A	machinist	39	"
L	Miller Winifred A—†	11–11A	housewife	32	"
M	Dolan Catherine—†	11–11A	"	48	
N	Dolan Edward H	11–11A	laborer	21	"
O	Dolan Frederick	11–11A	chauffeur	50	"
P	Dolan Joseph J	11–11A	"	22	..
R	*Allen Catherine—†	12	housewife	54	"
S	Allen Samuel	12	metalworker	55	"
T	Dufresne Cora J—†	12	housewife	74	"
U	Dufresne Edward P	12	retired	80	
V	LaPointe Emma—†	12	housewife	72	"
W	Hoban Laura—†	12	clerk	24	
X	Hoban Paul	12	"	26	
Y	Knight Catherine F—†	13	housewife	54	"
Z	Knight Harold R	13	chauffeur	45	"

1601

Letter	Full Name	Residence	Occupation	Age	
A	Knight Harold W	13	clerk	21	
B	Getz Mildred B—†	13	housewife	31	"
C	Shea James R	13	chauffeur	25	"
D	Shea Mary J—†	13	housewife	52	"
E	Cash Anna—†	13	"	55	
F	Cash Roderick	13	fireman	55	
G	Monagle Bernard J	14	laborer	55	
H	Monagle Margaret M—†	14	housewife	60	"
K	Glennon Thomas	14	retired	80	
L	Keep Lucy—†	15	saleswoman	55	"
M	Parks Anna—†	15	decorator	21	"
N	Merritt Winifred C—†	15	operator	42	19 Highland av
O	Tileston William J	15	guard	52	here
P	Gardiner Elizabeth—†	16	housewife	64	"
R	Gardiner Hugh	16	retired	65	"
S	Gardiner Hugh, jr	16	welder	40	

Anson Street—Continued

T	Hurley Catherine—†	17	tel operator	23	4 Lester pl
U	Hurley Cecelia L—†	17	housewife	59	4 "
V	Hurley Marie—†	17	clerk	23	4 "
W	Fennell John J	17	guard	50	here
X	Fennell John J, jr	17	clerk	21	"
Y	Fennell Sarah E—†	17	housewife	49	"
Z	Edwards Catherine—†	18	"	71	

1602

A	Edwards Harold	18	clerk	32	
B	Murray Alice—†	18	"	45	
C	Murray Dorothy—†	18	"	21	
D	Lynch Catherine—†	18	housewife	36	"
E	Lynch Patrick J	18	laborer	44	
F	Dolan James J	19	chauffeur	49	"
G	Reardon Mary B—†	19	housewife	43	"
H	*Crawford Elizabeth—†	19	"	37	70 Brookside av
K	Crawford Henry A	19	guard	39	70 "

Arborway

P	Morgan Catherine—†	350	at home	81	here
R	Morgan James F	350	U S N	47	"
S	Henry Catherine—†	352	tel operator	58	1377 Centre
T	Molloy Louise—†	352	forewoman	56	1377 "
U	Powers Catherine L—†	352	housewife	27	1377 "
V	Powers John J	352	splicer	28	1377 "
W	Shaw Virginia—†	352	clerk	25	1377 "
X	Shaw Perley	352	U S A	26	160 Templeton
Y	Keenan Rose—†	354	housewife	60	here
Z	Keenan Thomas	354	mechanic	55	"

1603

A	Keenan Thomas J	354	U S N	24	"
B	Lawler Catherine—†	354	housewife	50	62 Jamaica
C	Lawler Mary C—†	354	secretary	22	62 "
D	Lawler Patrick J	354	guard	57	62 "
E	Lawler Robert	354	U S N	24	62 "
F	Lawler William	354	engineer	27	62 "
G	Hogarty Elizabeth—†	356	housewife	50	15 Orchard
H	Hogarty John J	356	U S M C	23	15 "
K	Hogarty Peter F	356	buyer	50	15 "
L	Hogarty William	356	clerk	21	15 "

Arborway—Continued

M	Cunningham Heloise—†	358	housewife	28	here
N	Cunningham Thomas E	358	clerk	32	Cambridge
O	Greer Beatrice L—†	358	secretary	41	here
P	Leveroni Edna M—†	358	manager	25	"
R	Leveroni Frank	358	attorney	66	"
S	Leveroni John	358	"	21	"
T	Leveroni Louise—†	358	housewife	65	"
U	Leveroni Vivian—†	358	clerk	32	"
V	Kelley Agnes M—†	360	at home	53	"
W	Kelley Eleanor B—†	360	housewife	30	"
X	Kelley Ferdinand T	360	agent	31	"
Y	Cronin Barbara J—†	362	housewife	23	139 Rowe
Z	Cronin Frank J	362	fireman	24	139 "

1604

A	McCarthy Alphonsus	362	clerk	51	139 "
B	McCarthy Dorothy A—†	362	housewife	47	139 "
C	McCarthy Edgar	362	U S N	21	139 "
D	Porcellini Carmela—†	362	at home	79	Natick
E	Kirby Cecelia R—†	364	stenographer	47	here
F	Kirby Mary A—†	364	at home	51	"
G	McMorrow John J	364	broker	46	"
H	McMorrow Margaret M–†	364	housewife	42	"
K	Fayle Charles H	366	retired	75	
L	Laughlin Grace M—†	366	clerk	24	
M	Laughlin June L—†	366	secretary	22	"
N	Laughlin Marion F—†	366	housewife	45	"
O	Laughlin Walter F	366	clerk	25	
P	Curry Madeline I—†	368	teacher	53	"
R	Curry Mary L—†	368	at home	64	"
S	Joyce Agnes—†	370	"	75	
T	Joyce Ellen F—†	370	"	67	
U	Kenney John T	370	clerk	34	
V	Kenney Mary—†	370	teacher	32	"
W	Mullen Thomas H	370	retired	74	
X	Reilly Charles A	374	supervisor	41	"
Y	Reilly Margaret J—†	374	housewife	40	"
Z	Sydeman Abraham	376	manufacturer	83	"

1605

A	Trimbach Laura—†	376	housekeeper	61	"
B	Cronin Dennis	384	fireman	30	Somerville
C	Cronin Florence—†	384	waitress	25	here

Arborway—Continued

D	Gildea Charles F	384	clerk	49	here
E	Gildea Joseph H	384	"	38	"
F	Gildea Josephine F—†	384	teacher	41	"
G	Gildea Mary—†	384	at home	54	
H	Gildea Winifred B—†	384	secretary	45	"
K	Robinson Leo	388	manager	38	"
L	Robinson Maurice	388	broker	35	
M	Robinson Robert	388	U S A	25	
N	Robinson Rose—†	388	housewife	71	"
O	Robinson Samuel	388	U S A	32	
P	Godfrey Catherine L—†	392	at home	56	
R	Godfrey Margaret E—†	392	"	61	
S	O'Brien Lois G—†	392	housewife	51	"

Hampstead Road

T	Dailey Katherine A—†	1	housewife	46	here
U	Dailey Marion T—†	1	secretary	20	"
V	Dailey William F	1	foreman	47	"
W	Fitzgerald Patrick	1	laborer	40	45 Whiting
X	Fitzgerald Sarah—†	1	housewife	38	45 "
Y	Fitzgerald Thomas	1	merchant	39	45 "
Z	Daly Edmond A	3	manager	43	here

1606

A	Daly Esther T—†	3	housewife	38	"
B	Fitzgerald James P	3	clerk	27	"
C	Fitzgerald Madeline R—†	3	housewife	28	"
D	McAuliffe Michael J	3	guard	49	
E	Walsh Helen F—†	3	housewife	59	"
F	Walsh John O	3	carpenter	56	"
G	Kelly Rita P—†	5	housewife	29	"
H	Kelly Thomas J, jr	5	contractor	33	"
K	Flanagan Mary J—†	7	housewife	70	"
L	Flanagan Mary J—†	7	secretary	32	"
M	Hines Bridget G—†	9	housewife	78	"
N	Hines Sarah—†	9	secretary	39	"
O	Hines William J	9	electrician	57	"
P	Fox Eleanor E—†	9	secretary	23	"
R	Fox Harry A	9	salesman	55	"
S	Fox Harry A, jr	9	foreman	31	
T	Fox Mary A—†	9	housewife	54	"

Hampstead Road—Continued

u	Fox Mary J—†	9	secretary	21	here
v	Fox Robert J	9	laborer	28	"
w	White Emily—†	14	housewife	47	"
x	White Shirley A—†	14	clerk	22	
y	Finan Helen J—†	14	teacher	34	"
z	Finan Helena J—†	14	housewife	63	"

1607

a	Finan Mary C—†	14	at home	35	"
b	Finan William D	14	U S N	29	
c	Finan William F	14	retired	73	
d	Rorke Mary A—†	15	housewife	46	"
e	Rorke Thomas H	15	clerk	64	
f	Lane Catherine E—†	15	housewife	43	"
g	Lane James M	15	clerk	52	
h	Clement Beatrice L—†	16	saleswoman	40	"
k	Clement Raymond	16	cutter	45	
l	Jackson Joseph J	16	salesman	55	"
m	Batic Marion L—†	16	housewife	36	"
n	Batic Michael L	16	floorlayer	48	"
p	Bittihoffer Catherine F—†	16	dietitian	55	"
o	Lydon James E	16	attorney	33	"
r	Bittihoffer Ann M—†	16	housewife	22	"
s	Bittihoffer Thomas	16	clerk	25	..
t	Harney Helen T—†	24	at home	43	"
u	Byrne Catherine F—†	24	"	74	..
v	Sullivan John J	24	retired	74	
w	Sullivan Mary E—†	24	housewife	58	"
x	Hutchinson Rita—†	27	clerk	29	
y	Kenny Bernard F	27	messenger	69	"
z	Kenny Katherine—†	27	housewife	68	"

1608

a	Kenny Mildred K—†	27	hygienist	30	"
b	Bourdeau Dorothy L—†	27	housewife	35	"
c	Bourdeau Edward	27	electrician	38	"
d	Puccio Daniel J	31	merchant	35	"
e	Puccio Genevieve—†	31	housewife	26	"
f	Moran Anna A—†	35	supervisor	44	..
g	Moran Annie A—†	35	housewife	80	"
h	McComish Mary J—†.	35	"	46	..
k	McComish William	35	electrician	46	"
l	Cohan Margaret M—†	36	examiner	40	..

6

Hampstead Road—Continued

m	Cohan Mary T—†	36	at home	75	here
n	Cohan Timothy F	36	letter carrier	46	"
o	Costello John M	36	retired	76	"
p	Costello Leo J	36	realtor	36	
r	Costello Mary J—†	36	housewife	75	"
s	Noonan William J	36	attorney	43	"
t	Hall Louis	37	fireman	61	
u	*Hall Ragnhild J—†	37	housewife	50	"
v	Arnold Edward F	37	U S A	23	
w	Arnold Eugene C	37	musician	49	"
x	Arnold Josephine M—†	37	housewife	49	"
y	Devlin Catherine—†	37	at home	70	
z	Devlin Catherine V—†	37	clerk	26	

1609

a	Devlin Daniel J	37		41	
b	Lynch Mary M—†	37	"	36	"
c	Souther Henry	39	retired	72	Hingham
d	Souther Margaret—†	39	housewife	72	"
e	Truitt Ernest L	39	engineer	40	here
f	Truitt Helen M—†	39	housewife	50	"
g	Hardy Thelma E—†	39	clerk	22	"
h	O'Donnell Leonard J	39	salesman	24	"
k	O'Donnell Margaret—†	39	housewife	26	Cambridge
l	O'Donnell Margaret F—†	39	"	46	here
m	O'Donnell Patrick R	39	salesman	26	"
n	Blaney Daniel J	39	supt	60	"
o	Blaney Daniel J, jr	39	U S N	25	..
p	Blaney James C	39	"	22	
r	*Blaney Matilda—†	39	housewife	61	"
s	Klueber Elizabeth M—†	40	"	58	..
t	Klueber Gertrude R—†	40	secretary	28	"
u	Klueber Joseph A	40	contractor	68	"
v	Feeney Delia—†	40	housewife	66	"
w	Feeney Mary R—†	40	social worker	32	"
x	Feeney William V	40	teacher	31	"
y	Bowen Bridget J—†	43	housewife	74	1 S Worthington
z	Bowen Catherine A—†	43	operator	36	1 "

1610

a	Bowen Edward C	43	clerk	35	1 "
b	Smolinsky Anna E—†	43	housewife	40	1 "
c	Smolinsky John P	43	chauffeur	39	1 "

Hampstead Road—Continued

D	Green Ann E—†	44	bookkeeper	48	here
E	Green John J	44	engineer	45	"
F	Green Mary E—†	44	saleswoman	50	"
G	Glennon Maria—†	44	housewife	70	"
H	Glennon Marie C—†	44	teacher	41	"
K	Glennon Thomas	44	retired	73	"
L	Stratton Helen F—†	47	housewife	52	"
M	Stratton Helen W—†	47	secretary	21	"
N	Stratton William A	47	assessor	53	"
O	Blomberg Alma C—†	47	at home	77	"
P	Blomberg Edith M—†	47	"	72	
R	Blomberg Emma M—†	47	clerk	74	
S	Blomberg Hilma L—†	47	at home	83	"
T	Francis Idabelle—†	47	housekeeper	68	"
U	Savage Laura—†	47	clerk	41	"
V	Lucas Joseph	48	fireman	28	128 O
W	Lucas Margaret M—†	48	housewife	26	128 "
X	Melaugh Katherine F—†	50	secretary	25	here
Y	Reardon Charles W	50	laborer	45	"
Z	Reardon Charles W, jr	50	electrician	23	"

1611

A	Reardon Mary M—†	50	housewife	45	"
B	Fogarty Mary C—†	51	agent	37	"
C	Mooney Martin J	51	clerk	50	"
D	Mooney Muriel P—†	51	housewife	29	"
E	Mooney William E	51	U S N	39	
F	Rau Avis D—†	51	housewife	41	"
G	Rau Ernest P	51	foreman	47	"
H	Rau John P	51	U S A	21	"
K	Keating Elizabeth P—†	52	housewife	68	"
L	Keating John J	52	retired	69	
M	Keating Marion E—†	52	secretary	44	"
N	Fitzgerald Elizabeth J—†	54	housewife	59	"
O	Fitzgerald John E	54	photographer	23	"
P	Fitzgerald Mary L—†	54	teacher	29	"
R	Fitzgerald Mortimer F	54	printer	62	
S	Shea Pauline F—†	56	teacher	44	
T	Ramsdell Catherine B—†	56	housewife	50	"
U	Ramsdell Catherine M—†	56	secretary	25	"
V	Ramsdell Robert W	56	merchant	52	"
W	Ramsdell Robert W, jr	56	U S A	21	"

Hampstead Road—Continued

	x	Roming Louis	59	clerk	58	here
	y	Roming Sophia—†	59	"	56	"
	z	Murray Helen—†	59	typist	41	"
1612						
	a	Murray Mary A—†	59	housewife	79	"
	b	Burke Agnes—†	59	"	56	
	c	Burke Athene—†	59	bookkeeper	29	"
	d	Peacock Deane S	60	teacher	52	"
	e	Peacock Eleanor L—†	60	housewife	25	"
	f	Peacock Ruth C—†	60	"	48	
	g	Gambon Andrew J	61	accountant	53	"
	h	Gambon Andrew J, jr	61	U S M C	20	"
	k	Gambon Christopher	61	retired	79	
	l	Gambon Christopher L	61	student	26	
	m	Gambon Margaret M—†	61	clerk	22	
	n	Gambon Nellie A—†	61	housewife	58	"
	o	Gambon Thomas P	61	clerk	24	
	p	O'Brien Mary F—†	61	housewife	45	"
	r	O'Brien William P	61	retired	75	"
	s	O'Brien William P, jr	61	druggist	47	"
	t	*Marshall Evelyn P—†	61	at home	74	"
	u	Marshall Joseph P	61	bartender	38	"
	v	Brown Catherine M—†	67	housewife	35	"
	w	Brown Gerald F	67	electroplater	35	"
	x	Reynolds Alice—†	67	clerk	35	63 Downer av
	y	Reynolds Eugene J	67	electrician	37	63 "
	z	Reynolds James D	67	retired	67	here
1613						
	a	McEachern Angeline T—†	71–73	housewife	32	"
	b	McEachern John B	71–73	salesman	32	"
	c	Leonard Ann—†	71–73	housewife	52	"
	d	Leonard Patrick	71–73	clerk	55	
	e	Leonard Patrick J	71–73	U S A	20	
	f	Moscone Claire M—†	75–77	housewife	39	"
	g	Moscone Fred J	75–77	attorney	45	"
	h	Glynn Annette T—†	75–77	operator	44	"
	k	Glynn Catherine V—†	75–77	"	42	
	l	Glynn John J	75–77	retired	80	
	m	Glynn Stephen P	75–77	clerk	40	
	n	Fischer Albert A	76	wigmaker	76	"
	o	Fischer Bertha A—†	76	housewife	73	"

9

Hampstead Road—Continued

P	Meany John W	79	supervisor	33	here
R	Meany Sarah J—†	79	housewife	33	"
S	Lembo Anthony	79	painter	27	13 Havre
T	Lembo Carmella—†	79	dressmaker	32	13 "
U*	Lembo Michael	79	dairyman	65	13 "
V	Lembo Nancy—†	79	stitcher	28	13 "
W	Lembo Philomena—†	79	housewife	65	13 "

Rosemary Street

X	Bryant Edward	7	clerk	40	here
Y	Hafey Katherine—†	7	housewife	75	"
Z	McIsaac Mary—†	7	housekeeper	66	"
	1614				
A	Tileston Margaret—†	7	matron	65	
B	MacDonald Ellen J—†	9	housewife	73	"
C	MacDougall Frederick	9	salesman	46	"
D	MacDougall Mary P—†	9	secretary	45	"
E	Cain Ann—†	11	housewife	32	"
F	Ginty Anthony	11	stevedore	62	"
G	Ginty Margaret T—†	11	housewife	60	"
H	Fallon Anna C—†	15	"	35	
K	Fallon Patrick	15	brewer	36	
L	Reilly Alice M—†	15	secretary	42	"
M	Reilly John J	15	brewer	42	"
N	Dalton Edward G	17	bartender	43	"
O	Dalton Margaret M—†	17	corsetiere	42	"
P	McCarthy Anna E—†	17	teacher	35	"
R	McCarthy Elizabeth A—†	17	dietitian	25	"
S	McCarthy Helen J—†	17	teacher	32	"
T	McCarthy Joseph T	17	salesman	30	"
U	McCarthy Julia A—†	17	housewife	70	"
V	McCarthy Margaret E—†	17	stenographer	39	"
W	McCarthy Mary F—†	17	"	43	"
X	Woodard Marie E—†	19	housewife	40	17 Hillside
Y	Woodard Montague W	19	chauffeur	40	17 "
Z*	Keneavy Agnes T—†	19	housewife	47	here
	1615				
A*	Keneavy Martin J	19	laborer	51	
B	Moore James J	19	"	55	

Rosemary Street—Continued

c	*LaBonte Anna S—†	19	housekeeper	43	10 Boynton
d	Tremble Matthew R	21	mortician	29	here
e	Tremble Natalie R—†	21	housewife	30	"
f	McCabe Francis	21	rigger	47	"
g	McCabe Mary A—†	21	housewife	44	"
h	Haveron Bridget—†	25	"	58	
k	McLaughlin Joseph	25	laborer	45	"
l	McLaughlin Theresa—†	25	clerk	22	
m	Dolan Lillian A—†	25	"	22	
n	Dolan Lillian V—†	25	housewife	48	"
o	Dolan Thomas E	25	U S N	20	"
p	Dolan Thomas F	25	fireman	50	"
r	Green Anna H—†	27	housewife	49	"
s	Green Joseph	27	engineer	48	"
t	Hurley Helen L—†	27	housewife	30	20 Smith
u	Hurley William J	27	operator	31	20 "
v	*Walsh Kathleen—†	27	housewife	51	here
w	Cole Celia—†	29	"	48	"
x	Cole John J	29	laborer	55	"
y	Maloney Elizabeth M—†	29	housewife	51	9 Hall
z	Neale Frances S—†	29	"	57	here

1616

a	Neale Walter F	29	policeman	65	"
b	Neale Walter F, jr	29	U S A	23	
g	McDonald Gertrude C—†	33–35	housewife	32	"
c	McDonald Harold J	33–35	salesman	38	"
d	Barrett Sarah—†	33–35	housewife	80	"
e	McGinnis Francis J	33–35	chauffeur	52	"
f	Nash John	33–35	laborer	65	
h	Roche Catherine A—†	33–35	domestic	50	"
k	Roche Virginia E—†	33–35	"	25	

Saint Mark Street

m	Baird Euphemia—†	7	housewife	45	here
n	Baird James	7	student	21	"
o	Baird William	7	milkman	47	"
p	Arena Amelia—†	9	housewife	53	"
r	Arena Liborio	9	barber	63	
s	Arena Santo L	9	U S A	20	

Saint Rose Street

T	Daly Mary—†	5	housewife	52	here
U	Daly Parker	5	laborer	68	"
V	*Twohig Elizabeth—†	5	clerk	42	"
W	Twohig Mary—†	5	waitress	40	"
X	Bartsch Gustav E	10–12	driller	52	
Y	Bartsch Mary F—†	10–12	housewife	51	"
Z	Kelley Elizabeth A—†	10–12	"	42	

1617

A	Kelley William H	10–12	engineer	44	"
B	Rochefort Arthur	10–12	student	21	"
C	Rochefort Helen T—†	10–12	housewife	49	"
D	Rochefort Henry C	10–12	mechanic	52	"
E	Rochefort Mary C—†	10–12	student	27	"
F	Fleming Delia A—†	14–16	housewife	75	"
G	Fleming James	14–16	cutter	41	
H	Fleming Lillian F—†	14–16	bookkeeper	32	"
K	Fleming Mary A—†	14–16	manager	50	"
L	Brooks Delia J—†	14–16	housewife	63	"
M	Brooks James B	14–16	machinist	40	"
N	Brooks Mary F—†	14–16	clerk	30	"
O	Meade Gertrude—†	14–16	WAVE	32	
P	Crowell Margaret M-†	14–16	housewife	65	"
R	Crowell Mary E—†	14–16	clerk	29	"
S	Crowell Michael F	14–16	operator	67	"
T	Mitchell Eleanor M—†	18–20	clerk	23	"
U	Mullaney Dorothea B-†	18–20	secretary	21	"
V	Mullaney Lillian M—†	18–20	housewife	53	"
W	Groggett Bessie H—†	18–20	"	38	
X	Groggett Richard W	18–20	mechanic	41	"
Y	Normoyle Cornelius A	18–20	clerk	62	"
Z	Normoyle Cornelius A, jr	18–20	electrician	24	"

1618

A	Bartsch Joseph E	18–20	mechanic	26	"
B	Bartsch Margaret M—†	18–20	housewife	26	"
C	Cronin Catherine T—†	22–24	"	62	
D	Cronin Joseph F	22–24	salesman	31	"
E	Cronin Mary M—†	22–24	clerk	25	"
F	Hopey Evelyn G—†	22–24	at home	35	28 Beecher
G	Carey Gertrude—†	22–24	housewife	42	here
H	Carey John J	22–24	policeman	46	"
K	Carey Virginia M—†	22–24	clerk	22	"
L	Sullivan Annie—†	22–24	housewife	75	"

Saint Rose Street—Continued

M	Sullivan Margaret R—†	22–24	inspector	44	here
N	O'Leary Eleanor—†	22–24	housewife	45	"
O	O'Leary Thomas J	22–24	shipfitter	44	"
P	Harrington Catherine A—†	26–28	housewife	61	"
R	Harrington James F	26–28	guard	28	
S	Harrington John	26–28	operator	60	"
T	Callahan James A	26–28	teacher	27	
U	Callahan James J	26–28	inspector	60	"
V	Callahan Louise—†	26–28	housewife	48	"
W	Powers Robert	26–28	retired	69	
X	Cohane Mary—†	26–28	at home	74	
Y	Reynolds Catherine—†	26–28	housewife	37	"
Z	Reynolds John J	26–28	salesman	40	"
	1619				
A	Kelly Paul R	30–32	printer	33	
B	Kelly Veronica—†	30–32	housewife	33	"
C	Kelly Catherine—†	30–32	clerk	48	
D	Kelly Mary E—†	30–32	"	49	
E	Kelly Patrick	30–32	guard	42	
F	Fairbanks Agnes V—†	30–32	secretary	24	"
G	Quinn Annie K—†	30–32	housewife	62	"
H	Quinn Edward	30–32	retired	64	"
K	Quinn Francis M	30–32	U S N	29	
L	Nixon Annie—†	34–36	housewife	61	"
M	Nixon Catherine—†	34–36	clerk	31	
N	Nixon Edward	34–36	chauffeur	30	"
O	Nixon John J	34–36	guard	65	"
P	Hanberry Catherine R–†	34–36	housewife	25	58 Forest Hills
R	Hanberry John W	34–36	salesman	27	here
S	Hanberry Mary C—†	34–36	housewife	52	"
T	Hanberry William F	34–36	policeman	52	"
U	Joyce Francis T	34–36	clerk	28	101 Sydney
V	Joyce Mary R—†	34–36	"	24	here
W	Horan Mary—†	34–36	housewife	68	"
X	Horan Patrick J	34–36	retired	67	"
Y	Kilroy Edward	38	clerk	38	
Z	Kilroy Marion—†	38	housewife	28	"
	1620				
A	Harrington Catherine—†	38	"	35	
B	Harrington John	38	mechanic	42	"
C	McGraw Lucy M—†	42	housewife	54	"

Page.	Letter.	FULL NAME.	Residence, Jan. 1, 1946.	Occupation.	Supposed Age.	Reported Residence, Jan. 1, 1945. Street and Number.

Saint Rose Street—Continued

D	McGraw Margaret—†	42	operator	52	here
E	Owens Helen R—†	46	housewife	32	163 South
F	Owens John J	46	operator	46	163 "
G	Greaney Joseph L	48	clerk	35	here
H	Keough John	48	fireman	48	49 Saint Rose
K	Keough Nora—†	48	housewife	48	49 "
L	Kilroy Thomas E	48	laborer	26	49 "
M	Mitchell Ethel—†	50	housewife	50	here
N	Mitchell William D	50	welder	48	"
O	Lynch David W	50	retired	70	"
P	Lynch Elinor M—†	50	clerk	32	
R	Lynch Helen T—†	50	housewife	65	"
S	Rohan Kathleen M—†	50	"	28	
T	Hutton Helen—†	54		57	
U	Hutton Helen—†	54	clerk	31	
V	Hutton John	54	operator	58	"
W	Hutton John	54	U S A	29	
Y	Carroll Joseph B	62	clerk	33	
Z	Carroll Margaret F—†	62	housewife	34	"
	1621				
A	Bridges Ellen F—†	62	"	80	
B	Bridges Michael	62	mechanic	85	"
C	George Evelyn—†	62	domestic	46	Melrose
D	Carroll Mary E—†	62	at home	65	here
E	Downey Eileen—†	62	housewife	28	19 Goldsmith
F	Downey Francis V	62	decorator	30	19 "
G	Morton Anna C—†	62	at home	61	here
H	Kelly Charles T	66	technician	24	590 Park
K	Kelly Florence S—†	66	housewife	21	590 "
L	Kelly Eileen—†	66	"	34	here
M	Kelly Patrick	66	·clerk	35	"
N	Huber Ann G—†	70	housewife	42	"
O	Huber John A	70	chauffeur	47	"
P	Murray Edward	70	laborer	34	
R	Babb Charles	70	machinist	47	"
S	Babb Mabel—†	70	housewife	46	"
T	Foran Phyllis—†	70	"	21	
U	Foran William	70	machinist	23	"
V	Legere Lawrence	74	guard	22	Hingham
W	Legere Marion E—†	74	housewife	20	Pennsylvania
X	Campbell Alice J—†	74	"	30	here

Saint Rose Street—Continued

Y	Campbell Francis A	74	salesman	30	here	
Z	Tilley Arthur	74	machinist	29	"	

1622

A	Tilley Lorraine—†	74	housewife	26	"	
B	Sasche Emily J—†	78	clerk	42		
C	Sasche Walter	78	accountant	52	"	
D	Walsh Margaret J—†	78	at home	64	"	
E	McIntyre Russell E	78	foreman	52	"	
F	McIntyre Winifred—†	78	housewife	51	"	
G	Maguire James H	82	salesman	41	"	
H	Maguire Madeline G—†	82	housewife	38	"	
K	O'Brien Francis A	82	U S N	22		
L	O'Brien Marie H—†	82	housewife	54	"	
M	McCarthy Charles J	94	painter	39	"	
N	McCarthy Nora—†	94	housewife	35	"	
O	Young Elizabeth H—†	98	"	46		
P	Young Harold E	98	agent	42	"	
R	Stevens Emma—†	98	housewife	43	Worcester	
S	Stevens Lionel A	98	mechanic	43	"	
T	Powers Edward F	98	clerk	33	here	
U	Powers Frances V—†	98	housewife	29	"	

South Street

W	Leonard Albert F	133	shipper	62	here	
X	Leonard Elizabeth—†	133	housewife	59	"	
Y	Morris John F	133	janitor	62	"	
Z	Trainor Mathew J	133	clerk	33		

1623

A	Greeley Claire—†	141	at home	40	"	
B	Evans George	141	checker	44	37 Boynton	
C	Evans Sally—†	141	housewife	43	37 "	
D	Connare Catherine—†	141	"	28	here	
E	Connare James	141	printer	28	"	
F	Mullen Bridget M—†	145	housewife	52	"	
G	Mullen Peter	145	laborer	53	"	
H	Flynn Annie—†	145	at home	73	"	
K	Riley Annie T—†	145	"	57	78 Tower	
L	Aldridge Byron	145	technician	27	here	
M	Aldridge Mary—†	145	clerk	24	"	
N	Diggins John	145	janitor	63	"	

South Street—Continued

o	Diggins Joseph	145	chauffeur	25	here
p	Diggins Julia—†	145	laundress	32	"
r	Whelton Eleanor—†	145	stenographer	32	"
s	Logue Catherine—†	149	housewife	44	38 Custer
t	Logue Edward	149	chauffeur	40	38 "
u	Gately John K	149	U S A	20	New York
v	Gately Margaret—†	149	teacher	22	here
w	Gately Margaret C—†	149	housewife	50	"
x	Gately Thomas L	149	repairman	55	"
y	Clancy Helen—†	149	stenographer	32	"
z	Clancy Joseph P	149	clerk	46	"

1624

a	Clancy Mary—†	149	housewife	74	"
b	LeVie Forrest	153	U S A	33	"
c	LeVie Frances—†	153	housewife	33	"
d	McArdle Ellen—†	153	operator	50	"
e	Mullen Helen—†	153	at home	71	"
f	Corson Elizabeth—†	153	housewife	49	"
g	Corson Herbert	153	salesman	24	"
h	Corson Leroy	153	U S A	28	
k	Weintraub Abraham D	159	physician	33	"
l	Weintraub Mildred—†	159	housewife	29	"
m	Waible Hilda T—†	159	"	44	
n	Waible Leo J	159	salesman	50	"
o	Favalore Anna—†	159	at home	49	"
p	Hamrock Edward	159	clerk	32	"
r	McGee Mary—†	159	"	54	
s	McGee Terrance T	159	"	41	
t	McGee William C	159	"	39	
u	Greeley Mary E—†	159	housewife	85	"
v	Greeley Thomas F	159	salesman	64	"
w	Coady David J, jr	159	technician	35	"
x	Coady Evelyn—†	159	salesman	35	"
y	Cruickshank Alice—†	161	stenographer	25	"
z	Cruickshank James	161	electrician	30	"

1625

a	Barry Mary A—†	161	stenographer	63	"
b	Gaddis Delia—†	161	waitress	65	"
c	Gaddis Margaret—†	161	housewife	62	"
d	Murray Anne—†	161	housekeeper	63	"
e	O'Neill John J	161	accountant	22	"

South Street—Continued

		FULL NAME.	Residence	Occupation	Age	Reported Residence
	F	O'Neill Margaret—†	161	housewife	48	here
	G	Dwyer Arthur	161	musician	30	"
	H	Dwyer Theresa—†	161	housewife	65	"
	L	Luppold Bernard	161	cutter	62	
	M	Luppold Katherine F—†	161	housewife	60	"
	O	Nolan James J	163	draftsman	29	"
	P	Nolan Priscilla A—†	163	housewife	25	"
	R	Roche Christine A—†	163	"	40	
	S	Roche James L	163	inspector	39	"
	T	Duff Jemima—†	163	housewife	45	"
	U	Duff William G	163	meatcutter	44	"
	V	Foley Michael	163	porter	60	
	W	Foley Nellie J—†	163	housewife	55	"
	X	Cotter James	163	clerk	40	
	Y	Cotter Margaret—†	163	housewife	40	"
	Z	Swanborn Edwin	163	machinist	35	46 St Rose
1626						
	A	Swanborn Jean—†	163	housewife	30	46 "
	C	Downing Charles D	165	retired	28	here
	D	Downing Delia E—†	165	housewife	58	"
	E	Downing John T	165	technician	29	150 South
	F	Smith Anna G—†	165	cashier	35	here
	G	Smith Walter J	165	mechanic	50	"
	H	McKeown Daniel	165	laborer	73	"
	K	McKeown Mary—†	165	housewife	73	"
	L	McKeown Phillip	165	bookkeeper	41	"
	M	Mace Minnie—†	165	housewife	76	"
	N	Mace Norman F	165	operator	38	"
	O	Moroney John E	165	machinist	39	"
	P	Moroney Theresa E—†	165	clerk	39	
	R	O'Neill Daniel J	165	mechanic	41	"
	T	Flynn Margaret M—†	165	housewife	38	"
	S	Flynn Margaret T—†	165	at home	84	
	U	Flynn William H	165	technician	44	"
	Y	Dillon Melvin J	171	electrician	60	"
	Z	Dillon Sarah—†	171	at home	83	
1627						
	A	McFarland John	171	milkman	55	"
	C	Smith Carl F	185	printer	38	
	D	Smith Helen—†	185	stenographer	38	"
	E	Cheesman John	185	fisherman	50	"

South Street—Continued

	Letter	Full Name	Res.	Occupation	Age	Reported Residence
	F	Cheesman Mary E—†	185	housewife	48	here
	G	*Walker Alfred	185	operator	65	"
	H	*Walker Catherine—†	185	housewife	66	"
	K	Maier Amy G—†	185	"	45	
	L	Maier Harry T	185	salesman	47	"
	M	Morgan Anne G—†	185	housewife	58	"
	N	Morgan Helen G—†	185	teacher	51	
	O	Walker Thomas	185	salesman	40	"
	P	Thompson Catherine M—†	190	housewife	43	"
	R	Thompson Edward G	190	buyer	40	
	S	McCarthy Margaret E—†	190	housewife	37	"
	T	McCarthy William J	190	machinist	40	"
	U	Barry Gertrude L—†	190	housewife	51	"
	V	Barry Joseph P	190	clerk	54	
	W	Lawson Marie E—†	190	housewife	29	"
	X	Lawson Robert A	190	U S A	27	
	Y	Mudge Margaret—†	195	packer	34	
	Z	O'Hara Mary—†	195	"	36	
1628						
	A	Kelly Henry A	195	retired	79	
	B	Kelly Mary F—†	195	housewife	75	"
	C	Hogan Christine M—†	195	"	52	..
	D	Hogan James W	195	shipper	36	
	E	Hogan Thomas	195	secretary	63	"
	F	Larson Gustav F	195	foreman	41	"
	G	Larson Lillian A—†	195	housewife	40	"
	H	Collins Dennis J	195	laborer	54	
	K	Collins Helen M—†	195	clerk	32	
	L	Collins Patrick W	195	laborer	56	
	M	Golden Dorothy J—†	195	clerk	32	
	N	Morrison Edna L—†	195	tel operator	32	"
	O	Morrison Elise—†	195	housewife	63	"
	P	Morrison James	195	operator	67	"
	R	Dolan Catherine J—†	196	at home	70	"
	S	Ging Cecelia E—†	196	clerk	48	
	T	Ging John J	196	letter carrier	50	"
	U	Purtell Anna A—†	196	secretary	44	"
	V	Thompson John J	196	fireman	67	"
	W	Thompson Mary J—†	196	tel operator	38	"
	X	Thompson Theresa F—†	196	bookkeeper	33	"
	Y	Thompson Theresa M—†	196	housewife	65	"

z	LeStrange Thomas P	198	clerk	50	here

1629

A	McIntyre John J	198	longshoreman	39	"
B	McIntyre Margaret F—†	198	bookkeeper	45	"
c	Kenney Catherine M—†	198	housewife	53	"
D	Kenney Dennis F	198	chauffeur	55	"
E	Hines Edward J	198	laborer	24	
F	Hines John J	198	repairman	48	"
G	Hines Mary C—†	198	housewife	48	"
H	Wittig Carl L	199	supt	56	
K	Wittig Marjorie—†	199	housewife	53	"
L	Geary Inez M—†	199	waitress	47	
M	Geary Martin J	199	electrician	51	"
N	Moody Irwin R	199	machinist	23	"
o	Moody Mary A—†	199	bookkeeper	29	"
P	Moody Wesley P	199	clerk	30	69 Robeson
R	Garrity M Edith—†	199	housewife	35	here
s	Garrity Thomas	199	foreman	46	"
T	O'Brien Frederick J	199	machinist	28	"
U	O'Brien Margaret J—†	199	cashier	48	
v	Noonan Eileen—†	199	clerk	49	
w	Noonan Theresa—†	199	"	45	
x	Smith Frederick	199	inspector	65	"
Y	Smith Gertrude—†	199	housewife	55	"
z	Lavin Margaret M—†	200	secretary	26	"

1630

A	McCormack Frederick W	200	carpenter	22	"
B	McCormack Nora A—†	200	housewife	51	"
c	McCormack Patrick J	200	operator	63	"
D	Connaughton John J	200	gardener	58	"
E	Connaughton Katherine—†	200	housewife	48	"
F	Potter Dorothy R—†	200	"	39	"
G	Potter William E	200	guard	37	
H	Barrett Margaret—†	202	housewife	40	"
K	Barrett Patrick M	202	printer	44	
L	Linehan Anna M—†	202	housewife	43	"
M	Linehan John J	202	merchant	44	"
N	Morris Catherine N—†	202	housewife	39	"
o	Morris Eugene J	202	operator	40	"
o¹	Hunter Ann S—†	204	housewife	58	"
P	Hunter John	204	printer	66	

South Street—Continued

R	Hunter John, jr	204	printer	30	here
S	Blume Helen M—†	204	housewife	34	"
T	Blume John J	204	pressman	37	"
U	Callahan John F	204	bookbinder	30	New Jersey
V*	Daly Daniel F	204	laborer	70	here
W	Daly Daniel F	204	"	24	"
X	Harrington Daniel J	204	gardener	74	"
Y	Harrington Margaret M—†	204	housewife	64	"
Z	Harrington Mary A—†	204	tel operator	24	"

1631

B	Morgan Catherine—†	206	housewife	65	"
C	Morgan Michael	206	guard	67	
D	Morgan William M	206	plumber	26	"
E	Brennan Mary—†	206	housewife	33	"
F	Brennan Phillip	206	chauffeur	35	"
G	Morgan Helen—†	206	housewife	32	"
H	Morgan Lawrence	206	milkman	34	"
L	Healy Elizabeth—†	211	housewife	32	"
M	Healy Martin F	211	clerk	38	
N	Morrissey Mary—†	211	at home	36	"
O	Doherty Bridget—†	211	housewife	39	"
P	Doherty William	211	electrician	36	"
R	McCaffrey Catherine S—†	212	housewife	81	"
S	McCaffrey Sarah C—†	212	tel operator	48	"
T	Hawkins Catherine J—†	212	housewife	51	"
U	Hawkins Patrick J	212	operator	52	"
V	Hawkins Patrick J, jr	212	chauffeur	26	"
W	Hawkins Theresa K—†	212	tel operator	21	"
X	McMahon Helen—†	214	housewife	36	"
Y	McMahon Leo J	214	foreman	45	"
Z	Foley Bridget M—†	214	housewife	60	"

1632

A	Foley Edward F	214	electrician	27	"
B	Foley Timothy J	214	merchant	60	"
C	Ahearn Eleanor M—†	214	clerk	27	
D	Ahearn Marguerite T—†	214	housewife	51	"
F	Maroney Anna—†	215	at home	38	217 South
G	Roche Evelyn—†	215	operator	33	here
H	Famelitis Gloria—†	217	housewife	29	25 Queensberry
K*	Famelitis Nicholas	217	mechanic	39	25 "
L	Hemeon Helen—†	217	housewife	49	here

M	Hemeon Ralph	217	U S A	28	here
N	Hutchinson Catherine—†	217	housewife	42	"
O	Hutchinson James	217	clerk	21	"
P	Hutchinson Michael	217	porter	50	
R	Connolly Mary J—†	218–230	clerk	39	
S	Connolly Peter A	218–230	retired	73	
T	Connolly Thomas F	218–230	laborer	32	
U	Lund Marie D—†	218 230	cashier	39	
V	Keeley Catherine—†	218–230	at home	72	
W	Norton Catherine C-†	218–230	housewife	38	"
X	Norton Kenneth E	218–230	clerk	37	
Y	Lockhart Lina M—†	218–230	nurse	56	
Z	Wesley Sarah A—†	218–230	at home	79	..
	1633				
A	Adams Anna F—†	218–230	housewife	65	"
B	Adams Grace E—†	218–230	secretary	34	"
C	Calnan Anna—†	218–230	teacher	62	"
D	Calnan Gertrude—†	218–230	clerk	60	"
E	Fullerton Bertha H-†	218–230	at home	68	"
F	Mullen Mary T—†	218–230	"	52	78 Orchard
G	Lamb Frances C—†	218–230	teacher	58	here
H	McLellan Grace G—†	218–230	housewife	75	"
K	McLellan Herbert S	218–230	engineer	55	"
L	McDermott Bridget A—†	218–230	at home	62	..
M	McFadden George A	218–230	letter carrier	36	"
N	Hartung Crescentia B—†	218–230	at home	69	"
O	Ottiano Centa G—†	218–230	housewife	49	"
P	Ottiano James	218–230	engineer	49	"
R	Clifford Agnes A—†	218–230	housewife	40	"
S	Clifford Charles H	218–230	salesman	50	"
T	Faulkner James M	218–230	guard	41	
U	Faulkner Leonora—†	218–230	clerk	39	
V	Hill Louise—†	218–230	"	34	
W	Patterson Mabel—†	218–230	"	34	"
X	Vasin George B	218–230	U S A	30	287 Summit av
Y	Vasin Ruth—†	218–230	housewife	30	287 "
Z	Bowes John S	218–230	teacher	26	here
	1634				
A	Bowes Katherine—†	218–230	housewife	25	"
B	Bowes Mary E—†	218–230	"	68	
C	Gleason Margaret T-†	218–230	waitress	55	

South Street—Continued

D	Gleason Nora F—†	218–230	waitress	61	here
E	Shaw Roderick N	218–230	clerk	59	"
F	Shaw Sadie R—†	218–230	housewife	53	"
G	Chase Ivy B—†	218–230	nurse	48	
H	Falt Gertrude H—†	218–230	teacher	40	"
K	McGinnis Ellen A-†	218–230	housewife	54	"
L	McGinnis Patrick	218–230	operator	53	"
M	Kennedy Alice—†	218–230	housewife	42	"
N	Kennedy Thomas	218–230	policeman	44	"
O	Moore Esther—†	218–230	forewoman	47	"
P	Hobart Estelle—†	218–230	"	44	"
R	Pomner Gertrude A-†	218–230	at home	64	"
S	Pomner Harriet S—†	218–230	clerk	55	"
T	Nealey Marion F—†	218–230	housewife	40	S Acton
U	Nealey Ronald	218–230	engineer	40	here
V	Rogers Marie—†	218–230	clerk	31	"
W	MacKay Charles	218–230	supt	61	"
X	MacKay Minnie L-†	218–230	housewife	54	"
Y	Canfield Mabel M-†	218–230	nurse	50	
Z	Sheridan Abbie B—†	218–230	"	50	

1635

A	Keigher John	218–230	machinist	48	"
B	Keigher Margaret—†	218–230	housewife	42	"
C	MacDonald Mary L—†	218–230	social worker	53	"
D	Norton David	218–230	retired	55	
E	Norton Mary F—†	218–230	stenographer	47	"
F	Seymour Mildred E-†	218–230	secretary	30	30 Turner
G	Seymour Paul E	218–230	agent	39	30 "
H	McCann Joseph	218–230	U S A	27	here
K	McCann Rose—†	218–230	buyer	48	"
L	McTernan Alice—†	218–230	bookkeeper	35	"
M	McTernan Mary A-†	218–230	housewife	70	"
N	Killeen Catherine—†	218–230	clerk	35	
O	Killeen Edward C	218–230	policeman	42	"
R	Watson Gladys—†	218–230	secretary	45	"
S	Hopfgarten Rudolph	218–230	salesman	35	"
P	Watson Alice—†	218–230	housewife	76	"
T	Hickey Lucena—†	218–230	clerk	53	
U	Hickey Richard	218–230	retired	60	
V	Bowman Edna N—†	218–230	housewife	36	"
W	Bowman Harold L	218–230	accountant	39	"

x	Magner Thomas	218–230	foreman	51	here
y	Prendergast Daniel J	218–230	agent	61	"
z	Prendergast Rose N–†	218–230	housewife	55	"

1636

A	McKenna Francis J	218–230	clerk	58	12 Santuit
B	McKenna Helen M–†	218–230	housewife	55	here
c	Clougherty Margaret	218–230	"	53	"
D	Clougherty Michael T	218–230	salesman	61	"
E	Dolan Josephine—†	218–230	stitcher	60	
F	Fraser Mary—†	218–230	cook	29	
G	MacDonald John A	218–230	janitor	62	
H	Parkton Julia A—†	218–230	at home	79	
K	Riordan Sarah A—†	218–230	"	77	
L	Dove Joseph	218–230	retired	69	
M	Pierce Frank S	218–230	agent	74	
N	Pierce Olive M—†	218–230	housewife	73	"
o	Heil Marion—†	218–230	stenographer	43	"
P	Lewis Anna M—†	218–230	at home	67	"
R	Parker Everett	218–230	custodian	54	"
s	Parker Frances F—†	218–230	housewife	54	"
T	Tuffey John R	218–230	teacher	48	
u	VanVleck Anna—†	218–230	housewife	49	"
v	VanVleck Roy A	218–230	teacher	50	
w	Costello James J	218–230	bartender	42	"
x	Costello Margaret E–†	218–230	housewife	40	"
y	Corcoran Helen—†	218–230	stenographer	44	"
z	Fitzgerald Irene C–†	218–230	clerk	48	"

1637

A	Bruno Anna R—†	218–230	housewife	43	"
B	Bruno George F	218–230	merchant	55	"
c	Sullivan Francis R	218–230	salesman	65	"
D	Sullivan Mary M—†	218–230	housewife	65	"
E	Hazoury Edna J—†	218–230	"	61	
F	Hazoury Jacob A	218–230	tailor	63	
G	Moran Anna G—†	218–230	housewife	67	"
H	Moran James F	218–230	bookbinder	64	"
K	McLeod Arline R—†	218–230	secretary	21	"
L	McLeod Estelle A–†	218–230	housewife	54	"
M	McLeod Walter I	218–230	distributor	54	"
N	McDonagh Delia—†	218–230	seamstress	54	"
o	McDonagh Ellen—†	218–230	clerk	37	

South Street—Continued

P	McDonagh Mary—†	218–230	clerk	35	here .
R	Karam George	218–230	agent	39	"
S	Karam Sophie—†	218–230	housekeeper	67	"
T	Cullen Marion F—†	218–230	clerk	36	"
U	Cullen Walter G	218–230	electrician	40	66 Walk Hill
V	McNabb Helen—†	218–230	housewife	59	here
W	Peterson John	218–230	machinist	29	10 Stella rd
X	Peterson Myrtle E–†	218–230	stenographer	29	here
Y	Duffley Catherine—†	219	housewife	66	"
Z	Duffley Charles W	219	pipecoverer	72	"

1638

A	Bandino Alice—†	219	housewife	49	"
B	Bandino James	219	U S A	21	
C	Pearl Frances—†	219	housewife	43	"
D	Pearl Louis W	219	operator	47	".
E	Peterson Ada—†	221	housewife	48	"
F	Peterson Oscar	221	pipefitter	55	"
G	Pearl Anne—†	221	teacher	28	"
H	Pearl Harold	221	accountant	45	"
K	Pearl Louis	221	mechanic	47	"
L	Pearl Marianne—†	221	housewife	65	"
M	Burns Joseph A	221	U S A	20	
N	*Burns Mary E—†	221	operator	41	"
O	Burns William	221	carpenter	46	"
R	Bell Catherine—†	223	housewife	72	"
S	Bell John F	223	chauffeur	46	"
T	Harrison George	223	policeman	28	9 Chestnut
U	Harrison Mary—†	223	housewife	26	9 "
V	Seigler Anne—†	225	"	59	here
W	Seigler Morris	225	merchant	59	. "
X	McCorry Agnes—†	225	housewife	45	"
Y	McCorry James E	225	shipfitter	47	"
Z	Pallamary Dorothy M—†	225	housewife	59	"

1639

A	Pallamary Michael J	225	investigator	57	"
B	Pallamary Michael J, jr	225	musician	23	"
D	Brucker Emma—†	234	housewife	70	"
E	Brucker Louis	234	butcher	65	"
F	Parker Edward F	238	painter	40	
G	Parker Evelyn M—†	238	housewife	38	"
H	Dailey Joseph D	238	supervisor	39	"
K	Dailey Mary A—†	238	housewife	60	"

Spalding Street

L	Savage Bernard T	7	U S M C	25	here
M	Savage Emily W—†	7	housewife	61	"
N	Savage James P	7	meatcutter	71	"
O	Savage John J	7	student	26	
P	Hill Anna V—†	7	housewife	56	"
R	Owens Bridget—†	7	"	81	
S	Mee Catherine T—†	8–10	waitress	34	"
T	Mee Catherine V—†	8–10	housewife	57	"
U	Mee Margaret E—†	8–10	secretary	32	"
V	Mee William J	8–10	operator	61	"
W	Spillane Norah M—†	8–10	waitress	69	"
X	Scully Annie M—†	8–10	housewife	68	"
Y	Scully John J	8–10	U S A	26	
Z	Scully Patrick J	8–10	laborer	66	
	1640					
A	Single Charles A	8–10	U S N	26	
B	Single Mary F—†	8–10	at home	24	"
C	McKeon Daniel L	8–10	salesman	25	"
D	McKeon Gladys M—†	8–10	housewife	25	Wisconsin
E	Smith Dorothy T—†	8–10	clerk	27	here
F	Smith John C	8–10	machinist	57	"
G	Smith John C, jr	8–10	tel worker	28	"
H	Smith Margaret H—†	8–10	housewife	55	"
K	McManus Helen T—†	9	"	42	
L	McManus Michael J	9	laborer	48	
M	McGrath Margaret—†	11	housewife	44	"
N	McGrath Patrick	11	cook	55	
O	Condry Genevieve M—†	11	saleswoman	54	"
P	Condry Julia E—†	11	"	55	
R	Condry Mary E—†	₋11-	housewife	82	"
S	White Frank L	11	metalworker	65	"
T	White Mary—†	11	housewife	60	"
U	Grenham Catherine D—†	12	"	38	
V	Grenham Thomas J	12	planner	37	
W	Ennis Catherine M—†	12	housewife	23	"
X	Ennis Thomas J, jr	12	packer	25	
Y	MacDonald Annie—†	12	housewife	50	"
Z	MacDonald John R	12	mechanic	26	"
	1641					
A	MacDonald Joseph A	12	steamfitter	59	"
B	MacDonald Vincent H	12	pipefitter	25	"
C	Green Edward F	12	clerk	23	

Spalding Street—Continued

D	Green Edward M	12	retired	60	here
E	Green Evelyn M—†	12	housewife	27	"
F	Green Katherine J—†	12	packer	25	"
G	Dampolo Joseph	13	cutter	40	
H	Dampolo Mary—†	13	housewife	37	"
K	*Dampolo Rose—†	13	at home	70	330 Centre
L	Keane Helen—†	13	housewife	60	here
M	Perednia Catherine—†	13	clerk	25	"
N	Lyons Eleanor M—†	13	"	21	"
O	Lyons George F	13	U S A	23	
P	Lyons James A	13	chauffeur	62	"
R	Lyons James J	13	U S C G	25	"
S	Lyons Nellie—†	13	housewife	50	"
T	Dee Anthony	15	bricklayer	42	"
U	Dee Theresa—†	15	housewife	41	"
V	Drummey Dorothy A—†	15	"	37	
W	Drummey William	15	chauffeur	38	"
X	Bullen Catherine T—†	15	housewife	68	"
Y	McMurrough Dorothy—†	16	clerk	20	
Z	McMurrough Evelyn A—†	16	secretary	21	"

1642

A	McMurrough Frank E	16	mechanic	56	"
B	McMurrough Joseph	16	U S A	22	
C	McMurrough Mary E—†	16	clerk	24	
D	Faherty Anne J—†	16	housewife	71	"
E	Faherty John J	16	clerk	32	
F	Faherty Mary C—†	16	maid	33	
G	Kelleher Helen G—†	16	at home	70	"
H	Kelleher John H	16	operator	58	"
K	Kane Lawrence E	17	machinist	33	"
L	Kane Margaret J—†	17	housewife	32	"
M	Morrison Eugene L	17	brakeman	31	"
N	Morrison Margaret E—†	17	housewife	29	"
O	Massey Bartley G	17	clerk	24	
P	Massey Mary J—†	17	secretary	26	"
R	Massey Nora—†	17	housewife	59	"
S	Massey Paul J	17	U S N	22	"
T	Massey Thomas P	17	carpenter	29	"
U	Sullivan Charles F	19	shipper	46	31 Brighton
V	Sullivan Charles W	19	U S N	21	31 "
W	Sullivan John L	19	"	21	31 "

Letter.	FULL NAME.	Residence, Jan. 1, 1945.	Occupation.	Supposed Age.	Reported Residence, Jan. 1, 1945. Street and Number.

Spalding Street—Continued

x	Sullivan Mary E—†	19	housewife	51	31 Brighton
y	McGloin Francis	19	clerk	27	here
z	McGloin Mary—†	19	housewife	60	"

1643

a	McCarthy Eugene	19	porter	46	153 Hemenway
b	McCarthy Nancy N—†	19	housewife	42	153 "
c	Herwood Sarah—†	20	maid	34	here
d	Ward Mary—†	20	housewife	42	"
e	Ward Patrick	20	laborer	56	"
f	Crisp Edna R—†	20	stenographer	24	Fall River
g	Crisp Ernest F	20	guard	32	11 Myrtle
h	Lord Mary A—†	20	housekeeper	68	Fall River
k	Dempsey Alice V—†	20	stenographer	21	here
l	Dempsey Dennis J	20	laborer	52	"
m	Dempsey Jennie—†	20	housewife	50	"
n	Dempsey Mary A—†	20	clerk	22	
o	Cauley Patrick J	22	laborer	58	
p	Green Bertha—†	22	operator	44	"
r	Green Margaret—†	22	housewife	52	"
s	Bernard Helen—†	22	"	40	
t	Bernard John E	22	dairyman	42	"
u	McHugh James T	22	U S N	20	
v	McHugh Patrick F	22	laborer	47	
w	McHugh Sabina J—†	22	housewife	45	"

View South Avenue

x	McCarthy John	4–6	U S N	20	here
y	McCarthy John J	4–6	rigger	56	"
z	McCarthy Marie T—†	4–6	bookkeeper	22	"

1644

a	McCarthy Mary E—†	4–6	housewife	56	"
b	Harding John J	4–6	manager	51	"
c	Harding Nora T—†	4–6	housewife	51	"
d	O'Leary John J	4–6	electrician	24	"
e	O'Leary Margaret E—†	4–6	secretary	23	"
f	Walsh John J	4–6	operator	55	"
g	Walsh Mary A—†	4–6	housewife	52	"
h	Walsh Mary A—†	4–6	tel operator	26	"
k	Fitzgerald Catherine V—†	5–7	housewife	53	"
l	Fitzgerald Patrick F	5–7	laborer	55	

View South Avenue—Continued

M	Walsh Catherine—†	5–7	housewife	60	here
N	Walsh John	5–7	operator	63	"
O	Shiers Forrest W	5–7	"	61	"
P	Shiers Nellie M—†	5–7	housewife	58	"
R	Shiers Richard G	5–7	U S N	25	
S	Brennan Alice—†	8–10	housewife	50	"
T	Brennan William	8–10	salesman	53	"
U	Johanson Anna—†	8–10	housewife	65	"
V	Johanson Carl O	8–10	carpenter	64	"
W	Johanson Eric A	8–10	engineer	30	"
X	Lyons Anna M—†	8–10	housewife	61	"
Y	Lyons Thomas M	8–10	clerk	26	
Z	Walsh Joseph F	8–10	"	32	

1645

A	Walsh Mary L—†	8–10	housewife	31	"
B	Gerke Albert G	9–11	manager	62	"
C	Gerke Charles A	9–11	laborer	33	
D	Gerke George F	9–11	clerk	37	
E	Griffin Eleanor J—†	9–11	housewife	27	"
F	Griffin Thomas J	9–11	chauffeur	30	"
G	Altimar Frank	9–11	clerk	25	
H	Altimar Rose—†	9–11	housewife	23	"
K	Spellman Francis T	9–11	U S A	22	
L	Spellman Margaret—†	9–11	housewife	42	"
M	Spellman Thomas J	9–11	mechanic	49	"
N	O'Brien William T	9–11	retired	69